Storytelling
ART AND TECHNIQUE

Storytelling
ART AND TECHNIQUE
FOURTH EDITION

Ellin Greene and Janice M. Del Negro

Foreword by Jack Zipes

LIBRARIES UNLIMITED

AN IMPRINT OF ABC-CLIO, LLC
Santa Barbara, California • Denver, Colorado • Oxford, England

Library of Congress Cataloging-in-Publication Data
Greene, Ellin, 1927–
  Storytelling : art and technique / by Ellin Greene and Janice M. Del Negro. — 4th ed.
    p. cm.
  Includes bibliographical references and index.
  ISBN 978-1-59158-600-5 (pbk : acid-free paper) 1. Storytelling—United States. 2. Activity programs in education—United States. I. Del Negro, Janice. II. Title.
  LB1042.B34 2010
  372.67'7—dc22   2009026365

14 13 12 11 10   1 2 3 4 5

This book is also available on the World Wide Web as an eBook.
Visit www.abc-clio.com for details.

ABC-CLIO, LLC
130 Cremona Drive, P.O. Box 1911
Santa Barbara, California 93116-1911

This book is printed on acid-free paper ∞™

Manufactured in the United States of America

Every reasonable effort has been made to trace the owners of copyright materials in this book, but in some instances this has proven impossible. The editors and publishers will be glad to receive information leading to more complete acknowledgments in subsequent printings of the book and in the meantime extend their apologies for any omissions.

CONTENTS

FOREWORD

A CONTEMPORARY CLASSIC

Originally written and published in 1977 with Augusta Baker, *Storytelling: Art and Technique* is now in its fourth edition, and thanks to Ellin Greene and Janice Del Negro, it has become a vital, contemporary classic that has changed with the times and addresses the profound concerns of anyone interested in storytelling and the future of the great tradition of storytelling in America. While the intended audience for the first edition of *Storytelling* was constituted primarily of librarians serving children in public and school libraries, Augusta Baker and Ellin Greene stated clearly that the scope of their work was much larger. "Our emphasis throughout is on storytelling as an oral art," they wrote. "We believe that storytelling as a listening/language experience should not be lost. Our eye-minded society has forgotten the power of the spoken word and emphasized the visual, reducing written language to everyday speech, but in storytelling the full range of language is possible."

This statement was written during the revival or renaissance of storytelling in America during the 1970s, when change was in the wind. Indeed, the fear about the neglect of the spoken word expressed by Baker and Greene was soon overcome, and the full range of language was made possible through educational reforms and storytelling in schools, libraries, churches, youth centers, hospitals, parks, old age homes, theaters, and so on. If anything, one could argue that the cultural shifts in the 1970s and the rise of new technologies may have brought about too much storytelling in America, clouding our vision of what "genuine" storytelling means.

Janice Del Negro discusses the new problems confronting librarians and storytellers in her introductory chapter when she talks about our media-saturated, quick-fix, illiterate society. In the past thirty years, we have witnessed tumultuous changes in education and the arts that are related to commercialism, consumerism, and standardization. The budgets for public schools and libraries have been continually reduced. Arts programs in many schools and libraries have been curtailed if not eliminated. Testing and sports remain supreme throughout the educational system. Some of these straitjacket tendencies have adversely affected storytelling throughout America in manifold ways and are discussed by the French critic Christian Salmon in his provocative book *Storytelling: La machine à fabriquer et à former les esprits*, which can roughly be translated as *Storytelling: The Machine for Fabricating and Forming Minds*. Salmon, who spent a good deal of time in the United States as a researcher, became intrigued by the history and revival of storytelling in the 1970s. In his opinion, the revival eventually and ironically helped the advertising industry to learn how to use stories and myths to reinforce logos and brand names and to develop systematic storytelling by corporations, the culture industry, and politicians so that they could increase productivity and the effectiveness of management; to conceal the machinations of governments in collusion with big business; and to promote exploitative tactics in all domains of institutional life. Though Salmon's arguments may be at times exaggerated, his study, which belongs to a long tradition of foreign, or more precisely, serious French studies of American culture such as Alexis de Tocqueville's *Democracy in America* (1835–1840), sounds an alarm: what we Americans thrive on most, our great storytelling tradition, might be in danger and on the verge of being destroyed.

According to Salmon, the art of the story, in its origins, was formed to tell about and to clarify human experience. Now, through the training of storytellers and transforming storytelling into a commercial profession, the art of story has become the instrument that enables the state to lie and control opinions and huge conglomerates to use stories to advertise and sell products. Dazzling the mind through a barrage of storytelling linked to political and commercial manipulation has led to the formation of master narratives to which all listeners and viewers should subscribe if they want to feel acculturated and cultivated in American society. It is bizarre that the revival of storytelling in the 1970s has led to its perversion in the twenty-first century. Or, has it?

All is not doom and gloom if we take a look at the daily persistent endeavors of storytellers, artists, librarians, and educators who employ storytelling to develop the humanistic sensibilities of children and their critical literacy. Another book, *Telling Stories to Change the World: Global Voices on the Power of Narrative to Build Community and Make Social Justice Claims,* edited by Rickie Solinger, Madeline Fox, and Kayhan Irani, provides information about storytelling and theater projects that resist the co-option of traditional storytelling, projects about which we seldom hear. The editors have collected twenty-three essays about the ways in which social justice activists, artists, and project leaders all over the world demonstrate the power that stories have to generate hope and engagement, personal dignity and active citizenship, the pride of identity, and the humility of human connectedness. All the essays indicate that the beginning of the twenty-first century is a historical moment in which narrative is more broadly recognized than ever as a significant, simple, crucial vehicle for reawakening, disseminating, and sustaining social justice impulses.

Ellin Greene and Janice Del Negro's revised edition of *Storytelling* takes into consideration this historical juncture and the diverse changes in the media and educational and cultural institutions. All the chapters of the book have been revised, a new chapter on storytelling in the UK and the Republic of Ireland by Patrick Ryan, and a report on storytelling in modern China by Judith Heineman have been added along with thirteen new stories, additions to the superb bibliographies, recommendations of stories to tell for different age groups as well as one hundred books to read aloud, and a listing of storytelling recordings and audiovisual producers. In particular, Ellin Greene's revision of Chapter 8, "Storytelling to Young Children," deserves special mention because it elaborates on recent research on early brain development and how storytelling programs help babies, toddlers, and preschoolers make connections between the world around them and the world of the book. Library programs for the very young are crucial for language development and visual appreciation and for opening up new vistas for children and thereby stimulating their brains to make important connections so that the children can decipher the language, signs, and symbols of texts and the actual world itself. Greene's insightful suggestions for how to work with parents and children, what books to use, and how to organize programs that will have a positive impact, along with sample programs, will be welcomed by librarians intent on helping young children develop early literacy skills and acquire a love of books and reading.

Storytelling is a very practical book and immensely useful to any librarian, educator, or storyteller who wants to create a storytelling program. Ellin Greene and Janice Del Negro have based their work on years of experience as storytellers and librarians, and their advice and recommendations, intended to enable children and young adults to appreciate stories and become storytellers in their own right, are invaluable. They do not have an ideological ax to grind except to say that they want to instill in children and adults a respect for the profound art of storytelling at a time when storytelling is threatened by programs of functional literacy and commercial spectacles. Greene and Del Negro believe strongly in the personal and humane interaction demanded by rigorous storytelling programs and in the power of stories to change lives for the better. Their thoughtful commentaries and original programs designed for young people of different ages and for adults are intended to deepen the roots of the great storytelling tradition in America. Their collaborative book is indeed a classic in the best sense of the term. Steeped in the history of the past, *Storytelling* speaks to us in the present, mindful that the future of our culture depends on how we build on the past.

—*Jack Zipes*

PREFACE

THIS FOURTH EDITION of *Storytelling: Art and Technique* reflects the radical cultural and societal changes that have taken place since the first edition was published in 1977, including the onslaught of a technological tsunami; the development of an increasingly diverse society; the fact that a greater number of mothers work outside the home and its corollary, the attendance of more children in daycare or preschool; and the availability of more organized after-school activities for older children. Coupled with these are the research in early brain development that demonstrates the importance of interaction between child and adult during the first six years of life; the public library children's services person now being regarded as an education partner in emergent literacy and a new awareness of how the physical arrangement of the public library affects service to children; and the availability of professional storytellers (people who make their living telling stories) to children's librarians whose administrative responsibilities have increased and who face the public's demand for more storytimes for babies and toddlers, leaving them less time to spend on the selection and preparation of stories to tell to older children.

Public librarians have reordered their storytime priorities based on recent research that demonstrated that being read to in early childhood lays the foundation for literacy. Storytelling programs for infants and toddlers and their caregivers can be found in almost every public library in the United States with as many as twenty lap-sits or toddler storytimes scheduled weekly. Publishers have responded to the demand for more books for younger children, often reprinting old favorites in a board-book format suitable for infants and toddlers. Although there seem to be fewer *regularly* scheduled storytelling programs for children in the middle age-group, that is, between the ages of 8 and 11, it doesn't mean that librarians "no longer tell to any audience but preschoolers," as the main speaker proclaimed at a library conference in the Midwest attended by one of Janice Del Negro's students. This came as a surprise to the students as well as to librarians on the PUBYAC listserv who protested vigorously and chimed in with their descriptions of storytelling to everyone from grade-school students to adults from North Carolina to California, Illinois to New York.

Storytelling is still being taught in graduate schools of library and information science (where *Storytelling: Art and Technique* is often the textbook); is still an event at the American Library Association's Annual Conference; and is still actively being practiced in libraries, classrooms, and museums across the United States and around the world. In storytelling residencies and programs such as Neighborhood Bridges in Minnesota, children and young adults are learning to appreciate different traditions as they hear and learn the stories of other cultures, and to be conscious of how stories influence their thinking and the way they view life. In the frenetic isolation created by information overload, the act of storytelling creates a paradoxical eye in the storm—a still and quiet place in which listeners form community.

The primary purpose of *Storytelling: Art and Technique* is to give both beginning and experienced storytellers—especially those who work in a public library or school media center, and also adults who work with children in Head Start programs, daycare centers, museums, and other recreational places where children gather—a sense of the role of storytelling in human history; an understanding of the importance of story in a child's life; basic information about how to choose, prepare, and tell stories; program planning guidance; and ways to gain administrative and community support for storytelling as an important part of library service to children. Extensive bibliographies in Part IV: Resources for the Storyteller are provided for students and other readers who wish to pursue the art and technique of storytelling.

As in the previous three editions, the emphasis is on storytelling as an *oral* art. Our visually oriented society has forgotten the power of the spoken word, reducing written language to everyday speech, but in storytelling, the full range of language is possible. Aidan Chambers, in his *Introducing Books to Children* (Horn Book, 1983, p. 130) wrote:

> As children listen to stories, verse, prose of all kinds, they unconsciously become familiar with the rhythms and the structure, the cadences and conventions of the various forms of written language. They are learning how print "sounds," how to "hear" it in their inner ear. Only through listening to words in print being spoken does anyone discover their color, their life, their movement and drama.

Storytelling at its best is mutual creation. Children listen and, out of the words they hear, create their own mental images. This opening of the mind's eye develops the imagination. Many contemporary storytellers, in an effort to compete successfully with television and the visual arts, have turned away from the oral tradition, with the result that storytelling, particularly for younger children, is often limited to the sharing of picture books. As valuable as picture-book art is, we believe that listening can be a complete experience, even for young children.

Basically, *Storytelling: Art and Technique* is about the relationship between storytelling and the place of literature in a child's life. Through the stories themselves and through the interaction between teller and listener, traditional storytelling goes beyond the surface child to speak to the inner child. I am more concerned with touching this inner child, with nurturing the spirit-self, and with enriching and deepening a child's feelings, than with mere entertainment.

When Barbara Ittner asked me to consider writing a fourth edition of *Storytelling: Art and Technique*, I agreed provided I could have a co-author. Janice M. Del Negro immediately came to mind, and I was delighted when she agreed. I had met Janice at a storytelling event when I was teaching at the University of Chicago Graduate Library School in the 1980s and Janice was working as a children's librarian for the Chicago Public Library. Several years later I heard Janice give the keynote speech at the Ready to Learn: Kids Need Libraries conference at the University of North Carolina at Greensboro. At that time Janice was youth services consultant at the State Library of North Carolina. Her speech made a lasting impression on me: her down-to-earth philosophy; her love of children's literature, which grew out of her experiences at the New York Public Library; and her decision to become a children's librarian rather than an academic librarian, prompted by her work as a student assistant to children's literature professor Margaret Poarch at SUNY Geneseo GSLIS. Later I read an essay based on her earlier speech and knew I wanted to include it as the opening essay in the fourth edition of *Storytelling: Art and Technique*. Janice is the author of three highly acclaimed story books and numerous articles in professional publications, including "Augusta Baker" in *Notable American Women, A Biographical Dictionary, Volume Five, 1976–2000* (Harvard University Press, 2004). Director of the Center for Children's Books from 2001 to 2004, she brings extensive knowledge of children's literature to this work. Janice has served on many American Library Association (ALA) and Association of Library Services for Children (ALSC) committees and was chair of the 2007 Caldecott Award Committee. Currently she is a member of the Planning Committee for the Butler Children's Literature Center at Dominican University, where she is also a member of the faculty in the Graduate School of Library and Information Science. I trust Janice to continue and carry forward the philosophy of library storytelling set forth by Augusta Baker in the first and second editions of the book Jack Zipes declares "a contemporary classic."

Chapter 1 is a brief overview of the history of storytelling, from its beginnings in preliterate society to the storytelling renaissance that began in the 1970s. In Chapter 2 the focus is on storytelling to children in libraries. It includes biographical sketches of some of the early storytellers who gave impetus to the growth of storytelling in libraries and schools during the twentieth century. Well-known living storytellers have not been included. Much of the material in this chapter is based on unpublished manuscripts and papers from the files of the Office of Children's Services of the New York Public Library, with which I was closely associated for many years.

Chapter 3 restates the purpose and values of storytelling, and gives an update on current research. Storytelling is an art, and as such needs no justification. However, librarians and teachers often find themselves in the position of having to defend the inclusion of storytelling in their work to skeptical administrators and colleagues. Awareness of the educational values of storytelling, fortified by the findings in Kendall Haven's (2007) book, *Story Proof: The Science Behind the Startling Power of Story*, gives new tellers a sound basis for sharing stories with children.

Chapter 4 covers the principles of selection and the types of literature (both traditional and contemporary) that lend themselves to storytelling. Particular attention has been paid to selection because most librarians and teachers, unlike folklorists who gather their material directly from oral sources, are dependent on the printed word for their storytelling material. Knowing how to select the right story out of the vast body of literature today is one of the most important aspects of storytelling. This chapter also addresses currently controversial questions, such as story ownership and permission for a teller from one culture to tell stories from another culture.

Storyteller-author Linda Marchisio graciously granted permission to reprint her "Movement Warm-ups for Storytellers" in Chapter 5, which deals with basic techniques of learning and telling a story. Chapter 6 is concerned with how to prepare an audience for listening and how to present stories.

Chapter 7, "Storytelling to Children with Special Needs or in Special Settings," has been enriched by insights contributed by Susan Danoff and her colleagues Paula Davidoff and Julie Pasqual; by Gwyn Calvetti, David Ponkey, and Jill Beebout, all of whom have extensive experience storytelling to children with learning differences; and by museum storytellers Mary Grace Ketner, Maureen Korte, and Kim Sheahan. We are grateful to Valerie Marsh for permission to include in the section "Storytelling to Deaf or Hearing-Impaired Children" a signed version of "The Little Red Hen" from her book *Beyond Words: Great Stories for Hand and Voice*.

Chapter 8, "Storytelling to Young Children," has been greatly expanded, primarily because of recent research that demonstrates a connection between hearing stories read aloud or told during early childhood and becoming a lifelong reader. Librarians are conducting more parent/child programs and are frequently asked to present workshops on picture-book reading to Head Start and nursery school teachers and parents. Beautiful picture books roll off the presses daily, but all too often the stunning artwork is accompanied by a weak text. The picture books cited within the text and in the bibliographies have been chosen as much for beauty of language as for visual delight.

Beth Horner has expanded her tips on storytelling to young adults and the bibliographies in the *Third Edition* in Chapter 9, "Storytelling to Young Adults."

Chapter 10 focuses on children and young adults as storytellers. We are most grateful to author/storyteller Susan Danoff; Anne Shimojima, IMC director, Braeside School, Highland Park, Illinois; and Darlene Neumann, IMC director, Sherwood Elementary School, also in Highland Park, for their contributions to this chapter.

Program planning (with sample programs) is discussed in Chapter 11. It was exciting to hear about new programs, such as "Language of the Heart," a family storytelling program developed by Sue Sutton, youth services librarian at the West Bloomfield Township Public Library, West Bloomfield, Michigan. Aware of her community's rich cultural diversity, Sue persuaded volunteers to offer a 30-minute story program in their native language. Chapter 12 offers helpful advice about administration of storytelling programs and in-service education.

A new section, "An International Perspective," was added, with an essay, "Storytelling in Libraries and Schools in the United Kingdom and the Republic of Ireland," by Patrick Ryan, and a short report, "How Do You Say 'Storytelling' in Chinese? Shuo Shu (Shuo—to Talk/to Tell; Shu—Book)," by Judith Heineman, a member of the People to People Storytelling Delegation to China in April 2008. It is my hope that this section will be expanded in the next edition of *Storytelling: Art and Technique.* As author Ursula LeGuin has pointed out "the story—from *Rumpelstilskin* to *War and Peace*—is one of the basic tools invented by the mind of man, for the purpose of gaining understanding. There have been great societies that did not use the wheel, but there have been no societies that did not tell stories."[1]

In place of the Festschrift in honor of Augusta Baker that appeared in the *Third Edition*, the reader will find the full text of thirteen stories that appeal to children of various ages from the very young to teens and represent different story types, from folktale to literary fairy tale, from humorous to spiritual. Through the kindness of the publisher, the Festschrift will be available on the Libraries Unlimited website for a limited period of time. Some of the books from which stories in both the third and fourth editions were taken are no longer in print. Our warmest thanks to the publishers and authors for permission to reprint these stories to make them more readily available to the reader.

Part IV: Resources for the Storyteller has been reformatted and enlarged. The Professional Reading section contains titles that both the beginner and the seasoned storyteller will return to again and again for valuable background information and inspiration. It also includes a list of helpful web sources. The authors recognize that web addresses, although current when this edition went to press, are subject to change. We suggest that if a URL is no longer accurate, a web search for the article title will often yield positive results.

More than 700 titles have been added to the bibliographies; titles we consider to be the most helpful for librarian and teacher storytellers. Since the founding of publishing houses for storytelling materials, such as August House and Yellow Moon Press in 1979, and the growing understanding of the importance of storytelling in human development, there has been an explosion of storytelling for all ages, but especially for the young child. Janice and I have read as many of the new books—literally thousands—as time allowed and often called on storytelling colleagues for input.

Stories for different ages of listeners appear in this section, first to aid eager new storytellers looking for tried-and-true tales, followed by 100 read-alouds and more than 100 recordings and videos that can be used in programs.

I have tried to bring together what I have gleaned about the art and technique of storytelling from personal experience, readings, and friendship with some of the finest storytellers practicing today. I was privileged to have as students Carol Birch at Rutgers, the State University of New Jersey; Jeslyn Wheeless, Columbia University; and Beth Horner, the University of Illinois, Urbana, and it has been a joy for me to follow their careers as professional storytellers. An equal source of joy is the many unsung former-student heroes and heroines who now tell stories in their classrooms, school media centers, and public libraries. From colleagues Laura Simms and Susan Danoff, with whom I have conducted storytelling residencies, I have learned immeasurably. It would take too much space to name all the wonderful people I have met over the years through storytelling who have enriched my life.

This book would not have been possible without the help and encouragement of many people. I especially want to thank my steadfast friend Deirdre Smerillo for her technical assistance and Janice's graduate assistant, Marta Siuba, for assistance in preparation of the manuscript.

Thanks to the publishers who so generously supplied review copies of materials listed in the bibliographies. It is our hope that publishers will consider bringing back in print out-of-print titles listed herein.

Grateful acknowledgment is made to Robert Sink of the New York Public Library Archives for directing me to the photographs of children in the library taken by the noted photographer Lewis Hine for the Child Welfare Exhibit of 1911, and to the photographs of Pura Belpré and Augusta Baker.

Many thanks to Irfan Master, manager of the Kick into Reading project, for the photograph that accompanies Patrick Ryan's essay; to Polly Koenigsknecht; to photographer Mike Greer for the photographs of children and parents at the West Bloomfield Township Public Library storytimes; to

Anne Shimojima for the photograph of fourth-grade storyteller Bennett Preskill; and to José González for the photograph of Lucía González with puppets Perez and Martina.

I am deeply indebted to Clara N. Bohrer, director of the West Bloomfield Township (Michigan) Public Library for her generosity. Clara graciously shared her notes for the many speeches about the role of the public library in emergent literacy that she gave in 2004-2005 as president of the Public Library Association, descriptive material about her library's services for early childhood, and the photos by Mike Greer. Jill Bickford, coordinator of children's services, and Sue Barash and Sue Sutton, youth services librarians at West Bloomfield Township Public Library, were most helpful and contributed sample programs in Chapter 11.

I am also indebted to Elaine McConnell, director of Ocean County Library, and her staff, especially the librarians of my home branch, Point Pleasant, New Jersey, and in particular Taya M. Petino, Elsworth Rockefeller, and Robin Romance. All were extremely helpful and always gracious. In 2008 Ocean County Library received two prestigious awards: the National Medal from the Institute of Museum and Library Services and the John Cotton Dana Public Relations Award. I feel very privileged to live in a community that offers such excellent library service.

Our thanks go to Susan Danoff and Janet Thompson for reading the manuscript and for their invaluable suggestions. Special thanks also to Jeanne Lamb, coordinator of children's services, New York Public Library; Marilyn Iarusso, formerly assistant coordinator, children's services and storytelling specialist, New York Public Library; Carol Birch, recently retired head of services to children, Chappaqua Public Library; Sally Dow, head of children's services, Ossining Public Library; Carole Walton; and Jeslyn Wheeless for enriching the text with their contributions and insightful comments. To all the many other storytellers and students who suggested titles of books and stories for the bibliographies, our deepest appreciation.

Warmest thanks to Jack Zipes for taking time from his very busy schedule to write the foreword. Jack is a distinguished scholar and prolific author who shares our respect for genuine storytelling and who has devoted much of his life to empowering young people through the art, and, in particular, through Neighborhood Bridges, the program that strives to empower young people by making them storytellers of their own lives.

Words are inadequate to express my appreciation to Christine McNaull for her invaluable suggestions and painstaking help with the production of this book. Lastly, a sincere thank you to Barbara Ittner and to Catherine Barr for shepherding our book through the production stages with patience and grace.

—*Ellin Greene*

REFERENCES

1. LeGuin, Ursula K. "Prophets and Mirrors: Science Fiction as a Way of Seeing." *Language of the Night: Essays on Fantasy and Science Fiction*. Edited and with introductions by Susan Wood. Putnam, 1979.

Storytelling: Art and Technique is dedicated in
loving memory of Augusta Baker.

Ellin Greene and Janice M. Del Negro

FOR STORY'S SAKE:
READING AS ITS OWN REWARD

WE LIVE IN A MEDIA-SATURATED society that, on a surface level at least, increasingly defines individuals by their outer trappings: the images they cultivate, the goods they can afford, the toys they acquire. We live in an era that rewards the quick fix, the easy answer, and the software solution. The bottom line is all that matters, whether in budget or circulation figures—if you can't measure it, it's not valuable, and kids need to be paid off with bribes and incentives in order to participate in reading programs or other book-related activities. If they're not, reading program participation figures will go down, circulation figures will plummet, and book-buying budgets will dwindle accordingly.

How's that for a scenario? Nuclear winter is cozier.

I love books. I have always loved them. I have no memory of a time when I did not know how to read. My first conscious memory of actually reading a book is reading the poems in *A Little Pocket Book of Verse.* I think it belonged to my brother. "Tiger tiger burning bright, in the forests of the night, what immortal hand or eye dare frame thy fearful symmetry?" Or "Take her up tenderly, lift her with care, fashioned so slenderly, young and so fair." Or even "Young Lochinvar is come out of the West, of all the fine horses his was the best. So faithful in love and so dauntless in war, There ne'er was a knight like young Lochinvar." Did I know what those poems meant? I didn't have a clue, and it didn't matter.

My child-self inadvertently stumbled through the door of the public library and found solace and sustenance, in silence, in books, in language. The public library was an incredible haven, a respite from an inhospitable world. The Throgs Neck Branch of the New York Public Library was a converted storefront, with a children's side and an adult side. The library was warm, it smelled of books and dust and lemon wax, and there was always a place for me to sit. You could check out six books on a children's card then; when you turned thirteen you got an adult card and could check books out from the adult side, as many as twelve. I yearned to be thirteen.

Effie Lee Power said in her book *Library Services for Children* that the primary purpose of all storytimes is to interpret literature for children and to inspire them to read it for themselves. Power's point is, perhaps, not the only reason for telling stories to children, but in library land, where reading motivation is the Holy Grail, her point is definitely toward the top of the list. "The primary purpose of all storytimes is to interpret literature for children and to inspire them to read it for themselves." I had a different source of inspiration.

There was a librarian at the Throgs Neck Branch—a formidable woman. She was tall, black, and imposing—or maybe that was because I was none of those things. She was stern—or maybe that was because I was young. I never knew her name, but she knew mine. Looking back on it from the perspective of a youth services librarian, I realize that she had a very odd way of doing reader advisory. I would come into the library to return my books and she would say "Good afternoon, Miss Del Negro." I would mumble something completely unintelligible. She would examine the titles I had returned, and, not really looking at me, not really giving it too much visible attention, she would wave her hand toward a table in the children's room and say "There are some books over there you might like." I always looked, and I always liked them. I had some strange idea about reading through all the fiction in alphabetical order. I made a pretty good dent in it. Then one day the librarian came over to me and said, "I think you should look at these" and she pointed me at the 398s. I read them all, from folk tales to literary tales, from Andrew Lang, Joseph Jacobs, and Ashley Bryan to Eleanor Farjeon, Howard Pyle, and Oscar Wilde. When I found out there were actually branch libraries—what a novel idea—and that I could get to them with a bus pass—I checked out the 398s in every branch library I could get to by bus or train. That's a pretty fair number of libraries, and a pretty fair number of 398s.

Eileen Colwell once said that the child's imagination must be stimulated from an early age if she is to develop as a person; without it she is locked into a narrow environment bounded by what she is able to see and touch. In a converted storefront in the Bronx, I found not just a world, but a galaxy; not just a galaxy, but universes, too numerous to count but still close enough to touch.

Years later I found myself in graduate library school, planning to specialize in academic libraries, and met the second librarian who shaped my life. Margaret Poarch had been an army librarian before becoming a professor of children's literature. She was from the American South; two of her favorite phrases were "My country tis of thee!" and "Honey, don't get me started." My job as Margaret's assistant consisted, among less important things, of pulling books for her classes. I pulled truckloads of them. Every time I did, I would say "Gee, Margaret, I remember this book—I read it when I was a kid." After about three weeks of this, Margaret finally turned to me and said "Honey, you don't want to be an academic librarian. Academic libraries are borin'. You are a children's librarian, through and through." Margaret's tiny office in the Genesee Valley was very like that old library storefront—it was small, crowded, and full of books; it smelled of dust and lemon wax, and there was always someplace for me to sit, even if I had to move a stack of books off a chair in order to do it. It was Margaret who first introduced me to storytelling, and it was Margaret who told me it was the story that mattered, not the teller. "Know the story," she said. "If you know the story well enough, the rest will take care of itself. It's the story that matters, not the teller." That phrase has stayed with me all these years.

The philosophy of youth services in libraries was shaped by professional women with visionary ideals. A key element in that philosophy, a constant throughout a hundred years of public library history, was the notion that youth services in libraries existed in order to connect children to books, to the very best literature the profession could offer them. Carolyn Hewins, Anne Carroll Moore, Effie Lee Power, Augusta Baker—we are, many of us, ignorant of their names and sometimes of their vision as well. Their vision included the awakening of the desire for knowledge in children who have little or no such stimulation in their personal lives; providing a connection, a bridge to powerful, beautiful literature and beautiful language, and fostering a lifelong love of reading. This was both a professional and moral vision, a vision with focus and impact. Andrew Carnegie thought of the public library as the poor man's university; author Mollie Hunter once said "If you can read, you can educate yourself." She also said "'If' is a little word with a very big meaning."

Public libraries and youth services in particular lack strong support, if they are not under downright attack, from fiscally prudent if short-sighted private individuals and government agencies. The quest for equal access to educational opportunity for all children travels a long and tortuous route, with impediments in the shape of monolithic bureaucracies, hostile challenges, ignorance, and greed. Any quest worthy of the name requires a heroic figure, a hero, to meet and overcome all obstacles.

Youth services librarians are heroes worthy of the name. I've seen heroic deeds and miraculous accomplishments in the smallest storefronts. I've seen children's librarians coax non-readers into the world of books. I've seen smiling calm in the face of a roomful of adolescents bursting at the seams with an energy I only vaguely remember. I've seen libraries moved, rooms rearranged, computers installed, and new skills learned and acquired at lightning speed. I've seen quality services maintained in spite of budget and staff cuts that would cripple any corporate organization. I've seen literature-based programs created from tissue and glitter, story and song. I've seen children's rooms turned into rainforests with green construction paper and safety scissors. I've seen children's librarians stand their ground when a book is challenged, when a patron gets belligerent, when quality service is threatened.

In folktales, the hero seldom accomplishes much by herself. There is always some convenient animal helper, magical old man, or mystical wise woman to help the hero out of wells, up glass mountains, or into towers with no doors.

It's true for youth services librarians as well. The best of us realize that we accomplish little on our own, that everything we do is connected to everything else. Whether we are talking about the volunteer who cuts out nametags in the thematically appropriate shape for storytime, the clerk who patiently explains for the 200th time how a child gets her first library card, the page who actually displays books with attractive covers instead of the ones that just got back from the bindery—the library is a story within which all the characters are connected by blood, coincidence, or circumstance.

Ideally, every child you help has a supportive adult standing behind them—a parent, a grandparent, a teacher. Each of those adults is a possible ally in your journey to connect children and books, children and story. They are the magical helpers in the quest to communicate the importance of children, children's books, and storytelling to the unknowing in your community. Everybody knows somebody else, and that somebody else may be the person you need to know to more effectively deliver quality library services to children.

What about the child who doesn't have a supportive adult? The child who has no advocate? Well, we change roles within the story then. We shape-shift, if you will, from the hero of the tale to the convenient helper. Magic man or wise woman, we are there to open the door to books and story for those children who cannot easily access what we can provide. In order to serve them effectively we unite with all those "everybodies who know somebody else"; we work with parents and teachers, daycare centers and preschools, health care and other community agencies.

I am familiar with the sinking feeling that this is an overwhelming task, providing access to literature and story for all the youth in your community—the dragon is too fierce, the spell too strong, the wizard too powerful to be conquered by—what? A children's librarian disguised as a hero? Most of us did not become involved in children's services because it was going to be politically hazardous and fraught with difficult financial issues. Most of us became involved in children's work because we had an affinity for children, and for children's books.

In service to those affinities, I would like to present you with a radical notion. These two affinities—our affinity for children and our affinity for children's books—are our strongest traits, the magic cloak, the seven-league boots, the water of life that will help us succeed in our quest to connect children and books, children and story.

What is it that makes the public library unique? What is it that makes us different from any other community agency? Understanding that libraries are more than books, I say to you that it is books that make us unique, and, in the end, it is our knowledge of those books and our ability to connect them with readers that makes us effective.

We select books and tell stories in libraries for many reasons: to build bridges between children and books, between childhood and adulthood, between language and reading, between one culture and another. In the tradition of the library professionals who have gone before us, we tell stories to keep the art of library storytelling alive.

A century of storytelling in the library oral tradition is our heritage as youth services librarians. This heritage includes literary tales memorized with love and care; personal tales from our own lives; folktales from oral and written sources; and anything that promotes a love of language and an appreciation of the power of the written and spoken word.

Many librarians started telling stories because they heard a storyteller, felt a connection to the tale and the telling, and wanted to be a part of a remarkably resilient tradition. The profession has long held that using stories with children has a number of benefits, from the practical increase of attention spans to the lyrical soaring of the soul that occurs when art is experienced.

We have seen the power and authority of storytelling work its magic on the most reluctant listeners. The library literature on the promotion and use of traditional literature is based on the underlying certainty that stories will lead children to books, and that books will lead children to richer, fuller lives. Storytelling gives us heroes and heroines who win with wit against the powerful, with humor against the self-satisfied, and with generosity of heart against evil self-interest. Storytelling creates a community of listeners out of a group divided by age, gender, race, and economics. Promoting and telling tales from many cultures raises awareness of those cultures, and promotes pride in the cultural heritage of individual listeners. Telling tales from many cultures provides listeners with a common culture, a unity created from the diversity of many. The answer to the question "where can I find more stories?" is books.

Keeping up with the literature is the pivotal issue in library services for children. You cannot effectively utilize your collection unless you know what's in it. You cannot effectively do reader advisory unless you know what is in your collection. You cannot effectively do juvenile reference unless you know what is in your collection. You cannot effectively direct other adults who work with children to the resources and materials they require unless you know your collection. You cannot effectively defend your book budget unless you know your collection. How do you know your collection? You read it. Read all the picture books. Read as much fiction as you can. Scan the nonfiction—table of contents, photos, index. You cannot defend your collection if you do not know what's in it, and you cannot know what's in it if you don't read it. Knowledge of children's literature, its history and content, is critical when formulating a collection development policy. It is also critical in giving you a sound basis for selection. No one has so much money in their book budget that they can afford to buy mediocre materials, and there is a lot of mediocrity out there. Buy multiple copies of quality, don't waste money on mediocrity: mediocrity is not motivational. How do you know what constitutes quality material? Read reviews, read journal articles, read the books, and then use them with children.

When people come to us, to children's librarians, they expect us to know the books, the children, and the ways to connect them. When daycare centers, schools, and other community agencies come to us, they want the knowledge and expertise they expect professional children's librarians to have—what books work with kids and why. Parents come in and want to know how they can help their children become readers. Teachers come in and want books for a specific curriculum unit. Homeschooolers come in and want classic titles that reflect a certain value system. Children come in and want a good book, a funny book, a mystery or a book like the one they read last time. You can serve your patrons because you know the books and can talk about them in a knowledgeable fashion that inspires confidence in your selection and belief in your professional integrity.

Our second strength is our affinity for children. I think that part of what makes youth service librarians so effective with children is that we are probably the only adults they know who don't want anything from them. We're not their parents, so we have few expectations about their personalities or interests. We're not their teachers, so we don't pressure them about grades. We're not their coaches, so athletic prowess or lack thereof is not an issue. We're not their peers, so whether they are part of the right crowd is of little concern. We take them as they come, and as long as they are not defacing library property or engaging in obviously destructive behavior, we take them as they are. Our only concern is to connect them to the books and materials they need, the books that will help them write a paper, develop a self-concept, and formulate a worldview that is bigger than their backyard, their street, their side of the road.

Children need access to information of all kinds, in all formats, and youth services librarians are the ones who provide that vital access. Despite our best intentions, however, it seems we are sometimes less able than we should be to communicate our place in the big picture to the community at large. How do we reach the people we need to reach in order to confirm our place in the policy-making arena? Significant, lasting change comes from the grassroots level, and grassroots change comes from networking. Being a good children's librarian gives you an instant opening with your most natural allies—the parents of the children you serve. Put up your tent and pound your drum. Every child who has a positive library- and book-related experience has a message for the adults around him; every adult you convince about the importance of connecting children and books is a missionary for your cause. Push the books. Base all your programming on the literature. Talk about the importance of books and reading. Challenge your service area to become a reading community, a place where reading, readers, and books are valued. Make it a team effort. Do not waste your time on programming or events that do not promote your collection and the other resources you offer. Do literature-based programs and coordinate literature-based events that focus on the goal of creating a reading community.

I know what you're thinking. It's too much. The hero cannot possibly sort millet seed from sand. It's too big. The giant has seven heads and the hero only one. We can't do it. One cannot carry water in a sieve.

Well, many hands make light work, the hero has a magic sword, and doing whatever is necessary to get the job done is the definition of a professional. Keep the idea of the library connecting children to books and stories at the forefront of community events. Be aware. Be responsive. Love the children, the books, the stories, your work. Know the whys and wherefores of what you do: Why storytimes? Why toddler programs? Why booktalks? Why storytelling? Why outreach? We must tell the story of the importance of connecting children and books. We must communicate the importance of positive interaction with books and print. We must communicate and nurture the spirit of discovery, the joy in story, and the intellectual curiosity that turns children into self-aware, powerful adult seekers of knowledge, online, offline, and every place else.

Am I advocating a return to dusty storefronts with crowded shelves, a smell of lemon wax, and no PACs? As much as I might be sentimentally attached to the notion, I am not. I would not give up my computer for love or money, and I am infinitely thrilled by the World Wide Web and the opportunities that it provides. I think cruising the information highway (remember that phrase? now relegated to yesterday's info-byte junk pile)—I think cruising the info highway is very handy for lots of stuff, but as a friend of mine once told me when I was learning to drive in Chicago—never get emotionally involved with traffic.

The professional literature, the journals, the newspapers, are full of articles about technology and its impact; school and public library administrators are frantically pouring thousands of dollars into technology in a futile effort to be on the cutting edge; and computerized reading programs that give points for books read are dangerously close to becoming selection tools instead of motivational tools. We have high government officials who think we should pay kids a dollar or two for every book they read, parents who think reading certificates aren't enough of a reward for participating in the summer reading program, and school administrators who don't see the value of a well-equipped, on-site media center. What's a librarian to do?

Smile. Be enthusiastic. Be informed. Pick up a book, and make them an offer they can't refuse. "In the light of the moon, a little egg lay on a leaf. One Sunday morning the warm sun came up and—pop!—out of the egg came a tiny and very hungry caterpillar." . . . "My great great great grand-mother did great things. Elizabeth lived during the Revolutionary War, but she did not fight in it." . . . "The first week of August hangs at the very top of summer, the top of the live-long year, like the highest seat of a Ferris wheel when it pauses in its turning . . ."

Tell them a story. "Once there was and twice there wasn't . . ." or "Most folks don't know it but the animals didn't always live on earth. Way back before 'In the beginning' and 'Once upon a time,' they lived next door to the moon." . . . or "When wishes were horses and beggars could ride, in a stone castle by the sea there lived a rich laird" . . . or "Once there lived a woman who had a son, a boy so round and fat, and so fond of good things to eat that everyone called him Buttercup."

Never underestimate the power of a story. Ruth Sawyer—one of those professional women with vision that we don't talk about nearly enough—tells about an encounter she had with a child and a story in *The Way of the Storyteller*. Sawyer was sixteen and visiting Boston with her parents. Sawyer babysat for the seven-year-old daughter of their hosts. During the daytime all was well, but when night fell the child became frightened and uneasy until all the lamps were lit. At bedtime, she would not go to bed until Saw-yer promised to stay with her and keep a light burning. Sawyer offered a story, but the child resisted; she hated stories as much as she hated the dark, especially stories with witches, giants and ogres in them. "How about fair-ies?" Sawyer asked. "They're elegant." Then Sawyer told the story of the boy who gathered herbs by moonlight so his mother would be healed. "It will sound better if I put out the light." She told the story three times. The next night it was the same, and the next, until "dark came gently, with it the stars, the call of the screech owl, and all the little sounds of earth that came with spring. Together we felt the comfortable darkness fold us in." Years later Sawyer met the young girl in a cafeteria. Each was unsure of the other's identity at first, until the girl, now an eighth grader cried out: "I know who you are! You're the girl who made me like the dark."

Our sense of our profession's history and philosophy supports our quest. Return to that basic but irreplaceable premise: the right book for the right child at the right time. Develop something of an attitude as well. My friend Michael, a children's librarian, had it down cold. When asked by a well-meaning but apparently uninformed parent what the reward was for reading a book in the summer reading program, Michael, a most elegant dresser, would let his reading glasses slide down to the end of his nose, peer disdainfully over them, and reply precisely and succinctly: "Madam, reading is its own reward."

Ruth Sawyer would have approved.

> (Keynote Speech by Janice M. Del Negro, Children's Literature Conference, Champaign Public Library, November 7, 1997. Edited for this publication.[1])

REFERENCES

1. This speech was expanded into an article in *Story: From Fireplace to Cyberspace: Connecting Children and Narrative.* Eds. Betsy Hearne, et al. Allerton Institute 39. University of Illinois, GSLIS, 1998, available at https://www.ideals.uiuc.edu/handle/2142/662.

PART I:
HISTORY AND PRACTICE

1 STORYTELLING: A HISTORICAL PERSPECTIVE

Stories have been told as long as speech has existed, and sans stories the human race would have perished, as it would have perished sans water.
    —Isak Dinesen[1]

STORYTELLING HAS BEEN CALLED the oldest and the newest of the arts. Though its purpose and conditions change from century to century, and from culture to culture, storytelling continues to fulfill the same basic social and individual needs. Human beings seem to have an innate impulse to communicate their feelings and experiences through storying. We tell stories in order to make sense of our world. We express our beliefs, desires, and hopes in stories, in an attempt to explain ourselves and to understand others. In *The Completed Gesture*, a book about the importance of story in our lives, John Rouse writes, "Stories are told as spells for binding the world together."[2]

According to Ruth Sawyer, "The first primitive efforts at conscious storytelling consisted of a simple chant, set to the rhythm of some tribal occupation such as grinding corn, paddling canoe or kayak, sharpening weapons for hunting or war, or ceremonial dancing. They were in the first person, impromptu, giving expression to pride or exultation over some act of bravery or accomplishment that set the individual for the moment apart from the tribe."[3] One of the illustrations Sawyer gives is this Inuit chant from Greenland:

I, Keokok, have slain a bear,
    Ayi–ayi–ayi—
A great bear, a fierce bear,
    Ayi–ayi–ayi—
With might have I slain him.
    Ayi–ayi–ayi—
Great are the muscles of my arm—
Strong for spear throwing—
Strong for kayak going—
I, Keokok, have slain a bear.
    Ayi–ayi–ayi—[4]

In this early period everyone was a storyteller just as every young child today is a storyteller. The three-year-old tells a story using gestures, mime, dance, sound, and language, as in an earlier age when the expressive arts were one. As human societies became more complex, art specialties—drama, dance, music—developed. Song separated from narration. Those persons who possessed charisma, a greater command of language, a good memory, and a fine sense of timing became the community's storytellers. Stories changed from first-person to third-person narratives. One theory is that deeds were so exaggerated that modesty required the teller to attribute them to a third party, and thus the hero tale was born. Storytellers became the genealogists, historians, and keepers of the culture, as well as its entertainers.

The first written record of an activity that appears to be storytelling is found in an Egyptian papyrus called the Westcar Papyrus (recorded sometime between 2000 and 1300 B.C.E.) in which the three sons of Cheops, the famous builder of pyramids, take turns entertaining their father with strange tales. The earliest known heroic epic, *Gilgamesh*, was first told by the Sumerians, the inventors of the written word, and was taken over by the Babylonians when the Sumerian civilization collapsed in 2000 B.C.E. There are evidences of *Gilgamesh* in Homer's *Iliad* and *Odyssey*, in the Greek mythologies, and in Hebrew scriptures. The tellers of the Greek myths created supernatural beings with the power to rule the terrifying forces of nature, and yet these gods had human frailties. Abraham and his descendants, the Israelites, preserved the stories within the Sumerian epic, changing them as storytellers do, and so, out of the story of the great flood came Noah and the ark. Scholars see a relationship between the bull painted by the cave artists, the Bull of Heaven in the *Gilgamesh* tale, Zeus transforming himself into a white bull to seduce Europa, the Greek myth of Theseus and Minos's minotaur (who was half man, half bull), and the buffalo dance of Native American tribes.

Storytelling was also looked upon as a way of teaching social and moral values. Both Plato and Aristotle mention storytelling to children in this connection, and the *Panchatantra* (c. 400 C.E.), compiled for the education of the royal children of India, teaches:

Whoever learns the work by heart,
Or through the storyteller's art
Becomes acquainted;
His life by sad defeat—although
The king of heaven be his foe—
Is never tainted.[5]

Among Native Americans, children were present during storytelling and were expected to listen. Among the Xhosa and Zulu peoples of Africa, storytelling was considered training in listening and telling; children were expected to learn the stories they heard from their elders.

The first professional storytellers were bards, or singer-performers. Bards were of two types: praise singers who sang of the great deeds of the fore-bears and leaders of the group, and chronicler-historians who recited genealogies and sang about historic events. In the *Odyssey*, Homer describes a banquet scene at which a blind bard sings of the quarrel between Odysseus and Achilles. As was the custom, the bard accompanied himself on a lyre, held with both hands. John Harrell, in his engaging narrative *Origins and Early Traditions of Storytelling*, notes that after about 200 years the demand for new forms and new styles of storytelling led to the demise of this Homeric tradition. The Homeridai who accompanied themselves on the kithara were replaced by rhapsodes who, instead of singing with a kithara, stood holding a staff called a rhabdos, which freed one of the storyteller's hands. This allowed the storyteller to move about and to gesture and to use his rhabdos as a prop. "The new dramatic style," Harrell remarks, "encouraged embellishments and strivings for effects. With this increasingly personalized performance of the epics, the rhapsode became more and more a celebrity in his own right. . . . The rhapsodes were very popular and always drew audiences, especially at festivals where they held contests . . . and outdid themselves to gain first prize."[6] The abuse of this new style eventually led to reform, but, as Harrell points out, "All subsequent styles are variants of these original, basic modes, and within them lie our roots."[7]

Two schools of storytelling came into existence during the time of the Roman Empire: the Gaelic school of *ollamhs* in Ireland and the Cymric school of bards in Wales. Aspiring storytellers attached themselves to a master storyteller, sometimes staying for several years and studying under different masters. Master storytellers were elevated to positions of great power. They owned certain stories and no apprentice could tell these without permission. In Ireland, an *ollamh*, or master storyteller, knew 350 stories, had a special chair, and could wear five colors, only one less than royalty, while more common folk were allowed to wear only one, two, three, or four colors, depending on their social standing. An *ollamh* was also entitled to wear a cloak made of many-colored bird feathers. The master Welsh bard was the *pinkerdd* and his apprentices were known as the *mabinogs* because every apprentice had to learn the group of tales called the *Mabinogion*. The *pinkerdd* told from the front of the great hall while the *mabinogs* told from the back. In Sawyer, we read that the *pinkerdd* was under the protection of the king. He was assigned the tenth chair from the king and his value was the handsome sum of 126 cattle. He received "A harp from the king, a ring from the queen, cloth and a horse from the king, linen from the queen; and from the court, a man's maintenance."[8]

Bards were known in Asia, Europe, Africa, the South Pacific, and among the Aztecs and the Mayans. Stories traveled from Asia to Europe and back, carried by traders and wandering minstrels. Anglo-Saxon gleemen and, later, Norman minstrels traveled all over England and continental Europe and passed along their tales in song, dance, and story. In Germany there were the minnesingers, members of the music and poetry guilds; in Russia there were the *skomorokhi* who performed a similar function. Women as well as men were bards. Colwell remarks, "How great a number of minstrels there were, we do not know, but we read that the king employed 426 minstrels at the wedding of Margaret of England in 1290, and that amongst the many minstrels on the payroll of Edward I there were two women with the intriguing names of Matill Makejoye and Pearl in the Egg."[9] In Africa, there was the "resident storyteller" and the "traveling storyteller." The former was part of a chief's household; his only responsibility was to keep alive the exploits of his leader. The "traveling storyteller," however, went from village to village with tales, anecdotes, and fables and became the collector of an oral, narrative tradition.

In western Europe storytellers reached the height of their power during the Middle Ages from the tenth to the fourteenth centuries. During the latter half of the Middle Ages, guilds of storytellers were organized. At the time of Charles IV a charter and coat of arms recognized the artistry of storytellers. Storytelling competitions were held. It is known that competitions took place in Wales as early as the late twelfth century; they continue today.

Scholars began to write down the stories and, with the invention of the printing press in 1450, the oral tradition began to wane, especially among the upper classes and the new middle class who were able to afford books. The storyteller's role as historian, genealogist, and news-bearer was usurped by the print media and the ascendance of science, which served to question literary wisdom. Storytelling gradually lost its spiritual force and became mere entertainment. In France Marie-Catherine d'Aulnoy's fairy tales and Charles Perrault's sophisticated retellings of the old folktales amused the French court, while the common folk continued to listen and to tell tales to ease the monotony of work and to bring laughter and wonder into their lives. Among the common folk, storytelling was so closely associated with spinning and weaving that "to spin a yarn" and "to weave enchantment" were synonymous with "to tell a tale."

Irish storyteller and poet Padraic Colum believed that the extension of the day's rhythm into night also contributed to the decline of storytelling.[10] Before daylight was extended by artificial means, day and night rhythms were very different, and long, dark nights lent themselves to storytelling.

In time, storytelling was relegated to the nursery, where the tales were preserved for the folklorists to rediscover in the nineteenth century.

Jacob and Wilhelm Grimm revived an interest in the oral tradition when they collected stories from oral sources and published their collection *Kinder- und Hausmärchen* in 1812 and 1815. Their methodology has been criticized by modern folklorists but their work encouraged other nineteenth-century collectors, including Alexander Afanasyev (Russian), Joseph Jacobs (English), Peter Asbjørnsen and Jørgen Moe (Scandinavian), and Jeremiah Curtin (Irish). As scholars studied these collections they found striking similarities among the tales. Some folklorists attributed the similarities to universal emotions; the tales were fantasies that fulfilled human wishes and dreams. Others believed the tales were remnants of nature myths or ancient religious rituals. In the early 1900s Finnish folklorist Antti Aarne developed a classification system that assigned a type number to individual tales. American folklorist Stith Thompson carried this a step further and assigned a motif number to each significant element of a tale. His six-volume work, *Motif-Index of Folk-Literature*, was first published in 1932, with a revised edition published in 1955–1958. Both *The Types of the Folktale* by Aarne and Thompson's *Motif-Index of Folk-Literature* are essential tools for the storyteller. Margaret Read MacDonald followed Stith Thompson's classification in *The Storyteller's Sourcebook*, but she adapted it to meet the needs of teachers and librarians who work with children's collections.

As Anne Pellowski observed in her scholarly survey *The World of Storytelling*, ". . . the Grimm Brothers' tales must be considered as the single most important group of folk stories that affected storytelling for children. Their widespread appeal and their contemporaneous legitimacy helped educated European parents to believe it was important to continue telling stories to children, even though, in many cases, there was opposition from formal educational authorities."[11]

Fortunately, the great German educator Friedrich Froebel recognized the value of stories and made storytelling an important part of the kindergarten program that he founded in 1837. German emigrants to America took with them the idea of kindergartens, and in 1873 the first kindergarten was incorporated into a public school system in the United States. Instruction in storytelling was given in the kindergarten training schools, and in 1905 Sara Cone Bryant, a kindergarten teacher, wrote the first storytelling text to be published in the United States, *How to Tell Stories to Children*.

It is interesting to note that the two oldest storytelling organizations in the United States—the National Storytellers League (formerly, the National Story League) and the National Storytelling Network (founded as the National Association for the Preservation and Perpetuation of Storytelling, better known as NAPPS)—both began in Tennessee.

In July 1903 a group of teachers attending summer school at the State University in Knoxville, Tennessee, began meeting on the lawn at twilight to tell stories under the stars. By the end of summer school they had decided to form a storytellers league. The purpose of the league was "to discover in the world's literature, in history, and in life the best stories for education, and to tell them with love and sympathy for the children, and to bring together in story circles those who love to hear and tell a good story, the kindergartners, teachers, church workers, children's librarians, and those whose hearts are afire with this work, that they might impart its spirit to others."[12]

Richard T. Wyche was the league's main organizer and served as president from 1903 to 1919. It is worth noting that Wyche had been a student at the University of Chicago in 1901 when the great Norwegian storyteller, Gudrun Thorne-Thomsen, was teaching at the University of Chicago's Laboratory School (see Chapter 2). Wyche edited the league's journal, *The Storytellers' Magazine* (now *Story Art*, published quarterly), and wrote the second book of storytelling to be published in the United States, *Some Great Stories and How to Tell Them*.

One hundred and five years later, the National Storytellers League is still active, with seventeen leagues in fifteen states. Several leagues sponsor Junior Story Leagues. The League is divided into two districts: Eastern District and Western District. Its motto remains the same, "Service through storytelling." Members volunteer storytelling service in schools, libraries, museums, hospitals, nursing homes, adult daycare centers, and other community agencies. The League holds a national conference every two years; the Districts meet in the alternate years. Currently, the League is promoting a letter writing and petition signing campaign for a United States postage stamp to Honor the Art of Storytelling. For more information about NSL, contact Carol Satz, NSL President, 47 Burholme Drive, Hamilton, NJ 08691; email englearnr@aol.com or visit www.nslstorytellers.org. In addition, two leagues have websites: firesidestoryleague.org (Washington) and gardenstatestorytellersleague.org (New Jersey).[13]

For most of the twentieth century, storytelling in the United States was generally associated with children. Librarians and teachers kept the art alive (see Chapter 2). In 1973 a revival of appreciation and respect for storytelling for adults was ignited by Jimmy Neil Smith (then a journalism teacher at Science Hill High School in Johnson City, and later a restaurateur and mayor of Jonesborough, Tennessee). Smith was driving some of his students to nearby Elizabethtown to print the school newspaper when he tuned in his radio to storyteller-humorist Jerry Clower. The students' enthusiastic response to Clower's monologue started Smith thinking about organizing a storytelling festival. With the support of the Jonesborough Civic Trust he invited Clower who agreed to participate for the then hefty fee of

$1,000. In October of that year, about 300 people gathered on the lawns and porches of the historic old houses in Jonesborough to swap stories. From that small gathering grew an annual storytelling festival that today draws thousands of storytelling enthusiasts from around the world. When the National Storytelling Festival celebrated its 20th anniversary in 1992, Clower returned but this time performed for free!

In 1975 Smith founded the National Association for the Preservation and Perpetuation of Storytelling (NAPPS), renamed the National Storytelling Association (NSA) in the early 1990s. In 1998, in an effort to better serve the needs of the diverse storytelling community, NSA was divided into two separate organizations: the National Storytelling Network (NSN) and the International Storytelling Center (ISC). Both organizations are dedicated to advancing the art of storytelling, but the two organizations have taken two different approaches to accomplish their common goals.

The National Storytelling Network is a member-driven organization that provides direct services, publications (including *Storytelling Magazine*, published bimonthly, with a special Storytelling World issue), and educational opportunities to several thousand individuals and local storytelling guilds and associations. These services are designed to enhance the quality of storytelling at all levels—as entertainment, in a variety of businesses and industries, and wherever storytelling can make a contribution to the quality of life. The National Storytelling Network is divided into seven regions: Pacific, Western, North-Central, South-Central, Northeast, Mid-Atlantic, and Southeast. Within each region are state liaisons. The National Storytelling Network holds a national conference during the summer, hosted by a different NSN Region each year. The National Conference features a keynote speaker, workshops, and of course, lots of storytelling, both informal story swaps and the more formal storytelling concerts. The Oracle Awards in recognition of outstanding contribution to storytelling are presented on the last day of the conference. The National Storytelling Network also serves as the facilitator for Tellabration!, an international storytelling event traditionally held on the Saturday evening before Thanksgiving. Originated by NSN member, the late J. G. Pinkerton, the first Tellabration! was held in Connecticut in 1988. It is now celebrated on every continent except Antarctica. The National Storytelling Network is headquartered in Jonesborough, TN. For more information about NSN, call (800) 525-4514, email nsn@storynet.org, or visit www.storynet.org.

The International Storytelling Center, located on a three-acre campus in downtown Jonesborough, is dedicated to inspiring and empowering people around the world to remember, craft, and tell their stories and to use storytelling to build healthier communities, more effective workplaces, and enriched human lives. To accomplish its mission, ISC builds public awareness and credibility for storytelling, develops and delivers story-based products and services, and teaches people how to use storytelling to achieve their personal, organizational, and community goals. Areas of focus include education, health care, business/industry, community services, arts, culture, and media. The International Storytelling Center archives are housed at the Library of Congress. The internationally acclaimed National Storytelling Festival, co-owned by ISC and NSN, is solely produced by ISC and held the first full weekend every October in Jonesborough. For more information about ISC, call (800) 572-8392, email info@storytellingcenter.net, or visit www.storytellingcenter.net.[14]

You can read more about the storytelling revival in the United States beginning in the 1970s in Joseph Daniel Sobel's award-winning book, *The Storyteller's Journey: An American Revival*.[15] The impact of a professional storytellers' movement on storytelling in libraries and schools and on librarian and teacher storytellers is discussed in Chapters 2 and 6.

Storytelling is no longer just for children. Adults have reclaimed it for themselves. Perhaps storytelling fills the need for intimacy not easily found in our mobile society (and not offered by the electronic storyteller that invaded the family living room in the 1950s). Perhaps, as former student Tina-Jill Gordon (now curriculum director, Wall Township Schools, New Jersey) wrote in her doctoral dissertation, "It may be that as our world has metaphorically shrunk, we have had to confront the fact that we are part of a global community. As we seek to understand one another, what binds us together is beginning to seem more significant than what makes us different. Just as we have begun to recognize that the ecosystem of the earth is one interconnected system, perhaps we are beginning to realize that the human experience is similarly connected."[16]

REFERENCES

1. Isak Dinesen, "The Cardinal's First Tale," in *Last Tales* (Random House, 1957), p. 23. (Vintage Books edition, 1996)

2. John Rouse, *The Completed Gesture* (Unicorn/Skyline Books, 1978).

3. Ruth Sawyer, *The Way of the Storyteller* (Viking, 1942, 1962), pp. 45–46. (Penguin edition, 1977)

4. Ibid., p. 46.

5. *The Panchatantra*, trans. by Arthur Ryder (University of Chicago Press, 1925), p. 16. (University of Chicago Press, 1971), (Alternate translations are available from Penguin Classics, 2007, and Jaico Publishing House, 2005)

6. John Harrell, *Origins and Early Traditions of Storytelling* (York House, 1983), pp. 54-55.

7. Ibid., p. 61.

8. Sawyer, *The Way of the Storyteller*, p. 69.

9. Eileen Colwell, "Folk Literature: An Oral Tradition and an Oral Art," *Top of the News* 24 (January 1968): 177.

10. Padraic Colum, "Introduction," in *The Complete Grimm's Fairy Tales* (Pantheon edition, 1944), pp. vii–xiv. (Pantheon, 1976)

11. Anne Pellowski, *The World of Storytelling*, expanded and revised (H. W. Wilson 1990), p. 16.

12. Richard Alvey, *The Historical Development of Organized Storytelling to Children* (University Microfilms International, 1974), p. 28.

13. Carol Satz, President, NSL, and Gwendolyn Jones, Garden State Storytellers' League, personal communications (2008).

14. Jimmy Neil Smith, Director, ISC, Jonesborough, TN, and NSN Staff, personal communications (2008).

15. Joseph Daniel Sobel, *The Storytellers' Journey: An American Revival*, University of Illinois Press, 1999.

16. Tina-Jill Gordon, "Teachers Telling Stories: Seven-, Eight- and Nine-Year Old Children's Written Responses to Oral Narratives" (Ed. D. diss., Rutgers University, 1991), p. 2.

WEB RESOURCES

History of Storytelling
http://www.rif.org/educators/articles/storytelling.mspx
Reading Is Fundamental, Inc.

Origins of Storytelling
http://falcon.jmu.edu/~ramseyil/storyorigins.htm#B
Inez Ramsey, Professor Emeritus, James Madison University

Yale-New Haven Teachers Institute: The Oral Tradition:
http://www.yale.edu/ynhti/curriculum/units/1984/4/
Professional articles about different oral traditions.

2 STORYTELLING TO CHILDREN IN LIBRARIES

These women linked folklore and children's literature both literally and figuratively. They told folktales, myths, and legends in library settings while other women waited in the wings with books that would allow children to read the same stories in print. They linked children whose immigrant parents were illiterate, but rich in oral tradition, to a new multiculture of stories. And they, themselves, often learning stories from women who had been part of an oral tradition, "moved" those stories into a new literary milieu of children's books.
—Betsy Hearne[1]

CHANGES IN ATTITUDES TOWARD children and several social movements that occurred in the United States during the second half of the nineteenth century and the twentieth century encouraged organized storytelling, that is, formal presentations of stories, to groups of children. These movements included the development of playgrounds, settlement houses, and Sunday Schools; the founding of the YMCA in 1851 and the YWCA in 1866; and the founding of the Boy Scouts in 1910 and the Girl Scouts in 1912. In 1900 the American Library Association, formed in 1876, established a special division for librarians serving children.

BEGINNINGS

The exact date of the first library story hour is uncertain, but it was about 1900. By 1896 Anne Carroll Moore had given storytelling a place in the children's room of the new Pratt Institute Free Library in Brooklyn, New York. Storytelling had been tried experimentally as early as 1899 in the Carnegie Library of Pittsburgh, just a year after the organization of the department for work with children. The program had such spectacular success that Frances Jenkins Olcott, who was the director of children's work, incorporated the story hour as a regular part of the program. In an article published in *Carnegie Magazine* in 1933, Elizabeth Botset of the Carnegie Library of Pittsburgh gave credit to another Pittsburgh librarian, Charlotte Keith Bissell, for the origin of library story hours. According to Botset,[2] Bissell noticed a group of younger children listlessly leafing through picture books in the library. She wondered what the result would be if a librarian told stories to such children and why the story hour, so successful in hospitals, had not been tried in libraries to introduce books. During the same period the Buffalo (NY) Public Library experimented with storytelling on Sunday afternoons to stimulate interest in books and reading, and in 1899 started regular Saturday morning story hours. Similar experiments were carried out in other newly organized children's rooms. Effie Louise Power (better known as Effie Lee Power), the first children's librarian at the Cleveland Public Library (1898–1903) and later director of work with children at CPL (1920–1937), became supervisor of children's work at the St. Louis Public Library in 1911, where she established a storytelling program similar to the one at the Carnegie Library in Pittsburgh. Power's *Library Work with Children* (ALA, 1930), later updated and retitled *Work with Children in Public Libraries* (ALA, 1943), was the first textbook on children's librarianship. Power also compiled four story collections: *Bag o' Tales* (1934), *Blue Caravan* (1935), *Stories to Shorten the Road* (1936), and *From Umar's Pack* (1937). Her textbook and the anthologies greatly influenced what stories were told by librarian-storytellers and the role of storytelling in library work with children. Librarians were seeking ways to bring together children and books and to interpret literature in an artistic rather than in a pedantic manner. They were already beginning to recognize the great potential of storytelling when, in 1900, Marie Shedlock came to the United States to lecture on Hans Christian Andersen and to tell his tales.

MARIE SHEDLOCK (1854–1935)

Marie Shedlock was born in France and grew up in England. She was a teacher of young children for many years before becoming a professional storyteller in 1890. Shedlock's lectures on storytelling formed the basis of a book that became a classic in storytelling, *The Art of the Story-Teller.*

It was on Shedlock's first visit to the United States that Mary Wright Plummer, director of the School of Library Science at Pratt Institute in Brooklyn, heard her tell stories in French and English at one of a series of matinees at Sherry's, a fashionable New York City restaurant. She told Hans Christian Andersen's "Tin Soldier," "The Swineherd," and "The Princess and the Pea," and the telling was unforgettable. Plummer invited Shedlock to tell stories to the trustees, directors, and faculty of Pratt.

When Anne Carroll Moore, head of the children's room at Pratt, heard Shedlock she decided that there must be a story hour for the children, too, and so, on a snowy Saturday morning in January 1903, Marie Shedlock returned to Pratt. When the program was over, a little girl asked Miss Moore, "Is she a fairy, or just a lady?" In later years Moore wrote, "There was never any doubt in my mind after that morning that a children's library should have a regular story hour."[3]

Shedlock did not use the affected speech that was in vogue at the time, nor was she didactic. It was her inspiration, as she traveled around the United States telling stories and lecturing on storytelling, that gave impetus to the idea of storytelling as a true art. Shedlock inspired others to become storytellers, among them Anna Cogswell Tyler, Moore's assistant at Pratt, and Ruth Sawyer, one of America's best-known storytellers. After Shedlock's visit to Boston in 1902, regular library story hours were established, and in 1911 the Boston Public Library hired Mary W. Cronan, a kindergarten teacher trained in the Froebel method and an experienced storyteller. She was soon joined by her husband, John, and her sister, Margaret Powers. The trio told the legends of heroes and saints to the children of immigrants in schools, playgrounds, and museums, as well as in the library.[4]

In Pittsburgh, too, storytelling assumed a new importance. Pittsburgh librarians began to hold weekly story hours in their branches and to take stories to the playgrounds. By 1909 Edna Whiteman was appointed supervisor of storytelling at the Carnegie Library of Pittsburgh. Whiteman selected the most suitable versions of stories for telling, arranged programs, and told stories in the children's rooms of the branch libraries. In 1916 she prepared the first edition of *Stories to Tell to Children: A Selected List*. Unfortunately, the eighth and last edition of this helpful list (1974), revised and edited by Laura E. Cathon, Marion McC. Haushalter, and Virginia A. Russell, Margaret Hodges, Consultant, is out of print. The eighth edition, as well as earlier editions, is available online.

In the Cleveland Public Library, Carolyn Burnite, who took over the organization of work with children in 1904, established storytelling as an important, regular part of that work. Usually two story hours a week were held in each branch library. Because storytelling was regarded as one of the children's librarians' responsibilities, time was allowed for the preparation of stories. As time went on, more and more children came to hear the stories; in 1909 the library reported a record attendance of 80,996.

Even though she was convinced that a children's library should have a regular story hour, Anne Carroll Moore did not rush to select her first storyteller. In later years she wrote:

> Finding a story-teller of the right sort was not easy. Poor story-telling is more disastrous than poor story-writing, which can be skipped or left entirely alone without affecting anyone else. I had been conscious from the first months of my personal work in a children's room of the need for investing reading with dramatic interest and pictorial tradition, if it were to have any real meaning in the daily lives of hundreds of children who were coming to the library.[5]

For a year after Shedlock's visit to Brooklyn, Moore conducted an experimental story hour, inviting different people to tell stories as she and the children listened. She described one memorable story hour in her book *My Roads to Childhood*: *Views and Reviews of Children's Books*:

> I learned a very great deal from listening. In the spring of that year Miss Shedlock came back again and told Hans Christian Andersen's "Nightingale." It woke the story-teller for whom I had been waiting so long, and on May Eve, a Robin Hood story from Howard Pyle and a true story out of her own childhood marked the first of Anna Cogswell Tyler's distinctive contributions to story-telling.[6]

ANNA COGSWELL TYLER (1859–1923)

Anna Cogswell Tyler, Moore's assistant at Pratt, had heard Marie Shedlock tell stories to the boys and girls of Brooklyn on that exciting Saturday morning. Tyler had dramatic training but, bowing to family pressures, she did not go on the stage; storytelling, however, was the answer to this dramatic urge. In 1907, a year after Moore was appointed the first supervisor of work with children at the New York Public Library, she brought Tyler to the library to develop a storytelling program. By 1909 a strong storytelling program was in progress and Tyler had been appointed the first supervisor of storytelling for the library. In a 1909 report she wrote:

> We are striving to make a more direct application between the story told and the book itself. This we do by only telling stories that will interest the children in the special book from which the story is told. . . . The Assistant in Charge of Storytelling is giving more careful supervision to all those assistants telling stories in the libraries; helping in the choice of story, selecting the best versions to use, directing as far as possible their advance reading, and generally trying to so mould the work of the storyhour that it may assume a more definite, lasting and literary form, while trying in each case to fit the particular needs and interests of the children. Already the storyhour has assumed a more dignified and definite aspect both in the kinds of stories told and the manner in which the storyhour is being conducted. Each month the storyhour is fast losing its haphazard appearance and is entering upon its proper function in library economy—that of introducing children to the best kind of books, arousing a desire for a wider range in reading in boys and girls who, having fallen into the clutches of the series habit, seem unable to be interested in anything outside that rut until they listen to a well-told story of a great deed or a great romance, handle the book which contains it, learn to know where it may be found, and, the interest once aroused, the book is in constant demand.[7]

In 1909 the storytelling staff told stories to 28,325 children; in 1910, 1,008 story hours were held for 30,000 children in 36 branch libraries. Anna Tyler planned and held staff workshops, gave on-the-job training, and inspired the new storytellers with her own art. She knew the need

FIGURE 1. *Boys Reading Club, Yorkville Branch, New York Public Library, 1910. Photograph by Lewis Hine. Reprinted by permission of the Manuscripts and Archives Division. New York Public Library. Astor, Lenox, and Tilden Foundations.*

for inspiration, and so she held the first Spring Storytelling Symposium in 1909, at which fledgling storytellers could by the example of their own art inspire others to become storytellers. One of her innovative ideas was a weekly evening story hour for non-reading boys that was held in a branch library from November 1909 to May 1910. The boys' interest in books was stimulated, and the books used in the story hours began to circulate (Figure 1).

Tyler's influence spread throughout the profession as she held workshops and chaired storytelling committees for the Playground Association of America, Clark University, New York City's Board of Education, and others. In 1921 she compiled her favorite stories in *Twenty-four Unusual Stories*. On her retirement in 1922 she was succeeded as supervisor of storytelling by her assistant, Mary Gould Davis.

During this early period the Chicago Public Library was using the talent of an outstanding storyteller, Gudrun Thorne-Thomsen. Chief librarian Henry L. Legler was quoted in 1910 as saying, "We are now engaged in developing the branch library system of the city and no doubt storytelling will be made incidentally a feature of the work planned for the children's rooms. This work must be done by the children's librarians, the storytelling growing out of library work and merging into it in order that its most effective side be legitimately developed."[8]

GUDRUN THORNE-THOMSEN (1873–1956)

In 1944 a group of children's librarians at the New York Public Library listened to a small, quiet, unassuming woman tell "East of the Sun and West of the Moon." The story came alive as this master storyteller used only her lovely voice, perfect timing, and unobtrusive, spontaneous gestures to tell the tale. The storyteller was Gudrun Thorne-Thomsen.

Gudrun Thorne-Thomsen was born on April 8, 1873, in Trondheim, located on one of Norway's beautiful fjords. When she was four years old the family moved to Bergen, Norway's chief seaport, where she saw ships of many countries and listened to the sailors' tales from other lands. Her grandmother read to her and to the other children in the family and told them stories about the great Norse heroes and about trolls and *nissen*.

Gudrun's mother, Fredrikke Nielsen, was an actress, famous for her portrayal of the women in Henrik Ibsen's plays. The home Gudrun grew up in was an exciting place, frequented by musicians, poets, and writers, and alive with amateur theatricals, singing, and storytelling in which the entire family took part. It is little wonder that she grew up to love literature, to understand the strength and power of words, and to scorn careless speech.

When Gudrun was 15 years old, she moved to Chicago to live with her mother's sister. There she trained to be a teacher at the Cook County

Normal School and came under the influence of Colonel Francis W. Parker, whom John Dewey called "the father of progressive education." In 1893 she married Georg Thorne-Thomsen and the young couple made their home in Chicago.

Gudrun joined the staff of Colonel Parker's new school. Parker's innovative ideas in education attracted the attention of William Rainey Harper, then president of the University of Chicago. Harper invited Parker to bring his school to the university as part of the newly formed School of Education and to become director of the Laboratory Elementary School. John Dewey, already at the university as head of the Elementary School of the Department of Pedagogy, was appointed head of the Laboratory High School. The laboratory schools were Froebel-inspired, and storytelling was prominent in the curriculum. Harper, active in the Chautauqua movement and a storyteller himself, strongly supported the 1901 appointment of Gudrun Thorne-Thomsen to the faculty of the university as teacher of third grade in the elementary school, critic teacher, and instructor in the School of Education. She taught courses in oral reading, history, and literature for lower grades; reading in primary grades; children's literature; and storytelling.

During 1908–1909 Thorne-Thomsen was on leave from the University of Chicago to serve as a storyteller in branch libraries opened by the Chicago Public Library in park recreation buildings. These programs were jointly sponsored by the Chicago Public Library, the Chicago Association of Collegiate Alumnae, and the Chicago Woman's Club. The program was so successful that story hours became a regular part of the library's service to children. Thorne-Thomsen began retelling the old Norse folktales for children, and out of this came her first book, *East of the Sun and West of the Moon*, in 1912.

Her reputation as a gifted storyteller grew and Thorne-Thomsen was invited to lecture on storytelling throughout the Midwest, California, Oregon, and Hawaii. She annually lectured on storytelling and folklore at the Western Reserve Library School and the Carnegie Library School of Pittsburgh. In 1923 she and her husband joined the faculty of the Ojai Valley School near Santa Barbara, California, and she became the school's first principal.

Soon after her husband's death in 1936, Thorne-Thomsen retired as principal and launched a new career both as a visiting storyteller and as a recording artist for the Library of Congress and, later, for the Victor Company. Two books, *The Sky Bed* and *In Norway*, followed in the 1940s. In 1953 she was still training librarians in the art of storytelling in formal workshops and at informal gatherings.

"Perhaps the most wonderful thing of all," one of her students of that period reported, "was to make us feel that we could tell stories too; that it was not some difficult art to be mastered by only a few gifted individuals, but the rightful heritage of us all and a source of great joy."[9]

She died in 1956, but not before she knew—and took joy in the knowledge—that she would be honored with a day of storytelling at the storytelling festival to be held in Miami Beach during the 1956 American Library Association conference. "You librarians who work with children," she wrote in acknowledgment of the honor, "I congratulate you on keeping alive the art of storytelling."[10]

MARY GOULD DAVIS (1882–1956)

Mary Gould Davis was born in Bangor, Maine, on February 13, 1882, the seventh of eight children. Shortly thereafter, the family moved to the Cumberland Mountains of Kentucky and, although they finally settled in New York in 1896, Davis never lost her love for Kentucky and the mountain folk. Every night her mother read to the children, or their Irish nurse told them stories. It was a book-loving family, and half a century later Davis still shared these stories and poems with boys and girls. According to Davis, she had a "haphazard education" under the guidance of a governess and in private schools, and then began her career in the Brooklyn Public Library. In 1910 she went to the New York Public Library, where she became an assistant to Anna Cogswell Tyler, whom she succeeded.

The new supervisor believed that only training and experience can make storytelling effective and that a controlled story hour encouraged the children to listen with a deep quietness, and so New York Public Library story hours, under her direction, were formal and dignified, with fresh flowers, a "wishing candle," and books on the table. The story-hour line, the well-planned program, careful selection of stories—all were part of Davis's philosophy. An adult who heard her tell stories during this period described her telling and the children's reactions to her:

> For them she changed these stories from being something with which you kept children quiet at the end of the day into something they must have, a part of their heritage of wonder and laughter, of understanding, of perception. The telling of a tale deserved the creative effort and discipline which a work of art demands. I have often wished I could draw adequately the faces of one of the audiences. Over all of them, young and old, passed each emotion evoked by the tale—awe, solemnity, suspense, and the quick flicker of humor. Her voice was gifted, her timing perfect, her gestures controlled. There was never anything histrionic, for a story was never a medium for her own virtuosity, but her consummate skill was the medium for her story. "That Foolish Mr. Bun," "The Timid Little Hare," "Molly Whuppie" have been passed on with as vivid and distinct personalities as those of people we know well.[11]

Beginning in 1923 Davis found time to travel abroad—to England, Italy, Spain, the island of Skye in Scotland—to search out stories and to trace versions of those she already knew. *Truce of the Wolf* was her collection of tales from Tuscany and Umbria, and *Three Golden Oranges and Other Spanish Folk Tales*, with Ralph Boggs, was a collection of stories from Spain. In 1945 she collaborated with Ernest Kalibala in *Wakaima and the Clay Man*, a collection of East African folktales. She wrote a short biography of Randolph Caldecott, which was published on the occasion of the one hundredth anniversary of his birth, prepared new editions of the Andrew Lang "color" fairy-tale books, and contributed to many periodicals and encyclopedias. For several years she was editor of a department of the *Saturday Review of Literature*, "Books for Young People." From the classes she taught at the School of Library Service, Columbia University, storytellers carried her philosophy across the country and abroad. Davis retired from the New York Public Library in 1945 and died in April 1956.

The first day of the Miami Beach Storytelling Festival at the American Library Association conference, held in June 1956, was dedicated to Davis, and admiring librarians told stories there in her honor (Figure 2).

Another storyteller who was honored at the festival was Ruth Sawyer.

RUTH SAWYER (1880–1970)

Ruth Sawyer was born in Boston in 1880 but grew up in New York City where she was educated in private schools and in the Garland Kindergarten Training School. Her introduction to storytelling came from her Irish nurse, Johanna, who instilled in her a deep love of Irish folklore. Sawyer began telling stories and collecting folklore when she was sent to Cuba in 1900 to organize kindergartens. At Columbia University, where she had been awarded a scholarship, she studied folklore. She began to tell stories in schools, and then came the memorable experience of hearing Shedlock tell Andersen fairy tales. "It was Miss Shedlock who lighted the fuse that shot me into storytelling in earnest," she wrote.[12]

Sawyer's opportunity to delve seriously into the sources of folktales came first in 1905 and again in 1907 when the *New York Sun* sent her to Ireland to write a series of articles on Irish cottage industries, Irish folklore, and Gaelic festivals. During this trip, she heard what became perhaps her best-known story, "The Voyage of the Wee Red Cap." She told this story at her first library story hour at the Hudson Park branch of the New York Public Library in 1910, and thereafter it became a part of the library's Christmas tradition. Rarely did Sawyer miss the St. Nicholas Eve program, and rarely did she miss telling one of her Christmas stories. "Rich in feeling for Christmas, gifted with a beautiful singing voice, clear memory, keen sense of humor, faith in the unseen, and indomitable personal courage and

STORYTELLING FESTIVAL

Program Chairman, Mrs. Eulalie S. Ross, Public Library, Cincinnati, Ohio

Admission by ticket only (no charge). Tickets reserved in advance but not received and any tickets still available may be picked up at the Storytelling Festival ticket table in the lobby of the Fontainebleau Hotel Ballroom.

Tuesday, June 19, 10:00 a.m.
Fontainebleau Hotel—La Ronde Room

Stories told in memory of Mary Gould Davis

Mrs. Augusta Baker, New York Public Library: "The Goat Well" from *The Fire on the Mountain*, by Harold Courlander and Wolf Leslau.

Marjorie Dobson, Public Library, Indianapolis, Ind.: "The Peddler of Ballaghadereen" from *The Way of the Storyteller*, by Ruth Sawyer.

Shigeo Watanabe, New York Public Library: "The Old Man of the Flowers" from *The Dancing Kettle*, by Yoshiko Uchida. Mr. Watanabe will tell his story in Japanese.

Mary Strang, New York Public Library: *The Nightingale*, by Hans Christian Andersen from *The Art of the Storyteller*, by Marie L. Shedlock.

Wednesday, June 20, 10:00 a.m.
Fontainebleau Hotel—La Ronde Room

Storytelling Festival continued

Stories told in memory of Gudrun Thorne-Thomsen

Eileen H. Colwell, Public Library, Hendon, England: "Elsie Piddock Skips in Her Sleep" from *Martin Pippin in the Daisy Field,* by Eleanor Farjeon.

Stephanie Fraser, Enoch Pratt Free Library, Baltimore, Md.: "Miss Cow Falls a Victim to Mr. Rabbit" from *Uncle Remus, His Songs and His Sayings,* by Joel Chandler Harris.

Mrs. Rosemarie Höhne, Public Library, Cincinnati, Ohio: "The Wolf and the Seven Kids," by the Brothers Grimm. Mrs. Höhne will tell her story in German.

Marguerite A. Dodson, Public Library, Brooklyn, N.Y.: "The Great Bell of Peking" from *The Golden Bird,* by Katharine Gibson.

Thursday, June 21, 10:00 a.m.
Fontainebleau Hotel—La Ronde Room

Storytelling Festival continued

Stories told in honor of Ruth Sawyer Durand

Mrs. Frances Clarke Sayers, storyteller, author, and lecturer on children's literature, Los Angeles, Calif.: Hero Cycle from *The Wonder Smith and His Son,* by Ella Young; "Old Fire Dragaman" from *The Jack Tales,* by Richard Chase; "The Hare and the Hedgehog" from *Told Again,* by Walter de la Mare.

F I G U R E   2.   *Program for a storytelling festival presented by the Children's Library Association at the ALA Miami Beach Conference, June 19–21, 1956.*

capacity to share the interests of others, she has been able to give dramatic joy to thousands of as strangely assorted people as ever came together upon this earth."[13]

Sawyer told stories from one end of New York City to the other. She went to nearby states and later wrote:

> One of the best of my storytelling experiences was at the Boys' Club in Greenwich, Connecticut. There were about eighty boys in the club, confirmed crapshooters, pool-players and delinquents. I held them for the first three days by telling them stories of the Ringling Brothers Circus and the few days I had been traveling with it. From the circus we passed on to Kipling, Stockton, Mark Twain, and the boys started using the library.[14]

Later Sawyer went to Spain, and the stories she heard and retold were included in *Picture Tales from Spain*. Out of this experience, too, came *Tonio Antonio*. In Mexico she found material for *The Least One*. She collected Christmas stories from around the world and brought them together in *The Long Christmas*. *The Way of the Storyteller*, a book about storytelling as a creative art that continues to inspire both new and experienced storytellers, and *My Spain*, a "storyteller's year of collecting," followed.

Sawyer was awarded the Newbery Medal in 1937 for *Roller Skates*, a story based on her childhood experiences in New York City, and the Regina Medal in 1965 for "a lifetime of distinguished contribution to children's literature." That same year she received the Laura Ingalls Wilder Award from the Children's Services Division (now the Association for Library Service to Children) of the American Library Association, for books that "over a period of years have made a substantial and lasting contribution to literature for children." Sawyer's acceptance of this award was a memorable occasion for the many storytellers who saw her stand before the large audience, a frail woman of 85 years, and with a deep and resonant voice begin, "Once upon a time . . . ."

The beautiful voice was stilled forever when Sawyer died in 1970. Beryl Robinson, a Boston Public Library storyteller who had heard her often, wrote this remembrance of her:

> Ruth Sawyer's life brought rich gifts to children everywhere. Gifts of fun and laughter and wonder. Of thoughtfulness, deep absorption, and joy. Gifts that inspire courage and bring awareness of beauty. The stretching of the imagination, the opening of the heart, and the widening of the horizons that come whenever there is good storytelling, whether given richly by the master storyteller or read from a beautifully written page. But she was also a great teacher; and countless numbers of children in the future will share in her giving as their teachers and librarians follow the way of the storyteller she so brilliantly illumined for them.[15]

CHARACTERISTICS OF LIBRARY STORYTELLING

The close connection between storytelling and reading is characteristic of library storytelling. Thorne-Thomsen, who had a strong influence on the development of storytelling in libraries, believed that imaging exercises and listening to oral literature prepared children for reading. The imaging exercises that Thorne-Thomsen used in 1908 are similar to what psychologists today call "guided imagery." Children were asked to imagine the house they grew up in, the objects in the house, the faces they remembered. When children became stuck in decoding, Thorne-Thomsen advised their teachers to abandon any further effort at that task and, instead, to tell the children a story. As children listen to stories, they create images or pictures in their minds. We now know that even if a child can decode he may not be *reading*, that is, the words and sentences may have no *meaning* for him. To comprehend the meaning of printed material, the child must understand the oral language patterns and see the images that the printed words represent. This insight into the relationship of oral literature, imaging, and reading, shared by Gudrun Thorne-Thomsen, Francis Parker, and John Dewey, was lost for many years while schools emphasized the technical aspects of reading.

The early children's librarians thought of storytelling as a form of reading guidance. The purpose of the library story hour was to introduce children to the best kind of books and to broaden their reading interests. The Carnegie Library at Pittsburgh, for instance, became famous for its story-hour cycles on Greek myths, Norse mythology, and hero tales. At the New York Public Library, Anna Cogswell Tyler (quoted earlier) carefully selected stories from books on the library shelves on the assumption that story-hour listeners would want to read the stories for themselves. Circulation figures seem to bear this out. The children's librarian at the Cleveland Public Library noted in her annual report for 1909 that Hans Christian Andersen's *The Snow Queen* circulated 93 times at the two branch libraries where the story was told at story hour, compared with four circulations at the two branches where it had not been told. Such early reports show that the keeping of statistics to justify library programs is not new.

Storytelling in libraries was widely accepted though it was not without its critics. John Cotton Dana, then librarian of the Newark (NJ) Public Library and past president of the American Library Association, thought that storytelling was the responsibility of the schools and considered it an ill use of the librarian's time and energy. Writing for *Public Libraries* in 1908, Dana labeled librarian-storytellers "altruistic, emotional, dramatic, irrepressible childlovers who do not find ordinary library work gives sufficient opportunities for altruistic indulgence," and advised any library that could spare such misguided souls "to set them at teaching the teachers the art of storytelling."[16] Fortunately, Dana's opinion reflected a minority point of view and storytelling continued to flourish in libraries. Librarians went out into the schools, playgrounds, and other recreational centers to tell stories, as reported in Moore's "Report of the Committee on Storytelling," published in *Playground* in 1910.[17]

Before leaving this early period it is worth noting, as Richard Alvey points out in his doctoral dissertation on organized storytelling to children in the United States, that approximately one million immigrants entered the United States each year from 1900 to 1913.[18] Librarians looked on storytelling as a way of integrating many diverse heritages and of teaching English and the English language orally. Libraries in ports of entry, particularly New York and Boston, carried out extensive programs among immigrants. At the New York Public Library, story hours were occasionally told in a foreign language. These story hours were conducted by a library assistant of the nationality or by a foreign visitor.

Alvey also noted the conflict between storytelling as an art and storytelling as an educational device or as a way to increase book circulation. There were few librarians like Edna Lyman Scott, who publicly stated that storytelling was "an art in itself, with the great underlying purpose of all art, to give joy to the world," and that "only as storytelling [was given] its real place in the world of art [could it attain] its full significance."[19] Nevertheless, librarians who had been influenced by the artistry of Marie Shedlock and Gudrun Thorne-Thomsen believed that storytelling demanded creative effort and discipline. Both Shedlock and Thorne-Thomsen emphasized simplicity, careful selection, and reliance on the human voice alone to convey the nuances of the story. Librarian-storytellers considered themselves to be interpreters of literature for children; their goal was "to cultivate a capacity for literary appreciation in children." This attitude, which continues to the present day, was eloquently expressed by Alice M. Jordan, head of children's work at the Boston Public Library, in an article published in 1934 in the first Storytelling Issue of *The Horn Book Magazine*: "There is, as we know, a sensitiveness to the magic of words natural in some children, while in others it waits to be wakened. . . . Out of the repetition of melodious expressions as they reach the ear comes an appreciation of language not easily gained from the printed page."[20]

The first library story hours were planned for children age nine and older. By that age children were expected to have mastered the mechanics of reading, but librarians noticed that at about the same age children began to lose interest in reading. Picture-book hours for children ages five to seven started at the Carnegie Library of Pittsburgh as early as 1902 and other libraries soon followed.

Library story hours for children of school age reached a peak in the 1920s. In Boston, Jordan estimated that in 1920 the Cronans were telling stories to 1,800 library listeners per week as well as to 4,000 classroom

F I G U R E   3. *Getting tickets for story hour, Yorkville Branch, New York Public Library, 1910. Photograph by Lewis Hine. Reprinted by permission of the Manuscripts and Archives Division. The New York Public Library. Astor, Lenox, and Tilden Foundations.*

F I G U R E   4. *At the shelves after the story hour, Webster Branch, New York Public Library, 1910. Photograph by Lewis Hine. Reprinted by permission of the Manuscripts and Archives Division. The New York Public Library. Astor, Lenox, and Tilden Foundations.*

FIGURE 5. *Italian boys listening to Pinocchio, told in their native language by an Italian visitor at the New York Public Library, 1910. Photograph by Lewis Hine. Reprinted by permission of the Manuscripts and Archives Division. The New York Public Library. Astor, Lenox, and Tilden Foundations.*

FIGURE 6. *Story hour for Russian children at Rivington Street Branch, New York Public Library, 1910. Photograph by Lewis Hine. Reprinted by permission of the Manuscripts and Archives Division. The New York Public Library. Astor, Lenox, and Tilden Foundations.*

pupils in auditorium groups. Attendance at Carnegie Library story hours peaked in 1924 at nearly 150,000.

Shift in Emphasis from Oral Narration to the Printed Word

In 1919 Macmillan created the first juvenile department in a publishing house. Other publishers soon followed. *The Horn Book Magazine*, a literary journal, and *Elementary English Review* (now *Language Arts*) began publication in 1924. The influx of illustrators from Europe after World War I—artists influenced by the impressionists and expressionists, cubists, and other postimpressionists, who brought with them a rich tradition—and the development of better methods of reproducing art in books set the stage for the flowering of the American picture book.

In 1935 the Detroit Public Library began picture-book hours for preschoolers ages three to five. Library story hours for school-age children were scheduled less frequently as attendance declined. The proliferation of organized activities competed for the children's attention, and greater administrative demands made on children's librarians left less time for story-hour preparation.

This was the period, too, of the early-childhood movement. Lucy Sprague Mitchell spearheaded the "here and now" school of publishing—here and now meaning the familiar and immediate. Although perhaps still unaware of what was happening, the library profession—along with general society—was moving toward an emphasis on information. In 1939 Elizabeth Nesbitt, then associate professor of library science at Carnegie Library School, made an impassioned plea for the continuation of the library story hour and the importance of the storyteller as an interpreter of literature for the child. Nesbitt carefully distinguished between reading for information and reading for literary appreciation.[21]

The 1940s and 1950s saw an increase in the publication of informational books for children, accelerated in 1957 when the Russians launched Sputnik and interest in science skyrocketed. Library story hours for ages three to five flourished during the baby boom of the 1950s, but the time needed for preparation for the story hour for older boys and girls was viewed with suspicion in an increasingly technological society and a cost-effective economy. "Realists" questioned the value of imaginative stories in the child's development and spoke out against the violence in many of the folktales.

There were other changes taking place too. Beginning in the 1920s thousands of Puerto Ricans came to live in the United States. In an effort to serve the Spanish-speaking community better, the New York Public Library hired Pura Belpré, "the first public librarian who preserved and disseminated Puerto Rican folklore throughout the United States."[22] Belpré's work became increasingly important as the Puerto Rican population increased—from 69,967 in 1940 to 301, 375 in 1950.

PURA BELPRÉ (1903–1982)

Born on February 2, 1903, in Cidra, Puerto Rico, Pura Belpré was one of five children of Felipe Belpré Bernabe and Carlota Nogueras. Belpré recalled growing up "in a home of storytellers, listening to stories which had been handed down by word of mouth for generations. . . . As a child I enjoyed telling many of these tales that I heard. The characters became quite real to me. I remember during school recess that some of us would gather under the shade of the tamarind tree. There we would take turns telling stories."[23]

Her father was a building contractor whose search for work caused the family to move several times during Belpré's childhood. In spite of the many moves she was an excellent student and in 1919 she entered the University of Puerto Rico, intending to become a teacher. But a year later, on a trip to New York City to attend the wedding of her older sister Elisa, fate intervened.

Ernestine Rose, branch librarian of the 135th Street branch of the New York Public Library (later renamed the Countee Cullen branch), was looking for a bilingual assistant and offered the position to Elisa. When Elisa's husband refused to let his bride work, Elisa persuaded Pura to accept the position.

Initially, Belpré was assigned to work in both the adult and children's departments. She enrolled in the Library School of the New York Public Library and Columbia University where she studied Latin American literature, puppetry, and Portuguese. It was in the course in storytelling taught by Mary Gould Davis that she first told a folktale heard from her grandmother in Puerto Rico about the courtship of the pretty cockroach Martina and the gallant mouse Perez. Belpré yearned to tell the tales she remembered from childhood but couldn't find them in any books in the library's collections. At that time it was standard library practice to tell stories only found in books, but Belpré's folkloric story made such a deep impression on Davis and on her fellow classmates that she was given special permission to tell her unpublished tales at the branch story hours.

In 1929 Belpré was assigned to the 115th Street branch in southwest Harlem, then a predominantly Puerto Rican neighborhood. In her efforts to reach the Puerto Rican community she introduced bilingual story hours and obtained permission to allow the parents of the children to attend. The parents sat at the back of the story-hour room. Noting the children's enthusiastic response to a puppet show performed by Leonardo Cimino, brother of the children's librarian Maria Cimino, Belpré created her own juvenile puppet theater and began using puppets in her storytelling.

Belpré practiced outreach long before it became popular in the 1960s. She told stories and talked about library services at churches, community centers, neighborhood organizations, and schools. She initiated the library's celebration of *El Dia de Reyes* (the Feast of the Three Kings), which is observed on the sixth of January in Puerto Rico and throughout Hispanic America with Spanish *cuentos* (stories), *bailes* (dances), and *musica* (music). In 1932 Frederic Warne published *Perez and Martina: A Portorican Folk Tale*. It was Belpré's first book and the first Puerto Rican folktale published in the United States.

When the Puerto Rican population moved to the South Bronx and East Harlem, Belpré was transferred to the Aguilar branch on East 110th Street. There she continued her bilingual story hours, reading clubs, puppet theater, and outreach programs, and helped develop the library's Spanish-language collections.

In 1940 Belpré presented a paper, "Children: The Link Between the Spanish Adult and the Library," at the American Library Association conference in Cincinnati, Ohio. During her visit to Cincinnati she met the conductor, concert violinist, and musicologist Clarence Cameron White. Belpré married White in December 1943, and took a leave of absence from the library to travel with her husband and to write. Her first collection, *The Tiger and the Rabbit and Other Tales*, was published in 1946.

After the death of her husband in 1960, Belpré returned to the New York Public Library to fill the newly created position of Spanish children's specialist. By then more than 600,000 Puerto Ricans were reported to be living in New York City.

Belpré engaged her listeners with her quiet but animated manner of telling, her expressive eyes, and her warm smile. Puerto Rican folktales such as "The Albahaca Plant," "The Earrings," "Juan Bobo," and "Perez and Martina" were favorites with her Hispanic listeners, but she could just as easily hold them spellbound with a Howard Pyle story.

Her writing continued, and in the ensuing years she published *Juan Bobo and the Queen's Necklace: A Puerto Rican Tale*; a second edition of *The Tiger and the Rabbit and Other Tales*; a Spanish edition of *Perez y Martina*; Spanish and English editions of *Oté: A Puerto Rican Folk Tale; Santiago*, an original story; *Dance of the Animals: A Puerto Rican Folk Tale; Once in Puerto Rico*; and *The Rainbow Colored Horse*. In addition, she translated several English books into Spanish, made recordings, and compiled (with Mary K. Conwell) *Libros en Español: An Annotated List of Children's Books in Spanish*.

Belpré retired from the New York Public Library in March 1968, at the age of 65, but was persuaded by Augusta Baker to work two days a week in the South Bronx project. For the next decade she visited community centers and worked with neighborhood organizations. Once again, she incorporated puppetry into her storytelling. She designed "a collapsible puppet theater that was lightweight and easily transportable throughout the city" and "instructed the library staff in the arts of designing costumes, creating theatrical props, selecting appropriate story lines, preparing scripts, and acting with puppets."[24] The shows were tremendously popular with both staff and South Bronx residents.

Beginning in 1972 she began presenting puppet shows at El Museo del Barrio, assisted by the museum staff. Belpré designed the theater and made all of the puppets. A staff member described the puppet theater as

> unique in that it was constructed like a kiosco, and in the future will be transformed into a bohio in keeping with Puerto Rican culture. Mrs. White and her assistant are fully visible to the children watching the show. In this way the children are involved in the changes and different movements necessary in order to bring the puppets to life. This however, does not at all distract the children; in fact it seems to make it all the more interesting for them since they become involved with the little intricacies that make the puppets function.[25]

During this period Belpré was a frequent guest lecturer at colleges and universities throughout the United States. Wherever she went she told her Puerto Rican folktales and fostered a greater awareness of Puerto Rican culture.

On May 20, 1982, Pura Belpré was among the honorees at the sixth annual presentation of the Mayor's Awards of Honor for Arts and Culture, presided over by Edward I. Koch, then mayor of New York City. Belpré was honored for "her contribution to the Spanish-speaking community . . . and for enriching the lives of the city's Spanish-speaking children."[26] The following morning, when her brother went to wake her, he found that she had died in her sleep. Through her books and her storytelling art, Belpré left a legacy of rich Puerto Rican folklore that can be enjoyed by all children today.

FRANCES CLARKE SAYERS (1897–1989)

Frances Clarke Sayers was born in Topeka, Kansas, on September 4, 1897. It is said that she decided to be a children's librarian at the age of 14 after reading about the New York Public Library Children's Room in *St. Nicolas Magazine*. She grew up in Texas, studying at the University of Texas, Austin, and later at the Carnegie Institute of Technology (now Carnegie-Mellon University) in Pittsburgh, Pennsylvania. Among her instructors at Pittsburgh were library luminaries Ernestine Rose and Elva Sophronia Smith, and the great Norwegian storyteller Gudrun Thorne-Thomsen. She met Anne Carroll Moore, superintendent of work with children at the New

FIGURE 7. *Pura Belpré telling to Hispanic children, New York Public Library, ca. 1938, 1939. Reprinted by permission of the Manuscripts and Archives Division. The New York Public Library. Astor, Lenox, and Tilden Foundations.*

York Public Library, and was offered work in the Central Children's Room. From 1918 to 1923 she enjoyed the vitality of the city, meeting editors, authors, illustrators, but when her family moved to Los Angeles she went with them. A year of work at the LA Public Library was followed by a year in a position at the UCLA University Elementary School.

In 1925 she married Alfred Henry Sayers, a bookman and librarian whom she had met in New York. The couple moved to Chicago, where they lived until 1932 when they returned to California to be nearer to her family. She began writing children's books based on her childhood memories of growing up in Texas, lectured on children's librarianship at Berkeley library school and other universities, and wrote numerous articles in professional journals. An eloquent speaker, teacher, writer, and storyteller, passionate about children's librarianship, Sayers was rapidly becoming a leader in her field. Aware of her growing reputation, Franklin Hopper, director of the New York Public Library, invited her to become the new superintendent of work with children at NYPL when Miss Moore retired in 1941. Sayers remained in this position until 1952, when she returned to California and was offered a part-time lectureship in the UCLA English Department. When the UCLA School of Library Service opened in the fall of 1960, Director Lawrence Clark Powell, a Sayers convert to children's librarianship, proudly introduced her as a member of the faculty.

Summoned by Books: Frances Clarke Sayers, Essays and Speeches, compiled by Marjeanne Jensen Blinn with a Foreword by Lawrence Clark Powell, is *must* reading for every children's librarian and library director. For Frances Clarke Sayers, librarianship would always be "a magnificent profession." Her speeches and essays, written well over a half century ago, still have the power to jolt citizen complacency about the role of the public library and the importance of reading for a democracy to flourish.

New storytellers will find especially memorable her essays, "From Me to You," and "The Storyteller's Art." Sayers writes, ". . . for the storyteller works with words, words that clothe and change and charge all the emotion the heart endures, or is capable of enduring—the storyteller deals with the stuff of the spirit" and "The story that is told should be equal to the telling: for the spoken word, and the memory of the spoken word, remain with peculiar potency in the consciousness of the listener. The stories we choose to tell should also make an enduring contribution to the minds and imagination of the children with whom we share them."[27]

Perhaps no one captured Frances Clarke Sayers's storytelling style in print better than her colleague and friend Eleanor Cameron, in her article, "The Inimitable Frances":

> For not only was she a most gifted and impressive teacher of her subject but an absolutely superb storyteller, with her unforgettable voice, rich and reso-

nant and with a slightly Southern glide to it, that could hold any audience mouse-quiet, and a most subtle appreciation of the nuances of a story. These she brought out to the depth and extent of their possibilities, not by large gestures or movements of the body—abhorrent to the skilled storyteller, when all attention should be concentrated on the story itself—but by the rhythms of her telling, the variations of tone and emphasis. To me, she always evoked the impression that the story came out of her own essence—she the magical spider spinning her web out of her own imagination and experience. Though she would have been the first to remember that her art lay in faithfully handing on, simple as the medium, what the ages have given us.[28]

Videos of Frances Clarke Sayers reading/telling stories can be found on the Internet Archive.

Over the years Frances Clarke Sayers received numerous honors, including the Joseph W. Lippincott Award for Distinguished Service in the Profession of Librarianship (1965); the Clarence Day Award for *Summoned by Books* (1966); a Southern California Council Literature for Children and Young People Award (1969); the California Library Association Edna Yelland Award (1970); and the Catholic Library Association's Regina Medal for a lifetime dedication to the cause of excellence in children's literature (1973).

AUGUSTA BAKER (1911–1998)

Augusta Baker enjoyed a multifaceted career—as children's librarian, administrator, teacher, author, anthologist, reviewer, speaker, consultant, and radio and television presenter. But the first word that comes to mind to all who knew her is *storyteller*.

Born April 1, 1911, in Baltimore, Augusta grew up surrounded by books and stories. After attending the University of Pittsburgh for two years, she transferred to the State University of New York at Albany and received her B.A. in education in 1934. But teaching wasn't for her. She went on to earn a B.S. in library science and began her career as a children's librarian at the New York Public Library in 1937. In 1953 she went to Trinidad to organize children's work in the Trinidad Public Library. That same year she was appointed assistant coordinator of children's services and storytelling specialist at the New York Public Library. She served in that position until 1961 when she became coordinator of children's services, supervising 80 children's rooms.

During her 37 years at the New York Public Library, Baker founded the James Weldon Johnson Memorial Collection (books about black history and culture for children), located at the Countee Cullen Regional Branch; conceived and edited the first six editions of *The Black Experience in Children's Books*; coauthored the first two editions of *Storytelling: Art and Tech-*

nique with Ellin Greene; and edited three books: *The Talking Tree, The Golden Lynx*, and *Young Years*. She was the author of numerous articles, reviews, and forewords. Baker served on the board of directors and, in 1968, as president of the Children's Services Division (now ALSC) of the American Library Association. She also served on the ALA Council and executive board, and chaired several committees.

Baker retired from the New York Public Library in 1974, and in 1980 moved to Columbia, South Carolina, to be near her son and granddaughters. Almost immediately the University of South Carolina created the position of storyteller-in-residence for her. In addition to teaching a course in storytelling, she gave state workshops for the Department of Social Services, nursery schools, and area colleges. She retired from this position in 1994.

Since April 1986, the Richland County Public Library and the School of Library and Information Science, University of South Carolina, have sponsored "A(ugusta) Baker's Dozen," a two-day storytelling festival in honor of this extraordinary woman. On the Friday morning, fourth-grade students are bused in from all over the Columbia area to hear stories. A program of interest to adults, featuring a prominent author, illustrator, or publisher, is held on Friday evening. The next morning there is a storytelling program for families.

Baker was a guest instructor in storytelling at many universities, including Columbia, the New School for Social Research, New York University, Rutgers, the State University of New Jersey, Syracuse University, and the universities of Nevada, South Florida, and South Carolina. She held honorary doctorates from St. John's University and the University of South Carolina. In 2005, the University of South Carolina established the Augusta Baker Chair in Childhood Literacy, currently endowed at $1.5 million with the goal of reaching $3 million. For further information about the Chair, contact Ellen Shuler at ShulerE@gwm.sc.edu.

Author Betsy Byars once said that Augusta Baker was like the lace snail who left a trail of silken white lace behind, wherever she went. In recognition of her achievements she received many awards, including the first Dutton-Macrae Award (for advanced study in the field of library work with children and young people); the *Parents Magazine* Medal for Outstanding Service to the Nation's Children; the ALA Grolier Award (for outstanding achievement in guiding and stimulating the reading of children and young people); the Constance Lindsay Skinner Award, Women's National Book Association; the Clarence Day Award (for leadership given to the world of children's books); the Regina Medal, Catholic Library Association; and the Distinguished Service Award, Association for Library Service to Children, American Library Association.

Baker often spoke of the impact that storytellers have on children. "I meet adults on the street and they say, 'I was at your story hours,' and they turn to their children and say, 'This is the woman who used to read me stories when I was little.'" In her acceptance for the 1971 Constance Lindsay Skinner Award, she returned the compliment: "Through the years boys and girls have strengthened my love for storytelling as they have settled in their seats, fixed their eyes on me, and settled down as I have said 'Once upon a time.' This has been one of my best rewards and I give thanks for it."[29]

As indicated earlier, during the political and social upheaval of the 1960s librarians reached out into the community with a fervor matched only by their pioneer counterparts at the turn of the century. They held stair-step story hours in urban ghettos and worked with Head Start teachers. Some of the children who attended these programs came from cultures rich in the oral tradition. A greater number were born into families that had neither an oral nor a print tradition. Librarians sought simpler storybooks to use with preschoolers who were not used to being read to at home. Music, especially the singing of folk songs, was added to the story-hour program. Story hours became less literary, less structured. Film programs and multimedia story hours became increasingly popular with children who were growing up with television.

Impact of Professional Storytellers on Library Storytelling Programs

After attending the National Storytelling Association's first storytelling festival in 1973, cousins Connie Regan and Barbara Freeman decided to leave their positions as librarians in Chattanooga, Tennessee, to become traveling storytellers. Since 1975, thousands of librarians, teachers, and children have heard this popular duo, known as "The Folktellers." The Folktellers' success inspired others to leave their first profession to join the ranks of professional storytellers, that is, people who make their living solely or primarily through storytelling. Probably not since the Middle Ages have there been so many professional storytellers! They tell in coffeehouses, concert halls, theaters, churches, museums, and parks, as well as in schools and libraries. Their audiences include adults and children, and their performances are entertainment-oriented.

In an interview in *The Horn Book Magazine* Augusta Baker expressed her concern over the trend toward the use of personal stories in storytelling, popularized by many professional storytellers, and the emphasis on performance.[30] Children enjoy hearing personal anecdotes from people important in their lives. Anne Carroll Moore, one of the earliest advocates of storytelling in the library, told personal anecdotes in her informal story hours at Pratt Library.[31] But children also need to know their literary heritage. This is especially true for older children and young adults. (Former children's librarian and professional storyteller Beth Horner addresses this aspect of storytelling in Chapter 9.)

Pertaining to Baker's concern about the emphasis on performance, the shift in modern folklore scholarship from the study of the story itself to the study of the story within its context has served to reinforce the modern teller's focus on performance and the audience's reaction to it. Folklorists consider the physical and social environment in which the story is told essential for an understanding of its meaning, and the storyteller's voice, gestures, and interaction with the listeners are as important as the story itself.

Ellin Greene reflected on the professional storytellers' effect on librarian-storytellers in an article titled "There Are No Talent Scouts . . . ."[32] The title of the article comes from Mary Gould Davis, who used to tell her students at Columbia University Library School, "There are no talent scouts in the audience of children," meaning that the story is more important than the teller. In this respect the librarian-storyteller's presentation is closer to that of the traditionalist than to that of the professional storyteller where the emphasis is as much, or even more so, on the performance as on the story. The traditionalist tells stories absorbed from a storytelling community while the librarian-storyteller usually tells from a background in storytelling literature, although he or she may combine elements of both traditions. It was said of Gudrun Thorne-Thomsen, "when she told a story, it was like watching a tree grow; you felt it coming from such roots!"[33]

Introducing children to literature through reading aloud and storytelling and encouraging them to participate in the creative act of story listening and telling require different skills than performing for large audiences (see Chapter 6).

While guest storytellers have always been an inspirational part of the library tradition—one has only to think of Marie Shedlock, Gudrun Thorne-Thomsen, and Ruth Sawyer—the library storytelling program was never dependent upon guest storytellers. Storytelling should not be limited to "special occasions" when the budget allows for a professional teller. Children are enriched by the experience of hearing stories told by both guest storytellers and by their beloved librarian-storyteller.

Award-winning professional storyteller *and* children's librarian Carol Birch comments:

> The two platforms for storytelling offer different opportunities and challenges. For those of us who work with children within a single institution, our great opportunity derives from our relationships with listeners. Years of contact— along with years of stories—build on each other; both contribute to a larger story of connection that frames individual stories. For professionals who regularly tell stories to children with whom they work, our biggest challenge is time. There isn't time to polish a story because the next program that requires new stories comes at us fast. For those of us who travel extensively as guest

storytellers, our great opportunities are the gift of different audiences who provide feedback and the gift of time to polish stories. Our challenge is the road with its grind and the disconnect of travel."[34]

IMPACT OF EARLY-CHILDHOOD RESEARCH ON LIBRARY PROGRAMMING

Burton L. White's research while director of Harvard University's preschool project from 1965 to 1978 demonstrated the importance of interaction between children and their caregivers during the first three years of life, and that interaction's impact on language development, later cognitive functioning, personality, and social behavior. Other researchers, among them Howard Gardner and Brian Sutton-Smith, were exploring the young child's sense of story. Vivian Gussin Paley, a kindergarten teacher at the laboratory schools of the University of Chicago, was doing seminal work on the use of storytelling in the early-childhood classroom, for which she later received a MacArthur Foundation award.

Jean Piaget, the eminent Swiss psychologist who received recognition in Europe in the 1930s for his theories of cognitive development, was becoming more widely known to Americans through translations and interpretations of his writings. Piaget considered assimilation and accommodation to be the two most important processes for human functioning. The process of assimilation involves abstracting information from the outside world and putting the information into the organizing schemes that represent what the child already knows. Accommodation is the process by which the child modifies these schemes to fit his or her stage of developing knowledge. Betty Weeks, an early-childhood educator at the National College of Education in Evanston, Illinois, believed that listening to stories helps children with these processes. After listening to the story of Persephone, on a brisk March day with a tinge of spring in the air, a five-year-old remarked, "Mrs. Weeks, I don't think Persephone is with her mother quite yet."

In 1976 Bruno Bettelheim published his widely discussed *The Uses of Enchantment: The Meaning and Importance of Fairy Tales*. Bettelheim's Freudian interpretations of familiar folktales have been challenged, but his book served to call attention to the need for stories and storytelling during childhood.

THE CURRENT SCENE

Even before the rise of a professional class of storytellers, librarians had changed their priorities from story hours for older boys and girls to storytimes for younger children. Today, almost every public library offers picture-book programs for preschoolers and children in the primary grades. The availability of beautiful picture books for young children and of traditional folk and fairy tales in picture-book format encourages this practice.

In response to the growing evidence that children under the age of three were capable of responding to stories on a more sophisticated level than formerly thought, children's librarians began experimenting with toddler storytimes—storytelling programs designed for children from eighteen months to three years of age, accompanied by a caregiver. At the same time, the noticeable lack of storybooks appropriate for toddlers led publishers to bring out attractive board books by talented authors and illustrators. Most public libraries in the United States offer toddler storytimes. Many also offer programs for babies, accompanied by a caregiver. The latest research in early brain development supports the value of parent-child-centered programs in which the very young interact with books and caring adults. We have come full circle to the Mothers' Room programs of the 1930s!

In 2000 the National Institute of Child Health and Human Development (NICHD) published a report by the National Reading Panel, "Teaching Children to Read: Evidence-Based Assessment of the Scientific Literature on Reading and Its Implications for Reading Instruction." Based on the report's findings, the NICHD identified six early literacy skills (see p. 133). In response, librarians created a new program, Every Child Ready To Read@your library (ECRR), a partnership between the Public Library Association (PLA), the Association for Library Service to Children (ALSC), and NICHD. The goal of ECRR is to help parents raise children who love to read and love to use the library (see Chapter 8).

Today, only a relatively small number of libraries offer story hours for children over eight years of age on a *regular* (weekly, semi-monthly, or monthly) basis. The tendency is to invite a professional storyteller to visit the school or public library as the budget allows and to hold storytelling programs in between visits as special-occasion events. These programs are less likely to be publicized as "Story Hours" as the term has become associated with storytelling for young children. However, the decline of the formal story hour doesn't mean that older children aren't being exposed to storytelling. More family story programs are being held. Third graders through teenagers are being introduced to storytelling through storytelling workshops conducted by the local children's librarian or by a visiting professional storyteller, and they, in turn, are telling stories to younger children and to each other.

The whole-language movement made teachers more aware of children's literature and they were eager to learn effective ways of sharing literature with children. Through the work of Marie Shedlock and Gudrun Thorne-Thomsen, librarians and teachers realized the power of storytelling in passing on to children their literary heritage and this is still the primary purpose of storytelling to children in school and library settings. "True literacy comes from a deep-rooted love for stories ... stories that enable children access to the magical worlds of written texts and the infinite possibilities to which these texts invite them."[35] Unfortunately, the current emphasis on "teaching to the test" too often means literature-sharing in the classroom is neglected. Librarians can encourage parents to read aloud or tell stories to their young children every day; they can encourage teachers to read aloud or tell stories in their classrooms every day; they can teach older children and teenagers how to read aloud or how to tell stories to younger children in the library; they can conduct storytelling workshops for day-care staff and other adults who work with children; and they can use storytelling techniques in book talks and tell stories during class visits.

Annual storytelling events—such as the New York Public Library's storytelling symposium held early in May in honor of Marie Shedlock's birthday; "A(ugusta) Baker's Dozen: A Celebration of Stories," sponsored by the Richland County Public Library, the School of Library and Information Science at the University of South Carolina, and the South Carolina State Library every April; and the summer conference sponsored by the National Storytelling Network—offer inspiration to both novice and experienced storytellers. As the renowned librarian-storyteller Frances Clarke Sayers exclaimed, "It [storytelling] is a deathless art, lively and diverse, which like music, refreshes and revives those whom it touches even in its farthest reaches."[36]

REFERENCES

1. Betsy Hearne, "Ruth Sawyer: A Woman's Journey from Folklore to Children's Literature," *The Lion and the Unicorn* 24:2 (2000): 279–307.

2. Elizabeth Keith Botset, "The Once-Upon-a-Time Hour," *Carnegie Magazine* 6 (February 1933): 266–269.

3. Anne Carroll Moore, *My Roads to Childhood: Views and Reviews of Children's Books* (Doubleday, 1939), p. 145. (Horn Book, 1970)

4. Alice M. Jordan, "The Cronan Story Hours in Boston," *The Horn Book Magazine* 26 (November–December 1950): 460–464.

5. Moore, *My Roads to Childhood*, p. 145.

6. Ibid.

7. Anna Cogswell Tyler, in a report dated 1909 in the files of the Office of Children's Services, New York Public Library.

8. Anne Carroll Moore, "Report on Storytelling," *Library Journal* 35 (September 1910): 408.

9. Jasmine Britton, "Gudrun Thorne-Thomsen: Storyteller from Norway," *The Horn Book Magazine* 34 (February 1958): 27.

10. "Storytelling Festival at Miami Beach," *Top of the News* 13:1 (October 1956): 7.

11. Mary Rogers, in a letter in the files of the Office of Children's Services, New York Public Library.

12. Virginia Haviland, *Ruth Sawyer* (Walck, 1965), p. 22.

13. Anne Carroll Moore, "Ruth Sawyer, Story-Teller," *The Horn Book Magazine* 12 (January-February 1936): 34–38.

14. Ibid., p. 37.

15. Beryl Robinson, "Ruth Sawyer: 1880–1970," *The Horn Book Magazine* 46 (August 1970): 347.

16. John Cotton Dana, "Storytelling in Libraries," *Public Libraries* 13 (1908): 350.

17. Anne Carroll Moore, "Report of the Committee on Storytelling," *Playground* 4 (August 1910): 162ff. Reprinted in *Library Work with Children* by Alice I. Hazeltine (Wilson, 1917), pp. 297–315. (Paperback edition: Quill Pen Classics, 2008, pp. 287-307.)

18. Richard Gerald Alvey, *The Historical Development of Organized Storytelling to Children* (University Microfilms Intl., 1981), p. 16.

19. Ibid., p. 35.

20. Alice M. Jordan, "Story-Telling in Boston," *The Horn Book Magazine* 10 (May 1934): 182.

21. Elizabeth Nesbitt, "Hold to That Which Is Good," *The Horn Book Magazine* 16 (January–February 1940): 7–15.

22. Julio L. Hernandez-Delgado, "Pura Teresa Belpré, Storyteller and Pioneer Puerto Rican Librarian," *The Library Quarterly* 62 (October 1992): 425–440. The section on Pura Belpré is based on material in this article and on Ellin Greene's personal recollections.

23. Pura Belpré, "I Wish to Be Like Johnny Appleseed." n.d., Pura Belpré Papers, Centro de Estudios Puertorriquenos, Hunter College Eveline Lopez Antonetty Puerto Rican Research Collection.

24. Lillian Lopez, Interview by Julio L. Hernandez-Delgado, May 31, 1989.

25. Mary Segarra Diaz, *Quimbamba: Bilingual Education Quarterly* (January 1973): 13.

26. Susan Heller Anderson, "Six Patrons of the Arts Receive Mayor's Awards of Honor," *New York Times*, May 21, 1982.

27. Frances Clarke Sayers, "From Me to You"; "The Storyteller's Art" in *Summoned by Books: Essays and Speeches*, by Frances Clarke Sayers, compiled by Marjeanne Jenson Blinn (Viking, 1965), p. 96; p. 99.

28. Eleanor Cameron, "The Inimitable Frances," *The Horn Book Magazine* 62 (March/ April 1991): 181.

29. Augusta Baker, Acceptance speech 1971 Constance Lindsay Skinner Award.

30. Henrietta M. Smith, "An Interview with Augusta Baker," *The Horn Book Magazine* 71 (May–June 1995): 292–296.

31. Frances Clarke Sayers, *Anne Carroll Moore: A Biography* (Atheneum, 1972), p. 77.

32. Ellin Greene, "There Are No Talent Scouts. . . ." *School Library Journal* 29 (November 1982): 25–27.

33. Frances Clarke Sayers, "A Skimming of Memory," *The Horn Book Magazine* 52 (June 1976): 273.

34. Carol Birch, correspondence with Ellin Greene (February 15, 2008).

35. Tina-Jill Gordon, "Teachers Telling Stories: Seven-, Eight-, and Nine-Year-Year-Old Children's Written Responses to Oral Narratives" (Ed.D. diss., Rutgers University, 1991), p. 107.

36. Frances Clarke Sayers, "Storytelling," in *Anthology of Children's Literature*, by Edna Johnson, Evelyn R. Sickels, and Frances Clarke Sayers, 4th rev. ed. (Houghton, 1970), p. 1146.

WEB RESOURCES

Spinning Straw into Gold: Becoming a Storyteller at the Library: An Infopeople Workshop.
http://infopeople.org/training/past/2005/spinning/
Created by Gay Ducey, March–July 2005

3 PURPOSE AND VALUES OF STORYTELLING

In researching this book (Story Proof: The Science Behind the Startling Power of Story), I have reviewed over 350 research studies from fifteen separate fields of science. Incredibly, every one of those studies, as well as every other study they cite—every one—agrees that stories are an effective and efficient vehicle for teaching, for motivating, and for the general communication of factual information, concepts, and tacit information. Not one doubted or questioned the effectiveness of stories.

—Kendall Haven[1]

WHAT IS STORYTELLING? What is its purpose? What are its values? In an attempt to define storytelling, participants at a conference sponsored by the National Storytelling Association in 1989 spoke of "oral narration," "communication," "transmission of images," "revelation," "co-creation," "creating order out of chaos," and "worship." It seems easier to agree on what storytelling is *not*. Storytelling is not recitation, nor is it acting.

Lewis Carroll called stories "love gifts";[2] contemporary author Jean Little calls them "invitations to joy."[3] Both are apt descriptions, for telling a story is, indeed, giving a gift. Storytelling brings to the listeners heightened awareness—a sense of wonder, of mystery, of reverence for life. This nurturing of the spirit-self is the primary purpose of storytelling, and all other uses and effects are secondary.

Storytelling is a sharing experience. When we tell, we show our willingness to be vulnerable, to expose our deepest feelings, our values. That kind of nakedness that says we care about what we are relating invites children to listen with open minds and hearts.

Enjoying a story together creates a sense of community. It establishes a happy relationship between teller and listener, drawing people closer to one another, adult to child, child to child. This rapport carries over into other areas as well, for children tend to have confidence in the person who tells stories well.

Library storytelling grew out of a desire to introduce children to the pleasures of literature, to excite children about books and reading. This viewpoint was eloquently expressed by Elizabeth Nesbitt:

Story-telling provides the opportunity to interpret for the child life forces which are beyond his immediate experience, and so to prepare him for life itself. It gives the teller the chance to emphasize significance rather than incident. It enables her, through the magic quality of the spoken word, to reveal to the child the charm and subtle connotations of word sounds, all the evanescent beauty emanating from combinations of words and from the cadence, the haunting ebb and flow, of rhythmical prose. It is through the medium of interpretation that all of us, adults and children, come to genuine appreciation. . . . Story-telling, rightly done, is such an art.[4]

By making the connection between storytelling and books—by telling a story and indicating the book from which it comes and pointing out that hundreds of other wonderful tales can be found in books—the storyteller is introducing reading as a source of enjoyment throughout life. With so many children's books in print, it is possible for a child to read a great number without reading even one worthwhile book. Through storytelling and reading aloud we can introduce books of quality that otherwise might be missed. Too, children are often ready for the literary experience a book offers before they are able to read it on their own. *Charlotte's Web* is the classic example of a book that can be enjoyed on several levels. Reluctant readers, who may never read fiction or fantasy, can also have a share in literature through the experience of hearing stories told or read aloud.

In our multicultural, multilingual classrooms and libraries, there will be children who are experiencing difficulty making the transition from oral to written narrative, as well as children from homes where books and reading are not valued. Storytelling can provide a transition, a bridge to reading. Storytelling allows these children to lose themselves in a story in the same way that fluent readers lose themselves in a book. And because the words go directly from the ear to the brain, story listening is an invaluable experience for beginning readers, reluctant readers, or children who have difficulty comprehending what they are reading.

From listening to stories, children develop a richer vocabulary. A kindergarten teacher who was telling "One-Eye, Two-Eyes, and Three-Eyes" to her class for the second time said the mother was very "angry." The children corrected her: "She was FURIOUS." The way the children emphasized "furious" made it clear that their first meeting with the word was in the story and it had make a strong impression on them.

The storyteller works with words. The sound of words, the way an author puts words together to form a rhythmic pattern, pleases the ear and evokes a physical response from the young child. Research indicates that there is a connection between the development of motor ability and language competence. That there is such a relationship comes as no surprise to anyone who has ever held an infant and shared aloud Mother Goose rhymes. The young child responds to the rollicking verses with rhythmic movements of the body.

> To market, to market, to buy a fat pig,
> Home again, home again, jiggety-jig;
> To market, to market, to buy a fat hog,
> Home again, home again, jiggety-jog.

The enjoyment of sound and rhythm is enhanced by the sensuous pleasure of close body contact.

But Mother Goose rhymes have more to offer than rhythm and repetition. A Mother Goose rhyme is a mini-drama. Consider, for example, "The Old Woman and Her Pig." This simple tale has characters, conflict, and action that lead to a climax and satisfying resolution. The old woman must persuade her obstinate pig to go over the stile so that she can get home. She appeals to quite ordinary objects—a stick, fire, water, rope—and to common animals—a dog, ox, rat, cat—for help. These usually inanimate objects and dumb animals act with wills of their own, entering into the conflict. The conflict is resolved when the old woman fills the cat's request for a saucer of milk, thus starting a sequence of events that culminates in the pig's jumping over the stile.

Children find pleasure in the way an author uses words to create mood, to evoke response, to create images that please the inward eye, as in the following three excerpts:

Whenever fairies are sad they wear white. And this year, which was long ago, was the year men were tearing down all the old zigzag rail fences. Now those old zigzag fences were beautiful for the fairies because a hundred fairies could sit on one rail and thousands and thousands of them could sit on the zigzags and sing pla-sizzy pla-sizzy, softer than an eye wink, softer than a baby's thumb, all on a moonlight summer night. And they found out that year was going to be the last year of the zigzag rail fences. It made them sorry and sad, and when they are sorry and sad they wear white. So they picked the wonderful white morning glories running along the zigzag rail fences and made them into little wristlets and wore those wristlets the next year to show they were sorry and sad.

From "How to Tell Corn Fairies When You
See 'Em," in Carl Sandburg's *Rootabaga Stories*.[5]

Long, long ago the wind and the water were the closest of friends. Every day Mrs. Wind would visit Mrs. Water, and they would spend the day talking. Mostly they enjoyed talking about their children. Especially Mrs. Wind. "Just look at my children," Mrs. Wind would say. "I have big children and little children. They can go anywhere in the world. They can stroke the grass softly, and they can knock down a tree. They can go fast or they can go slowly. Nobody has children like mine."

From "Why the Waves Have Whitecaps," in Julius
Lester's *The Knee-High Man and Other Tales*.[6]

But that wasn't the end of Elsie Piddock; she has never stopped skipping on Caburn since, for Signed and Sealed is Signed and Sealed. Not many have seen her, because she knows all the tricks; but if you go to Caburn at the new moon, you may catch a glimpse of a tiny bent figure, no bigger than a child, skipping all by itself in its sleep, and hear a gay little voice, like the voice of a dancing yellow leaf, singing:

> "ANdy
> SPANdy
> SUGARdy
> CANdy
> FRENCH
> ALmond
> ROCK!
> Breadandbutterforyoursupper'sallyourmother'sGOT!"

From "Elsie Piddock Skips in Her Sleep," in
Eleanor Farjeon's *Martin Pippin in the Daisy Field*.[7]

Storytelling encourages the art of listening. Children experience the whole of a piece of literature, uninterrupted by questions or discussion. If the stories they hear are worth listening to, they are eager to learn the key that unlocks the symbols. Studies of children who read early indicate that hearing stories told or read aloud in early childhood is a common factor.

Story listening may have an even greater significance in the young child's life. Howard Gardner writes in *The Arts and Human Development*:

> . . . story hearing and telling is a very special, almost religious experience for the young child, one which commands his absolute attention and seems crucial in his mastery of language and his comprehension of the world. The child identifies fully with the characters and episodes in the stories and integrates them with situations encountered in the remainder of his working day, even as he incorporates names, events, rhythms, melodies, sounds, even entire passages into his night-time monologues. The central role played by story hearing and storytelling in the lives of most young children leads me to speculate that the narrative impulse plays an important role in organizing the child's world; and the auditory and vocalizing systems may require a certain amount of stimulation which, though available from many sources, seems particularly well satisfied by literary experience.[8]

Hearing stories told gives children practice in visualization. As children listen they create the scenes, the action, the characters. The ability to visualize, to fantasize, is the basis of creative imagination. It also appears to have a positive effect on social and cognitive development. Children with a strong predisposition toward imaginative play seem to empathize with other children more readily. This is of special significance to educators who fear that test-driven education has emphasized cognitive skills at the expense of affective development. The noted Russian author and specialist in children's language and literature Kornei Chukovsky believed the goal of storytelling to be "fostering in the child, at whatever cost, compassion and humaneness—this miraculous ability of man to be disturbed by another being's misfortunes, to feel joy about another being's happiness, to experience another's fate as one's own."[9]

Literature gives children insight into the motives and patterns of human behavior. Bruno Bettelheim, in his book *The Uses of Enchantment: The Meaning and Importance of Fairy Tales*, discusses the role of fairy tales in helping children master the psychological problems of growing up:

> A child needs to understand what is going on within his conscious self so that he can also cope with that which goes on in his unconscious. He can achieve this understanding, and with it the ability to cope, not through rational comprehension of the nature and content of his unconscious, but by becoming familiar with it through spinning out daydreams—ruminating, rearranging, and fantasizing about suitable story elements in response to unconscious pressures. By doing this, the child fits unconscious content into conscious fantasies, which then enable him to deal with that content. It is here that fairy tales have unequaled value, because they offer new dimensions to the child's imagination which would be impossible for him to discover as truly on his own. Even more important, the form and structure of fairy tales suggest images to the child by which he can structure his daydreams and with them give better direction to his life.[10]

In stories, children meet all kinds of people. Although folktale characters tend to be one-dimensional (which makes it easier for young children to distinguish between good and evil and other opposites), what a variety of characters live in the tales—beauties and monsters, simpletons and wise folk, scoundrels and those without guile. What a wide range of human emotion—jealousy, love, hatred, contentment, greed, cunning, anger, compassion!

Some parents worry about the violence in many folktales. In today's society even young children are exposed to violence on television or in real life. It may be of some comfort to know that psychologists believe the chants and rhythms in folktales contain the violence, enabling children to handle it. The words "Once upon a time . . . " also signal to the child that the story took place in a make-believe time and place, and that the child is safe within its confines.

Historically, storytelling has been used to educate as well as to entertain. Stories such as "Little Red Riding Hood" and "The Wolf and the Seven Little Kids" warned children to beware of strangers. "Little Eight John" and similar tales attempted to teach acceptable social behavior while other stories passed on the values of the culture. Meifang Zhang, a teacher of English at Shanxi University, Shanxi Province, China, and a former exchange scholar-researcher at the University of South Carolina in Columbia, observed that the ancient tales of her native land encouraged traditional Chinese values—respect for elders, obedience to parents, precedence of the group over the individual, and conformity to rules—whereas the new writers for children encourage individual initiative and performance. As an example, Zhang cites "Who Will Be Our Future Monitor?" by Wang Anzi, in which an obedient girl is belittled and an aggressive boy is praised. The rationale for such stories is that modern China needs *bold* thinkers.[11] (Unfortunately, this example seems to perpetuate a sexual stereotype.) Jack Zipes has written extensively about the historical/sociocultural context of folk and fairy tales. His remarkably successful program, Neighborhood Bridges (www. neighborhoodbridges.org), is designed to help young people recognize and counterbalance such influences and "become storytellers of their own lives."[12]

Storytelling is a way of keeping alive the cultural heritage of a people. It is akin to the folk dance and the folk song in preserving the traditions of a country for the foreign-born child and of building appreciation of another culture for the native-born child. Storytellers find that whenever they tell a story from the cultural background of their listeners, there is an immediate excitement.

In her book *Journey to the People*, Ann Nolan Clark wrote:

> Children need to know children of other nationalities and races so that, inheriting an adult world, they find a free and joyous interchange of acceptance and respect among all peoples. . . . There is need for awareness that each group of people has its own special traditions and customs. There is need that respectful recognition be given these special traditions and customs. There is need for acceptance of these differences. There is tragic need for loving communion between children and children, children and adults, adults and adults—between group and group.[13]

Folklore is living proof of the kinship of human beings. Among various nations, similar stories are found, but they assume a variety of forms according to the culture in which they developed. Paul Bunyan is related to Ti-Jean. More than 300 years ago the French colonists brought the Ti-Jean stories to America; they soon became French-Canadian tales, and now they are part of the spoken tradition of the country. Glooscap was the hero-trickster of a great mythology shared by the Native Americans of Canada,

Maine, and Massachusetts, and these stories show a likeness to both Norse and European folktales.

RESEARCH UPDATE

There was much anecdotal information about the values of storytelling to children when the third edition of *Storytelling: Art and Technique* was published but scant "hard" research. Slightly more than a decade later, Kendall Haven published *Story Proof: The Science Behind the Startling Power of Story*. In 1984, Haven gave up a career in oceanography for storytelling because he thought science and story were incompatible. Fortunately for us, his curiosity as a scientist led him to research story. Haven reviewed more than 350 research studies from fifteen separate fields of science (cognitive sciences, neurological science, developmental psychology, and neural net modeling). His book cites both quantitative and qualitative research, anecdotal examples and demonstrations, and includes an extensive bibliography. As a result of his research and his work as a storyteller for more than twenty-five years, Haven believes that science and story *are* compatible and that story is the most effective way of teaching and learning.

Three key truths have emerged from recent neurological research:

1. One hundred thousand years of human reliance on story has evolutionarily rewired the human brain to be predisposed to think in story terms and to use story structure to create meaning and to make sense of events and others' actions.

2. Cells that fire together wire together. The more a child (or adult) engages their story neural net to interpret incoming sensory input, the more likely they are to do it in the future.

3. This evolutionary predisposition is reinforced by the dominant use of story throughout childhood. Children hear stories, see stories, have stories read to them, and read stories themselves. This dominance of story exposure through the key years of brain plasticity results in adults irrevocably hardwired to think in story terms.[14]

Modern scientific and medical techniques have given us an understanding of how the human brain develops in the embryo and during the first years of life. Even before the baby is born the embryo is producing millions of neurons. The neurons branch out and establish synapses. Haven notes, "By a baby's second day of life, all of its sensory organs function (vision develops last) . . . For the next eighteen months a baby's brain is a learning machine—learning for the sake and joy of learning—with no need for context or relevancy for the incoming information."[15] Researchers who have explored the link between babies' neural processing and story structure conclude that we are born preprogrammed to think in, make sense in, and create meaning from story elements. The significance of this for all who tell or read stories to the very young, including librarians, teachers, parents, and other caregivers, is addressed in Chapter 8.

Haven cites numerous studies that confirm that exposure to stories and story structure improves comprehension and content recall, and develops vocabulary, language fluency, and reading and writing skills. As librarians, our primary interest lies in the relationship between story and reading, story and literacy. Worth mentioning, however, is "a particularly interesting and innovative bit of research," related by Haven: "Canadian researchers found a strong positive correlation between early storytelling activity and later math abilities. They suggested that time spent on early stories (telling, reading, and listening to stories) during preschool years improves *math* skills upon entering school. (O'Neill, Pierce, and Pick, 2004, p. 4). That says that learning story structure develops logical and analytical thinking as well as language literacy!"[16]

What is happening when we say a listener is "caught up in the story"? Every storyteller has noticed during a successful telling the faraway look in a child's eyes, indicating that something more than hearing words is taking place in the child's mind. Modern research techniques confirm physiological changes occur as children and adults listen to stories: blood pressure and body temperature lower, breathing slows, and the brain becomes more active in certain areas during this altered state of mind.

Interest in the storylistening trance, as this phenomenon is called, inspired Brian W. Sturm, associate professor in the School of Information and Library Science at the University of North Carolina at Chapel Hill, to interview twenty-two listeners immediately following storytelling performances at eight different storytelling events in the Midwest. Six characteristics of the storylistening trance emerged from the data he collected: a sense of realism (the listeners experienced a story "as if" it were real); a lack of awareness of one's surroundings; engaged receptive channels (visual, auditory, kinesthetic, and emotional); a lack or loss of control of the experience (feeling transported into the story); a "placeness" (feeling inside the story); and a sense of time distortion—time seemed to pass faster than chronological time for some listeners, more slowly for others. Sturm discusses these six characteristics in some depth—as well as the influences on the storylistening trance, such as the storyteller's style of telling, story content, length of the story, sense of comfort, technical problems, and the like—in his intriguing article "The 'Storylistening' Trance Experience."[17]

Storyteller Patrick Ryan has also written about this phenomena. Ryan describes how classic formulae devices within narratives, such as "'Once upon a time,' repetitive phrases or actions (Goldilocks trying three different things three times each, always with the same result)" and the storyteller's voice, gestures, and vocal techniques help to create altered mental states.

Ryan points out the value of the liminal state for the child. "Liminal states develop the child's sense of temporality by the incongruities between time-lines experienced in narrative and real world time. . . . The liminal state internalizes experiences and information, associating narratives with knowledge and experiences that the child already has, so developing new concepts, views, and observations that are stored for future reference. This brings enlightenment and engagement, even enchantment. . . . It remains vital to provide storytelling, oral story reading, and silent reading experiences throughout childhood and teenage years, so that all young people have a chance to enter liminal states, to develop and experience 'flow'—the place where they may be 'away with the fairies.' This 'once upon a time' state is where true engagement with story occurs."[18]

Past studies on the comparative effectiveness of storytelling presented in different media—the told story, the acted-out story, and the story presented on film—suggested that young children seem to remember the story best when some kind of interaction with the story takes place, such as in creative dramatics. When young children act out a story, they more easily identify with the characters in the story. Viewing a story on film seems least effective for recall of content. However, a later study by Laurene Brown found significant differences in *what* children took away with them from a story presented in two different media. Children ages six, seven, nine, and ten either watched *A Story, A Story* on a television monitor or heard it read aloud from the picture book. In retelling the story, the children who saw the television version used more active verbs. The book audience seemed more attentive to the sounds of language and retained more of the author's vocabulary in their retellings. For example, they called the characters by their book names, "Anansi" and "Osebo," whereas the viewers called them simply "man" and "the leopard." In interpreting the story, the book audience relied on the text and on personal knowledge and past experience.

Brown's study indicates that the oral medium helps develop language and the skills requisite to reading. The television medium, on the other hand, develops "visual literacy, skill at reading moving pictures, vividness of mental imagery, and ability to remember picture information and to produce images themselves."[19] Many educators believe that television is destroying children's ability to imagine. Brown, an educational psychologist, disagrees, and takes a positive approach toward both media. Knowing the strengths and weaknesses of each medium in literacy development is valuable for librarians and teachers.

Haven conducted an experiment in 1998 in which he presented the same two stories at six assemblies for primary-grade students at five Las Vegas schools. At each assembly, he read one story and told the other, alternating which story he read and which he told and the order of the stories. The teachers were asked not to discuss the stories or the performances with the students for twenty-four hours, at which time the students were asked to draw one picture from one of the stories as part of a class "thank you" packet. Seventy-three percent chose to draw a picture from the told story versus twenty-seven percent for the read story. From this Haven concluded that the told story enhanced memory.

Haven cites an unpublished doctoral work in which Janner (1994) presented the same story to four fourth-grade classes. "To one, he read the story; to the second, he gave copies of the story and had students read it; to the third, he showed a video of the story; and to the fourth, he told the story. One month later he interviewed selected students from each class to see how the medium of delivery affected their long-term memory of the story. The students who most accurately recalled the story and its images came from the class that had seen the video. However, they typically required extensive prompting to activate those remembered images. The students who were the most enthusiastic and excited about their recollection of the story, who most readily recalled the story without prompting, who held the most vivid and expansive images of the story, and who were best able to verbalize their memory (and version) of the story were those from the class to whom he told the story." To Haven, the studies, though small, indicated "the preeminence of story as a teaching and learning vehicle."[20]

Giving Children Time to Read and to Reflect on Their Reading

Research suggests that children need opportunities to discuss the stories they have heard and to use what they have heard to construct their own meanings. Charlotte Huck, author of *Children's Literature in the Elementary School* and a pioneer in bringing children's literature into the classroom, advised: "If we want children to become readers, we must give them real time to read, to become involved in books, and to have a chance to share books with their friends. If they are not reading outside school (and many are not) then we must reorder our priorities and give them time to read books of their own choosing inside school."[21]

Traditionally, librarians read a story straight through in order to maintain its literary integrity. Nursery school teachers, on the other hand, often interact with children during read-aloud sessions by asking questions and encouraging comments. When parents read aloud, they hold their children on their laps, focus attention on the book, and interrupt the reading to talk about what is happening. The parent's interruptions occur at places in the story where the child might not have the experience required to understand. The parent fills in, asks questions, or "scaffolds" the learning. The child's questions, quizzical looks, or misstatements show the adult what the child needs to know in order to understand the story. What we have learned from the research about the importance of interacting with the child has encouraged librarians to use more participation stories with younger children. Young children enjoy joining in the refrains, and it sharpens their listening and memory skills.

Children can be encouraged to use language by discussing stories, but there is a danger in the kind of questions asked. Aidan Chambers suggests open-ended questions, such as "Tell me about the parts you like most," "Tell me about the parts you didn't like," "Was there anything that puzzled you?" and "Did you notice anything in the story that made a pattern?"[22] During her school residences, storyteller Susan Danoff asks the children to describe the images ("pictures in your head") that they see as they listen to the story. Danoff also asks the children if they remember any special words, and how the story makes them feel. Such questions are much more appropriate than asking "Where was Cinderella when she lost her slipper?" and other questions of "fact." The ability to visualize—to make images—has been identified as an important strategy in reading comprehension. The child who can make mental images from the words on the page is better able to understand and remember what has been read. He is able to construct inferences and to make predictions. Olga Nelson found that after listening to a told story, fourth-grade students in three separate classrooms reported images that were "clear, vivid, varied, complex, multilayered, and interactive."[23] Nelson found that the images varied greatly from child to child. Visual images were reported most often, but the children also experienced auditory, olfactory, tactile, and gustatory images.

ACTIVITIES THAT EXTEND THE STORYTELLING EXPERIENCE

The whole-language movement of the 1980s and 1990s made literature more central to the school curriculum, though one could still find an overuse of workbooks and non-related activities. This is even more true since the No Child Left Behind Act was passed and "teaching to the test" is often the norm. (As this book goes to press there is serious discussion of the need to make changes in the government's program.) An activity that deepens a child's appreciation of a story is appropriate, but too often activities that have little or nothing to do with the *meaning* of the story are tacked on. To tell the story "The Blind Boy and the Loon" and then to have the children construct igloos of flour and salt or to talk about the coloration of the loon is not what the story is about. Having the children dramatize the story might be appropriate, however.

Many stories lend themselves to creative drama, and children of all ages enjoy this activity. Maria Asp and Jack Zipes consider creative drama fundamental for the Neighborhood Bridges program cited earlier, and some of the theater games and exercises used are described in detail in Zipes's book *Speaking Out: Storytelling and Creative Drama for Children.*

You might have the children retell the story to a partner or in groups of three or four. Or you might invite the children to paint their favorite character or scene, or to express visually (that is, through art) how the story makes them feel. One of the most enthusiastic promoters of reading and storytelling is Caroline Feller Bauer. Her books (see Appendix) are a treasury of activities that help children make the story their own.

As a visiting storyteller, you may be asked by the teacher or staff person how to help the children build on the storytelling experience. Storyteller Doug Lipman suggests leaving a list of appropriate follow-up activities. For example, the teacher or staff person might tell or read aloud a variant of the tale, other stories from the same culture, or another story by the same author. Lipman recommends having older children and young adults analyze the story by focusing on one or more of the following elements: similarities, motifs, plots, themes. After this activity, the students might try to create a new story by keeping the plot but changing the setting and characters, or by keeping the theme and characters but changing the plot. Or the students might make up further adventures for one of the characters in the story.

Do not feel you must engage the children in some activity after a story. In their wonderful book *Stories in the Classroom*, Bob Barton and David Booth say, "Sometimes the children are making meaning from the collective hearing/reading of the story. They may call upon the experience later. There may be no need for external response at the moment. Reflective journals, putting the story into writing, remembering the story at a later date; all are modes of responding that help children build a story frame."[24]

IMPORTANCE OF READING ALOUD

Becoming a Nation of Readers: The Report of the Commission on Reading (1985) concluded that the single most important activity for building the knowledge required for eventual success in reading is reading aloud to children.[25]

Children read to by a warm, caring adult associate reading with pleasure. In fact, parents and teachers have discovered that many children go through a stage in learning to read when they *refuse* to read themselves because they fear the reading aloud will stop!

Hearing stories read aloud gives children "a sense of story." If the stories are chosen from different genres (folktales, fiction, fantasy, biography, poetry, and nonfiction), children learn that each form of literature has its unique language, style, and structure. They learn patterns of language and develop an understanding of plot and characterization. This helps them with their own writing.

As a doctoral student at Rutgers, Tina-Jill Gordon explored the dynamic between teachers telling stories and the written narrative responses to these stories by children who are beginning writers. During the nine-week study, Gordon discovered that children "recall many details of the stories which they hear via storytelling" and that "telling oral literature stories to children inspires them to write about the stories, to imitate the stories, and to use the stories as a trigger for creating their own stories."[26] Well-known writers, such as Eudora Welty and Robert MacNeil, attest to the importance of hearing stories during their childhood. In her memoir, *One Writer's Beginnings*, Welty recalls: "Long before I wrote stories, I listened for stories. . . . Listening children know stories are there. . . . When their elders sit and begin, children are just waiting and hoping for one to come out, like a mouse from its hole."[27] MacNeil's mother read aloud to him often. Of *Winnie-the-Pooh* he wrote: "This was my first experience of being drawn into the spell cast by a storyteller whose words spin gossamer bonds that tie your heart and hopes to him. It was the discovery that words make another place, a place to escape to with your spirit alone. Every child entranced by reading stumbles on that blissful experience sooner or later."[28]

In *Books Kids Will Sit Still For 3: A Read-Aloud Guide*, Judy Freeman lists Thirteen Reasons to Read Aloud and Read Alone:

1. To bond together, either one on one, as parent and child, or together as part of a larger group.
2. To figure out how to handle new or difficult or challenging life situations.
3. To open up a global window and see how people do things in other parts of the world.
4. To visualize text and stories and exercise the mind's eye or imagination.
5. To develop empathy, tolerance, and understanding.
6. To grow language skills, exploring narrative, dialogue, the use of language, vocabulary, and the relationship between the written and spoken word.
7. To better recall and comprehend the narrative structure, plot elements, and sequence of events in a story.
8. To be exposed to eloquent, elegant, interesting, or unusual examples of language, writing styles, and words, and to hear the author's "voice" out loud, spoken with expression and fluency.
9. To share emotions, from laughter to tears.
10. To develop critical thinking skills: making inferences, drawing conclusions, identifying key words and ideas, comparing and contrasting, recognizing cause and effect, sequencing, and defining problems versus solutions.
11. To experience sheer enjoyment and the love of stories, both old favorites and brand-new ones, for their own sake.
12. To hone writing skills. As children's author Richard Peck writes in *Past, Perfect, Present Tense: New and Collected Stories* (Dial, 2004), "Nobody but a reader ever became a writer." And "You have to read a thousand stories

before you can write one." And "We write by the light of every story we ever read. Reading other people's stories shows you the way to your own."

13. To grow from an avid listener into an avid reader, learner, and thinker.[29]

That sums it up beautifully!

WHAT SHOULD BE READ ALOUD?

Once you are hooked on *telling* stories, reading aloud may seem less satisfying, but reading aloud is a good way to introduce long stories that have complex sentence structure or more description than action, stories with wordplay that might slip past the children, picture book stories, literary fairy tales that must be word perfect (such as Sandburg's *Rootabaga Stories*) or that require more time to learn than you have time to give, or chapter stories. Read aloud from books that children might miss because the text is too difficult for them to read on their own at the time they are interested in the story. By reading a short selection or chapter, you may entice a few of the children into reading the entire book for themselves.

Choose a variety of story types. Younger children like stories about animals, humorous tales, and stories about children who are like themselves. Older children like adventure stories, mysteries, and science fiction. Do not waste your time and the children's time by reading ordinary, dull, uninspiring, vocabulary-controlled stories. Read only what you enjoy, so that your enjoyment is transferred to the listeners.

The length of the material should be suitable to the maturity of the group. It is best to choose stories that can be read in one sitting if the children are young or if you find yourself with a different group of children each time you read, as often happens in a public library. Whole books can be read as serials, a chapter or two at a time. Myths, legends, hero tales, and tall tales lend themselves well to reading aloud. Poetry almost demands to be read aloud. Reading a poem aloud catches elements that may be missed when the poem is read silently.

One hundred of our favorite titles for reading aloud are listed in the Appendix. For further suggestions, see the aforementioned title by Judy Freeman, *Books Kids Will Sit Still For 3: A Read-Aloud Guide,* which includes more than 1,700 suggestions and *The Read-Aloud Handbook, Sixth Edition*, by Jim Trelease.

IS THERE AN ART TO READING ALOUD?

Reading aloud is an art, and like storytelling, requires careful selection and preparation. Read the material aloud by yourself to become aware of the rhythms and mood as well as the plot and characters. Know your material so well that you do not struggle over words and ideas and can look frequently at your listeners in order to involve them in the story.

Read in a natural voice but with expression and feeling. Vocal variety will keep your listeners interested. Strengthen your technical equipment—pleasant, flexible voice; clear enunciation; skillful pacing. The timing and the pause are as important in reading aloud as in storytelling. This is storytelling with the book. The reader appreciates, interprets, and calls attention to what the author has created with as much imaginative skill as possible. You might find it helpful to listen to authors reading from their own works (see "A Sampling of Storytelling Recordings" in the Appendix).

IS STORYTELLING MORE IMPORTANT THAN READING ALOUD?

Both storytelling and reading aloud are important to creating and sustaining children's interest in books and reading. Augusta Baker said that reading aloud does for a literate society what the telling of folktales does for a folk society. However, the teller, unhampered by the necessity of reading from a book, is able to communicate more fully with the listeners by using eye contact. And, as the great Irish *shanachie* Seumas MacManus wrote in the preface to his *Hibernian Nights*, "While the read story may possess the value of the story alone, the told story carries, superimposed on it, the golden worth of a good storyteller's captivating art and enhancing personality—trebling its wealth."[30] Reading aloud gives the potential storyteller a sense of security and confidence. Once you know you want to be a storyteller, close the book and begin! You will find the experience exhilarating!

REFERENCES

1. Kendall Haven, *Story Proof: The Science Behind the Startling Power of Story* (Libraries Unlimited, 2007), p. 4.

2. Lewis Carroll, *Alice's Adventures in Wonderland & Through the Looking Glass.* Illus. by John Tenniel, 2 books, boxed set (Morrow, 1993).

3. Jean Little, "Invitations to Joy," a speech delivered at the Canadian Children's Book Centre, Annual Lecture #1, 1988.

4. Elizabeth Nesbitt, "Hold to That Which Is Good," *The Horn Book Magazine* 16 (January–February, 1940): 14.

5. Carl Sandburg, "How to Tell Corn Fairies When You See 'Em," in *Rootabaga Stories* (Harcourt, 1951), p. 210. (Kessinger edition, 2008)

6. Julius Lester, "Why the Waves Have Whitecaps," in *The Knee-High Man and Other Tales* (Dial, 1972), p. 21. (Puffin edition, 1992)

7. Eleanor Farjeon, "Elsie Piddock Skips in Her Sleep," in *Martin Pippin in the Daisy Field* (Lippincott, 1937), p. 81. (Candlewick edition, 2000)

8. Howard Gardner, *The Arts and Human Development* (Wiley, 1973), p. 203 (Basic Books edition, 1994)

9. Kornei Chukovsky, *From Two to Five*, trans. and ed. Miriam Morton (University of California Press, 1963), p. 138.

10. Bruno Bettelheim, *The Uses of Enchantment: The Meaning and Importance of Fairy Tales* (Knopf, 1976), p. 7 (Vintage Books, 1989)

11. Meifang Zhang and W. Gale Breedlove, "The Changing Role of Imagination in Chinese Children's Books," *The Reading Teacher* 42 (February 1989): 406–412.

12. To learn more about Neighborhood Bridges, read *Creative Storytelling: Building Community, Changing Lives* by Jack Zipes (Routledge, 1995) and *Speaking Out: Storytelling and Creative Drama for Children*, by Jack Zipes (Routledge, 2004). Because of space limitations only five titles about the historical and cultural context of folk and fairy tales by this prolific scholar are listed in the Resources for Storytellers section.

13. Ann Nolan Clark, *Journey to the People* (Viking, 1969), pp. 27, 89.

14. Haven, Kendall. *Story Proof: The Science Behind the Startling Power of Story*, Libraries Unlimited, 2007, p. 27.

15. Ibid., p. 24.

16. Ibid., p. 4.

17. Brian Sturm, "The Storylistening Trance Experience" in *Journal of American Folklore* 113 (449): 287–304.

18. Patrick Ryan, "Once Upon a Time into Altered States: Temporal Space, Liminality, and Flow" in *Time Everlasting: Representations of Past, Present and Future in Children's Literature*. Papers from the IBBY/NCRCL Conference held at Roehampton University, London, November 11, 2006, NCRL papers 13, ed., Pat Pinsent, Pied Piper Publishing Ltd., pp. 41, 42.

19. Laurene Krasny Brown, "What Books Can Do That TV Can't and Vice Versa," *School Library Journal* (April 1986): 38–39.

20. Kendall Haven, *Story Proof: The Science Behind the Startling Power of Story*, Libraries Unlimited, 2007, pp. 120-121.

21. Charlotte Huck, "Literacy and Literature," *Language Arts* 69 (November 1992): 523.

22. Aidan Chambers, *Booktalk* (The Bodley Head, 1985), p. 170.

23. Olga Georgia Nelson, "Fourth-Grade Children's Responses to a Storytelling Event: Exploration of Children's Reported Images and Meaning Sources" (Kent State University, 1990).

24. Bob Barton and David Booth, *Stories in the Classroom: Storytelling, Reading Aloud and Roleplaying with Children* (Heinemann, 1990), p. 92.

25. R. C. Anderson, E. H. Hiebert, J. A. Scott, and I. A. G. Wilkinson, *Becoming a Nation of Readers: The Report of the Commission on Reading* (Center for the Study of Reading, 1985), pp. 74–75.

26. Tina-Jill Gordon, "Teachers Telling Stories: Seven-, Eight- and Nine-Year-Old Children's Written Responses to Oral Narratives" (Ed.D. diss., Rutgers University, 1991). Dr. Gordon is currently director of curriculum, Wall Township, NJ, Schools.

27. Eudora Welty, *One Writer's Beginnings* (Harvard University Press, 1983), p. 4. (Harvard University Press paperback edition, 1998)

28. Robert MacNeil, *Wordstruck: A Memoir* (Viking, 1989), p. 17 (Random House edition, 1992)

29. Judy Freeman, *Books Kids Will Sit Still For 3: A Read-Aloud Guide* (Libraries Unlimited, 2006), p. 43.

30. Seumas MacManus, "About Storytelling," in *Hibernian Nights* (Macmillan, 1963), p. vi. (Barnes & Noble edition, 1994)

WEB RESOURCES

Making the Case: The Research on Storytelling Is a "State-of-the-Heart"

http://www.ala.org/ala/mgrps/divs/aasl/aaslpubsandjournals/
knowledgequest/kqwebarchives/v36/365/365pollicino.cfm

Elizabeth Pollicino, May/June 2008.

National Council of Teachers of English (NCTE): Position Paper on Storytelling

http://www.ncte.org/positions/statements/teachingstorytelling

The Value of Storytelling in Education

http://www.katedudding.com/value-storytelling-education.htm

Kate Dudding

SELECTION

Out of a rich reading background to select the story that exactly fits the day or the hour or the mood . . . that is to be a happy and successful storyteller. The ability to make the Story Hour a natural part of the life of a children's room, the experience that tells us how to group the children, how to protect them and ourselves from interruption, how to make the book that we tell the story from theirs as well as ours, how to recognize and direct the enthusiasm, the imagination and the faith that the story kindles—all these things become second nature after awhile. But the power to choose—that is very much harder to come by!
—*Mary Gould Davis*[1]

THE POWER TO CHOOSE involves knowledge of self, knowledge of storytelling literature, and knowledge of the group to whom one is telling.

Storytelling flows from a deep desire to share, the desire to be open about something that has touched one deeply. The choice of story and the manner in which it is told reveal one's inner self. Although the storyteller may be recreating a traditional tale, it is his or her experience of life that enters the telling and makes the story ring true. A soft-spoken, gentle young student chose to tell for her first story Grimm's "Fisherman and His Wife." Although she knew the plot perfectly, she was unable to hold the children's attention because she could not bring to her telling any understanding of the emotional makeup of the greedy wife. She made the wife's requests sound so reasonable that the dramatic conflict was lost and the children were bored. Some time later in the course, she told, successfully, Andersen's "Swineherd," a tale technically more difficult to learn and to tell. She was successful because her empathy with the emotions dealt with in the story gave color to her telling.

The storyteller must take the story from the printed page and blow the breath of life into it. This cannot be done unless the story has meaning for the one who is telling it, because children are quick to sense one's true feelings about a story. The storyteller, then, must enjoy the content, mood, or style and must have a desire to share this enjoyment. Frances Clarke Sayers, who recalled listening to the story "The Gingerbread Boy" as a child, remarked of the storyteller, "She told it as though she were relating a tale as great in magnitude as 'Hamlet,' as indeed it was for me, because it was for her. It was mystery, and tragedy, and delight."[2]

This knowing whether a story is right for you and your listeners is attained through trial and error—through the experience of telling and listening. But it also implies an enjoyment of storytelling literature and a wide knowledge of its background. A folktale is more likely to feel "right" if the storyteller has a thorough knowledge of the literature and the characteristics, customs, and ideals of the people or country from which the story has come. A literary fairy tale, on the other hand, requires that the storyteller empathize with the author. It is this genuine appreciation on the part of the storyteller that brings an intangible, personal quality to the telling of the story.

Finding stories one likes to tell may take more time than learning them. The storyteller reads constantly in search of new material. Rereading is important, too, because a story that may not appeal to the storyteller at first reading may appeal at another time.

There is a wide variety of literature to choose from: the great body of traditional literature (folktales, myths and legends, hero tales, fables, and drolls) and modern literature (such as the literary fairy tale, fantasy, fiction, and nonfiction, including biography). A long story can be broken down and told serially, or a single incident from a book may be selected for telling.

Poetry can be woven into the fabric of the story hour—offering fresh insights on the central theme, sharpening the senses—or it can stand on its own. It is made to be shared and not taught. The blending of poetry and folktales or fairy tales is a natural marriage, for both develop a child's imagination. Their combination in a single story program can change the pace, create a mood, or add variety to the program. A poem can crystallize the meaning of a story or extend the story by reminding the listeners of a character or event in the tale. However, include a poem only if you truly like it, for false interest, dislike, and discomfort are all readily apparent to children.

Subject matter and concept must be considered in choosing poems, for these are the qualities that can place a poem beyond the comprehension and understanding of a child. On the other hand, many poems written for adults are appropriate to use in story programs for older boys and girls. As in the selection of stories, one must read widely in the area of poetry in order to make wise and appropriate selections.

There are poetry collections and poems for all ages, from Mother Goose to the Robin Hood ballads, from which to make a choice. Poems that have story content, strong rhythm, and descriptive language lend themselves well to the storytime. Quiet, gentle poems can set the mood for a special program. A nonsense poem sets the stage for a humorous story. Haiku's 17-syllable verse is often just right for a break between stories.

WHAT MAKES A STORY TELLABLE?

A good story for telling is one that has something to say and that says it in the best possible way. It is a story that has vision as well as integrity and that gives a child something to hold. There should be sound values—compassion, humor, love of beauty, resourcefulness, kindliness, courage, kinship with nature, zest for living—but they should be implicit in the story, because a good story teaches without preaching.

Some of the characteristics of a good story are:

1. A single theme, clearly defined
2. A well-developed plot

   A brief opening introduces the main characters, sets the scene, arouses pleasurable anticipation, and then, almost immediately, the story plunges into action.

   Action unfolds through word pictures, maintains suspense, and quickly builds to a climax. Each incident must be related in such a way that it makes a vivid and clear-cut image in the listener's mind. One event must lead logically and without interruption to the next. There should be no explanations or descriptions except where they are necessary for clearness.

   Avoid stories with flashbacks, subplots, or long, descriptive passages that interfere with the flow of the story. The essential movement of the story must depend on events, not on attitudes.

   The ending resolves the conflict, releases the tension, and leaves the listener feeling satisfied.
3. Style

   Look for vivid word pictures, pleasing sounds, rhythm.
4. Characterization

   The characters are believable, or, in the case of traditional folktales, they represent qualities such as goodness, evil, beauty.
5. Faithfulness to source material

   Beware of the watered-down adaptation and the vocabulary-controlled tale.
6. Dramatic appeal

   Children need and enjoy a perfectly safe edge of fear and sadness. Marie Shedlock called storytelling "drama in miniature." She believed in satisfying the dramatic instincts of the child so that no child need say, as did one little girl, "It was no good; no one was killed. There were no lions, no tigers, no nothing at all."

7. Appropriateness for the listener

A story's appeal depends on a child's age, previous story-listening experience, and interests. Restlessness often results from a poor choice. This criterion is developed at greater length in the pages that follow.

The youngest listeners, children from birth to age three, like Mother Goose rhymes, simple folk songs, lullabies, and lilting poetry. They enjoy stories with interesting sound patterns, such as *Goodnight Moon* by Margaret Wise Brown, and books that invite participation, such as *It Looked Like Spilt Milk* by Charles Shaw. Toy books and movable books fascinate toddlers. There are many titles to choose from today. In addition to familiar stories about the little dog Spot, try *Go Away, Big Green Monster!* by Ed Emberley, and *The Very Hungry Caterpillar* by Eric Carle. Children from three to five years old respond to rhythm and repetition; simple, direct plots in which familiarity is mixed with surprise; short dialogue; clear and simple images; action that quickly builds to a climax; and a satisfying ending. Young children blend fantasy with reality. In such a story as "The Three Bears," for instance, the chair and the bowl of porridge are familiar to children. Having them belong to the bears adds mystery and adventure to the story, but the situation is simple, and there are enough everyday events in it so that the children are not confused. They accept the unreal because it is close enough to the real world they know. The rhythm in stories for young children comes primarily from the repetition of words and phrases in a set pattern. Such phrases as "Not by the hair of my chinny-chin-chin," "Then I'll huff and I'll puff and I'll blow your house in" in "the Three Little Pigs" and similar repetition in "The Three Billy Goats Gruff," "The Gingerbread Man," and "The Old Woman and Her Pig" elicit a delighted response. Young children also enjoy stories like "The Bed," in which the sounds of animals are introduced. They enjoy stories in which children like themselves have adventures, such as *Alfie Gets in First*, by Shirley Hughes, *Knuffle Bunny: A Cautionary Tale*, by Mo Willems, and *The Snowy Day*, by Ezra Jack Keats.

Six-, seven-, and eight-year-olds have a peak interest in traditional folktales and fairy tales, such as "One-Eye, Two-Eyes and Three-Eyes," "Cinderella," and "Mother Holle." F. André Favat found a close correspondence between the child's psychological characteristics at this stage in development and the characteristics of the folktale (i.e., egocentrism, and a belief in magic, animism, and retributive justice).[3] Through the story content children work through their inner fantasies and come to terms with the "real" world. Listening to these tales, they are Jack the Giant Killer or

Molly Whuppie. The art form of the folktale also is very satisfying. In his introduction to *The Complete Grimm's Fairy Tales*, Padraic Colum discusses the patterns and rhymes in the folktales that make them so memorable. In "Rapunzel," for example, "the maiden has long hair and the witch confines her in a tower, and we do not know whether the tower makes it proper she should have long hair, or whether her long hair makes the tower part of the story." Good storytellers make the patterns evident. Mediocre storytellers "confuse the pattern by putting incidents in the wrong place, by using unfitting metaphors, by making a hurried beginning or a hurried end, by being unable to use the chiming words that made special, or, as we would say now, that featured some passage: 'puddle' with 'path,' 'tooth' with 'lose,' for example."[4]

Nine- to eleven-year-olds enjoy the more sophisticated folktales, such as "Clever Manka" and "Wicked John and the Devil." They like trickster tales, and such tales appear all over the world. The stories about Anansi the spider and Waikama the rabbit from West Africa are the forerunners of the West Indian Anansi tales and the American Brer Rabbit stories. Raven and Coyote are Native American tricksters. In his introduction to *More Tales of Uncle Remus*, Julius Lester wrote, "Trickster's function is to keep Order from taking itself too seriously."[5] Perhaps that explains the special appeal of these stories for this age group.

Children in the middle grades also seem to have an affinity for scary ghost stories—the grosser the better! This interest continues right into the teen years. "Mr. Fox," "Mary Culhane and the Dead Man," and any of the tales in Alvin Schwartz's Scary Stories series are sure to hold your listeners spellbound.

Children over nine are looking for something that will appeal to their developing powers of reason and judgment and to their concern about competency. George Shannon's popular Stories to Solve books, Nina Jaffe and Steve Zeitlin's *While Standing on One Foot: Puzzle Stories and Wisdom Tales from the Jewish Tradition*, and many of the African tales, such as "The Fire on the Mountain," present a challenge. Many of the African tales are of interest at this age because they all do not end "And they lived happily ever after"; these tales correspond more closely to the older child's growing understanding of the consequences of one's actions.

Take, for example, a tale from the Congo, perhaps best known in its picture-book edition, *The Magic Tree*, illustrated by Gerald McDermott. Storyteller Laura Simms recorded it under the title "Magoolie," on *Stories Old as the World, Fresh as the Rain*. It is the story of twin brothers. Their mother loves the strong, handsome twin and rejects the scrawny, weak twin. When the rejected son reaches manhood, he leaves home and, unwittingly, frees a people imprisoned in a magic tree. The people's queen, after making Mavungu (Magoolie) handsome and rich, takes him for her husband.

Mavungu is happy for a while, but after some time he desires to visit his mother and brother. Unable to dissuade him, his wife warns him not to reveal the source of his beauty and wealth. On the first visit Mavungu heeds his wife's words, but on his second visit his tongue is loosened by too much beer and he reveals the secret. As he speaks, his fine clothes turn to rags and his face becomes ugly. Though he searches, he cannot find his wife and people. The storyteller asks, "Why did he betray those who loved him? Why did he trust those who did not care?" In the typical Western European tale, at the moment of Mavungu's greatest despair, a helper would have appeared in the guise of an old crone or an animal and shown Mavungu how to find his way back to his wife and happiness. The African tale, however, leaves the young person with much to ponder.

Older children also enjoy hero tales, myths, and legends. This is the time to introduce the retellings of the *Odyssey* by Padraic Colum and the legends of Robin Hood and King Arthur as retold by Howard Pyle. The exaggerated humor of the tall tale is appreciated. Stories about Davy Crockett, Paul Bunyan, Pecos Bill, and John Henry should be told as if they were the "gospel truth."

Slightly older children, the eleven- to thirteen-year-olds, are experiencing sexual awakening and are involved in a search for personal identity. The romantic stories of Eleanor Farjeon, the bittersweet fairy tales of Laurence Housman, the more elaborate tales from the *Arabian Nights*, the modern fairy tales of Jane Yolen, and the sly humor of Natalie Babbitt's stories about the Devil are enjoyed by these young people, who are ready to appreciate the plot, the beauty of language, and the deeper meanings that lie behind the words. The subtlety of African tales such as "The Woodcutter of Gura" is lost on children in the younger age groups, but they are fine choices for young-adult and adult audiences. *A Treasury of African Folklore* by Harold Courlander is an excellent sourcebook. Its subtitle describes the range of material that is included in this book: "The Oral Literature—Myths, Legends, Epics, Tales, Recollections, Wisdom, Sayings, and Humor of Africa." It is a must for the storyteller's shelf.

Stories of coming-of-age, such as those found in Joseph Bruchac's *Flying with the Eagle, Racing the Great Bear*, and *The Girl Who Married the Moon* by Joseph Bruchac and Gayle Ross, speak to young people about courage and responsibility.

WHAT KINDS OF STORIES ARE NEEDED IN A STORYTELLER'S REPERTOIRE?

A storyteller must be flexible, as it is often necessary to change a program at the last minute. The makeup of the group may not be what the storyteller expected, or the time allotted for the program may have to be shortened or expanded. In building a repertoire, new tellers will want to include story types: action stories, romances, hero tales, "why" or *pourquoi* stories, humorous stories, short "encore" stories, and stories that appeal to a wide age range.

Though storytellers will need to have different types of stories in their repertoires for different occasions, they often find that they feel more comfortable with certain kinds of stories than with others. Stories from one's own ethnic or cultural background are usually a happy choice for the beginning storyteller.

The novice would do well to turn to folktales, stories that have been passed down through word of mouth and polished over centuries of telling. These traditional tales have the essentials of a good short story: terseness, simplicity, and vigor. They begin simply, come to the point, and end swiftly and conclusively. They are full of action, and the action is carried forward by the main characters. There are no unnecessary words, but only the right ones, to convey the beauty, the mood, the atmosphere of the tale.

These stories come from the folk—workers, peasants, just plain people. They are as old as the human race. Though they were told primarily to amuse, they also contain the key to the ideas, customs, and beliefs of earlier peoples, for life then was told in a tale, not explained in a philosophy. Thus the folktale is enhanced by simplicity and directness—and this is the way it should be.

The qualities and atmosphere of the country in which folktales originate and the differences that natural environment makes in the development of imaginative literature can be seen in a comparison of two excerpts from folktales:

> Across the wide sea-ocean, on the further side of high mountains, beyond thick forests, in a village that faced the sky, there once lived an old peasant who had three sons.
>
> From "The Little Humpbacked Horse,"
> in Post Wheeler's *Russian Wonder Tales.*[6]

At once we are in Russia, that land of vast distances. What a different mood this scene evokes:

> Ol-Ambu followed a path that led to the grassland. Where the forest ended and the plains spread out before him, he stopped. He looked over the sea of brown grass with acacia trees and thornbushes scattered over it. And his eyes fell upon the largest giraffe he had ever seen.
>
> From "Ol-Ambu and He-of-the-Long-Sleeping-
> Place," in Verna Aardema's *Tales for the Third Ear:
> From Equatorial Africa.*[7]

Likewise, the storyteller can convey to children the kinship of peoples by telling variants of well-loved tales, such as "Cinderella" ("Yeh-Shen," "Vasilisa the Beautiful," "The Rough-Face Girl") and "Rumpelstiltskin" ("Tom Tit Tot," "Whuppety Stourie," "The White Hen").

The storyteller of some experience, or the beginning storyteller who has an affinity for certain authors, will also tell literary fairy tales. The literary fairy tale is a consciously created work of art by a known author. It bears the stamp of individuality that immediately sets it apart from others. Hans Christian Andersen, Eleanor Farjeon, Laurence Housman, Carl Sandburg, Oscar Wilde, and contemporary writers Natalie Babbitt, Isaac Bashevis Singer, Barbara Picard, and Jane Yolen are among those who have distinguished themselves in this genre.

The modern fairy tale does not invariably end happily; often it leaves one thoughtful and sad. Told sensitively, reflecting the writer's own attitudes, many of the literary stories are vivid, accurate commentaries on society and the individuals who struggle within it. Characters in these modern imaginative stories are individuals with distinct personalities, as opposed to the stock characters we meet in the folktale.

Literary fairy tales tend to be longer and more descriptive than folktales. The words are filled with the beauty of sound, for the writer of the literary fairy tale is a word stylist. If the order of the words is altered, the beauty may be lost.

Some literary fairy tales are almost like folktales. Their writers base their styles on folklore and do it so successfully that their stories may have as universal appeal as the folktales themselves. Howard Pyle was a writer who used the manner of the folktale. His collection *The Wonder Clock* is built on what folklorists call the framing story. His preface begins, "I put on my dream-cap one day and stepped into Wonderland." The whole of this preface, with its power to set the stage and to convey atmosphere, should be told before each of the stories. Then let the old clock strike and tell the story that you have selected.

Howard Pyle used the rhythm of folklore and its repetition. For example, in "The Swan Maiden," the king's son mounts the wild swan and then:

> On flew the swan, and on and on, until, by and by, she said: "What do you see, king's son?"
>
> "I see the grey sky above me and the dark earth below me, but nothing else," said he.
>
> After that they flew on and on again, until, at last, the Swan Maiden said, "What do you see now, king's son?"
>
> "I see the grey sky above me and the dark earth below me, but nothing else," said he.
>
> So once more they flew on until the Swan Maiden said, for the third time, "And what do you see by now, king's son?"

But this time the prince said, "I see the grey sky above me and the dark earth below me, and over yonder is a glass hill, and on the hill is a house that shines like fire."

"That is where the witch with the three eyes lives," said the Swan Maiden.

From "The Swan Maiden," in
Howard Pyle's *The Wonder Clock*.[8]

In *Tales Told Again*, Walter de la Mare has taken nineteen familiar folktales and touched them subtly with his genius. An English countryside seems the perfect setting for his humorous elaboration of the old fable in which the hedgehog beats the quick-footed but slow-witted hare; the hedgehog has his wife (who looks exactly like him) wait at one end of the field while he remains at the other. Every time the hare arrives at either end of the field, he sees the hedgehog, or so he thinks, and hears his laughing taunt, "Ahah! So here you are again! At last!"

What Kinds of Stories Appeal to Groups in Which There Is a Wide Age Range?

Stories that can be enjoyed on different levels are good choices for the storytime group composed of mixed ages. Younger children enjoy the plot and action; older children enjoy the subtleties of humor and the interplay among characters. Younger children, hearing the story "Two of Everything" from *The Treasure of Li-Po*, by Alice Ritchie, marvel at the pot that can make two of anything the old couple puts into it, whereas older children—and adults—are amused by the couple's plight when another wife steps out of the pot! In Harold Courlander's "Uncle Bouqui Rents a Horse," young children find the mental image of two large families and livestock loaded on the horse great fun. Older children appreciate the outwitting of Uncle Bouqui. In presenting these stories, the storyteller should emphasize the aspects of the story that will appeal most to a particular group of listeners.

Where Can a Storyteller Find Stories That Have Known Appeal to Children?

One of the best sources is *Stories: A List of Stories to Tell and to Read Aloud*, published by the New York Public Library. *Stories* is an annotated list, arranged alphabetically by story title. The concise annotations evoke the flavor of the stories. The list is based on a program of regular story hours held over a period of more than a hundred years and represents the children's choices. *Stories* also includes a bibliography of Resource Materials: books on storytelling techniques and program planning, reference tools, a sampling of storytelling recordings, and a short list of films and videos on storytelling. It is indexed by type of stories, such as "Action and Participation Stories," "For Younger Children," "'Jump' Stories," "Literary Stories," "Music, Song & Dance," and "Short Stories (less than 5 minutes)." Folktales are indexed by country. The list was last published in 1990, but you may still be able to order a copy from the New York Public Library. Storytellers continue to hope that a new edition of this invaluable list will be published in the not-too-distant future.

Many of the books listed at the end of the chapters (see especially Chapters 8, 9, and 10) and in the extensive Resources for Storytellers include bibliographies of stories suggested for telling. Collections compiled by storytellers with broad experience are also an excellent source for beginning storytellers. Storytellers are very much aware of the differences between written and spoken language. Some recently published collections, such as those by Margaret Read MacDonald (see Resources for Storytellers) and *Ready-To-Tell Tales*, edited by David Holt and Bill Mooney, offer stories in a form closer to oral speech. These collections are helpful to the beginning storyteller, but there is a danger, too. It is the danger of oversimplification. Every storyteller must make a story his or her own. Each person has a distinct pattern of speaking, a distinct rhythm, and each person will interpret characters and events in a story differently. If you slavishly "copy" the reteller's version, the story will not be *yours*. Use these retellings as models, but, whenever possible, go to the sources given in the text and analyze what the reteller has done. This is part of becoming a storyteller.

HOW DOES A STORYTELLER DEVELOP CRITICAL ABILITY?

The storyteller is someone who appreciates literature as a whole and knows good language, form, and substance. Critical ability is developed by reading widely and by constantly comparing recommended versions included on storytelling lists with newly published material. Careful attention should be given to the notes in collections by such reputable compilers as Joseph Jacobs, Harold Courlander, and Richard Chase, and by reputable translators including Erik Haugaard and Elizabeth Shub.

Critical listening is developed by reading aloud various versions of the same story and selecting the one that sounds best. Listening to recordings made by fine storytellers (see Resources for Storytellers) gives one a sense of good pacing and the importance of word tone.

HOW DOES A STORYTELLER RECOGNIZE THE BEST VERSION OR TRANSLATION OF A STORY?

Every year dozens of new translations or new retellings of the old tales come into our hands. We need to test them first in the light of our own personal knowledge of storytelling literature, based on continual study and reading, and then consider their vitality and their holding power with children.

The folktales we share with children are polished retellings of "raw" folklore. They are not only less violent, they are more homogenized. However, the versions we choose must catch the flavor of the people from whom the tales come and must give a feeling for what those people value. The language should flow in the cadence of the original tongue.

The West Indian tales are a mixture of Carib and Arawak Indian, African, and European cultures. These stories are lively, dramatic, witty, and humorous. Philip Sherlock, author-editor of three collections of these tales, has modified the local pattern of speech without losing the rhythm and color of the islands. The Brer Rabbit stories as told by Joel Chandler Harris suffer from author-created dialect, while those from Julius Lester's *The Knee-High Man and Other Tales* and *The Tales of Uncle Remus* series, William J. Faulkner's *The Days When the Animals Talked*, and *The People Could Fly* by Virginia Hamilton, are good examples of tellable tales from the rich tradition of African American folk literature. *Bo Rabbit Smart for True* is retold by Priscilla Jaquith in the poetic, lilting language of Gullah.

Look for collections in which the compiler gives the sources of the stories and adds explanatory notes about the background of the tales. Look too, whenever possible, for collections that explain the context of storytelling in the culture from which the stories come, such as *The Magic Orange Tree and Other Haitian Folktales*, by Diane Wolkstein.

The World Folklore Series published by Libraries Unlimited includes background information, photographs of the people and the country, and notes about the stories and the tellers. Such information will add a subtle richness to your telling.

In selecting epics or hero tales, storytellers must be thoroughly familiar with different versions. Often they will have to make their own arrangement of the material, weaving together episodes from the various stories told about the hero, whether Robin Hood, King Arthur, or Cuchulain, that have come down by way of tradition.

Myths should reflect the people from which they originated. Compare Penelope Proddow's translation of *Demeter and Persephone* with Nathaniel Hawthorne's version in his *Tanglewood Tales*. Hawthorne embroiders the tale and diminishes the gods. Proddow retains the story's classic beauty.

Language should be beautiful, colorful, and descriptive. Compare the following excerpts from two versions of "The Golden Goose":

> There was once a man who had three sons, the youngest of whom was called the Simpleton. He was laughed at and despised and neglected on all occasions. Now it happened one day that the eldest son wanted to go into the

forest, to hew wood, and his Mother gave him a beautiful cake and a bottle of wine to take with him, so that he might not suffer from hunger or thirst. When he came to the wood he met a little old grey man, who, bidding him good-day, said: "Give me a small piece of the cake in your wallet, and let me drink a mouthful of your wine; I am so hungry and thirsty." But the clever son answered: "If I were to give you my cake and my wine, I should have none for myself, so be off with you," and he left the little man standing there and walked away. Hardly had he begun to cut down a tree, when his axe slipped and cut his arm, so that he had to go home at once and have the wound bound up. This was the work of the little grey man.

From L. Leslie Brooke's *The Golden Goose Book.*[9]

There was once a man who had three sons, the youngest of whom was called Dummling.

One day, the eldest son decided to go into the forest to cut some wood. Before he started, his mother packed a lunch for him so that he might not suffer from hunger or thirst.

In the wood at midday, he stopped work and sat down to eat. Just then, a little old man appeared before him and said, "May I have a crust of bread and some milk? I am so hungry and thirsty."

But the young man said, "If I do, I shan't have enough for myself. Be off with you!"

He left the little man standing there and went on his way. But he had not been long at work, chopping down a tree, before he cut himself and had to go home to have it bandaged.

Now this was no accident. It was brought about by the little man, who had magic powers, and had decided that anyone as selfish as this fellow should be punished.

From "The Golden Goose," in *Favorite Fairy Tales to Read Aloud.*[10]

The second version has had a stamp of approval put upon it by a "distinguished panel" of experts that includes two educators and one librarian. But how much of the color and beauty of style will be lost to the child who hears this version rather than the other!

Another pitfall to avoid is the vocabulary-controlled book. Consider Hans Christian Andersen's "Ugly Duckling":

It was so beautiful out in the country. It was summer. The oats were still green, but the wheat was turning yellow. Down in the meadow the grass had been cut and made into haystacks; and there the storks walked on their long red legs talking Egyptian, because that was the language they had been taught by their mothers. The fields were enclosed by woods, and hidden among them were little lakes and pools. Yes, it certainly was lovely out there in the country!

The old castle, with its deep moat surrounding it, lay bathed in sunshine. Between the heavy walls and the edge of the moat there was a narrow strip of land covered by a whole forest of burdock plants. Their leaves were large and some of the stalks were so tall that a child could stand upright under them and imagine that he was in the middle of the wild and lonesome woods. Here a duck had built her nest. While she sat waiting for the eggs to hatch, she felt a little sorry for herself because it was taking so long and hardly anybody came to visit her. The other ducks preferred swimming in the moat to sitting under a dock leaf and gossiping.

Finally the eggs began to crack. "Peep . . . Peep," they said one after another. The egg yolks had become alive and were sticking out their heads.

"Quack . . . Quack . . ." said their mother. "Look around you." And the ducklings did; they glanced at the green world about them, and that was what their mother wanted them to do, for green was good for their eyes.

> From "The Ugly Duckling," in *Hans Christian Andersen: The Complete Fairy Tales & Stories*, trans. by Eric Christian Haugaard.[11]

Now read the same part of the story from a Read-It-Myself book:

Once upon a time there was a mother duck. The mother duck had some eggs. "Quack, quack," said Mother Duck. "I must sit on my eggs. I must sit on my eggs a long time. One day the eggs will crack. Then little ducklings will jump out of the eggs."

So Mother Duck sat and sat. She sat on the eggs a long time. Then one egg began to crack. "Crack, crack" went the egg. "Crack, crack, crack." A little duckling jumped out.

"Jump, jump," went the duckling.

Mother Duck was so happy. "Quack, quack," said Mother Duck. "Quack, quack, quack." "Peep, peep," said the duckling. Soon another egg began to crack.

> From Hans Christian Andersen's *The Ugly Duckling*, adapted by Frances K. Pavel.[12]

The story continues in this vein until all the eggs are hatched.

Yes, the child can easily read the second version, but as Clifton Fadiman has said, "What the child-mind measurers call a feeling of mastery is often only a feeling of boredom."[13]

The storyteller rejects the versions with undistinguished language and uses the ones with smooth, rhythmic style and language that add to the musical flow of the story.

WHAT IS FRACTURED STORYTELLING?

Fractured stories are modernized renditions of traditional tales. They are often witty or bizarre. The tale may be told from the viewpoint of another character in the story; for instance, *The True Story of the Three Little Pigs by A. Wolf, as Told to Jon Scieszka*. The story may be reversed as in *The Three Little Wolves and the Big Bad Pig* by Eugene Trivizas, or the tale may be placed in a modern setting with characters speaking contemporary slang. Fractured tellings, such as those found in *The Stinky Cheese Man and Other Fairly Stupid Tales* by Jon Scieszka and *Roald Dahl's Revolting Rhymes*, are fun to share with older listeners who are familiar with the traditional versions. Younger listeners need to hear the traditional versions. They are part of every child's literary heritage.

WHAT SHOULD I DO WHEN PARENTS OR TEACHERS OBJECT TO MY TELLING STORIES WITH WITCHES, GHOSTS, AND DEVILS IN THEM?

The adults' objections usually come from a misunderstanding of the nature of folktales. Most folktale characters are symbols. The princess is usually a symbol of beauty, the witch a symbol of evil, but the meaning of the symbol varies from culture to culture. For example, in western European folktales, the dragon is a dangerous creature who devours human beings and must be slain, while to the Chinese the dragon is a symbol of good fortune. Try to educate the adults gently and calmly; be considerate of their feelings and beliefs.

Keep your listeners in mind when you choose your stories. If you choose your stories from a variety of cultures, your older listeners will begin to understand (subconsciously, at least) that folktale characters are symbols. This won't take away the magic, but it can get them thinking about cultural differences.

IS IT ALL RIGHT FOR A STORYTELLER FROM ONE ETHNIC OR RACIAL GROUP TO TELL A TALE FROM ANOTHER GROUP?

This question is asked in almost every workshop. The best answer I've ever heard is the one given by Julius Lester in his foreword to *The Tales of Uncle Remus: The Adventures of Brer Rabbit*:

> The most important element in telling these tales, or any folktale, is, do you love the tale? After all, what is a tale except a means of expressing love for this experience we call being human. If you love the tale, and tell it with love, the tale will communicate. If the language you speak is different from the language I speak, tell the tale in your language. Tell the tale as you would, not I, and believe in the tale. It will communicate its riches and its wonders, regardless of who you are. Trust the tale. Trust your love for the tale. That is all any good storyteller can do.[14]

Endeavor to seek out stories with a traceable, known history, with references and notes that indicate the source(s) of the folktale, changes made by the reteller, and the cultural context of the story. Betsy Hearne, storyteller and scholar, has described the importance of source notes and cultural respect in her *School Library Journal* articles, "Cite the Source"[15] and "Respect the Source."[16]

REFERENCES

1. Mary Gould Davis, "The Art of Storytelling," paper delivered at a meeting of the American Library Association, Washington, D.C., 15 May 1929.

2. Frances Clarke Sayers, *Summoned by Books: Essays and Speeches* (Viking, 1965), p. 96. (Viking Compass, 1969).

3. F. André Favat, *Child and Tale: The Origins of Interest* (National Council of Teachers of English, 1977). (NCTE Research Report No. 19).

4. Padraic Colum, "Introduction," in *The Complete Grimm's Fairy Tales* (Pantheon, 1944), p. ix. (Pantheon paperback, 1980).

5. Julius Lester, "Introduction," in *More Tales of Uncle Remus* (Dial, 1988), p. xiii. [See Also *Uncle Remus: The Complete Tales* (Dial, 1999)].

6. Post Wheeler, "The Little Humpbacked Horse," in Wheeler, *Russian Wonder Tales* (Beechhurst, 1946), p. 67. (Kessinger, 2008).

7. Verna Aardema, "Ol-Ambu and He-of-the-Long-Sleeping Place," in Aardema, *Tales for the Third Ear: From Equatorial Africa* (Dutton, 1969), pp. 59–60.

8. Howard Pyle, "The Swan Maiden," in Pyle, *The Wonder Clock* (Harper, 1887, 1915), pp. 232–233. (Kessinger, 2008).

9. L. Leslie Brooke, *The Golden Goose Book* (Warne, 1905), unpaged. (Kessinger, 2008).

10. "The Golden Goose," in *Favorite Fairy Tales to Read Aloud* (Grosset, 1958), pp. 5–6.

11. Hans Christian Andersen, *Hans Christian Andersen: The Complete Fairy Tales & Stories*, trans. by Eric Christian Haugaard, foreword by Virginia Haviland (Doubleday, 1974), p. 216. (Puffin, 1994).

12. Hans Christian Andersen, *The Ugly Duckling*, adapted by Frances K. Pavel (Holt, 1961), pp. 1–4.

13. Clifton Fadiman, "Holiday Handbook of Children's Reading," *Holiday* 30 (November 1961): 148.

14. Julius Lester, "Foreword," in *The Tales of Uncle Remus* (Dial, 1987), p. xxi. (Puffin, 2006). [See Also *Uncle Remus: The Complete Tales* (Dial, 1999)].

15. Hearne, Betsy. "Cite the Source: Reducing Cultural Chaos in Picture Books, Part I." *School Library Journal* 39.7 (1993): 81-83.

16. Hearne, Betsy. "Respect the Source: Reducing Cultural Chaos in Picture Books, Part II." *School Library Journal* 39.8 (1993): 33-37.

WEB RESOURCES

Professor D. H. Ashliman
http://www.pitt.edu/~dash/ashliman.html

Homepage for Professor Ashliman and contains links for an online library and other resources, including *Folk and Fairy Tales: Web Site Links* **http://www.pitt.edu/~dash/**

folklinks.html. Links for search engines, reference works, electronic texts, directories of folk and fairy tale sites, film and fairy tales, and the like.

Folklore and Mythology
http://www.pitt.edu/~dash/folktexts.html
A folk and mythology electronic texts library organized by theme, author, figure, and plot.

Library of Congress American Folklife Center
http://www.loc.gov/folklife/
Contains collections of Native American song and dance, ancient English ballads, and stories from the lives of many people across the United States.

Project Gutenberg
http://www.gutenberg.org/wiki/Main_Page
More than 25,000 free books available online.

5 PREPARATION

I think stories must be acquired by long contemplation, by bringing the imagination to work, constantly, intelligently upon them.
—Ruth Sawyer[1]

STORYTELLING IS AN ART, and like all arts, it requires training and experience. However, anyone who is willing to take the time to find the right story and learn it well, and who has a sincere desire to share enjoyment of the story, can be a successful storyteller. A good part of our daily conversation is composed of stories, incidents, and anecdotes, for we are all storytellers a few steps removed from platform storytellers. Our language is somewhat less formalized, but we are still sharing our experiences and emotions.

BASIC APPROACHES TO LEARNING A STORY

Storytelling is an individual art and each storyteller must discover his or her own best method of learning a story. However, there seem to be two basic approaches: the visual and the auditory. In the visual approach, the storyteller sees the story in a series of pictures, much like the pictures in a slide show. In learning the story of "The Woman Who Flummoxed the Fairies,"[2] for example, the storyteller might see the following pictures:

1. the woman baking cakes and pastries for a wedding or a christening
2. the fairies longing for a bit of her cake and plotting to steal her away to be their baker
3. the woman baking cakes in the castle kitchen for the great wedding
4. the fairies hiding in flower cups and under leaves along the woman's path home
5. the fairies flying out at the woman and letting fern seeds drift into her eyes to make her sleepy
6. the woman asleep on the fairy mound
7. the woman waking up in fairyland and pretending to be happy and willing to bake a cake for the fairies
8. the woman asking the fairies to fetch things from her kitchen so that she can bake a cake for them

9. the fairies fetching the eggs, sugar, flour, butter, bowl, wooden spoons, and egg whisk, till they are tired out

10. the woman asking first for her cat, then for her dog, her babe, and finally her husband

11. the woman beating the cake batter, the baby screaming, the cat purring, the dog snoring, and the husband looking bewildered

12. complete bedlam—the woman giving the baby the spoon to bang with, the husband pinching the dog and treading on the tail of the cat

13. the fairies exhausted by the noise

14. the woman asking for an oven

15. the fairies letting her and her family go home after she promises to leave the cake by the fairy mound for the fairies

16. the woman and her family at home and content

17. the woman leaving the cake behind the fairy mound and finding the little brown bag of gold pieces the fairies left for her

18. the woman baking a cake every week for the fairies and receiving a bag of gold pieces in return

19. everyone living happily ever after[2]

The visual approach works well in learning a folktale because language is subordinate to action in this type of story. In the auditory approach, the storyteller is conscious of the sound of words and their arrangement. A break in the rhythm is a warning that the telling is off track. Those who use this approach often record the story before learning it. Playing back the recording in relaxed moments or while doing undemanding chores facilitates the learning process. A word of caution may be in order for the neophyte. Be sure that you want to be a storyteller *before* you record because the recording will bring out every imperfection of your voice and timing. Do not be discouraged. If the story you have chosen to learn has been recorded by a professional storyteller, you may prefer to listen to that recording until you have gained confidence in yourself. There are many outstanding recordings of stories available (see Resources for Storytellers). However, some new storytellers find it distracting, in the early stages of learning, to listen to someone else telling a story because the beginner has a tendency to copy the recorded teller's pacing and inflections.

The beginning storyteller who has a great deal of self-confidence may wish to video the story. The video captures facial mannerisms and gestures as well as imperfections of voice and timing. It is a harsh learning tool but a very helpful one, provided you do not let it rob you of the pleasure of sharing the story. Using a video recording is probably more helpful to the experienced storyteller who wants to perfect style and technique.

This is an appropriate place to mention mechanical devices, other than recorders, that storytellers may find helpful. Some storytellers claim that typing a story makes a "carbon copy" of it on the mind. Others find that outlining the story impresses it on the mind, and the outline serves as a quick memory refresher when the story is told at a later date.

Cue cards can be a useful aid. As you read, whenever you come across a story you enjoy and want to learn, fill out a 4-by-6-inch index card with the following information: title, author, source, running time, characters, scenes, synopsis, and any rhymes or characteristic phrases you wish to memorize (see Figure 8).

Choreographing, that is, marking the story to indicate voice inflections, pace, and timing, is another technique. Storyteller Carol Birch commented in the first edition of *Storytelling: Art and Technique* (Bowker, 1977): "When

Title:	"The Frog Prince"
Author:	Brothers Grimm
Source:	*Tales from Grimm*, trans. and illus. by Wanda Gág (Coward, 1936)
Running time:	8 minutes (determined by reading the story aloud)
Characters:	Princess, Frog Prince, King
Scenes:	Well under the linden tree
	Dinner table at the palace—repeated
	Bedroom of the Princess—repeated
Synopsis:	When the Princess loses her golden ball in the well, the frog rescues it on condition that the Princess will allow him to eat from her golden plate and sleep in her own little bed. The Princess is forced to keep her promise. On the third morning the spell is broken, and the frog changes into a handsome young Prince. When the Princess and the Prince grow up, they marry and live happily ever after.
Rhymes:	"Youngest Daughter of the King
	Open the door for me
	Mind your words at the old well spring
	Open the door for me."
Audience: 6–8-year-olds	

FIGURE 8. *Sample cue card.*

first learning a story, I am very formal about modulation. I search for the best way to create the effect I want. In this way I shape a story from the beginning, noting places to pause, lines that come quickly, words that need emphasis, places to raise or lower my voice. This is like a musician working with phrasing and tempos, for a story changes with each telling, as music changes with each performance." (See example from Laurence Housman's "The Wooing of the Maze,"[3] Figure 9.)

Carol no longer feels the need to work on stories in this way, but her intent was to make the narrative sections more compelling. She writes,

> Although storytellers generally color what characters say, they often speak narrative sections in a colorless way in an attempt to keep from distorting the author's voice or the omniscient narrator's voice. But it is the storyteller's voice that makes the telling "distinctive."
>
> John Houston's description of film directors is comparable to the creativity of storytellers—each artist takes a controlling part in the creation of a small world. A picture is made and a frame is put around it. Whether a story

That same day the Princess, sitting upon her throne and having crown and scepter in her hands, caused the gardener to be called into her presence. The courtiers thought it was very strange that the *GRAND* Princess should have a thing of such importance to make known to a *haughty* *like sucking on a lemon* gardener that it was necessary for her to receive him with crown and throne and scepter, as if it were an affair of state. *gossipy guilt*

To the gardener, when he stood before her, she said, "Gardener, it is my wish that there should be fashioned *sly* for me a very great maze, so intricate and deceitful that no man who has not the secret of it shall be able to pene- *wistful* trate therein. In*most* is to be/a little tower/and foun-) *see each detail* tains/and borders of *sweet* sweet-smelling flowers and herbs. But the man who fashions this maze and has its secret *unsure* must remain in it forever lest he should betray his knowl- *halting* edge to others. So it is my will that(you)should devise *breathless* such a maze for my delight and be yourself the prisoner *hopeful* of your own craft when it is accomplished.") *intense, she is prisoner to her heart – he has the key*

FIGURE 9. *Choreographed portion of "The Wooing of the Maze," in* The Rat-Catcher's Daughter: A Collection of Stories *by Laurence Housman, selected by Ellin Greene. Choreographed by Carol Birch. Used by permission of Carol Birch.*

is filmed, written or told, the narrator's controlling presence ultimately puts "a frame around" every person, place, and event in the story. Nonetheless, storytellers often say a typical line in a fairytale like "the king walked into the room" without affect—without any frame or point of view. The line actually comprises a whole scene in and of itself. If you shift an impersonal line like this into personal memory, it becomes easier to envision the energy in such a line. Remember how your father heard you come home and rushed in eagerly to see you? How furiously he strode in knowing you had snuck out of the house again? Or, how quietly he tiptoed in to envelop you in his arms? The verbs in folktales might not be as descriptive as the verbs in the examples above, but the storyteller needs to envision similarly concrete actions and attendant emotional nuances. When we delve into memory, suddenly our awareness might include particular scents, temperatures, and the slant of light, your clothing, his clothing, as well as perceptions of quiet furies or wild joys. When a story comes from a printed source, it is the storyteller's imagination working with *cues from the text* that provides the details memory brings to personal stories. Please understand the words do not have to change. The storyteller can still say "the king walked into the room" but how it is said speaks to the dynamism of the scene. Storytellers diminish the power of a story when they paint narrative sections in shades of gray and save bold or subtle hues only for lines spoken by characters. All of it is color *full!*

Long ago in *The Way of the Storyteller*, Ruth Sawyer instructed storytellers to learn a story image by image, not word by word. In following this, I realized that using images meant using the imagination to explore a story. Using the imagination lifts a text off the page. From examining details, large discoveries emerge. Instead of holding a story in the tiny section of our brains that is linear and structures rote memorization, the story is held viscerally with associative memories of sensation. Storytellers can move beyond frozen moments of performance techniques to the more fluid, mutable, and innumerable responses of emotional honesty *in support of the text*. The substance and resonance of the story remain. But listeners are also afforded a storyteller who presents a true measure of himself in concert with a story.

Looking back to my contribution to the first edition of this wonderful book by my storytelling teacher, mentor, mom, and seer, the shift in my approach becomes obvious. What never changed was my certainty that narrative sections needed to sound spoken. Back then I choreographed the text to ensure that important words and images that gave vitality to sentences, paragraphs, and sections of the story were highlighted. Early on I knew the text needed to be spoken by someone, but it took years before I realized that I was the speaker. It took years before I *consciously* presented a true measure of myself in concert with the story. Consciousness opened another dimension of story to explore, play, or work. The poet William Snodgrass said the only reality a poet can ever surely know is the self he cannot help being. If an artist rejects his own reality and speaks in the voice of any borrowed authority, his words will be less than alive.

The oral tradition is more fluid than the absolute uniformity of the print tradition. Subsequent printings of a story are exactly the same. In the oral tradition, subsequent tellings of a story are not exactly the same. Improvisation plays a vital role in storytelling. Improvisation includes the beauty of tradition, while growing out of experience, originality, and the generative power of the interactions between an audience and the storyteller. The oral tradition celebrates an inherent fluidity, creativity, and natural development in the life of a story. As Ruth Sawyer wrote in *The Way of the Storyteller:* "Sorry indeed are the performance and the performer when all that is given is what a public stenographer could note down on paper . . . when all that is given in the telling is no more than what may lie already on the printed page." (Sawyer: 32)

Knowing the words of a story in rote memorization is comparable to walking on a tightrope. Walking a tightrope must be a thrilling art; certainly it is exhilarating to watch a performer exhibit such singular control and acrobatic skill. Nonetheless, it fails as a productive metaphor for the relationship of the storyteller to the story or the audience. Too breathless. Too performance oriented. The focus is the walker's skill; the relationship between artist and audience is skewed by a heightened awareness of the void between them; part of the attraction comes from the tension created at watching someone dare death. Above all, storytelling is about relationship, not performing with an audience sitting tensely below.

Nor is storytelling like mountain climbing. To hear some people speak you would believe storytelling required a great deal of equipment, that it's all uphill, and that people can die. Both metaphors are at odds with the goal of being grounded, well prepared for the journey. Storytellers need to know more than the words. We need to internalize the map of the story so that we know how to take a detour, which side roads are worth traveling down if there is time, and what vistas lay ahead. These things need to be known before we invite others to travel with us. Then, when others are moving through the landscape with us, our focus can be on enjoying the trip *with them.*

I do not memorize stories, and yet I know them absolutely. Someone asked the great Arturo Rubinstein how he memorized black marks scattered across a page. His response speaks directly to storytellers: the goal is not to memorize a piece but to know *where the tune is going.*

Learn the shape of the story, where its tune is going. Take cues from the text, research all you can. Imagine all you need to know about the faces and hearts of the characters, the stresses and conflicts they encounter, and the possibilities for victory they can achieve. *And tell that.* Move beyond stock castle, beyond stereotyped woodcutters and warriors, beyond typical journeys. Localize, particularize, specify, clarify and you'll know the story beyond all question of memorizing and forgetting.[4]

BASIC STEPS IN LEARNING A STORY

Allow time each day over a period of at least two to three weeks to make a new story your own. Live with your story until the characters and the setting become as real to you as people and places you know. Know it so well that it can be told as if it were a personal reminiscence.

Read the story from beginning to end several times. Read it for pleasure first. Then read it over with concentration. Analyze the story to determine where the appeal lies, what the art form is, what word pictures you want your listeners to see, what mood you wish to create. Before learning a story, Gudrun Thorne-Thomsen would ask herself a number of questions. What is it about the story that I want to share with children? Is it the humor? The rhythmic language? The sense of wonder? Beauty? What is its essential quality? Whatever the particular quality and appeal of the story, the storyteller must respond to it, sense it, feel it intimately before giving it out again.

Read the story aloud and time it. Time it again when you begin to tell it. Some variation in time of reading and telling is to be expected, but if the telling takes much less time than the reading, it may indicate that parts were omitted or that you are speaking too quickly. If it takes much longer, you may have added to the tale or you may be speaking too slowly.

Learn the story as a whole rather than in fragments. Master the structure of the story. Perceive the story line. The story line consists of the beginning, which sets the stage and introduces the characters and conflict; the body, in which the conflict builds up to the climax; and the resolution of the conflict. Do not alter the essential story line. Note how the action starts, how it accelerates, how and where the transitions occur. Note sequences of names and events. Know absolutely what the successive steps are in the course of action. Test yourself by closing the book and making a list of these steps in proper order.

Master the style of the story. To retain the original flavor and vigor, memorize rhymes or characteristic phrases that recur throughout the story, such as these two:

Be bold, be bold, but not too bold,
Lest that your heart's blood should run cold.

From "Mr. Fox," in Joseph Jacobs's *English Fairy Tales*.[5]

Now with cold grows faint her breath,
Fire will conquer frosted death.

From "The Magic Ball," in Charles J. Finger's *Tales from Silver Lands*.[6]

Observe the sentence structure, phrases, and unusual words and expressions. The beginning and ending are important. You may want to memorize them. "Crick crack," says the storyteller on the Caribbean island of Martinique, and the children reply, "Break my back." "Once there was and twice there wasn't, when genies played polo in the old Turkish bath, when the camel was a salesman and the flea a barber . . ." is one traditional way of beginning a Turkish tale. "He was then married to the king's daughter, and the wedding lasted nine days, nine hours, nine minutes, nine half minutes, and nine quarter minutes, and they lived happy and well from that day to this" is a characteristic Irish ending.

Make the story your own. Become familiar with the characters and the scenes. Build in your imagination the setting of your story. What are the main characters like—are they clever, kind, greedy, timid, mischievous? How are they dressed? How do they speak—in vernacular, short sentences, pompously? Visualize the happenings. Reproduce these happenings as though you were seeing and experiencing them. Imagine sounds, tastes, scents, colors. Only when you see the story vividly yourself can you make your audience see it. Eulalie Steinmetz Ross advised:

> Bring to the telling of the story any experience, any memory, any knowledge from life that will give breadth and depth to its interpretation. Hear the Sleeping Beauty Waltz as the French fairy tale weaves its spell of enchantment. See the Chicago skyline as the background for Carl Sandburg's "Two Skyscrapers Who Decided to Have a Child." Remember the lines of Robert Frost's poem, "Stopping by Woods . . ." as you tell Mary Wilkins' "The Silver Hen." Train yourself to see, and you unconsciously give your audience time to see also. The pace of the story will come to fit the action and the scene. You must give the story depth and conviction, setting and atmosphere, before you can make it live for your audience.[7]

Miming the actions, characters, and emotions develops a kinesthetic sense of the story that enhances the telling. Exaggerate your gestures and movements. When you tell to an audience you will not exaggerate, but through the process of exaggeration you will have freed your body.

Timing is the dramatic part of storytelling. Each story has its own pace; for example, "Sleeping Beauty" is slow and stately, "The Gingerbread Man" is sprightly, "Robin Hood" is strong and firm. Good timing makes the difference between the neophyte and the accomplished storyteller. Herein lies the value of listening to recordings by notable storytellers.

The following are a few suggestions about timing:

1. Pause before any change of idea, before any significant word.
2. Emphasize words that carry meaning.
3. In general, take poetic and imaginative passages slowly; take rapidly the parts narrating action.
4. Build toward the climax. Change pace as you near it so that your listeners may know the pleasure of anticipation. Some climaxes are made more impressive by a gradual slowing down, others are highlighted by speeding up the rate of telling. Knowing whether to slow down or speed up comes with experience and sensitivity.

5. Conversation should be taken at a speed that is appropriate for the character speaking. Beginning storytellers often are afraid of using pauses, but when they are handled well, pauses can add drama and meaning, and they do not suggest nervousness or hesitancy.

6. Remember that the pause and a dropped voice can be more effective than the shout.

Practice telling the story aloud—to yourself, your pet, your family and friends, to anyone who will listen! Any hesitation reveals weak areas in your knowledge of the story. Practice wherever and whenever you can—while waiting in the doctor's or dentist's office, while traveling on public transportation, while doing undemanding chores. Ignore the stares of strangers, friends, family! Practice, practice, practice. As a final aid, just before going to sleep at night, read the story as printed in the book, slowly and aloud.

Practice in front of a mirror to catch distracting mannerisms. Gestures should be natural to the story and to the storyteller. The art of storytelling should not be confused with the art of acting. The storyteller interprets and expresses the ideas, moods, and emotions of the story, but never identifies with any character. The storyteller is not an actor but the medium through which the story is passed. There should be no studied gestures, no gimmicks, no tricks of changing voices to suit each character in the story. These only tend to detract from the story. Storytelling is a folk art and does not lend itself to the grand gestures of the stage.

Tone of voice should relate to what is going on in the story. The storyteller develops a sensitivity to words. Feel the appropriate emotion when you sound words, so that the word "dull," for example, has a dullness about it. Train your ear to hear rhythmic phrases. Chant the skipping-rope rhyme in "Elsie Piddock Skips in Her Sleep" as if in time to a jump rope.

BREATHING AND RELAXATION EXERCISES

How you use your breath is important. Place your voice somewhere near the middle of the chest rather than in the head or upper chest. Breathing from the upper chest or head will give you a lighter, weaker tone; breathing from the abdomen will give you rich, full tones, connoting strength and vigor. Instead of assuming different voices for different characters, suggest characters by the amount of breath used. For example, instead of using a high-pitched, squeaky voice for the wee little bear in "The Story of the Three Bears," use a lighter breath. However, once you have differentiated the characters in any way you must be consistent throughout the story.

"Life is in the breath; therefore he who only half breathes, half lives" is a yogic proverb storytellers should heed. The person who breathes deeply has more life, is more "alive." Yogic breathing exercises relax the body and bring vitality. Here are Ellin Greene's directions for the "Complete Breath":

1. Sit in a cross-legged posture. Slowly exhale through the nose. Simultaneously contract the abdomen as far as possible to help empty all air from the lungs.

2. Slowly inhale through the nose. Simultaneously attempt to push out the abdominal area. This movement permits air being inhaled to enter the lower area of the lungs.

3. Continue the slow, quiet inhalation. Simultaneously contract the abdomen slightly and attempt to expand the chest as far as possible.

4. Continue the slow, quiet inhalation. Simultaneously raise the shoulders slowly as high as possible. This permits air to enter the high area of the lungs.

5. Hold breath with shoulders raised for a count of five.

6. Slowly and quietly exhale deeply, relaxing shoulders and chest as you exhale and contract abdomen.

7. When exhalation is completed, repeat.

There are many exercises besides yoga to relax the body. Choose one that relaxes you. For example, rotate head on shoulders; relax throat by yawning; swing arms, then legs; rotate ankles. Here are two longer exercises that students find very relaxing:

1. Stand tall; raise your arms over your head; stretch high; tense every muscle. Think of yourself as a puppet on a taut string. Then, one by one, let your hands flop, bend your elbows, bring bent arms to your sides, bend forward from your waist, and hang limp with relaxed knees. Let your arms and hands dangle. Slowly come to an upright position. Repeat.

2. Lie on your back. Close your eyes and breathe slowly. Think of yourself as a rag doll filled with sawdust. Imagine that the sawdust is slowly seeping out of you, from toes to head. Let your whole body go limp. Remain in this position for five to ten minutes.

SPEECH EXERCISES

To overcome lazy habits of articulation, it is necessary to exercise the speech organs in much the same way that we exercise for muscular coordination in athletics or instrumental music. Regina Brown, an actress and former staff member of the New York Public Library, worked for many summers

Movement Warm-Ups for Storytellers

Whether you need to calm down, loosen-up or energize before a performance, a few movement warmups can do the trick. Gentle yet invigorating exercise can release pre-performance tension, get you breathing properly (which is important for voice support), loosen your muscles so your body language will match naturally with your verbal portrayal of the story, and give you a nice refreshed positive attitude. Sounds great? Sounds impossible? It is great! It's not impossible! You can do it without dance training in five minutes time.

Here are a few gentle, natural exercises suited to a storyteller's pre-performance needs. These exercises are designed to be done standing without messing up your clothing. All the exercises are meant to make you feel good. If anything hurts, don't do it! With the stretching exercises don't bounce. Throughout all the exercises, breath in through your nose and out through your mouth. Once you know the sequence, it will only take you five minutes.

1. YAWN STRETCH

Standing up, yawn and stretch with as many parts of your body as you can (your back, neck, legs, arms, etc.) Open your mouth wide as you yawn. Think of stretching luxuriously on a lazy morning in bed. Do this several times.

2. ALIGNMENT

Stand with your feet parallel to one another, your weight balanced between your toes and heels, your feet directly under your pelvis; not wider, not narrower than your own body width. Gently tuck your buttocks under and draw you abdomen up and in. Imagine an eye hook in the top of your head that is attached to a cord that extends to the ceiling. Let the cord lengthen your whole spine, but keep your shoulders down and relaxed and your feet grounded on the floor. Try to feel long, yet relaxed. This position leaves plenty of room for your lungs and diaphragm, which support your voice. It also presents a positive self-image.

3. BREATH

Still standing aligned, take at least two full breaths in through your nose and out through your mouth. Close your eyes. Relax on each exhale. Breathe from your diaphragm. This means that the breath movement takes place in the abdomen, not the chest.

4. NECK

a) Chin Down: On your next exhale, let your chin come down toward your chest, but still keep the rest of your body upright and aligned. Stay in this position for two exhales. B) Neck swings: Leaving chin close to chest, move in gentle neck swings from right to left. Exhale each time you swing right. Do six repeats. c) Over Shoulder: Slowly lift head back to upright and look over your right shoulder. Stay for two exhales. Look over your left shoulder. Stay for two exhales. d) Side to Side: In a smooth slow manner, switch from looking over your left shoulder to looking over your right shoulder. Exhale as you look to right. Inhale as you return to the left. Repeat six times.

5. BACK STRETCH

a) Clasp hands behind your back and raise your arms as high as you can. Your shoulder blades will push close together. Hold this position for two exhales. Unclasp hands. B) Clasp hands over your head. With straight arms, bring them as far behind your head as you can. They won't go very far. Hold for two exhales. Unclasp hands.

6. SIDE STRETCH

Reach right arm over your head toward the left. This stretches your right side. Hold for two exhales. Now, stretch your left arm over your head toward the right side. Hold for two exhales. This stretches the left side. Remember not to bounce.

7. SHAKE-OUT

Start by shaking your arms in a loose and jiggly manner. Then add other body parts. Add the shaking of your shoulders, add the shaking of your back and buttocks, add the shaking of your legs by shifting your weight from side to side.

Keep shaking loosely until you are shaking your whole body. Shake until your muscles feel slightly warm. Stop and stand aligned. Relax.

8. TOE PRESS WALK

Standing aligned, roll onto the ball of your right foot, bending your right knee slightly. Switch and roll onto the ball of your left foot. Keep switching right, left, right, left, similar to walking in place but always keeping your toes on the floor. Pick up the rhythm of your natural walking speed. Let your arms swing freely as if you were outside enjoying a country walk. Smile and think a positive thought about yourself.

9. ALIGNMENT

Align yourself as described in exercise #2. Close your eyes and relax on each exhale. Exhale twice. Open your eyes and really look around and see your space fully. Exhale and nod your head in affirmation that you are ready.

You can do voice warm-ups either before or after the movement warm-ups. It's up to your preference. I prefer to do my voice warm-ups after the movement exercises, then I go back and do exercise #8, the shake-out, one more time just before I go before my audience.

Try experimenting with the exercises. Adapt them in ways that suit your body best. Always remember to breathe when you exercise. Take time to make sure your body is in alignment.

You might like to try doing movement warm-ups everyday, even if you are not going to be performing. They are a great way to start the day. Or end it, if you want to wash away the tensions of a bad day.

Remember that your posture and body movement are physically connected to your breath and voice. Your body posture and movements affect people's interpretation of what you are saying. Body posture and movement affect your own self image and your mental attitude. Body, mind and spirit tell the story. Prepare your whole self for storytelling.

FIGURE 10. *Movement warm-ups for Storytellers. Reprinted by permission of Linda Marchisio, MALS, storyteller-author (email Ljclsj@cox.net).*

as a storyteller in the parks and playgrounds. Here are some of her favorite exercises:

Tongue Exercises

1. Stick out tongue toward nose and try to touch nose; point tongue.
2. Stick out tongue toward chin and touch chin; point tongue.
3. Stick out tongue from right side of mouth; point tongue.
4. Stick out tongue from left side of mouth; point tongue.
5. Rotate tongue—encircle lips first to right, then to left.
6. Trill tongue.
7. Repeat "Around the rugged rock the ragged rascal ran" three times.

Lip Exercises

1. Pout, relax; pout, relax.
2. Spread lips and say ee.
3. Round lips and say oo.

Jaw Exercises

1. Move jaw from side to side.
2. Move jaw up and down.
3. Rotate jaw first to left, then to right, then open and close mouth slowly.

Take time to learn your stories. Marie Shedlock advised her students to learn no more than seven stories a year. She herself learned only three stories a year, but they were learned to perfection. Even if you only learn three stories a year, in ten years you'll know thirty stories. A repertoire of thirty stories of different types will serve you well. Don't be afraid to repeat your stories. Children enjoy hearing them again and again. Tell them at library story programs, to school classes, and during visits to youth organizations.

LEARNING A FOLKTALE

1. Learn the folktale as a whole, using the visual approach described earlier in this chapter. Do not memorize word for word.
2. Follow the steps described above in the section "Basic Steps in Learning a Story."

The art of telling a folktale was, perhaps, best expressed by Mary Gould Davis in these words:

> It needs no technique to tell a folk story. What it really needs is a knowledge of literature, a thorough enjoyment of the tale, and a picture in either the mental or the physical eye of the country that the tale comes from. The greatest enemy to the successful telling of a folktale is self-consciousness. There is no self behind a folk story—there is only a slow, natural, almost inevitable growth. If we put self into it we take away from its simplicity, its frankness, its almost ruthless reality. It should be our first care to select the editor or translator who has had the courage and the wisdom to let the story reflect not his own scholarship or his power as a writer, but the country from which it comes. Every bit of knowledge that we, as storytellers, have about that country helps us.[8]

LEARNING A LITERARY FAIRY TALE

The literary fairy tales are more difficult to tell, and take longer to prepare because their beauty and vitality lie in their wording, which must be retained as nearly as possible. The storyteller is interpreting a piece of creative writing. Each word and its placement in the sentence has special value and importance in relation to the story as a whole. These stories must be memorized, but the storyteller must know them so well that the artificiality and mechanization of the memorization process are overcome. The storyteller reads and rereads the story until the memorization of it becomes an unconscious one and not one of rote learning.

Reading other stories by the same author will help the storyteller discover the rhythm of the author and will reinforce perception of his or her style. Authors have a very personal way of speaking. When we hear "O Best Beloved" we immediately think of Rudyard Kipling. We recognize Laurence Housman's voice in such passages as:

> Now anyone can see that a man who practiced so cunning a roguery was greedy beyond the intentions of Providence. . . . The gnome laughed to himself to see how the trapper was being trapped in his own avarice. . . . And now the rat-catcher was the richest man in the world: all his traps were made of gold, and when he went rat-hunting he rode in a gilded coach drawn by twelve hundred of the finest rats. This was for an advertisement of the business. He now caught rats for the fun of it and the show of it, but also to get money by it; for, though he was so rich, ratting and money-grubbing had become a second nature to him; unless he were at one or the other, he could not be happy.
>
> From "The Rat-Catcher's Daughter," in *The Rat-Catcher's Daughter: A Collection of Stories by Laurence Housman* selected by Ellin Greene.[9]

About the literary fairy tale, Mary Gould Davis wrote:

> This type of story has always seemed to me very much dependent upon personality. If it does not kindle in us a responsive spark, if we do not feel that between the writer and us there is a peculiar understanding, then—no matter how carefully we learn it, how faithfully we tell it—it remains a dead thing. But when that spark is kindled, as instinctively, as unconsciously as the musician strikes the right note, we reproduce the style, the "power with words" of the author. We know, for instance, that it is a kind of betrayal to begin the story of "The Elephant's Child" with "Once Upon a Time." We may interest and please the children with the adventures of the young elephant and the crocodile; but, if we use that old traditional folk beginning, we know that we have struck the wrong key—we have left something out. And if we search ourselves thoroughly enough, we will find that the thing we have left out is no more and no less than Mr. Kipling! There is only one way in which to begin the story of "The Elephant's Child" and that is the way Kipling begins it—"In the High and Far Off Times, O Best Beloved. . . ." The quality in us that makes it possible for us to tell a stylist story successfully is closely akin to the quality that lets us read poetry successfully. A sense of rhythm and a sense of words—they go hand in hand. They are sister to the art of music and the art of dancing. They are the necessary part, I think, to the art of storytelling.[10]

Knowing and enjoying other stories by the same author brings an intangible quality to the telling. Give yourself time to get to know your author. Know in October that you want to tell an Andersen story in April. Steep yourself in Andersen as you learn your story.

Memorize the literary fairy tale, then forget it has been learned word for word and tell it naturally rather than in a recitative manner. It is far better to read such stories aloud than to spoil them with inept telling.

SHOULD A STORYTELLER WHO DOES NOT LIKE A STORY OR WHO IS OFFENDED BY PARTS OF A STORY ADAPT IT?

The best thing to do, if you dislike a story or find parts of it offensive, is to choose another story. It will be easier to learn as well as to tell. An adaptation by an inexperienced teller often changes or distorts the meaning of the story. This is unfair to the story and to the listeners. Should we let a little bird warn the Gingerbread Boy so he can run home to safety, or should we have the Fox eat him? We know the version the children prefer.

A young librarian was constantly asked by the neighborhood children in a branch of the New York Public Library to read Wanda Gág's *Millions of Cats*. One day she was ill and another librarian took her place in the reading-aloud area. The children asked her to read their favorite. When the librarian reached the part in the story where the cats fight and scratch so that only one poor little cat is left, the children all shouted, "No! That isn't the way the story goes." Questioning revealed that the first storyteller had permitted the cats to argue a bit and then run away and hide under bushes, leaving the forlorn little cat alone. When questioned, she stated that she changed that part of the story because she did not approve of violence in a children's book. The librarian was advised to select stories thereafter of which she approved, for storytellers must believe in and enjoy the stories they select for telling.

In his book *Once Upon a Time: On the Nature of Fairy Tales*, Max Lüthi discusses the internal consistency in the folktale and the importance of keeping that consistency. For example, the cruel punishment of the stepsisters in the Grimm version of "Cinderella" (pigeons peck out their eyes) is consistent with their self-inflicted wounds (cutting off part of their heel or toe in order that their foot will fit the slipper), whereas the haughty but less cruel stepsisters in Perrault's version are not only forgiven, but are married off to rich lords and invited to live at the palace. When storytellers retell a tale, they must be aware of this need for balance.

HOW DOES A STORYTELLER CUT A STORY?

Occasionally a storyteller may wish to shorten a story because it is too long for the time allowed, or the form is not best for dramatic effect, or the action is slowed down by long descriptive passages. Cutting a story requires knowledge of storytelling literature and knowledge of children's reactions to hearing stories. Such knowledge comes with experience. The experienced storyteller knows what to leave out. The beginning storyteller has a tendency to cut out all description and atmosphere and to reduce the story to a mere outline. An experienced storyteller cautions, "Don't have the characters acting on an empty stage." Select a good version of a story and stick with it. Such versions can be found in recommended lists or in collections compiled by storytellers. The storyteller who has gained a sense of security will know when a small alteration in some phrase would make for smoothness, a descriptive passage might be shortened, a section might be summarized, or superfluous details and unnecessary complications of plot (two or more threads of narrative) deleted.

HOW DOES A STORYTELLER AMPLIFY A SHORT STORY?

The storyteller needs to flesh out the scenes and characters of a "barebones" story, using imagination to create vivid word pictures. In retelling the Haitian folktale "Uncle Bouqui Rents a Horse," Harold Courlander made the telling more interesting to the children by enumerating the people on the horse rather than simply stating, "And they were all on the horse."

The experienced storyteller is able to combine different versions of a story successfully. In doing so, it is wise to write out the story and learn the rewritten version. As in cutting a story, the storyteller must keep the story whole, presenting a single point of view and developing the events in logical sequence.

A good example is Ashley Bryan's *The Cat's Purr*, based on an old West Indian folktale, "Why Cats Eat Rats." Bryan deemphasized why cats eat rats and created a plausible origin of the cat's purr. The original folktale and its source are printed at the end of Bryan's book.

SHOULD A STORYTELLER USE HIS OR HER OWN WORDS OR THE AUTHOR'S WORDS?

Use the author's words if they are better than yours. Increase your own vocabulary. How many synonyms can you find for "beautiful," for "brave"? In telling stories in our own words, we often reuse the same words, especially adjectives. Be careful not to intersperse the story with "uh," "and now," and other speech mannerisms we can catch if we listen to ourselves. Respect the spare quality of such stories as those found in Joseph Jacobs's *English Fairy Tales*, and do not embellish them with your own additional words. Avoid slang when telling a traditional tale.

Are our colloquialisms appropriate to the story? The storyteller's own words should never change the meaning, the rhythm, or the cadence of a story. In telling Sandburg's "The Huckabuck Family and How They Raised Pop Corn in Nebraska and Quit and Came Back," a new storyteller changed "squash" to "pumpkin" because she thought that the children might not know "squash" pie, but that "everyone knows pumpkin pie." This showed her insensitivity to the sound of words. She didn't realize that Sandburg, the poet, had achieved a rhythm with "squash." This is made obvious by reading the following passage out loud, as written, and then reading it substituting the word "pumpkin" for "squash."

> And this was the year Pony Pony was going to bake her first squash pie all by herself. In one corner of the corn crib, all covered over with pop corn, she had a secret, a big round squash, a fat yellow squash, a rich squash all spotted with spots of gold.
>
> From "The Huckabuck Family and How They Raised Pop Corn in Nebraska and Quit and Came Back," in Carl Sandburg's *Rootabaga Stories.*[11]

"Squash" and "pumpkin" have an entirely different feeling—this is a sensual thing. Children do not grow linguistically or intellectually if we constantly revise downward.

WHAT SHOULD A STORYTELLER DO ABOUT FOREIGN WORDS?

For correct pronunciation refer to a dictionary or to a resource person, such as the language specialist, on your staff.

SHOULD A STORYTELLER USE DIALECTS?

Webster's New College Dictionary (3rd ed., 2008) defines dialect as: "1. a variety of a language that is distinguished from other varieties of the same language by features of phonology, grammar, and vocabulary, and by its use by a group of speakers who are set off from others geographically or socially. 2. a provincial, rural, or socially distinct variety of a language that differs from the standard language, esp. when considered as substandard."

Vernacular is a speech pattern that is the native language of a place or the plain variety of speech in everyday use by ordinary people. Regional vernacular is acceptable, while dialect used to indicate social or racial inferiority is offensive and misleading.

Syncopation of speech, with its rhythmical stress, is part of a storyteller's interpretation. In *God's Trombones*, James Weldon Johnson said, "He [the black poet] needs to find a form that will express the racial spirit by symbols from within rather than by symbols from without—such as the mere mutilation of English spelling and pronunciation."[12] Black writers such as Virginia Hamilton and Julius Lester have achieved a form that is larger than dialect, that flows freely, and expresses the imagery, the idioms, the humor and pathos, the unique turns of thought crucial to the storytelling voice.

The heavy Irish dialect in the out-of-print editions of Seumas Mac-Manus was translated by MacManus himself when he wrote *Hibernian Nights*. He retained the flavor of the original tales by the use of imagery, musical narrative, humor, and colloquialisms in dialogue.

Few storytellers are able to use dialect to good advantage. Ruth Sawyer told Irish stories superbly because she had been imbued with the richness of the Irish tongue from early childhood by an Irish nurse. But even this great storyteller did not sound natural when she assumed a German accent to tell a German folktale. Much practice is required to capture dialect and to use it in a relaxed and comfortable manner. It is better in most cases, therefore, to avoid dialect and, instead, retain the rich expressions, the cadence, the flavor, and the inflection of the particular speech patterns.

Regional vocabulary is not only acceptable but often necessary in storytelling. For example, in telling the story "Wicked John and the Devil," from Richard Chase's *Grandfather Tales*, the storyteller must refer to "sweet milk" rather than "milk," because the former places the story geographically. As a matter of fact, the author of this story once pointed out to his audience that in Appalachia the person asking for milk rather than "sweet milk" might be served buttermilk!

AFTER WORKING ON A STORY FOR SOME TIME, HOW DOES A STORYTELLER OVERCOME BOREDOM?

There seems to be a point in the learning process when a plateau is reached and all effort is drudgery. Accept this and let the story go for a few days or a week, then return to it. Recall the emotions the story originally aroused in you. When you tell the story to children and you see the wonder in their faces or the laughter in their eyes you will feel that all the time spent on learning it was worthwhile.

WHAT ARE THE QUALITIES OF A GOOD STORYTELLER?

The early storytellers had qualities that are just as important today. One must have a keen enjoyment of one's material and a burning desire to share one's enthusiasm with others. Elizabeth Nesbitt, a storyteller long associated with the Carnegie Library of Pittsburgh, said:

> Storytelling, like anything else, cannot achieve its rightful best unless it is done with understanding, integrity, and acceptance of the fact that it requires thought, care, time, and knowledge in selection and preparation, and recognition of the necessity for a special kind of artistry in the telling. The art of storytelling is a spontaneous, unsophisticated art. [13]

It holds, therefore, that storytelling is an individual art, and that each storyteller will bring a special kind of appreciation, imagination, and interpretation to the telling. Extensive reading and building of background are necessary, for the storyteller must think of the story as a part of the whole literature to which it belongs, and of the storyteller as the medium through which the story comes to life.

All creative artists share the same qualities—enthusiasm, spontaneity, imagination, perception, insight. A good storyteller is also a vital human being who finds joy in living, and who can reach the heart and mind of a child. Taste and appreciation grow as the storyteller is exposed to art, to music, and to dance; the entire range of feelings, intellect, and spirit comes alive. Good storytellers, like good wine, age well. The words of the story may not change, but what the storyteller brings to the story changes with the experience of living. Ellin Greene will never forget standing at the back of the auditorium of Donnell Library Center, New York Public Library (there were no seats left for staff in the standing-room-only crowd), the evening that Ruth Sawyer, age 78, put aside the microphone and held her audience spellbound with her deep, rich voice and consummate telling.

Children demand the best, and they walk away from anything less. Good storytelling presupposes a willingness to work hard. In "Storytelling—A Folk Art," a chapter in *The Way of the Storyteller*, Ruth Sawyer says that she has no basic recipe for good storytelling. The most important requirement for her is the right approach and the recognition that storytelling is a folk art. She does, however, list certain invariables—experience, building of background, creative imagination, and a gift for selection.

Marie Shedlock had these qualities, as have other great storytellers. Ruth Sawyer was inspired by Shedlock and remembers:

> The qualities that Miss Shedlock brought to her art, and of which she gave so abundantly to all who listened, have remained for us the high mark of perfect storytelling. Voice and the spoken word were the medium for the art, and she used them with that same care and appreciation with which a painter uses line, color, and perspective. She had a wonderful voice, perfectly pitched, flexible. She never droned. Her sense of timing was always right: she knew the value of a pause. Her power to build expectation as the story grew combined both the traditional art and that of the conscious and trained artist. She belonged to those stories she told as the traditional storyteller belonged to those which had been handed down to him, an enduring legacy. Everyone who remembers her telling of the fairy tales of Hans Christian Andersen knows how deeply rooted was this kinship.[14]

REFERENCES

1. Ruth Sawyer, *The Way of the Storyteller* (Viking, 1942), p. 142. (Penguin, 1977).
2. Sorche Nic Leodhas, "The Woman Who Flummoxed the Fairies," in Leodhas, *Heather and Broom: Tales of the Scottish Highlands* (Holt, 1960), pp. 35–43.
3. Laurence Housman, "The Wooing of the Maze," in *The Rat-Catcher's Daughter: A Collection of Stories by Laurence Housman*, selected by Ellin Greene (Atheneum, 1974), p. 59.
4. Carol Birch, personal correspondence with Ellin Greene (2008). Herein, Carol draws on, and expands, what she wrote in her essay, "Who Says?" in *Who Says: Essays on Pivotal Issues in Contemporary Storytelling*, edited by Carol L. Birch and Melissa A. Heckler (August House, 1996), and in her award-winning *The Whole Story Handbook: Using Imagery to Complete the Story Experience* (August House, 2000). Both her essay and her book should be read in full.
5. Joseph Jacobs, "Mr. Fox," in Jacobs, *English Fairy Tales* (Dover, 1898), p. 154. (Create Space paperback edition, 2008).
6. Charles J. Finger, "The Magic Ball," in Finger, *Tales from Silver Lands* (Doubleday, 1924), p. 45. (Scholastic paperback edition, 1989).

7. Eulalie Steinmetz Ross, in a manuscript in the files of the Office of Children's Services, New York Public Library. Appears in slightly altered form in *The Lost Half-Hour: A Collection of Stories*, ed. Eulalie Steinmetz Ross (Harcourt, 1963).

8. Mary Gould Davis, "The Art of Storytelling," paper delivered at a meeting of the American Library Association, Washington, D.C., 15 May 1929.

9. Laurence Housman, "The Rat-Catcher's Daughter," in *The Rat-Catcher's Daughter: A Collection of Stories by Laurence Housman*, pp. 3, 5, 6–7.

10. Davis, "The Art of Storytelling."

11. Carl Sandburg, "The Huckabuck Family and How They Raised Pop Corn in Nebraska and Quit and Came Back," in Sandburg, *Rootabaga Stories* (Harcourt, 1951), pp. 170, 173.

12. James Weldon Johnson, *God's Trombones* (Viking, 1927), p. 8. (Penguin, 2008).

13. Elizabeth Nesbitt, "The Art of Storytelling," *Catholic Library World* 34: (November 1962): 143–145.

14. Ruth Sawyer, "Storytelling: Fifty Years a-Growing," in *Reading Without Boundaries*, ed. Frances Lander Spain (New York Public Library, 1956), p. 61.

WEB RESOURCES

Aaron Shepard's Storytelling Page
http://www.aaronshep.com/storytelling/index.html
Adaptations of Shepard's stories, guide to storytelling, articles and quotes about storytelling, and a recommended reading list on storytelling, folklore, and mythology.

Better Kid Care: Storytelling
http://www.nncc.org/Literacy/better.storytell.html
Part of the Better Kid Care Project. Offers General guidelines for storytelling, selecting and preparing stories, and four methods of telling.

6 PRESENTATION

"Begin at the beginning," the King said, gravely, "and go on till you come to the end; then stop."
        —Lewis Carroll, Alice in Wonderland[1]

A SMALL BOY SAT between two adults at the village soda fountain. He had just been collected from his first library story hour, and a celebration was in order. The storyteller sat three stools away, unrecognizable in winter scarf and hood. The curious adults were trying in vain to pry some statement of reaction to the story hour from the boy, a most reluctant informer, until at last one of them complained with some asperity, "You could at least tell us how the teacher told the stories? Did she read them from a book? Did she tell them from memory?" "Oh, mother," he explained with a long sigh, "she just told them from herself."[2]

No storyteller ever received higher praise, for the ultimate goal is to tell a story so simply and directly that it appears to be told "from yourself." All the emphasis should be placed upon the story rather than upon the story-teller, who is, for the time being, simply a vehicle through which the beauty and wisdom and humor of the story come to the listener.

Master storyteller and teacher Augusta Baker advised beginning story-tellers: "Let the story tell itself, and if it is a good story and you have pre-pared it well, you do not need all the extras—the costumes, the histrionics, the high dramas. Children of all ages do want to hear stories. Select well, prepare well, and then go forth, stand tall, and just tell."[3]

TELLING THE STORY

Before beginning, call up the essential emotions of the story as you first felt them. When you tell from the part of you that was touched by the story, the story becomes yours.

Breathe deeply and begin. No matter what the opening words of the story are, the tone should be intimate.

Look directly at your listeners. As you tell, let your gaze move from one to another so that each child feels involved in the telling of the story. Break direct eye contact only to look at an imaginary scene or object you want your listeners to see, or when you engage in dialogue between two or more characters during the telling.

Speak in a pleasant, low-pitched voice with enough volume to be heard easily by listeners in the last row. Speak clearly, distinctly, smoothly, and at a pace suitable for the story.

Gestures, if used at all, should be natural to the teller and to the action of the story. If gestures draw attention to themselves they are wrong. Exaggerated gestures usually indicate a futile attempt to draw attention away from inadequate preparation. Do not stand motionless as if you were a stick of wood, but do not dramatize the action of the story, for example, "marching up and down the road," "bowing," and so forth. The children may be fascinated with your movement, but they will not remember your story.

Avoid nervous mannerisms, such as biting your lips or pulling at a strand of hair. Stand with your two feet firmly on the floor. Do not rock.

Use your hands naturally. Don't jam them in your pockets. Don't stand with arms crossed in a hostile posture. If you do not know what to do with your hands, hold them behind your back. "Keep your listeners in the *what* of the story, not in the how of the telling," advises an experienced storyteller.

The storyteller establishes the mood of the storytelling program. Physical appearance, a pleasant expression, a smile, personal warmth, and pleasure in the story—all these give a sense of enjoyment.

Sometimes new storytellers wonder what to wear. Dress comfortably and simply. Children appreciate a bright scarf or attractive jewelry, but nothing should distract from the story. In a large hall, wearing something colorful will focus attention on the storyteller. However, there is no need to wear a "costume." Beware of jangly bracelets, long beads, and other potential distractions. One well-known storyteller wore long strands of beads. She always asked that she be reminded to remove them before the story hour. Otherwise she would begin to handle them during her telling, and the children would be as interested in whether the beads would break as they would be in the story.

A storytelling program can be held anywhere. A separate room may be desirable, but it is not indispensable. What is needed is a setting that is informal and an atmosphere that is relaxed and intimate. In the classroom, children may remain in their regular, assigned seats, but an informal seating arrangement is preferred. A semicircle of listeners facing the storyteller seems to be the most effective arrangement. The storyteller can be heard and seen easily by all the children. Do not let the semicircle be too wide, or the storyteller's head will have to turn from side to side like a spectator's at a tennis match. If there are twenty-eight children in the group, it is better to have four rows of seven chairs than two rows of fourteen chairs. Seat the children on chairs or on the floor so that no child is directly behind another. The children should face away from the sunlight or any windows where traffic or other distractions may divert their interest. The storyteller will sit or stand, depending on the size of the group and visibility. It may be more comfortable to sit when telling to a small group or to younger children, but standing gives better eye span, and therefore better control. It also gives the storyteller freedom of movement. The exception is when you are telling to very young children, or when you are sharing picture books with young children. In such a situation it is best for the storyteller to sit on a low stool or chair so that the storyteller and the pictures are at the children's eye level (see Chapter 8). If the storyteller is comfortable and confident, the children will be too. The arrangement of storyteller and listeners in Figure 11 will permit everyone to see and hear the storyteller easily.

Ask the children to put aside anything they are carrying (books, marbles, purses, dolls, and so on) on a separate table or under their chairs. If they have books in hand, they will surely peek into them during the storytelling. They really are not disinterested in your telling, but some children can focus on two things at once. This can deflate you as a storyteller, and it may distract other listeners.

If there is a separate room for storytelling programs, check the heat and ventilation before the program begins. A room that is too warm and without sufficient air will make children drowsy.

If there is no separate room, use a screen to give a sense of privacy. Locate the storytelling area away from room traffic, circulation desk, and telephone.

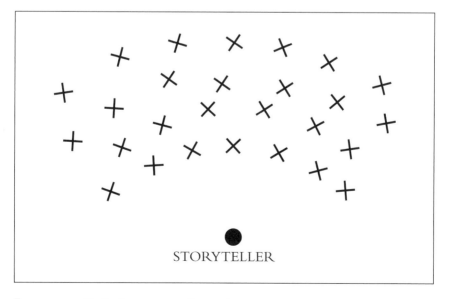

FIGURE 11. *Seating arrangement for storytime.*

Place on the "story table" the books from which you are telling, some fresh or dried flowers or leaves, realia relating to the stories, and, if fire regulations allow, the "wishing candle" (see p. 100).

Introduce the book from which the story is taken. This can be done naturally by picking up the book, either before or after the story, and saying, "This story is from . . ." All children, whether or not they are readers, like to hear a good story told well. After they have heard it, book-loving children want to read it again for themselves. Even girls and boys who are not natural readers will turn to a book once it has been "opened" for them by the warmth and intimacy of a storyteller's voice and personality.

No explanations of the story are necessary. Occasionally the storyteller may wish to give a short introduction. Some books, such as Eleanor Farjeon's *The Little Bookroom*, Howard Pyle's *The Wonder Clock*, and Harold Courlander's *Uncle Bouqui of Haiti*, have natural introductions. Introductions should be interesting and simple; you are not giving a lesson. You can develop your own short introduction (for example, "In Haiti there are two very important men. One is named Bouqui and he is a fat, good-natured fellow. The other is his best friend, Ti-Malice, a skinny little fellow who always tricks Bouqui. One time, Bouqui . . .") and then go straight into the story. The ages of your listeners will determine the type and extent of your introduction. If you are telling a long story serially, prepare a short summary to refresh the children's memory and to introduce the story to newcomers. If you tell one incident from a long book, briefly introduce the characters and the situation in which they find themselves.

No definitions of "strange" words are necessary. Frequently, inexperienced storytellers feel that they must define all unfamiliar words in order for children to understand the story. They forget that the context of the story and the child's imagination are enough to supply definitions. If children do not understand a word, they will ask, or if they look puzzled and the word is essential for meaning, the storyteller can substitute a synonym the next time the word is used in the story. For example, if the storyteller is telling Asbjørnsen's "The Squire's Bride" and realizes that the children do not know what a bay mare is, the storyteller can substitute the word "horse" in the following sentence: "Some pulled at the head and the forelegs of the mare (horse) and others pushed from behind, and at last they got her up the stairs and into the room."

Then there are words that give atmosphere, and it really doesn't matter what they mean. In her delightful article "The Pleasant Land of Counterpane," Claudia Lewis recalls her childhood encounter with Robert Louis Stevenson's poem "The Land of Counterpane."

> [The poem was] magical simply because of that bewildering word counterpane. Yes, of course, my mother explained to me what it meant, and in some

rational part of my mind I knew very clearly what it meant. Yet it was not a word current in the everyday speech of the people around me; and it suggested a baffling combination of windowpane and kitchen counter. At the same time, what a splendid-sounding word it was! I must have closed off that rational corner of mine and let my thoughts go romping off with whatever textural images and associations the word called up, and fortunately for me, my mother did not drill in the meaning. I was left to enjoy the poem, and enjoy it I did, in my own way. It would be difficult for me to describe just what "the pleasant land of counterpane" was to me (and still is). This is a case of the quality of a particular word spilling over and giving color to a whole poem, or rather, to the poem one reconstructs inwardly in heightened imaginative dimensions.[4]

If a storyteller becomes bogged down in a vocabulary lesson, the pleasure is diminished for the children, who should be allowed to relax and enjoy the story.

In planning a satisfying program, the storyteller must be concerned with a variety of practical problems as well as with the content. Some of these concerns are reflected in the following questions.

SHOULD THE STORY GROUP BE LARGE OR SMALL?

When no visuals are used there is no need to restrict group size. However, a group of twenty to thirty children is a comfortable size, especially for the beginning storyteller. The ability to project to large groups comes with experience. If you anticipate large groups or if you plan to tell out of doors, you will need to learn how to project your voice without distorting its quality.

Occasionally, the storyteller is asked to tell stories at a school assembly. Although this can be done effectively, it is difficult to create an intimate "from me to you" feeling in an assembly setting. If you have such a request, you might ask to tell to several smaller groups of children rather than to a large assembly. Telling to several groups on the same day may be physically more demanding of the storyteller, but it makes for a more satisfying storytelling and listening experience.

HOW IS A LISTENING MOOD CREATED?

The mood is created by attractive surroundings—a well-ventilated room, comfortable seating, and the story table with appropriate, authentic realia, clean books, some fresh flowers or leaves, and the wishing candle, if it is to be used. The rituals of the story line and the wishing candle also help to establish a listening mood. However, it is the storyteller who is most important in setting the mood. The storyteller's manner should be dignified but friendly. It should say, "Listen deeply, for I have something special to share with you."

WHAT IS THE "STORY LINE" AND WHAT ARE ITS ADVANTAGES?

The "story line" can be used wherever there is a separate storytelling area. Have the children assemble in a line away from the area. This gives the children a chance to quiet down before the program. It gives the storyteller a chance to assess the group. This is the time to ask the children to put away personal items and to collect tickets, if used.

Children like the formality and it creates a mood of wonder, as described in this excerpt from the psychoanalysis of a 24-year-old woman, who recalled going to story hour when she was about 7 years old:

> This just reminded me of my greatest happiness and excitement as a child. And that was going every Friday afternoon after school to storytelling in the Public Library. It was not just ordinary storytelling. First, all of the children lined up and waited. Then they led us down into a room in the cellar with chairs all arranged in rows. The room had the most immense and useless windows you ever saw. Not only were they completely out of reach, but the shades were always drawn tight so that the room was dark except for the glow of two immense candles on a desk at the front. And behind the desk, illuminated by the candlelight, was the prettiest face imaginable. I am quite sure there was a body attached to the face. But I do not remember it. She must have been the librarian ... but then I never thought of her as being a mere librarian any more than a child can conceive of its mother as a little baby. She was a real fairy that came to tell us stories. I loved the first story best always because there were two more to come. I hated, hated, hated, having to go upstairs when all the stories were done.[5]

HOW IS THE WISHING CANDLE USED?

As previously indicated, stricter fire regulations may prohibit the use of the wishing candle. Where allowed, the wishing candle can add a touch of magic to the occasion. The lighting of the wishing candle indicates the start of the program. Before lighting the candle, the storyteller may say, "Once the candle is lit, no one speaks but the storyteller." Wishes are made silently at the end of the program. Choose one child—perhaps a birthday child—to blow out the candle while the storyteller holds the candle and everyone makes silent wishes. Be sure to use a dripless candle to avoid being sprayed with wax when the candle is blown out!

FIGURE 12. *Augusta Baker lights the wishing candle at a storytelling program at the Chatham Square Branch of the New York Public Library. Reprinted by permission of the Manuscripts and Archives Division. The New York Public Library. Astor, Lenox, and Tilden Foundations.*

HOW SHOULD I INTRODUCE MY STORY?

"Once upon a time," or words to that effect invite the children into the story world. The words and your manner of speaking let the children know that they are about to enter a different realm, where extraordinary things happen but where they are perfectly safe. With younger children, storyteller Maggie Kimmel draws a magic circle around the group where all within are safe. With older children, you might open your story hour with Shel Silverstein's poem "Invitation" from *Where the Sidewalk Ends*.

Sometimes you will want to provide some information about the country or people from which the story comes. Knowledge gained through background reading, authors' notes, travel, and personal experiences enriches the telling when shared with the children. If you are telling a literary fairy tale, share with the children something about the author's life, perhaps an incident from the author's childhood.

Ask yourself, what is the purpose of my introduction? To get the attention of the listeners? To set the stage? To let the audience adjust to my voice and manner of speaking? Then act accordingly, but keep your introduction short, just enough to whet the children's appetite for the story they are about to hear.

HOW CAN A STORYTELLER AVOID HAVING A DRY MOUTH?

1. Swallow to get the saliva glands working. (When Luciano Pavarotti asked Joan Sutherland what to do about this problem, she advised him to bite his tongue. This has the same effect as swallowing.)
2. Whenever possible, before telling a story, get off by yourself. Do some yoga or other relaxation exercises (see Chapter 5). If privacy is not possible, take a few deep breaths and yawn discreetly before you begin your story.

DO I NEED PERMISSION TO TELL A STORY?

If you are telling stories in a public library or school as part of your work as a librarian, teacher, or school library media specialist, you do not need permission to tell. However, always acknowledge your sources and credit the reteller or compiler of the collection from which the story is taken. If you are a professional storyteller, and especially if the audience is charged an admission fee, you will need to get permission from the person who owns the copyright. Whether you are a paid storyteller or not, if you tell a story on radio or television and the story is protected under copyright, you will need written permission from the author and/or publisher.

To acquire permission, email or write the copyright holder with your request, or telephone the publisher directly. The website of the Children's Book Council (http://www.cbcbooks.org/) has a list of trade publishers with contact information. Ask for the person in charge of copyright permission. Give complete bibliographic information for the story: title; author, reteller, or editor's name; name of collection in which the story appears; publisher; and date of publication. Most permission departments require a copy of the entire story along with the title and copyright page of the collection. Indicate how you wish to use the material: the occasion, event site, number of performances, and so forth. Enclose a stamped, self-addressed envelope with your request. You might want to enclose a draft permission agreement although most publishers prefer to use their own permission form. A request to use a story should be sent to the publisher well in advance of the scheduled date of the program as the permission process can take several weeks.

DOES THE PRESENTATION OF A STORY DIFFER WHEN IT IS TOLD TO DIFFERENT AGE GROUPS?

In telling to different age groups, the storyteller's facial expressions, attitude, or approach to the story may be different. The listeners play an important role. Children will be responding to the story line, adults and teens to the subtle humor or poignancy of a tale. The subtle interplay between husband and wife in "Two of Everything" is lost on children but not on adults. In telling "Uncle Bouqui Rents a Horse" to adults, the last sentence, "'It's *certainly a day* to remember,' Madame Bouqui said," is spoken with a sarcastic inflection. Of course there are many stories that can be told successfully to different age groups without changing the presentation. "Mr. Sampson Cat" is one of them.

HOW CAN A STORYTELLER TELL IF THE CHILDREN ARE ENJOYING THE STORY?

When children are enjoying a story their faces express interest, curiosity, delight. Sometimes they show their pleasure by listening quietly with little or no expression on their faces. A deep sigh and a faraway look at the end of the story usually mean that you have reached that child. Some children do not seem to be paying attention at all; yet these same children will ask you for the story several weeks after you have told it. The new storyteller must remember that a story that is a roaring success with one group can leave another cold. Do not be discouraged. Continue to work on any story you really like. Accept failure along with your success.

WHAT DOES A STORYTELLER DO IF THE CHILDREN SEEM DISINTERESTED?

Restlessness often occurs when the story chosen is inappropriate for the group or when the storyteller has failed to capture the imagination of the children at the beginning. Sometimes the storyteller can recapture the children's interest by telling with greater conviction. However, if this fails, it is best to summarize the remaining part of the story and bring the story hour to a close, or if possible, to tell a different type of story. The story program should be remembered with joy.

If you know beforehand that you will be telling to children who have little or no experience in listening to stories, you might want to try Leslie Morrow's approach. Morrow, a professor in the Department of Learning and Teaching at the Graduate School of Education, Rutgers—The State University of New Jersey, is well known for her work in emergent literacy. When she first starts storytelling to such children, Morrow uses 70 percent manipulatives and 30 percent pure telling. Manipulatives include flannel board figures, puppets, stick figures, dolls, and other realia. Gradually she changes the percentages, so that by the end of the school year the percentages are reversed, and the children are actively listening.

WHAT IS THE BEST WAY TO HANDLE DISRUPTIONS?

The storyteller must be aware of the audience. Because the storyteller respects both story and listeners, no one should be allowed to disrupt what promises to be an enjoyable listening experience. Do not permit two little girls who are giggling and whispering to each other to sit together. They will surely whisper in the middle of the story even though they are following it closely.

Weave discipline into your telling. For example, in coping with restless listeners, you might insert as part of your story, "You two boys in the back could never guess. . . ." One storyteller, who was telling a story about a beautiful princess, used this ploy with success beyond her expectations. As she told her story she looked directly at a little girl who was chewing bubble gum and interjected, "And the princess did not chew gum." The girl was so surprised she swallowed her gum!

The following example may be helpful in handling a difficult situation: As you start to tell the story, you are aware that one boy is surreptitiously punching another. For a few seconds you tell the story directly to them.

Your tone of voice is firm. You look away in order to give the boys a chance to behave, but they continue to punch each other. Now they are challenging you. As you continue the story, you take a few steps toward them. Your tone of voice and body language are clearly understood by the boys. You move away again and continue the story. The third time they misbehave, you stop the story and tell them they will have to leave if they continue to disrupt the storytelling. You apologize to the other children that this has happened, then go on with the story. If the two boys do not settle down, you ask them to leave. The storyteller has a responsibility to the group and cannot let a few children spoil the listening experience.

What Should I Do If I Forget My Story?

Because the book from which you are telling your story will be close by on the story table, place a small marker in the first page of your story. If you forget your story, pick up the book and open it to the marker, which will guide you to your story. (Without a marker you might search nervously through the book and lose your poise.) Many times a glance at the place in the story where you forgot will set you free again, and you can put the book back on the table. If not, *read* the rest of the story. More often than not, if you know the story well and you have a moment of forgetfulness, you can improvise until the story comes back to you. If you forget an essential part of the story say, "Did I tell you that . . .?" Most times, if you don't indicate you have forgotten your story, your audience won't know. Nervous laughter or "I forgot to tell you that . . ." give you away.

How Does a Storyteller Conclude the Story Program?

End with the ending of the story. When the story is over, its spirit remains. Honor the story with a minute or two of silence (Marie Shedlock recommended five minutes of complete silence after a story.) Do not ask questions about the story or try to elicit comments. Let the children leave with their own private thoughts. Do not invade their privacy. After the few minutes of silence, a simple "Thank you for coming"—not a corny "We have been down the road to fairyland"—is a good conclusion to a program held in a public library or recreation center. Now is the time to announce the next storytelling program. Direct the children to books. Let the children go two or three at a time to avoid disrupting other areas of the library. Be available after the program to discuss stories with children who take the initiative, who *want* to talk.

WHAT IS THE DIFFERENCE BETWEEN A PERFORMER (PLATFORM)-STORYTELLER AND A LIBRARIAN- OR TEACHER-STORYTELLER?

In the current renaissance of storytelling, the subtle line between performance and telling is becoming increasingly hard to define. Constance A. Mellon, then Associate Professor at East Carolina University, suggested that the difference lies in the relationship between the teller and the listener. "And the focus of that relationship is the story."[6]

Performer-storytellers have a dramatic style. Usually they have had some theatrical and voice training, have stage presence, and enjoy being "on stage" and telling to a large audience. Mary Gould Davis called the librarian- or teacher-storyteller who enjoys telling stories to children but who does not like to give a performance "the children's storyteller." She wrote, regarding the two types of storytellers:

> Almost anyone who knows and loves a good tale . . . can tell it effectively to a small, intimate group. To make a story effective to a large group in a more or less formal atmosphere requires what Marie Shedlock calls "the art of the storyteller": an interpretive art as subtle and as challenging as that of the musician or the painter. To broaden and to perfect this art one can give years of study and comparison, of travel to the countries from which the stories come. One can study the latent possibilities of the human voice, inflection, emphasis, the use of the pause. But, because in the minds of the children the important thing is not the storyteller but the *story*, one can, with no training nor experience whatsoever, take the book, tell the *right* tale and hold the boys and girls in a "listening silence."[7]

More than half a century later, Kay Stone wrote in the same vein:

> As with a traditional audience, children are not passive listeners, and they still live in a predominantly oral milieu. They do not demand a flamboyantly oral/visual performance (though many adults think it necessary). They do demand sincerity and openness, and they tend to suffer honest fools gladly. Like a traditional audience they do not stop to ask, "Was that profound and meaningful, or just amusing?" If a story is well told, they will absorb other levels of meaning that appeal to their levels of experience and understanding.[8]

I FEEL INTIMIDATED BY VISITING PERFORMER-STORYTELLERS. HOW CAN I GAIN CONFIDENCE AS A LIBRARIAN- OR TEACHER-STORYTELLER?

There are different levels of proficiency in storytelling, just as there are in any art. As a non-performer-pianist is not in competition with the concert pianist, the librarian- or teacher-storyteller is not in competition with the visiting performer-storyteller. You are sharing your love of stories and giving children a pleasurable listening experience. All that is asked of you is that you tell the best you can and that you continue to stretch and grow as a teller.

Carol Birch is both a performer-storyteller and a librarian-storyteller. She enjoys wearing both hats and notes that the two platforms offer different opportunities and challenges. She wisely remarks, "When we reject the narrow measuring stick of the star system and respect our own process, art spirits thrive. On a continuum of informal to formal performance spaces, each of us has a unique place that another literally cannot fill. At our singular place on the continuum, our voice is usually more effective and potent than anyone else's could be because of our relationship to a place and the people in that place."[9]

To become an accomplished storyteller you need to experiment with different methods of learning and with different styles of telling. There is no one *right* way to tell a story. Stories may be interpreted in many ways. All that matters is that the style fit the teller. Two students told "Tom Tit Tot." One imbued the story with mystery and all kinds of psychological implications. The other told the tale as if she were the "gatless" young girl herself. Both tellings were successful because they were appropriate for the story and for the teller.

Listen to a recording of the same story told by two different tellers. For example, if you listen to "The Steadfast Tin Soldier" as told by Frances Clarke Sayers and then as told by Mary Strang, you will realize how two master storytellers bring differences to the telling—in tone of voice, pacing, characterization, and emphasis. It is similar to hearing the same piece of music played by different orchestras and conductors.

A story is not really yours until you have told it to at least three different audiences. Children respond differently from adults, and children respond differently according to their moods. You may be startled when the children laugh at something that you, the adult, did not think funny. By telling the story to different groups you discover more about the story and you learn how best to pace it. Performer storytellers have the advantage of telling the same story many times and to many different audiences.

WHAT IS THE DIFFERENCE BETWEEN TELLING A STORY TO AN INDIVIDUAL CHILD AT HOME AND TELLING A STORY TO A GROUP OF CHILDREN?

The adult telling a story to an individual child at home is very much aware of that child's interests, fears, likes, and dislikes. This knowledge makes it easier to choose a story that will appeal. The telling is informal and interruptions are permitted since there is no time schedule to keep. Telling to a group of children is more formal—the larger the group, the more formal the presentation, usually; but there are exceptions, such as storytelling around a campfire. The storyteller does not expect all the children in the group to have the same listening experience or to like the tale equally well.

It would not be appropriate to tell a story to one or two children in exactly the same manner that it would be told to a group of children. The experience might be too intense, too emotionally demanding of the child. In a group, a child is freer to let his or her mind engage in imaginative play.

IS THERE A PLACE FOR SPONTANEOUS STORYTELLING?

Absolutely! Storytelling should not be limited to the scheduled story program. If you are prepared and an opportunity presents itself, such as a quiet day in the public library, at school when a story would relate naturally to the classroom discussion, or at the end of an activity when the children need a change of pace, tell a story or read aloud. Fortunate are those children who attend a school where it is customary for the classroom teacher to read aloud to the children one half-hour every day, often at the end of the day. Such children will grow up with literature as much a part of their life as video games.

REFERENCES

1. Lewis Carroll, *Alice's Adventures in Wonderland* (Harcourt, 1999), p. 182.
2. Eulalie Steinmetz Ross, Manuscript in the files of the Office of Children's Services, the New York Public Library.
3. Henrietta M. Smith, "An Interview with Augusta Baker," *The Horn Book Magazine* 71 (May–June 1995): 296.
4. Claudia Lewis, "The Pleasant Land of Counterpane," *The Horn Book Magazine* 42 (October 1966): 543.
5. From the personal files of Augusta Baker.
6. Constance A. Mellon, "Storyteller or Performer? You Can't Tell the Difference Without a Scorecard," *School Library Journal* 33:2 (October 1986): 122. Excerpted from *By Word of Mouth* (Winter 1986).
7. Mary Gould Davis, "The Art of Storytelling," paper presented at a meeting of the American Library Association, Washington, D.C., 15 May 1929.
8. Kay Stone, "'To Ease the Heart': Traditional Storytelling," *National Storytelling Journal* 1 (Winter 1984): 5.
9. Carol Birch. Personal communications with Ellin Greene (2008).

WEB RESOURCES

Audio Stories
http://www.storyteller.net/stories/audio

Free downloadable stories.

Circle of Stories
http://www.pbs.org/circleofstories/

"Circle of Stories uses documentary film, photography, artwork and music to honor and explore Native American storytelling."

iTales
http://www.itales.com/

A site where both professional and amateur storytellers can upload and listen to stories from around the world. Also features several free podcasts.

7 STORYTELLING TO CHILDREN WITH SPECIAL NEEDS; STORYTELLING IN SPECIAL SETTINGS

Before Cushla was born, I would have laid claim to a deep faith in the power of books to enrich children's lives. By comparison with my present conviction, this faith was a shallow thing. I know now what print and picture have to offer a child who is cut off from the world, for whatever reason. But I know also that there must be another human being, prepared to intercede, before anything can happen.
—Dorothy Butler[1]

DOROTHY BUTLER'S *CUSHLA AND HER BOOKS* is an inspirational account of the remarkable role stories played in the life of Butler's grandchild, who has multiple disabilities.

Mainstreaming has brought many more children with special needs into the library's storytelling audience. The skills needed for effective storytelling to these children are, however, rarely covered in the library-school curriculum or in the standard storytelling literature.

The Americans with Disabilities Act (ADA), which mandates accessibility for persons with disabilities to all public facilities and activities, has increased librarians' awareness of the necessity to accommodate special needs children in storytelling programs and other events. To inform librarians of the implications of the ADA for staff training and program planning, as well as facilities and costs, the ALA/ALSC Library Service to Children with Special Needs Committee offered the support publication "Programming for Serving Children with Special Needs." More recently, the ALSC Library Service to Special Population Children and Their Caregivers Committee compiled a list of resources, *Children with Disabilities and Library Programs*, which is available on the ALA website at www.ala.org.

Additional information can be found at U.S. Department of Education, such as *Rights and Responsibilities of Parents of Children with Disabilities* by Bernadette Knoblauch and Kathleen McLane, published by the Educational Resource Information Center, and the website of the Office of Special Education Programs and Rehabilitation (www.ed.gov/about/offices/list/

osers/osep/index.html). Earlier books such as *Meeting the Needs of People with Disabilities: A Guide for Librarians, Educators, and Other Service Professionals* by Ruth A. Velleman, and *Meeting the Needs of Children with Disabilities: Families and Professionals Facing the Challenge Together* by Helen Warner contain valuable information.

The storyteller who tells to children with special needs must have all the qualities of a good storyteller—only more so. Extra warmth and extra sensitivity to the group's needs are necessary in order to sustain good listening. The emphasis must be on the whole child and whatever method of storytelling works best with that child. Storytellers who have the opportunity to work with special needs children consider it a joy and a challenge. As noted in the examples that follow, effective storytelling has the capacity to reach children with visual and hearing impairments, children who struggle with reading and writing, children who have behavioral issues, children who have processing and communication difficulties, and children with attention deficit.

STORYTELLING TO BLIND OR PARTIALLY SIGHTED CHILDREN

A pleasing, musical voice is a great asset to all storytellers, but it is vital for the storyteller who tells to the visually impaired. Since facial expressions and body movement are lost to blind or partially sighted listeners, the storyteller's voice quality and choice of words are extremely important. For blind children, the beauty of language comes through the sound. Rhythmic, expressive language, such as that found in poetry and songs, is often especially successful with these groups.

Storytelling is an asset to language development, so choose stories with vivid mental images. Craig Werner, a blind child and now a teacher of children's literature, writes that the stories he enjoyed most as a child were those with long descriptive passages, such as the fairy tales of Hans Christian Andersen. He concludes that imagination is the most important faculty involved in understanding and appreciating a good story.[2]

STORYTELLING TO CHILDREN WITH COGNITIVE DIFFICULTIES

Children with mental disabilities function intellectually below the average. They tend to be even more literal-minded than most children and have difficulty understanding abstract concepts. They enjoy simple stories about animals and familiar things. Look for strong plot, obvious humor, simple vocabulary, and concrete language rather than abstractions. Choose picture-book stories in which the pictures tell the story.

Be prepared to substitute synonyms for unfamiliar words. Use pictures and realia to illustrate unfamiliar words.

The tight structure of the folktale, with its definite beginning, middle, and ending, is particularly satisfying to these children, and cumulative folktales (see Resources for the Storyteller) are enjoyed as much for their repetition and rhythm as for their plot. Participation stories are also popular, especially those in which the children are invited to respond to animal sounds. Having the children retell the story in another form, through creative drama or dance, for example, reinforces the story.

STORYTELLING FOR CHILDREN WITH LEARNING DIFFERENCES

Talking with teachers in advance of classroom visits, observing classes before beginning a residency, and learning as much as possible about the children's needs is important for the visiting storyteller. Likewise, classroom teachers will find that incorporating storytelling into their day can add color and depth to a lesson. Here are just a few examples of classroom storytelling with children who have learning differences.

Storytellers Joanne Epply-Schmidt and Luray Gross have worked extensively with students and teachers at the Bridge Academy in Lawrenceville, New Jersey, a small school devoted to educating children with learning disabilities whose educational needs exceed the expertise of their districts. While most of these students have language-based disabilities, not all do, and many have a complex constellation of learning needs. During a period of three months, the storytellers visited middle school classes twice a week, sharing stories; focusing on listening skills, comprehension, sequencing, and discussion; and teaching the children to tell.

Epply-Schmidt writes, "Our first unit introduced the students to the art of storytelling and the art of story listening. Auditory and attention skills are a significant challenge for many of the students, so listening itself could not be taken as a given. By the second week the enthusiasm of hearing stories was evident. The language arts teacher was delighted by the students' capacity to retell the story in proper sequence even several days after hearing it."[3]

The storytellers proceeded to tell and discuss more complex tales, discovering that even children who had trouble putting their thoughts into words became increasingly articulate and engaged in their discussion of stories. Finally, all of the students learned to tell and perform a short folktale, many far surpassing the expectations of their teachers and parents—and perhaps most importantly—themselves. According to Epply-Schmidt, the classroom teacher felt that the storytelling program reinforced all aspects of the language arts curriculum. "Yet it was the transformation in each child, the confidence, emotional growth, and well earned self-esteem that came from working with stories that was the most satisfying outcome."[4]

Gwyn Calvetti is a speech and language pathologist who uses storytelling with elementary and middle school students in LaCrosse, Wisconsin. Most of Calvetti's students have severe speech and language needs and struggle with learning and using language effectively. Calvetti finds that storytelling improves her students' comprehension and increases their overall achievement on developmental reading assessment tests.

To aid in comprehension Calvetti begins with a folktale, such as "Mrs. Chicken and the Hungry Crocodile." Using a pre-made blank cartoon page with empty boxes, she tells her students, "I'll draw while you tell me the story again." The students retell the story while Calvetti draws simple stick figures; then the children retell the story using Calvetti's drawings as cues. "Anything that gives a kinesthetic or visual link helps," says Calvetti. For example, after telling "The Crab and the Jaguar," play a recording of sea sounds and let the children look at and touch a variety of seashells, coral, and other "treasures of the sea" that the crab might have seen. Calvetti recommends cut-and-tell stories and string stories for this audience. She also engages her listeners by having them draw a scene from a story they have heard. The children must agree on the chronology of events and move the pictures around until they are in the proper order.

Calvetti recommends small groups when working with special needs children. She also reminds storytellers that eye contact can be difficult for some special needs children. Giving listeners a part to play in the tale can help engage them.[5]

In the Storytelling Arts programs that Susan Danoff ran in some of New Jersey's low-income and special needs schools, many storytellers encountered children with attention difficulties though not all had been formally diagnosed with Attention Deficit Disorder (ADD) or Attention Deficit Hyperactivity Disorder (ADHD).

When the storytellers visited, teachers often noted in questionnaires that their most active and inattentive students not only sat still during storytelling but also attended to the story and responded appropriately. Often these were the very same children whom the storytellers had pegged their most attentive listeners.

After many years of collecting numerous responses from teachers indicating the positive impact of storytelling on these children, Danoff says, "I believe that the dynamics of storytelling, particularly the emotional connections that stories forge between teller and listener, help to engage children on a very deep level. Brain research tells us that the emotional component of learning is crucial, and storytelling simultaneously engages both the emotions and the intellect. In the thirty years that I've been telling stories in classrooms, there is rarely a time that a teacher doesn't mention how a particular child, usually the most inattentive child in the class, has surprised her by listening attentively and sitting quietly for stories. Those same children often become stars during storytelling, giving them the opportunity to gain positive feedback."

Danoff also says that children who have visual processing problems and struggle with decoding can be insightful listeners and excellent retellers. These children may struggle with reading, but when it comes to listening and remembering what they hear, they shine in class. It's important to present challenging and age-appropriate material to children with learning differences. "One of my favorite classes at Martin Luther King Middle School in Trenton was a language arts class for children with learning differences. In storytelling class when discussion, insight, and recall were central activities, these students were among the strongest I taught."[6]

STORYTELLING TO CHILDREN WHO ARE INATTENTIVE

As noted with learning differences, it is essential for storytellers working with children who have behavioral disorders to be able to observe classes and seek guidance and feedback from classroom teachers before and after presentations. Storytelling programs can be beneficial, particularly if they are repeated on a regular basis so that children can learn to understand the storytelling culture, build trust with the storyteller, and learn the behaviors appropriate for story listening, participating, and retelling. This takes time, and sometimes the reactions of listeners may be different from other children. For example, children may not seem to be listening if they are not comfortable with eye contact. Storytellers need to adjust their expectations.

Paula Davidoff, a New Jersey storyteller who has worked for many years with children of all ages who have behavioral issues writes, "One of the most important things a storyteller who is planning to work with emotionally disturbed children needs to realize is how much time it takes to gain their trust. These children have had numerous experiences with adults whose behavior has been inconsistent and condescending, and they have little reason to believe that what we as teachers and storytellers have to offer is worth their attention and respect. The stories themselves play an important part in building this respect by creating a metaphorical space in which the teller and audience have shared experiences that they can use to connect to each other and that the students can connect to their lives."[7]

New Jersey storyteller Julie Pasqual spent two years making weekly visits to an elementary school for students with behavioral disorders. The class she remembers most fondly was a group of ten- to twelve-year-old boys she thought of as "my old men," because, as she puts it, "With their world-weary faces and dead eyes . . . they all looked about one hundred years old." Eight months later, these children were totally transformed during storytelling. They were smiling, joining in, and volunteering to tell their own stories. "The transformation that took place in that class might seem like something from a fairytale. But there were no magic wands or secret potions. It was the telling of tales that allowed a class of emotionally scarred students to trust, open their minds, and risk expressing themselves."[8]

When working with younger children, involve the children in the telling. *Listen and Help Tell the Story* by Bernice Wells Carlson contains stories and activities that can be used effectively, as does Naomi Baltuck's *Crazy Gibberish*. The ALA/ALSC Library Service to Children with Special Needs committee suggests following the reading or storytelling with "an art activity in which the children illustrate an aspect of the story. The illustrations can be displayed to provide recognition of the children's efforts. Simple, clearly defined, yet creative, art and craft activities, such as sponge painting and easy cardboard construction, may also reinforce positive behavior."[9] Paula Davidoff adds, "Creative drama activities also work well. These activities also give the teller/teacher/therapist a window into the child's interpretation and understanding of the story."[10]

David P. is a storyteller from California who works with at-risk adolescents recovering from a wide range of emotional trauma. His specialty is telling myths, legends, and sagas to young adults over a number of weeks. He advises storytellers to avoid talking down to their listeners. Young adult audiences can be hostile and resistant; they often see storytelling as an activity for babies. David P. wins listeners' attention with "The Twelve Labors of Hercules," or a complex Irish tragedy. These epic tales are "clearly not stories for babies, but tales designed to enlighten kings."[11] David P. himself favors the hero sagas and mythic cycles of Viking, Irish, and Finnish cultures, as well as Arthurian legend. The amount of background he provides depends upon the group; he always provides some context for his telling. Questions are taken after the story is complete, and while David P. ruefully points out that his listeners are always ready to tell him when he has made a mistake, he also points out that the comments often evolve into real questions about details in the stories themselves. David P. is very clear: questions are taken *after* the story is complete in order not to break the purposeful rhythm of the telling. David P. describes his listeners as hyperaware and sensitive to nuance, declaring that the pause is everything, the "hypnotic spaces as important as the words."[12]

The issues physically and emotionally abused adolescents confront are hugely out of scale, that is, they do not see their stories mirrored in the everyday world. The epic tales David P. tells have themes and concepts large enough to encompass the out-of-scale world of these young adults, and make them part of the whole. David P. says his listeners already know the world is dangerous, they know the world is not safe. The tales of brave heroes who overcome great trials, the cast-off younger brother who defeats the giant, or the distressed princess who finds her own happiness, provide these listeners with a context in which to place their own history, a context that offers them both insight and hope.

STORYTELLING TO DEAF OR HEARING-IMPAIRED CHILDREN

Jill Beebout is a storyteller and state-certified American Sign Language (ASL) interpreter. From 1999 until 2005 she worked with Illuminations . . . Theatre with the Deaf (now Illuminations Arts) in Houston, Texas. Starting out as a storyteller for Illuminations, Beebout became the Storytelling Coordinator in 2000 and created/directed the program "Hand Held Tales: Stories in ASL & English." During her time there she told stories to audiences of hearing and non-hearing listeners, from preschoolers to the elderly. All the storytelling programs were produced bilingually, in voice and in American Sign Language (ASL), with one deaf and one hearing teller.

Beebout points out that the storyteller should not assume that a non-hearing audience will be behind in language or vocabulary—they may be behind in reading, but not necessarily language, and they are most often conceptually on level. Almost any age-appropriate story will work with a non-hearing audience, with the possible exception of scary stories that rely on scary sounds or overhearing disembodied voices. Physical stories with lots of action work well, as do animal tales and *pourquoi* stories. Fewer characters are sometimes best, as a large number of characters interacting can be confusing.

Rhymes are difficult, nonsense words are brutal, and puns, which play on words, don't translate well into any language, including ASL. A story that has a long or complicated rhyme is difficult to sign. The repetition becomes tedious to both the signer and the audience. If, however, the repetition is very short, like the rhyme in Wanda Gág's *Millions of Cats*, your audience can join in with the signing of the rhyme.

A fluent signer is a gift to the non-hearing audience. Beebout offers these tips for the librarian storyteller working with a sign-language interpreter.

1. If possible, make sure the signer sees the text of a story before interpreting.
2. Remember that the signer may be a beat behind the teller; that is, there is a lag in response time for the deaf audience that the teller must keep in mind.
3. The signer and teller should stand close together so that the deaf audience can see them both.

4. The teller should introduce the interpreter and both should move forward naturally to communicate the story.

Beebout mentions that hearing people sometimes think that interpreters over-dramatize, but she reminds us that ASL is an independent language with a grammatical structure completely independent from English: "The grammar of ASL is in my facial expression. I am doing with my face what the storyteller is doing with her voice."[13]

Telling stories on your own to children with impaired hearing requires clear visual presentation. Sit or stand with the light on your face and draw drapes to keep out bright sunshine and minimize glare. Make use of facial expressions and body movement. Speak more slowly and in a moderate tone of voice, but do not mouth each word, as this distorts normal rhythm. A lip-reader is looking for the thought, not single words. Male storytellers should remember that lips can be read more easily if there is no mustache or beard.

Children with impaired hearing cannot use their eyes and ears simultaneously. They cannot look at pictures and read lips or watch signing at the same time. If you are using a picture book, close the book (instead of holding it open with the pages turned toward the children) as you tell. Then open the book to show the picture, or show the pictures after each section of the story as appropriate. Picture-book stories with action, repetition, and humor, such as *Mr. Gumpy's Outing* by John Burningham, *The Very Hungry Caterpillar* by Eric Carle, and *Rosie's Walk* by Pat Hutchins, work well with younger children.

Children with hearing problems usually tire more quickly when they are required to pay close attention to looking or listening. Extra concentration is called for; therefore, one story—or two short stories—may be sufficient for the storytelling period.

With one million deaf or hearing-impaired children in the United States, it is likely that at some time you will encounter hearing-impaired children in your story hour. The inclusion of some sign language in story programming is welcoming and fun, and the hearing children will enjoy learning the signs as well. If you have never seen anyone sign stories, watch Connie Regan-Blake tell "I Know an Old Lady" on the video *Pennies, Pets and Peanut Butter: Stories for Children* (see Resources for the Storyteller). Many community colleges offer courses in signing, and the public library will have dictionaries in American Sign Language. There are numerous online sites to assist with learning signs.

Consider the following suggestions when signing to a group:

1. Speak and enunciate normally.
2. Keep your hands fairly close to your lips without covering your mouth.

The Little Red Hen

*F*ar ago, there was a Little Red Hen. She was friends with a duck, a cat, and a dog. The Little Red Hen worked hard all day long. But the duck, the cat, and the dog did not! They did not like to help.

One fine spring day, Little Red Hen found some grains of wheat. She took them home. She asked, "Who will help me plant these grains of wheat?".

"Not I," said Duck.

"Not I," said Cat.

"Not I," said Dog.

"Very well then, I'll plant the seeds myself," said Little Red Hen. And she did.

One fine summer day, Little Red Hen went out to the garden. She saw that the wheat was growing. She asked, "Who will help me water the wheat and pull the weeds?"

"Not I," said Duck.

"Not I," said Cat.

"Not I," said Dog.

"Very well then, I'll water the wheat and pull the weeds myself," said Little Red Hen. And she did.

One fine fall day, Little Red Hen went out to the garden. She saw that the wheat was very tall and golden. She asked, "Who will help me cut down the wheat?"

"Not I," said Duck.

"Not I," said Cat.

"Not I," said Dog.

"Very well then, I'll cut the wheat myself," said Little Red Hen. And she did. Little Red Hen scooped the wheat into her wagon and asked, "Who will help me take this wheat to the mill. It must be ground into flour."

"Not I," said Duck.

"Not I," said Cat.

"Not I," said Dog.

"Very well then, I'll take it myself." said Little Red Hen. And she did.

One fine winter day, Little Red Hen walked into her kitchen. She saw the wheat flour. She said "This day is a good day to bake. I will bake a loaf of bread* with the wheat flour. Who will help me bake the bread?"

"Not I," said Duck.

"Not I," said Cat.

"Not I," said Dog.

"Very well then, I'll bake it myself," said Little Red Hen. And she did.

Soon Duck smelled the baking bread. Soon Cat smelled the baking bread. Soon Dog smelled the baking bread.

When the bread was all done, Little Red Hen said, "Who will help me eat the bread?"

"I will!" said Duck.

"I will!" said Cat.

"I will!" said Dog.

"But who planted the wheat? Who watered the wheat and pulled the weeds? Who cut the wheat? Who took the wheat to the mill to be ground into flour? Who baked the bread?" asked Little Red Hen.

"Not I," said Duck.

"Not I," said Cat.

"Not I," said Dog.

"Very well then, I'll eat the bread myself. And she did.

FIGURE 13. *Signing "The Little Red Hen," from* Beyond Words: Great Stories for Hand and Voice *by Valerie Marsh (Alleyside Press, 1995). Reprinted by permission of Valerie Marsh.*

Little

"L"-shape hands, index tips out, then move close together.

Red

Brush lower lip twice with RH "R" sign.

Hen

"Three"-shape RH. Tap thumb on chin.

Duck

Snap thumb, index and middle fingers together at mouth.

Cat

Place thumb and index of RH "9" at side of upper lip Pull away twice.

Dog

Pat right thigh twice, then snap fingers twice.

Not

RH knuckle left, "A"-shape. Place extended thumb under chin, then move out.

Did

Move open hands, palms down, from side to side. Then swing RH open "B," tips forward, twice.

Help

Place LH "A," thumb up, in RH palm. Raise both hands.

Wheat

LH, palm up, "5" shape, fingers cupped. Brush fourth finger of RH "W" up against LH fingers. Repeat.

Palm left, "I"-shape RH, then place thumb side on chest.

3. Use facial expressions and body language.

4. Wear clothes that will make your hands easily visible.

5. Make clarity, not speed, your goal.

6. Be aware of the abilities of your audience, adjusting your speed and content accordingly.

Remember that American Sign Language is not just a collection of hand motions. According to the National Institute on Deafness and Other Communication Disorders, "American Sign Language (ASL) is a complete, complex language that employs signs made with the hands and other movements, including facial expressions and postures of the body. It is the first language of many deaf North Americans, and one of several communication options available to deaf people. ASL is said to be the fourth most commonly used language in the United States."[14]

One of the earliest trade children's books about American Sign Language is *Handtalk: An ABC of Finger Spelling and Sign Language* by Mary Beth Miller, in collaboration with Remy Charlip and George Ancona. Another is Laura Rankin's *The Handmade Alphabet,* which shows human hands forming the sign for each letter with an alphabetically keyed object on the same page. *Simple Signs* by Cindy Wheeler introduces twenty-eight signs for words used by young children, such as "cookie," "more," and "love."

Key signs for ten nursery tales and ten original stories can be found in the older title *Beyond Words: Great Stories for Hand and Voice* by Valerie Marsh. (See Figure 13 for an example.) Gallaudet College Press still publishes nursery rhymes and favorite nursery tales in Signed English (Signed English uses American Sign Language signs in English word order).

During storytelling for an audience that includes both hearing and hearing-impaired young children, teach the finger plays in sign language to everyone. This creates a sharing environment in which the hearing-impaired children can help the other children with the signs. Almost any finger play works well for signing because of the simple vocabulary. Children who are used to signing are very adept with their hands and seem to enjoy string stories very much. String stories tend to have simple story lines and the audience can participate with their own strings after the first telling. Give each child a loop of string after you tell the story; then teach them the moves. Always encourage them to take the string home and learn new moves.

Simple songs, such as "The Alphabet Song," are excellent to use with mixed audiences using sign language. If the songs are repeated often enough, soon all those attending will be "singing" them with their hands.

Explore your community for counselors or teachers of deaf or hearing-impaired children, for community college classes in sign language, or for local or state advocacy groups for the deaf. You will find guidance and discover new ideas and materials. The rewards you receive from sharing stories with these children will be many.

STORYTELLING IN SPECIAL LOCATIONS

Storytelling is a practical, flexible tool for the traveling librarian—it requires no props, takes up no space, and can be carried anywhere.

STORYTELLING IN HOSPITALS

Time passes slowly for the hospitalized or chronically ill child. The storyteller, equipped with all types of stories—picture books, simple folktales, a short literary tale to read aloud, even a puppet or two—can help ease the child's concerns and bring the gift of shared pleasure.

The librarian storyteller visiting a hospital may tell or read to an individual child or to a group of children; a group will most likely include a wide age range. A beginning storyteller once went to a hospital to share picture books with young children. Her audience turned out to be a group of fifth- and sixth-grade boys. Fortunately, she knew a story that pleased them. Then she confessed her predicament and invited them to share her own delight in picture-book art. Because she had not talked down to them, the boys thoroughly enjoyed their introduction to the picture-book world.

There is a special need for reading aloud and storytelling in the clinic waiting room. Often parents must sit with their children a long time, waiting to be called by the doctor. The children become restless, and very often are overexcited by the time the doctor is ready to examine them. Experience has shown that the medical staff usually welcomes a "quiet time" before the examination. Librarians have discovered that the clinic is a wonderful place to introduce parents and other caregivers to the library and its services.

STORYTELLING OUTDOORS

In many communities storytellers from the public library visit parks and playgrounds to tell stories on a regular schedule, especially during the summer months. Summer storytelling programs bring librarians into contact with readers and nonreaders; these encounters are often a child's introduction to the public library and to books.

Storytellers at recreational centers and camps use the outdoors as the setting for storytelling. In addition to scheduled periods set aside for storytelling, informal storytelling is carried on while the children are resting or between activities.

Camp programs recognize that storytelling around a campfire at night has a magic of its own. Use the locale, whether woods, seashore, or mountains. A starry night is the perfect time to tell legends of the stars and sky beings. Ghost stories are a favorite, but these are best reserved for older listeners; younger children enjoy scary stories in more familiar surroundings. On a rainy evening suggest that the youngsters take turns telling stories indoors; these round-robins encourage children to become storytellers.

Summer storytelling in parks presents a real challenge. Often the groups are very large and have a wide age span—from toddlers to grandparents. Mothers bring their children, recreation leaders see the storytelling crowd and bring their group to join it (sometimes in the middle of the story), teenagers stop to listen, dogs bark around the periphery. Every possible distraction can be present. Such situations demand poise, a strong voice, and a careful selection of stories. The storyteller must be flexible and unflappable.

Find a quiet, shady, secluded area, away from swimming and wading pools and noisy play areas. Invite the children to sit on the ground in a semicircle with the smaller children in front. Give the children plenty of leg room. The storyteller usually stands so that the children can hear the story and see the storyteller more easily.

Plan the program for about twenty-five to thirty minutes. Bring along a few picture books with large, colorful pictures in case you need to begin your program with stories for the youngest. Tell two or three short, surefire stories, full of dramatic action and a good helping of humor. Folktales are a wise choice. Keep the program relaxed and informal.

STORYTELLING IN MUSEUMS

Many museums carry out a regular storytelling program for children. This practice can be traced back to 1911 in the Boston Museum of Fine Arts and to 1918 in the Metropolitan Museum of Art (one of the places where Marie Shedlock lectured on storytelling). The purpose of these early story hours was to stimulate children's interest in art in general and in particular in works of art in the galleries. No matter how vivid the printed descriptions identifying art objects are in the galleries, the art does not speak without some context. Young people can develop a personal involvement with art if they feel an emotional connection with a character in a painting, or know why or how a certain object was used in the past. Art museums are emphasizing the education aspect of their mission, and storytelling has become a powerful means of connection between the language of words and the language of images.

Museums have devised imaginative ways to incorporate stories into their calendar of events. Whenever feasible, the storytelling takes place in the galleries where the audience is close to objects that draw on the same cultural traditions as the stories being told. Some museums focus a day of storytelling on a work in their collection. An example is the day of medieval stories about knights and princesses planned by Susan Kuliak of the Art Institute of

Chicago and held on April 23, St. George's Day, to connect visitors to Bernardo Martorell's painting *St. George Killing the Dragon.* If a large number of visitors prevents gallery presentations, audiences meet in atriums, auditoriums, or special rooms away from the art. Wherever the audience gathers, storytellers try to make vivid connections among the stories, the intentions and techniques of the artists, the purposes and meanings of the artifacts, and the cultures they represent.

In April 1995 the Children's Museum of Indianapolis opened a permanent interactive educational exhibit called "Life Stories: African-American Voices That Teach Us All." The exhibit was intended to:

> . . . help families of all backgrounds understand and appreciate the role of storytelling and oral tradition, both in the African-American community as well as their own. . . . The exhibit is designed as a composite neighborhood street made up of several settings. Each stage or setting provides a different context in which a group of stories are told. As visitors amble down the "street," they may visit a family and "eavesdrop" on the Sunday dinner conversation or hear a bedtime story. They might stop by the barber shop to hear the latest "stories" or watch TV and shoot the breeze. Maybe they'll get lucky and arrive at "the stoop" just as the three neighborhood storytellers get ready to spin a couple of good yarns. They might climb in the car and become an active participant in the story that "Aunt Janice" has to tell as she taxis kids all over the neighborhood. Or perhaps they will go into the storefront church to hear the story of why the oral tradition is so important to the African-American community. Before they leave, each visitor will have an opportunity to visit the story bank to deposit a story from their own family or to withdraw a good story to take home.[15]

The exhibition was developed with large participation from the local African American community. The stories were gathered from oral history interviews as well as traditional folklore.

Mary Grace Ketner takes storytelling into the galleries of the Institute of Texas Cultures, a museum in San Antonio that focuses on the lives and folkways of the various ethnic groups of Texas, with the informal mission of "letting Texans know that there were all kinds of folk in Texas, not just cowboys and oil men."[16] The museum sponsors the Texas Folklife Festival where there has been a storytelling stage since the 1970s.

One of Ketner's roles at the institute was that of "sitting storyteller." There was no formal schedule; one morning a week during school tours Ketner would go into the galleries and invite docents to bring their tours to hear an exhibit-related story. This was a simple and effective way to make connections to exhibits and to the school curriculum.

Mid-Winter Tales was a once-a-week storytelling project held for four to six weeks that featured a different storyteller each week. Storytellers were selected to represent a diverse group of cultures (African American, Latino, and so forth) or would focus on the tales of an assigned ethnic group. The program was highly successful, the museum hosting crowds of children during what were traditionally slow winter months. Another community favorite is a storytelling program for Halloween organized around a Tyrannosaurus Rex named Sue entitled "Bone-Chilling Tales with Sue."

Storytelling is almost always connected to exhibits, such as "Children from Around the World," which included tales from different countries along with a craft component. More recently the institute has begun to offer live videoconference programs, among which the most popular is world folktales, wherein Ketner tells stories from around the world, taking questions from students in distance classrooms. Teachers began using the program as a reward or a special event for classes; the institute received more out-of-state than in-state requests.

Maureen Korte is the education director at the Iowa State Historical Museum. She is committed to including storytelling in museum programming, "because stories are history and history makes all of us real."[17] Korte says that half of history is story, and that stories are how we preserve history. Museums keep historical stories in context so history is undistorted.

Korte tells stories herself, or the museum does research and then hires theater companies and storytellers to create the specific storytelling performances needed. Storytelling in the museum is connected to exhibits and special events, such as the Fall to Winter Storytelling Festival, a Bastille Day Fest, Hay Days (stories about horses, harvest, and farm life); all programs are connected to the cultural origins of Iowa's population.

The importance of storytelling has been absorbed into the museum's programming. For example, the museum did research for a program called "Haunted Iowa," and hired eight storytellers to portray Iowans who had had paranormal experiences. The storytellers, in period costume, were placed in various locations in the museum that coordinated with their stories. Another of the museum's research projects resulted in the Des Moines Metropolitan Opera production of *George Washington Carver*.

In addition to the general public, Korte's audience includes all K–12 students in the state of Iowa. She is working with drama coach Ruth Ann Gaines and speech coach Ginger Johnson to establish a young adult storytelling guild in an inner-city high school. Planned storytelling workshops will help recruit students to a program that seeks to provide a foundation for self-worth through an introduction to both the art of storytelling and tales from students' own ethnic origins. Korte wryly points out that while plans are often subject to funding, most projects don't necessarily require money, just sweat.

Storyteller Kim Sheahan is the assistant director of education at the Spurlock Museum in Urbana, Illinois. The museum collection covers six continents and a million years of history. Sheahan's job is to create and present in-house and outreach educational programs and special events related to permanent and traveling exhibits. Adults as well as children seek these outreach programs, which extend not only to schools, but to local organizations of all kinds, including the Rotary, local women's clubs, exchange clubs, and service organizations such as the Council of Volunteers.

Sheahan tells stories in the museum "because it allows me to do what a museum educator is supposed to do, which is make the artifacts come alive. Stories give the artifacts context, take them out from behind the glass."[18] Sheahan feels that storytelling focuses the energy and attention of children, and gives the artifacts context within important cultural traditions.

Sheahan tells stories from as many cultures represented in the museum as is humanly possible. She is concerned about finding stories that are authentic, "that have a lineage, a paper trail of references."[19] It must be very clear that a folktale is a tale handed from teller to reteller to teller, and that the story being told is one person's version, not a replication of a cultural event.

Formal concerts (Winter Tales, Halloween, Day of the Dead, and the like) balance between education and entertainment. Everything except for the formal concerts is connected to an artifact. Sheahan is constantly building programs, and plans to put curriculum support modules online. Program offerings include Greek mythology, Cinderella Around the World, Trickster Stories, Kid Heroes, and Tall-Tale Heroes. Examples of artifacts coupled with stories include "The Wedding of the Mouse" with a Japanese wedding kimono; "Meng's Bitter Weeping" with the Chinese warriors from the first emperor's tomb; "The Spider Weaver" with African kente cloth; "Only One Cowry" with African currency and items decorated with cowry; and "The Doomed Prince" with papyrus and the human mummy from Egypt.

As a librarian and member of a community agency serving children, you may be asked to tell stories at a museum or to train museum docents in storytelling. If you are asked to give a workshop for museum docents, you will need to familiarize yourself with the museum collections. Spend time gathering story collections and selecting individual stories that complement artifacts in the museum; only then will you be ready to meet with the docents. The emphasis of your workshop should be on selecting, learning, and presenting stories. Introduce the docents to a basic text, such as *Storytelling: Art and Technique*, and to resources such as D. L. Ashliman's *A Guide to Folktales in the English Language* and Margaret Read MacDonald's *The Storyteller's Sourcebook*. Give examples of matching a story with an artifact, and prepare a short annotated bibliography to get the docents started.

Museum staff have observed that visitors who are untrained in looking at art or artifacts usually spend only a few seconds before a particular piece, but when they listen to a story told in front of a carefully chosen object, they may spend as long as twenty minutes sitting or standing in one place in the museum. During this time they are listening, imagining, concentrating. Art objects alone cannot represent the rich diversity and the creativity of our ancestors. Storytellers, too, help keep the people of the past alive—their energy and sense of humor, their virtues, the physical attributes they admired, the dangers they faced, and the dreams they wished to pass on to those who follow.

STORYTELLING ON RADIO AND TELEVISION

To sustain a story on the air for twenty minutes or more with the use of only one instrument, the voice, although it may sound easy, is really a most demanding act. The storyteller's voice must have great range and flexibility. . . . He must convey the "feel" of each new character at once solely by the use of his voice.[20]

If you tell stories on radio or television, choose them for their broad appeal, literary quality, action, and a minimum of detail. Folktales are excellent choices, though modern and personal stories and literary fairy tales can be used. The tales should appeal to as wide an audience as possible. Select a story that requires no cutting or a minimum of cutting to fit the time allotted.

A fifteen-minute radio show is a good length; television producers usually want a thirty-minute show. Television spots must be planned with visuals, so the story should be selected with this in mind. Shortening a story by even two minutes requires substantial cutting, so try to find an appropriate story that will fit the allotted time with very little adjustment. Nevertheless, it is important to learn how to cut a story, if necessary. Do not eliminate all description, because this kind of background information is necessary in order to create a mood and establish atmosphere and visualization. A word here and there, an unnecessary phrase, a digression, can be easily eliminated. For example, cut "Once upon a time there was" to "Once there was"; eliminate adjectives where they seem superfluous. The result will be a tightened story, which becomes a script to be told or read as naturally as possible.

If the story you have chosen is not long enough for the allotted time, stretch the program with poetry or song or both. A lively theme song can be used as an introduction and as a fade-out to set the mood for the program.

Plan programs well in advance. Obtain the permission of the publisher to use any copyrighted materials that are needed for the program. Be sure to give credit to the author, illustrator, and publisher of any book used, regardless of whether it is protected by copyright.

During the broadcast it is very important for the storyteller to watch the director or manager for cues and to follow directions. Be prepared to improvise, especially during the last few minutes of the program. Do not speak too quickly, but do not drag out the story. Enunciate clearly, use a natural manner and voice, avoid over-dramatization, but do not eliminate all the drama in your telling, especially on radio. Use the dramatic pause and perfect its timing. Have a glass of water handy for that unexpected tickle in the throat. (The glass of water and any notes you have can be hidden from the camera by placing them behind your books.) Look directly into the camera, not at the monitor, and remember that the microphone picks up the slightest noise—a cleared throat, a sigh, the rattle of papers. It is difficult for most storytellers to tell a story to a microphone or to a camera, so try to picture a group of listeners as you tell. Let the enjoyment of the story come through in your voice if the medium is radio, and through your voice and facial expression if the medium is television.

STORYTELLING ONLINE

Storytelling online gained ground during the first decade of the twenty-first century. Library forays into the Web environment resulted in stories being told not over the telephone as in the old Dial-a-Story days, but online through audio and video streaming.

Technological improvements make the accumulation and dissemination of storytelling programs, whether full or samples, easier as time goes by. Libraries with the technological know-how were quick to move into the online arena. For example, the Enoch Pratt Free Library (http://www.prattlibrary.org/home/storyIndex.aspx) has put storytellers from across the United States online through a grant from the Institute of Museum and Library Services. Various public libraries have their own librarian-storytellers telling and reading stories on library websites. The Denver Public Library uses podcasting to put their children's librarians online reading and telling stories (http://podcast.denverlibrary.org/index.php?post_category=Folk%20and%20Fairytales).

Although learning how to put stories online may appear daunting, audio and video recording and editing software is standard on many new computers and is also available as freeware, so with care the financial output is small.

REFERENCES

1. Dorothy Butler, *Cushla and Her Books* (Horn Book, 1980), p. 107.
2. Craig Werner, "A Blind Child's View of Children's Literature," *Children's Literature* 12 (1984): 209-216.
3. Joanne Epply-Schmidt, personal communications to Susan Danoff, January 10, 2009.
4. Won-Ldy Paye, Margaret H. Lippert, and Julie Paschkis, *Mrs. Chicken and the Hungry Crocodile* (Holt, 2003).
5. Gwyn Calvetti, telephone interview with Janice Del Negro, August 7, 2008.
6. Susan Danoff, personal communications with Ellin Greene, December 2008.
7. Paula Davidoff, correspondence with Ellin Greene, December 2008.

8. Julie Pasqual, "My Old Men" in her Notes from the Field (http://juliepasqual. blogspot.com/2007/06/notes-from-field-part-i.html).

9. Evelyn Walker, ed., *Programming for Serving Children with Special Needs*, prepared by the Library Service to Children with Special Needs Committee, Association for Library Service to Children (American Library Association, 1994), p. 12.

10. Paula Davidoff, correspondence with Ellin Greene, December 30, 2008.

11. David P., telephone interview with Janice Del Negro, August 10, 2008.

12. Ibid.

13. Jill Beebout, telephone interview with Janice Del Negro, August 10, 2008.

14. National Institute on Deafness and Other Communication Disorders, www.nidcd. nih.gov/index.aspl, accessed October 16, 2008.

15. Rita C. Organ, former curator/programmer of African American materials, Children's Museum of Indianapolis, Indiana, correspondence with Ellin Greene (1995).

16. Mary Grace Ketner, telephone interview with Janice Del Negro, August 14, 2008.

17. Maureen Korte, telephone interview with Janice Del Negro, August 12, 2008.

18. Kim Sheahan, telephone interview with Janice Del Negro, August 15, 2008.

19. Ibid.

20. Lilian Okun, *Let's Listen to a Story; Radio Scripts for Children* (Wilson, 1959), pp. 11–12.

WEB RESOURCES

The Art of Storytelling: Enriching Art Museum Exhibits and Education through Visitor Narratives by Matthew Fisher, Beth A. Twiss-Garrity, and Alexandra Sastre
http://www.archimuse.com/mw2008/papers/fisher/fisher.html
Produced by Archives and Museum Informatics

CELLnotes (Center for Early Literacy Learning): Children's Active Participation in Reading and Storytelling Can Enhance Early Literacy Learning by Carol M. Trivette and Carl J. Dunst
http://www.earlyliteracylearning.org/cellpapers/cellnotes_v1_n2.pdf

Programming for Children with Special Needs
http://www.alsc.ala.org/blog/?p=800

Telling Tales: A Guide to Developing Effective Storytelling Programmes for Museums Researched and Written by Emily Johnsson, Edited by Claire Adler
www.mlalondon.org.uk/uploads/documents/Hub.pdf
London Museums Hub 2006

8 STORYTELLING TO YOUNG CHILDREN

Children who are not spoken to by live and responsive adults will not learn to speak properly. Children who are not answered will stop asking questions. They will become incurious. And children who are not told stories and who are not read to will have few reasons for wanting to learn to read.
—*Gail E. Haley*[1]

THE TEACHER/ADMINISTRATOR of a nursery school offered an example that illustrates Haley's point. A four-year-old boy came to her school not knowing the names of common objects. The teacher described the mother as caring but noticed that she spoke very little to her son. The boy would point to an object and his mother would give it to him without naming it. She answered his questions simply "yes" or "no," without expanding. As she helped him dress she did not name any article of clothing. Consequently, the child did not connect names to objects. When the teacher asked him for a crayon, play block, or other object, the child did not understand her request. He did not know that what he wore on his feet are called socks and shoes. The teacher learned that the mother did not read or tell stories to her son. This mother cared for her son's physical needs but was unaware of her role in his literacy development.[2]

During the past forty years a great deal of research has been done on how children become literate and the relationship between listening and speaking, reading, and writing. Research on the how and why of storybook reading development has focused on parent-child interactions or teacher-child interactions with storybook readings and the child's independent "readings." In a summary of her work with two- to five-year-olds, Elizabeth Sulzby writes, "The acquisition of literacy can be said to involve a transition from oral language to written language. First, early storybook reading by parents includes aspects of both oral and written language. Second, as children gain experience, storybook reading becomes more like conventional conceptualizations of written language. Third, children's earliest interactions with storybooks are mediated by an interactive adult and gradually become the performance of a text-as-monologue by the adult for the listening and observing child. Finally, storybook reading becomes a task which the child performs for another person or for himself/herself alone. As the child becomes a more independent 'reader' (long before s/he is reading conventionally from print), the language s/he produces for the storybook becomes more truly 'written language.'"[3]

Storybook readings introduce children to book language. Children learn the nature of the book and of print—what Don Holdaway calls "a literary set for learning to read."[4] They learn that in our culture a book is read from left to right and from top to bottom. They learn about "word-space-word" arrangement and punctuation. Most important, they learn that the squiggly marks on the page have meaning. At first, non-reading children "read" the pictures. Gradually, they learn that the words tell the story.

As noted in Chapter 2, the first library story hours were planned for children ages nine and older, the age when children were expected to know *how* to read. Librarians wanted to encourage young readers and considered storytelling a form of reading guidance. Picture-book hours for younger children, ages five to seven, soon followed.

The parent and child literature-sharing programs for infants and toddlers and their caregivers began in 1935 with the "Mothers' Room" program started by Clarence Sumner, director of the Youngstown (Ohio) Public Library. Sumner was a visionary who saw the Mothers' Room as "the 'builder' and 'feeder' for the Children's Room, being the logical first unit in the program of the public library."[5] The Mothers' Room was designed to encourage literature-sharing activities between mothers and preschoolers, not with the purpose of teaching young children to read, but "to impress upon their minds the pleasures of literature."[6] The Mothers' Room collection included picture storybooks and books and magazines on parenting. Lectures were presented every other week on children's reading, child care, and family relations. The movement spread nationwide, but after World War II, for reasons still not clear, librarians focused their attention on the three- to five-year-olds. Undoubtedly, one reason was the influx of picture-book artists from Europe and the improved technology that made possible the making of beautiful picture books for young children.

Library story hours for three- to five-year-olds began in the late 1930s and were firmly established as part of regular library work by 1940. When the federal government initiated Head Start in 1965, attention once more turned to the role of the parent or primary caregiver as the child's first teacher. The Harvard Preschool Project (1965-1978) clearly demonstrated the importance of the first three years of life in intellectual, emotional, social, and language development. Such programs substantiated the research and writings of Swiss psychologist Jean Piaget on early learning. This new information convinced librarians of the need to shift their orientation away from the librarian-child-centered preschool story hours toward infant and toddler parent-child-centered programs.

Brain Development in Infancy

At birth, a baby's brain is still developing. Dean Falk, paleoanthropologist and author of *Finding Our Tongues: Mothers, Infants and the Origins of Language,* explains: "Walking on two legs (bipedalism) caused our ancestors to diverge from those of chimpanzees some 5-7 million years ago, and was accompanied by two important but conflicting trends: the changes in the pelvis that facilitated walking caused birth canals to become increasingly narrow, and brain size steadily increased as our early relatives continued to evolve. The result was that childbirth became increasingly difficult for pre-historic mothers, and only babies that were born smaller and more helpless survived. Because of their delayed development, these little late bloomers lost the ability to cling unsupported to their mothers, a skill monkey and ape infants very quickly develop. Before the invention of baby slings, mothers had little choice but to carry babies on their hips or in their arms. These mothers must have put their babies down beside them during pauses for resting and gathering food, as contemporary women sometimes do. When separated from their mothers, the babies would have fussed, as they do today, and busy prehistoric moms would have tried to soothe their babies voice-to-voice, which is probably how the first lullabies were invented. Modern babies everywhere are extraordinarily musical, so it is not surprising that people sing lullabies and play songs to them throughout the world. Baby talk, or 'motherese,' which is unique to our species and exists in some form in all human cultures, would also have developed as a part-time replacement for cradling arms. Because motherese helps modern infants learn the rhythms and rules of their languages through repetition, exaggerated vowels, simplified vocabulary, and its musical quality, it is reasonable to suggest that our ancestors' first words and, eventually, their first language were among the evolutionary spinoffs of the very first baby talk. And this all occurred because feet that had become tailored for walking and helpless little hands lost the ability to cling."[7]

The infant is born with billions of brain cells, or neurons, but most of these neurons are not yet connected in networks. These connections, called synapses, are created as the infant interacts with the environment through the senses of touch, taste, smell, sight, and hearing. "In a new brain, synapses form at a rate of three billion a second. By eight months of life, there are one thousand trillion connections. These gradually begin to decline and by age ten or so, half of the connections die off leaving about five hundred trillion that last most of life. Information flows easily into the brain through 'windows' that open for varying duration. These windows of development occur in phases from birth to age twelve when the brain is very actively learning from the environment. It is during this period, and especially the first three years, that the foundations for thinking, language, vision, attitudes, aptitudes, and other characteristics are laid down" (Source: U.S. Department of Health and Human Services Early Head Start National Resource Center @ Zero to Three). Synapses used repeatedly in the child's everyday life are reinforced; those not used repeatedly are eliminated.

Holding baby while singing a lullaby, playing patty-cake with baby, talking to baby about everyday things, and reading to baby really can make a difference. According to a study by Reading Is Fundamental (RIF), at age six the child who has been read to from birth has an average vocabulary of 20,000 words. By contrast, the six-year-old who has had little experience with books in early childhood has an average vocabulary of 3,000 words. This differential impacts on a child's success both in school and in life.

Steve Herb, then Education Librarian at Pennsylvania State University, wrote in *School Library Journal*, July 1997, that "the foundation for emergent literacy is in preschool experiences with language. And the only sound means of transmitting those experiences is through human interaction, the social aspects of learning. We've learned that the roots of literacy appear to be strongly grounded in orality (speaking and listening) and playfulness. In fact, playful oral language experiences prepare children to understand and experiment with written language."[8]

The emphasis on parent-child-centered programs was greatly accelerated in 2000 with the creation of Every Child Ready to Read @ your library (ECRR), a partnership between the Public Library Association (PLA), the Association for Library Service to Children (ALSC), and the National Institute of Child Health and Human Development (NICHD). The goal of ECRR is to help parents raise children who love to read and love to use the library. ECRR established public libraries as a partner in the education continuum. "The thinking behind ECRR," as stated by authors Saroj Nadkarni Ghoting, consultant to the program, and Pamela Martin-Diaz in their book *Early Literacy Storytimes @ your library: Partnering with Caregivers for Success*, is that "library staff are ideally suited to inform parents and caregivers about early literacy research. . . . To inform parents and caregivers about the research behind early literacy, a series of workshops was developed for libraries. Fourteen demonstration sites were chosen to evaluate the effect of these workshops on the early literacy behaviors of participants. These sites presented the workshops both in and out of the library and to parents and to childcare providers. The full evaluation and a list of demonstration sites are available at http://www.pla.org/earlyliteracy.htm. In addition to workshops, these sites have applied this early literacy information to other aspects of library service by

- enhancing storytimes with the inclusion of early literacy information for adults;

- incorporating early literacy skills into reading programs;
- doing more outreach programs;
- changing the library environment to be more language rich;
- incorporating early literacy information into the one-on-one interaction (via reference and readers' advisory interviews); and expanding collections."[9]

KEY POINTS OF EVERY CHILD READY TO READ @ YOUR LIBRARY

- Parents and caregivers play the most important role in developing their own children's literacy skills. Parents are with their children every day. Librarians' intermittent contacts with the children are not enough to effect real and lasting change.
- Librarians must make *outreach* efforts a priority. Families most in need of literacy information don't come to the library.
- Librarians must partner with others in the community who advocate early literacy. Schools are a good first choice.
- To change the lives of children, librarians must make parent/caregiver education a top priority.

Librarians need to know what early literacy is, the language of early literacy, how the physical space in their library promotes—or does not promote—early literacy, and must be comfortable talking with parents about the parents' role in developing their child's early literacy skills, as they present toddler story times.

Research conducted by NICHD identified six early literacy skills that are precursors to learning to read:

1. Print motivation—a child's interest in and enjoyment of books
2. Phonological awareness—the ability to hear and play with the smaller sounds in words
3. Vocabulary—knowing the names of things
4. Narrative skills—the ability to describe things and events and to tell stories
5. Print awareness—noticing print, knowing how to handle a book, and understanding how to follow the written words on a page
6. Letter knowledge—knowing letters are different from each other, that the same letter can look different, and that each letter has a name and relates to specific sounds

Author-experts Ghoting and Martin-Diaz suggest what to tell parents/caregivers about each of the six skills. Their comprehensive guide includes sample programs for children from newborns to age five that integrate early literacy information into the programs, and sample parent tip take-home pages. Just remember to have fun. Don't turn the storytime into an academic lesson!

Clara N. Bohrer, PLA president (2004-2005) and director of the West Bloomfield Township Public Library, Michigan (one of the fourteen ECRR demonstration sites), made emergent literacy a major part of her platform. Bohrer defines early literacy as "what children learn about reading and writing before they actually can read or write." In speaking about the six skills in her presentations to librarians, she would ask: "What can you do to reinforce the skills during storytimes?" Here are some of her suggestions:

1. Print Motivation—Share the enjoyment of reading children's books with parents. Remind them that children love to imitate their parents so parents have to not only read to their children, but they must also read in front of their children.

2. Vocabulary—Choose books that will expand the vocabularies of children, discuss unfamiliar words before reading, have children repeat words that may not be familiar—do it in a fun way.

3. Print Awareness—When you read, make a point of showing the cover, open the book facing the children. State and talk about the title and author. From time to time point to the text as you say the words. Use nametags; have parents write out the tags, do it with their child, and maybe the child can say it or spell it out.

4. Narrative skills—Choose books that are cumulative or sequential. Read without much interruption so children can hear entire sequence. Then reread with the children saying what comes next. Give children an opportunity to respond orally to simple questions about the story or pictures. Occasionally, at the end, have the children act out the story with movement.

5. Phonological awareness—Use books that rhyme and can be sung. Use nursery rhymes, fingerplays, songs and music in storytimes. Play rhyming games. Use books that have a nice rhythm and rhyme in the language of the text.

6. Letter knowledge—Use ABC books; point to the letters and say the names. Have the children join in. Use books about shapes and colors.[10]

The photos and the sample Babytime program in this chapter are from the West Bloomfield Township Public Library. West Bloomfield is a northwest suburb of Detroit with a culturally diverse population of 64,860. Twenty-three languages are spoken in the school system. The Main Library and the Westacres Branch (the libraries are 3.5 miles from each other) were renovated and redesigned between 1997 and 2001, following a two-year planning process that included input from both the community and the library staff. More space was allotted for youth services, including a separate programming room, and more programming was planned for children from birth to five. The environment was made more childlike, yet with an appeal to children through Grade 5. More opportunities were created for caregiver/child interaction beyond reading with the emphasis on developmentally appropriate activities, including play and a puppet theatre.

PARENT AND CHILD LITERATURE-SHARING PROGRAMS

The new understanding of how the human brain develops, and the importance of timing (the first three years are prime learning time) reignited interest in programs like the Mothers' Rooms of the 1930s. Today, almost all public libraries offer storytimes for preschoolers and toddlers and many offer literature-sharing programs for infants accompanied by a parent/caregiver. These programs are called by various names: lap-sits, baby play, baby time, storytime for prewalkers/pretalkers (birth–24 months), storytime for walkers/talkers, toddler times (2- to 3-year-olds), prereaders/preschool storytime (4- to 5-year-olds). When the audience includes children from birth to age 5 or older accompanied by parents/caregivers they are usually called Family Storytimes.

The goals of the parent and child literature-sharing program are:

1. to inform parents/caregivers of early literacy research and give them an awareness of the role they play in emergent literacy;
2. to acquaint parents/caregivers with quality books and non-print materials developmentally appropriate for young children;
3. to give parents/caregivers participatory experiences in sharing literature with their children and an opportunity to observe effective storytelling;
4. to introduce the public library as a resource center for parents/caregivers;
5. to provide a place for first-time parents to meet;
6. to give infants and toddlers a joyous experience so that they will associate books and libraries with pleasure.[11]

Encourage parents to make storybook reading a part of their children's everyday life. The research shows that children who are read to early on and who associate books with pleasure are likely to become lifelong readers. From listening to stories, children learn story structure, patterns of language, the connection between the squiggly lines on the page and words, and the connection between words and meaning. Even though infants and toddlers may not understand much of what is read to them, they are learning to connect the world of books to the world around them. This helps them later as they learn to read and write. Mem Fox, bestselling author and an international literacy consultant, writes, "If every parent understood the huge educational benefits and intense happiness brought about by reading aloud to their children, and if every parent—and every adult caring for a child—read aloud a minimum of three stories a day to the children in their lives, we could probably wipe out illiteracy within one generation."[12]

Before starting a parent and child literature-sharing program, carefully consider the practical issues. Is there a quiet, self-contained area away from distractions where the parents and infants and toddlers can listen to stories and enjoy other appropriate storytime activities together? Are there enough books and other materials to support the program? Is there enough staff? Librarians who have conducted many parent and child literature-sharing programs estimate that a thirty-minute storytime may require two hours of preparation time (of course you can repeat a program during another series or on visits to early childhood centers).

Many librarians have found it is impossible to schedule the number of storytimes demanded by older, better-educated parents who want the best for their children. At the other extreme, there are communities where teenage parents—some still children themselves—are unaware of library services that could help them, and communities where people are totally unaware of what the library has to offer because they are newly arrived from countries in which library service is not well developed. Hard decisions have to be made. If you cannot offer as many storytimes within the library as you would like, consider offering a series or limiting attendance to one series only. You might schedule workshops for day-care and Head Start staff in selection and presentation of literature to young children, so they can conduct their own programs, or you might make a demonstration video to show to parents and child caregivers.

The earliest introduction to literature is through the ear—lullabies, nursery rhymes, and the like—but lap reads can begin as soon as the infant is able to support his or her own head, at about three months. In *Family Storybook Reading*, authors Denny Taylor and Dorothy Strickland say: "Books are like lullabies: they caress a newborn baby, calm a fretful child, and help a nervous mother."[13] During the parent and infant literature-sharing program you can introduce parents to board books, story rhymes, play songs, and singing games that they can enjoy with their young children at home. Infants delight in looking at the photos of babies in *The Baby's Book of Babies* by Kathy Henderson and the soft watercolor paintings in *Time for Bed* by Mem Fox. They appreciate the sharp figure-ground contrast in Tana Hoban's board books *Black on White* and *White on Black*.

Children younger than eighteen months of age are not ready for much story listening in a group, but enjoy interacting with the parents or caregivers in turn-taking games, such as "pat-a-cake" and "peek-a-boo"; chanting nursery rhymes; singing; and looking at clear, bright pictures. They relish the sounds of language. Use Mother Goose nursery rhymes, perhaps accompanied by flannel-board figures, and simple stories with familiar objects, such as *Goodnight Moon* by Margaret Wise Brown, and *"More More More," Said the Baby: 3 Love Stories* by Vera Williams.

BABY TIMES

Here is a sample "Finger Fun for Babies" program based on one offered at the Portland Public Library in Maine and contributed by Phyllis Fuchs, formerly children's librarian at the Curtis Memorial Library in Brunswick, Maine. Fuchs writes that the program requires energy to maintain a brisk pace throughout the 20-minute session and she recommends having two presenters who offer the rhymes alternately. Each rhyme is introduced with a cheerful descriptive phrase intended to get everyone ready; for example, "Here's a bouncing one," or "Get ready for a fall." Each rhyme is repeated twice and accompanied by appropriate actions.

1. Pat a cake, pat a cake, baker's man . . .
2. "Let's twinkle." Twinkle, twinkle little star . . . opening and shutting fingers for twinkles.
3. "A bouncing one"—Ride a cock horse to Banbury Cross . . .
4. This little piggy went to market . . .
5. "Get ready for a big jump!" Leg over leg the dog went to Dover . . .
6. "Get ready for a fall." Humpty Dumpty . . .
7. Hickory, dickory, dock . . .
8. "Get your rowing arms ready." Row, row, row your boat . . .
9. Five little ducks went swimming in the water . . . with a clap for each quack.
10. Diddle diddle dumpling, my son John. . . . This becomes a bouncing rhyme.
11. The eensie weensie spider . . .

12. Trot trot to Boston. . . . A lap rhyme with a drop between the adult's legs for the child.

13. Tommie Thumb is up and Tommie Thumb is down, Tommie Thumb is dancing all around the town. . . . This song and finger play continue using all the fingers in turn: Peter Pointer, Toby Tall, Ruby Ring, and Baby Finger.

14. The wheels on the bus . . .

15. Depending on the time, the presenter might ask for a request or two.

16. At this point, the presenter might invite the babies to choose a book from a pile placed in the middle of the floor and take it to the adult so child and adult can look at a book together.

17. After a few minutes for sharing books, the presenter closes the program with a song, such as "If You're Happy and You Know It, Clap Your Hands."

The following is a Babytime/Walkers program presented by Sue Barash, youth services librarian, West Bloomfield Township Public Library, Michigan:

THEME: Exploring the Senses
WELCOME SONG: "Welcome, Welcome Everyone"

> Welcome, welcome everyone,
> Now you're here, let's have some fun.
> First we'll clap our hands just so,
> Then we'll bend and touch our toes.
> Welcome, welcome everyone,
> Now you're here, let's have some fun.

Dance Little Babies
> Dance, dance, dance little _____(insert a child's name)
>   Additional lines: clap, jump, bounce, spin
> While we sing this song.

> (We go around the room with this until we've inserted every child's name. It helps us learn each other's names, and the children love to hear their own names in the song!)

STORY: *Crunch Munch* by Jonathan London
LAP PLAY: "Open, shut them"/"This Little Piggy"/"Hickory Dickory Doc"
SHARED STORY: *Who's Peeking?* by Charles Reasoner
ACTIVE MOVEMENT: "I Wish I Were a Bunny"—bunny, frog, bird, fish
"Row Your Boat"
"If You're Happy and You Know It, Clap Your Hands"

F I G U R E   14. *Babytime I, storytime for babies from birth to 12 months. Mike Greer Photography, www.mikegreer.com. Reprinted by permission of the West Bloomfield Township Public Library, West Bloomfield, Michigan.*

FIGURE 15. *Babytime II, storytime for babies 12 to 24 months, conducted by Pat Reynolds, Youth Services Librarian (now retired). Mike Greer Photography, www.mikegreer.com. Reprinted by permission of the West Bloomfield Township Public Library, West Bloomfield, Michigan.*

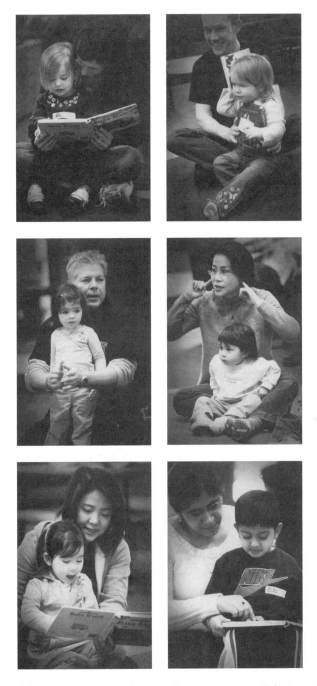

FIGURE 16. *Fathers as well as mothers enjoy listening to stories at Babytime and Toddler Time. Mike Greer Photography, www.mikegreer.com. Reprinted by permission of the West Bloomfield Township Public Library, West Bloomfield, Michigan.*

Sensory: Scarf Songs: "This Is the Way We Wave Our Scarves"

Each parent is given a set of two scarves. First, the babies or young toddlers explore the feel and color of the scarves, then we sing "This Is the Way We Wave Our Scarves" to the tune of "Here We Go Round the Mulberry Bush" (see words below) as the parents and/or children wave the scarves around. We sing the song twice.

This is the way we wave our scarves,
wave our scarves, wave our scarves.
This is the way we wave our scarves, so early in the morning.
Wave up high and touch the sky,
touch the sky, touch the sky,
Wave up high and touch the sky, so early in the morning.
Wave down low and touch your toes,
touch your toes, touch your toes.
Wave down low and touch your toes, so early in the morning.

Where Is Baby? (Sung to the tune of "Frère Jacques")
Where is baby, where is baby?
There she is! There she is!
I'm so glad to see you.
I'm so glad to see you.
Peek-a-boo! I see you!
Peek-a-boo! I see you!
    (Repeat)

March to "Walking, Walking" (*Songs for Wiggleworms* CD 5/song no. 30, Old Town School of Music, available through Amazon.com)

Bubbles: Each parent/caregiver is given a small bottle of bubble water and everyone has fun blowing and observing bubbles.

Parachute: Babies crawl underneath a parachute being lifted up and down while songs with a theme of community or good feelings, such as "May There Always Be Sunshine" by Jim Gill (*Jim Gill Sings the Sneezing Song and Other Contagious Tunes*) is played.

Goodbye Song: (*Songs for Wiggleworms* CD 5/song no. 38, Old Town School of Music, available through Amazon.com)

For more program ideas for Baby Times see appropriate titles listed under "Resources for Planning Early Childhood Services for the Storyteller," in this chapter.

TODDLER TIMES

By age two or younger, children are able to follow a simple story plot. As Hannah Nuba observes in "Books and Babies,"

> The age of two is ideal for introducing books to children in a library group setting. By age two, children have developed a strong command of language. They love picture books about familiar experiences, with lilting repetitions and colorful, recognizable illustrations.
>
> Two-year-olds are very concrete in their thinking and not ready to deal with subtle plot lines, abstractions, or fine distinctions. Book experiences for the toddler have until now been mainly on the lap of a caring adult. In the library setting, children still need to see the book close up, page by page, with the librarian occasionally tracing a finger under the text (as parents should do at home) to show the letter-sound-meaning connection.
>
> As the children take their cues from the sounds, the printed symbols on the page, the meaning and enjoyment of the story, the illustrations, and repeated listening experiences, a lifelong link between reading and pleasure will have been forged."[14]

Young children's approach to picture books is a literal one. They expect the pictures to tell them the story. They like to pore over details, such as the bear motif that L. Leslie Brooke incorporates in his pictures throughout the story of "The Three Bears" in *The Golden Goose Book.* Since they cannot read, children's pleasure comes through the senses, especially through their eyes and ears. They need pleasing word sounds and pictures. Stories with rhythm, repetition, and nonsensical words delight. This is the perfect time for Mother Goose.

Toddlers enjoy books that they can interact with—books with pictures that have a flap to lift and books that surprise children with pictures that pop up. *Go Away, Big Green Monster!* by Ed Emberley is an instant hit with the two- and three-year-olds who enjoy the empowerment the story gives them. Toddlers like stories that ask them to anticipate or guess, such as *The Very Hungry Caterpillar* by Eric Carle, and Eric Hill's popular series about the little dog Spot. They enjoy picture books with a simple story line involving commonplace objects and everyday events, like Ezra Jack Keats' stories about Peter. The world is still new to toddlers and they are fascinated by things that older children take for granted.

If you are a beginning storyteller and have not had much experience with very young children, the thought of trying to hold the attention of a group of two- and three-year-olds may be daunting. The trick is to remember to have fun. Little children differ in the ways they like to listen to stories. Some will listen quietly, some will want to join in, while others may get up and wander about. The "wanderers" are the reason it is important to enclose the children within a safe space. A circle works best, with each child sitting in front of the parent or other caregiver.

A typical toddler storytime might include the following components:

theme song or music to settle the group (use same each week in a storytime series)

attention-getter, such as the use of a puppet

name song, where everyone is greeted by name by the librarian or puppet

hand play or action rhyme

story

activity song, rhyme song, circle song

second story

ending song

book sharing, where children and parents or other caregivers look at books together

It isn't necessary to center your program around a theme, but many educators believe that a theme helps young children to focus and refocus their attention, thus reinforcing learning. Toddlers like themes about feelings (happy, sad, surprised, mad); simple concepts (colors, opposites); noises/sounds; things that move; nature/the seasons; achieving independence; and family. Whether or not you use a theme, be sure your program has variety and rhythm. Here are four sample toddler storytime programs with a theme. For additional program ideas, see appropriate titles listed in "Resources for Planning Early Childhood Services for the Storyteller," in this chapter.

TODDLER STORYTIME PROGRAM

THEME: Moon

WELCOME SONG: "Hello, everybody, hello"

STORY: *Kitten's First Full Moon* by Kevin Henkes

POEM: "Silverly" from *Here's a Little Poem* by Jane Yolen and Andrew Fusek Peters

STORY: *Emily's Balloon* by Komako Sakai

MOVEMENT ACTIVITY: Play with balloons. (Distribute inflated balloons and let the toddlers and caregivers toss them about to background music.)

STORY: *Goodnight Moon* by Margaret Wise Brown

CLOSING SONG

TODDLER STORYTIME PROGRAM

THEME: Away We Go! (trains)
WELCOME SONG: "Hello, everybody, hello"
STORY: *Hey Mr. Choo-choo, Where Are You Going?* by Susan Wickberg
FINGERPLAY: "Here Comes the Choo-Choo Train"

> Here comes the choo-choo train (elbows slide along sides, arms make forward circles)
> Puffing down the track.
> Now it's going forward . . .
> Now it's going back. (reverse circles)
> Hear the bell a-ringing. (one hand above head, make bell-ringing motion)
> Ding . . . Ding . . . Ding . . . Ding
> Hear the whistle blow. (cup hands around mouth)
> Whooooo-Whoooooo!
> Chug, chug, chug, chug (make side circles slowly, then pick up speed)
> ch . . . ch . . . ch . . . ch . . . ch . . . ch . . . ch . . .
> Shhhhhh (fold hands in lap)
> Everywhere it goes.

STORY: *Two Little Trains* by Margaret Wise Brown
STORY: *Jiggle, Joggle, Jee!* by Laura E. Richards
GOODBYE SONG

TODDLER STORYTIME PROGRAM

THEME: Rabbits
WELCOME SONG: "Hello, everybody, hello" (If you have a rabbit puppet have the puppet greet each of the children by name during the song.)
STORY: *Thunder Bunny* by Barbara Helen Berger
FINGERPLAY: "Little Rabbit"

> I saw a little rabbit go hop, hop, hop (hop in place)
> I saw his long ears go flop, flop, flop (hands above head, "flop" wrists over and back)
> I saw his eyes go blink, blink, blink (blink eyes)
> I saw his little nose go twink, twink, twink (wiggle nose)
> I said, "Little Rabbit, won't you stay?" (make a beckoning motion)
> He looked at me and hopped away! (hop quickly)

STORY: *Rabbit's Gift* by George Shannon
SONG: "If You're Happy and You Know It, Clap Your Hands"
STORY: *The Runaway Bunny* by Margaret Wise Brown
CLOSING SONG

TODDLER STORYTIME PROGRAM

THEME: Mother Goose

Play selections from Maurice Ravel's *Mother Goose Suite* as the children enter the storyhour room through the maze in *Johnny Crow's Garden*. (The idea of a maze comes from Susan Pine, Materials Specialist, Office of Children's Services at the New York Public Library. Pine duplicated the maze in *Johnny Crow's Garden* and decorated it with Mother Goose characters for a program for young children at the Bloomingdale branch.)

SONG: Sing a song from *Jane Yolen's Mother Goose Songbook*.

STORY: *Johnny Crow's Garden* by L. Leslie Brooke

Meet Mother Goose characters. Recite several Mother Goose rhymes as you introduce "Little Miss Muffit," "Humpty Dumpty," "Old King Cole," and so forth, using flannel-board figures. Say the rhyme twice. Have the children act it out the second time around.

STORY: *The Owl and the Pussycat* by Jan Brett

SONG: Close with a song or two from *Jane Yolen's Mother Goose Songbook*.

THE PRESCHOOL STORYTIME

The preschool storytime is designed for children ages four and five. Usually the children attend alone while the parents and caregivers use the time to browse in the parenting collection or in the adult department. In *Booksharing: 101 Programs to Use with Preschoolers*, Margaret Read MacDonald makes "a plea for the inclusion of parents as participants in preschool programs,"[15] but, traditionally, the preschool storytime was considered to be the child's introduction to literature and art in a group setting *on the child's own*. Whether to open up the preschool storytime to adults will depend on your community's needs and your own feelings about this. Preschoolers behave differently when their parents are in the listening area. One thing you want to avoid is having the parents and caregivers congregate adjacent to the listening area, distracting the children (and the storyteller!) with noisy conversation. If possible, at the first preschool storytime in a series, have another librarian meet with the parents and caregivers to explain the purpose and goals of the preschool storytime and to introduce them to outstanding picture books for young children and some techniques in reading aloud. If no staff member is available, a video, produced by the library staff and covering the same points, can be shown. A third alternative is to encourage the parents and caregivers to browse in the parenting and adult sections of the library. Emphasize to the parent or caregiver the importance of remaining in the library building, as little children sometimes become upset or frightened and it is only a familiar, beloved face (and arms) that will comfort them.

The preschool storytime should provide the following:

1. first lessons in group experiences on their own;
2. the ability to sit quietly, to listen to words with open ears, to look at pictures with seeing eyes;
3. an introduction to the best in children's literature;
4. opportunities to select books for home reading.[16]

Hold the program in a separate room or a quiet corner of the children's room and make it as attractive as possible. Display the picture books you will use in the program and related realia, if any, on a low table. The story-teller usually sits on a stool or low chair, with the children seated on a rug or cushions in a semicircle around the teller. With this arrangement, the children can see the pictures as the storyteller reads the story with the pages of the book turned outward. This means that the storyteller must be thoroughly familiar with the story, but the storyteller does not memorize the text. In preparation, read the book aloud at least twice—first for the story line, and second for the placement of the words in relation to the pictures. Hold the book as you would for a group of children, pictures at their eye level, and practice until you feel comfortable. Most people are comfortable reading the text from the side, with the book cradled in one arm; others have mastered the art of reading the text upside down as they hold the book at the top of its spine and turn the pages. If the group is large (twelve to fifteen is the ideal size but larger groups can be handled with help), move the book in a sweeping motion so that all of the children in the group can see the pictures. If you practice holding the book in front of a mirror you will quickly learn how to hold it without tilting the pictures. Turn the pages slowly, to give the children time to enjoy the pictures.

Read the story naturally and unhurriedly. A gentle, quiet voice will encourage the children to listen attentively. Read with feeling and expression.

Young children enjoy hearing the same stories over and over. You can add a new dimension to familiar stories by presenting a flannel-board or video version of a book read previously. Telling the story without using the pictures will encourage the child's growing power to imagine. The nursery tales that come from the oral tradition are meant to be *told*. Modern imaginative stories in which the pictures are an integral part of the story (such as *Where the Wild Things Are* by Maurice Sendak) should by read word for word. The pictures and words are so closely interwoven that they should be presented as a unity.

The preschooler is irresistibly attracted to poetry. Kornei Chukovsky, author of *From Two to Five* and a poet himself, writes, "There is hardly a child who does not go through a stage in his preschool years when he is not an avid creator of word rhythms and rhymes."[17] Keep a fine anthology on the storyteller's shelf, such as *Talking Like the Rain: A First Book of Poems* by X. J. Kennedy and Dorothy M. Kennedy.

Be flexible and willing to accommodate the children's attention span and mood. If the children become restless, change the pace with a song, a finger play, or a stretch. Little children are fascinated by handkerchief stories and stories told with objects, such as nesting dolls or paper cutting. See *The Family Storytelling Handbook*, by Anne Pellowski, for instructions.

Be prepared for interruptions. Acknowledge the child with a smile or nod, then go on with the story. Be gentle but firm. Anyone who has seen the film *The Pleasure Is Mutual* will recall the scene where the preschoolers are about to take over the storytime with their exuberance. The storyteller interrupts their enthusiastic comments with a firm "But when you do go . . ." and jumps right into the story.

The preschool storytime usually lasts about twenty-five to thirty minutes. You may want to extend the program with a *related* activity, such as dramatic play or creative movement based on the story, or by having the children retell the story using flannel-board figures. Lastly, encourage the parents/caregivers to help their children select books to borrow from the library.

Some libraries offer preschool storytimes throughout the year, but most librarians find it more feasible to offer a six- to eight-week series three or four times a year. If there are many preschoolers in your community, you may have to limit a child's attendance to one series. Some children's librarians now offer preschool storytimes for large groups of thirty to eighty children. The large group storytime is more performance-oriented and requires special skills. Carefully consider the pros and cons of such a program, both for the listeners and for the storyteller, before undertaking it.

The program is usually held mid-morning or early evening so as not to interfere with afternoon nap time. "Pajama parties" for preschoolers and older toddlers and their parents are popular evening programs.

A typical preschool story program will include three or four stories, with a finger play, poem, or song in between the stories. There are many finger play collections, but *Ring a Ring O'Roses: Finger Plays for Pre-School Children*, published by the Flint Public Library, Michigan (one of the first libraries to hold preschool storytimes), is an excellent resource.

The program can be arranged around a theme or not, as you feel comfortable. If you like to work with themes, browse in Margaret MacDonald's *Booksharing: 101 Programs to Use with Preschoolers; A to Zoo: Subject Access to Children's Picture Books*, 7th edition, by Carolyn W. Lima and John A. Lima; and *The Storybook Sourcebook II: A Compendium of 3,500+ New Ideas and Resources for Storytellers* by Carolyn N. Cullum.

Here are three sample preschool story hours:

PRESCHOOL STORY PROGRAM

THEME: Elephants
MUSIC: Selections from Camille Saint-Saëns's *Carnival of the Animals*
WELCOME SONG
STORY: *Little Elephant* by Tana Hoban and Miela Ford
FINGERPLAY: "An Elephant Goes Like This and That"

> An elephant goes like this and that
>   (rocking sideways, hands stiff out to sides)
> He's terribly big and he's terribly fat
>   (continue rocking motion, taking stiff steps)
> He has no fingers (wiggle fingers)
> He has no toes (wiggle toes)
> But OH MY GOODNESS WHAT A NOSE!

Make trunk with arms clasped and walk around swinging it.
STORY: *The Elephant and the Bad Baby* by Elfrida Vipont
ACTION SONG: "One Elephant"

> One elephant went out to play
> On a spider's web one day.
> He had such enormous fun,
> He asked another elephant to come.[18]

Form a circle. One child goes to the middle and chooses another to join after song. Each then chooses another until only parents are left as the circle.
STORY: *Tabu and the Dancing Elephants,* retold by Rene Deetlefs
CLOSING SONG

PRESCHOOL STORY PROGRAM

THEME: Gardening
SONG: "Inch by Inch: The Garden Song," by David Mallett
STORY: *Wild Wild Sunflower Child Anna* by Nancy White Carlstrom
FINGERPLAY: Repeat these words from *Wild Wild Sunflower Child Anna* as you do appropriate actions:

> Digging in the garden
> Kneeling on her knees
> Leaning on elbows
> Whispering to the seeds
> Anna sifts the soil lightly through her fingers
> Anna talking, Anna walking
> Sunshine

Grow, grow
Grow in the garden, Anna

STORY: *To Be Like the Sun* by Susan Marie Swanson
    Share a few poems or riddles from *Busy in the Garden* by George Shannon
STORY: *Planting a Rainbow* by Lois Ehlert
CLOSING SONG: "Everything Grows" by Raffi

PRESCHOOL STORY PROGRAM

THEME: Farm Animals
WELCOME SONG: "Hello everybody, how are you?"
STORY: *The Cow Who Clucked* by Denise Fleming
SONG: "Hairy Harry" on Playtime Songs GW CD 1-58467-014-2
STORY: *Dooby Dooby Moo* by Doreen Cronin
SONG: "Old MacDonald Had a Farm"
STORY: *Book! Book! Book!* by Deborah Bruss
GOODBYE SONG

REFERENCES

1. Gail E. Haley, Caldecott Award acceptance for *A Story, A Story* in *Newbery and Caldecott Medal Books: 1966–1975*, ed. Lee Kingman (Horn Book, 1975) p. 225.

2. Personal communications to Ellin Greene from Barbara Tillson, Teacher/Administrator, The Church in Brielle, New Jersey, Nursery School (May 10, 2008).

3. Elizabeth Sulzby, "Children's Emergent Reading of Favorite Storybooks: A Developmental Study," *Reading Research Quarterly* 20 (Summer 1985): 462.

4. Don Holdaway, *The Foundations of Literacy* (Heinemann, 1979).

5. Clarence W. Sumner, *The Birthright of Babyhood* (Nelson, 1936), p. 41.

6. Ibid., p. 42.

7. Communication from Dr. Dean Falk (October 16, 2008).

8. Steven L. Herb, "Building Blocks for Literacy: What Research Shows," *School Library Journal*, 43(7), p. 23.

9. Saroj Ghoting and Pamela Martin-Diaz, *Early Literacy Storytimes @ your library, Partnering with Caregivers for Success* (American Library Association, 2005), Preface, ix, pp. 3-4.

10. Clara N. Bohrer. Clara gave several presentations on Emergent Literacy and the Public Library during her PLA presidency and generously shared her notes with Ellin Greene.

11. Ellin Greene, *Books, Babies, and Libraries: Serving Infants, Toddlers, Their Parents and Caregivers* (American Library Association, 1991). Sections of this chapter are taken from the author's book and are reprinted here with the permission of the author and the publisher.

12. Mem Fox, *Reading Magic: Why Reading Aloud to Our Children Will Change Their Lives Forever,* updated and revised edition (Harcourt, 2008), p. 12.

13. Denny Taylor and Dorothy S. Strickland, *Family Storybook Reading* (Heinemann, 1986), p. 23.

14. Hannah Scheffler Nuba, "Books and Babies," in *Infancy: A Guide to Research and Resources* (Garland, 1986), p. 145.

15. Margaret Read MacDonald, *Booksharing: 101 Programs to Use with Preschoolers* (Library Professional Pub., 1988), pp. 3–4.

16. Augusta Baker, *Once Upon a Time. . .* (New York Library Association, 1955), p. 3.

17. Kornei Chukovsky, *From Two to Five*, trans. and ed. by Miriam Morton, Foreword by Frances Clarke Sayers (University of California Press, 1963), p. 64.

18. MacDonald, *Booksharing*, p. 145.

RESOURCES FOR PLANNING EARLY CHILDHOOD SERVICES FOR THE STORYTELLER

BOOKS

American Library Association, Association for Library Service to Children. Preschool Services and Parent Education Committee. *First Steps to Literacy: Library Programs for Parents, Teachers, and Caregivers.* American Library Association, 1990. ISBNs 0-8389-0521-8 and 9780838905210

Butler, Dorothy. *Babies Need Books*: *Sharing the Joy of Books with Children From Birth to Six*. Revised edition, with drawings by Shirley Hughes. Heinemann, 1998. ISBNs 0-435-08144-6 and 9780435081447

Carlson, Ann. *Flannelboard Stories for Infants and Toddlers, Bilingual Edition*. American Library Association, 2005. ISBNs 0-8389-0911-6 and 9780838909119

Chukovsky, Kornei. *From Two to Five*. Revised edition trans. and ed. by Miriam Morton. Foreword by Frances Clarke Sayers. University of California Press, 1988. ISBNs 0-520-00237-7 and 9780520002371

Cullinan, Bernice E. *Read to Me: Raising Kids Who Love to Read*. Revised and updated with an introduction by Dorothy S. Strickland. Scholastic, 2000. ISBNs 0-439-08721-X and 9780439087216

Cullum, Carolyn N. *The Storybook Sourcebook II: A Compendium of 3,500+ New Ideas and Resources for Storytellers*. Neal-Schuman, 2007. ISBNs 1-55570-589-8 and 9781555705893

Dailey, Susan M. *Sing a Song of Storytime*. Neal-Schuman, 2007. ISBNs 1-55570-576-6 and 9781555705763

Diamant-Cohen, Betsy. *Mother Goose on the Loose*. Neal-Schuman, 2006. ISBNs 1-55570-536-7 and 9781555705367

Ernst, Linda L. *Lapsit Services for the Very Young II: A How-to-Do-It Manual.* Neal-Schuman, 2001. ISBNs 1-55570-391-7 and 9781555703912

———. *Baby Rhyming Time.* Neal-Schuman, 2008. ISBNs 1-55570-540-5 and 9781555705404

Falk, Dean. *Finding Our Tongues: Mothers, Infants and the Origins of Language.* Basic Books, 2009. ISBNs 0-465-00219-6 and 9780465002191

Feinberg, Sandra. *Learning Environments for Young Children: Rethinking Library Spaces and Services.* American Library Association, 1998. ISBNs 0-8389-0736-9 and 9780838907368

Fox, Mem. *Reading Magic: Why Reading Aloud to Our Children Will Change Their Lives Forever.* Updated and revised edition. Illus. by Judy Horacek. Harcourt, 2008. ISBNs 0-15-603510-3 and 9780156035101

Ghoting, Saroj, and Pamela Martin-Diaz. *Early Literacy Storytimes @ your library, Partnering with Caregivers for Success.* American Library Association, 2005. ISBNs 0-8389-0899-3 and 9780838908990

Greene, Ellin. *Books, Babies, and Libraries: Serving Infants, Toddlers, Their Parents and Caregivers.* American Library Association, 1991. ISBNs 0-8389-0572-2 and 9780838905722

Hansen, Charles A., and Cynthia S. Stilley, eds. *Ring a Ring o' Roses: Fingerplays for Preschool Children.* Flint, MI: Flint Public Library, 2002. ISBNs 0-9654589-0-3 and 9780965458900

Harris, Robie H. *Hello Benny! What It's Like to Be a Baby.* Illus. by Michael Emberly. Simon & Schuster/McElderry Books, 2002. ISBNs 0-689-83257-5 and 9780689832574

———. *Go! Go! Maria! What It's Like to Be 1.* Illus. by Michael Emberly. Simon & Schuster/McElderry Books, 2003. ISBNs 0-689-83258-3 and 9780689832581 (see also other titles in this series)

MacDonald, Margaret Read. *Booksharing: 101 Programs to Use with Preschoolers.* Library Professional Publications, 1988. ISBNs 0-208-02159-0 and 9780208021595

Marino, Jane. *Sing Us a Story: Using Music in Preschool and Family Storytimes.* H. W. Wilson, 1994. ISBNs 0-8242-0847-1 and 9780824208479

Nichols, Judy. *Storytimes for Two-Year-Olds, Third Edition.* Illus. by Lori D. Sears. American Library Association, 2007. ISBNs 0-8389-0925-6 and 9780838909256

Nuba, Hannah, Michael Searson, and Deborah Lovitky Sheiman, eds. *Resources for Early Childhood: A Handbook.* Routledge, 1994. ISBNs 0-8240-7395-9 and 9780824073954

Paley, Vivian Gussin. *The Boy Who Would Be a Helicopter: The Uses of Sto-rytelling in the Classroom*. Foreword by Robert Coles. Harvard University Press, 1990. ISBNs 0-674-08030-0 and 9780674080300

Pellowski, Anne. *The Family Storytelling Handbook: How to Use Stories, Anecdotes, Rhymes, Handkerchiefs, Paper and Other Objects to Enrich Your Family Traditions*. Illus. Lynn Sweat. Macmillan, 1987. ISBNs 0-02-770610-9 and 9780027706109

Reid, Rob. *Children's Jukebox*. 2nd ed. American Library Association, 2007. ISBNs 0-8389-0940-X and 9780838909409

———. *Something Musical Happened at the Library: Adding Song and Dance to Children's Story Programs*. American Library Association, 2007. ISBNs 0-8389-0942-6 and 9780838909423

Tashjian, Virginia. *Juba This and Juba That: Favorite Children's Songs to Sing, Stories to Tell, Rhymes to Chant, Riddles to Guess, and More!* 2nd ed. Illus. Nadine B. Westcott. Little, Brown, 1995. ISBNs 0-316-83234-0 and 9780316832342

Taylor, Denny, and Dorothy S. Strickland. *Family Storybook Reading*. Foreword by Bernice E. Cullinan. Heinemann, 1986. ISBNs and 0-435-08249-3 and 9780435082499

Wells, Rosemary. *Read to Your Bunny*. Scholastic, 1997. ISBN 9780590302845 (also see Scholastic/Weston Woods DVD 678 *Reading to Your Bunny*, inspired by the book; ISBNs 0-439-84928-4 and 9780439849289

WEBSITE RESOURCES

American Library Association, PLA, and ALSC's Every Child Ready to Read Preschool Literacy Initiative
http://www.ala.org/ala/mgrps/divs/alsc/ecrr/index.cfm
www.pla.org/earlyliteracy.htm

Association for Library Service to Children, Born to Read: How to Raise a Reader
http://www.ala.org/ala/mgrps/divs/alsc/initiatives/borntoread/index.cfm

Beginning with Books Center for Early Literacy
www.beginningwithbooks.org
Publishes information about their program and an annual list, *Best Books for Babies*, available from Beginning with Books, 5920 Kirkwood St., Pittsburgh, PA 15206. Tel. 412-361-8560.

Brooklyn Public Library
www.brooklynpubliclibrary.org/first5years

Brooklyn Public Library has produced a video, *Reading with Babies* (*Leyendo con Bebes*).

Duluth Public Library

www.duluth.lib.mn.us

Early Literacy Resources: Books, Articles, Studies and Web Sites. This list was originally prepared for "Early Literacy @ your library," a program at the Minnesota Library Association Annual Conference, September 2003, and subsequently updated.

National Center for Infants, Toddlers and Families Zero to Three: Parents

www.zerotothree.org/ztt_parents.html

Designed for parents, this site offers good information on brain development in young children and stages of child development.

Read to Me: An Intergenerational Reading Program

www.readtomeprogram.org

A parent-baby reading program that focuses on teen parents and moms.

Reading Is Fundamental

www.rif.org

The oldest and largest nonprofit children's literacy organization. Lots of information for parents and educators.

300+ TITLES TO SHARE WITH YOUNG CHILDREN

MOTHER GOOSE, NURSERY RHYMES, FINGER PLAYS, ACTION RHYMES, LULLABIES, POETRY AND SONG, STORIES IN RHYME COLLECTIONS

Beaton, Clare. *Playtime Rhymes for Little People*. Barefoot, 2001. ISBNs 1-84148-425-3 and 9781841484259

Calmenson, Stephanie. *Welcome Baby! Baby Rhymes for Baby Times*. HarperCollins, 2002. ISBNs 0-688-17736-0 and 9780688177362

Chorao, Kay. *The Baby's Lap Book*. Dutton, 1991. ISBNs 0-525-44604-4 and 9780525446040

———. *The Baby's Bedtime Book*. Dutton, 1984. Reissued 2004. ISBNs 0-525-47327-0 and 9780525473275

———. *The Baby's Playtime Book*. Dutton, 2006. ISBN 0-525-47576-1

Clark, Emma Chichester. *I Never Saw a Purple Cow and Other Nonsense Rhymes*. Little, Brown, 1990. ISBNs 0-316-14500-9 and 9780316145008

Cole, Joanna, and Stephanie Calmenson. *Pat a Cake and Other Play Rhymes*. Illus. by Alan Tiegreen. Morrow, 1992. ISBN 0-688-11038-X

Crews, Nina. *The Neighborhood Mother Goose*. Greenwillow, 2004. ISBNs 0-06-051573-2 and 9780060515737

Cousins, Lucy. *The Little Dog Laughed and Other Nursery Rhymes*. Dutton, 1990. ISBNs 0-525-44573-0 and 9780525445739

deAngeli, Marguerite. *Marguerite deAngeli's Book of Nursery and Mother Goose Rhymes*. Doubleday, 1954, o.p.

Delacre, Lulu. *Arrorro, mi nino / Latino Lullabies and Gentle Games*. Musical arrangements by Cecilia Esquivel and Diana Saez. Lee & Low, 2004. ISBNs 1-58430-159-7 and 9781584301592; CD 9781600601231

dePaola, Tomie. *More Mother Goose Favorites*. Grosset & Dunlap, 2007. ISBNs 0-448-44494-1 and 9780448444949

Dillon, Leo, and Diane Dillon. *Mother Goose: Numbers on the Loose*. Harcourt, 2007. ISBNs 0-15-205676-9 and 9780152056766

Dyer, Jane. *Animal Crackers: A Delectable Collection of Pictures, Poems, and Lullabies for the Very Young*. Little, Brown, 1996. ISBN 0-316-19766-1

Engelbreit, Mary. *Mary Engelbreit's Mother Goose: One Hundred Best-Loved Verses*. Introduction by Leonard S. Marcus. HarperCollins, 2005. ISBNs 0-06-008171-6 and 978006-0081713

Griego, Margot C., et al. *Tortillitas para Mama: And Other Spanish Nursery Rhymes, Spanish and English*. Illus. by Barbara Cooney. Holt, 1981. ISBN 0-8050-0285-5

Hall, Nancy Abraham, and Jill Syverson-Stork. *Los pollitos dicen: Juegos, rimas y canciones infantiles de paises de hable hispana / The Baby Chicks Sing: Traditional Games, Nursery Rhymes, and Songs from Spanish-Speaking Countries*. Illus. by Kay Chorao. Little, Brown, 1994. ISBNs 0-316-34010-3 and 9780316340106

Hart, Jane, comp. *Singing Bee! A Collection of Favorite Children's Songs*. Illus. by Anita Lobel. Lothrop, 1982. ISBNs 0-688-41975-5 and 9780688419752

Hughes, Shirley. *Rhymes for Annie Rose*. Lothrop, 1995. ISBN 0-688-14220-6

Jaramillo, Nelly Palacio. *Grandmother's Nursery Rhymes: Las Nanas de Abuelita*. Illus. by Elivia. Holt, 1994. ISBNs 0-8050-2555-3 and 9780805025552

Kennedy, X. J., and Dorothy M. Kennedy. *Talking Like the Rain: A First Book of Poems*. Illus. by Jane Dyer. Little, Brown, 1992. ISBNs 0-316-48889-5 and 9780316488891

Lach, William, ed. *I Imagine Angels: Poems and Prayers for Parents and Children*. Metropolitan Museum of Art/Atheneum, 2000. ISBNs 0-87099-949-4 and 9780870999499 (MMA); ISBNs 0-689-84080-2 and 9780689840807 (Atheneum)

Lamont, Priscilla. *Ring-a-Round-a-Rosy: Nursery Rhymes, Action Rhymes, and Lullabies*. Little, Brown/Joy Street, 1990. ISBNs 0-316-51292-3 and 9780316512923

Lindbergh, Reeve. *On Morning Wings*. Adapted from Psalm 139. Illus. by Holly Meade. Candlewick, 2003. ISBNs 0-7636-1106-9 and 9780763611064

Lines, Kathleen. *Lavender's Blue: A Book of Nursery Rhymes*. Illus. by Harold Jones. Oxford University Press, 2007. (Originally published 1954) Paperback edition. ISBNs 0-19-278225-8 and 9780192782250

Lobel, Arnold. *The Random House Book of Mother Goose*. Random, 1986. ISBNs 0-394-86799-8 and 9780394867991

Marks, Alan. *Over the Hills and Far Away: A Book of Nursery Rhymes*. North-South, 1994. ISBNs 1-55858-285-1 and 9781558582859

———. *Ring-a-Ring o' Roses and a Ding, Dong, Bell: A Book of Nursery Rhymes*. Picture Book Studio, 1992. ISBNs 0-88708-187-8 and 9780887081873

Mayo, Margaret. *Wiggle Waggle Fun: Stories and Rhymes for the Very, Very Young*. Illus. by twenty-four different artists. Knopf/Borzoi Books, 2002. ISBNs 0-375-81529-5 and 9780375815294

Moore, Lilian, comp. *Sunflakes: Poems for Children*. Illus. by Jan Ormerod. Clarion, 1992. ISBNs 0-395-58833-2 and 9780395588338

Moses, Will. *Mother Goose*. Penguin/Philomel, 2003. ISBNs 0-399-23744-5 and 9780399237447

Opie, Iona, ed. *Here Comes Mother Goose*. Illus. by Rosemary Wells. Candlewick, 1999. ISBNs 0-7636-0683-9 and 9780763606831 (See also *My Very First Mother Goose*)

Orozco, Jose-Luis, *Diez Deditos: Ten Little Fingers and Other Play Rhymes and Action Songs from Latin America*. Selected, arranged, and translated by Jose-Luis Orozco. Illus. by Elisa Kleven. Dutton, 1997. ISBNs 0-525-45736-4 and 9780525457367

Philip, Neil. *The Fish Is Me: Bathtime Rhymes*. Illus. by Claire Henley. Clarion, 2002. ISBNs 0-618-15939-8 and 9780618159390

Prelutsky, Jack. *Read-Aloud Rhymes for the Very Young*. Illus. by Marc Brown. Introduction by Jim Trelease. Knopf, 1986. ISBNs 0-394-87218-5 and 9780394872186

Raffi. *The Raffi Singable Songbook*. Illus. by Joyce Yamamoto. Crown, 1988. ISBNs 0-517-56638-9 and 9780517566381

Sharon, Lois, and Bram. *Sharon, Lois and Bram's Mother Goose: Songs, Finger Rhymes, Tickling Verses, Games and More*. Illus. by Maryann Kovalski. Little, Brown, 1986. ISBNs 0-316-78281-5 and 9780316782814

Watson, Wendy. *Wendy Watson's Mother Goose*. Lothrop, 1989. ISBNs 0-688-05708-X and 9780688057084

Wilner, Isabel. *The Baby's Game Book*. Illus. by Sam Williams. Greenwillow, 2000. ISBNs 0-688-15916-8 and 9780688159160

Wyndham, Robert. *Chinese Mother Goose Rhymes*. Illus. by Ed Young. Putnam/Sandcastle, 1989. ISBNs 0-399-21718-5 and 9780399217180

Yolen, Jane, ed. *Here's a Little Poem: A Very First Book of Poetry*, collected by Jane Yolen and Andrew Fusek Peters. Illus. by Polly Dunbar. Candlewick, 2007. ISBNs 0-7636-3141-8 and 9780763631413

―――. *This Little Piggy: Lap Songs, Finger Plays, Clapping Games, and Pantomime Rhymes*. Illus. by Will Hillenbrand. Musical arrangements by Adam Stemple. With CD. Candlewick, 2005. ISBN 0-7636-1348-7

SINGLE TITLES

Andrews, Sylvia. *Dancing in My Bones*. Illus. by Ellen Mueller. HarperCollins, 2001. ISBNs 0-694-01316-1 and 9780694013166

Banks, Kate. *Close Your Eyes*. Illus. by Georg Hallensleber. Farrar, 2002. ISBNs 0-374-31382-2 and 9780374313821

―――. *Mama's Coming Home*. Illus. by Tomek Bogacki. Farrar/Foster, 2003. ISBNs 0-374-34747-6 and 9780374347475

Beaumont, Karen. *Baby Danced the Polka*. Illus. by Jennifer Plecas. Dial, 2004. ISBNs 0-8037-2587-6 and 9780803725874

Boyd, Lizi. *Lulu Crow's Garden: A Silly Old Song with Brand-New Pictures*. Little, Brown, 1998. ISBNs 0-316-10419-1 and 9780316104197 (based on *Johnny Crow's Garden* by L. Leslie Brooke. Warne, 1903.)

Calmenson, Stephanie. *Jazzmatazz!* Illus. by Bruce Degen. HarperCollins, 2008. ISBNs 0-06-077289-1 and 9780060772895

Christelow, Eileen. *Five Little Monkeys Jumping on the Bed*. Clarion, 1989. ISBN 0-89919-769-8. Also available in Spanish, ISBNs 0-618-56442-X and 9780618564422 (board book). See also other titles about these five playful monkeys.

Cote, Genevieve. *With You Always, Little Monday*. Harcourt, 2007. ISBNs 0-15-205997-0 and 9780152059972

Cronin, Doreen. *Wiggle*. Illus. by Scott Menchin. Atheneum, 2005. ISBNs 0-689-86375-6 and 9780689863752

Cruise, Robin. *Only You*. Harcourt, 2007. ISBNs ISBN 0-15-216604-1 and 9780152166045

Fox, Mem. *Ten Little Fingers and Ten Little Toes*. Illus. by Helen Oxenbury. Harcourt, 2008. ISBNs 0-15-206057-X and 9780152060572

———. *Time for Bed*. Illus. by Jane Dyer. Harcourt/Gulliver, 1993. ISBNs 0-15-288183-2 and 9780152881832

Frasier, Debra. *On the Day You Were Born*. Harcourt, 1991. ISBNs 0-15-257995-8 and 9780152579951. Book and musical CD, 2005, ISBNs 0-15-205567-3 and 9780152055677

Ginsburg, Mirra. *Asleep, Asleep*. Illus. by Nancy Tafuri. Greenwillow, 1992. ISBNs 0-688-09153-9 and 9780688091538

Glazer, Tom. *On Top of Spaghetti*. Illus. by Tom Garcia. Doubleday, 1982. ISBNs 0-385-14250-1 and 9780385142502

Greene, Ellin, adapter. *Mother's Song: A Lullaby*. Illus. by Elizabeth Sayles. Clarion, 2008. ISBNs 0-395-71527-X and 9780395715277

Grimes, Nikki. *Welcome, Precious*. Illus. by Bryan Collier. Orchard Books/Scholastic, 2006. ISBNs 0-439-55702-X and 9780439557023

Hillenbrand, Will. *Fiddle-I-Fee*. Harcourt/Gulliver, 2002. ISBNs 0-15-201945-6 and 9780152019457

Ho, Minfong. *Hush! A Thai Lullaby*. Illus. by Holly Meade. Orchard Books/Scholastic, 1996. ISBN 0-531-088850-2

Hoberman, Mary Ann, adapter. *Miss Mary Mack: A Hand-Clapping Rhyme*. Illus. by Nadine Bernard Westcott. Little, Brown, 1998. ISBNs 0-316-93118-7 and 9780316931182

Isadora, Rachel. *Peekaboo Bedtime*. Putnam, 2008. ISBNs 0-399-24384-4 and 9780399243844. Also available as board book.

———. *Peekaboo Morning*. Putnam, 2002. ISBNs 0-399-236023 and 9780399236020. Also available as board book.

Jacques, Florence Page. *There Once Was a Puffin*. Illus. by Laura McGee Kvasnosky. Dutton, 1995. ISBNs 0-525-45291-5 and 9780525452911

Kleven, Elisa. *Sun Bread*. Dutton, 2001. ISBNs 0-525-46674-6 and 9780525466741

Kuskin, Karla. *Green as a Bean*. Illus. by Melissa Iwai. HarperCollins, 2007. ISBN 9780060753323

Lear, Edward. *The Owl and the Pussycat*. Illus. by Jan Brett. Putnam, 1991. ISBNs 0-399-21925-0 and 9780399219252

Love, Maryann Cusimano. *You Are My Miracle.* Illus. by Satmi Ichikawa. Philomel, 2005. ISBNs 0-399-24037-3 and 9780399240379

Mahy, Margaret. *Down the Back of the Chair.* Illus. by Polly Dunbar. Clarion, 2006. ISBNs 0-618-69395-5 and 9780618693955

Martin, Bill, Jr. *Baby Bear, Baby Bear, What Do You See?* Illus. by Eric Carle. Holt, 2007. ISBNs 0-8050-8336-7 and 9780805083361 (see also other books in this series)

Marzollo, Jean. *Pretend You're a Cat.* Illus. by Jerry Pinkney. Dial, 1990. ISBNs 0-8037-0773-8 and 9780803707733

Meyers, Susan. *Everywhere Babies.* Illus. by Marla Frazee. Harcourt, 2001. ISBNs 0-15-202226-0 and 9780152022266

Murphy, Mary. *I Kissed the Baby.* Candlewick, 2003. ISBNs 0-7636-2122-6 and 9780763621223

Ormerod, Jan. *Jan Ormerod's To Baby with Love.* Lothrop, 1994. ISBNs 0-688-12558-1 and 9780688125585

———. *101 Things to Do with a Baby.* Lothrop, 1984. ISBNs 0-688-03801-8 and 9780688038014

Peddicord, Jane Ann. *That Special Little Baby.* Illus. by Meilo So. Harcourt, 2007. ISBNs 0-15-205430-8 and 9780152054304

Pinkney, Brian. *Hush, Little Baby.* Greenwillow, 2006. ISBNs 0-06-055993-4 and 9780060559939

Richards, Laura E. *Jiggle, Joggle, Jee!* Illus. by Sam Williams. Greenwillow, 2001. ISBNs 0-688-17833-2 and 9780688178338

Shannon, George. *Dancing in the Breeze.* Illus. by Jacqueline Rogers. Bradbury, 1991. ISBNs 0-02-782190-0 and 9780027821901

———. *Oh, I Love!* Illus. by Cheryl Harness. Bradbury, 1988. ISBNs 0-02-782180-3 and 9780027821802

Spinelli, Eileen. *Rise the Moon.* Illus. by Raul Colon. Dial, 2003. ISBNs 0-8037-2601-5 and 9780803726017

Sweet, Melissa. *Fiddle-I-Fee: A Farmyard Song for the Very Young.* Little, Brown/Joy Street, 1992. ISBNs 0-316-82516-6 and 9780316825160

Tafuri, Nancy. *I Love You, Little One.* Scholastic, 1998. ISBNs 0-590-92159-2 and 9780590921596. Also available as a board book.

Thompson, Lauren. *The Apple Pie that Papa Baked.* Illus. by Jonathan Bean. Simon & Schuster, 2007. ISBNs 1-4169-1240-1 and 9781416912408

Weiss, George David, and Bob Thiele. *What a Wonderful World.* Illus. by Ashley Bryan. Simon & Schuster/Atheneum, 1995. ISBNs 0-689-80087-8 and 9780689800870

Weiss, Nicki. *If You're Happy and You Know It.* Greenwillow, 1987. ISBNs 0-688-06444-2 and 9780688064440

————. *Where Does the Brown Bear Go?* Greenwillow, 1989. ISBNs 0-688-07862-1 and 9780688078621

Westcott, Nadine Bernard. *Peanut Butter and Jelly: A Play Rhyme.* Dutton, 1987. ISBNs 0-525-44317-7 and 9780525443179

Wheeler, Lisa. *Jazz Baby.* Illus. by Gregory Christie. Harcourt, 2007. ISBNs 0-15-202522-7 and 9780152025229

Wickberg, Susan. *Hey Mr. Choo-choo, Where Are You Going?* Illus. by Yumi Heo. Putnam, 2008. ISBNs 0-399-23993-6 and 9780399239939

Zelinsky, Paul O. *The Wheels on the Bus.* Dutton, 1990. ISBNs 0-525-44644-3 and 9780525446446

Zolotow, Charlotte. *Sleepy Book.* Illus. by Stefano Vitale. HarperCollins, 2001. Newly illustrated edition, ISBNs 0-06-027873-0 and 9780060278731

Zuckerman, Linda. *I Will Hold You 'Til You Sleep.* Illus. by Jon J Muth. Scholastic/Arthur A. Levine, 2006. ISBNs 0-439-43420-3 and 9780439434201

ALPHABET AND COUNTING BOOKS, BOARD BOOKS, CONCEPT BOOKS, TOY BOOKS

Ahlberg, Janet, and Allan Ahlberg. *Peek-a-Boo.* Viking, 1997. ISBNs 0-670-87176-1 and 9780670871766 (board book)

Ashman, Linda. *Babies on the Go.* Illus. by Jane Dyer. Harcourt, 2003. ISBNs 0-15-201894-8 and 9780152018948 (board book)

Asim, Jabari. *Whose Toes Are Those?* Illus. by LeUyen Pham. Little, Brown, 2006. ISBNs 0-316-73609-0 and 978031673609 (board book). *Whose Knees Are These?* is a companion book. ISBNs 0-316-73576-0 and 9780316735766

Aston, Dianna Hutts. *An Orange in January.* Illus. by Julie Maren. Dial, 2007. ISBNs 0-8037-3146-9 and 9780803731462

Baer, Edith. *The Wonder of Hands.* Photos by Tana Hoban. Simon & Schuster, 1992. ISBNs 0-02-708138-9 and 9780027081381

Bang, Molly. *Ten, Nine, Eight.* Greenwillow, 1983. ISBNs 0-688-00906-9 and 9780688009069

Barton, Bryan. *My Car.* Greenwillow, 2001. ISBNs 0-06-029624-0 and 9780060296247

Brown, Margaret Wise. *Goodnight Moon.* Illus. by Clement Hurd. HarperCollins, 1947. New ed. ISBN 0-694-01675 (board book, larger size than original)

———. *The Runaway Bunny.* Illus. by Clement Hurd. HarperCollins, 1942. New ed. ISBNs 0-694-01671-3 and 9780694016716 (board book, larger size than original)

———. *Two Little Trains.* Illus. by Leo and Diane Dillon. HarperCollins, 2001. ISBNs 0-06-028376-9 and 9780060283766

Brown, Ruth. *Ten Seeds.* Knopf, 2001. ISBNs 0-375-80697-0 and 9780375806971

Bunting, Eve. *Flower Garden.* Illus. by Kathryn Hewitt. Harcourt, 1994. Red Wagon Books edition, 2008. ISBNs 0-15-201968-5 and 9780152019686 (board book)

Campbell, Rod. *Dear Zoo.* Simon & Schuster/Little Simon 25th Anniversary edition, 2007. ISBNs 1-4169-4737-X and 9781416947370 (board book)

Carle, Eric. *The Very Hungry Caterpillar.* Philomel, 2007. ISBNs 0-399-24745-9 and 9780399247453 (oversized board book edition with CD of Eric Carle reading the story)

Charlot, Jean. *A Child's Good Morning Book.* Harper Festival, 1996. Originally published: Scott, 1952. ISBNs 0-694-00882-6 and 9780694008827 (board book)

Crews, Donald. *Freight Train.* Greenwillow, 1978. ISBNs 0-688-80165-X and 9780688801656

Curtis, Jamie Lee. *Today I Feel Silly and Other Moods that Make My Day.* Illus. by Laura Cornell. HarperCollins, 1998. ISBNs 0-06-024560-3 and 9780060245603

Dyer, Jane. *Animal Crackers/Nursery Rhymes.* Little, Brown, 2002. ISBNs 0-316-19687-8 and 9780316196871 (boxed set of 3 board books)

Ehlert, Lois. *Planting a Rainbow.* Harcourt, 1988. Red Wagon Books edition, 2003. ISBNs 0-15-204633-X and 9780152046330 (board book)

Emberley, Ed. *Go Away, Big Green Monster!* Little, Brown, 1992. ISBNs 0-316-23653-5 and 9780316236539

Field, Rachel. *Prayer for a Child.* Illus. by Elizabeth Orton Jones. Simon & Schuster/Little Simon Inspirations, 2005. ISBNs 0-689-87886-9 and 9780689878862 (board book)

Fleming, Denise. *The Everything Book.* Holt, 2000. ISBNs 0-8050-6292-0 and 9780805062922

Fujikawa, Gyo. *Ten Little Babies.* Sterling, 2008. ISBNs 1-4027-5700-X and 9781402757006 (board book)

George, Kristine O'Connell. *Book!* Illus. by Maggie Smith. Clarion, 2001. ISBNs 0-395-98287-1 and 9780395982877

Gravett, Emily. *Monkey and Me*. Simon & Schuster, 2008. ISBNs 1-4169-5457-0 and 9781416954576

———. *Orange Pear Apple Bear*. Simon & Schuster, 2007. ISBNs 1-4169-3999-7 and 9781416939993

Grindley, Sally. *Shhh!* Illus. by Peter Utton. Little, Brown, 1991. ISBNs 0-316-32899-5 and 9780316328999

Henderson, Kathy. *The Baby's Book of Babies*. Photos by Anthea Sieveking. Dial, 1988. ISBNs 0-8037-0634-0 and 9780803706347

———. *Look at You! A Baby Body Book*. Illus. by Paul Howard. Candlewick, 2006. ISBNs 0-7636-2745-3 and 9780763627454

Henkes, Kevin. *Sheila Rae's Peppermint Stick*. Greenwillow, 2001. ISBNs 0-06-029451-5 and 9780060294519 (board book)

Hill, Eric. *Where's Spot?* Putnam, 1980. ISBNs 0-399-20758-9 and 9780399207587 (lift-the-flap book)

Hindley, Judy. *Eyes, Nose, Fingers and Toes*. Illus. by Brita Granstrom. Candlewick, 2004. ISBNs 0-7636-2383-0 and 9780763623838

Hoban, Tana. *Black on White* and *White on Black*. Greenwillow, 1993. ISBNs 0-688-11918-2 and 9780688119188; ISBN 0-688-11919-0 (board book)

———. *What Is That?* Greenwillow, 1994. ISBNs 0-688-12920-X and 9780688129200 (board book)

Isadora, Rachael. *I Touch*. Greenwillow, 1985. ISBNs 0-688-04255-4 and 9780688042554; ISBNs 0-688-10524-6 and 9780688105242 (board book). *I Hear* and *I See* are companion books.

———. *Uh-Oh!* Harcourt, 2008. ISBNs 0-15-205765-X and 9780152057657

Keats, Ezra Jack. *Over in the Meadow: A Counting-Out Rhyme*. Penguin Group/Viking, 1999. ISBNs 0-670-88344-1 and 9780670883448

Kersten, Hamilton. *Red Truck*. Illus. by Valerie Petrone. Viking, 2008. ISBNs 0-670-06275-8 and 9780670062751

Krause, Ruth. *The Carrot Seed Board Book*. Illus. by Crockett Johnson. HarperCollins, 1993. ISBNs 0-694-00492-8 and 9780694004928 (board book)

Lyon, George Ella. *Trucks Roll!* Illus. by Craig Frazier. Atheneum, 2007. ISBNs 1-4169-2435-3 and 9781416924357

MacDonald, Suse. *Alphabatics*. Simon & Schuster/Bradbury, 1986. ISBNs 0-02-761520-0 and 9780027615203

McPhail, David. *Emma's Pet*. Dutton, 2003. ISBNs 0-525-47047-6 and 9780525470472 (board book)

Martin, Bill, Jr., and John Archambault. *Chicka Chicka Boom Boom*. Illus. by Lois Ehlert. Simon & Schuster, 1989. ISBNs 0-671-67949-X and 9780671679491

Milich, Zoran. *The City ABC Book*. Kids Can Press, 2001. ISBNs 1-55074-942-0 and 9781550749427

Miller, Margaret. *What's on My Head?* Little Simon, 1998. ISBNs 0-689-81912-9 and 9780689819124 (oversized board book)

Munari, Bruno. *Bruno Munari's ABC*. Chronicle, reissued 2006. ISBNs 0-8118-5463-9 and 9780811854634. See also *Bruno Munari's Zoo*. Chronicle, reissued 2006. ISBNs 0-8118-4830-2 and 9780811848305

Murphy, Mary. *I Like It When . . .* Harcourt/Red Wagon Books edition, 2005. ISBNs 0-15-205649-1 and 9780152056490; ISBNs 0-15-205649-1 and 9780152056490 (board book)

Numeroff, Laura. *If You Give a Mouse a Cookie*. Illus. by Felicia Bond. HarperCollins, 1985. ISBNs 0-06-024587-5 and 9780060245870 (See also other books in this series)

Oxenbury, Helen. *Tom and Pippo Read a Story*. Aladdin Books, 1988. ISBNs 0-689-71252-9 and 9780689712524 (board book). (See also other books in this series about Tom and his toy monkey, Pippo)

Peddicord, Jane Ann. *That Special Little Baby*. Illus. by Meilo So. Harcourt, 2007. ISBNs 0-15-205430-8 and 9780152054304

Polacco, Patricia. *Mommies Say Shhh!* Philomel, 2007. ISBNs 0-399-24720-3 and 9780399247200 (board book)

Porter-Gaylord, Laurel. *I Love My Daddy Because . . .* and *I Love My Mommy Because . . .* Illus. by Ashley Wolff. Dutton, 1991. ISBNs 0-525-44624-9 and 9780525446248 (board book); ISBNs 0-525-44625-7 and 9780525446255 (board book)

Rand, Ann. *Sparkle and Spin*. Illus. by Paul Rand. Chronicle, 2006. (reissue, Harcourt, 1957) ISBNs 0-8118-5003-X and 9780811850032

Ryder, Joanne. *Won't You Be My Hugaroo?* Illus. by Melissa Sweet. Harcourt, 2008. ISBNs 0-15-206298-X and 9780152062989 (board book)

Scott, Ann Herbert. *On Mother's Lap*. Illus. by Glo Coalson. Clarion, 2000. ISBNs 0-618-05159-7 and 9780618051595 (board book)

Shannon, George. *Tomorrow's Alphabet*. Illus. by Donald Crews. Greenwillow, 1996. ISBNs 0-688-13505-6 and 9780688135058

———. *White Is for Blueberry*. Illus. by Laura Dronzek. Greenwillow, 2005. ISBNs 0-06-029276-8 and 9780060292768

Shaw, Charles. *It Looked Like Spilt Milk*. HarperCollins, 1947. ISBNs 0-06-025566-8 and 9780060255664

Smith, Maggie. *One Naked Baby: Counting to Ten and Back Again.* Knopf, 2007. ISBNs 0-375-83329-3 and 9780375833298

Sweet, Melissa. *Fiddle-I-Fee.* Adapted and illus. by Melissa Sweet. Little, Brown, 2002. ISBNs 0-316-75861-2 and 9780316758611 (board book)

Tafuri, Nancy. *Have You Seen My Duckling?* Greenwillow, 1984. ISBNs 0-688-02797-0 and 9780688027971

————. *I Love You, Little One*. Scholastic, 1998. ISBNs 0-590-92159-2 and 9780590921596 (also see other books by this author–illustrator)

Walsh, Ellen Stoll. *Mouse Paint*. Harcourt/Red Wagon Books edition, 1995. ISBNs 0-15-205533-9 and 9780152055332 (oversized board book)

Wellington, Monica. *All My Little Ducklings.* Dutton, 1995. ISBNs 0-525-45360-1 and 9780525453604 (board book)

Wells, Rosemary. *Read to Your Bunny*. Scholastic, 1997. ISBNs 0-590-30284-1 and 9780590302845

Williams, Sue. *I Went Walking*. Harcourt/Red Wagon Books edition, 1996. ISBNs 0-15-200771-7 and 9780152007713 (board book)

Zelinsky, Paul. *Knick-Knack Paddywhack!* Dutton, 2002. ISBNs 0-525-46908-7 and 9780525469087

MODERN STORIES (IMAGINATIVE AND REALISTIC) TO SHARE WITH OLDER TODDLERS AND PRESCHOOLERS

Alarcon, Karen Beaumont. *Louella Mae, She's Run Away!* Illus. by Rosanne Litzinger. Holt, 1997. ISBNs 0-8050-3532-X and 9780805035322

Arnosky, Jim. *All Night Near the Water*. Putnam, 1994. ISBNs 0-399-22629-X and 9780399226298

Averbeck, Jim. *In a Blue Room*. Illus. by Tricia Tusa. Harcourt, 2008. ISBNs 0-15-205992-X and 9780152059927

Bang, Molly. *When Sophie Gets Angry, Really, Really Angry*. Scholastic/ Blue Sky, 1999. ISBNs 0-590-18979-4 and 9780590189798

Becker, Bonny. *A Visitor for Bear*. Illus. by Kady MacDonald Denton. Candlewick, 2007. ISBN 978076362807

Bemelmans, Ludwig. *Madeline.* Viking, 1958. ISBNs 0-670-44580-0 and 9780670445806

Berger, Barbara Helen. *Thunder Bunny*. Philomel, 2007. ISBNs 0-399-22035-6 and 9780399220357

Bergman, Mara. *Snip Snap! What's That?* Illus. by Nick Maland. Greenwillow, 2005. ISBNs 0-06-077754-0 and 9780060777548

Bernstein, Ruth. *Little Gorilla.* Clarion, 1986. ISBNs 0-395-28773-1 and 9780395287736

Boelts, Maribeth. *Before You Were Mine.* Illus. by David Walker. Putnam, 2007. ISBNs 0-399-24526-X and 9780399245268

Bruss, Deborah. *Book! Book! Book!* Illus. by Tiphanie Beeke. Scholastic, 2001. ISBNs 0-439-13525-7 and 9780439135252

Buckley, Helen E. *Grandfather and I* and *Grandmother and I.* Illus. by Jan Ormerod. Lothrop, 1994. ISBN 0-688-12533-6; ISBNs 0-688-12531-X and 9780688125318

Burningham, John. *Mr. Gumpy's Motor Car.* HarperCollins, 1993. ISBNs 0-690-00799-X and 9780690007992

Burton, Virginia Lee. *The Little House.* Houghton Mifflin, 1978. ISBNs 0-395-18156-9 and 9780395181560

———. *Mike Mulligan and His Steam Shovel.* Houghton Mifflin, 1939. ISBNs 0-395-06681-6 and 9780395066812

Carlstrom, Nancy White. *Wild Wild Sunflower Child Anna.* Illus. by Jerry Pinkney. Macmillan, 1987. ISBNs 0-02-717360-7 and 9780027173604

Chodie-Irine, Margaret. *Ella Sarah Gets Dressed.* Harcourt, 2003. ISBNs 0-15-216413-8 and 9780152164133

Cooney, Barbara. *Miss Rumphius.* Viking, 1982. ISBNs 0-670-47958-6 and 9780670479580

Cronin, Doreen. *Dooby Dooby Moo.* Illus. by Betsy Lewin. Atheneum, 2006. ISBNs 0-689-84507-3 and 9780689845079 (see also other books by this author-illustrator team.)

Daugherty, James. *Andy and the Lion.* Viking, 1938. ISBN 0-670-12433-8

deBrunhoff, Jean. *The Story of Babar.* Random House, 1937. ISBNs 0-394-80575-5 and 9780394805757

Dorros, Arthur. *Abuela.* Illus. by Elisa Kleven. Dutton, 1991. ISBNs 0-525-44750-4 and 9780525447504

Duvoisin, Roger. *Veronica.* Knopf, 2006. (Reissue 1961). ISBNs 0-375-83566-0 and 9780375835667

Ehlert, Lois. *Growing Vegetable Soup.* Harcourt, 1987. ISBNs 0-15-232575-1 and 9780152325756

Ets, Marie Hall. *Play with Me.* Viking, 1955. ISBNs 0-670-55977-6 and 9780670559770

Falconer, Ian. *Olivia*. Atheneum, 2001. ISBNs 0-689-82953-1 and 9780689829536 (also see other stories about Olivia.)

Fleming, Denise. *The Cow Who Clucked*. Holt, 2006. ISBNs 0-8050-7265-9 and 9780805072655

————. *In the Small, Small Pond*. Holt, 1993. ISBNs 0-8050-2264-3 and 9780805022643

————. *In the Tall, Tall Grass*. Holt, 1991. ISBNs 0-8050-1635-X and 9780805016352

Ford, Miela. *Little Elephant*. Illus. by Tana Hoban. Greenwillow, 1994. ISBNs 0-688-13140-9 and 9780688131401

————. *Sunflower*. Illus. by Sally Noll. Greenwillow, 1995. ISBNs 0-688-13301-0 and 9780688133016

Fox, Mem. *Hattie and the Fox*. Illus. by Patricia Mullins. Bradbury, 1987. ISBNs 0-02-735471-7 and 9780027354713

————. *Wilfrid Gordon McDonald Partridge*. Illus. by Julie Vivas. Kane/Miller, 1985. ISBNs 0-916291-04-9 and 9780916291044

Freeman, Don. *Corduroy*. 40th Anniversary Edition. Viking, 2008. ISBNs 0-670-06336-3 and 9780670063369

Ginsburg, Mirra. *Across the Stream*. Illus. by Nancy Tafuri. Greenwillow, 1982. ISBNs 0-688-01204-3 and 9780688012045

Hamilton, Kersten. *Red Truck*. Illus. by Valeria Petrone. Viking, 2008. ISBNs 0-670-06275-8 and 9780670062751

Harper, Isabelle, and Barry Moser. *My Dog Rosie*. Scholastic, 1994. ISBNs 0-590-47619-X and 9780590476195

Henkes, Kevin. *The Biggest Boy*. Illus. by Nancy Tafuri. Greenwillow, 1995. ISBNs 0-688-12829-7 and 9780688128296

————. *A Good Day*. Greenwillow, 2007. ISBN 978006114018

————. *Kitten's First Full Moon*. Greenwillow, 2004. ISBN 0-06-0588-4

————. *Lilly's Purple Plastic Purse*. Greenwillow, 1996. ISBNs 0-688-12898-X and 9780688128982 (also see other books about this lovable character.)

————. *Wemberly Worried*. Greenwillow, 2000. ISBN 0-688-17027-7

Hesse, Karen. *Come on Rain!* Illus. by Jon J Muth. Scholastic, 1999. ISBNs 0-590-33125-6 and 9780590331258

Hoffman, Mary. *Amazing Grace*. Illus. by Carolina Binch. Dial, 1991. ISBNs 0-8037-1040-2 and 9780803710405

Hughes, Shirley. *Alfie Gets in First*. Lothrop, 1982. ISBNs 0-688-00848-8 and 9780688008482

Hutchins, Pat. *Little Pink Pig*. Greenwillow, 1994. ISBNs 0-688-12014-8 and 9780688120146

———. *Rosie's Walk*. Simon & Schuster/Macmillan, 1968. ISBNs 0-02-745850-4 and 9780027458503

Johnson, Paul Brett. *On Top of Spaghetti*. Lyrics by Tom Glazer. Scholastic, 2006. ISBNs 0-439-74944-1 and 9780439749442

Juster, Norton. *The Hello, Goodbye Window*. Illus. by Chris Raschka. Hyperion/di Capua, 2005. ISBNs 0-7868-0914-0 and 9780786809141

Keats, Ezra Jack. *Peter's Chair*. Harper, 1967. ISBNs 0-06-023111-4 and 9780060231118

———. *The Snowy Day*. Viking, 1962. ISBNs 0-670-65400-0 and 9780670654000

———. *Whistle for Willie*. Viking, 1964. ISBNs 0-670-76240-7 and 9780670762408

Kerr, Judith. *The Tiger Who Came to Tea*. HarperCollins, 2002. ISBNs 0-06-051780-8 and 9780060517809. Originally published London: W. Collins, 1968.

Lobel, Arnold. *Frog and Toad*. HarperCollins, 1996. ISBN 0-06-44167-9 (boxed set, 4 books)

London, Jonathan. *Froggy Gets Dressed*. Illus. by Frank Remkiewicz. Viking, 1992. ISBNs 0-670-84249-4 and 9780670842490 (also see other stories about Froggy.)

McCloskey, Robert. *Blueberries for Sal*. Viking, 1948. ISBNs 0-670-17591-9 and 9780670175918

———. *Make Way for Ducklings*. Viking, 1941. ISBNs 0-670-45149-5 and 9780670451494

McDonald, Megan. *When the Library Lights Go Out*. Illus. by Katherine Tillotson. Atheneum, 2005. ISBNs 0-689-86170-2 and 9780689861703

McPhail, David. *Big Brown Bear's Birthday Surprise*. Harcourt, 2007. ISBNs 0-15-206098-7 and 9780152060985

Marshall, James. *George and Martha*. Houghton Mifflin, 1972. ISBNs 0-395-16619-5 and 9780395166192 (also see other stories about George and Martha)

Minarik, Else H. *Little Bear's Visit*. Illus. By Maurice Sendak. HarperCollins, 1961. ISBNs 0-06-024265-5 and 9780060242657 (also see other stories about Little Bear)

O'Connor, Jane. *Fancy Nancy*. Illus. by Robin Preiss Glasser. Harper, 2006. ISBNs 0-06-054209-8 and 9780060542092

————. *Fancy Nancy Bonjour, Butterfly*. Illus. by Robin Preiss Glasser. HarperCollins, 2008. ISBNs 0-06-123588-1 and 9780061235887

————. *Snow Globe Family*. Illus. by S. D. Schinder. Penguin Putnam, 2006. ISBNs 0-399-24242-2 and 9780399242427

Polacco, Patricia. *Oh, Look!* Philomel, 2004. ISBNs 0-399-24223-6 and 9780399242236

Potter, Beatrix. *The Tale of Peter Rabbit.* Warne, 1987 new ed. with new reproductions. ISBNs 0-7232-3460-4 and 9780723234609 (also see other "Tale of . . ." classics by this beloved author–illustrator)

Pryor, Ainslie. *The Baby Blue Cat Who Said No.* Viking, 1988. ISBNs 0-670-81780-5 and 9780670817801 (also see other books about the Baby Blue Cat)

Rankin, Joan. *The Little Cat and the Greedy Old Woman.* Simon & Schuster/McElderry, 1995. ISBNs 0-689-50611-2 and 9780689506116

Ringold, Faith. *Tar Beach.* Crown, 1991. ISBNs 0-517-58030-6 and 9780517580301

Rylant, Cynthia. *The Stars Will Still Shine.* HarperCollins, 2005. ISBNs 0-06-054639-5 and 9780060546397

Sakai, Komako. *Emily's Balloon.* Chronicle, 2003. ISBNs 0-8118-5219-9 and 9780811852197

Schwartz, Amy. *What James Likes Best.* Atheneum, 2003. ISBNs 0-689-84059-4 and 9780689840593

Sendak, Maurice. *Where the Wild Things Are.* Harper & Row, 1963. ISBNs 0-06-025492-0 and 9780060254926

Shannon, George. *April Showers.* Illus. by Jose Aruego and Adriane Dewey. Greenwillow, 1995. ISBNs 0-688-13121-2 and 9780688131210

Swanson, Susan Marie. *To Be Like the Sun.* Illus. by Margaret Chodos-Irvine. Harcourt, 2008. ISBNs 0-15-205796-X and 9780152057961

Thomson, Pat. *Drat That Fat Cat!* Illus. by Ailie Busby. Scholastic, 2003. ISBNs 0-439-47195-8 and 9780439471954

Van Laan, Nancy. *So Say the Little Monkeys.* Illus. by Yumi Heo. Atheneum, 1998. ISBNs 0-6898103-8-5 and 9780689810381

Vipont, Elfrida. *The Elephant and the Bad Baby.* Illus. by Raymond Briggs. HarperCollins, 1986. ISBNs 0-698-20039-X and 9780698200395

Waddell, Martin. *Can't You Sleep, Little Bear?* Illus. by Barbara Firth. Candlewick, 1992. ISBNs 1-56402-007-X and 9781564020079 (also see other stories about Little Bear)

———. *Farmer Duck*. Illus. by Helen Oxenbury. Candlewick, 1992. ISBNs 1-56402-009-6 and 9781564020093

Wahl, Jan. *Little Gray One*. Illus. by Frané Lessac. Morrow, 1993. ISBNs 0-688-12037-7 and 9780688120375

Wells, Rosemary. *Edward Unready for School*. Dial, 1995. ISBNs 0-8037-1884-5 and 9780803718845 (also see other stories about Edward Unready)

Willems, Mo. *Knuffle Bunny: A Cautionary Tale*. Hyperion, 2004. ISBNs 0-7868-1870-0 and 9780786818709

———. *Knuffle Bunny Too: A Case of Mistaken Identity*. Hyperion, 2007. ISBNs 1-4231-0299-1 and 9781423102991

Williams, Linda. *The Little Old Lady Who Was Not Afraid of Anything*. Illus. by Megan Lloyd. HarperCollins, 1986. ISBNs 0-690-04586-7 and 9780690045864

Williams, Vera B. *A Chair for My Mother*. Greenwillow, 1982. ISBNs 0-688-00914-X and 9780688009144 (also see other titles in this series)

———. *"More More More," Said the Baby: 3 Love Stories*. Greenwillow, 1990. ISBNs 0-688-09173-3 and 9780688091736

Yashima, Taro. *Umbrella*. Viking, 1958. ISBNs 0-670-73858-1 and 9780670738588

Yolen, Jane. *Owl Moon*. Illus. by John Schoenherr. Philomel, 1987. 20th Anniversary edition, 2007. ISBNs 0-399-24799-8 and 9780399247996

FOLK AND FAIRY TALES TO SHARE WITH OLDER TODDLERS AND PRESCHOOLERS: COLLECTIONS

Baumgartner, Barbara, reteller. *Crocodile! Crocodile! Stories Told Around the World*. Illus. by Judith Moffatt. Dorling Kindersley, 1994. ISBNs 1-56458-463-1 and 9781564584632

Brooke, L. Leslie, illus. *The Golden Goose Book*. Afterword by Neil Philip. Houghton Mifflin, 1992. ISBNs 0-395-61303-5 and 9780395613030

Gág, Wanda, translator-illustrator. *More Tales from Grimm*. Univ. of Minnesota, 2006. (Reissue: 1936, Coward-McCann) ISBNs 0-8166-4938-3 and 9780816649389

———. *Tales from Grimm*. Univ. of Minnesota, 2006. (Reissue: 1936, Coward-McCann) ISBNs 0-8166-4936-7 and 9780816649365

Galdone, Paul. *Nursery Classics: A Galdone Treasury.* Clarion, 2001. ISBNs 0-618-13046-2 and 9780618130467. Complete texts and illustrations of "The Three Little Pigs," "The Three Bears," "The Little Red Hen," and "Cat Goes Fiddle-i-fee."

Haviland, Virginia. *The Fairy Tale Treasury.* Illus. by Raymond Briggs. Dell, 1986. ISBNs 0-440-42556-5 and 9780440425564 (thirty-two of the best loved tales for young children)

Hutchinson, Veronica. *Candlelight Stories.* Illus. by Lois Lenski. Minton, Balch, 1926. o.p.

————. *Chimney Corner Stories.* Illus. by Lois Lenski. Minton, Balch, 1925. o.p.

————. *Fireside Stories.* Illus. by Lois Lenski. Minton, Balch, 1927. o.p.

Lester, Julius. *The Knee-High Man and Other Tales.* Illus. by Ralph Pinto. Dial, 1972. ISBNs 0-8037-4593-1 and 9780803745933

Oxenbury, Helen, reteller and illus. *The Helen Oxenbury Nursery Story Book.* Knopf, 1992. ISBNs 0-394-87519-2 and 9780394875194 (an appealing collection of ten nursery tales, including such favorites as "Henny-Penny," "The Turnip," and "Goldilocks and the Three Bears")

Rockwell, Anne, ed. *The Acorn Tree and Other Folktales.* Greenwillow, 1995. ISBNs 0-688-10746-X and 9780688107468

————. *The Old Woman and Her Pig.* Crowell, 1979. ISBNs 0-690-03928-X and 9780690039283

————. *The Three Bears and Fifteen Other Stories.* Crowell, 1975. ISBNs 0-06-440142-1 and 9780064401425

Sierra, Judy. *Can You Guess My Name? Traditional Tales Around the World.* Illus. by Stefano Vitale. Clarion, 2002. ISBNs 0-618-13328-3 and 9780618133284

————. *Nursery Tales from Around the World.* Clarion, 1996. ISBNs 0-395-67894-3 and 9780395678947

Windham, Sophie, reteller. *Read Me a Story: A Child's Book of Favorite Tales.* Scholastic, 1991. ISBNs 0-590-44950-8 and 9780590449502 (fifteen familiar nursery tales)

SINGLE TITLES

Aardema, Verna, reteller. *Borreguita and the Coyote.* Illus. by Petra Mathers. Knopf, 1991. ISBNs 0-679-80921-X and 9780679809210. A clever little lamb outwits a hungry coyote.

————. *How the Ostrich Got Its Long Neck.* Illus. by Marcia Brown. Scholastic, 1995. ISBNs 0-590-48367-6 and 9780590483674. (A *pourquoi* story from Kenya, reminiscent of "The Elephant's Child" by Rudyard Kipling.)

Andersen, Hans Christian. *The Ugly Duckling.* Illus. by Jerry Pinkney. HarperCollins, 1999. ISBNs 0-688-15932-X and 9780688159320

———. *The Ugly Duckling.* Retold by Stephen Mitchell. Illus. by Steve Johnson and Lou Fancher. Candlewick, 2008. ISBNs 0-7636-2159-5 and 9780763621599

Aylesworth, Jim. *The Gingerbread Man.* Illus. by Barbara McClintock. Scholastic, 1998. ISBNs 0-590-97219-7 and 9780590972192

Barton, Byron. *The Little Red Hen.* HarperCollins, 1993. ISBNs 0-06-021675-1 and 978006-0216757

———. *The Three Bears.* HarperCollins, 1991. ISBNs 0-06-020423-0 and 9780060204235

Brett, Jan. *Goldilocks and the Three Bears.* Putnam, 1990. ISBNs 0-399-22004-6 and 9780399220043

———. *The Mitten: A Ukrainian Folktale.* Adapted and illus. by Jan Brett. Putnam, 2009. ISBNs 0-399-25296-7 and 978039925969.

Brown, Marcia. *Once a Mouse.* Simon & Schuster, 1972. ISBNs 0-684-18490-7 and 9780684184906

———. *Stone Soup.* Simon & Schuster, 1979. ISBNs 0-684-92296-7 and 9780684922966

Dayrell, Elphinstone. *Why the Sun and Moon Live in the Sky.* Illus. by Blair Lent. Houghton Mifflin, 1968. ISBNs 0-395-53963-3 and 9780395539637

Deetlefs, Rene. *Tabu and the Dancing Elephants.* Illus. by Lyn Gilbert. Dutton, 1995. ISBNs 0-525-45226-5 and 9780525452263

deGerez, Tree. *When Bear Came Down from the Sky.* Illus. by Lisa Desimini. Viking, 1994. ISBNs 0-670-85171-X and 9780670851713

Galdone, Paul. *What's in Fox's Sack?* Houghton Mifflin, 1987. ISBNs 0-89919-062-6 and 9780899190624

Greene, Ellin. *The Little Golden Lamb.* Illus. by Rosanne Litzinger. Clarion, 2000. ISBNs 0-395-71526-1 and 9780395715260

Grimm, Jacob, and Wilhelm Grimm. *The Bremen Town Musicians.* Trans. by Anthea Bell. Illus. by Lisbeth Zwerger. Penguin, 2007. ISBNs 0-698-40042-9 and 9780698400429

———. *The Elves and the Shoemaker.* Retold and illus. by Bernadette Watts. North-South, 1986. ISBNs 1-55858-035-2 and 9781558580350

———. *Little Red-Riding Hood.* Illus. by Trina Schart Hyman. Holiday, 1983. ISBNs 0-8234-0470-6 and 9780823404704

———. *The Wolf and the Seven Little Kids*. Illus. by Felix Hoffman. Harcourt, 1959. o.p.

Harper, Wilhelmina. *The Gunniwolf*. Illus. by Barbara Upton. Dutton, 2003. ISBNs 0-525-46785-8 and 9780525467854

Kimmel, Eric A. *Anansi and the Moss-Covered Rock*. Illus. by Janet Stevens. Holiday, 1990. ISBNs 0-8234-0689-X and 9780823406890

MacDonald, Margaret Read. *Conejito: A Folktale from Panama*. Illus. by Gerado Valerio. August House, 2006. ISBNs 0-87483-779-0 and 9780874837797

———. *Go to Sleep, Gecko! A Balinese Folktale*. Illus. by Geraldo Valerio. August House, 2006. ISBNs 0-87483-780-4 and 9780874837803

Moser, Barry. *The Three Little Pigs*. Little, Brown, 2001. ISBNs 0-316-58544-0 and 9780316585446

Percy, Graham, illus. *The Cock, the Mouse, and the Little Red Hen*. Candlewick, 1992. ISBNs 1-56402-008-8 and 9781564020086

Pinkney, Jerry. *The Little Red Hen*. Dial, 2006. ISBNs 0-8037-2935-9 and 9780803729353

———. *Little Red Riding Hood*. Little, Brown, 2007. ISBNs 0-316-01355-2 and 9780316013550

Rounds, Glen, reteller and illus. *Three Little Pigs and the Big Bad Wolf*. Holiday, 1992. ISBNs 0-8234-0923-6 and 9780823409235

Sandburg, Carl. *The Huckabuck Family and How They Raised Popcorn in Nebraska and Quit and Came Back*. Farrar, Straus & Giroux, 1999. ISBNs 0-374-33511-7 and 9780374335113

———. *The Wedding Procession of the Rag Doll and the Broom Handle and Who Was in It*. Illus. by Harriet Pincus. Harcourt, 1978. ISBNs 0-15-695487-7 and 9780156954877

Shannon, George. *Rabbit's Gift*. Illus. by Laura Dronzek. Harcourt, 2007. ISBNs 0-15-206073-1 and 9780152060732

Slobodkina, Esphyr. *Caps for Sale*. HarperCollins, 1947. ISBNs 0-201-09147-X and 9780201091472

So, Meilo. *Gobble, Slip, Slop: The Tale of a Very Greedy Cat*. Knopf, 2004. ISBNs 0-375-82504-5 and 9780375825040

Taback, Simms. *Joseph Had a Little Overcoat*. Viking/Penguin Putnam, 1999. ISBNs 0-670-87855-3 and 9780670878550

———. *There Was an Old Lady Who Swallowed a Fly*. Viking, 1997. ISBNs 0-670-86939-2 and 9780670869398

———. *This Is the House that Jack Built*. Putnam, 2002. ISBNs 0-399-23488-8 and 9780399234880

Thurber, James. *Many Moons*. Illus. by Marc Simont. Harcourt, 1990. ISBNs 0-15-251872-X and 9780152518721

Young, Ed, trans. and illus. *Lon Po Po: A Red-Riding Hood Story from China*. Putnam, 1989. ISBNs 0-399-21619-7 and 9780399216190

———. *Seven Blind Mice*. Putnam, 1992. ISBNs 0-399-22261-8 and 9780399222610

Zemach, Margot. *The Little Red Hen: An Old Story*. Farrar, 1993. ISBNs 0-374-44511-7 and 9780374445119 (The classic nursery story reinterpreted through humorous pictures.)

MUSICAL RECORDINGS: A SAMPLING

American Folk Songs for Children. Sung by Pete Seeger. Smithsonian/ Folkways SF 45020

Babes, Beasts, and Birds. Sung by Pat Carfra. Lullaby Lady Productions/ dist. by Alcazar JOL 3

Baby and Me: Playsongs and Lullabies to Share with Your Baby. Sung by Rachael Buchman. A Gentle Wind GW 1055

Baby Games: 6 Weeks to 1 Year. Created by Priscilla Hegner, with musical arrangements by Dennis Buck. Kimbo Educational KIM 9102/9102C

The Baby Record Featuring Bob McGrath and Katharine Smithrim. Kids Records KRLIKRC 1007

Baby's Bedtime. Lullabies from Kay Chorao's book, sung by Judy Collins. Lightyear Entertainment LIGHT 5105. (Other titles in this series include *Baby's Morningtime*, sung by Judy Collins, LIGHT 5104 and *Baby's Nursery Rhymes*, sung by Phylicia Rashad, LIGHT 5107.)

BabySong. Sung by Hap and Martha Palmer. Educational Activities AR 713/AC713

Bean Bag Activities. Kimbo Educational KIM 7055/7055C

Birds, Beasts, Bugs and Little Fishes. Sung by Pete Seeger. Smithsonian/ Folkways SF 45021

Camels, Cats and Rainbows. Sung by Paul Strausman. A Gentle Wind GW 1009

Did You Feed My Cow? Fred Koch and a group of children present the songs of Ella Jenkins. Red Rover Records RRR-333

Early, Early Childhood Songs. Sung by Ella Jenkins. Smithsonian/Folkways SF 45015

Friendship Stew: Songs from Here, There, and Around the World. Sung by Pam Donkin and Greta Pedersen. Magical Music Express GW 2001

Golden Slumbers: Lullabies from Far and Near. Harper Children's Audio ISBNs 0-89845-104-3 and 9780898451047 (Traditional lullabies performed by Pete Seeger and Oscar Brand.)

Hello Everybody! Playsongs and Rhymes from a Toddler's World. Sung by Rachael Buchman. A Gentle Wind GW 1038 ISBN 0-939065-61-4

A Hop, Skip, and a Jump: Activity Songs for the Very Young. Sung by Pam Donkin. A Gentle Wind GW1069

I Wanna Tickle the Fish. Performed by Lisa Atinson. A Gentle Wind GW1042

If You're Happy and You Know It Sing Along with Bob. Vols. 1 and 2. Sung by *Sesame Street's* Bob McGrath. Kids' Records KRL/KRC 1009 and KRL/KRC 1014

It's Toddler Time. Sung by Norm Michaels and Lynn Roberts. Kimbo Educational. KIM 0815/0815C

Jim Gill Sings Do Re Mi on His Toe Leg Knee. Jim Gill Music www.jimgill.com

Jim Gill Sings the Sneezing Song and Other Contagious Tunes. Jim Gill Music www.jimgill.com

Magical Earth. Performed by Sarah Pirtle. A Gentle Wind GW1058

Mainly Mother Goose: Songs and Rhymes for Merry Young Souls. Performed by Sharon, Lois & Bram. Elephant Records EF 301 (also listen to other titles by this popular trio from Canada)

More Singable Songs. Performed by Raffi. KSR 8104/8104C

A Place to Be. Performed by Jay Unger and Lyn Hardy. A Gentle Wind GW1006

Playtime Songs. Award-winning performers. A Gentle Wind GW 1063

Singable Songs for the Very Young. Performed by Raffi. KRS 8102/8102C

Sleeptime Serenade. Performed by Linda Schrade. A Gentle Wind GW1048

Songs and Games for Toddlers. Bob McGrath. Kids Records KRL 1016/KRC 1016

Songs for Wiggleworms #5. Old Town School of Music

Songs to Grow On for Mother and Child. Sung by Woody Guthrie. Smithsonian/Folkways SF 45035

Toddlers on Parade. Sung by Lynn Roberts. Kimbo Educational KIM 9002/9002C

Toddlers Sing Storytime. Music for Little People.

You'll Sing a Song and I'll Sing a Song. Sung by Ella Jenkins. FC 7664C

9 STORYTELLING TO YOUNG ADULTS

World myths are psychologically large enough for this audience [young adults]. The characters and storylines are ripe with images big enough to grip this self-conscious age group and transport them out of the anxious present into bigger ideas of who they are and who they can become. Myths help young adults TRUST the coming adult world, reassures them they are not alone. For ages and ages, human beings have made the transition to adulthood and lived to tell fantastic stories.
—*Megan Wells*[1]

YOUNG ADULTS OFTEN QUESTION the appropriateness of storytelling as an activity for them, but many of the values of storytelling discussed in Chapter 3 are pertinent to the developmental needs of adolescents. For example, literary fairy tales, with their underlying meanings, moral philosophies, and sometimes bittersweet moods, are especially meaningful to young people who are becoming aware of their individuality, and who find their values in conflict with society. These tales give the adolescent courage to explore his or her inner space—dreams, images, and feelings—and, through imagination, to construct a self.

In her article "To Tell or Not to Tell: Storytelling for Young Adults," Beth Horner recommends "a gradual exposure to storytelling by integrating it into successful existing programs or into situations in which the young adult is a captive audience, such as the school assembly or classroom."[2] Classroom projects, such as collecting family or community stories, using stories as a springboard to creative writing, or learning to tell stories to young children (see Chapter 10), create an interest in storytelling for its own sake.

Initially, many adults are intimidated by the prospect of telling stories to adolescents. Adolescents appear innately critical because they are looking at the world through an increasingly discerning eye. However, this age group can also be the most satisfying and rewarding group with which to share stories. "At a time when the young person feels bombarded by inner changes and the world's expectations and constraints; at a time when the adult feels bombarded by the resulting changes, questions, and criticisms, the coming together of storyteller and listener is even sweeter, and the naturally occurring rapport developed between teller and listener even more powerful."[3]

According to Swiss psychologist Jean Piaget's theory of intellectual development, adolescence marks the stage of "Formal Operations." Formal operations is the stage at which one is able to logically consider abstract ideas. Thus adolescents are able to consider ideas beyond their own experience and to look at issues from differing viewpoints. At this stage in life the individual begins to challenge accepted ideas and beliefs, to draw away from the values and expectations of authority figures. Working to form an identity, but not yet ready to be completely independent, the young adult tends to rely on his or her peer group for beliefs and values. Facing adulthood with its responsibilities can be overwhelming. Add to these factors the elements of hormonal changes and physical growth, and adolescence becomes a developmental period fraught with challenges.

This being said, it is not surprising that young adults prefer stories that provide a strong intellectual challenge, are psychologically complicated, poke fun at accepted values or authority figures, and contain characters who are multidimensional rather than all good or all evil. The storytelling experience allows young adults to look at darker aspects of life and provides an opportunity for them to face fearful beings and situations, including family and societal conflict, safely. In her fine *Storytelling for Young Adults: A Guide to Tales for Teens*, Gail de Vos states: "Listening to stories can serve as an outlet and testing ground for the strong emotions that young adults are experiencing, and, in many instances, trying to camouflage."[4] Stories that speak to this audience hint at the complications of emotional and physical love, address feelings of powerlessness, and include characters embarking on quests or life journeys.

In this chapter, Beth Horner, a professional storyteller and former youth services librarian, discusses the elements of a successful storytelling program for young adults: story selection, introduction and presentation, and program flow.

STORY SELECTION

The story qualities that appeal to young adults are the qualities of traditional literature, and that influence can clearly be seen in popular media. Young adults form a hard-core fan base for contemporary fantasy and science fiction, whether novels, films, or television shows. Traditional literature is the well from which much contemporary fantasy springs,[5] which makes the more complex traditional tales, such as romances, hero tales, ghost stories, and epics a rich source for storytelling to young adults.

FANTASY, SCIENCE FICTION, AND FOLKTALES

Tales of the fantastical attract young adults, which is why adroitly selected folktales work so well with this age. Original re-imaginings of traditional folk and fairy tales are written from within the contemporary gestalt, and new interpretive nuances transform old tales into new stories that resonate with present-day listeners, such as stories found in collections by Vivian Vande Velde, Datlow and Windling, and Virginia Hamilton. The science fiction quest tale—for new planets, galaxies, or life forms—is the hero's journey set in an interstellar future.[6]

Literary and fantasy tales for young adults include stories easily adapted for storytelling, as do carefully selected tales of science fiction. Robert J. Sawyer and Ursula LeGuin are masters of the short form. The fantasy and science fiction stories of Ray Bradbury and Isaac Asimov are highly recommended; try Bradbury's "All Summer in a Day" and Asimov's "The Ugly Little Boy." If you are unfamiliar with this genre, start with the best: Go to the website of the Science Fiction and Fantasy Writers of America (www.nebulaawards.com) for a list of the Nebula-winning short stories. Other sources of masterful science fiction include *The Science Fiction Hall of Fame, Volume I: The Greatest Science Fiction Stories of All Time, Chosen by the Members of the Science Fiction Writers of America*. For an international take on science fiction and fantasy, look at *The SFWA European Hall of Fame: Sixteen Contemporary Masterpieces of Science Fiction from the Continent*; and *Speculative Japan: Outstanding Tales of Japanese Science Fiction and Fantasy*.

Locus Online (www.locusmag.com) is "a semi-autonomous web version of *Locus Magazine*, which focuses on news of the science fiction publishing field and coverage of new science fiction books and magazines."[7] *Science Fiction Weekly* (www.scifi.com/sfw) is "the leading electronic publication covering the world of science fiction with news, reviews, original art and celebrity chat."[8]

Folktale Variants and Re-Imaginings

Cultural variations of traditional tales are of interest because they provide a different take on what is considered an old story, but these tales are best told in the middle of a program rather than at the beginning. There are many ways to find multiple variants, including resource books such as Margaret Read MacDonald's *The Storyteller's Sourcebook*.[9] Tales can be found simply by browsing in the picture-book section of the library. There one finds such gems as *Moss Gown*, a Cinderella variant from the southeastern United States; *Lon Po Po: A Red Riding Hood Story from China*; and *Mufaro's Beautiful Daughters*, a Cinderella variant from Africa. One might not think of the picture-book collection (ordinarily considered appropriate for younger children) as a source, but the stories in these books are often of great interest to young adults. In addition, the illustrations in today's picture books are both eye- and interest-catching.

The place of females in folktales has been energetically and often humorously transformed, and old tales featuring strong females continue to be actively sought by contemporary tellers. When seeking tales for older audiences, do not overlook the large number of fine picture books with young adult appeal, such as *Brave Margaret* and *Cupid and Psyche*. Current trends in folktales for youth include picture-book retellings that feature girls, women, and witches with their fair share of wit, wisdom, and courage. Other retellers seek out traditional tales of active women, such as the brave (but not beautiful) sister in the Italian *Count Silvernose* and the adventurous, multiethnic heroines of *The Serpent Slayer and Other Tales of Strong Women*.[10]

The trend for retelling traditional tales through a contemporary lens, incorporating modern values and perspectives, appears to be growing: a Google search of "retold + fairy + tales" leads to Amazon.com and a dizzying assortment of novel-length retellings of traditional tales for adults and young adults. Mass-market fairy tale series from Ace and Tor are commissioned from well-known writers of fantasy such as Jane Yolen and Charles de Lint, and the Windling and Datlow anthologies of retold folk and fairy tales are consistently popular in the fantasy field. Graphic novel series such as *Grimm Fairy Tales* by Ralph Tedesco and Joe Tyler and *Nightmares and Fairy Tales: Once Upon a Time* by Serena Valentino twist the traditional folktale into contemporary noir, while mystery and horror burgeon in series such as *30 Days of Night* by Steve Niles and *The Dark Tower* graphic novels by Peter David, Stephen King, Robin Furth, and Jae Lee. While this format may not lend itself to a storytelling repertoire per se, it does provide confirmation of the types of tales that work with young adults.

GHOST, HORROR, AND SUSPENSE TALES

One of the most popular types of stories for young adults is the tale of suspense. Suspense tales are good program openers because they immediately dispel any thought that storytelling is too childish for young adult audiences. Young adulthood is an age when one faces real unknowns, difficult situations, and an unclear future; therefore, the suspense tale is particularly intriguing. Surefire suspense stories include folktales such as "Mr. Fox" by Joseph Jacobs; "Sop Doll" by Richard Chase; "Mary Culhane and the Dead Man" by Molly Bang; "The Weeping Lass at the Dancing Place" by Sorche Nic Leodhas; and "The Devil's Dulcimer" by Janice Harrington. Literary tales often require editing to move from written to oral telling, but such tales can be equally effective. "The Monkey's Paw," "The Tell Tale Heart," "Occurrence at Owl Creek Bridge," and "Mama Gone" are four excellent examples.

Edgar Allan Poe, Judith Gorog, Maria Leach, Sorche Nic Leodhas, Robert San Souci, Janice M. Del Negro, and Jane Yolen have all edited or authored particularly good folk or literary collections containing tales with varying levels of suspense. Recommended recordings include *The Tell-Tale Heart and Other Terrifying Tales, Chillers, Tales from the Other Side,* and *Mama*

Gone and Other Tales to Trouble Your Sleep. All of these individual, collected, and recorded tales deal with powerful life concerns, choices, and challenges within the parameters of a horror or suspense story.

Objections to stories with ghosts and witches do sometimes occur, yet the reason there are so many tales of the supernatural is that these stories are psychologically important to human development. According to psychologists, listeners and readers vicariously experience whatever the main character in a story experiences. When the main character overcomes fear and defeats a frightening being or situation, listeners learn to face and defeat the challenges in their own lives as well. This is an essential part of learning to live in a complicated world. Making a brief statement to this effect before or after telling one of these stories might help you and your listeners feel more relaxed. You might even remark that the reason there are so many headless creatures in stories is that the thing we fear more than anything in the world is losing our heads! This lighthearted approach usually puts listeners at ease so that they can listen and enjoy the story. At the same time, we need to respect the wishes of our listeners and sponsors. If, prior to the program, the sponsor requests stories without witches or ghosts, honor that request. There are many suspenseful tales that include neither.

It is often fun to add a "jump" at the end of a suspense or ghost story. To add a jump, lower your voice as you approach the frightful moment/phrase, pause before the phrase, then hit the phrase hard, fast, and loud! If done well, every listener jumps. This causes laughter and creates a shared experience among the listeners. The jump in a story is "the great leveler." If everyone jumps, then everyone laughs—at themselves and at each other. No one is more cool or less cool than anyone else, a rare occurrence in the young adult world. Listeners relax, and they are then open to even more stories.

URBAN-BELIEF TALES

An offshoot of the suspense tale is the urban-belief tale. The urban-belief tale (also referred to as the urban legend and the urban myth) is a story usually set in a contemporary setting, grounded in some element of truth or plausibility and told as actual fact. These tales are popular with young adults for two reasons. First, they often contain elements of suspense or eeriness, as is the case with "The Vanishing Hitchhiker" and "The Hook" tales. Second, urban legends are particularly intriguing because they seem plausible. Therefore, there is always the question: Did that actually happen? The beehive hairdo, for example, was indeed an actual hairdo. Babysitting can often be a little scary in an unfamiliar home. People do sometimes put odd items into a microwave. Urban legends have an additional advantage: they often have a delightful "grossness" factor that really appeals to younger adolescents.

Teens who have heard variations of these stories often share their own versions and a rapport is established between teller and listener. "La Llorona, the Wailing Woman," an urban legend found in the Southwest U.S., Mexico, and Central and South America, is widely known by teens in many variations. A Google search of "La Llorona" results in multiple versions and a number of sources for this tale; an online search for "urban legends" is also fruitful. Holt and Mooney's *Spiders in the Hairdo: Modern Urban Legends* and Pat Mendoza's *Between Midnight and Morning: Historic Hauntings and Ghost Tales from the Frontier, Hispanic, and Native American Traditions* contain unusual, not often heard tales; additional sources of urban legends include collections by Jan Brunvand, Daniel Cohen, and Alvin Schwartz.

HUMOR, INCLUDING FRACTURED TELLINGS OF WELL-KNOWN TALES

Shared humor is a strong bonding tool. However, *what* is funny varies from age group to age group, and from culture to culture. Humor is usually best understood by one's peer group and sometimes best shared in one's peer group, so selecting a humorous story can be tricky. As mentioned earlier in this chapter, young adults find irreverent, satirical tales funny because they poke fun at accepted standards. For example, our culture's emphasis on physical beauty as a requisite for happiness is turned on its head by Natalie Babbitt's sly wit in "The Very Pretty Lady."

Tales with a humorous surprise ending, such as "Those Three Wishes" by Judith Gorog or "The Barking Mouse" retold by Antonio Sacre, are of interest to this age group because this group enjoys the unexpected. Irreverence, cleverness, surprise, and the defeat of the oppressor by the oppressed are particularly appreciated. Examples of stories with these elements include "The Debate in Sign Language," which includes gesture; and the Indonesian story "The Mousedeer and the Buffalo Chip," which includes manure! In "The Two Old Women's Bet," the women compete to see whose husband is the most foolish. Noodlehead stories, such as those found in Isaac Bashevis Singer's *When Shlemiel Went to Warsaw*, allow young people to laugh at themselves and to feel superior at the same time.

Irreverence is definitely appreciated by young adults, but they are also fascinated by literary, poetic, and even cultural variations of well-known tales. All speak to that stage of seeing things from different points of view and branching away from the well-known or generally accepted. Consider *Fables for Our Time* by James Thurber, *Fables You Shouldn't Pay Any Attention To* by Florence P. Heide, and selections from *American Literature in Parody* edited by Robert P. Falk. Jane Yolen's *Sleeping Ugly*, Vivian Vande Velde's *Tales from the Brothers Grimm and the Sisters Weird* or *The Rumpelstiltskin Problem*, and story collections by William J. Brooke are amusing take-offs on folk and fairy tales familiar from childhood.

Poetic versions of well-known tales are found in *Disenchantments: An Anthology of Modern Fairy Tale Poetry* by Wolfgang Mieder, and *Transformations* by Anne Sexton. A few satirical pieces such as "And Although the Little Mermaid Sacrificed Everything to Win the Love of the Prince, the Prince, Alas, Decided to Wed Another" are included in Judith Viorst's poetry collection *If I Were in Charge of the World*. *Trail of Stones* by Gwen Strauss, *The Poets' Grimm: 20th Century Poems from Grimm Fairy Tales*, Roald Dahl's *Revolting Rhymes*, *Story Hour*, and *If the Shoe Fits: Voices from Cinderella* all contain interpretations of fairy tales through poetry.

MYTHS, HERO TALES, AND LEGENDS

Young adults enjoy the grand adventure story. They are fascinated by tales with multidimensional characters who are journeying, seeking, facing challenges, and defining who they are, just as the young adult listener is doing. These tales include myths about the Greek, Roman, Aztec, African, or American Indian gods, goddesses, demigods, and spirits; Arthurian legends; and epics such as *Beowulf* and the *Odyssey*. As daunting as they may appear, it is possible to work these epic tales into learnable, tellable tales. An excellent example of condensing an epic is Syd Lieberman's 13-minute retelling of Beowulf's first adventure on his recording *The Tell-Tale Heart and Other Terrifying Tales*. Storyteller Ron Adams is a retired teacher who told Egyptian, Greek, and Norse mythology to his English classes at Collinsville High School in Illinois. He finds that *Mythology* by Edith Hamilton has easily told forms of the myths that are clearly edited with strong plot lines. Adams also recommends *Bulfinch's Mythology* and *The Golden Bough*. Barbara McBride-Smith, storyteller and elementary school librarian, combines mythology and irreverence in her excellent, satirical retellings of myths on her recordings *Greek or Whut?* and *Medusa and Other Good Ol' Greeks* as well as in her collection *Greek Myths Western Style*. McBride-Smith recommends *d'Aulaire's Book of Greek Myths* (Delacorte, 1992); Rosemary Sutcliff's telling of the *Iliad* in *Black Ships Before Troy* (Delacorte, 1993); and Neil Philip's *The Adventures of Odysseus* (Orchard, 1997) as well as collections by Robert Graves, Alfred J. Church, and Padraic Colum. Collections with a non-European focus include Katrin Tchana's *Changing Woman and Her Sisters: Stories of Goddesses from Around the World*; Joseph Bruchac and Gayle Ross's *The Girl Who Married the Moon*; Tim Tingle's *Spirits Light and Dark*; and Olga Loya's *Momentos Mágicos, Magic Moments*.

RIDDLE TALES

Intrigued by an intellectual challenge, young adults enjoy riddle tales such as "Clever Manka," "The Smuggler," and "Sir Gawain and the Loathly Lady," an Arthurian tale about obtaining power over one's own destiny that centers around the question "What is it that women most desire?"

Nina Jaffe and Steve Zeitlin have edited two collections of very tellable riddle tales titled *The Cow of No Color: Riddle Stories and Justice Tales from Around the World* and *While Standing on One Foot: Puzzle Stories and Wisdom Tales from the Jewish Tradition*. George Shannon's *Stories to Solve* series includes bite-sized riddle stories perfect when one has only a moment to tell an intriguing tale.

In *Fair Is Fair: World Folktales of Justice*, attorney Sharon Creeden expands the riddle to legal questions, presenting age-old folktales that pertain to various aspects of justice and law and relating them to present-day legal issues.

HISTORICAL AND CURRENT TOPICAL TALES

Historical and current topical stories are extremely powerful and, if well edited and well told, of particular interest to young adults. Coming into their own as participants and responsible members of society, they learn from historical tales and are often living with the issues of the current topical tales.

Look to history and historical figures for storytelling material, and be prepared to structure what you find. The historical story intrigues because it tells of events (often heroic and, just as interesting, often commonplace) that actually took place. These tales often portray real-life issues that teens deal with on a daily basis. There are numerous sources on the library shelf. Consider excerpts from *Selma, Lord, Selma: Girlhood Memories of the Civil Rights Days* by Sheyann Webb, Rachel West Nelson, and Frank Sikora. This firsthand account of two African American teenagers' experiences during the turbulent civil rights uprisings and marches in Selma, Alabama, in the 1960s is vividly and clearly told. Another true and exciting story, "Where the Girl Rescues Her Brother," tells of a young Cheyenne woman who rescued her brother from Crow scouts during a battle near Rosebud Creek in present-day Montana. Joseph Bruchac and Gayle Ross tell us that the battle took place only a few days before the Lakota and Cheyenne victory against the forces of Lieutenant Colonel George Armstrong Custer at Little Bighorn.

Excellent examples of taking historical and topical material and structuring it for vibrant, immediate, and dynamic telling can be found on the recordings *Tribes and Bridges*, three stories by LaRon Williams, Antonio Sacre, and Susan O'Halloran of growing up African American, Cuban American, and Irish American in the United States; *The Pipeline Blues* by Beth Horner, a humorous, true tale of political and environmental triumph in one midwestern U.S. town; *Hidden Memory: Japanese American Internment* by Anne Shimojima; *Nepantla: Twelve Wheels on Mars* by Syd Lieberman, the tale of NASA's landing of the rovers on Mars; *Intrepid Birdmen: Fighter Pilots of WWI* by Syd Lieberman; and *The Silver Spurs: A True Tale of the American*

Civil War by Beth Horner. Storyteller Kathryn Tucker Windham tells tales of living and working in the pre- and post-segregation American South.

TALES OF LIFE'S CONFLICTS AND ISSUES

Love, depression, family conflict, war, acceptance by others, grief, and similar issues are the subject of many folk and literary tales and are of particular importance to adolescents. Wait until the middle or later part of a program before telling these stories to young adult listeners; by that time, they will be more comfortable with the idea of storytelling and will be better able to listen and absorb these more sensitive tales. "Oliver Hyde's Dishcloth Concert" by Richard Kennedy delves into the loss of a loved one, depression, and the importance of one's community when facing life's difficult times. "Cap o'Rushes" in Joseph Jacobs' *English Folk and Fairy Tales* is a King Lear tale of family conflict, betrayal, and learning the meaning of true family love (see storyteller Patrick Ryan's version, "More than Salt" on p. 310). "The Young Woman of Vietnam," a retelling of the Chinese folktale "The Half Carpet" is a poignant but slightly humorous story of cross-generational conflict and acceptance; "The Apple Tree" speaks to family acceptance of a wayward son. "Whitebear Whittington," "Owl," "Count Alaric's Lady," and "Beauty and the Beast" address different aspects of romantic love. "City Girls" is a real-life story dealing with the trials and tribulations of "fitting in" within the context of race, economic status, and family secrets.

Personal tales can also have tremendous impact on young adult listeners, who often relate to the unique yet universal experiences of others when structured in oral narrative. Elizabeth Ellis, a former children's librarian and now a professional storyteller, is one of the most effective tellers of the personal tale in the United States today. Her book *Inviting the Wolf In*, written with co-author Loren Niemi, discusses the need for exploring difficult life lessons. Ellis, however, also tells personal tales that combine humor and pathos in such a way as to touch the full spectrum of human emotion in one tale. Her recordings *Mother and Daughter Tales* and *Valentine's Day at Wal-Mart* are two fine examples of the personal made universal.

INTRODUCING AND PRESENTING THE PROGRAM

An effective introduction anticipates anything that might block the listeners from enjoying the story, and indicates to the listeners that the storyteller respects them, their experiences, and their opinions. If your young adult listeners are new to storytelling, you must immediately dispel any notion that storytelling is "just for little kids," so that they can relax and enjoy the program. For example, you can briefly discuss the function of storytelling in society. Explain that this ancient art was originally a form of entertainment for adults and that there is a current revival of storytelling for adults with many festivals, concerts, and recordings that are not for children. For example, mention "Tellabration," celebrated throughout the United States on the Saturday evening before Thanksgiving. Present this material in an informative rather than a defensive manner. This kind of introduction will assure young adults that you do not consider them to be children, that you respect them, and that you will treat them as adults. If you plan to accompany any of your stories with a musical instrument, you might ask the group to observe this storytelling style with an analytical eye and decide whether the addition of music detracts from or enhances the story. After the story ask for their opinions. Such follow-up again indicates your respect for their intelligence and viewpoint.

If a story has an odd name or strange phrase that you know will distract your listeners, mention it ahead of time, indicating the source of the phrase or name, and suggest that they simply "ride with it" when it shows up in the story. For example, before telling the story "Sop Doll," mention the term "job of work" and explain that different cultures use different words or phrases to describe the same thing and that "job of work" simply refers to what we call "a job." Explain that one of the characters makes a very odd sound and says something that might at first seem to be gibberish. Suggest that they listen closely and see if they can figure out the meaning. After the story, ask for their interpretations of the term "sop doll" and then explain that "doll" is a colloquialism for paw or hand and that "sopping bread" is similar to "dunking doughnuts."

PROGRAM FLOW

Storyteller Elizabeth Ellis coined a rubric—HAHA, AH HA, AAAH, AMEN—for arranging story types for optimum ease of flow, or, in her own words, to "open the human heart." According to Ellis:

> HAHA stories let us laugh so we can relax and listen; these stress-busting stories are for the body.
> AH HA stories activate our curiosity. From jump tales to pourquoi stories, the mind loves to reason things out.
> AAAH stories engage our emotions with deeper meaning; these tales satisfy the hungry heart.
> AMEN stories remind us of ancient wisdom or modern insight. The Spirit shines through these stories.[11]

Ellis's ideal program is a journey that flows from HAHA to AMEN, touching on all the complex emotions in between.

The flow of a storytelling program is certainly important. A sample program could begin with a suspense tale told in a straightforward manner, avoiding exaggerated voice changes or an overly dramatic style, thus easing the listener into the storytelling experience. Young adults accept the suspense tale as appropriate for adults, immediately become engrossed, and can relax and listen to the program instead of punching their buddies and rolling their eyes to indicate to their peers that they are not taken in by a children's activity. Some storytellers start with a jump story that startles the listeners and causes them to laugh at themselves and each other, and to thus relax even more. Good rapport is now established. You may choose to cement this rapport by next telling an urban-belief tale before moving on to other types of stories.

Once listeners realize that they are going to enjoy the program and have confidence in the teller, they will relax and be able to absorb and enjoy a wider variety of story content and styles; they will become interested in the stories and the storytelling process. The middle and later part of the program can include any number of the types of stories mentioned earlier, stories that might take more intellectual concentration to absorb or that ask for deeper emotional involvement. Include at least one quieter, sub-tler, more sensitive tale that speaks to some of the conflicts and issues with which teens grapple. These stories do not necessarily get an overt reaction, but often they are the ones best remembered and the ones that have the most impact.

Lastly, it often works well to close the program with a humorous tale. By the end of the program, there is a better understanding of what both the teller and listeners consider funny. Ending with a humorous story closes the program on an upbeat, satisfying note.

REFERENCES

1. Megan Wells, "Waking the Mythic Mind," *The Storytelling Classroom: Literacy Development in the Storytelling Classroom*, ed. Jane Stenson (Libraries Unlimited, 2009).

2. Beth Horner, "To Tell or Not to Tell: Storytelling for Young Adults," *Illinois Libraries* 65 (September 1983): 458–464.

3. Beth Horner, "Storytelling to Young Adults." Workshop presented at the National Storytelling Conference, June 1998. A portion of chapter 9 consists of material presented by Beth Horner in her workshops and reflects her extensive experience in storytelling to young adults.

4. Gail de Vos, *Storytelling for Young Adults: A Guide to Tales for Teens* (Libraries Unlimited, 2003.) p.3

5. Betsy Hearne and Christine Jenkins, "Sacred Texts: What Our Foremothers Left Us in the Way of Psalms, Proverbs, Precepts, and Practices," *Horn Book* 75.5 (1999): 536–558.

6. Janice M. Del Negro, *A Trail of Stones and Breadcrumbs: Evaluating Folktales Published for Youth in the 20th Century, 1905–2000* (dissertation, Graduate College of the University of Illinois at Urbana-Champaign, 2007).

7. *Locus* Online, www.locusmag.com.

8. *Science Fiction Weekly*, www.scifi.com/sfw.

9. Margaret Read MacDonald, *The Storyteller's Sourcebook: A Subject, Title and Motif Index to Folklore Collections for Children, 1961–1982* (Neal-Schuman Publishers in association with Gale Research, 1982). *The Storyteller's Sourcebook: A Subject, Title, and Motif Index to Folklore Collections for Children, 1983–1999* (Gale Group, 2001).

10. Janice M. Del Negro, *A Trail of Stones and Breadcrumbs: Evaluating Folktales Published for Youth in the 20th Century, 1905–2000* (dissertation, Graduate College of the University of Illinois at Urbana-Champaign, 2007).

11. Personal communications from Elizabeth Ellis to Janice Del Negro, January 1, 2009.

STORIES, RECORDINGS, AND COLLECTIONS TO SHARE WITH YOUNG ADULTS

FANTASY, SCIENCE FICTION, AND FOLKTALES

Folktale Variants

Bruchac, Joseph, and Ross, Gayle. *The Girl Who Married the Moon.* Troll Communications, 1994. ISBN 9780816734801

Hooks, William H. *Moss Gown.* Illus. by Donald Carrick. Houghton Mifflin/Clarion, 1987. ISBN 9780899194608

Kimmel, Eric. *Count Silvernose: A Story from Italy.* Illus. by Omar Rayyan. Holiday House, 1996. ISBN 9780823412167

Louie, Ai-Ling. *Yeh-Shen: A Cinderella Story from China.* Illus. by Ed Young. Putnam/Philomel, 1982. ISBN 9780698113886

Martin, Rafe. *The Rough Faced Girl.* Illus. by David Shannon. Putnam, 1998. ISBN 9780698116269

Moser, Barry. *Tucker Pfeffercorn.* Little, Brown, 1994. ISBN 9780316585422

San Souci, Robert. *Brave Margaret.* Simon & Schuster, 1999. ISBN 9780689848506

Steptoe, John. *Mufaro's Beautiful Daughters.* Scholastic, 1988. ISBN 9780590420587

Young, Ed. *Lon Po Po: A Red Riding Hood Story from China.* Putnam/Philomel, 1989. ISBN 9780399216190

Fantasy and Science Fiction

Asimov, Isaac. "The Ugly Little Boy." *Tomorrow's Children: Eighteen Tales of Fantasy and Science Fiction.* Doubleday, 1966. ISBN 9780860078210. Also in Isaac Asimov and Theodore Sturgeon, *The Ugly Little Boy and the Widget, the Wadget and Boff,* Tor Books, 1989. ISBN 9780812559668

Bradbury, Ray. "All Summer in a Day." *R Is for Rocket–S Is for Space.* Bantam, 1990. ISBN 9781904619789

Craft, M. Charlotte. *Cupid and Psyche.* Illus. by Kinuko Y. Craft. Harper-Collins, 1996. ISBN 9780688131630

Datlow, Ellen, and Windling, Terri, eds. *Swan Sister.* Simon & Schuster, 2003. ISBN 9780689846137

————. *A Wolf at the Door and Other Retold Fairy Tales.* Simon & Schuster, 2000. ISBN 9780689821394. Additional collections include *Snow White, Blood Red*, Morrow, 1993; *Black Thorn, White Rose*, Morrow, 1994; and *Black Swan, White Raven*, Avon, 1997.

King, Stephen. *The Gunslinger Born* (The Dark Tower Graphic Novels, Book 1, with Peter David, Robin Furth, and Jae Lee). Marvel Comics, 2007. ISBN 9780785121442

Morrow, James, and Kathryn Morrow, eds. *The SFWA European Hall of Fame: Sixteen Contemporary Masterpieces of Science Fiction from the Continent.* Tor Books, 2008. ISBN 9780765315373

Niles, Steve. *30 Days of Night.* IDW, 2004. ISBN 9781932382174

Silverberg, Robert, ed. *The Science Fiction Hall of Fame, Volume I: The Greatest Science Fiction Stories of All Time, Chosen by the Members of the Science Fiction Writers of America.* Tor Books, 2003. ISBN 9780765305367

Tedesco, Ralph, and Joe Tyler. *Grimm Fairy Tales.* Zenescope Entertainment, 2007. ISBN 9780978687403

Valentino, Serena. *Nightmares and Fairy Tales: Once Upon a Time.* SLG Publishing, 2004. ISBN 9780943151878

Van Troyer, Gene, ed. *Speculative Japan: Outstanding Tales of Japanese Science Fiction and Fantasy.* Kurodahan Press, 2007. ISBN 9784902075267

Vande Velde, Vivian. *Tales from the Brothers Grimm and the Sisters Weird.* Harcourt, 1995. ISBN 9780152002206

GHOSTS, HORROR, AND SUSPENSE TALES

Bang, Molly. "Mary Culhane and the Dead Man" in *The Goblins Giggle and Other Stories.* Peter Smith, 1988. ISBN 9780684132266

Bierce, Ambrose. "Occurrence at Owl Creek Bridge" in *In the Midst of Life: Tales of Soldiers and Civilians.* Citadel Press, 1993. ISBN 9780806505510

Bruchac, Joseph, and Jacob Bruchac. *When the Chenoo Howls: Native American Tales of Terror.* Illus. by William Sauts Bock. Walker & Co., 1998. ISBN 9780802786388

Burch, Milbre. *Mama Gone and Other Stories to Trouble Your Sleep*. Kind Crone Productions, 2007. ISBN 9780979527173

Chase, Richard. "Sop Doll" in *Jack Tales*. Houghton, 1943. ISBN 9780395669518

Del Negro, Janice M. *Passion and Poison: Tales of Shape-Shifters, Ghosts, and Spirited Women*. Marshall Cavendish, 2007. ISBN 9780761453611

Deyer, Bob, and Beth Horner. "The Phantom Black Carriage." Told by Beth Horner on *An Evening at Cedar Creek*. Wellspring CS 4902

The Folktellers. *Chillers*. MamaT Artists, 1990. ISBN 9789999158640

Hamilton, Virginia. *The Dark Way: Stories from the Spirit World*. Harcourt, Brace, 1990. ISBN 9780152223410

Hayes, Joe. *La Llorona / The Weeping Woman*. Cinco Puntos Press, 2004. ISBN 9780938317395

Jacobs, Joseph. "Mr. Fox" in *English Fairy Tales* by Joseph Jacobs. Dover, 1989. ISBN 9780486218182; told by the Folktellers on *Chillers* by Mama-T Artists MTA-2

Jacobs, W. W. "The Monkey's Paw" in *The Oxford Book of English Ghost Stories*. Ed. by Michael Cox and R. A. Gilbert. Oxford University Press, 1986. ISBN 9780192826664

Keding, Dan. *Stories from the Other Side*. Turtle Creek Recordings TC 1003

Leodhas, Sorche Nic. "The Weeping Lass at the Dancing Place" in *Twelve Great Black Cats and Other Eerie Scottish Tales* by Sorche Nic Ledhas. Dutton, 1971. ISBN 9780525415756

Lieberman, Syd. *The Tell-Tale Heart and Other Terrifying Tales*. August House, 1995. ISBN 9780874834307

Manning-Sanders, Ruth. "The Skull" in *The Book of Ghosts and Goblins*. Dutton, 1969. ISBN 9780416110500; retold by Beth Horner on *Encounter with a Romance Novel: Women in Everyday Life*. Wellspring CS 4902

Tingle, Tim. *Spirits Light and Dark: Supernatural Tales from the Five Civilized Tribes*. August House, 2006. ISBN 9780874837780

Vande Velde, Vivian. *All Hallows' Eve: 13 Stories*. Harcourt Brace, 2006. ISBN 9780152055769

Yolen, Jane. "Mama Gone" in *Vampires*. HarperCollins, 1991. ISBN 9780060268008

———. *Twelve Impossible Things Before Breakfast*. Harcourt Brace, 1997. ISBN 9780152015244

URBAN-BELIEF TALES

Brunvand, Jan Harold. *The Choking Doberman and Other "New" Urban Legends.* Norton, 1986. ISBN 9780393303216

———. *The Vanishing Hitchhiker: American Urban Legends and Their Meaning.* Norton, 1989. ISBN 9780393951691

Cohen, Daniel. *Southern Fried Rat and Other Gruesome Tales.* M. Evans, 1982. ISBN 9780380706556

Holt, David, and Bill Mooney, comp. *The Exploding Toilet: Modern Urban Legends.* August House, 2004. ISBN 9780874837544

———. *Spiders in the Hairdo: Modern Urban Legends.* August House, 1999. ISBN 9870874835250

Schwartz, Alvin. *Scary Stories to Tell in the Dark: Collected from American Folklore.* HarperCollins, 1981. ISBN 9780064401777; also available on Harper Children's Audio CPN 1794

HUMOR, INCLUDING FRACTURED TELLINGS OF WELL-KNOWN TALES

Babbitt, Natalie. "The Very Pretty Lady" in *The Devil's Storybook.* Farrar, Straus, Giroux, 1974. ISBN 9780374417086

Brooke, William J. *A Telling of the Tales: Five Stories.* Illus. by Richard Egielski. HarperCollins, 1990. ISBN 9780060206888

———. *Untold Tales.* HarperCollins, 1992. ISBN 9780060202712

Chase, Richard. "The Two Old Women's Bet" in *Grandfather Tales.* Houghton Mifflin, 1973. ISBN 9780395066928

Falk, Robert P., ed. *American Literature in Parody.* Greenwood, 1977. ISBN 0-8371-9741-4

Garner, James Finn. *Politically Correct Bedtime Stories: Modern Tales for Our Life and Times.* Macmillan, 1998. ISBN 9780025427303

Gorog, Judith. "Those Three Wishes" in *A Taste for Quiet and Other Disquieting Tales.* Putnam/Philomel, 1982. ISBN 9780399209222; also in *Ready-To-Tell Tales* by David Holt and Bill Mooney. August House, 1995. ISBN 9780874833812

Heide, Florence P. *Fables You Shouldn't Pay Any Attention To.* Lippincott, 1978. ISBN 9780397317820

Horner, Beth. "The Mousedeer and the Buffalo Chip" on *An Evening at Cedar Creek.* Wellspring, CS 4902

Lieberman, Syd. "The Debate in Sign Language" by *Joseph the Tailor and Other Jewish Tales.* August House, 1995. ISBN 9780874834260

Mieder, Wolfgang, ed. *Disenchantments: An Anthology of Modern Fairy Tale Poetry.* University Press of England, 1985. ISBN 9780874513271

Sacre, Antonio. "The Barking Mouse" in *Ready-To-Tell Tales*. Ed. by David Holt and Bill Mooney. August House, 1995. ISBN 9780874833812

Sexton, Anne. *Transformations*. Houghton Mifflin, 1972. ISBN 9780618083435

Singer, Isaac Bashevis. *When Shlemiel Went to Warsaw and Other Stories*. Trans. by Isaac B. Singer and Elizabeth Shub. Illus. by Margot Zemach. Farrar, Straus, Giroux, 1986. ISBN 9780440493068

Thurber, James. *Fables for Our Time*. HarperCollins, 1983. ISBN 9780060909994

Vande Velde, Vivian. *The Rumpelstiltskin Problem*. Houghton Mifflin, 2000. ISBN 9780618055234

Viorst, Judith. "And Although the Little Mermaid Sacrificed Everything to Win the Love of the Prince, the Prince, Alas, Decided to Wed Another" in *If I Were in Charge of the World and Other Worries*. Simon & Schuster, 1981. ISBN 9780689707704

Yolen, Jane. *Sleeping Ugly*. Putnam, 1981. ISBN 9780590461054; told by Milbre Burch on *Touch Magic . . . Pass It On*. Weston Woods WW 741C

MYTHS, HERO TALES, AND LEGENDS

Bulfinch, Thomas. *Bulfinch's Mythology*. Random House, 1988. ISBN 9780451627995

D'Aulaire, Ingri, and Edgar Parin d'Aulaire. *D'Aulaire's Book of Greek Myths*. Delacorte, 1992. ISBN 9780440406945

Erdoes, Richard. *American Indian Myths and Legends*. Pantheon, 1984; Peter Smith 1977. ISBN 9780844669267

Frazer, Sir James George. *The Golden Bough*. Macmillan, 1985. ISBN 9781853263101

Hamilton, Edith. *Mythology*. Little, Brown, 1942. ISBN 9780451628039

Hamilton, Virginia. *In the Beginning: Creation Stories from Around the World*. Harcourt, Brace, 1988. ISBN 0-15-2387-404

Hazeltine, Alice I. "The Return of Odysseus" in *Hero Tales from Many Lands*. Illus. by Gordon Laite. Abingdon, 1961. ISBN 9780687169436

Lieberman, Syd. "Beowulf" in *The Tell-Tale Heart and Other Terrifying Tales*. August House, 1995. ISBN 9780874834307

Loya, Olga. *Momentos Mágicos/Magic Moments*. August House, 1997. ISBN 9780874834970

McBride-Smith, Barbara. *Greek Myths, Western Style*. August House, 1998. ISBN 9780874835243

————. *Medusa and Other Good Ol' Greeks*. Pandora Productions 102.

Tchana, Katrin. *Changing Woman and Her Sisters: Stories of Goddesses from Around the World*. Holiday House, 2006. ISBN 9780823419999

————. *The Serpent Slayer*. Illus. by Trina Schart Hyman. Little, Brown, 2001. ISBN 9780316387019

HISTORICAL AND TOPICAL TALES

Bruchac, Joseph, and Gayle Rose. "Where the Girl Rescued Her Brother" in *The Girl Who Married the Moon: Tales from Native North America*. BridgeWater, 1994. ISBN 9780816734801

Horner, Beth. *The Pipeline Blues*. www.BethHorner.com

————. *The Silver Spurs: A True Tale of the American Civil War*. www. BethHorner.com

Lieberman, Syd. *Intrepid Birdmen: Fighter Pilots of WWI*. www.SydLieberman.com

————. *Twelve Wheels on Mars*. www.SydLieberman.com

Loya, Olga. *Nepantla: Caught Between Two Worlds*. www.racebridges-forschools.com

O'Halloran, Susan, Antonio Sacre, and La'Ron Williams. *Tribes and Bridges*. www.ohallorancommunications.com

Shimojima, Anne. *Hidden Memory: Japanese American Internment*. www. Racebridgesforschools.com

Webb, Sheyann, Rachel West Nelson, and Frank Sikora. *Selma, Lord, Selma: Girlhood Memories of the Civil Rights Days*. University of Alabama Press, 1980. ISBN 9780817300319

TALES OF LIFE'S CONFLICTS AND ISSUES

Alexander, Sue. *Nadia the Wilfull*. Dragonfly, 1992. ISBN 9780679834809

Chase, Richard. "Like Meat Loves Salt" in *Grandfather Tales* by Richard Chase. Houghton Mifflin, 1973. ISBN 9780395066928

————. "Whitebear Whittington" in *Grandfather Tales* by Richard Chase. Houghton Mifflin, 1973. ISBN 9780395066928

Ellis, Elizabeth, and Loren Niemi. *Inviting the Wolf In: Thinking About the Difficult Story*. August House, 2001. ISBN 9780874836233

Hearne, Betsy. *Beauties and Beasts*. Oryx Press, 1993. ISBN 9780897747295

Holt, David. "The Apple Tree" in *The Hairyman and Other Wild Tales*. Weston Woods, 1982. ISBN 9780897199391

Kennedy, Richard. "Oliver Hyde's Dishcloth Concert" in *Richard Kennedy: Collected Stories*. HarperCollins, 1987. ISBN 9780060232559

Lipman, Doug. "The Young Woman of Vietnam" in *Folktales of Strong Women*. Yellow Moon, 1983. ISBN 9780938756118; also told by Beth Horner on *Encounter with a Romance Novel: Heroines in Everyday Life*. Beth Horner Productions BEB5301

O'Halloran, Susan. "City Girls" in *Journeys of the Heart*. www.susanohalloran.com

Picard, Barbara. "Count Alaric's Lady" in *The Faun and the Woodcutter's Daughter*. Crowell, 1964. ISBN 9780200719995; also in: Greene, Ellin. *Storytelling: Art and Technique*. 3rd ed. Bowker, 1996. ISBN 9780835234580

Ryan, Patrick. "More than Salt." (See pp. 310–313)

Wolkstein, Diane. "Owl." *The Magic Orange Tree and Other Haitian Folktales*. Schocken, 1984. ISBN 9780394933900

RIDDLE TALES

Bauer, Caroline Feller. "The Smuggler." *Handbook for Storytellers*. Books on Demand. ISBN 9780838902936

Creeden, Sharon. *Fair is Fair: World Folktales of Justice*. August House, 1996. ISBN 9780874834000

Fillmore, Parker. "Clever Manka." *The Shoemaker's Apron*. Harcourt, 1920. ISBN 9780548983713; also in Greene, Ellin. *Storytelling: Art and Technique*. 3rd ed. Bowker, 1996. ISBN 9780835234580

Hastings, Selina. *Sir Gawain and the Loathly Lady*. Illus. by Juan Wijngaard. Lothrop, 1985. ISBN 9780688058234

Jaffe, Nina, and Steve Zeitlin. *The Cow of No Color: Riddle and Justice Tales from Around the World*. Illus. by Whitney Sherman. Holt, 1998. ISBN 9780805037364

———. *While Standing on One Foot: Puzzle Stories and Wisdom Tales from the Jewish Tradition*. Illus. by John Segal. Holt, 1993. ISBN 9780805025941

Shannon, George. *Stories to Solve: Folktales from Around the World*. Greenwillow Press, 1985. ISBN 9780688129477

10 CHILDREN AND YOUNG ADULTS AS STORYTELLERS

I never knew how much thought went into telling a story. It's hard, but it was fun. I was so nervous when I first got up to tell my story, but by the end of the week I actually enjoyed telling it. If I can do that I think I can do anything.
—*Eighth grader*[1]

CHILDREN IN THE MIDDLE and upper grades enjoy telling stories to younger children, and younger children respond enthusiastically. The ten-year-old who shuns the library storytime as a program "for babies" may rediscover the power of stories as he or she relates them to peers or younger listeners.

The child as teller may seem a contemporary idea but in fact it was practiced in early library work with children. For instance, in 1917 the New York Public Library had 46 reading clubs with a membership of nearly 1,000 boys and girls. That year a special meeting was held to welcome Marie Shedlock to Staten Island. Each club sent a representative to the meeting. One young representative made this tribute to Marie Shedlock:

> Three or four years ago we were content to read stories and plays, but during the past two winters we have tried to tell stories ourselves and thus, Miss Shedlock, our ambition has been aroused to further your great work in reviving the art of storytelling.[2]

Across the country creative librarians and teachers are introducing children to the art of storytelling, and a cadre of professional storytellers are making possible more storytelling residences in schools.

FOURTH GRADE IS THE BEST GRADE JUST BECAUSE OF STORYTELLING!

Anne Shimojima, director of the Instructional Media Center at Braeside School in Highland Park, Illinois, has told stories to her students for many years, using a variety of activities to expand the storytelling experience. Anne writes:

Storytelling is an important and integral component of the library program. In kindergarten, the students act out stories, providing the dialogue while I do the narration. In first grade, the classroom teachers and I lead discussions about story elements—character, setting, problem, and resolution. Second grade provides time for a year-long unit on folklore, and students fill out story maps, put the story into correct sequential order, create a class picture book retelling of a story, or take part in an exciting Battle of the Folk Tales, a team activity in which they answer questions for points. Third graders enjoy the Jack Tale unit and the culminating activity in which they rewrite and illustrate a story that is filmed for a DVD. Fourth graders listen to fairy tales to develop their listening skills. But, by far, the most popular activity is the unit in which I teach fourth graders to become storytellers themselves.

I chose the fourth grade because after five years of listening to stories, they have an enthusiastic love of story and the time that the curriculum-heavy fifth grade doesn't allow. But when I first suggested to my fourth-grade students that they learn how to become storytellers, they didn't greet the idea very enthusiastically. I was surprised. They had been coming to the library media center and hearing stories told from their very first week in kindergarten, and I knew that they loved storytelling. Then I told them that they would be telling stories to the first graders. That did it. They smiled and started asking questions excitedly. I realized that they had just been nervous, but the idea of telling to younger students won them over.

Over the years, I have developed the following activities to use with our student storytellers in the library. Each takes from forty-five minutes to one hour.

Our first session begins with my telling a story that they have heard in third grade. I purposely pick a story that they know, because I want them to focus on how I am telling the story, not how it ends. Afterward, I ask them to comment on the telling—what did they notice? I make a list of their responses. I want them to be conscious of how I wait for everyone to be ready before I start, pace, expression, gesture, and eye contact. The purpose of this session is to make them more conscious of the storyteller and the telling, not the story.

The second session focuses on visualization. I tell a story, first encouraging the students to see the images in their imaginations. Then they fill out a worksheet on which they describe how they saw different characters in their minds. How old was the main character? What was he wearing? What color was his hair? What about a second character? After hearing their responses aloud, I lead the students through a creative visualization exercise. We turn down the lights and they close their eyes. They imagine walking through a meadow and into a forest to a bench. An old person is sitting there and gives a gift—a bag—holding something the student needs right now. The person leaves and I invite the students to look in the bag. When we turn the lights back on, the students share what they saw in their imaginary bags.

In the third session, we concentrate on the use of voice and expression. Students practice saying the same sentence in different ways, to reflect different feelings, and emphasizing different words to change the meaning. Then we have some fun with tongue twisters to emphasize the importance of clear speaking.

Before I expect the students to start working on a story to tell, I want to help them become more comfortable with the idea of speaking before the group. Our fourth session moves into personal storytelling. Students choose a topic from a list (e.g., tell about a time you did something you feel proud of; tell about something funny with a brother or sister; tell about something memorable with a pet; tell about something interesting that happened on vacation, and the like), and I give them ten minutes to think about their stories. Then we sit in a circle on the floor and each student takes two to three minutes to tell his or her story to the class. I always start with an example from my own life to model the activity for them.

For the fifth session each student brings an object from home, something that he or she has feelings about. We go around the room, each student telling how he or she got the object and why it is important. Students bring stuffed animals, family photographs, trophies, and other treasured mementos. One thing I like about this activity is that it gives me a peek into what they hold dear. Again, I start the activity with a story about an object from my own life.

The sixth session is our joke-telling session. I select appropriate jokes, type them up, and put them into a shoebox. First the students are put into pairs and each pair pulls a two-person joke from the box. They have a few minutes to learn the joke and everyone acts out their jokes for the class. Then each student selects and learns a joke alone to tell to the class. Although they can take the papers up with them, they are encouraged to try to do it without reading.

The seventh session is based on an idea from *Every Child a Storyteller: A Handbook of Ideas* by Harriet R. Kinghorn and Mary Helen Pelton. I have rewritten several well-known folk tales, "Goldilocks and the Three Bears," "Little Red Riding Hood," "The Three Billy Goats Gruff," and "The Three Little Pigs." Each story has a narrator, but all dialogue is omitted. The students are put into small groups, one group per story. Each child takes a character's part and adds the dialogue. After twenty minutes to prepare and practice, each group performs its story for the class. I encourage the students to be creative. Some exchanges went like this:

From "The Three Little Pigs":
Third pig: How much are your bricks?
Brick seller: One hundred dollars.
Third pig: Do you take credit cards?

From "Little Red Riding Hood":
Little Red (noticing that Grandma looks different): Grandma, what happened?
Grandma: I decided to make a couple of changes.

From "The Three Billy Goats Gruff":
Troll (after the first goat crosses): Oh, that would have made some great goatburgers!

From "Goldilocks and the Three Bears":
Goldilocks (after trying the second bed): This bed is a waterbed! I don't like waterbeds!

Now it is time for the students to choose a story to learn. All the stories I offer to the students are folk tales, stories of the oral tradition that have come down through the years. I use stories I have rewritten plus stories from books that give permission for classroom use and copying, and I ask publishing companies for permission to copy stories for this unit. Each story is put into a file folder. Students must read at least three stories before choosing one to learn. At this first reading they are asked to write what country the story came from, who the main character is, why they like the story, what the main idea is, and what the most important thing about the story is, e.g., it's funny, it teaches a lesson, or it makes you jump.

In the classroom, teachers direct the students to fill out a character study sheet for the main character of the story, fill out a story map, read the story aloud to a partner, write out the first and last sentences and any special chants, and tell the story to a partner. The students are urged to practice their stories at home as well. I emphasize several points. They should not memorize the story, but become very familiar with the main plot points and what happens first, second, third, and so on. They should tell the story in their own words. They should make eye contact with their listeners, and speak loudly, clearly, and with expression.

After the students are given a week to learn their stories, I place them in small coaching groups. Each student tells his or her story to the group. The students give positive feedback, and then I make suggestions for improvement. At this point I make a note of how long each story lasts. This is useful information when I create the small groups for telling, as I will be able to make each group last approximately the same amount of time. I emphasize to all the students that they must practice, practice, practice, and they must do their practicing out loud. The classroom teachers are providing additional support in the classroom, giving their students time to practice with each other and sometimes in front of the whole class.

Finally the big day arrives. I organize the entire first and fourth grades into small groups. At the appointed time, the fourth graders pick up their first graders; take them to their telling space (in classrooms, the library, and hallways); tell their stories; and return the younger students to their classrooms. I circulate among the groups to make sure all is going well. The first and fourth grade classroom teachers are each sitting in on a group. After the telling, the storytellers fill out a response sheet: How did the telling go? How did the students behave? What was the best thing about telling? What will you do differently next time?

The second telling is to second graders. Again, small groups are made and the same procedure is followed. The tellers fill out another response sheet after this telling.

The students are usually excited and enthusiastic about their storytelling experiences. Here are some of their comments:

It went like a roller coaster. It went by so fast.
It was so fun. Telling the story was the best part even if it is scary to tell it.
After we stretched one boy said, "Is it over?" We said no. Then he said, "Good!"

FIGURE 17. *Fourth-grade storyteller Bennett Preskill keeps his first-grade listeners engaged with his lively telling of a tall tale, "Jack and the Two-Bullet Hunt." Photograph by Anne Shimojima. Reprinted by permission of Anne Shimojima, IMC Director, Braeside School, Highland Park, Illinois.*

It went great because all the kids were listening and we were all tremendous and I want to do it again.

I felt like a grownup telling a story to them. I wish I would get a chance to do it every day!

Fourth grade is the best grade just because of storytelling!

The best thing about telling stories to younger children is that they actually listened to you.

It's really fun that the little children were laughing and that felt good to me.

The best thing about telling stories to younger children is that if you mess up they don't care.

I felt like a real storyteller!

The classroom teachers love the unit. They tell me that student storytelling has noticeably helped their students improve in their oral presentations and their confidence before the class. Perhaps the biggest joy for me is to see our fourth graders blossom in front of the younger students. As often happens, having older students work with younger students brings out the best in the older ones. They take good care of the little ones—walking them down the hallways, leading stretches between stories, and trying their best, because of the small faces turned up and listening intently. I hope that they feel a little more empowered and discover that, while listening to stories is enjoyable, telling stories is the most fun of all.[3]

STORYTELLING RESIDENCIES IN SCHOOLS

Many state arts councils sponsor Artists-in-Education programs and storytellers are eligible to participate.

One of the most comprehensive educational programs, Storytelling Arts, Inc., was founded and directed by Susan Danoff from 1996 to 2007. During the 1980s Susan had worked as the first storytelling teaching artist for the New Jersey State Council on the Arts, Artists-in-Education program, and she was both delighted and amazed by the intense interest and response of low-income urban school children to storytelling. She saw the potential for storytelling to teach literacy skills and motivate students who were not being served by more conventional teaching methods. She founded the New Jersey nonprofit corporation Storytelling Arts in order to offer teacher training and long-term storytelling programs for low-income and special needs populations.

From 1998 to 2007 Susan and the nine other storytellers with whom she collaborated served approximately 18,000 students in preschool through high school in programs that ran from 15 to 35 days a year. In these programs, the tellers designed curriculum around storytelling by creating cohesive follow-up activities and customizing programs to support the classroom teachers' goals of improving comprehension, writing, retelling, thinking, and listening skills. Programs were supported by foundation and government grants, school funding, and charitable contributions. Susan also developed extensive professional development programs for teachers, and she continues to offer week-long summer institutes for teachers at Princeton University and to provide professional development for schools.

Although Storytelling Arts programs were custom-designed for each site by storytellers with very different telling styles, the storytellers discovered that storytelling addresses the same behavioral and academic issues, regardless of age. In her book *The Golden Thread: Storytelling in Teaching and Learning,* Susan discusses how and why storytelling seems to have a positive impact on trusting relationships between students and their teacher, community building, imagination, and literacy skills. Susan writes:

> Children who come from cultures where the oral tradition is more important than the written are deeply engaged by storytelling. That is why when I visit classrooms in urban New Jersey schools, I always have the feeling that the language of story is the language that the children know, understand, and feel comfortable with. These children need to hear live stories from their teachers in order to learn. The personal voice of story can bring a new dimension to what would otherwise appear to them as cold and lifeless because they have not learned to hear the voice inside the text, the voice that the storyteller can teach them to hear. Most children enjoy hearing stories, but for children who do not easily connect to the written word, stories can be the bridge to literacy.[4]

At the preschool level, when storytellers had the opportunity to work with the same children on a weekly basis, students heard new stories and retold familiar ones. The storytellers used interactive techniques involving chanting, singing, movement, and dramatization to teach comprehension skills, story structure, prediction, visualization, and vocabulary building—all skills that prepare children for reading when they get to elementary school. As the storytellers visited on a regular basis, they found that the children's interest in stories did not diminish; it grew.

One Head Start teacher in East Orange, New Jersey, said that her students asked every day if storyteller Jim Rohe was coming. "Finally," she said, "I made a chart with the days of the week, and learned that Mr. Rohe came on Thursdays. The children learned the days of the week because they were waiting for the storyteller." One of Susan Danoff's Trenton Head Start classes fell in love with "The Three Bears." At the beginning of the school year these three-year-olds could barely understand a story. Between Susan's visits, they reenacted "The Three Bears" numerous times, and by January, all were able to sit and listen to stories for a full half hour.

Storytelling Arts programs in elementary school through junior high school focused on using storytelling to engage children in discussion and writing. In a three-year program at Schoenly Elementary School in

Spotswood, New Jersey, kindergarten students had weekly storytelling sessions with Helen Wise, during which time they learned to listen, retell, and improvise with stories. When these students graduated to first grade with storyteller Tara McGovan and continued to practice these skills, teachers noticed that the children's writing changed dramatically from previous years to include beginnings, middles, endings, detail, and dialogue.

In long-term programs with adolescents, storytellers used storytelling and writing activities to engage students in discussions of compelling life issues and to help them articulate their own stories both orally and in writing. After a program at Mercer County Detention Center designed and implemented by Paula Davidoff and Joanne Epply-Schmidt, one student wrote eloquently about what the program meant to him:

> I was the most stubborn person when this first started. But slowly and gradually I opened up and let the full impact of what this program was going to do for me take its course. As I progressed, I grew. This class showed me in its own little way that tribulation produces perseverance, and perseverance character, and character hope. I don't know what hope means to you, but to a 17-year-old incarcerated boy, hope is the only thing I hold dear, besides family. Hope is the thing that keeps me motivated daily. Hope keeps my head above water. Hope gives us that chance to live our dreams and turn them into a reality.[5]

In other programs with juveniles in detention and children classified with behavioral disorders, storytellers selected stories that spoke metaphorically to issues in children's lives. The stories offered choices and possibilities that the students may not have perceived before, thus providing the hope that this young man writes about.

PRE-PLANNING THE RESIDENCY

It is essential that the "storyteller-in-residence" meet with the school principal in advance of the program. After the school principal decides on the number of weeks in the residency and selects the classes that will participate, the principal, the teachers involved, and the storyteller plan the schedule of dates and times and discuss how the visiting storyteller and classroom teachers will work together to make the program effective and relevant to the curriculum.

The storytelling residency is most successful when it is a true collaboration between the classroom teacher and the storyteller. The classroom teacher must not perceive the storytelling residency as a convenient time to grade papers or take a break. In most schools it is illegal for the teacher to leave the classroom with a visiting artist who is not a certified teacher. Teachers often comment that as they watch their students engage in storytelling, they can often gain valuable insights into their students' learning issues that they do not have time to notice when they are intent on teaching the lesson. It is important for the storyteller to recognize that the teacher remains the most important person in the classroom. Engage the teacher in the activities, ask the teacher to help model for the students, and encourage the teacher to connect the storytelling activities to ongoing classroom activities and lessons and to tell or read aloud stories to the children *everyday*.

School administrators often request some tie-in with the school curriculum. For instance, the children might study the folktales of a particular country or geographical region, or stories from different regions of the United States to complement a social studies program. Children can learn research skills and how to use the library's resources as they select, research, and learn a tale. To succeed, this program requires an extensive collection of folk and fairy tales. If improving writing skills is the primary goal, there are numerous writing activities that can be modeled through using stories. For example, hearing a story and then having the children write the images they remember most demonstrates that we all choose different moments in a story, and even if we choose the same moment we see it differently—a natural lead-in to creative writing in the language arts curriculum.

Residency programs usually require a teacher workshop component so that the program will have lasting value after the storyteller's work is completed. Ideally, these workshops are part of a regularly scheduled in-service program. Although some storytellers have reported conducting workshops during the lunch period, this is prohibited in schools where teachers' unions require that teachers not be asked to work during free periods and lunchtime. If it is not possible to hold short weekly workshops, schedule a sixty- to ninety-minute workshop early in the residency. Like the workshops for the classroom, it is important to find out what will be most useful to the teachers as a first step. They need to listen to stories, experience the high degree of engagement, and explore how and why they can use stories to teach.

When one of the goals of the residency is to help children gain confidence and ease in speaking before a group, the children first tell in their classrooms, then to younger children or peers in their schools. At the end of the residency, schools often sponsor a festival night for parents and teachers featuring the young tellers. The visiting storyteller and the classroom teachers should be equally involved in planning this event.

LET THE FESTIVAL BEGIN!

Sherwood Elementary School in Highland Park, Illinois, has held an annual student storytelling festival since 1997. The first festival was a two-day event held in May. It is now a three-day festival that is held Wednesday-to-Friday in February because the end of the school year is so busy. Each fourth- and fifth-grade student tells a story, performed individually or in tandem. The school has a dual-language program, so some stories are told in Spanish followed by the same story told in English. Library Media Center Director Darlene Neumann coaches the children as they choose, learn, and tell their stories.

A professional storyteller opens the festival on Wednesday morning. Sometimes the guest teller will give a workshop for classes or for the storytelling clubs. Sherwood has storytelling clubs from second through fifth grades. A few first graders, coached by older tellers, participate in the second-grade club. If there are no workshops, the student tellers tell on Wednesday following the guest storyteller and all day Thursday and Friday from 8:50 A.M. to 3:10 P.M., excluding lunch. The day is divided into half-hour slots. Teachers can sign up their classes for audience. Sometimes there is an evening performance.

The festival is held in the Instructional Media Center (IMC), which is warm, bright, and comfortable. The IMC is large enough to hold three classes for audience plus families and other visitors. Nearly all of the tellers' proud parents attend. At the latest festival, audience members ranged from two-year-old twin siblings of a fourth-grade girl to an eighty-two-year-old great-grandmother of a fifth-grade boy. Preschoolers listen in amazement as older siblings tell stories, and kindergarteners look forward to the time when they can tell a story. As one kindergarten student left, she asked, "Does the *M* in IMC stand for *Magic*?"

Neumann credits the success of the festival to integration of storytelling skills into the curriculum, administrative support, cooperation from staff and parents, and financial support from the Parent-Teacher Organization. No small part of its success is due to the fact that Neumann, a professional storyteller herself, thoroughly enjoys working with the children to help them listen and tell. She has told at festivals, international schools, and public libraries, and has conducted storytelling workshops at library and educational conferences and universities. Her student tellers have presented at the Illinois Storytelling Festival, senior centers, and public libraries, and the Sherwood Festival has inspired other teachers in Illinois to develop student storytelling programs.

WHEN THE TROUPE TOLD TALES

For twenty-five years, Bob Rubinstein, a language and performing arts teacher at Roosevelt Middle School, Eugene, Oregon, taught a class in "Folktales and Storytelling," and directed the Roosevelt Troupe of Tellers. The Troupe of Tellers consisted of twelve sixth to eighth graders, selected from students who had taken the storytelling course or who had had onstage acting experience. The Troupe's training was twelve weeks long and was part of the school day. Two weeks were spent in preparation and ten weeks in performance. During the preparation period the students received intensive training in audience presentation and learned a minimum of four stories—three short tales (each about three minutes long) suitable for listeners in kindergarten through second grades, and a longer story (five to eight minutes) suitable for older listeners.

During its 25 years of existence, the Troupe told stories and performed story-theater for more than 70,000 children in classrooms, public libraries, camps, and hospitals in the Eugene-Springfield-Bethel area. They presented workshop performances to educators, librarians, and university students in Oregon and Washington. In 1983 they received one of the state of Oregon's "Great Kids" Awards in recognition of their community service, and in 1993 they presented a performance workshop at the University of Washington in Seattle for the NSA National Storytelling Conference, with people attending from throughout the United States and other countries.

Due to insufficient funding, 1995 was the last year for this fine program, "still considered a national model for how young people can learn to tell and grow through telling as well as for how valuable storytelling can be in the school curriculum." Fortunately, a video, *When the Troupe Tells Tales*, featuring members of the Roosevelt Middle School Troupe of Tellers and their director, Robert Rubinstein, is still available. The young tellers talk about their experiences choosing, preparing, and telling a story, what it's like to work as a team, and how this has changed their lives.[6]

Another well-known group was the Poetry Troupe, begun by Isabel Wilner when she was the librarian at the laboratory school at Towson State University in Maryland. A group of elementary school children went into the campus classrooms to read aloud to the college students. The children's favorite poems—and information about the troupe—were published in *The Poetry Troupe: An Anthology of Poems to Read Aloud*, compiled by Wilner.

A basic guide for anyone interested in starting a storytelling group or troupe is *Raising Voices: Creating Youth Storytelling Groups and Troupes*, by Judy Sima and Kevin Cordi. Written by two veteran storytellers with years of experience teaching storytelling to children and young adults, this award-winning book leads you through the process step-by-step and presents fun activities that teach and strengthen storytelling skills (Storytellers' Bingo, A Storytelling Scavenger Hunt, and Crazy Mixed-up Fairy Tales, to mention just a few); plus it includes reproducibles and an extensive Storytelling Resources section (books; audio and video tapes; sources for puppets, props, and instruments; storytelling websites; and organizations, publishers, and distributors specializing in storytelling materials).

"REACH FOR A STORY" PROJECT

A number of years ago, Emily Holman, then coordinator of children' services at the Ocean County Library in New Jersey, and storyteller Ellin Greene (serving as a consultant) planned and directed a storytelling project for the children's staff and for fourth to sixth graders in the county. The project, called "Reach for a Story," had ten goals:

1. To introduce children to the art of storytelling for their own enjoyment and for the entertainment of others
2. To motivate children to read and to use the resources of the library
3. To nurture the child's creative imagination
4. To increase the child's communication skills—listening, speaking, reading, and writing
5. To introduce children to folk literature and modern imaginative stories
6. To guide children in the selection of tellable tales
7. To teach children the techniques of learning and telling stories
8. To build in children appreciation of cultural differences and similarities
9. To encourage parents, teachers, librarians, and other professionals to use storytelling in their work with children
10. To increase the visibility of the library and its program for children

It was decided that each of the seven regions in the county system would hold a mini-festival, rather than a "contest," at which time *all* the children participating in the project would tell a story. The regional librarians, the storytelling consultant, the coordinator of children's services, and the young tellers would then select a representative from each region to tell at a grand festival to be held at the main library during Children's Book Week. The selections were made on the basis of the requirements for a good program (variety in theme, length of stories, and styles of telling) as well as on the proficiency of the teller. Every child who participated in the project received a certificate of recognition and a copy of the consultant's story anthology, *Midsummer Magic*. In addition, the seven representatives at the grand festival were presented with a book bag imprinted with a specially designed logo, "Reach for a Story," and a copy of Virginia Haviland's *Favorite Fairy Tales Told Around the World* to encourage continuation of their newly learned craft. Three of the seven tellers later appeared on local cable television to talk about their experiences in learning to be a storyteller and each told a story. Many of the children also told stories to classes in their schools. One of the tellers, Aimee Amodio, later became a professional storyteller and author.

The storytelling consultant presented two workshops for the children in each region. In between the workshops the regional librarians met with the young tellers. Interesting and colorful facts about medieval storytellers (such as those presented in Chapter 1) stirred the children's imagination.

After asking the children why they thought people told stories and where they thought stories came from, the consultant told them *A Story, A Story* using only the text of Gail Haley's picture book. Then the consultant and the children talked about the "pictures" people see in their mind's eye as they listen to a story, and the children shared some of their "pictures" before looking at Haley's illustrations. It is always surprising to hear the many different images the same words evoke.

Next the consultant told a variant of a familiar folktale, such as "Cinderella" or "Rumpelstiltskin." Time permitting, the children were encouraged to become "folklorist-detectives," a term coined by Professor Jane Bingham of Oakland University. In this activity the children find variants of a tale or compare several picture-books editions of the same story. Thus the children learn that storytelling is a way of seeing. To help the children visualize the happenings in a story, the consultant told "Hafiz, the Stonecutter," from Marie Shedlock's *The Art of the Story-Teller*, and asked the children to list the happenings in the story in their proper order. (The unillustrated Shedlock version was chosen over the more familiar picture-book version by Gerald McDermott primarily because the Shedlock version encourages children to make their own images, but also because it has an upbeat ending and a message that strikes a sympathetic chord with young tellers—"Be Yourself.") The children and the consultant discussed the story's circular pattern and the repetition of important phrases—the children were becoming aware of story form and the necessity of events occurring in logical sequence. Then the children made storyboards (see Figure 18) by drawing pictures of the happenings on their lists.

The storytelling consultant and the children talked about the many different kinds of stories—folktales, literary fairy tales, myths and legends, hero tales, tall tales, humorous stories, jokes, and ghost stories—and the qualities that make a story tellable (see Chapter 4). The children browsed in collections of tellable tales pulled from the folktale shelves before the workshop began. Individual consultations concluded the workshop.

Some children immediately found a story to work with; others took home one or two story collections to read before the next workshop. To find a story they would enjoy telling required browsing through several collections and reading many stories, one of the goals of the project. A few children found stories in places not anticipated by the staff. For instance,

FIGURE 18. *Storyboard by Colleen Dolcy, Ocean County Library, New Jersey. Reprinted by permission.*

one girl chose a story about Detective Mole from Robert Quackenbush's easy-to-read mysteries. Another chose a short humorous tale, "What Hershel's Father Did," from *Cricket Magazine*.

The storyboard was presented as a memory jogger. Another memory aid used was the cue card (see Chapter 5). The children were encouraged to make both a storyboard and a cue card for their stories (cue card forms were provided). These were discussed the following week when the children met with their librarians. The librarians listened to the children's first attempts at storytelling and, when necessary, assisted them in finding a different story if the original choice wasn't working out.

At the second workshop the children worked on vocal tone and facial expression, language, and the use of kinesics in storytelling. They practiced phrasing, or what storyteller Kathryn Farnsworth calls "where to take a breath," by marking up a story to indicate the shortest possible phrases.[7] They said tongue twisters and "acted out" their stories. Bob Barton, in his *Tell Me Another*, recommends the use of call-and-response stories, chanting word play, drama games, and the like. Such approaches offer fun as well as opportunities for practice. The children enjoyed relaxation and voice exercises—jumping jacks, head and shoulder rolls, yawning, "ugly exercises," and imagining themselves as puppets (see Chapter 4).

The children and the consultant talked about the importance of the beginning and ending of a story. With everyone speaking at the same time, to avoid self-consciousness, they said the first and last lines of each of their stories to suggest different states of emotion—surprise, boredom, sadness, anger, anxiety, pleasure. Then they listened to each teller say the lines as he or she thought they should be said.

The teller identified the most important moment in the story and pantomimed the emotion of that moment, with the group guessing the emotion. They talked about effective—and ineffective—use of gestures, facial expressions, and body movements.

Finally, the group gave a critique of the tellings. By asking, "What did you like about the way (storyteller's name) told the story?" and "Can you suggest anything (storyteller's name) might do to make the telling even better?" the consultant kept the group's criticism positive. Negative criticism, if any, should be offered by the group leader in private—and gently. Children, like adults, learn through experience.

The librarians met with the children a week later to hold a rehearsal for the mini-festivals. As often as possible the rehearsal took place in the same room as the mini-festival. In this way the children became familiar with the size and seating arrangement of the room and could practice projecting their voices in the more formal setting. They asked themselves, "Can the person sitting in the last row hear my story? Did I tell my story slowly enough so that the listeners had time to see the happenings in the story?" In several schools the librarian or media specialist arranged for the children to tell their stories during a class visit to the library. These experiences helped to polish the tellings. The regional librarians were astonished at the progress the young tellers made in such a short period of time, and at their poise and pleasure in telling before a group. Incidentally, the girls outnumbered the boys two to one, but the boys told with vigor and obviously enjoyed the experience. Parents noted an increase in self-confidence and in reading for pleasure. The children learned courtesy and how to be good listeners as well as good tellers.

Were there negative features? Yes, a few. Despite early resolutions to discourage competitiveness, a few teachers and librarians still conceived the festivals as contests. The consultant agrees with educator Bryon Padgett that there is no place in storytelling for "competitiveness that makes most kids feel anxious, unloved, and defeated, or vainly victorious."[8]

The biggest problem was the uneven size of the groups in the regions. Some groups had as few as four children while others had as many as twenty-two. The ideal size is ten to twelve tellers. At the time, public transportation was almost nonexistent in Ocean County and redistribution would have created a hardship. Instead, the regional librarian and the consultant each worked with half of the larger-sized groups. The rewards far outnumbered the problems.

STORYTELLING BUILDS COMMUNICATIONS SKILLS AND SELF-ESTEEM

Robert Rubinstein, founder and former director of the Roosevelt Troupe of Tellers, kept in touch with many of the members of the Troupe after the program ended. In an article published in *Middle Ground,* the National Middle School Association magazine,[9] Rubinstein wrote about how the experience had made a difference in their lives. All of the members grew in self-confidence, self-esteem, and self-expression. What they learned carried over into other aspects of their school work and after-school activities such as drama and musical productions. Rubinstein cites many examples in his article, including the following: A tall, gangly boy of fourteen who had no friends and could barely read or write learned to communicate and make friends. A severely hearing-impaired boy learned to overcome his difficult-to-understand speech and added signing to his tellings, captivating his listeners. After high school this young man performed as a member of the National Theatre of the Deaf and later became an actor in Hollywood. Another member of the troupe became a drama and language arts teacher at Roosevelt Middle School.

As noted earlier in this chapter, other storytellers who have taught children to tell report similar gains. One can only hope that more schools and libraries will offer children this opportunity.

More Fun Activities for Teaching Storytelling Skills

Start with group activities to relax the children, such as "And Then What Happened." The children and teacher or leader sit in a circle; the leader holds a soft ball and begins a story. Then he or she passes the ball to the next person and that person takes up the tale. This continues until the last person in the circle receives the ball and brings the story to its conclusion. A variation of this activity is done with a ball of yarn. The person who starts the story (and each teller who follows) tosses the ball, at an appropriate moment, to anyone in the circle to continue the story. Before tossing the ball, however, each person keeps hold of the yarn as it unwinds. At the end of the story each person is holding a piece of the yarn, symbolizing that each part of the story belongs to a teller. If anyone drops his or her strand, the pattern is broken, showing the importance of each element in the story.

Another fun activity is to have the group tell a story, using the "good/bad" pattern. The first child tells something good that happened to him or her that day. The group responds, "That's good!" The second child continues the tale, turning the good fortune to bad, and the group responds, "That's bad!" The story goes on, alternating good and bad fortune, while maintaining a logical sequence of events. Before doing this activity, you might want to read aloud Margery Cuyler's *That's Good! That's Bad!*

Teach the children strategies for learning a story, such as visualization, story webs (circles of keywords or brief phrases from the story) connected with lines to show the story sequence; story maps to show the setting and where events take place; or storyboards (to show the events of the action). A storyboard may contain dialogue but usually consists of simple line drawings.

Have the children work in pairs. First they can tell each other about their story. Encourage the listener to ask questions about the characters, setting, and action. Then have the children tell the story without words, by miming it. Lastly each child can tell the story to his or her partner, and the partner can act as a "coach" or "prompter" if the teller forgets any part of the story.

Sometimes it helps to have the children outline their story. Folktales, the easiest stories to learn because they have a tight structure, consist of a beginning in which the main character(s) and the problem are introduced, a middle that tells what happens to the character(s), and an ending that tells how the character(s) solved the problem.

Children need to know how to introduce a story and how to end it. They need to know that it's all right to have the story end in silence, with the listeners still in the story world; how to bring the listeners back to the present; and to accept applause when it is given.

STORY SOURCES AND RESOURCE GUIDES

Good stories for children to tell are short, easy to sequence, and have lots of dialogue. Anne Pellowski interviewed many children and teenagers who were storytelling when she wrote *The Storytelling Handbook: A Young People's Collection of Unusual Tales and Helpful Hints on How to Tell Them.* Her book contains the type of stories young people like to tell—stories with an unusual twist.

Martha Hamilton and Mitch Weiss, known professionally as Beauty and the Beast, have been telling stories and teaching children to tell stories for over twenty-five years. This husband–wife team has won numerous awards for books and recordings. Their latest textbook, *Children Tell Stories: Teaching and Using Storytelling in the Classroom, Second Edition,* belongs on every teacher's bookshelf. You'll find everything you need to know to get started, extensive bibliographies, and an inspiring DVD featuring Hamilton and Weiss, child storytellers, and teachers and children's literature specialists talking about the values of storytelling. The appendixes include "Suggested Stories for Students to Tell," with stories from anthologies and picture-book stories listed by difficulty for telling.

Susan Danoff's *The Golden Thread: Storytelling in Teaching and Learning* discusses why storytelling belongs in the classroom and addresses issues of student/teacher relationships, classroom community, imagination, and literacy. Storytellers and teachers will find this book useful in addressing the most fundamental issues relating to storytelling and education.

Lastly, Jack Zipes's *Creative Storytelling: Building Community, Changing Lives* and its companion, *Speaking Out: Storytelling and Creative Drama for Children,* about his experiences in various storytelling projects and the remarkably successful Neighborhood Bridges program in Minneapolis and St. Paul, are *must* reading for anyone serious about storytelling and children. Unfortunately, few librarians and teachers have the resources to duplicate this program, but both books are inspiring and offer many ideas that can be adapted on a smaller scale.

REFERENCES

1. Martha Hamilton and Mitch Weiss, *Children Tell Stories: A Teaching Guide* (Richard C.

Owen, 1990), p. 15.

2. Report in the files of the Office of Children's Services, New York Public Library.

3. Communication from Anne Shimojima to Ellin Greene (April 2008).

4. Susan Danoff, *The Golden Thread: Storytelling and Learning* (Storytelling Arts Press, 2006), pp. 116–117.

4. From the files of Susan Danoff.

5. Robert E. Rubinstein (director), *When the Troupe Tells Tales* [videotape], by the Roosevelt Middle School Tellers (1993). Available from Robert Rubinstein. Email: info@robertrubinstein.net.

6. Kathryn Farnsworth, "Storytelling in the Classroom—Not an Impossible Dream," *Language Arts* 58 (February 1981): 165.

7. Bryon Padgett, "The Care and Feeding of a Child's Imagination," *Ms.* (May 1976): 61.

8. Robert E. Rubinstein, "When the Troupe Told Tales," *Middle Ground,* The National Middle School Association Magazine, April 2005.

RESOURCE BOOKS CITED IN THIS CHAPTER

Barton, Bob. *Tell Me Another: Storytelling and Reading Aloud at Home, at School and in the Community*. Heinemann, 1986. ISBN 9780435082314

Danoff, Susan. *The Golden Thread: Storytelling in Teaching and Learning*. Storytelling Arts Press, 2006. ISBN 9780977722808

Hamilton, Martha, and Mitch Weiss. *Children Tell Stories: Teaching and Using Storytelling in the Classroom, Second Edition*. Richard C. Owen Publishers, 2005. ISBN 9781572746633

Kinghorn, Harriet R., and Mary Helen Pelton. *Every Child a Storyteller: A Handbook of Ideas*. Illus. by Myke Knutson. Libraries Unlimited, 1991. ISBN 9780872878686

Pellowski, Anne. *The Storytelling Handbook: A Young People's Collection of Unusual Tales and Helpful Hints on How to Tell Them*. Illus. by Martha Stoberock. Simon & Schuster, 1995. ISBN 9780689803116

Sima, Judy, and Kevin Condi. *Raising Voices: Creating Youth Storytelling Groups and Troupes*. Libraries Unlimited, 2003. ISBN 9781563089190

Wilner, Isabel. *The Poetry Troupe: An Anthology of Poems to Read Aloud*. Atheneum, 1977. ISBN 9780684151984

Zipes, Jack. *Creative Storytelling: Building Community, Changing Lives*. Routledge, 1995. ISBN 9780415912723

———. *Speaking Out: Storytelling and Creative Drama for Children*. Routledge, 2004. ISBN 9780415966610

WEB RESOURCES

Aaron Shepard's RT Page Scripts and Tips for Reader's Theater
http://www.aaronshep.com/rt/index.html

Coaching Youth Storytellers by Kevin Cordi
Kennedy Center ArtsEdge
http://artsedge.kennedy-center.org/content/3266/

Creative Dramatics
http://www.cwu.edu/~robinsos/ppages/resources/Creative_Dramatics/
Creative_Drama_Biblio.htm

Internet Resources for Conducting Readers Theatre
http://www.readingonline.org/electronic/carrick/

Youth Storytelling
http://www.youthstorytelling.com

PROGRAM PLANNING

"Well," said Charlotte, vaguely, "I'm working on a plan."

"That's wonderful," said Wilbur. "How is the plan coming, Charlotte? Have you got very far with it?" Wilbur was trembling again, but Charlotte was cool and collected.

"Oh, it's coming all right," she said lightly. "The plan is still in its early stages and hasn't completely shaped up yet, but I'm working on it."

"When do you work on it?" begged Wilbur.

"When I'm hanging head-down at the top of my web. That's when I do my thinking, because then all the blood is in my head."

—E. B. White, Charlotte's Web[1]

A SUCCESSFUL STORYTELLING program requires careful planning, flexibility, and creativity.

PLANNING

Planning ahead allows the storyteller to select stories to learn and to arrange them in a program that is a satisfying whole. Know the number of programs you are going to give during the year and the types of programs, such as picture-book hours for the five- to seven-year-olds, storytimes for children in grades three to five, programs for pre-teens, family storytimes, holiday and special celebrations, and any others. (Note: Program planning for children under the age of five is discussed in Chapter 8. Programs for young adults are discussed in Chapter 9.)

In planning the story program consider the ages and interests of the children, their cultural or racial heritage, their listening capacity, and the scheduled length of the program. Selecting stories for children of similar background is not difficult, but often story groups are composed of children of varying ages and interests. A program that includes a variety of types of stories and provides a change of pace and mood will appeal to the greatest number of children. Now is the time to go back to the cue cards that you made from your readings. You have the titles, types of stories, sources, and synopses at your fingertips. In building your repertoire you have chosen different types of stories, stories of varying lengths and moods, and stories of universal appeal.

FLEXIBILITY

The storyteller learns with experience to judge the mood of the children and to adjust the program accordingly. Sometimes the choice of stories, though planned in advance, must be changed at the last minute. The public library storyteller does not always know who will be at the story program and therefore must be prepared to make changes.

Because it is more difficult to establish a listening mood for the imaginative literary fairy tale than for the robust action of the folktale, it is usually best to tell the folktale first if your program includes both types of stories.

When telling to a group of children of mixed ages, tell a story for the younger children first. The older children will be receptive if you explain that the story was chosen especially for the younger children. Next tell your main story and end with a short humorous tale. Take care that the story chosen for the younger children is not so simple in concept that it causes the older children to feel that they are too old for the entire program. The story for the older children must meet their interests and yet not be so far above the heads of the younger ones that they get nothing out of it. One storyteller, caught in a situation where the schedule was changed just prior to his arrival, found himself facing an audience of first and sixth graders. He carried it off by first telling a story that appealed to a mixed age group. Next he invited the sixth graders to learn "Mr. Wiggle and Mr. Waggle," an action story for young children, "to tell to your younger brothers and sisters or when you babysit." He ended the program with a story for the older children that contained elements familiar to the younger listeners. It is also possible to explain at the beginning of the program that the first story is for the younger children and that they may leave, if they wish, after it is told (providing, of course, that the adults responsible for the children are in the building).

Three shorter stories seem to work well with younger children or children who are not used to listening to stories. The first story should catch the children's fancy; the second story may ask for a more thoughtful response or be more moving emotionally; the third should be easily comprehended and satisfying. If the children seem to need a break between the second and third stories, tell a short participatory story or simply have the children stretch. Sometimes a participatory story at the end provides a welcome release of any built-up tension. With older children who are used to listening, try two longer stories with some riddles or a stretch in between the tales.

Occasionally a teacher may request a story on a curriculum-related subject. Do this whenever you can; however, the storyteller must be free to select material for the storytime rather than to tell a story for didactic purposes. Although storytelling may be used legitimately to support and enhance the curriculum, the teacher should respect the storyteller's right to choose the story.

HOW LONG SHOULD THE STORY PROGRAM BE?

The outdated phrase "story hour" was always misleading because the story hour rarely lasted sixty minutes. The age of the children, their past experience in story listening, and the library's or center's schedule all influence the length of the program. It may be as short as thirty minutes or as long as an hour. Sometimes a craft activity follows the story listening, lengthening the program. The length of time should be stated to eliminate the coming and going that breaks the mood, and as a courtesy to parents who are providing transportation to and from the storytime. Begin on time and end as close to the announced time as possible. School-age children today are likely to be involved in various after-school activities, making the traditional weekday 4 o'clock story hour at the public library a thing of the past. Storytimes are more likely to be held on Saturday or Sunday. Many parents do not want their children to be out after dark; during the winter months the program may have to be shortened or planned as an evening program for the family.

CREATIVITY

Creativity enters the picture in how you combine the various elements in the program. Some storytellers like to plan their program around a theme, such as the season, a particular cultural heritage, or a holiday or special event. Other programs may celebrate the birthdays of writers of children's books with the telling of their stories or reading of their poems. Hearing an author or a poet speak in his or her own voice adds richness to the program. Virginia Hamilton recorded stories from her collection *The People Could Fly*. E. B. White's recording of *Charlotte's Web* is an example of effective reading aloud without voice changes for the different characters, while Jim Dale's reading of the Harry Potter series is that rare example of a narrator who can give each character a different voice and be consistent throughout the reading. Arna Bontemps, Carl Sandburg, and Shel Silverstein recorded their poetry for children. Several poets read one of their poems on the compact disc that accompanies the book *Poetry Speaks to Children*. (See *A Sampling of Storytelling Recordings* in Resources for the Storyteller.) For ideas about combining poetry with miscellany refer to *Days to Celebrate: A Full Year of Poetry, People, Holidays, History, Fascinating Facts, and More* by Lee Bennett Hopkins.

The program may simply consist of stories that are unrelated in theme and yet balanced by type and mood. You might begin by gathering together some of your favorite picture books or thinking about your favorite stories. If you build the program around stories and books that you enjoy, your listeners will enjoy them too. As Janice Del Negro tells her students, "The second most important thing to remember about story programming is that every program has an arc: lead your listeners in gently, hold them with humor and action, and fare them well with something warm for the way home. The first most important thing to remember about story programming is to have fun."[2]

The sample programs in this chapter are intended to help you get started. Books and recordings used in the programs are listed alphabetically by title at the end of this chapter.

THE PICTURE-BOOK PROGRAM

The picture-book program for five- to seven-year-olds is probably the easiest storytelling program to plan and conduct. By this age most children have participated in group activities and have developed some social skills. They have listened to stories and are familiar with story patterns. They are ready for picture books with more narrative than those used in the pre-school storytime. Interest in the folktale peaks during this period and many beautiful editions of the traditional tales are available. If the book has many pages of text that have no pictures, learn the tale and tell it without the pictures, just as you would to an older group. Share the pictures *after* the telling. The folktales were meant to be *told*; they can stand on their own without illustration. Modern imaginative stories in which the text and pictures are interwoven should be read with the pictures facing toward the children as the story unfolds. If the text is long, read the page with the book turned toward you, then show the illustration to the children after each page.

Children this age enjoy literary fairy tales such as *Many Moons* by James Thurber, *The Huckabuck Family and How They Raised Popcorn in Nebraska and Quit and Came Back* by Carl Sandburg, and the fairy tales of Hans Christian Andersen. Use poetry, action rhymes, or participation stories in between the longer stories. See *Juba This and Juba That* by Virginia A. Tashjian for suggestions. This change of pace offers a break from intensive listening.

Hold the picture-book program in the storytelling room or in a quiet area of the children's room away from traffic and noise. The program is usually held after school hours or on Saturday and lasts thirty to forty-five minutes. Before the children arrive, arrange the storyteller's table with the books you will read, some fresh flowers or appropriate realia, and, if fire laws permit, the wishing candle. A group of twenty to thirty children is a comfortable number, and thirty to forty minutes is a reasonable period of time for quiet listening. Tell the children that once the candle is lit, no one speaks but the storyteller. At the end of the program, let the children make a wish and blow out the candle. (For safety reasons, do not use the wishing candle with toddlers or preschoolers. Young children are fascinated by the flame and may reach out to touch it, not realizing the danger.) After the program, encourage the children to browse at the tables where you have placed the story books and other picture books that they might like to borrow for reading at home. This is an opportunity to talk informally with the children and any parents who are present, to listen to the children's comments about books, and to suggest other titles that the children might enjoy.

The emphasis in this section has been on picture-book storytelling, but listening can be a complete experience even for young children. Occasionally, *tell* a short story in between the picture-book presentations. You can find lots of good tales to tell in "Stories of Special Appeal to 5- to 8-Year-Olds" in the Resources for the Storyteller chapter.

SAMPLE PICTURE-BOOK PROGRAMS

THEME: Lions/Acts of Kindness

STORY: *Library Lion* by Michelle Knudson

STORY: "The Lion and the Mouse" from *Aesop's Fables* by Michael Morpurgo

ACTION STORY: "The Lion Hunt" in *Juba This and Juba That* selected by Virginia A. Tashjian

STORY: *Andy and the Lion: A Tale of Kindness Remembered or the Power of Gratitude* by James Daugherty

THEME: Apple Gala/Fall (You may wish to make this a story-craft program.)

Place some fall leaves and a few apples of different varieties on the storyteller's table along with the books.

STORY: Show the children two or three books about Johnny Appleseed, such as *The True Story of Johnny Appleseed* by Margaret Hodges, *Johnny Appleseed: The Story of a Legend* by Will Moses, and *Johnny Appleseed, a Tall Tale* by Steven Kellogg. Let the children choose which book they would like you to read. Next show them Jane Yolen's *Johnny Appleseed: The Legend and the Truth* and share some things that are true about John Chapman and some things that are not.

STORY: *The Apple Pie That Papa Baked* by Lauren Thompson

STORY: *Leaf Man* by Lois Ehlert

CRAFT: Time permitting, make an apple craft or provide materials (construction paper leaves in different shapes and colors, light cardboard, and safety scissors) for the children to make a collage of their own.

MUSICAL PICTURE-BOOK PROGRAM[3]

STORY: *The Philharmonic Gets Dressed* by Karla Kuskin

Suggest that the orchestra may have been getting ready to perform "Peter and the Wolf."

MUSIC: Play Boris Karloff's introduction to Sergei Prokofiev's classic musical tale in which a different instrument represents each character in the story. (Musical Heritage Society CD 5171273)

STORY: *Peter and the Wolf* by Ian Beck (This classic edition is out of print. Other picture-book editions are available.)

STORY: Show the children Chris Raschka's *Peter and the Wolf.* The Caldecott Medalist has changed the setting and turned the story into a zany stage performance. Have fun with the story; if there is time, the children might like to act it out.

STORYTIMES FOR CHILDREN AGES FIVE TO EIGHT

THEME: Cinderella stories

STORY: *Billy Beg and His Bull, An Irish Tale* retold by Ellin Greene

STORY: *The Korean Cinderella* by Shirley Climo

Both of the above stories feature an animal helper. Have other variants of Cinderella—ones that feature a different kind of helper—on the storyteller's table and talk with the children about the version(s) they knew before the versions they heard at storytime.

THEME: Caribbean stories

STORY: *The Dancing Granny* by Ashley Bryan (see p. 292)

STRETCH: Dance like Granny—"Shake It to the East, Shake It to the West"

STORY: "The Magic Orange Tree" from *The Magic Orange Tree and Other Haitian Folktales* by Diane Wolkstein

CRIK? CRAC! Explain to the children that every Haitian story begins with these words. The storyteller calls out Crik? (pronounced "creek"), and if the audience is ready to listen, they respond Crac! (pronounced "crack"). After Crac!, before beginning the story, the teller may sing the orange tree song so the audience hears the melody. The audience joins in singing the song throughout the story. For the music, see pages 196–197 in *The Magic Orange Tree and Other Haitian Folktales* by Diane Wolkstein.

STORYTIME FOR CHILDREN AGES EIGHT TO TEN

THEME: The Truth Will Out

STORY: "More than Salt" retold by Patrick Ryan (see p. 310)

STRETCH: Cross the middle-of-the-body stretches to relax and energize the group

Participation Story: Tell any story from *More True Lies: 18 Tales for You to Judge* by George Shannon and ask the children to judge.

Story: "The Princess on the Pea" from *Twelve Tales: Hans Christian Andersen*

STORY PROGRAM FOR A MIXED-AGE GROUP

Theme: Tall Tales

Story: *Willa and the Wind* by Janice M. Del Negro (see p. 305)

Stretch: If the children need a stretch, have them move about the room like the wind

Story: "Jack and the Two-Bullet Hunt" in *From Sea to Shining Sea: A Treasury of American Folklore and Folksongs* by Amy L. Cohn and Suzy Schmidt (see p. 303)

Song(s): End with everyone singing a folksong or two from the above-mentioned book

STORY PROGRAM FOR AGES ELEVEN TO FIFTEEN

Theme: Riddling

Story: Briefly talk about the tradition of riddling and pose a few riddles from *Lightning Inside You: And Other Native American Riddles,* edited by John Bierhorst

Story: "Clever Manka" from *The Shoemaker's Apron* by Parker Fillmore

Participation Story: Tell any story from *Still More Stories to Solve* by George Shannon and ask the children to solve it

Story: "The Court Jester's Last Wish" from *While Standing on One Foot: Puzzle Stories and Wisdom Tales from the Jewish Tradition* by Nina Jaffe and Steve Zeitlin

Family Storytelling Events

Family storytelling events are usually scheduled for early evening, about 7:00 or 7:30 p.m., in an effort to balance the family's need to complete dinner and arrive at the program without feeling rushed with the need for concluding the program at a reasonable time to get children home and to bed. The early hour allows time for a few minutes of visiting, browsing, and selecting books to take home, because this audience often leaves immediately after the program.

The program is often planned for children ages six and older and their parents—older children need the occasional family excursion in which they are the center of the group—but a wide range of ages is to be expected as younger children often attend.

If there are quite a few younger children in the audience and if a second staff member is available, this person can take the younger children aside and have a picture-book program. Another possibility is to have volunteers—high school students or other parents—who will read to the younger children. The librarian-storyteller should be prepared to adjust to a mixed-age audience complete with younger-child distractions. Flexibility is key.

Allow about forty minutes for the actual storytelling. A program of two stories with some poetry or music or three short stories allows flexibility for creative planning. A mixture of story types is advisable—literary and folk, serious and humorous, quiet and active are all to be considered. Choose stories that can be appreciated on both a child and an adult level. Spencer Shaw, an internationally known storyteller, held groups spellbound with his telling of "A Lover of Beauty," the story of Pygmalion and Galatea from *Greek Myths* by Olivia Coolidge, when he conducted his family evening story hours in the Nassau County libraries in New York. In speaking of the values of these story hours, Shaw said, "Parents experience a new relationship with their children: an emotional bond which finds release in shared laughter, shared adventure, shared confidences. Children experience a new understanding of the parents' concerns. Together, they enjoy a storyteller's art."[4]

In "Storytelling Programs for the Family," Carol Birch shares the obstacles and solutions she experienced during the "Family Storytelling Hour with Carol" at the Craft and Folk Art Museum in Los Angeles, a program she conducted monthly for two years. The pattern Carol established was (1) a ritualistic, opening story; (2) a specific sharing time; (3) a story with broad appeal; (4) a more difficult story; (5) a participation story; and (6) a short scary or funny story to close. Carol had families sit together during the story hour, rather than the usual "children in front, adults in the back." This arrangement encouraged family members to touch and interact and to share the experience.[5]

THE MULTIMEDIA PROGRAM

The multimedia program combines two or more art forms, each of which can stand on its own (storytelling, film, music, dance), into a creative whole. This type of program appeals to many storytellers, especially the librarian or school library media specialist who feels there is not enough time to learn a sufficient number of stories to sustain a regularly scheduled storytelling program. In truth, it takes as much time to plan and select materials for a multimedia program as it takes to learn more stories. However, some people prefer the varied activity involved in preparing this type of program—such as previewing films and listening to recordings—to selecting and learning a story. The cultural experience that this kind of program offers children justifies the choice.

Storytelling can combine very well with other art forms, provided the program is carefully thought out and the various parts are related. The most effective programs usually are those that center around a theme, subject, or person. A school library media specialist planned a multimedia program with a spring theme for kindergarten children. She read *When the Root Children Wake Up* by Helen D. Fish, using the opaque projector to show the pictures on the center of three screens. On the side screens she showed slides of buds bursting and flowers in bloom as she played a recording of "The Waltz of the Flowers" from Tchaikovsky's *Nutcracker Suite*. Spontaneously, these young children went up to the screen to touch the flowers—they looked so real—and began to dance to the music. It was a beautiful experience for both the librarian and the children.

The preparation of this kind of program involves careful selection of materials. For a multimedia program to be successful there must be a flow, a rhythm. The parts should complement each other, but each segment should be strong enough to stand on its own. If you use a film, choose one that is artistic. Remember that the story is as important as the film, dance, or other art form used; generally, it is best for the story to come first.

Music and stories are natural partners. Music can be used to introduce or conclude the program, set the mood or change the pace. Play a selection from the recording *Tribal Winds: Music from Native American Flutes* before or after telling *Love Flute*, Paul Goble's hauntingly beautiful retelling of the legend of the very first love flute. Play a recording of the "Sleeping Beauty Waltz" before telling the fairy tale. Softly playing music from "A Midsummer's Night's Dream" while telling Barbara Picard's "Count Alaric's Lady" will help listeners see the fairies dancing in the moonlight. This technique was perfected by Spencer Shaw. In his article, "Recorded Magic for Story Hours," Shaw noted that the music must be "integrated artistically . . . [It] blends with the words and mood so that it never becomes a foreign, musical intrusion. The story is the thing. The music merely heightens the emotional impact in certain passages or makes specific word pictures more meaningful."[6]

Songs can introduce or reinforce a story, or serve as a link between stories. Jeslyn Wheeless has combined storytelling and singing since the beginning of her career. "I grew up with family members who loved to sing, and I came of age during the folk music revival of the '60s," she explains.[7] When she began telling stories, it seemed natural to play her guitar and accompany a folksong following a story. For instance, Jeslyn told "Ashpet" from Richard Chase's *Grandfather Tales*, then sang "Sourwood Mountain," an Appalachian folksong, and taught the audience amusing hand motions to do while singing the chorus. Before long she added an Appalachian lap dulcimer to her collection and found it more authentic on some mountain tunes. Jeslyn's CD *Hoot Owl Blues: Tales and Tunes to Conjure Up a Mood*, an ALA Notable Children's Recording for the year 2000, is a sample of the way she presents story hours. "The Conjure Wives" is followed by an original blues song, "Hoot Owl Blues," with guitar accompaniment. "Wiley and the Hairy Man" leads into "A Dog Named Blue" on the dulcimer. Jeslyn called Wiley's dog "Blue" in the story to make the song connection more fun.

Whenever possible, involve the community in your program. If you are aware of a young person who plays an instrument, for instance, consider asking that person to play when appropriate. For a Family Program she called "Stories for a Generous Heart," Carol Birch told *The Cello of Mr. O*, Janet Cutler's inspiring story about the healing power of music, based on a true happening. Birch invited a high school student cellist to play. The young man chose to play "Albinoni's Adagio" in G Minor for Cello, which Vedran Smailovic played in Sarajevo, Bosnia, every evening, at 4 P.M. for twenty-two days in protest of the war and in memory of the twenty-two people who were killed instantly when a mortar shell fell on the bread line they were waiting in.

For several years Sue Sutton, youth services librarian at the West Bloomfield (MI) Public Library, has held a Family Storytime called "Language of the Heart." Aware of her community's rich cultural diversity, Sue contacted various organizations and international schools and asked if anyone would be interested in presenting a thirty-minute story program in their native language. There were many volunteers! Publicity handouts were given to the native storytellers to circulate to their community organizations and international schools. The flyer begins "Each family has a 'Language of the Heart,' the language that your family speaks at home. Our children go to school and grow up with children who speak many different languages . . . " and goes on to invite parents/caregivers to bring the entire family "to enjoy stories, songs, rhymes, and fingerplays in their native language or come because you would like your children to listen and learn about other languages and cultures." The program is held once a month from 7:00 to 7:30 P.M. on a Wednesday evening. Each program is presented by Sue and a native language speaker. Sue meets with the guest storyteller two or three times before the program is scheduled to go over the content and to make sure that the guest feels comfortable in the library setting. One guest storyteller gave a puppet performance of "The Three Billy Goats Gruff" with all dialogue in Japanese. A French woman told "The Gingerbread Man" in French. She had made a galette bretonne (a flat round French pastry) that she rolled on a stick as she told the story to the delight of her listeners. Afterward she shared her recipe for the pastry. The Russian storyteller told *A Little Story About a Big Turnip* by Tatiana Zunshine with children in costumes acting out the parts. Later in the program the storyteller explained the meaning of Russian artifacts, including Matyroshka nesting dolls, and the children created Matryoshka paper dolls using crayons, scissors, and glue sticks. In 2007–2008 the library presented "Language of the Heart" storytimes in Arabic, Chinese, French, German, Hebrew, Hindi, Japanese, Russian, and Spanish!

PREPARATION

Preparing a well-balanced program is not sufficient in the case of a multimedia story hour. The storyteller must also pay careful attention to the physical and mechanical requirements of the program. Check the condition of any films and recordings to be used. Reserve any audiovisual equipment needed. Arrange for a competent projectionist if you need help. Be prepared for equipment failure.

Arrange for a room that can be darkened if you plan to show a film. Check electrical outlets. Allow time to set up the equipment before the program begins. Arrange the seating so that you will be able to switch from one medium to another without having the children move.

Just before the program check the audiovisual equipment again. Focus the film you plan to show and adjust the sound. Now relax, and enjoy the program with the children.

SAMPLE MULTIMEDIA PROGRAMS

Program in honor of Pura Belpré, Spanish folklorist and storyteller. This program is often held around Three Kings Day (January 6) or during Hispanic Heritage Month (September 15th through October 15th). It can be planned for children only or for a family storytime.

THEME: Bilingual program in honor of Hispanic culture
> If fire laws permit, start by lighting the Storyteller's Candle.

STORY: *The Storyteller's Candle/La velita de los cuentos* by Lucia Gonzalez
> This is a story about Pura Belpré. After the story tell more about Pura Belpré's work at the New York Public Library (see Chapter 2).

STORY: *Perez and Martina* by Pura Belpré
> (Pura Belpré recorded "Perez and Martina" in Spanish and in English on CMS 505; if available, play a section of the recording)

SONGS: If the Belpré recording is not available, sing a few Hispanic songs or do a craft

CRAFT: Make a paper fan like Martina's

ACTIVITY: Break the piñata
> If the program is a family storytelling event, serve light refreshments.

Figure 19. *Lucía González, author of* The Storyteller's Candle, La velita de los cuentos, *with her puppets Perez and Martina. José Luis González, photographer. Reprinted by permission of Lucía González.*

Story Program in Honor of Eleanor Farjeon, a Hans Christian Andersen Award-Winning Author

OPENING: Speak briefly about Eleanor Farjeon and about the Hans Christian Andersen Award.

POETRY: Read from *Eleanor Farjeon's Poems for Children* or play a few poetry selections from Ellin Greene's recording *Elsie Piddock Skips in Her Sleep*. Invite the children to share the images the poetry evoked in their minds.

STORY: "Elsie Piddock Skips in Her Sleep," from *Martin Pippin in the Daisy Field* by Eleanor Farjeon. (After the telling, share Charlotte Voake's illustrations in the picture book edition *Elsie Piddock Skips in Her Sleep*, published by Candlewick Press.)

Program in Honor of the Author/Poet, Carl Sandburg

OPENING: Read a few selections from *Carl Sandburg: Adventures of a Poet* by Penelope Niven.

SOUND BITE: Play a few minutes of the recording *How to Tell Corn Fairies When You See 'Em, and Other Rootabaga Stories* to give your listeners an idea of the poet's slow rhythmic pacing.

STORY: Tell "The Huckabuck Family and How They Raised Popcorn in Nebraska and Quit and Came Back" from *Rootabaga Stories* or read aloud David Small's award-winning picture book.

STORY: If time permits, tell another story from *Rootabaga Stories* or a selection from the recording *Sandburg Out Loud*.

Program in Celebration of Black History Month

Display several books by or about well-known African American persons on the storyteller's table. As the audience assembles, distribute photocopies of the words of three spirituals—"This Little Light of Mine," "Oh, When the Saints Go Marching In," and "He's Got the Whole World in His Hands"—from Ashley Bryan's award-winning book *Let it Shine*.

OPENING SONG: "This Little Light of Mine."

POETRY: Read a poem or two by Langston Hughes, and tell a bit about his life based on the book *Langston Hughes: American Poet* by Alice Walker.

CONVERSATION: Talk about Martin Luther King, Jr., and the civil rights movement. Share parts of *My Brother Martin: A Sister Remembers Growing Up with the Rev. Dr. Martin Luther King, Jr.,* and *March On! The Day My Brother Changed the World* by Christine King Farris, the older sister of Dr. King.

STORY: Read aloud *Boycott Blues: How Rosa Parks Inspired a Nation* by Andrea Davis Pinkney.

CLOSING SONG: "He's Got the Whole World in His Hands" from *Let it Shine*.

Program with a Midsummer Theme

OPENING: Play incidental music from "A Midsummer Night's Dream" by Felix Mendelssohn as the children enter the room.

CONVERSATION: Talk about Midsummer folklore. (See *Midsummer Magic: a Garland of Stories, Charms, and Recipes* by Ellin Greene.)

STORY: "Count Alaric's Lady" from *Midsummer Magic*.

Dance Program for a Mixed-Age Group

OPENING: Play "Waltz of the Flowers" from the *Nutcracker Suite* by Tchaikovsky as the children enter the room. Have books about dance, such as *A Very Young Dancer* by Jill Krementz, on the storyteller's table.

STORY: "Nella's Dancing Shoes" from *Italian Peepshow* by Eleanor Farjeon.

STORY: Tell or read aloud sections from one of the picture book editions of *The Nutcracker* by E. T. A. Hoffmann.

CLOSING: Play another selection from the *Nutcracker Suite* as the children leave.

REFERENCES

1. E. B. White, *Charlotte's Web*, 50th Anniversary Retrospective Edition. Illus. by Garth Williams. Watercolors of Garth Williams, artwork by Rosemary Wells. With an afterword by Peter F. Neumeyer (HarperCollins, 2002), p. 63.

2. Janice M. Del Negro, Class Lecture, Dominican University, LIS 718 Storytelling for Adults and Children, Spring 2007.

3. "The Best Picture Books Featuring Music in Your Library" in Ron Reid's *Something Musical Happened at the Library: Adding Song and Dance to Children's Story Programs* (American Library Association, 2007) is an excellent source for planning musical picture-book programs.

4. Spencer G. Shaw, "A Story Falls in the Silence," *Wilson Library Bulletin* (October 1964): 179.

5. Carol L. Birch, "Storytelling Programs for the Family," *National Storytelling Journal* 1 (Summer 1984): 14–18.

6. Spencer G. Shaw, "Recorded Magic for Story Hours," *Top of the News* 15 (October 1958): 43–47.

7. Jeslyn Wheeless, personal communications to Ellin Greene (December 9, 2008)

WEB RESOURCES

Fairy Tales, Folk Tales and Mythology WebRing
http://www.webring.com/hub?ring=fairytale

Integrating Folklore, Folk Music, and Traditional Culture Instruction into K-12 Education
http://www.cyberplayground.net/Teachers/folkAlanJabbour.html
This site from the Educational Cyber Playground features definitions and practical links.

Junior Great Books: Folktales
http://www.greatbooks.org/programs-for-all-ages/junior.html
Search "folktales."

BOOKS AND RECORDINGS USED IN SAMPLE PROGRAMS LISTED ALPHABETICALLY BY TITLE

Note: ISBNs are for hardcover book editions. Several titles are available in a paper edition with a later publication date, but paper editions generally do not lend themselves to program presentation.

Aesop's Fables by Michael Morpurgo. Illus. by Emma Chichester Clark. Simon & Schuster/Margaret K. McElderry Books, 2004. ISBN 9781416902904

Andy and the Lion: A Tale of Kindness Remembered or The Power of Gratitude by James Daugherty. Viking, 1937. Paw Prints, 2007. ISBN 143520056X

Billy Beg and His Bull: An Irish Tale retold by Ellin Greene. Illus. by Kimberly Bulcken Root. Holiday House, 1994. ISBN 9780823411009

Boycott Blues: How Rosa Parks Inspired a Nation by Andrea Davis Pinkney. Illus. by Brian Pinkney. Greenwillow, 2008. ISBN 9780060821180

Carl Sandburg: Adventures of a Poet by Penelope Niven. With Poems and Prose by Carl Sandburg. Illus. by Marc Nadel. Harcourt, 2003. ISBN 0-15-204686-0

The Cello of Mr. O by Janet Cutler. Illus. by Greg Couch. Dutton, 1999. ISBN 9780525461197

The Dancing Granny retold and illus. by Ashley Bryan. Atheneum, 1977. ISBN 9780689305481

Days to Celebrate: A Full Year of Poetry, People, Holidays, History, Fascinating Facts, and More by Lee Bennett Hopkins. Illus. by Stephen Alcorn. Greenwillow, 2005. ISBN 9780060007652

Eleanor Farjeon's Poems for Children by Eleanor Farjeon. Lippincott, 1951. HarperCollins, 1984. ISBN 9780397320912

Elsie Piddock Skips in Her Sleep by Eleanor Farjeon. Illus. by Charlotte Voake. Candlewick, 2000. ISBN 9780763607906 (also in *Martin Pip-*

pin in the Daisy Field by Eleanor Farjeon. Illus. by Isobel and John Morton-Sale. Lippincott, c. 1937, 1965.)

Elsie Piddock Skips in Her Sleep: Stories and Poems by Eleanor Farjeon. Narrated by Ellin Greene. A Gentle Wind GW1025CD. ISBN 0-939065-74-6

English Folk and Fairy Tales by Joseph Jacobs. Illus. by John Batten. Everyman Library, 1940. Includes *English Fairy Tales* and *More English Fairy Tales.* ISBN 9780891900764

From Sea to Shining Sea: A Treasury of American Folklore and Folk Songs by Amy L. Cohn and Suzy Schmidt. Scholastic, 1993. ISBN 9780590428682

Grandfather Tales: American English Folk Tales selected and edited by Richard Chase. Illus. by Berkeley Williams, Jr. Houghton Mifflin, 2003. ISBN 9780618346912

Hoot Hour Blues: Tales and Tunes to Conjure Up a Mood. Performed by Jeslyn Wheeless, storyteller-folksinger, and Ben Wheeless, guitarist. ALA Notable Children's Recording 2000. Order CD or cassette from wheelessj@aol.com.

How to Tell Corn Fairies When You See 'Em, and Other Rootabaga Stories. Caedmon TC 1159

The Huckabuck Family and How They Raised Popcorn in Nebraska and Quit and Came Back by Carl Sandburg. Illus. by David Small. Farrar, Straus and Giroux, 1999. ISBN 9780374335113 (also in *Rootabaga Stories*)

Italian Peepshow by Eleanor Farjeon. Illus. by Edward Ardizzone. Walck, 1960.

Johnny Appleseed: The Legend and the Truth by Jane Yolen. Illus. by Jim Burke. HarperCollins, 2008. ISBN 9780060591359

Johnny Appleseed: The Story of a Legend by Will Moses. Philomel, 2001. ISBN 9780399231537

Juba This and Juba That: Stories to Tell, Songs to Sing, Rhymes to Chant, Riddles to Guess, and More! 2nd ed., by Virgina A. Tashjian. Illus. by Nadine Bernard Westcott. Little, Brown, 1995. ISBN 9780316832342

The Korean Cinderella by Shirley Climo. Illus. by Ruth Heller. Harper-Collins, 1993. ISBN 9780060204327

Langston Hughes: An American Poet by Alice Walker. Illus. by Catherine Deeter. HarperCollins, 2002. ISBN 9780060215194

Leaf Man by Lois Ehlert. Harcourt, 2005. ISBN 9780152053048

Let it Shine: Three Favorite Spirituals by Ashley Bryan. Atheneum, 2007. ISBN 9780689847325

Library Lion by Michelle Knudson. Illus. by Kevin Hawkes. Candlewick Press, 2006. ISBN 9780763622626

Lightning Inside You and Other Native American Riddles edited by John Bierhorst. HarperCollins, 1992. ISBN 9780688095826

A Little Story About a Big Turnip by Tatiana Zunshine. Pumplin House, 2004. ISBN 9780964601000

The Magic Orange Tree and Other Haitian Folktales by Diane Wolkstein. Drawings by Elsa Henriquez. Knopf, 1978. ISBN 9780394833900

Many Moons by James Thurber. Illus. by Marc Simont. Harcourt, 1990. ISBN 9780152518721

March On! The Day My Brother Changed the World by Christine King Farris. Illus. by London Ladd. Scholastic, 2008. ISBN 9780545035378

More True Lies: 18 Tales for You to Judge by George Shannon. Illus. by John O'Brien. Greenwillow, 2001. ISBN 9780688176433

My Brother Martin: A Sister Remembers Growing Up with the Rev. Martin Luther King, Jr. by Christine King Farris. Illus. by Chris King Soentpiet. Simon & Schuster, 2003. ISBN 9780689843877

The Nutcracker by E. T. A. Hoffman. Adapted by Janet Schulman. Illus. by Renee Graef. With audio CD narrated by Claire Bloom. Music by Peter Ilyich Tchaikovsky. HarperCollins, 1999. ISBN 9780060278144

Passion and Poison: Tales of Shape-Shifters, Ghosts, and Spirited Women by Janice M. Del Negro. Illus. by Vince Natale. Marshall Cavendish, 2007. ISBN 9780761453611

Perez and Martina by Pura Belpré. Illus. by Carlos Sanchez. Warne, c. 1932, renewed 1960. Viking, 1991. ISBN 9780670841660

Peter and the Wolf by Ian Beck. Random House, 1994. ISBN 9780385403436. Paperback edition (book and tape), Random House, 1977. ISBN 9780552204200

Peter and the Wolf by Chris Raschka. Atheneum, 2008. ISBN 9780689856525

Peter and the Wolf by Sergei Prokofiev. Narrated by Boris Karloff. Compact Disc 5171273. A Vanguard Classic CD distributed by Musical Heritage Society. The CD also includes Leopold Mozart's *Haydn's Toy Symphony* and Tchaikovsky's *Nutcracker Suite*.

The Philharmonic Gets Dressed by Karla Kuskin. HarperCollins, 1982. ISBN 9780060236229

Rootabaga Stories by Carl Sandburg. Illus. by Maud and Miska Petersham. Harcourt, c. 1922, 1950. Kessinger Publishing, 2008. ISBN 9781436607442

Sandburg Out Loud: A Selection of Carl Sandburg's Rootabaga Stories, Poetry and Folksongs Collected in the American Songbag. Told and sung by Carol Birch, Angela Lloyd, and Bill Harley with music by David Holt. August House, 2002. Compact Disc ISBN 0-87483-676-X; Cassette ISBN 0-87483-677-8

Shoemaker's Apron: A Second Book of Czechoslovak Fairy Tales and Folk Tales (1920) by Parker Fillmore. Illus. by Jan Matulka. Kessinger, 2008. ISBN 9780548983712

Still More Stories to Solve: Fourteen Folktales From Around the World by George Shannon. Illus. by Peter Sís. Greenwillow, 1994. ISBN 9780688046194

The Storyteller's Candle/La velita de los cuentos by Lucía González. Illus. by Lulu Delacre. Children's Book Press, 2008. ISBN 9780892392223

The True Tale of Johnny Appleseed by Margaret Hodges. Illus. by Kimberly Bulcken Root. Holiday, 1997. ISBN 9780823412822

A Very Young Dancer by Jill Krementz. Knopf, 1976. ISBN 9780394408859

When the Root Children Wake Up by Audrey Wood. Illus. by Ned Bittinger. Scholastic, 2002. ISBN 9780590425179 (Note: The classic edition by Helen D. Fish is o.p.)

While Standing on One Foot: Puzzle Stories and Wisdom Tales from the Jewish Tradition by Nina Jaffe and Steve Zeitlin. Illus. by John Segal. Holt, 1993. ISBN 9780805025941

Wiley and the Hairy Man by Judy Sierra. Illus. by Brian Pinkney. Dutton, 2001. ISBN 9780525674771

Willa and the Wind by Janice M. Del Negro. Illus. by Heather M. Solomon. Marshall Cavendish, 2005. ISBN 9780761452324

12 ADMINISTRATION OF THE STORYTELLING PROGRAM AND IN-SERVICE EDUCATION

People who work with children need to understand the importance of stories in the lives of children and the unique contribution that library storytelling can make in bringing children and books together, in helping children acquire language and literacy skills, and in giving children an appreciation of their literary and cultural heritage.
        —*Augusta Baker*[1]

IN A TIME OF BUDGET CUTS and diminishing staff, public librarians and school library media specialists may need to convince their administrators as well as other members of their staffs that the storytelling program is a basic part of library service to children. Research in brain development and literacy acquisition supports the use of storytelling as a pedagogic tool, but immeasurable intangibles, felt by the storyteller, are difficult to convey to others. Exposure to the art is one of the best ways to win over skeptics.

INTRODUCING STORYTELLING TO THE LIBRARY COMMUNITY

Invite administrators, librarians who serve adults, principals, and teachers to observe a storytelling program where they can see for themselves the response of the children. Public librarians and school library media specialists can reach parents at PTO meetings. Family Storytelling Events (see Chapter 11) will convince many parents of the value of storytime, and they will voice support of this program to both administrators and board members.

Plan a storytelling festival as a special event of the public library's children's department and invite both staff and community. Be sure to invite school administrators and faculty.

Seek invitations to tell stories to community groups; be alert to the possibility of inclusion in community programs. Suggest to your administrator the possibility of presenting a storytelling workshop at a staff or faculty in-service meeting. The administrator of a public library with a storytelling specialist on the staff can offer this specialist's services to other organizations in the community. Likewise, school administrators can share the expertise of their school library media specialists with teachers, aides, and others interested in storytelling.

Always prepare a formal report on the success of your story programs.

WORKDAY PREPARATION FOR SELECTING AND LEARNING STORIES

Administrators sometimes raise a question about the time needed to prepare for traditional library storytelling. Certainly time should be allotted to search for stories, because the reading of many books adds to the librarian's expertise in guiding readers. This reading cultivates and deepens the critical ability of the storyteller, who then gains in the appreciation of literary values, as well as the expertise to identify written tales that make effective oral narrative. Books are important tools of the librarian's profession, and therefore some time should be given to their examination and use. Realistically, much of the storyteller's preparation is done on his or her own time, but so is that of other professionals.

NON-CIRCULATING BOOKS TO SUPPORT THE STORYTELLING PROGRAM: PROFESSIONAL COLLECTION

A strong collection of reference books about storytelling and its related subjects is necessary for the storyteller's background reading (see Resources for the Storyteller). Such basic collections as Asbjørnsen and Moe's *East of the Sun and West of the Moon*, edited and illustrated by Ingri and Edgar Parin d'Aulaire; *The Glass Slipper: Charles Perrault's Tales of Times Past*, translated by John Bierhorst; the Lucy Crane, Lore Segal, and Ralph Manheim translations of the collected tales of the Brothers Grimm; and the M. R. James and Erik Haugaard translations of Hans Christian Andersen stories are necessary for comparative judgments of other translations. Clean books are necessary for the storytelling table and for display. These extra copies are part of the storyteller's professional library and are as necessary as the administrator's books on school or public library administration.

SCHEDULING STORYTELLING PROGRAMS

When scheduling a storytelling program, consider the availability of space and staff. Storytelling programs should be part of the library's long-range programming plan, and so the day of the week as well as the frequency of the program is often governed by the overall schedule of events. Be aware of events in the community to avoid conflicting programs seeking the same audience. It is often necessary to experiment with program days and times until the best one evolves. Public library storytelling programs for young children are usually scheduled mid-morning or in the afternoon during the week. Programs for school-age children are often scheduled at 4 P.M. when the most children are in the library, or at an appropriate time on Saturday or Sunday. Evening storytelling events for families are increasingly popular. The school library media specialist usually schedules storytelling within the school day. Parents, teachers, and even older children trained in storytelling (see Chapter 10) may be available to tell stories to children who do not go home for lunch or who are not bused home immediately after school. The classroom teacher can schedule time for telling or reading aloud within the school day and can be alert to every opportunity for informal, spur-of-the-moment storytelling.

FREQUENCY OF STORYTELLING PROGRAMS

Many factors enter into the decision to have weekly, monthly, semimonthly, or the occasional special storytelling event. A neighborhood with few organized activities for children might very well need more-frequent programs for six- to ten-year-olds than one with highly organized recreational and school activities and overscheduled children—those whose after-school hours are mostly taken up with dance lessons, violin lessons, choir practice, scouts, and other activities. The number of available storytellers is an important factor—over-scheduling can make what should be an enjoyable experience into a chore. Unless the librarian-storyteller has a fairly lengthy repertoire, a weekly storytelling program should be undertaken only when more than one storyteller is available. Of course, some programs include reading aloud and storytelling, which is always a winning combination.

Public libraries with multiple branches and multiple children's librarians can consider the feasibility of rotating storytellers and programs from branch to branch. One of the benefits of the swapping plan is that each storyteller involved has an opportunity to tell the same stories more than once. Even though each storyteller is telling stories weekly, there is more time to prepare new stories. This schedule also brings guest storytellers to the children.

ADULT ATTENDANCE AT STORYTELLING PROGRAMS

Teachers who bring their classes to the library for storytelling should stay to listen, not grade papers or perform other chores. The teacher models active listening and provides an example of appropriate audience behavior. Occasionally a visiting storyteller or a student observer may be in the group. Observing experienced storytellers is an important part of the training of beginners and should be permitted. Too many adults in the group, however, may affect the mood and could suppress children's spontaneous responses to the story; the sensitive librarian or teacher will know when to make an exception. On the other hand, family storytelling events with children and adults in attendance are ideal opportunities to create community. For example, in a predominantly Spanish-speaking community in New York City, adults attended storytelling programs with their children. The librarian storyteller was able to establish a rapport with parents recently arrived from Puerto Rico and to help them feel at home in the library. The parents in turn enriched the library by sharing their culture and strongly supporting the library's storytelling program.

EFFECTIVE PUBLICITY

The most effective publicity for both adults and children is positive word of mouth. One-to-one publicity is always effective, and children seem to remember this better than printed forms of publicity. A personal invitation to attend the next storytelling program makes the child feel especially wanted. The same "over-the-desk" conversation with parents is always worthwhile.

Press releases and articles in community and local papers will draw community-wide attention. Radio stations are usually willing to make spot announcements about community programs. Announcements on the library website and email announcements to a virtual mailing list are also highly effective. A well-designed poster or flyer can be placed in restaurants, community centers, grocery stores, staff rooms of schools and recreation centers, churches, and other public places frequented by adults.

The what-when-where facts must be included in all publicity. Program information should include the ages for which the storytelling is planned, the place and time of the program, and where additional information is available. Specify a time limit, such as 4:00 to 4:45 P.M., as this informs children and parents of the length of the program.

Consider using designs and illustrations from public domain picture archives such as those available from Dover Press in-print and online. If a copyrighted illustration is desired, it is necessary to get permission for its use from the publisher. Do not be intimidated by this process because it is relatively simple. The website of the Children's Book Council (www. cbcbooks.org) contains contact information for the major trade publishers of children's books. A brief note explaining the one-time use for which the library wants the image will suffice, and many publishers are quite generous.

Explore and use the artistic talents of your co-workers and friends. Invite the art class in a school to submit designs. The use of chalkwalks, sandwich boards, balloons, and other fun publicity is described in Caroline Bauer's *New Handbook for Storytellers*.[2]

If there is a public relations officer on the staff of the library or recreation center, publicity probably will be handled by that person. It then becomes the responsibility of the storyteller or organizer to get the necessary information to the public relations officer as early as possible.

"One-librarian-shows" are not unusual, so if you find yourself in a position where even the flyer design is up to you, take a less-is-more approach. Designing an effective flyer or webpage is like effective storytelling: keep it simple. Answer the who, what, when, and where questions. Use simple bold fonts. Make sure your graphics have an identifiable color or logo—some sort of visual brand that will identify your announcement before anyone even reads it. Remember the eye is attracted to contrast, whether on a webpage or a flyer, so consider the impact of font and background colors. A dark background with light lettering can be an eye-catching combination.[3]

THE IMPORTANCE OF COMMUNITY NETWORKING

Networking with those in the community whose goals dovetail with those of the library is critical. The dissemination of publicity depends largely upon your knowledge of key people in the community and your ability to gain their interest and cooperation. An up-to-date file or database of community organizations and people, complete with addresses, phone numbers, email addresses, and any other vital information is a necessity. Generally speaking, the response is best when publicity is directed to one person in the organization—the principal or school library media specialist, the director of the day-care center or recreation center, the president of the parents' organization, or the minister of the church. Newspapers and television and radio stations also respond best when the publicity is sent to a specific person with whom you have established contact. Email announcements, flyers, posters, press releases, and letters should be sent to this person with a request for posting, distribution, and public announcements.

THE PERSONAL TOUCH

A personal visit with the key people in an organization is very important. This is an opportunity to describe the storytelling program and the philosophy behind it. Some people must be convinced of the importance of storytelling before they will publicize a program. Invite these adults to attend a family or outdoor storytelling program for a mixed-age group so that they will feel more knowledgeable and involved. Building good personal relationships will gain support for your program and can save time too as it often makes it possible to ask for publicity for future events via email or over the phone.

PLANNING A STORYTELLING FESTIVAL

Storytelling festivals are inspirational in nature and are usually planned for a large audience with varying storytelling experience. They may or may not include workshops for the attendees.

SELECTION OF STORYTELLERS AND STORIES

Consider only the best storytellers. They may be members of the library staff or invited guests; the latter will almost certainly require additional funds. Select storytellers who have different styles and techniques, so that the program will have variety both in content and length of stories. The stories should represent the best versions of folktales, the finest literature, and the well-crafted personal tale.

THE PHYSICAL SETTING

Select a quiet room that can be made attractive and that has good acoustics. Use flowers and beautifully illustrated books as background. Arrange the books in groups, perhaps by theme, and vary the sizes and colors within each group. Simplicity and an uncluttered appearance are important.

Place the books from which the stories will be told on the story table with fresh flowers and the wishing candle, if one is to be used.

Arrange the chairs so that everyone can see the storyteller. Avoid using small, juvenile chairs for adult audiences; this is not cute and it can be very uncomfortable for some adults.

THE PROGRAM

Plan each segment of the program to last no longer than an hour or an hour and a half. Open with a few remarks about storytelling and the program. Introduce each storyteller by a short characterization of either the story to be told or the storyteller. Give the program dignity and integrity—no coy "let's pretend we are children" remarks.

Leave time at the end of the program for the audience to chat informally with the storytellers.

Planning a Storytelling Workshop

Establish the objectives of the storytelling workshop. What do you want to happen to the participants as a result of attending the workshop?

Define the audience you want to reach. Are they librarians, teachers, recreational leaders, staff, volunteers?

Plan a budget. How much money is needed? Will participants be charged a registration fee?

How much time is available—a half day, a full day, several half-day sessions, a weekend?

How many leaders are available? Will it be a one-leader workshop? One leader plus an inspirational keynote speaker? One leader and several resource persons?

Will the participants meet as one large group or will the group be divided into smaller interest groups?

What aspects of storytelling will be covered?

What kinds of presentations and activities will be most effective in achieving the objectives?

Hour-and-a-half or two-hour sessions are long enough to get into a topic and cover major points without tiring the audience. Keep the workshop groups reasonably small (fifteen to twenty-five persons). Larger groups can be accommodated, but the presentations will tend to be lectures. It is hard to have a good discussion in a large group and impossible for everyone to tell a story and receive feedback.

Provide an opportunity for the participants to hear good storytelling. If possible, arrange for children to be present at one of the storytelling demonstrations so that beginning storytellers can see an experienced storyteller interacting with children and handling some of the typical situations that arise.

Design an attractive web announcement or flyer stating the time, place, program, and registration information.

Send the announcement to the expected audience, whether via email or snail mail, in ample time to complete registration at least two weeks before the date of the workshop. Publicize your workshop on the library website as well as through email, direct mail, professional journals, local organizations, library systems, newspapers, and radio.

If you plan to sell any storytelling materials at the workshop, order the materials on consignment from the publishers or a jobber far in advance of the workshop date. Arrange for at least two people to handle the sales table, and be sure to have cash, including change, on hand.

Allow enough time to arrange for any technology or audiovisual materials you plan to use, to gather exhibit materials, and to prepare a bibliography. If you plan to use a film, reserve the projector well in advance. Be sure to have a projectionist available so that the workshop leader does not have this responsibility. Set up the equipment, and adjust the focus and sound before the workshop begins.

Arrange for comfortable meeting rooms. If a meal is to be served, plan an attractive but light menu. Coffee, tea, and juice served during the registration period are always welcome.

Have an attractive exhibit of books and other storytelling materials prominently displayed in a comfortable area. The exhibit should extend the participants' knowledge of storytelling literature. Allow time for browsing.

The introduction by the workshop leader or keynote speaker sets the tone for the workshop. The atmosphere should be relaxed, friendly, and supportive so that the participants are at ease when they tell a story or participate in discussion. The workshop leader should outline to participants what they will be doing and the time schedule.

Any workshop—and especially one planned for 100 or more people—takes a tremendous amount of planning and coordination with all departments involved, from maintenance staff to top administration. The hard work that goes into a workshop should not show on the day of the workshop. Take care of the nitty-gritty beforehand so that the workshop runs as smoothly as possible, but always be prepared for the unexpected. The Youth Services consultants at the North Carolina State Library keep a tackle-box full of oft-needed workshop items such as scissors, tape, glue, markers, and the like. Be ready with a short story to fill in the rough spots.

TELL THE PROGRAM'S STORY TOO

Include an evaluation in participants' handouts in order to discover responses to the program setting, design, and content. How well were the program objectives reached? Take pictures during the program, and include pictures and positive comments from the evaluations in your report to your director or board, as well as in follow-up publicity sent to local media and posted on the library website.

IN-STAFF WORKSHOP FOR BEGINNING STORYTELLERS

An in-staff workshop for beginning storytellers can be held once a week over a period of four to five weeks with each session lasting approximately two hours. The workshop leader should be an experienced storyteller.

Session 1   Purpose and values of storytelling
Selection of materials
Demonstration of storytelling
Bibliography of storytelling literature is distributed
Participants are asked to read widely from books listed on the bibliography and to select stories they want to learn

Session 2   Selection of materials (continued)
Discussion of stories selected by participants
Preparation and presentation—techniques of learning and telling stories
Demonstration of storytelling
Participants are asked to prepare a short, traditional tale (3 to 5 minutes) for presentation at the next session

Session 3   Stories are told by participants
General and constructive criticism is offered by the workshop leader and other participants (the leader must see that comments or criticisms are constructive and of such a nature that everyone can learn from them)
Discussion of any problems arising from participants' experience in preparing their stories

Session 4   Program planning
Administration
Model storytime by workshop leader
Participants are asked to prepare a longer and more complex story (7 to 10 minutes) for presentation at the next session

Session 5   Participants tell their stories and discuss their programs
General and constructive criticism is offered by the workshop leader and participants
Evaluation of workshop

Depending on the size of the group, it may be necessary to have additional sessions so that everyone has a chance to tell a story. If possible, the workshop leader should observe each participant as he or she tells a story to a group of children. This also presents an opportunity for the workshop leader to discuss in private any specific criticisms or suggestions for the beginning storyteller.

ONE-DAY WORKSHOP

One-day workshops planned for a larger audience with a wider range of experience often include several resource persons in addition to the workshop leader. A suggested program for such a workshop follows.

MORNING SESSION

Have an inspirational keynote speaker who will set the tone. Divide the audience into small interest groups, such as:

1. Multicultural Stories
2. The Black Heritage in Storytelling
3. Poetry in the Story Hour
4. The Illustrator as Storyteller
5. The Literary Fairy Tale

Assign a specialist to each group to direct the discussion and act as resource person and demonstration storyteller. Allow an hour and a half for the morning interest groups.

LUNCHEON

AFTERNOON SESSION

The interest groups can be repeated so that each participant can hear about two aspects of storytelling, or the workshop can be arranged so that participants stay in the same group all day. This allows groups to go into greater depth of subject matter and also gives more time for demonstration and audience participation. Allow time for a question-and-answer period. An alternative plan is to have shorter afternoon interest groups and to end the workshop with a storytelling demonstration by the various specialist leaders to the entire audience.

STORYTELLING WORKSHOP FOR DAY-CARE OR HEAD START STAFF

This kind of workshop is often held at the day-care or Head Start center, and is an excellent networking opportunity for you to make connections with others who work with young children in your community.

A sample workshop can focus on the library/day-care center partnership; an introduction to the world of children's book resources; evaluation and selection of books; and a description of services the library offers of particular interest to workshop attendees.

1. Introduce yourself as a representative of the library and talk about the library/day-care partnership in helping children develop a love of books and reading.
2. Emphasize the connection between hearing stories in early childhood and language development. Cite some of the supporting research.

3. Talk about the criteria for selecting stories to read aloud or to tell and illustrate your points with a variety of Mother Goose books, picture books, and simple folktales.

4. Demonstrate techniques of reading aloud and storytelling. If time allows, have the participants practice reading aloud in small groups.

5. Briefly describe the variety of services available to the organization from the library.

Above all, show the books and tell the stories, for well-selected books and stories will make your points for you. Make sure to leave time for questions and for looking at the books and other materials you have provided.

WORKSHOP FOR FIRST-TIME PARENTS

The research on early childhood brain development has led to a new emphasis in working with first-time parents. The following are sample steps for a new parent workshop.

1. Welcome the parents to the library.

2. Talk about the importance of sharing literature with children from birth on, citing research that shows a connection between being read to during early childhood, emergent literacy, and later success in school (see Chapter 8).

3. Ask parents if they remember a favorite book, story, or nursery rhyme from their own childhood.

4. Show examples of the types of books published for young children today: board books, cloth books, concept books, wordless picture books, Mother Goose and nursery rhymes, finger plays, and picture storybooks.

5. Read all or part of some books in different categories to model how to read aloud.

6. Allow time for questions and answers about the library's services for parents and young children.

7. Display resources on parenting and books for babies and toddlers and encourage the parents to browse.

THE CARE AND FEEDING OF GUEST STORYTELLERS

Sarah Howard, coordinator of children's and youth services at the Daniel Boone Regional Library system in Columbia, Missouri, has a "Tip Sheet" for libraries hosting storytelling and other programming events. This

26-point list outlines the steps for hiring a storyteller and planning and carrying out a successful event.

PROGRAMMING TIP SHEET

- Date
- Time and length
- Age range
- Location
- Potential audience size
- Number of shows per day
- Celebration/topic for program
- References
- Negotiation of total fee
- Performer description and photo
- Sound needs
- Space needs
- Other equipment needs (table, podium, computer)
- Time needs (set up, tear down)
- Other needs (food, transportation)
- Contact/contract information: map, additional venue information
- Internal paperwork and information sharing
- Public relations/marketing
- Registration; friendly reminder to performer re: program details
- Room set-up
- Performer needs
- Audience needs
- Introduction
- Statistics, notes, and evaluations
- Thank you note(s)

Howard has very practical advice for hosting storytellers as well. Make sure there is a designated area for performers to both leave their equipment and prepare for the program. Be aware that some tellers need a quiet time before a program in order to focus. If possible, make sure the storyteller can sell books or recordings. Libraries are not the highest-paying gigs, so the additional income provided by resource sales can be an inducement. Don't forget that a grant written with other community agencies, libraries, or schools can result in a higher-paying gig for the storyteller at a lower fee for the hosting participants.

FIGURE 20. *Example of an effective publicity poster (bottom) and one that does not project a positive image of storytelling (top). From* The National Storytelling Journal, *Summer 1984, p. 17.*

Howard points out that it is of no use to have a storyteller the audience cannot hear or see. Excellent sound is a must, and excellent lighting is a close second. Be aware of ambient noise and traffic around the location of the program. Try to ensure that the entrance to the space is behind the audience to avoid the distraction of late arrivals or early departures. The hosting library is responsible for keeping order during the program; your storytellers should not have to be house managers during their own shows. Make sure to set up the chairs so that everyone has a fairly clear line of sight, and reinforce agreed-upon age ranges at the door. Before welcoming everyone to the program, ask storytellers how they want to be introduced.

The most important thing? Feed your storytellers! Some will want to eat before the program, some will want to eat after, but all will want to eat. Regardless of whether you accompany your storyteller to meals, the provision of a list of local restaurants will be welcome.

REFERENCES

1. Augusta Baker, "Foreword" to *Storytelling: Art and Technique*, 3rd ed. (R. R. Bowker, 1996), p. xiv.

2. Caroline Feller Bauer, *New Handbook for Storytellers: With Stories, Poems, Magic and More* (American Library Assn., 1993), pp. 29–39.

3. *wikiHow: The How-to Manual That You Can Edit* at www.wikihow.com

RESOURCES

Doucett, Elisabeth. *Creating Your Library Brand: Communicating Your Relevance and Value to Your Patrons*. ALA Editions, 2008. ISBN 9780838909621

The Federal Library and Information Center Committee. *Tips for Planning Library Programs*. Library of Congress Bicentennial, 1800–2000. www.loc.gov/flicc/bicen/tips.pdf

Fisher, Patricia H., and Pride, Marseille M. *Blueprint for Your Library Marketing Plan: A Guide to Help You Survive and Thrive*. ALA Editions, 2005. ISBN 9780838909096

Houseal, Nancy. *Plan It and They Will Come (Hopefully)*. SelectioNotes: Kentucky Department for Libraries and Archives, September/October 2002. www.kdla.ky.gov/onlinepubs/selectionotes/SeptOct2002/Feature502.htm

Meskauskas, Debora. *Planning Special Events: Blueprint for Success*. Friends and Foundations of California Libraries. www.librarysupport.net/librarylovers/eventips.html

O'Keefe, Steve. *Complete Guide to Internet Publicity: Creating and Launching Successful Online Campaigns.* John Wiley, 2002. ISBN 9780471105800

Wagner, Pat. "Designing Promo Materials That Are Legible." *MLS: Marketing Library Services*, v. 20, no. 2, March–April 2006, pp. 1, 4–5.

Web & Graphic Design Libraries. Web and graphic design tips, articles, and software at www.design-lib.com

Wolfe, Lisa A. *Library Public Relations, Promotions, and Communications: A How-To-Do-It Manual for Librarians.* 2nd ed. Neal-Schuman, 2005. ISBN 9781555704711

PART II:
AN INTERNATIONAL PERSPECTIVE

Storytelling in Libraries and Schools in the United Kingdom and the Republic of Ireland

BY PATRICK RYAN

Patrick Ryan was born and raised in Springfield, Illinois, the eldest of six children of Irish/German parentage. He and I met in the early 1980s when I was teaching at the University of Chicago Graduate Library School. Pat served as a student assistant at a conference I presented on Midwestern Folklore. Our paths crossed at local storytelling events, but Pat and I got to know each other really well when he and Beth Horner worked as my research assistants for The Illustrator as Storyteller Conference, sponsored by a grant from the National Endowment for the Arts, in 1994–1995. At that time Pat was teaching fourth grade at St. Thomas Apostle Elementary School in Chicago (previously he had taught third and fifth grades at the University of Chicago Laboratory School). I vividly recall the day this ebullient young man strode into my office and announced that he had just cleared out his files and was leaving to teach at an international school in London for two years. Pat had taken a summer course in folklore at Bretton Hall College in Yorkshire in 1979 and had learned to do field work. Summers when he wasn't teaching in Illinois he returned to collect stories and visit with storytellers and folk music friends, so England was familiar territory. Pat taught at the international school for five years and by then "England was home." He now lives in London and can be reached at pryan@glam.ac.uk.

Pat is a professional storyteller and a part-time postdoctoral research fellow at the George Ewart Evans Storytelling Centre at the University of Glamorgan, Cardiff, where he earned his Ph.D. in 2004. Over the years we would get together when he was in the USA and once in London. Pat got to know my elderly mother and my friends, who eagerly looked forward to his visits to Point Pleasant. He even got to meet my Welsh cousin living in Pontypridd! As my mother once exclaimed, "Everyone should have a Patrick in their life!" Pat has presented workshops at the National Storytelling Network annual conference and been a guest storyteller at many storytelling festivals, including the annual NSN Festival. He has given storytelling workshops not only in the USA and the UK, but in several European countries, Hong Kong, and Australia. He is the author of Shakespeare's Storybook: Folk Tales that Inspired the Bard *(Barefoot, 2006) and numerous articles for professional journals.*

I invited Pat to write a chapter in this fourth edition of Storytelling: Art and Technique *because I thought his work in the United Kingdom and the Republic of Ireland would be of interest to American storytellers. Pat presents an overview of storytelling in modern Britain and describes notable projects in which he and his colleagues were involved. It is my hope that storytellers, librarians, and teachers in the USA will be inspired to adapt some of the ideas presented here, especially the* Kick into Reading *program, working with football (soccer) teams and libraries, as a way to get sports-minded kids into books and reading.*
　　　　—Ellin Greene

IN BRITAIN AND IRELAND storytelling in libraries and schools since the end of the nineteenth century has followed a trajectory similar to that in America. Marie Shedlock's and her peers' impact upon the first children's librarians in the United Kingdom inspired later librarian-storytellers, who continued developing storytelling for all ages in libraries, schools, and other venues. The interaction between library and school storytellers and professional storytellers continues to this day.

HISTORICAL BACKGROUND

STORYTELLING IN LIBRARIES—MAIN ROOTS OF THE BRITISH REVIVAL

In 1921 Eileen Colwell (1904–2002) was one of the first university-trained children's librarians and led the development of children's library services, with storytelling a key element from the start. Colwell's story hours, book talks, library clubs, and children's book groups were models of good practice, and her work with the Youth Libraries Group (YLG) provided training and raised standards of storytelling.[1] This eventually led to her telling and advising on storytelling for BBC radio in the 1940s and 1950s and television in the 1960s. Colwell collaborated with the poet laureate John Masefield, who dreamed of establishing a storytelling festival and storytelling houses across the country, which he described in *So Long to Learn, Chapters of an Autobiography.*[2] This inspired revival English storytellers such as Ben Haggarty and groups such as the Company of Storytellers and Common Lore, who were prime movers in establishing platform storytelling and storytelling festivals in 1980s England.

Colwell influenced Grace Hallworth, who founded the first children's library in her native Trinidad before settling as children's librarian for Hertfordshire. Hallworth took up much of Colwell's work in the YLG. Her study visits to libraries in New York and Toronto also inspired her library work and storytelling. Colwell's and Hallworth's publications popularized traditional stories, influencing other librarian-, teacher- and emergent revival storytellers.[3] Hallworth was keen to develop children's abilities to tell stories, emphasizing story *sharing* sessions above story*telling* performances, something she continues to do in retirement in Tobago.

In the 1970s Janet Hill, a librarian based in Lambeth, an inner-city neighborhood in London, pioneered taking storytelling out of libraries into public venues such as parks, recreation centers, and sports clubs (and in Hertfordshire, librarians adapted this idea with storytelling on canal boats). The diverse ethnic population in Lambeth also inspired multicultural programs with story content from traditions originating outside Britain and the recruitment of storytellers from various backgrounds. These programs brought storytelling to wider audiences, attracting children and families not usually drawn to reading and libraries. Many now-prominent professional storytellers in England first worked on Hill's summer storytelling projects. Her book *Children Are People, The Librarian in the Community*[4] described her philosophy and programs. Inspired by this, as well as by Colwell and Hallworth, Liz Weir, children's librarian for Belfast during the height of the recent Troubles, sent teams of librarian storytellers to community centers, parks, and sport and recreation centers every summer so that all children in a divided community not only continued being served by libraries, but were also brought together. Her program was reported in the National Association for the Preservation and Perpetuation of Storytelling's *Yarnspinner* newsletters, bringing many American tellers, myself included, in contact with Weir and the developing Irish storytelling scene.

ARTS CENTERS AND EXPERIMENTAL THEATER—OTHER 'ROOTS' TO THE BRITISH REVIVAL OF STORYTELLING

Librarian-storytellers contributed to the "storytelling revival" in Britain and Ireland throughout the twentieth century. However, to understand contemporary storytelling in these islands, one must also acknowledge theater influences—especially subsidized national theater, educational drama companies, and experimental theater.[5] Groups such as the Welfare State and Common Lore, one a political-community drama group, the second a theatre-in-education group, and arts centers such as the Netherbow Centre in Edinburgh (now the Scottish Storytelling Centre) and the Verbal Arts Centre in Derry, which each supported the development and exploration of traditional and written cultures of Scotland and northwestern Ireland respectively, have conducted various storytelling projects over recent decades. Some of the most experienced professional storytellers arose from these and similar organizations. Their work has been replicated, adapted, or expanded in response to changes in education, library management, and social and cultural developments such as immigration, de-industrialization, and deprivation.

THE INFLUENCE OF EDUCATIONAL AND GOVERNMENT ARTS POLICIES IN THE UK AND IRELAND

One also has to acknowledge influential educational and government arts policies on contemporary British and Irish storytelling. Mandates regarding literacy, multiculturalism, disaffected youth, and communities blighted by recession and post-industrialization provided arts organizations and individual storytellers and other artists with opportunities to address these concerns, both within and outside of formal education. Rather than single performances or one-day residencies, policy initiatives and funding encouraged long-term residencies with storytellers delivering several sessions to the same group over a specific period. These programs developed participants' skills, confidence and self-esteem, their sense of identity and/or community, and other social aims.

NATIONAL ORACY PROJECT AND THE NATIONAL CURRICULUM

In the 1980s the National Oracy Project (NOP) explored the importance of speaking and listening in writing and reading, for all curriculum subjects, not just in English. (The term "oracy" was coined in the 1960s as an equivalent to "literacy" and "numeracy," emphasizing that speaking and listening are also key skills.) The NOP's experimental projects included storytelling performances, workshops, and residencies that established practices that are still followed today. The NOP analyzed how initiatives with storytellers, dramatists, and writers in schools affected children's speaking and listening. It also developed oracy strategies across all curriculum subjects, setting models of good practice for academics, teacher trainers, and teachers. The acknowledged importance of speaking and listening arising from the NOP, as well as international research, encouraged teachers to tell stories and get students telling. It also prompted schools to use storytellers more.

Much of this was incorporated in a new national curriculum developed in the late 1980s for England and Wales, and a common curriculum for Northern Ireland. (The four national regions have distinctly different education systems and legislation.) In the English subject curriculum emphasis was placed on speaking and listening, with oral exams in English and foreign languages mandated for secondary school leaving qualifications. In the late 1990s a National Literacy Strategy, a more prescriptive English curriculum, was introduced in English primary schools. Over the same period, the Republic of Ireland also saw a new national curriculum providing opportunities to integrate storytelling. Less restrictive than that of the United Kingdom, it is predisposed to using "real books" and "oracy" to teach literacy, and includes oral examinations in English, Irish, and foreign languages for secondary school leaving certifications.

ARTS COUNCILS, STORYTELLING ORGANIZATIONS, AND OTHER AGENCIES

The arts councils of England, Wales, Scotland, Northern Ireland, and the Republic of Ireland all run writers-in-schools programs, and some jurisdictions run programs such as writers-in-libraries and writers-in-prisons. The programs vary, but councils subsidize or pay entirely the cost of one-day and, in some cases, long-term residencies. They maintain databases listing verbal artists, including storytellers, who do performances and/or workshops.

After a successful National Year of Reading in 1998-1999 the National Literacy Trust was established and did much to increase reading activities for pleasure, including storytelling, outside the classroom. At the same time, the Irish Arts Council expanded its Writers-in-Schools program under the wing of Poetry Ireland; concurrently, Ireland witnessed massive investment in public libraries. This had positive impacts on storytelling and storytellers.

Coincidentally with arts council and organizational developments, in the 1990s storytelling organizations formed throughout Britain and Ireland (and also other European countries). The Society for Storytelling (SfS) in England and Wales, the Scottish Storytelling Forum (later the Scottish Storytelling Centre), and Storytellers of Ireland/*Aos Scéal Éireann*[6] brought storytellers and those interested in storytelling together for professional support, discussion and debate (often heated), training, networking, and to share expertise. These organizations were also partly established to influence arts councils' policies on funding or encourage councils to prioritize storytelling. Longer-running organizations promoting children's books, librarianship, teaching, literature, and creative writing also promoted storytelling in their specialist areas by having storytellers perform or lead workshops for conferences or member training. These organizations include the National Association of Writers in Education, the National Literacy Trust, the Reading Agency, the International Board of Books for Young People (IBBY) UK, Children's Books Ireland, Poetry Ireland Writers-in-Schools Scheme, the School Library Association, and the Youth Libraries Group.

Arts centers across the UK and Ireland started hosting regular storytelling events, long-term projects, and sometimes large festivals. Both professional and teacher-librarian storytellers were well placed for creating a wide variety of programs described as applied storytelling: storytelling practiced within educational or community contexts, rather than solely as entertainment. Details of these centers, organizations, and institutions are listed at the end of this chapter.

EXAMPLES OF NOTABLE STORYTELLING PROJECTS

Educational and arts policies, combined with a restructuring of Local Education Authorities (LEAs—i.e., school districts) gave schools greater freedom for spending budgets and networking with other professionals. Thus many developed partnerships with individual tellers and writers and with institutions providing verbal artists. This increase in long-term residencies required storytellers to find skills and material supporting unusual programs that were more than performances.

The following are projects I am most familiar with, either because I was involved or close colleagues were and we drew from each other's experiences. I should emphasize that this is a small sample of storytelling found throughout Britain and Ireland. Indeed, many European countries see similar levels and variety of storytelling activity. This limited list of British and Irish projects will, I hope, provide a useful overview. Readers can refer to websites and books for detailed reports on these and other projects.

NORTHERN IRELAND: THE VERBAL ARTS CENTRE AND YARNSPINNERS

The Verbal Arts Centre (VAC) was established by Sam Burnside, poet and educator, in 1992 in order to integrate verbal artists into the community. The VAC has placed poets, novelists, short-story writers, playwrights and dramatists, journalists, storytellers, stand-up comics, satirists, debating and public speaking societies, and creative writing and book groups as participants in projects in schools, libraries, old people's homes, hospitals, hospices, community centers, and sports clubs, and also in their specially designed center in a rebuilt Victorian school on the mediaeval Derry walls. Its projects, festivals, and public events brought new audiences to storytelling, often simultaneously integrating a divided community.

The VAC was aided by groundwork Liz Weir laid throughout the 1970s and 1980s, both with the summer storytelling program described above and her establishment of Yarnspinners clubs: storytelling nights for adults first held in the Linen Hall Library and later replicated in libraries and arts centers across Northern Ireland and the Republic of Ireland. She also ran Ulster Storytelling Festival at the Ulster Folk and Transport Museum, an open-air museum near Belfast. This was the first modern storytelling festival in all of Ireland, and one of the first in the UK. Weir left Belfast Libraries to become a full-time storyteller, and her work (as well as her reputation in libraries, the communities of Northern Ireland, and the BBC) was well established when the VAC opened. Immediately enlisted as VAC storyteller-in-residence, she did much, through the VAC and independently, to raise standards and expand uses of storytelling throughout Ireland.

The VAC rapidly built on this, with storytelling programs such as "Blue Horizon" (a residency in a community center for adults with mental disabilities), "Sharing Tales" (a cross-generational project with primary school children collecting and retelling stories learned from hospitalized senior citizens), and "To Shorten the Road," the first International Storytelling Festival in Ireland. The Irish festivals not only brought professional performers to adult audiences; a major component always included local and traditional storytellers, elders, and schoolchildren, making them qualitatively different from UK festivals.

Storytelling in Ireland—A Reawakening

In 1994 the VAC commissioned me to report on the state of storytelling throughout Ireland, with an eye to using this as a policy document guiding future work. The arts councils of Northern Ireland and the Republic of Ireland were conducting major reviews so as to re-prioritize projects and funding, and recognized that new, increasing storytelling activities deserved consideration. The VAC was seen as key to this review and to future arts council initiatives. This was the year that the ceasefire and peace process began, and hopes were that all-island policies, particularly in arts and culture, could support that process. Storytelling was an art form practiced and popular throughout all communities on both sides of the border.

The subsequent report, *Storytelling in Ireland—A Re-Awakening*,[7] published in early 1995, was disseminated to more than 500 key figures (many contributors to the study) and through a conference of "Celtic" practitioners from Scotland, Ireland, and Cornwall. The document influenced not only the VAC's direction but also that of newly formed organizations such as Storytellers of Ireland/*Aos Scéal Éireann* and the Scottish Storytelling Centre. Emphasis at the VAC very much focused on *processes* of creative verbal arts *within* community and educational contexts. As such, it provided inspiration for many applying storytelling in educational and community work.

Word in Action

The Department of Education for Northern Ireland (DENI) funded the Developing Schools Project (DSP) to support schools identified as "disadvantaged." Paddy Ward, English adviser for the Western Education and Library Board (the local education authority serving northwest and western regions of Northern Ireland, including the cities of Derry and Enniskillen) asked the VAC to administer a storytelling project, *The Developing Schools Storytelling Project: Word in Action*,[8] with DSP funds.

Six secondary schools took part across Derry, Strabane, and Omagh. Catholic and Protestant schools were involved. I was the resident teller, with contributions from Liz Weir and Billy Teare, and, to a lesser extent, visiting tellers Michael Wilson and Godfrey Duncan (aka TUUP: The Unprecedented Unorthodox Preacher) (both based in England). The project aimed to use storytelling to raise students' self-esteem and confidence, and to improve oracy across the curriculum. It was also intended to model new or different practices that teachers might adapt, so refreshing their own skills. The final objective was to impress administrators, school governors, and parents so that senior management continued supporting storytelling after core funding finished. Schools had a storyteller for six full days per term, for three terms (April 1997 through February 1998).

In the first term, most work was conducted through English Departments. Schools took different approaches as to how they used the storyteller. Some wanted to develop students' speaking and listening skills, others linked oracy work to creative writing or literature. Some produced short stories, poems, or reports, or created anthologies for younger readers. Others had students tell stories for invited primary school children. In the second and third terms, storytelling was used across all curricular subjects, particularly History, Geography, Religious Education, Science, Math, and Physical Education. Some stories brought topics to life (for example, legends relating to historical periods such as the Irish Famine, World War I, or the Siege of Derry). This proved immensely effective. One student reported:

> You know that story we had to make up in History class about the Famine? You said not to write it down, but I wrote it for English homework. I wrote six pages—I never wrote more than three pages before. And I got a B+. I never got a B before.[9]

And related to the same lesson, his English teacher informed us:

> I work with the History teacher, and do a reading and creative writing lesson based on what the boys have just learned about the Famine. For the first time, they didn't have to revise and look things up again. The boys had loads of facts at their fingertips, facts they remembered about the Irish Famine which they picked up from the storytelling.[10]

Other activities demonstrated thought processes and strategies through using riddles. Math teachers commented that "The storytelling has contributed to an awareness of the importance of logical thinking. Riddles and conundrums as input for number and algebra was excellent . . ."[11] Many stories shared themes regarding issues of fairness, equality, and universal values (such as religious beliefs, sportsmanship, and so on). All teachers and students reported that the storytelling developed students' self-esteem and confidence, having a major impact on learning. As Michael Wilson observed when participating toward the end of the project, not all schools were practicing storytelling to the same degree, but a "culture of storytelling" was definitely established within all.[12]

Listen Up!

In 2001 Paddy Ward again used DENI funding for the VAC to develop *Listen Up!*, a project built on ideas gleaned from *Word in Action* and incorporating primary schools as well. Rather than try and provide storytelling experience for every child in the school (which *Word in Action* attempted), *Listen Up!* focused on one class or small group of classes for twelve half-day visits over four to six weeks. Storytellers involved were mostly Liz Weir and myself, but in later years Billy Teare, Frances Quinn, Bernadette Layden, Sheila Quigley, and Joe Brennan also took part. Tellers told stories and used activities to teach the children how to remember and tell stories, create stories orally, and perform stories.

As before, schools chose different approaches. Some focused on creative and shared writing, others on performances to peers, younger students, or their families. There was an equal mix of Protestant and Catholic schools involved, though more primary schools than secondary took part. When *Listen Up!* ended in 2005, thirty schools had participated, including two special needs schools (a center for Belfast high school students excluded for challenging behavior, and a Belfast primary school for children with learning disabilities).

The aim to develop students' confidence and self-esteem was definitely achieved. Many teachers, and some secondary school students, reported that pupils involved saw their reading ages rise by 2.3 to 3.0 years on tests. Sadly, funding ran out, with no opportunity to set up a controlled study to validate this finding or evaluate the sustainability of the results. Two videos document the first two years of the scheme, and are used in conferences and training days.[13] The experience of *Listen Up!* suggests future research in the area of storytelling residencies and literacy would be worthwhile.

T3—Teachers Telling Tales

One criticism by Northern Ireland senior management, however, was that after storytelling residencies finished, teachers did not carry on storytelling and leading activities as they did when the storytellers worked beside them. This was disputed by participants, for often, unselfconsciously, teachers incorporated strategies such as story mapping, shared writing, and poetry raps in their work.

In light of this, the Esmeé Fairbairn Foundation provided funding for an experiment in teacher training, monitored and assessed by university academics. This became known as *T3—Teachers Telling Tales*. All the fourth year Bachelor of Education students at Saint Mary's and Stranmillis University Colleges and all PGCE (Post Graduate Certificate in Education) students at Ulster University (in short, around 400 trainee primary school teachers in Northern Ireland) were provided a twelve-hour course in storytelling, team-taught by Liz Weir and myself. Some were offered a practicum, where they observed other professional tellers and then went out in "teams" to tell stories in schools, youth clubs, and libraries, or so was the intention. The plan was to follow, in their first two years as full-time teachers, all these student teachers who attained positions in Northern Ireland, providing further training through verbal arts projects placed in their schools. It was hoped this would provide teachers with confidence to work with tellers and other artists as equal partners, and, even more, to incorporate storytelling as a regular part of their teaching style and methodology.

Unfortunately, due to the complexity of the plan, combined with administrative problems and a major reorganization of the education and library systems of Northern Ireland, it proved too difficult to carry out *T3* as originally envisaged. Response from teacher training institutions, as well as from the student teachers, indicated a need for such courses being integral to teacher training. The culture of storytelling remains strong in Northern Ireland, and tellers working there regularly witness teachers who took part in *T3* and other programs demonstrating that they incorporate storytelling in teaching.

ENGLAND: UNUSUAL STORYTELLING PARTNERSHIPS

The proximity and the crossover of storytellers in Ireland and the UK meant that programs cross-fertilized each other. So successful was *Word in Action* that it was adapted for four secondary schools in inner London as *Steps to Storytelling*. Inno Sorsi, Arti Prashar, and I delivered the program, using storytelling to develop oracy across the curriculum in inner-city schools. This was not the first long-term residency I did in England. In the early 1990s the Wirral School Library service, near Liverpool, had writers—Brian Jaques and Levi Tafari—and myself working for two or three half-days in ten primary schools. Storytelling workshops preceded the writers' visits, and work concluded with a display of children's writing at a festival in the town hall. Similar residencies in secondary and primary schools developed throughout the 1990s.

Expanding the Frame

In 1998 the National Literacy Strategy, referred to as the Literacy Hour, was implemented in England's primary schools. (Other parts of the United Kingdom developed separate strategies to teach reading.) This prescriptive approach was controversial, but did include folktales, fairy tales, myths, and legends in each grade. A pilot project, "Expanding the Frame," with storytellers Helen East, Kevin Graal, Inno Sorsy, and me, ran in seven schools across London. The storytellers developed stories, lesson plans, materials, and activities for Literacy Hours over four weeks. We delivered initial literacy hours for four weeks, with teachers observing and assisting. The teachers then carried out our lesson plans between visits. The report and video arising from this supported teachers wishing to incorporate oracy, and storytelling, in the Literacy Hour.

Read One Tell One Share One

The new Labour government in 1997 was elected on a strongly pro-education platform and immediately initiated new education programs, with emphasis on early childhood literacy. Kensington and Chelsea Libraries in London asked me to run "Read One Tell One Share One," a course for parents, grandparents, and childcare workers, teaching how to tell and read stories to young children. Library staff team-taught with me, introducing participants to library services for families. We found diverse responses, all positive and revealing. The smallest branch library saw the largest demand for the program, and in Brompton (a neighborhood full of diplomats and wealthy families), almost all participants were nannies, au pairs, childcare givers, baby sitters, and governesses.

One father claimed storytelling was brilliant, and wished someone had suggested it before; he reported that his two-year-old used to resist sleep, but now that he told the toddler a story every night he went straight to sleep through the night. We were happy taking credit for storytelling, but assured him and other parents that it was also about routines and giving children a sense of security through special attention. One mother said she loved sharing picture books with her son but was afraid to: she was dyslexic and so made up stories from pictures. We told her that was absolutely fine, but she still worried. She was concerned, fearing that her son, coming across these books at school, would get into trouble if he told the teacher the books were "wrong," being different from his mother's "readings." We suggested she inform the teacher of what she did, along with her reasons, explaining that in doing so she would help her child by giving the child and teacher extra support. We assured her that teachers were under an obligation of confidentiality, which the parents didn't realize.

Parents also were surprised to learn of the range of library services. They didn't know these were free, that librarians had shelves with specialist material for parental advice on issues such as bereavement, family breakup, illnesses, and the like, and that the library had citizen advice services regarding benefits, advocacy, and so on. One parent was so taken with this news that she marched in a huge troupe of her extended family to sign up for library cards *en masse.* Storytelling, therefore, brought a much higher return to libraries than had been envisaged. Programs similar to Read One Tell One Share One have now run in other libraries.

Prisons and Young Offenders Units

Librarians and arts councils have also been instrumental in bringing storytellers and writers into prisons, most often with storytelling workshops encouraging incarcerated fathers and grandfathers to read, tell or make up stories, and record these on video or audio cassette, so they maintain regular contact with their children. The fathers are also encouraged to tell and read to their children on family visiting days.[14]

Some storytelling-in-prison is purely for needed entertainment, but more often it links to education: literacy, creative writing, or the mentioned parenting course. Young Offender Units have also incorporated storytelling, poetry readings, writers' visits, book groups, and creative writing workshops to support learning and social development. "Voyage into Books" was a multi-platform program run by East and West Sussex Libraries for the National Year of Reading. Several projects used tellers and/or writers to serve disadvantaged groups: minority communities, young offenders, single and teen-aged mothers, and immigrants and asylum seekers. A stand-up comedian, performance poet, and I worked with young offenders over three weeks in Lewes prison. We got the young men (mostly fourteen to twenty years of age) to create stories and poems and perform them.

This was in one of the oldest Victorian prisons in the UK, holding adult prisoners in a separate wing. Its age and shortage of resources caused challenges. Storytelling workshops were scheduled for the same period when the young men could access the gym for physical training and play (for safety reasons, they couldn't share facilities with adult offenders). Storytelling, comedy, and poetry proved so popular that the boys opted out of PE (although we verbal artists all pointed out to organizers that this was cruelly unfair to young men who, incarcerated for whatever reasons, still needed physical activity). The boys were particularly interested in ghost stories, and we explored the fact that, more than content, how a story is told makes it scary. After working on this, guards reported the next morning that the young men spent all night telling scary stories, scaring themselves so much they asked that lights be kept on; some disadvantages of a gothic Victorian prison proved advantageous to storytelling. When gently teased and asked if this was true, the boys grudgingly admitted it but proudly pointed out the "screws" (guards) were even more scared and it was their idea to keep the lights on.

Kick into Reading

Libraries were encouraged to make unusual partnerships during the National Year of Reading; many teamed up with local professional sports teams, especially football (soccer), basketball, and ice hockey. The National Literacy Trust (NLT) built upon this with Reading the Game, an initiative using sports figures to promote reading by all ages.

F I G U R E   21. *Paul Thompson, Arsenal Football Club community coach, holds the rapt attention of his young listeners at a Kick into Reading program at Islington Libraries as fellow community coach Samir Singh (center) and storyteller Pat Ryan (far right) look on. Irfan Master, photographer. Courtesy of the National Literacy Trust and the Arsenal Football Club, Islington, North London.*

One library and football club partnership led to an extremely successful program that has become one of the most effective and unusual storytelling projects in England. Oxfordshire Libraries teamed up with Oxford United Football Club, and invited me to an event to celebrate the project in 2001. Coaches and academy players (apprentice footballers) had done shared reading with local schoolchildren. For the celebration, the children heard Oxford United footballers reading and me telling stories.

Peter Rhoades-Brown, former Chelsea player and Oxford United's coach responsible for community work, and I enjoyed working together and suggested that librarians re-run the scheme. This they did, with Rhoades-Brown and I telling stories to rural schools visiting small branch libraries.[15] Rhoades-Brown recommended that other soccer clubs could and should do the project. Kick into Reading (KiR) became an ongoing program. The NLT took it over and coordinated KiR across London, and then England. To date twenty-two clubs have taken part (many four or five times) and we've reached more than 24,000 children and thousands of adults in the past six years.[16]

KiR happens over three to four weeks in a local soccer club and library service. Two training days are provided with mostly football-in-the-community coaches who teach soccer taking part, but academy players (apprentices) and first team players often work with us, meaning that from ten to fifteen club members are involved. Fifteen storytelling sessions over five days are scheduled in branch libraries, with thirty to sixty children aged eight to eleven attending. Librarians or literacy officers recruit schools, targeting those seldom using the library, with low literacy test scores, or in socially disadvantaged areas. Two to five footballers come with the storyteller for each story time, and take it in turn to tell or read traditional and personal stories, picture books and football poems, riddles, and word play and singing games. There is time for question and answers and to collect autographs and take pictures. Library staff distribute membership forms and information on library activities; footballers often give the children signed posters or club memorabilia to take with them. The children, and parents and siblings, are invited back to the club on a Saturday, for another storytime, followed by tours of the grounds (including changing rooms, VIP suites, and training facilities), a meeting with some star players, and free tickets to that day's match.

KiR aims to provide positive role models for children, especially male role models for boys, to encourage reading and library use, although women coaches and players have always taken part. A hundred percent of the teachers report that after KiR, children do more independent reading, and librarians report that 73 percent of the children who did not belong to the library join afterward, with a noticeable 25 percent increase in library use by all children doing KiR compared with those who do not take part. But clubs, coaches, players, and families all report positive outcomes that we did not anticipate when the program began. These include:

- Coaches telling stories and using storytelling activities on their own initiative during coaching sessions, for summer programs and holiday camps, and on classroom visits
- Players finding more confidence for public speaking, and a few exploring teaching as an alternative to their soccer career when that ends
- Academy players showing improvement in their studies and exams, particularly in English and communication
- An improved image of footballers and the soccer club in the community
- More families attending matches, and more children signing up for soccer schools and coaching sessions

Not only has KiR seen increased library membership and use by children: parents and siblings and teachers and football club staff have also used libraries more. Coaches and footballers have been known to sign up to or renew library membership in front of the children! Library staff, educators, and sports people have developed new social and professional networks that support all their work and strengthen the community. Jim Sells, who manages KiR for the National Literacy Trust, maintains that real literacy arises and thrives in strong, well-socially networked communities and that programs like this help create or strengthen those networks.

An example of how coaches and footballers take on traditional stories and wordplay, quickly adapting them to their own style, was provided by Norwich City Football Club. When training the players and coaches I often use Nancy Schimmel's "Just Enough to Make a Story," a Yiddish folktale, to demonstrate how memories are stories and become stories, and I then do an exercise where they share memories of things that have happened to them. Many develop these memory stories into narratives they can perform at KiR story times, as they commonly relate funny incidents when they played soccer as lads, to which the children relate easily. I then present Simms Taback's *Joseph Had a Little Overcoat* as a picture book they might read aloud, and explain they may retell the folktale or read aloud the picture book. One coach reworked the story into a football tale:

> Glenn Roeder, the manager for Norwich City Football Club, decided the team wasn't playing so well. They needed a bit of motivation, a morale booster. So he decided what was wanted was a new kit. So he went down the back lanes of old Norwich and found a proper tailor, and explained he wanted a whole new uniform for all the players.

This tailor gladly took the job on, being a big Canaries (team's nick-name) fan, and took the money Glenn Roeder gave him to go out and buy loads of green cloth and loads of yellow cloth, the colors of Norwich City Football Club. He brought it back to the shop and laid it out and cut it and stitched and sewed and sewed and stitched and made a whole bunch of green and yellow shirts with the Norwich badge on them.

When he presented these to the team they were delighted and proud. They wore the shirts in every match. And they played really well. That season, the team went up to the top of the league!

But you know what football kit is like when you wear it every game for a whole season. It gets faded and stained. So Glenn Roeder had a look at it, thought about how it had inspired the players, and went back to the tailor to ask him if he had any more of that green and yellow cloth to make new kit for the next season.

Well, the tailor didn't have so much of the cloth left. There wasn't enough to make shirts. But there was just enough to make new shorts! He took the cloth he had left and laid it out and cut it and stitched and sewed and sewed and stitched and made a whole bunch of green and yellow shorts.

When he presented these to the team they were delighted and excited. They wore the shorts in every match. And they played really well. That season, the team was promoted to a new league!

But you know what football kit is like when you wear it every game for a whole season. The shorts were all faded and stained. So Glenn Roeder had a look, saw this, thought about how the uniform had inspired the players, and went back to the tailor to ask him if he had any more of that green and yellow cloth to make new kit for the next season.

Well, the tailor hardly had any of that cloth left. There wasn't enough to make shorts. But there was just enough to make new socks! So he took the wee bit of gold and yellow material he had, laid it out and cut it and stitched and sewed and sewed and stitched and made a whole bunch of green and yel-low socks.

When he presented these to the team they were so pleased. They wore the socks in every match, played really well. That season, they won the championship!

But you know how after a whole season football kit gets faded and stained. So Glenn Roeder went back to the tailor to ask if he had any more green and yellow cloth to make new kit.

"Sorry, I haven't," the tailor told him. "You'll have to give me money to buy more material. But you know, I've so enjoyed talking to you and the players and hearing all they have to tell me, and following all the matches that I've got something else I've made for you."

And he pulled out a book, with all the stories about Norwich Football Club that the manager and players had told him, and stories made of all his own memories about Norwich City Football Club, and it even had a green and yellow cover on the book! And the book that he made is right here.

(*And the coach pulls out a copy of* One Hundred Years of Norwich City Football Club *to show the children.*)

This project has revealed many interesting quirks in teaching and learning. Early on, Peter Rhoades-Brown observed:

> Kids, I love watching your faces when you're listening to the stories. I can see you're really into the story, thinking about what just happened, guessing what's going to come next, you're working it all out in your head. It's the same as when you're playing football: you're thinking ahead, about where the ball is, where it's going, where you are, where the other players are, remembering what's happened, thinking what's coming next. You're using the same part of the brain, same part of the imagination. Listening to stories, reading, playing football, it's all the same, really, all using the same parts of the brain.[17]

This revelation, that thought processes for playing or watching sport, telling and listening to a story, and reading a story are the same, supports studies in cognition and neurology, and has often been confirmed by children's responses to KiR story times. Coaches and footballers are refreshingly blunt when answering children's questions: when asked why they're telling stories instead of playing football, one player said it was because boys don't read and so he was there to convince them to do so. The boys took great offense and started listing all they had recently read. The teacher sheepishly admitted afterward that she wasn't aware those boys were reading independently, nor knew of their reading material. Clearly, classroom measurements of literacy still need revision, to display what the children truly can and, most likely, prefer to read.

In another session a coach spoke about the special language sports commentators use when talking about football, and two eight-year-old boys, who were so excited by having someone from their local club in the same room that they scrambled to the front of the group, proclaimed excitedly that sports journalists use lots of alliteration and similes. The coach challenged them to prove this, and the boys gave excellent examples, all describing football events. The teacher nearly fell off her chair, and acknowledged she didn't think the boys had absorbed that English lesson, but she had never offered them the chance to use their favorite topic in their examples of descriptive language.

Another exciting phenomenon has been girls displaying more football knowledge than boys. In quizzes and word games in the KiR story hour, they win hands down regarding football trivia. Boys (and teachers) have been suitably impressed by the girls' knowledge and enthusiasm. There are plans to expand KiR with more football clubs, as well as have rugby, cricket, and Olympic sports such as wrestling and boxing doing similar work. There are requests to establish KiR in other parts of the UK, and in other countries, in all cases with football and other popular sports.

Storytelling in Museums, Galleries, and Historic and Nature Sites

Historical and archaeological sites, nature reserves, parks, museums, and art galleries all feature storytelling. Some have staff trained to tell stories to visitors, while others engage storytellers-in-residence to perform and/ or to train staff. Stories might range from local ghost stories and historical legends, to creation myths, stories about the environment, and biographical tales about great personages or common folk associated with the locale. The British and Victoria and Albert Museums engage storytellers from ethnic traditions to tell tales relating to exhibits. Tate Britain and Tate Modern regularly host children's literature conferences and festivals, asking writers and tellers to develop and perform material relating to their displays: tellings of classical myths, as depicted by Turner, legends and fairy tales, represented by the Pre-Raphaelites, and biographical stories relating to nineteenth- and twentieth-century artists and their works. London Transport Museum and Greenwich Heritage Centre have storytellers-in-residence to research and bring to life local history and ghost stories, and the National Trust, which owns and maintains many historic country houses (including Beatrix Potter's Lake District home) employ tellers to bring to life the history and stories relating to their estates.

One unique project in 1995 was at Croydon Clocktower, a library, gallery, and arts center completely modernized with award-winning architecture in a rebuilt Victorian library (the first in Britain with a library designed and purposely built for children). Their first art exhibition was "Cock and Bull Stories: A Picasso Bestiary." This brought together a huge range of Picasso's oeuvre—paintings, prints, ceramics, sculpture, and drawings— from his estate and various institutions' collections. These were categorized not by period or medium, but by animal groups as they all depicted creatures. Birds, Dogs, Cats, Mythical Beasts, Insects, Horses, Cattle and Apes all were featured.

Joan Barr and I were engaged to develop stories, and Terry Mann, a musician and composer, was commissioned to create music for the exhibition. Our brief was to create performance pieces inspired by the art, by aspects of Picasso's life that inspired particular works, or by traditional myths that inspired him. For example, one day Picasso's son was playing with his toy cars in the studio while his father worked. Inspired, Picasso took two metal cars, undersides together, to form a baboon's head; a round earthenware pot became the baboon's body; and the car's curving steel spring formed her backbone and long tail. The rest of her body and the figure of her baby were modeled from clay, and the whole piece was cast in bronze. The result was "Baboon and Young," Picasso's playful image of mother. His minotaurs, basilisks, and fabulous beasts gave opportunities to relate mythology. We provided special performances for the opening and during the exhibition's run. But mostly we visited schools, sharing the stories and leading workshops prior to students visiting the exhibition. We introduced Picasso, his life, and his work through stories. An audio recording of the stories and music was produced to accompany the exhibition.

SUMMARY

This small representation of storytelling projects is only a glimpse of the vast array across the UK and Ireland, and indeed, Europe. The George Ewart Evans Centre for Storytelling at the University of Glamorgan in Wales, the Scottish Storytelling Centre, and other universities across England and Scotland have begun to formalize storytelling training. They also conduct rigorous academic research into performance and applied storytelling. This bodes well for future developments in library and school storytelling.

REFERENCES

1. Eileen Colwell, *How I Became a Librarian* (Nelson, 1956).
2. Mary Medlicott and Mary Steele, *Eileen Colwell: An Excellent Guide, Writings in Celebration* (Daylight Press, for the Society for Storytelling, 1999) and *Once Upon a Time . . . Memories of An Edwardian Childhood* (privately published, 1998).
3. John Masefield, *So Long to Learn, Chapters of an Autobiography* (Heinemann, 1952) pp. 231–237. Also see Philip W. Errington, "The Law of My Being: John Masefield, Eileen Colwell and Storytelling," in *Eileen Colwell: An Excellent Guide, Writings in Celebration*, ed. Mary Medlicott and Mary Steele (Daylight Press, for the Society for Storytelling, 1999).
4. Eileen Colwell, *Storytelling* (The Bodley Head, 1980; new ed. The Thimble Press, 1991). Also see Grace Hallworth and Julia Marriage, *Stories to Read and Tell* (National Book League, 1978), Grace Hallworth, *Listen to This Story: Tales from the West Indies* (Methuen, 1977), *Mouth Open, Story Jump Out* (Methuen, 1984), and *Cric Crac: A Collection of West Indian Stories* (Heinemann, 1990).
5. Janet Hill, *Children Are People, The Librarian in the Community* (Hamish Hamilton, 1973).
6. Michael Wilson, *Storytelling and Theatre* (Palgrave Macmillan, 2006), pp. 13–17.
7. Society for Storytelling, PO Box 2344, Reading, RG6 7FG, England; www.sfs.org.uk. The Scottish Storytelling Centre, 43-45 High St., Old Town, Edinburgh, EH1 1SR, Scotland. www.scottishstorytellingcentre.co.uk. Storytellers of Ireland/Aos Scéal Éireann, www.storytellersofireland.org.
8. Patrick Ryan, *Storytelling in Ireland, A Re-Awakening* (Verbal Arts Centre, 1995).
9. Patrick Ryan, *Word in Action, A Report on the Developing Schools Project Storytelling Residency* (Verbal Arts Centre, 1998).
10. Ibid., p. 11.
11. Ibid., p. 11.
12. Ibid., p. 11.
13. Michael Wilson, *Storytelling and Theatre* (Palgrave Macmillan, 2006), pp. 101–103.

14. *Listen Up!* and *Listen Up! 2*, The Verbal Arts Centre and the Nerve Centre, Western Education and Library Board, Derry-Londonderry, Northern Ireland, 2001 and 2002.

15. Patrick Ryan, "Secure Storytelling—Storytelling in Prisons and Young Offenders' Units," *All Our Children: Library Services to Children at Risk*, ed. Anne Marley (YLG publication).

16. Patrick Ryan, "A Beautiful Game, Oral Narrative and Soccer, *Children's Literature and Education* (vol. 33, no. 2, June 2002): 149–163.

17. *The Kick into Reading Story—So Far* DVD documenting project (National Literacy Trust, 2007); http://www.literacytrust.org.uk/Football/index.html.

18. Patrick Ryan, personal interview with Peter Rhoades-Brown, 2003.

WEB RESOURCES

The Book Trust
www.booktrust.org.uk

Children's Books Ireland
www.childrensbooksireland.com/

The George Ewart Evans Centre for Storytelling
http://storytelling.research.glam.ac.uk/

La Maison des Contes et des Histoires
www.contes-histoires.net

La Maison du Conte de Bruxelles
www.lamaisonducontedebruxelles.be

The National Association for Literature Development
www.e-latest.org.uk/

National Association of Writers in Education
www.nawe.co.uk

The National Centre for Research in Children's Literature
www.roehampton.ac.uk/researchcentres/ncrcl

National Literacy Trust
www.literacytrust.org.uk

Poetry Ireland, Writers in Schools
www.poetryireland.ie/education/writers-in-schools.html

The Reading Agency
www.readingagency.org.uk

School Library Association
www.sla.org.uk

The Scottish Storytelling Centre
www.scottishstorytellingcentre.co.uk

Seven Stories, the Centre for Children's Books
www.sevenstories.org.uk

Society for Storytelling
www.sfs.org.uk

Storytellers of Ireland/Aos Scéal Éireann
www.storytellersofireland.org

Youth Libraries Group of the Chartered Institute of Library and Information Professionals
http://www.cilip.org.uk/specialinterestgroups/bysubject/youth

How Do You Say "Storytelling" in Chinese?

Shuo Shu (Shuo—to Talk/to Tell; Shu—Book)

BY JUDITH HEINEMAN

IN 2008 MARCIA K. DARTLEY, director, People to People Citizen Ambassador Programs, and Nancy Kavanaugh, former executive director of the National Storytelling Network, invited me to serve on the Storytelling Delegation to China. Nancy was to lead the group, but unfortunately she took a nasty fall just prior to the trip and had to cancel. I, too, was unable to serve as a delegate as I was anticipating total knee replacement and not up to such a vigorous trip. With the Summer Olympics on everyone's mind and the keen interest by Americans in China and Chinese culture I asked if another delegate would be willing to write a short report for the fourth edition of *Storytelling: Art and Technique*. In the report that follows, Judith Heineman addresses the topics suggested by Kavanaugh as the designated delegation leader:

- What are the means of collecting Chinese folk stories that are only in the oral tradition?
- How do Chinese folktales mirror the customs, fears, prejudices and dreams of the Chinese people?
- What has been the role of the storyteller throughout Chinese history?
- Are Chinese schools teaching children the traditional stories? At the university level, are there programs in Chinese folklore?

Judith also includes a delightful retelling of a Chinese love story relating to food, "Across the Bridge Noodles" (Guo Qiao Mi Xian).

Judith Heineman is a professional storyteller, co-founder of the Chicago Storytelling Guild, an Illinois Humanities Council "Road" Scholar, and an Illinois ArtsTour Artist. She is founder and producer of the Mohegan Colony Storytelling Festival held each summer in Crompond, New York.

Judith also is the producer of Tellabration, Chicago, Illinois, held annually on the Sunday before Thanksgiving in Hyde Park. For more information about Judith, visit http://www.storytelling.org/heineman.

—Ellin Greene

■

In China, there is a story or legend lurking behind every living thing and inanimate object. The People to People Ambassadors Program, founded in 1956 by President Eisenhower, promises professionals programs that "join common interests in uncommon places . . . through journeys that enrich the world." My trip to China in April 2008 on a Storytelling Delegation more than fulfilled this promise.

—*Judith Heineman*

THE DELEGATION CONSISTED OF TEN storytelling professionals from across the United States and four guests. Delegates met with professors, folklorists, publishers of *Story Press* magazine, retirees, and school children in Beijing, Shanghai, and rural Guiyang.

Lihui Yang, professor of folklore and mythology, Institute of Folklore and Cultural Anthropology at Beijing Normal University, presented an overview of storytelling in China, from its development in ancient China to its present-day Story Villages.

Storytelling became popular in the warring states era (475–221 B.C.). Stories, especially fables, were widely used for persuading, debating, and amusing listeners. Stories were often spoken and sung in combination, as in chanting. Gradually they became prose. During the Song period (906—1280 A.D.) stories became a major form of entertainment in city life. The professional storytellers told at temples, entertainment booths, pubs, fairs, tea houses, and in private homes of the leisure class and at court.

Professor Lihui, author of *Handbook of Chinese Mythology* (Oxford University Press), is the first woman to receive a Ph.D. in folklore in China. Professor Lihui directed the Story Village Project that was part of a twenty-year national story-collecting effort carried out by the China Folk Literature and Art Society. More than two million stories and three million folk songs have been collected.

Professor Lihui mentioned Luo Chengshuang, born in 1944, as one of the ten greatest storytellers in China. Chengshuang knows 400 stories and 600 folk songs. From 1966 to 1976 he was not allowed to tell stories or to sing folksongs because of the Cultural Revolution. Storytelling was revived after 1980, and more attention was paid to traditional culture. The Zao Tao Ji Cheng Project, begun in 1984, required local intellectuals to gather stories. In Hebei province, in the Wudang mountains, lies a Story Village.

In 1986 the Chinese government chose this village to develop as a tourist attraction. The village had 876 people: 185 knew 20 stories, 35 knew 50, 11 knew 100, 200 knew 8, 400 knew 1. Stories were told at conventional times: winter nights, bedtime, rainy days, funerals, neighbors gathering after a day's work, farmers working in the fields. Stories were used to educate children and to perpetuate story tradition. In 1990 a national story contest was organized that generated a lot of press coverage, and visitors and officials came to hear these storytellers. As a result, pride and respect for these villagers emerged. Their economy strengthened and they created roads to the outside world. In 1998 Chengshuang competed in the national story contest against the best storytellers in China and won. It was the most important event in his life. Chengshuang became a national treasure. Today his "golden time" is over and he feels a little lost, according to Professor Lihui. Other Story Villages have been created and fewer visitors come to see him.

At a meeting in Beijing, Professor Liu Kuili, president of the China Folklore Society, told the delegates that for ten years starting in 1986 researchers collected stories from 3,000 counties, mostly in rural areas where farmers have more time to communicate. They have collected 25,000 volumes of stories. Professor Kang Li, fellow member of the China Folklore Society, said there are two types of research going on: vertical and horizontal. Vertical research looks at the historicity of a story. Horizontal research studies different versions of the same story. Scholars look at a very old story—for instance, one that originated a thousand years ago—and research how and why the story changed over time and what social problems are reflected in the story. They would like to know why the story is told in a particular geographical area of China.

We asked whether Chinese storytellers tell campus ghost stories and if there is thought to be value in it. We were told that the researchers do not judge whether the value of a story is good or bad— "It is not for us to judge, we make no changes." They try to get the story down verbatim. Collecting is the only task at present. When they find a storyteller who knows more than a thousand stories, he or she becomes the subject of research.

The epic was developed orally, and the researchers are trying to find young people to carry it on. Storytelling is most active in rural areas. For example, there is a village where all the inhabitants come from the same original family—they keep the same last name to show respect to their family and they tell the story of their ancestors. They are eager to keep their history alive.

We wanted to know how research helps teachers and librarians to pass on stories to children. We were told that Dr. Yue Tao, a highly respected professor, has written a textbook that is divided seasonally and certain stories are told only at specific times of the year. His book is widely used.

Today, young children make up the largest group of story listeners and they are the main consumers of storybooks. Professor Lihui's own six-year-old daughter thrives on stories. She reads in her spare time and before naps. After dinner she watches stories online and at bedtime she listens to stories on the radio or to those that her mother tells her. After 1980, when radios became available and affordable, stories were easy to access. In Professor Lihui's daughter's Beijing elementary school, children are exposed to stories throughout the day. They listen to stories on CDs before naps and they are encouraged to retell stories and act them out. Teachers do not want rote recitations.

Professor Lihui spoke of Li Xiaocui, an excellent young teller who comes from a storytelling family. Li attended a storytelling contest when she was four. She was deeply influenced by the experience and immersed herself in learning stories through books and new sources such as television and campus ghost stories, a popular new genre.

The one-child rule is still strictly enforced. Therefore, parents who want to give every advantage to their only children sign them up for after-school enrichment classes. After-school classes are offered in art and reading. Students express themselves through painting, paper tearing, and drama, retelling and acting out fairy tales and fables such as "The Fox and the Tiger"/"Hu Jia Hu Wei." The literal translation is "Like a Fox that Borrows the Might of the Tiger." In addition, use of shadow puppetry is very popular. Students have a shadow screen and create silhouettes from leather or cardboard. They tell stories in teams. The first to know a new story gets to tell it. Students are especially encouraged to make up new endings and to tell original stories. Another strong reason parents sign their children up for this class is to have fun, to encourage self-expression, to foster stage presence, to overcome shyness, and to feel comfortable in front of a group. The main problem Professor Lihui cited is that most of the stories are foreign in origin, such as the tales collected by the Brothers Grimm, Aesop's fables, Disney stories, and Japanese stories, although "The Monkey King" is well known.

We visited the kindergarten of the Beijing National Development and Reform Commission School and found many of Professor Lihui's descriptions a reality. This is a well-equipped progressive school that encourages creativity and independent thinking. Storytelling is used extensively not only to teach English, but also to foster public speaking and to keep traditions alive. Our arrival was videotaped and the room was arranged in an open horseshoe so that there was a performing area in front. The principal and teachers greeted us with enthusiasm and refreshments at each of the child-size tables.

Each classroom has a reading nook with a cushion, and children feel free to go there and read stories during class time. The image of a Chinese student sitting obediently at attention paying silent respect to a teacher is no longer the model. The children we saw were chatting animatedly and snacking while their teachers were speaking to the class. They were enthusiastic about joining in on the delegates' stories. One delegate was swamped by the children when she invited them to participate in her story. She expected them to remain standing by their seats!

The kindergartners and first graders had prepared stories to tell our delegation. Their stories were enhanced by costumes and props that the teacher assisted the children in making. Two students narrated Aesop's "The Tortoise and the Hare" by heart in Chinese. The girl playing the Tortoise wore a pillow decorated as a cracked shell, and the Hare wore bunny ears. It needed no translation. Next, they acted out the universally known "Are You My Mother?", wearing hand-drawn baby animal headbands. Two children then attempted to tell the story in English. When one girl lost her place, she stood with poise until she remembered the rest. The children told four stories and four U.S. tellers had the chance to reciprocate. I had the privilege of telling a tale from India and using the children in my story. All of the stories were well received. Lixin, our guide, did the simultaneous translating.

At the Huai Hai Primary School in Shanghai, fifth and sixth graders told a fable, a folktale and stories in English, and a classic tale in Chinese acted out by five students in costume. About 15 girls presented a traditional Chinese dance whose graceful movements were enhanced by costumes with long flowing sleeves. Delegates were escorted by two student guides who practiced their English during the visit. One student, whose English name was Judy, won a storytelling contest in English. She told Aesop's fable of "The Lion and the Mouse" with appropriate facial expressions, gestures, and change of voice—she roared ferociously and squeaked like a mouse, a universal language.

A significant presentation that epitomizes storytelling training among young tellers, and the old and the new in China, was the performance in Chinese of the classical legend "Tuiqiao," or "Push or Knock." These very modern students, dressed in classical costumes (over jeans) complete with topknots and soldiers holding standards, told the story with reverence. The essence of the story was impressive: Jia Dao, a poet-monk is wrestling with a word choice for a poem he is composing—push or knock—when he inadvertently bumps into an official. He is almost arrested until he explains that he was distracted while writing a poem and can't decide between the two words. The official is also a poet and is intrigued. He invites Jia Dao into his carriage to continue the discussion. What struck me was how well rehearsed the students were and how the rest of the class supported them with focus and appreciation on the esoteric subject of word choice, so essential in writing poetry and crafting engaging stories. Their attention to detail and selection of this tale reinforced how storytelling is nurtured on a variety of levels in Chinese schools.

However, the school that won my heart was one in a poor, remote village outside Guiyang, in Guizhou province, not far from where the earthquake occurred in May 2008. As the delegates left the bus, students lined the entrance and drummed us in. Little children greeted each of us with a bouquet of wildflowers. Many of us were tearful at the warm welcome. Every desk in the school was brought into the courtyard to serve as a dais for the honored guests. Delegates presented many gifts including books for the new library. Sadly, they will remain unread for now because young English teachers want to be in the big cities. After watching modern and classical dance performances, the delegates interacted with the children in a spontaneous way—doing paper folding, hand puppetry, and singing. It was hard to leave.

I was curious to know if the Chinese tell personal narrative, a popular art form in the United States. I was delighted to learn that they do. At Jui Xian Qiao Community, a senior retirement community in Beijing, a retired teacher told a poignant story of a troubled student whom she befriended in his youth. When he was released from a mental hospital she was the first person he wanted to find. It took him a long time to track her down because it had been ten years since he was her student and during that time she had moved thirty miles away. She had had a profound influence on this young man and was the bright spot in his life; he needed to find her. They met again and he was overjoyed that the teacher remembered him. The teacher wanted to emphasize the power a teacher can exert over a student and the importance of continuing to share knowledge and kindness. Her dedication and passion were evident. In retirement, she still volunteers her teaching.

Every chance we had, especially during sightseeing excursions, we pumped our guides for stories. We learned that food, too, has its legends. A visit to Kunming in China's southwestern Yunnan Province would not be complete without tasting one of its most renowned dishes called "Across the Bridge Noodles," or "Guo Qiao Mi Xian"—literally, "crossing bridge rice thread-noodle." It is made even more savory when one knows the love story attached to its creation. The version that follows was told to me by our national guide, Lixin, while I was awaiting my flight to Kunming. My first meal there was this popular dish and I was grateful I knew the story.

A long time ago in Kunming, City of Eternal Spring, where the climate is always temperate, lush vegetables grew and farm animals were plentiful. Farmers tilled their land far from their homes. One farmer had to cross a long wooden bridge each day to get to his plot of land. His wife loved him very much. Each day she, too, would rise early and start preparations to make him a healthful lunch that would keep up his strength. She would boil the bones of chickens for hours and when it was ready, she would add chopped vegetables and thin strips of meat. Then off she would go, crossing the long wooden bridge to bring her husband a hot lunch. But, by the time she arrived his lunch was always cold.

"How can I bring my worthy husband the hot lunch he deserves?" she thought to herself. She tried wrapping her coat around the container, but her husband's lunch was still cold when she arrived. She tried running over the bridge, but it was still cold when she reached him. She tried not to show her disappointment and her kind husband never scolded her or even frowned, but she knew in her heart how much he would have enjoyed a hot meal for he still had many more hours of work.

One day she decided to make the broth extra rich. Instead of using just the bones, she cleaned a whole chicken, cut it in pieces, covered them with water, and let them simmer while she went about her other chores. By the time she returned to check on the broth, a layer of chicken fat had congealed over the top, keeping the contents warm. She carefully put the chopped vegetables into separate containers, including thin rice noodles she had made that morning, and carried them separately from the soup. This time when she arrived the broth was still hot. She opened the container of broth, broke the seal of fat that had congealed on top, removed the fat, added the vegetables and the thin rice noodles, and swirled them through the hot broth with her chopsticks. The soup smelled so good and tasted good as well. It made her happy to see the pleased look on her husband's face. When she got to the bridge she turned and waved. She could feel the warmth of her husband's smile all the way over the bridge and home.

Soon word spread to all the other wives in the village and they too began to prepare their husbands' lunch in the same way. From that time forward, all the husbands enjoyed hot lunches and considered their wives to be as clever as they were loving.

China is seeking many creative ways to boost its national economy and storytelling is one of its components. In Beijing, storytelling has a special role in the historic Hutong area. Lanes are narrow and only the rickshaw drivers can get through. Rickshaw tours have become more popular since the drivers have been encouraged to tell local stories. This clever marketing tool contributes to the development of folklore while increasing new customers and increasing tourism.

We learned how much in common we have with our Chinese folklorist counterparts. We share the same passion to preserve our respective cultures' stories and histories and desire to pass them on both informally and formally with well-trained presenters.

PART III:
STORIES

THE GINGERBREAD MAN

Source: Nursery Tales Around the World. Selected and retold by Judy Sierra. Illustrated by Stefano Vitale. Clarion Books, 1996.

Culture: United States

Telling Time: 6 minutes

Audience: Ages 3 to 5

Comment: "The Gingerbread Man" is a variant of Tale Type 2025, *The Fleeing Pancake,* told in England and many European countries. Judy Sierra has slightly retold the version in *Stories to Tell to Children* by Sara Cone Bryant (Houghton Mifflin, 1907). Frances Clarke Sayers wrote about the strong impression this tale made on her as a child. Over one hundred and thirty years after it first appeared in print in the children's magazine *St. Nicholas* (May 1875), it is still a favorite with young children.

ONCE UPON a time there was a little old woman and a little old man, and they lived all alone in a little old house. They hadn't any little girls or any little boys at all. So one day the little old woman made a boy out of gingerbread. She made him a chocolate jacket and put gumdrops on it for buttons. His eyes were made of fine fat currants, his mouth was made of rose-colored sugar, and he had a gay little cap of orange sugar candy. When the little old woman had rolled him out and dressed him up and pinched his gingerbread shoes into shape, she put him in a pan. Then she put the pan in the oven and shut the door, and she thought, "Now I shall have a little boy of my own."

When it was time for the Gingerbread Boy to be done, she opened the oven door and pulled out the pan. Out jumped the little Gingerbread Boy on the floor, and away he ran—out the door and down the street! The little old woman and the little old man ran after him as fast as they could, but he just laughed and shouted,

> Run, run, as fast as you can,
> You can't catch me, I'm the Gingerbread Man!

And they couldn't catch him.

The little Gingerbread Boy ran on and on until he came to a cow by the roadside. "Stop, little Gingerbread Boy," said the cow. "I want to eat you."

The little Gingerbread Boy laughed and said,

> I have run away from a little old woman,
> And a little old man,
> And I can run away from you, I can!

And as the cow chased him, he looked over his shoulder and cried,

> Run, run, as fast as you can,
> You can't catch me, I'm the Gingerbread Man!

And the cow couldn't catch him.

The little Gingerbread Boy ran on and on and on till he came to a horse in the pasture. "Please stop, little Gingerbread Boy," said the horse. "You look very good to eat."

But the little Gingerbread Boy laughed out loud. "Oho! Oho!" he said.

> I have run away from a little old woman,
> And a little old man,
> And a cow,
> And I can run away from you, I can!

And as the horse chased him, he looked over his shoulder and cried,

> Run, run, as fast as you can,
> You can't catch me, I'm the Gingerbread Man!

And the horse couldn't catch him.

By and by the little Gingerbread Boy came to a barn full of threshers. When the threshers smelled the Gingerbread Boy, they tried to pick him up, and said, "Don't run so fast, little Gingerbread Boy. You look very good to eat."

But the little Gingerbread Boy ran harder than ever, and as he ran he cried out,

> I have run away from a little old woman,
> And a little old man,
> And a cow,
> And a horse,
> And I can run away from you, I can!

And when he found that he was ahead of the threshers, he turned and shouted back to them,

> Run, run, as fast as you can,
> You can't catch me, I'm the Gingerbread Man!

And the threshers couldn't catch him.

Then the little Gingerbread Boy ran faster than ever. He ran and ran until he came to a field full of mowers. When the mowers saw how fine he looked, they ran after him, calling out, "Wait a bit, wait a bit, little Gingerbread Boy, we wish to eat you!"

But the little Gingerbread Boy laughed harder than ever and ran like the wind. "Oho! Oho!" he said.

> I have run away from a little old woman,
> And a little old man,
> And a cow,
> And a horse,
> And a barn full of threshers,
> And I can run away from you, I can!

And when he found that he was ahead of the mowers, he turned and shouted back to them,

> Run, run, as fast as you can,
> You can't catch me, I'm the Gingerbread Man!

And the mowers couldn't catch him.

By this time the little Gingerbread Boy was so proud that he didn't think anybody could catch him. Pretty soon he saw a fox coming across a field. The fox looked at him and began to run. But the little Gingerbread Boy shouted across to him, "You can't catch me!" The fox began to run faster, and the little Gingerbread Boy ran faster, and as he ran he chuckled and said,

> I have run away from a little old woman,
> And a little old man,
> And a cow,
> And a horse,
> And a barn full of threshers,
> And a field full of mowers,
> And I can run away from you, I can!
> Run, run, as fast as you can,
> You can't catch me, I'm the Gingerbread Man!

"Why," said the fox, "I would not catch you if I could. I would not think of disturbing you."

Just then the little Gingerbread Boy came to a river. He couldn't swim across, and he wanted to keep running away from the cow and the horse and the people.

"Jump on my tail, and I will take you across," said the fox.

So the little Gingerbread Boy jumped on the fox's tail, and the fox swam into the river.

When he was a little way from the shore, the fox turned his head and said, "You are too heavy on my tail, little Gingerbread Boy. I fear I shall let you get wet. Jump on my back."

The little Gingerbread Boy jumped on his back.

A little farther out, the fox said, "I am afraid the water will cover you there. Jump on my shoulder."

The little Gingerbread Boy jumped on his shoulder.

In the middle of the river the fox said, "Oh dear, little Gingerbread Boy, my shoulder is sinking. Jump on my nose, and I can hold you out of the water."

So the little Gingerbread Boy jumped on his nose.

The minute the fox got on shore, he threw back his head, and gave a snap.

"Dear me!" said the little Gingerbread Boy. "I am a quarter gone!" The next minute he said, "My goodness gracious, I am three-quarters gone!"

And after that, the little Gingerbread Boy never said anything more at all.

PEREZ AND MARTINA:
A PUERTO RICAN FOLKTALE

Source: Perez and Martina: A Puerto Rican Folktale, by Pura Belpré. Warne, 1932.

Culture: Hispanic American

Telling Time: 14 minutes

Audience: Ages 5 to 10

Comment: Pura Belpré told this story exactly as she heard it from her grandmother when she was growing up in Puerto Rico. The story of the pretty cockroach and the gallant mouse is known throughout Hispanic America. There are many variants, including the Cuban version in which Perez is rescued. Pura Belpré preferred this version and said the children did not find the ending sad. *Perez and Martina* was first published in 1932 and has remained a classic in children's literature ever since. Lucía González, recipient of the Pura Belpré Honor Medal, pays homage to this gifted storyteller and librarian in her bilingual picture book *The Storyteller's Candle/La velita de los cuentos*, illustrated by Lulu Delacre, Children's Book Press, 2008. You may wish to share Lucía's book with your listeners before telling "Perez and Martina."

∎

MANY YEARS AGO in a little house with a round balcony, there once lived a Spanish cockroach called Martina. She was a pretty cockroach with black eyes and soft brown skin. She was very refined and exceedingly proud of her descent.

Martina was a splendid housekeeper so that her pots and pans were always bright and shining. One day, as she was sweeping her patio, she found an old rusty coin. She picked it up and polished it until it was as bright as the Sun.

"Why," said Martina, "It is a peseta! What shall I buy with it?" She thought and thought but she could not think of anything to suit her taste.

"Oh well," said she, "It is time now for my siesta. After my siesta I shall be able to think much better." So she tip-toed to her house and putting away her little broom, and taking off her little apron, she sat on her balcony and was soon fast asleep.

When she awoke, she again thought what to buy with her money. "It cannot be a dress," said she, "for I had a dress made to order not long ago." "Perhaps a box of candy but candy never lasts me long. What shall I buy with it? Oh, I know, I must get a box of powder."

So she bought a box of powder, and that day she powdered her little face as she had not done for a long time. Then she put on her best dress, took a little fan and sat on her chair again. "I wonder," said she as she sat there, "if Perez the Mouse will come to visit me today."

Now Perez was a gallant little mouse who lived in the same town as Martina. There was no one else who could bow just as Perez could. No one else danced and talked as he did, and many a one wondered if Perez had not come from royal descent.

As Martina sat there and wondered about these things, old Señor Cat came to see her. "Buenos dias, Señorita Martina," said Señor Cat. "How pretty you look today! Señorita will you marry me?"

"Oh, perhaps," said Martina, "If you tell me how you would talk to me in the future."

"Oh yes," said Señor Cat, "I will talk to you like this, Miaow, miaow, miaow!"

"Oh no, no, Señor Cat," said Martina, "You will frighten me."

Señor Cat departed with tears in his eyes, but Martina remained on her balcony.

After a while she had another visitor. This time it was an old, proud cock who had always admired her.

"Buenos dias, Señorita Martina," said he.

"Buenos dias, Señor Cock," said Martina.

"Pretty Martina, will you marry me?" said Señor Cock.

"Oh perhaps," said Martina, "If you tell me how you would talk to me in the future."

"Yes," said Señor Cock, standing straight and flapping his wings, saying, "Qui-qui-ri-qui, qui-qui-ri-qui, qui-qui-ri-qui."

"Enough, enough," said Martina rising from her chair. "No Señor Cock, I will not marry you. You don't think I can stand that noise in my house for ever!"

Señor Cock bowed low and, like Señor Cat, departed, his eyes filled with tears and feeling his little heart almost torn to pieces.

Across Martina's patio there lived a family of ducks, who had a very accomplished son. Every day he would watch Martina as she came down to sweep her patio. Today he decided to pay her a visit, and as she walked toward her balcony he made a little speech all for her.

But when he reached her balcony he could only say "Buenos dias, Señorita Martina, will you marry me?"

"Oh, Buenos dias, Señor Duck," said Martina, "perhaps, if you tell me how you would talk to me in the future."

"Señorita, I will talk you like this—Quack, Quack, Quack, Quack."

"Oh no, Señor Duck, day after day do I listen to your Quack, Quack, across my patio. It is too tiresome to listen to the same thing over and over again, especially when there is nothing in it to delight you."

"No, Señor Duck, I will not marry you."

Señor Duck hid his head on his white wing and cried, because Señorita Martina would not marry him.

At the end of the street where Martina lived, there was a forest and in this forest there was a pool. In the pool lived an old lazy frog who had always advised Martina, and had watched her take her walk in the forest.

"I wonder," said he, "why she has not come today? I will go and pay her a visit," said he, leaping from the water and reaching the street.

He had hardly gone a few paces when he met Señor Cricket.

"Buenos dias, Señor Cricket," said Señor Frog.

"Buenos dias, Señor Frog," said Señor Cricket.

"Where are you going?

"To see Señorita Martina," said he. "I have a question to ask her."

"So have I, so have I," said Señor Cricket, "let's go together."

Soon they reached Martina's balcony.

"Buenos dias, Señorita Martina," said both at the same time, "Will you marry me?"

"Oh, but Señores, you forget your manners, I cannot talk to both of you at the same time."

"Señor Cricket, will you talk first?"

"Señorita Martina, will you marry me?" "Oh perhaps," said Martina, "If you will tell me how you would talk to me in the future."

"Oh, I will talk to you like this—Coqui, Coqui, Coqui."

"Señor Cricket, what makes your voice so sad? You will make me cry! No, I will not marry you."

Now Señor Frog, is your chance to speak.

"Señorita Martina, will you marry me?"

"Oh, perhaps," said Martina, "if you tell me how you would talk to me in the future!"

"Señorita, I will talk to you like this—Borom, Borom, Borom, Borom."

"No, no," said Martina, "I will not marry you! I do not like your voice and besides I have heard that you frogs talk constantly day and night."

It was getting late and Martina decided to go into the house, but before she did so, she happened to look down the street, and whom should she see coming but Perez the Mouse, gaily dressed in his best clothes, and wearing a straw hat with a long plume.

Martina sat again on her chair and fixed her little dress. She watched Perez as he walked slowly down the street.

She saw him as he took off his hat and bowed now and then to his friends in the street. Soon he reached Martina's balcony. He took off his hat and made a low bow.

"Buenos dias, Señorita Martina," said Señor Perez. "It is a lovely day. Will you come out and walk with me a while?" But Martina said she preferred her balcony and invited him to come and sit with her. Perez went slowly in, and as he walked he sang:

> De España un ratoncito soy
> Y en una cueva vivo
> Puedo por las tardes
> Ver la Puesta del Sol
> A veces veo al Rey y a la
> Reina pasar.

> I am a little mouse from sunny Spain,
> In Royal Mansion's halls is my domain.
> At night I watch the sun set in the sky,
> And sometimes see the King and Queen pass by.

"Señorita," said Perez, "For a long time I have been thinking of asking you a question. Will you marry me?"

"Oh, perhaps," said Martina. "If you tell me how you would talk to me in the future."

Señorita," said Perez, "I will talk to you in the language of my forefathers. Like this—Chui, Chui, Chui, Chui."

"Oh, how lovely! It sounds just like music," said Martina. "Yes, Señor Perez, I will marry you."

And they were married and a great wedding it was. They danced and sang, and Martina did many a Spanish dance for her Perez.

Christmas was coming, and Martina thought to give Perez a pleasant surprise. "What shall I make for him?" said she. "There is a Christmas dish that I am sure Perez has never tasted. I will make it for him."

So she went to the kitchen and took a kettle. Then she put in some rice and some cocoanut juice, some almonds and some raisins. She mixed these up and put in some sugar.

Then she put in some water and put it all in the kettle to boil. Then she went around the house making it tidy for the grand affair.

She had hardly departed when Perez the Mouse came in. He immediately smelled the new dish. "It is an entirely new smell," said Perez.

He followed the smell to the kitchen. There he found the kettle but it was too high for him to see what was inside. So he brought in a stool, and stepped upon it.

He peeped in. "If it tastes as good as it looks," said Perez, "I am certainly going to have a great treat."

He then stuck in his paw and tasted it. When he did so he knew he had never tasted anything like that before.

He peeped in again. Then he noticed a fat almond getting brown all over. "Oh, if I could only get it," said Perez.

"One good pull and it will be mine." He pulled once, but it did not come out. He pulled again and it shook a little. "Once more and I shall have it," said Perez. He gave it a good pull but unfortunately he lost his balance and fell into the kettle. He screamed and called for help. But who could help him?

Martina was the only one who could and she was away sweeping her patio. After a while she came back to see how her dish was coming along and took a wooden spoon to give it a good stirring. When she looked inside the kettle, she saw her Perez cooked to death.

She cried and called for him. "Oh, Señor Perez, come back to me." She went to her room and put on a black dress, and a black mantilla.

She took her guitar off the wall, and sat in her chair playing and singing and weeping. And her little voice was heard all over the place as she sang:

> El Ratoncito Pérez cayó en la olla
> Y la cucaracha Martina
> Lo canta y lo llora
> Lo canta y lo llora
> Lo canta y lo llora
> Lo canta y lo llora
>
> Little Perez, the mouse fell into a boiling pot,
> And Martina sings and cries for him,
> Sings and cries for him,
> Sings and cries for him,
> Sings and cries for him.

And to this time, she still sings, she still plays, and she still weeps for her little Perez to come back to her!

THE OLD WOMAN WHO LOST HER DUMPLING

Source: Japanese Fairy Tale Series No. 24. Rendered into English by Lafcadio Hearn. T. Hasegawa, 1902.

Culture: Japanese

Telling Time: 8 minutes

Audience: Ages 5 to 9

Comment: This story is one of five translated by Lafcadio Hearn for T. Hasegawa's *Japanese Fairy Tales*. Hearn was born in 1850 in Leucadia, Greece (pronounced Lefcadia, hence his name) of a Greek mother and Irish father. At the age of two he was sent to Ireland and raised by a great-aunt until at the age of nineteen he moved to America where he built a reputation as a gifted journalist, author, and literary critic. In 1890 he went to Japan as a newspaper correspondent but soon gave that up to become a teacher of English. He married Koizumi Setsu, daughter of a samurai, became a Japanese citizen, changed his name to Koizumi Yakumo, and devoted the rest of his life to interpreting Japanese culture and civilization to the Western world. Hearn died in 1904.

An *Oni* is an ogre. *Jizō* is the Japanese guardian deity of children and travelers.

This is a fun story to tell to a mixed age group. For a picture-book story program, consider Blair Lent's Caldecott Medal Book *The Funny Little Woman*, retold by Arlene Mosel.

■

LONG, LONG AGO there was a funny old woman, who liked to laugh and to make dumplings of rice-flour.

One day, while she was preparing some dumplings for dinner, she let one fall; and it rolled into a hole in the earthen floor of her little kitchen and disappeared. The old woman tried to reach it by putting her hand down the hole, and all at once the earth gave way, and the old woman fell in.

She fell quite a distance, but was not a bit hurt, and when she got up on her feet again, she saw that she was standing on a road, just like the road before her house. It was quite light down there, and she could see plenty of rice fields, but no one in them. How all this happened, I cannot tell you. But it seems that the old woman had fallen into another country.

The road she had fallen upon sloped very much, so after having looked for her dumpling in vain, she thought that it must have rolled farther away down the slope. She ran down the road to look, crying:

"My dumpling, my dumpling! Where is that dumpling of mine?"

After a little while she saw a stone *Jizō* standing by the roadside, and she said:

"Oh Lord *Jizō*, did you see my dumpling?"

Jizō answered:

"Yes, I saw your dumpling rolling by me down the road. But you had better not go any farther, because there is a wicked *Oni* living down there who eats people."

But the old woman only laughed and ran on farther down the road, crying, "My dumpling, my dumpling! Where is that dumpling of mine?" And she came to another statue of *Jizō*, and asked it:

"O kind Lord *Jizō*, did you see my dumpling?"

And *Jizō* said:

"Yes, I saw your dumpling go by a little while ago. But you must not run any farther, because there is a wicked *Oni* down there who eats people."

But she only laughed and ran on, still crying out: "My dumpling, my dumpling! Where is that dumpling of mine?" And she came to a third *Jizō*, and asked it:

"O dear Lord *Jizō*, did you see my dumpling?"

But *Jizō* said:

"Don't talk about your dumpling now. Here is the *Oni* coming. Squat down here behind my sleeve, and don't make any noise."

Presently the *Oni* came very close, and stopped and bowed to *Jizō*, and said:

"Good-day, *Jizō San!*"

Jizō said good-day, too, very politely.

Then the *Oni* suddenly snuffed the air two or three times in a suspicious way, and cried out: "*Jizō San, Jizō San!* I smell a smell of mankind somewhere—don't you?"

"Oh!" said *Jizō*, "perhaps you are mistaken."

"No, no!" said the *Oni* after snuffing the air again, "I smell a smell of mankind."

Then the old woman could not help laughing—"*Te-he-he*"—and the *Oni* immediately reached down his big hairy hand behind *Jizō*'s sleeve, and pulled her out, still laughing, "*Te-he-he!*"

"Ah! ha!" cried the *Oni*.

Then *Jizō* said:

"What are you going to do with that good old woman? You must not hurt her."

"I won't," said the *Oni*. "But I will take her home with me to cook for us."

"*Te-he-he!*" laughed the old woman.

"Very well," said *Jizō*; "but you must really be kind to her. If you are not, I shall be very angry."

"I won't hurt her at all," promised the *Oni*, "and she will only have to do a little work for us every day. Good-bye, *Jizō San*."

Then the *Oni* took the old woman far down the road, till they came to a wide deep river, where there was a boat. He put her into the boat, and took her across the river to his house. It was a very large house. He led her at once into the kitchen, and told her to cook some dinner for himself and the other *Oni* who lived with him. And he gave her a small wooden rice-paddle, and said:

"You must always put only one grain of rice into the pot, and when you stir that one grain of rice in the water with this paddle, the grain will multiply until the pot is full."

So the old woman put just one rice grain into the pot, as the *Oni* told her, and began to stir it with the paddle; and, as she stirred, the one grain became two—then four—then eight—then sixteen, thirty-two, sixty-four, and so on. Every time she moved the paddle the rice increased in quantity, and in a few minutes the great pot was full.

After that, the funny old woman stayed a long time in the house of the *Oni*, and every day cooked food for him and for all his friends. The *Oni* never hurt or frightened her, and her work was made quite easy by the magic paddle—although she had to cook a very, very great quantity of rice, because an *Oni* eats much more than any human being eats.

But she felt lonely, and always wished very much to go back to her own little house, and make her dumplings. And one day, when the *Oni* were all out somewhere, she thought she would try to run away.

She first took the magic paddle, and slipped it under her girdle; and then she went down to the river. No one saw her; and the boat was there. She got into it, and pushed off, and as she could row very well, she was soon far away from the shore.

But the river was very wide, and she had not rowed more than one-fourth of the way across, when the *Oni*, all of them, came back to the house.

They found that their cook was gone, and the magic paddle, too. They ran down to the river at once, and saw the old woman rowing away very fast.

Perhaps they could not swim; at all events they had no boat, and they thought the only way they could catch the funny old woman would be to drink up all the water of the river before she got to the other bank. So they knelt down, and began to drink so fast that before the old woman had got half way over, the water had become quite low.

But the old woman kept on rowing until the water had got so shallow that the *Oni* stopped drinking, and began to wade across. Then she dropped her oar, took the magic paddle from her girdle, and shook it at the *Oni*, and made such funny faces that the *Oni* all burst out laughing.

But the moment they laughed, they could not help throwing up all the water they had drunk, and so the river became full again. The *Oni* could not cross, and the funny old woman got safely over to the other side, and ran away up the road as fast as she could.

She never stopped running until she found herself at home again.

After that she was very happy, for she could make dumplings whenever she pleased. Besides, she had the magic paddle to make rice for her. She sold her dumplings to her neighbors and passengers, and in quite a short time she became rich.

THE DANCING GRANNY

Source: The Dancing Granny, retold and illustrated by Ashley Bryan. Atheneum, 1977.

Culture: West Indian

Telling Time: 13 minutes

Audience: Ages 6 to adult

Comment: Retold from "He Sings to Make the Old Woman Dance" (Antigua, English Antilles). In *Folk-Lore of the Antilles, French and English,* Part II by Elsie Clews Parsons. American Folk-Lore Society, 1936, p. 314. Ashley Bryan brings all his joy of life into his vibrant retelling of this delightful tale.

When Dan Wheeless traveled in Ghana in 2004, he visited a village in order to help with the building of a school. He mentioned to some of the women there that his mother, Jeslyn, was a storyteller, and that one of her favorite stories was about a dancing Granny. He told them he couldn't remember the story well enough to tell it to them, but he did remember the song, "Shake it to the east, shake it to the west, shake it to the very one that you love the best." The women immediately began singing the song with additional words and a dance to go along with it! Dan took this to mean that the story's roots were indeed African.

■

THERE WAS AN OLD WOMAN who lived in a hut. Everyone called her Granny Anika.

She sang her songs and she stirred her pot. She licked the ladle and tasted her stew. Umm-yum! She beat the sides of the calabash, pom-pa-lom! pom-pa-lom!

Granny Anika was a happy old lady. She woke up singing. All day long she sang and beat out rhythms on anything within reach. She rapped with sticks, she drummed with spoons, she tapped with ladles, and she hummed dance tunes to the beat of her knives.

> *Shake it to the East,*
> *Shake it to the West.*

But what Granny Anika loved the best of all was to dance. She danced in the morning. She danced at noon. She danced till the sun set. And then at night she dreamed dance dreams and danced in her sleep till dawn.

That old lady was never too busy or tired to do a little dance. She cleared a vegetable patch near her hut and sang as she hoed the ground. She kept step to the chop, chop, chop of her hoe.

The seeds stirred in the earth to the vibrations of Granny's song and dance. The vegetables came up strong to the gentle slap, pitter-pat of Old Anika's bare feet.

Granny Anika was proud of her grounds. She set in a good variety of seeds and raised all of her provisions. She sang:

> *Mama loves peas,*
> *Papa loves corn,*
> *Baby loves beans*
> *Sure as you're born.*
> *Put in potatoes,*
> *Granny loves yam,*
> *Don't forget okra,*
> *Beets and jam.*

Jam! Well, Granny picked sweet berries from bushes and made a thick brew, which she spread on sliced yam and called jam.

Granny Anika did her share of work, and she did her dance. Uh-huh! She snapped her fingers and clapped her hands. Uh-huh! She knew her song, and she got along.

Uh-huh!

One day Spider Ananse came strutting on by Granny Anika's hut.

You couldn't imagine a lazier fellow than Brother Ananse. He'd strut and stroll all day long, looking like he was doing something important. But Spider wouldn't work.

No kind of tune could make the hoe feel lighter in Brother Ananse's hands. And no kind of beat eased his long, slim feet on a spade dug into the ground.

Spider Ananse preferred resting and loafing and lounging and wandering around until he found someone he might trick for his dinner.

Spider watched Granny Anika working in her field. She was bent over the hoe doing a jig as she dug. She didn't see Spider Ananse climb into a tree.

Spider Ananse peeped out at Granny from behind the tree trunk. "Hmm ..." he thought, "I won't get a thing from that great garden patch if Granny doesn't go."

Brother Ananse began to sing. He sang one of his catchiest tunes. He broke off a twig and rapped out a marked dance beat on a dead branch.

> *Pom-pa-lom!*
> *Pom-pa-lom!*
> *Papa's here*
> *And Mama's gone.*

I sing, you dance, my dee-dee.
You dance, I sing, my swee-tee.
I'll trouble you, my dee-dee,
I'll trouble you, my la-dy.

Granny heard the tune and hummed it to herself. "Umm-hmm! Sweet, sweet, sweet," she sang.

Then the music and the beat got to Granny's feet. She held her hoe like a partner and swung with it to the right. She swung to the left.

Spider Ananse sang out:

Shake it to the East,
Shake it to the West.
Shake it to the very one
That you love the best.

Granny Anika skipped like a little girl. She flung out her arms, dropping the hoe, and danced off the field.

Spider Ananse sang louder and louder and rapped harder and harder.

Granny Anika wheeled to the East. She wheeled to the West. She let the music take her, and the dance carried her off. Away she wheeled northwards, head over heels, until she disappeared from sight.

Then Brother Ananse dropped down from the tree laughing till he shook.

"There goes the dancing Granny." He laughed. "Man! She sure looked like a tumbleweed as she wheeled by."

Spider helped himself to all the corn he could carry and carted it off to his house.

His wife said, "Good corn."

His mother said, "Sure as you're born."

That night they all sat down to heaping platefuls of steaming corn.

When Granny Anika finally came out of her dance right side up, she was eleven miles north of her village.

"O my! O my!" she cried. "I know that voice. It was Brother Ananse. He sure can sing. Now why didn't he come dance with me? Anyway, I got a good dance to the North."

Back home, Granny went to her field and saw that her corn crop was ravished.

"Eh, eh! That good-for-nothing, no' count Spider Ananse! He sure tricked me. So, that's why he didn't try to match my steps! But I'll catch him. Next time he comes I won't let the music sweet me so."

Sure enough, Spider Ananse soon came round again to plunder Granny's vegetable patch.

"Umm-yum," he thought as he looked out over the pretty field. "If the corn tasted so good, I wonder how Granny's peas and beans might be."

Spider Ananse climbed into the tree and began to sing:

> *Ah mini lah lee lee*
> *Again I'm in the country*
> *'Cause Nana's corn*
> *Tastes good to me.*
> *I see those beans,*
> *I see those greens,*
> *I see those beets,*
> *Fit for kings and queens.*

"See what you see and see what you like and have a fit too," said Granny, "'cause that see and that fit is all you're going to get. You can sing for beans and sing for peas for all I care. It's going to take two to dance to your tune today." Granny shuffled her feet lightly. "Yeah! Take a good look. You'll see that your Mama lives right here, and she don't plan to go nowhere. Uh-uh, no wheres away. Not this here day."

Spider laughed and did some variations on his rapping. Then he went into his big song:

> *Pom-pa lom!*
> *Pom-pa-lom!*
> *Papa's here*
> *But Mama's gone.*
> *I sing for peas,*
> *I sing for corn.*
> *You plant, I'll pull,*
> *Sure as you're born.*

Granny Anika held her hoe tightly and dug her toes into the ground. Spider sang on:

> *I sing, you dance, my dee-dee.*
> *You dance, I sing, my swee-tee.*
> *I trouble you, my dee-dee,*
> *I trouble you, my la-dy.*

Granny kicked up her feet and dropped the hoe. Spider sang:

> *O! Shake it to the East*
> *Shake it to the West,*

> *Shake it to the very one*
> *That you love the best.*

Granny's feet could no longer resist Spider's beat. She wheeled to the East, she wheeled to the West. Then head over heels, she cartwheeled southwards.

"Man, if Granny don't spin like a thistle on the breath of a whistle," laughed Spider, dropping out of the tree. He watched the dancing Granny twirl out of sight.

Then Spider filled his bag with peas and beans and strutted all the way home.

Spider's wife said, "Good beans, good peas."

Spider's mother said, "If you please."

That night they all sat down to heaping gourds of hot beans and peas.

Granny Anika found herself twelve miles south of her village before she danced Spider's tune out of her feet.

When she got back home, she saw that Spider Ananse had stolen her peas and beans.

"How can I catch that thieving rascal?" she said. "Brother Ananse sings the danciest tunes. I just can't stay still when the music sweets me so. That I know. Trouble is, Spider knows it too.

Spider Ananse came again and climbed into the tree. He stayed well out of reach of Granny, but his voice reached Granny Anika well.

> *Put your hands on your hips*
> *And let your backbone shake.*

Once Spider got into his song, Granny couldn't resist. She danced to the North. She danced to the South. And when Spider sang the pom-pa-lom part, Granny was into her steps.

> *Shake it to the East,*
> *Shake it to the West.*

Granny was now dancing her best and pleased as could be with her style. Even Spider Ananse had to admire her as she went, head over heels, cartwheeling westwards.

"That dancing Granny turns like a windmill!" he exclaimed. "She sure can twirl her arms and legs in time to the tune."

Spider took all the potatoes he could carry and toted the sack home.

Spider's wife said, "Good potatoes."

Spider's mother said, "Tastier than tomatoes."

That night they all sat down to a heaping mound of roasted potatoes.

Granny had a good dance, it's true. She came to a stop thirteen miles to the west of her village and returned home.

The fourth time Spider Ananse came by, he started singing before he was well into the tree.

> *Pom-pa-lom!*
> *Pom-pa-lom!*
> *Papa's hungry*
> *And Mama's not home.*

Granny started her dance. She swayed to the South. She swayed to the North.

> *Shake it to the East,*
> *Shake it to the West.*

"Sweet, sweet, sweet," sang Granny to the beat.

Spider didn't even have to finish his song. Granny heard well, and the tune was wheeling in her. Off she went, heels over head, wheeling eastwards.

Spider Ananse shook his head and said, "No one can outdance dancing Granny. She spins like a top."

He filled his basket with beets and beat it on back home.

Spider's wife said, "Good beets."

Spider's mother said, "Sweeter than sweets."

That night they all sat down to big bowls of boiled beets.

Granny Anika danced to a stop, right side up fourteen miles to the east of her village.

"My," she said, "that was the sweetest dance of all."

When she got home, Granny sat by her hut. She tapped her foot as she looked out over her ravished field.

"Look at that, will you?" she said. "Trickster Spider's done taken my corn, my peas and beans, my potatoes and my beets. I'll never catch that clever character as long as he swings on that sweet song."

So Granny Anika gathered in all that was left of her vegetables. There was nothing more in the fields for Brother Ananse to steal.

When Spider Ananse sauntered by again, he was so sure of himself that he started singing his song long before he reached the tree. Now what did he do that for?

Granny Anika was waiting for just such a chance. Quickly she swung her hoe and caught Brother Ananse around the waist. She pulled him to her and held onto him as if he were the first dance partner she ever had.

"Let go! Let go of me," Spider cried.

"I've got you now, you singing brother," said Granny. "Dance with me. To the East, to the West, to the North, to the South. Sing your song."

Granny Anika pinched Spider, and he began to sing:

> *Pom-pa-lom!*
> *Pom-pa-lom!*
> *I ate your peas,*
> *I ate your corn.*

"Sure as you're born, you did. Now dance, Brother! Dance!" sang Granny to the song. "I'll teach you that two can trip to that tune too."

Granny Anika led Spider Ananse in the dance. They whirled and they twirled to the wheeling beat. Every time Spider tried to stop, Granny squeezed him tighter.

They danced to the North.

They danced to the South.

Now Spider's feet felt the sweet beat of Granny's steps. Together they sang:

> *Shake it to the East,*
> *Shake it to the West,*
> *Shake it to the very one*
> *That you love the best.*

They wheeled to the East.

They whirled to the West.

They heeled to the North.

They twirled to the South.

Off they went capering and cartwheeling away!

> *Pom-pa-lom!*
> *Pom-pa-lom!*

Spider Ananse didn't get one vegetable from Granny Anika that day, but he sure got one good dance with the old woman.

Dancing Granny never had a better partner than Spider Ananse. They danced more miles together than Granny had ever danced alone. And if Spider's still singing, then they're still dancing.

> *"Dance Granny! You move like the river."*
> *"Dance Spider! Let's dance forever."*
> *"Dance, Granny! As the lead bends*
> *"The dance goes on, but the story ends."*

ANANSE THE SPIDER IN SEARCH OF A FOOL

Source: The Ox of the Wonderful Horns and Other African Folktales, retold and illustrated by Ashley Bryan. Atheneum, 1971. Also in *Ashley Bryan's African Tales, Uh-Huh*, retold and illustrated by Ashley Bryan. Atheneum, 1998.

Culture: West African

Telling Time: 15 minutes

Audience: Ages 8 to adult

Comment: The stories of Ananse originated in Ghana among the Ashanti people and were carried to the New World by Africans sold into slavery. Ananse has the ability to appear as spider or man, depending on the circumstances. He is a honey-tongued trickster who can sweet-talk Granny to leave her crops for dancing, as in the previous story, or bring stories to Earth by capturing four fearsome creatures, the price demanded by Nyame the Sky God. Rarely is Ananse outwitted, but in the following tale Ananse learns "that when one seeks to make a fool of another, he is bound to make a bigger fool of himself." In his retelling, Ashley Bryan uses a traditional Ashanti beginning and ending. You can hear him perform "Ananse the Spider in Search of a Fool" on his CD *Ashley Bryan: Poems and Folktales*. Audio Bookshelf, 1994.

■

WE DO NOT MEAN, we do not really mean, that what we are going to say is true.

Hear my account of Spider Ananse and the fish traps.

Spider Ananse once lived by the sea. There were plenty of fish in those waters. Yes, there were fish to be caught for those who had traps made and set. But Ananse was not one to be working like that.

"I'd like to catch and sell fish," he thought, "the regular type and the shell-fish, too. But if I'm to do that, I must hire a fool to make, set, and pull the traps." Spider was sure he'd have no trouble finding a fool. Once he did, he planned to make great catches of fish, which he'd sell in the market for cash. He would keep all the money for himself and grow rich in the fish business.

"I'll pay the fool a few regular fish and maybe even some shellfish," he told himself. "But as for money, of course, the fool will get none!" So Spider Ananse set out to find a fool. He walked about the fishing village, calling, "I want a fool. I want a fool." He saw a woman cooking. "I am looking for a fool," he said.

"A fool," she said, mocking him and shaking her wooden spoon. Spider ran off to the shore, where on the beach he saw a busy fisherman.

"I am looking for a fool," said Spider.

"A pool?" asked the fisherman.

"No! A fool," said Spider.

"A tool?" asked the fisherman.

"A fool, a fool," howled Spider as he hurried off. "A fool indeed," he muttered, "but deaf." And everywhere Ananse looked it was the same. No one listened to him. Nowhere could a fool be found.

After a long time, Ananse met Osana the Hawk. This time Ananse began in a new way. "Come," he said, "let's go and set fish traps." But Osana had heard that Ananse was hunting a fool to go fishing, so he said, "Oh, I have no need to set fish traps. I have plenty of meat to eat." Later Ananse met Anene the Crow. "Let us go and set fish traps," Ananse said.

"Why not?" said Crow. "I'll go with you." "Wait here," said Spider Ananse, almost bursting with joy. "I won't be long." He ran home to get his knife.

While Ananse was gone, Anene the Crow rested in the shade of a silk-cotton tree. And when Hawk was sure that Spider was gone, he flew down.

"Watch out for Ananse," Osana warned. "Don't go with him on this fish trap-setting trip. He's looking for a fool. He wants someone else to do the work. But he plans to sell all the regular fish, and the shellfish as well, and keep all the cash from the catch for himself." "Bakoo!" said Anene the Crow. "I did not know. But now I do. Thank you Osana. Don't say any more. I will go with Ananse, and we shall see who does the work and who gets the money." Spider Ananse soon returned with his knife. He and Crow set out at once for the bush to cut palm branches for traps.

When they came to a palm tree, Crow said to Spider, "Ananse, give me the knife. I will go cut the branches. You can sit here and take the weariness of my hard work." Spider replied, "Anene, do you take me for a fool? No! I will do the cutting. You will sit aside and take the weariness of my work." So Ananse the Spider did all of the cutting, while Anene the Crow sat aside sighing and yawning in weariness.

When Ananse had finished cutting the palms, Anene helped him tie them into a neat bundle.

Then Crow said, "Ananse, let me carry the bundle. You can trek after me and take the aches and pains of this backbreaking work." "Oh, no," said Spider. "You must take me for a fool! Here! You help steady the load on my head. I will carry, and you can take the aches." So Crow followed sighing and yawning and groaning beautifully, every step of the way. And Ananse carried.

When they reached Spider's hut, Crow helped Spider set the load on the ground.

"Now let me make the fish traps," said Crow. "Yes, let me. I'll show you how. You can take the fatigue of my labors." Spider replied, "Anene, never! Everyone knows that I'm a great weaver. Leave the trap making to me. You take the fatigue." Crow chose the most comfortable mat in Spider's hut and stretched out on his back. There he lay, sighing and yawning and groaning and bawling, more woefully than ever.

"Fool," said Spider. "Have you no sense? Just listen to your moaning. It sounds as if you were dying." Spider Ananse began to spin. He spun and he wove and he made palm mesh for the fish traps. He worked till they were well made and ready to be set.

"Let me carry the fish traps to the water," said Crow. "It's your turn to take the tiredness of all this trap making." Spider said, "No, no, Anene! None of your tricks. I'll take the traps, and you can take the tiredness of the task." They set out for the shore. Spider walked carefully, balancing the traps. Crow staggered behind sighing and yawning and groaning and bawling all the way.

At the beach, Crow said, "Father Spider, a beast lives in the sea. Let me stand in the water and set the fish traps. If the beast should bite me, then you can take the death." Spider said, "Anene, I swear that that is not a bit fair. I shall set the traps. If the beast bites me, then you shall die." So Spider Ananse toiled in the sea, setting the fish traps.

No beast bit. And Anene watched comfortably. Then the two returned to Spider's hut and slept.

The next morning they arose at dawn and hurried down to the sea. They opened the traps and found two fish as their catch.

Crow said, "Ananse, these two fish are for you. Tomorrow, when the traps have caught four, it will be my turn to take them." Spider exclaimed, "What a cheat you are! Do you take me for a fool? No sir! These two are yours. Tomorrow, I'll take the four." Anene the Crow took the fish and cooked them. He made a fine dish of fufu and fish and ate it all himself. The next day Spider and Crow examined the traps and found four fish.

Crow said, "Ananse, these four fish are yours. I'll take the next batch, whatever the catch. With this bait, we're bound to get eight." Spider said, "I'm no fool! I withdraw my claim to these four. You take these and tomorrow I'll have the eight." Crow took the fish and fried the four. He made a fine dish of fufu and fried fish and ate it all himself.

The next day when they inspected the traps, Spider counted eight fish as their catch.

"Take them, Ananse," said Crow. "I'll go back to the hut and wait for tomorrow's catch of sixteen." Spider said, "I am no fool, Anene. You take the eight fish. I'll have tomorrow's sixteen." Crow took the fish and baked the eight. He made a fine dish of fufu and baked fish and ate it all himself.

The next morning sixteen fish were caught in the traps.

And by now the fish traps were well worn out.

Anene the Crow said, "Ananse, these fish traps are rotten. They will not catch fish any longer. But each trap will fetch a price in the marketplace.

You take the sixteen fish and give me the rotten fish traps to sell." "Oh, no!" said Spider. "You take the fish and sell them if you can. I shall sell the rotten fish traps and keep the cash." Crow picked up the sixteen fish, and Spider picked up his rotten fish traps. Together they went to the nearby village market.

A crowd soon surrounded Crow. People bargained and bid and bought his fish. In no time at all he had sold the sixteen. If he had had more, he would have sold more. But he did well, just the same, for he had a great mound of gold dust in his feathered purse.

When the crowd broke up, Spider Ananse still sat with his unsold traps.

Crow said to him, "Don't just sit there with your wares. Take up those perfectly rotten fish traps and let people discover that you have them. Walk around and talk about your treasured traps. Cry out! Let the villagers hear your voice. Make a loud noise. Don't think you can sell by sitting in silence." Crow's fiery speech so inspired Spider that he leaped to his feet, lifted his traps, and sang out in a burst of pride and enthusiasm:

> "Rotten fish traps for sale
> Rare, bedraggled, and old
> Treat your son and yourself
> Pay in cowries or gold."

The village chief was astonished to hear such a ridiculous cry from the market place. Never before had his people been so insulted by a stranger.

"But where does this fellow come from?" he asked. "Send him to me!" Spider Ananse went quickly at the call, calculating a sale in cowries and gold. He was still busy making these calculations when the chief thundered:

"Do you suppose this is a village of fools?"

Spider trembled.

"Your friend Crow came and sold fine fish for a good profit. Did you sit by and not take notice? Then why do you seek to dispose of your useless, rotten fish traps among us?" The chief was so angry that he called his men and said, "Flog him!" Spider Ananse tried to flee, but he tripped over the loose palm strips of his rotten fish traps. As he flailed about to free himself, he became more entangled in the mesh until he was caught like a fish in his own fish traps.

As the blows drummed on Spider's back, he cried, "*Pui-pui, pui-pui!* Why do they beat p-po-poor me?" Tears of pain flowed from Ananse's eyes. Then suddenly they became tears of shame. For, at last, Spider Ananse realized that when one seeks to make a fool of another, he is bound to make a bigger fool of himself.

This is my story. Whether it be bitter or whether it be sweet, take some of it elsewhere and let the rest come back to me.

JACK AND THE TWO-BULLET HUNT

Retold by Amy L. Cohn and Suzy Schmidt

Source: From Sea to Shining Sea: A Treasury of American Folklore and Folksongs, by Amy Cohn and Suzy Schmidt. Scholastic, 1993.

Culture: United States/Southern Appalachian Mountains

Telling Time: 5 minutes

Audience: Ages 6 to adult

Comment: Fourth-grade Bennett Preskill chose to learn and tell this tall tale to the first graders as part of his work in Anne Shimojima's storytelling class. Anne slightly adapted the tale for her students. She writes, "Since this was a fairly complicated story, my goal was to make it flow as easily and simply as possible. I used language and phrases that worked rhythmically for me. The children loved the story. It provides a lot of opportunities for gesture as well as the repetitive phrase, "he still didn't have that RABBIT."

■

ONE TIME AWAY back years ago, there was a boy named Jack. He and his folk lived off in the mountains and they were awful poor, just didn't have a thing. Jack had two brothers, Will and Tom, and they are in some of the Jack Tales, but this one, there's mostly just Jack in it.

Jack was awful lazy sometimes, just wouldn't do any lick of work. His mother and his daddy kept tryin' to get him to help, but they couldn't do a thing with him when he took a lazy spell. But they kept tryin'.

So one cold December morning Jack's daddy stood beside Jack in the yard. Looked at rabbit tracks in the snow, looked at Jack, and said, "Son, at the end of them tracks is your breakfast."

Jack got his old single-barrel and the only two shells he had and started out. Jack walked on, walked on. After following the tracks around the hill apiece, he started gettin' tired and stopped to rest. Just then he heard a fluttering sound above him. He looked up and saw nine wild turkeys land on a tree limb in a big sweetgum.

"Can't pass them up," said Jack and fired away. Jack was so close that the charge split the tree limb and the turkeys caught their toes in the crack and beat each other to death flapping their wings. All Jack had to do was climb up and get 'em.

"I got nine turkeys," said Jack, "but I still don't have that rabbit." So he traveled on, traveled on. The tracks led him down the hill, and he stepped along after 'em.

"Whoa," cried Jack, sliding down through the snow, "what's that?" A big grizzly bear and a wild boar came tumbling toward him, fighting for dear life.

Well, Jack didn't think he had a chance. He just threw his gun down, closed his eyes, and threw out his arms hopin' to protect himself. The bear ran right into one of 'em, and Jack's hand went down its throat and out the other end. So Jack grabbed the bear's tail and turned him inside out.

When the old boar saw there wasn't anything else around to fight, he started butting Jack from behind with his six-inch tusks. Jack got so tired of landing flat on his rear that he gave up. "I'll just hide behind this tree," said Jack, "'till it's all over." But the boar kept comin'. When that boar rammed his six-inch tusks into the five inch tree, Jack bent down, picked up a rock, and bashed 'im down with it. "Yer caught," said Jack. "Now I got nine turkeys and two flavors of the big game, but I still don't have that rabbit."

So Jack ambled on, ambled on, along after those rabbit tracks 'til he got to the creek bank. He looked on up the creek, and there, flying right close together, were nine wild ducks. Jack looked on down the creek. "Whoa," he said, "there's nine wild geese." Then Jack heard a buzzing sound. He turned and stood face to face with a coiled up rattlesnake. Hadn't more than a second to think what to do so he just fired away, and Jack's old gun blew right up.

Well, the barrel went up the creek and killed the nine wild ducks. The stock went down the creek and killed the nine wild geese. The bullet ricocheted off a stone and hit the rattlesnake between the eyes. The kick of the gun knocked Jack head over heels backward right into the creek.

"Whoa," said Jack, wiping his eyes, "there's that durn rabbit." He paddled out of the cold water, intent on catchin' it. But when he came out on land his pockets were so full of fish he couldn't hardly move. The weight of those fish made a button pop off Jack's overalls. "Whoa," said Jack, and watched the button fly over and kill that rabbit.

Well, Jack took the rabbit, the fish, the rattlesnake, the geese, the ducks, the boar, the bear, and the turkeys and put out for home to cook his breakfast. And the last time I went to see him, he was a-doin' real well.

WILLA AND THE WIND

Source: Willa and the Wind, by Janice M. Del Negro. Marshall Cavendish, 2005.

Culture: Contemporary, based on a Norwegian folktale

Telling Time: 15 minutes

Audience: Ages 5 to 9

Comment: Adapted from "The Lad Who Went to the North Wind" from *Popular Tales from the Norse*, by Peter Christen Asbjørnsen, Edinburgh, 1859.

WILLA WAS BORN in a windy valley in the windy middle of nowhere. She lived in a small house on a small farm with her big sister, and as long as the wind blew and the clouds rained, the two sisters always had enough.

But one summer the wind took a holiday. The sun scorched the corn-fields dry and burned the girls' noses red.

"Willa," called Sis. "Go out to the barn and fetch some cornmeal so we can have cornbread and honey for breakfast."

"It's too hot," Willa grumbled, but off she went.

On her way back to the kitchen, the north wind swooped down out of the mountains. He was on holiday, but not from making mis-chief. WHOOSH! He blew birds, leaves, and Willa across the barnyard. WHOOSH! He blew the last bit of cornmeal right out of the bowl and WHOOSH!, he flew off hooting in a cloud of yellow dust.

"You ornery sack of no-good wind!" Willa shouted. "You bring that cornmeal back!"

"Well, don't have a hissy fit," said Sis. "If you want it that bad, go get it."

"I'm going, I'm going." Willa stomped down the road, bound for the mountains and the home of Old Windy, the north wind.

Old Windy lived in a great stone house on the side of a great stone mountain. Anyone else would have been afraid, but Willa marched up the stone steps to that front door and pounded on it. Old Windy himself whis-tled down from the top of the house, blew open the door with a great blast and roared, "WHO ARE YOU AND WHAT DO YOU WANT?"

"Don't yell at me, you no-good, no-account thieving windbag. I am Willa Rose Mariah McVale, and I want the cornmeal you stole, so give it back!"

Old Windy huffed and puffed, started and stopped, and finally spluttered, "GO AWAY!" Then he slammed the door.

"Hmphf," said Willa, and pounded on the door again.

Back and forth they went, Willa pounding and Old Windy shouting, until finally that breathless wind leaned against the door frame and said, "LOOK, LITTLE GIRL, I AM A FAIR WIND. TAKE THIS IN TRADE FOR YOUR CORNMEAL." From one of his deep pockets, he pulled a cotton handkerchief.

Willa narrowed her eyes. "Now why would I want that old thing? I have a hanky, thank you."

"IN ALL THE PLACES I'VE BLOWN, THERE'S NOT ANOTHER HANDKERCHIEF LIKE THIS ONE," said Old Windy. "LAY IT FLAT AND SAY 'HEADWIND, TAILWIND, GALE WIND ROUGH, GIVE FOOD AND DRINK, MORE THAN ENOUGH,' AND YOU WILL NEVER GO HUNGRY."

Willa tucked the hanky in her apron pocket and started home. The sun set behind the trees, and Willa knew it would be dark before she reached the safety of her sister's kitchen. She saw an inn by the side of the road, and she knocked on the door.

"Please, sir," Willa asked the innkeeper. "May I sleep by your fire tonight?"

"Well, girl, the fire burns with or without you in front of it," he said.

Willa went in and settled by the hearth. Then she unfolded the wind's handkerchief, and whispered,

"Headwind, tail wind, gale wind rough, give food and drink, more than enough." Sure as the wind blows, the hanky was spread with the finest food and drink, and Willa sat and ate her fill.

When the innkeeper heard the words and saw the magical feast, his heart turned moldy with greed.

That night, while Willa slept, the innkeeper crept to where she lay, and gently, gently, pulled the wind's hanky from her pocket, and left one of his own in its place.

Willa woke in the morning none the wiser, and, handkerchief in her pocket, she hurried home. Sis was tending the bees.

"Welcome home," she said. "Where's the cornmeal?"

"I have something better than cornmeal," said Willa, and she spread the handkerchief on the ground and chanted the magic words.

Nothing happened.

"It's a handkerchief," said Sis.

Willa thought about having a fit and falling in it, but instead she marched off to pay a second visit to Old Windy.

Old Windy's great stone house loomed above her. Willa went up to the door and pounded on it. Old Windy came whistling down the stone stairs, flung open the stone door, and howled, "WHO ARE YOU AND WHAT DO YOU WANT?"

"You know very well who I am. I want that cornmeal you stole because that hanky you gave me isn't worth a spoon of spit."

"I'D THANK YOU TO REMEMBER THAT I AM AN HONEST WIND. HERE. TAKE THIS AND GO AWAY."

Reaching behind him, he drew forth . . . a billy goat.

Willa looked at the goat. She looked at Old Windy.

"Why, exactly, do I want this goat? He'll eat everything he's not supposed to, he doesn't give milk, and he smells like a goat."

"IN ALL THE PLACES I'VE BLOWN, THERE'S NOT ANOTHER GOAT LIKE THIS ONE. TICKLE THE GOAT AND SAY THE WORDS 'HEADWIND, TAILWIND, GALE WIND BOLD, FILL EMPTY POCKETS FULL OF GOLD,' AND FROM HIS MOUTH THIS GOAT WILL DROP ENOUGH GOLD COINS TO FILL YOUR TWO CUPPED HANDS."

Willa thanked the north wind and started home. Darkness fell, and once again she turned off the road to the inn.

"Well, girl," the innkeeper said, "you may have a place by the fire, for that burns with or without you, but the goat must go to the barn."

Willa led the goat to the barn, but before she left, she tickled under his chin and whispered Old Windy's words, and sure as the wind blows, that goat opened his mouth and dropped enough coins to fill Willa's two cupped hands. She returned to the inn, where she paid for a fine supper and a fine night's rest.

She would not have slept so soundly had she known the innkeeper had seen her with the wondrous goat, and wanted it for his own. So, in the middle of the night, the innkeeper took Willa's goat and left one that looked exactly like it in its place.

In the morning, Willa was none the wiser. She took the animal by its tether and led it home.

Sis was feeding the chickens. She took one whiff and held her nose.

"Willa, wherever you got it, you can't keep it!"

"Oh, we'll keep it, all right," laughed Willa. "Watch! Headwind, tailwind, gale wind bold, fill empty pockets full of gold."

But sure as the wind blows, what that goat dropped had nothing to do with gold.

Willa left Sis spreading fertilizer in the garden and tore back to Old Windy's. She went up to the great front door and she pounded on it. Old Windy came whistling down from the top of the house, threw open the door, and blasted,

"WHO ARE YOU AND . . . OH, IT'S YOU."

Willa looked at him sternly.

"Now, look, I don't know what kind of sneaky shenanigans you're up to, but that hanky you gave me isn't worth a spoon of spit and that goat you gave me isn't worth a bag of bees. Besides, they only worked once, and what kind of trade is that?"

Old Windy didn't even blink. He reached into his deep sleeve and pulled out a wooden whistle.

"What do you think I am?" Willa asked. "Wooden whistles are as easy to find as twigs on trees."

"IN ALL THE PLACES I'VE BLOWN, THERE'S NOT ANOTHER WHISTLE LIKE THIS ONE," the north wind said. "ALL YOU NEED SAY IS 'HEADWIND, TAILWIND, GALE WIND SPIN, TURN WIND, SPIN WIND, WITHOUT END.'"

"Then what?" asked Willa.

"THEN BLOW THE WHISTLE. YOU WILL WHISTLE UP A WHIRL OF A WIND THAT WILL SPIN WHOEVER, WHATEVER, WHICHEVER AROUND UNTIL YOU WHISTLE IT DOWN."

He handed her the whistle.

"ON YOUR WALK HOME TONIGHT, CONSIDER THAT I AM AN HONORABLE WIND."

Willa pocketed the whistle and started home. A wisp of an idea blew her mind clear, and she headed straight to the inn.

"Well, girl!" the innkeeper said. "Have you come for another fine meal?"

Willa sighed. "Alas, I have no money. I have come only to beg a place by your fire."

Eyeing the wooden whistle peeking from her pocket, the innkeeper said, "The fire burns whether you are in front of it or not."

That night, Willa lay down by the fire, whistle in her pocket, and it wasn't long before she breathed the deep, loud sighs of sleep.

Now the innkeeper hadn't seen Willa do anything with the whistle, but he was certain that if the hanky was magic, and the goat was magic, then the whistle was magic, too. In the light of the windy dawn he crept to where Willa slept. Gently, gently, out of her pocket, he stole the wooden whistle.

He ran outside and blew on it. Nothing.

He blew again. Nothing.

He blew himself blue. Still nothing. He threw the whistle down and stamped his feet.

Willa, watching from the door, whisked out of the inn, scooped up the whistle, chanted the magic words, and blew. The whistle sounded sweet and clear.

A small breeze tickled the back of the innkeeper's neck. The breeze circled from inn to barn and back again. A wisp of wind whirled the magic handkerchief out of the innkeeper's pocket. A tiny tornado twirled the goat out of the barn. A huff of hurricane swirled him around and around until

. . .

"Mercy!" cried the innkeeper. "Mercy!"

"You don't deserve it," Willa said with a sniff.

She tucked the handkerchief into her pocket and took the goat by its tether. Then, and only then, did she blow on the wooden whistle and whistle down the wind.

"Behave yourself from now on," said Willa, "or I'll come back and whistle you dizzy."

Sis was frowning at the dusty garden when Willa stepped into the yard, whispered the words, and blew on her whistle. The wind picked up; gray clouds spun across the hot sky, and the rain began to fall.

"Willa, you brought the wind—and the rain!" laughed Sis.

"And that's not all," said Willa.

Ever since then, in that windy valley in the windy middle of nowhere, even in the driest summers in the hottest years, the wind whistles softly and the rain falls, cool and sweet.

MORE THAN SALT

Source: "More Than Salt," retold by Patrick Ryan.

Culture: Italian

Telling Time: 10 minutes

Audience: Ages 6 to adult

Comment: This is one of my favorite stories. There are versions of it all over the world, and of course it was an inspiration for Shakespeare's "King Lear." The English folk tale "Cap-o-Rushes" was one of the first I remember hearing and one of the first stories that I ever told as a storyteller. Friends in London have told me wonderful versions from their traditions in Bangladesh, Pakistan, and India, and Duncan Williamson and Betsy White both had marvelous versions in the Scots Traveller tradition, and I've found several written versions going back to the fourteenth century from many countries in Europe. This version I heard from an Italian teacher when I was telling stories in schools in Veneto and Veneto-Friuli. —Patrick Ryan

Note: You can hear Patrick tell "Cap-o-Rushes" on the CD that accompanies his *Shakespeare's Storybook, Folk Tales that Inspired the Bard* (Barefoot, 2001).

■

LONG AGO a certain King was thought to be the wisest, cleverest man in the world. Even so he once asked a stupid question. Well, he did not think it was a stupid question. The King had a problem. He knew one day he would grow old, and he wished to decide who would help him to rule his kingdom and then take his place when he died.

Now he had three children, all daughters, beautiful princesses who were wise and clever and good. Any one of them would have gladly helped her father govern, and each would have been an excellent queen. But only one could become queen, and the King could not decide which child it would be. So he decided to ask them a question.

He gathered the girls around him and said, "My darling dears, I am old and sick, and soon I shall die."

"Oh no, father!" the princesses cried. "You're not so old!"

"I am," he assured them, "but that is not my problem. I wonder who shall help me rule the kingdom? I wonder who shall be queen when I am gone? So I have decided to ask you a question—and listen well! Whoever gives me the best answer then she shall be queen when I am gone."

So it was that the King put his question: "My children tell me this—how much do you love me?"

Now imagine a father asking that question! A parent should know the answer without asking! Even so he asked and they had to answer, for like children everywhere they always answered their parents' questions politely.

The first princess replied, "Father, I love you more than bread!"

Bread, pondered the King, is a good answer, for bread is food, and food gives us life. Without food, without bread, we cannot live.

The second princess answered, "Father, I love you more than wine!"

The King considered this. Well, wine makes us merry, but also it can make us sad . . . But then, no matter what it does, it always makes life more interesting.

And so he was pleased with the first two. But it was the turn of his third daughter to answer the question, and she was his favorite and the most clever. He wanted her to give the best answer. But this princess thought her father was being very foolish. Maybe she replied honestly, perhaps she was just cheeky, for the third princess responded, "Father, if you must know, I love you more than salt."

The King heard this and flew into a rage. "More than salt!" he shouted. "More than salt is not good enough! The poorest people of my kingdom have salt. Say a better answer!"

But the princess refused. Like father like daughter, each was as stubborn as the other.

"Then you don't love me enough!" the King decided. "You're not my child, you no longer belong to this family. May you be locked up in the highest chamber of the tallest tower, never to see another, never to taste anything but bread and wine!"

"Fine!" pouted the youngest princess.

To the horror of his family, his servants, and his people, this was done. The third princess was taken to the highest chamber of the tallest tower of the palace. Every door was bricked up, each window was sealed, save for one tiny opening in her chamber at the top. That window did not look out on a fine view, over palace gardens, or the fine avenues of the capital city, nor did it look toward the mountains or sea. It looked down on a tiny, scrappy yard that kitchen servants would sit in as they chopped and peeled vegetables or scrubbed pots and pans.

She was left alone there with her books and bread and wine, which servants lifted up in a basket to her through the tiny window. The King forbade that any one should speak to her or mention her name. So she was forgotten. But she truly didn't care. The third princess was happy with her own company, and she had her books to read and found it amusing to watch the servants at work, though they ignored her and never spoke to her nor looked in her direction.

The princess also loved to sing and had a voice to do so. Her sweet voice carried out of the window and through the palace, though all pretended not to hear. The servants always made sure that, whatever room the King was in, the windows were shut tight or musicians were nearby to drown out the singing with the blasts of trumpets or thumping drums.

One day a young cook was in the yard peeling potatoes when the princess started to sing. It was a lovely song and she sang it well, and it was a song that the cook knew too. And the way it is with songs we know, we hear a well-known one and without thinking begin singing along. And this is what he did—soon the cook and the princess were singing together. When she finished, the cook sang a song and the princess joined in on that. They sang back and forth all day, harmonizing with each other.

When people sing together and like the same music, they quickly begin talking to each other and soon become friends. So it was with the cook and the princess. He forgot the King's commands regarding the princess. They were happy singing and talking together and each looked forward to the times they spent in song.

One day the princess asked, "Cook, my friend, tell me something."

"Anything, princess," he said.

"Do you always cook the King's supper?"

"Oh yes," the cook answered proudly. "I am the best cook in the palace! I always make the King's meals!

"That's very interesting!" she quietly considered.

The next day the princess asked another question. "Cook, dear friend, tell me. Do you always put salt in my father's food?"

"But of course," exclaimed the young man. "I'm a good cook! Food tastes bad without salt, and bad food wouldn't make a meal fit for a King! I always use salt."

"That's very interesting!" murmured the princess, reflecting on what he said.

On the third day the princess asked, "Cook, dear friend, you are my friend! Let me ask you—do you think . . . maybe . . . perhaps . . . one day—well, could you make the King's supper *without* salt?"

The cook was horrified. "Oh, but princess, that would make the food taste very bad. If I did that, he might be angry. The King might lock me in the tower too! He might even chop off my head!"

"Yes, he might," agreed the princess. "But I don't think so. You are my friend. For me, your friend, would you do this? Would you please think about it at least?"

The cook agreed to do this. As he thought about it, he did think what the King had done to the princess was not fair. It was not right. And she was his friend, and friends always help each other if they are true friends. So he decided to make the King's supper that night without salt!

The King took one bite of his supper and found it terrible. He ordered the cook to come to him.

"What have you done to this food, it is awful!"

"I have made your supper without salt!" the cook informed him.

"What? Do you try to poison me?" asked the King.

"No, I'm just doing what your majesty wishes," the cook answered innocently.

"I never told you not to use salt!"

"You told your daughter that salt was not good enough, that everyone, even the poorest people have salt. If this is so, then salt is not good enough, not special enough for a King. So being a King's cook I must make sure your food is the best, made without a handful of salt, with not a pinch of salt, not even a grain of salt!" explained the young man, with a twinkle in his eye. "So from now on, all your food will be prepared without salt and fit for a King!"

The King suddenly understood. He understood what the cook said and what his daughter had meant. Salt is what all must have, what all need—and all need and must have love. Her answer had been the best.

So the King himself went to the tower. He unbricked the door with his own hands, and climbed up the tall tower's stairs on his hands and knees, and bowed before his youngest child to beg her forgiveness. And of course she forgave her father.

From that time on she stood by his side, helping him to rule the kingdom wisely and well. And next to her always sat the young cook, for he was her true friend.

And that was good, and it wasn't bad!

LING-LI AND THE PHOENIX FAIRY: A CHINESE FOLKTALE

Source: Ling-Li and the Phoenix Fairy: A Chinese Folktale, retold by Ellin Greene. Clarion Books, 1996. A Notable Book in Social Studies.

Culture: Chinese

Telling Time: 11 minutes

Audience: Ages 8 to 12

Comment: The Chinese phoenix is entirely different from the fabled bird in Greek mythology that symbolized immortality. In Chinese mythology, there is not one phoenix, but two. Together they symbolize union. The presence of the phoenix was a sign that the reigning ruler was honorable and just. When the Chinese philosopher Confucius complained that "the phoenix appears no more," he meant that the government was corrupt and there was no prospect for improvement.

The flower that reminded Ling-Li of the phoenix bird in its flight to the sun is related to a common wildflower in the United States, known as jewelweed.

■

ONCE, LONG AGO, in a small village in the mountainous region of China, there lived a girl who was exceptionally clever with her hands. In weaving or embroidery, no one could match her skill. She was pretty, too—as beautiful as the poppy that grows in the fields—and thrifty besides. Her name was Ling-Li.

Opposite Ling-Li's house there lived a boy named Manchang. Ever since they were little, the two children played together. And as the one was known for her thriftiness and skill in homespun crafts and the other for his diligence and skill in farming, the two became close friends. Their parents noticed how well suited they were for each other and, according to ancient custom, arranged their betrothal.

Manchang's parents were very poor. All they could afford to give as a betrothal gift was two baskets of double-eared corn, a large green cabbage, a sheaf of violet peas with striped pods, and two strings of red chili peppers. But to Ling-Li these vegetables were the most beautiful gifts in the world. She carefully placed them where she could look at them first thing in the morning when she awoke and last thing at night before she went to sleep.

Manchang and Ling-Li were to be married in the autumn. Ling-Li's parents wanted to sell everything they could spare in order to buy wedding clothes for their daughter. But Ling-Li would not have it. "I can make my own wedding robe," she said. With money he had saved, Manchang bought Ling-Li several catties of raw cotton, and she set to work.

In the same village there lived a girl called Golden Flower. She, too, was to be married that autumn, to the son of a wealthy family. The groom's parents sent Golden Flower expensive gifts—intricately engraved bracelets of ivory, beautiful brocaded jackets, and dazzlingly embroidered satin robes. Golden Flower tried on this and that. All day long she kept changing her clothes, making up her face, and gazing at her reflection.

All the other girls in the village admired Golden Flower's new clothes, but Ling-Li did not so much as cast a glance at them. She spun the cotton Manchang had given her, wove the thread into cloth, and made it into a wedding robe. Then she embroidered the robe with patterns of the double-eared corn and the green cabbage, the red chili peppers, and the violet peas. The corn looked as if it were made of gold, the cabbage of jade, the chili of red coral, and the violet peas of dragon's gall. The more she embroidered, the more intricate the patterns became, and the more beautiful they looked.

Day after day Ling-Li stitched busily from morning till evening. Sometimes she pricked her finger with the needle and a drop of blood fell onto the robe, and there she would embroider a red flower. Sometimes she became tired and beads of sweat soiled the cloth, and here she would embroider butterflies.

For three whole months she worked, and at last the robe was finished. It was lovelier than the changing clouds in the sky and more colorful than a meadow in full bloom.

On the day the robe was finished, Golden Flower happened to pass by Ling-Li's house. When she saw the robe she was overcome with envy.

"Ling-Li," she said, "I'll give you ten embroidered satin robes and six brocaded jackets for your wedding robe."

"No," Ling-Li replied, "I won't exchange, for nothing can compare with this robe of mine."

But Golden Flower was used to having her way. Before Ling-Li had time to realize what was happening, Golden Flower snatched up the robe and ran out the door. "I'll wear it for a day, then I'll return it to you," she called over her shoulder.

Ling-Li hurried after her. Suddenly, Golden Flower tossed the robe onto a wall that ran alongside the road. Ling-Li looked around for a bamboo stick to fetch the robe down, but before she could find one, a flock of magpies swooped down from the sky and whisked the robe away.

Ling-Li stamped her feet and shouted at the birds, but the magpies only soared higher and disappeared into the clouds, taking the brightly colored garment with them.

Ling-Li was so angry she could have cried. Golden Flower put up a show of sympathy and even offered Ling-Li one of her silk dresses to wear at her wedding, but Ling-Li refused. "None of your silk dresses can compare to my homespun wedding robe," she replied indignantly. Golden Flower, secretly pleased by the theft, shrugged her shoulders and went home.

Ling-Li determined to trap the magpies and get back her wedding robe. From the thread she had left over, she wove a large net.

Early the next morning the magpies flew over Ling-Li's house. They perched on the roof and chattered incessantly. As soon as Ling-Li heard them she ran into the garden, spread her net, and threw a handful of grain onto it. The magpies flew down to peck at the grain. With a pull of her robe, Ling-Li caught them in the net, but as she drew the net toward her the magpies suddenly flapped their wings and flew off, lifting the net and Ling-Li into the sky.

Flying at high speed, they soared toward the rising sun. All Ling-Li could hear was the sighing of the wind. The rice fields below her looked like patches of red and green, disappearing into the distance.

The magpies flew on and on until they reached the peak of a high mountain. There they gently set Ling-Li on the ground. All around her were green trees where birds of every kind—larks, golden orioles, peacocks, parrots, and doves—hopped from branch to branch. The magpies tore the net into shreds to free themselves.

As soon as the magpies joined the others, all the birds began to sing. Startled by the sound, Ling-Li looked up and saw a spirit maiden, dressed in a beautifully embroidered robe, approaching her. Ling-Li was puzzled, for the robe was the one that the magpies had taken from her.

The spirit maiden spoke in a kind voice. "Ling-Li, your robe is beautiful, but I have one even more beautiful. Will you exchange?"

"I'm sorry," Ling-Li replied, "but I cannot, for this is my wedding robe that I've made myself."

"Oh," said the spirit maiden, "then I'll return it to you at once." And she took off the robe and gave it back to Ling-Li. "Thank you for letting me wear it. May you and your husband live in harmony and have a rich, full life together." Before Ling-Li could reply, the spirit maiden turned and disappeared.

As Ling-Li stood there, thinking herself in a dream, she saw a dazzlingly colored phoenix fly out of the woods. Immediately, the other birds took wing and followed it.

"It must have been the Phoenix Fairy, the Queen of the Birds," thought Ling-Li. Then, taking her wedding robe, she tripped merrily down the mountain toward home.

Halfway there she met Manchang, beside himself with worry. Early that morning, as he was working in the fields, he had seen the flock of magpies carrying the net with Ling-Li dangling from it. He immediately gave chase, but the birds flew so fast he was soon left behind.

Ling-Li told him everything that had happened. Manchang in return told her that the bridal chamber had been cleaned and whitewashed and that all was ready for the wedding.

The next day, dressed in her lovely embroidered wedding robe made with her own hands, Ling-Li became Manchang's bride. And no couple was ever happier.

After the wedding Ling-Li was more industrious and thrifty than ever. At the break of day with the call of chattering magpies, she would put on her embroidered robe and go out into the fields to work. Whenever she felt too warm, she would take the robe off and carefully lay it on the ground. Then the magpies would appear and circle overhead, on the lookout in case someone should try to steal it.

One day while Ling-Li was helping Manchang with the harvest, she took off her robe and laid it on a ridge. Just at that moment Golden Flower was returning from town to visit her parents. As she walked along the ridge, she saw the embroidered robe lying there. Stealthily she snatched it up and flung it across her shoulders. But as she was thrusting her hands into the sleeves, a flock of magpies swooped down from the sky. With loud caws they encircled the thief and pecked at her. Shielding her face with her hand, Golden Flower ran and hid herself from her persistent pursuers. In all the confusion the embroidered robe was torn to shreds. Golden Flower's face, too, was gashed, and even after her wounds healed her face showed ugly scars.

The varicolored shreds of cloth looked like thousands of beautiful flowers as they danced in the breeze, chased by butterflies. They drifted farther and farther away and then gradually fluttered to the ground, strewn all over the fields and newly upturned soil.

The following spring, clusters of tender plants appeared in the fields. Whenever Ling-Li saw these plants she felt a pang in her heart, for they reminded her of her lost robe. She dug the plants up one by one and planted them in her garden. By summer they were full grown, with reddish-brown stems, shiny green leaves, and blood-red flowers.

To Ling-Li the flowers looked like the colorful phoenix bird with outstretched wings in its flight to the sun.

RUBIES

Source: Passion and Poison: Tales of Shape-Shifters, Ghosts, and Spirited Women, by Janice M. Del Negro. Marshall Cavendish, 2007.

Culture: Literary tale with Italian setting

Telling time: 10 minutes

Audience: Young adults to adults

Comment: "Rubies" is a story of seduction, betrayal, ghosts, and vengeance. The plot turns on one gold ring, so be careful of the details! "Rubies" is very loosely based on the Child ballad "Lady Isabel and the Elf Knight," multiple versions of which can be found online at http://www.springthyme.co.uk/ballads/balladtexts/4_LadyIsabel. html.

■

OH, THE SEDUCTION had been so smooth. It had happened right beneath their noses, in front of their eyes, and none of them ever saw what he was doing. Rafael, a traveling trovatore, had been visiting the house for months, singing and telling stories. He did not appear to treat Helene differently from the other young women of the household. He sang love songs to all of them, kissed all their hands, admired all their jewels—especially their jewels. He was like a black-eyed raven, unable to resist anything that glittered, though he wore little jewelry himself—one gold ring, set in one pierced ear, like a pirate.

The cousins thought him most romantic, but it was the daughters of the house who mattered. There were two: Giovanna was the elder, Helene the younger. Both sisters had their choice of sparkling gems to adorn their olive skin and dark hair, but even the costliest gems paled against Helene's beauty. Only her mother's rubies did her justice. There were bracelets, and earrings, and dozens of hairpins with shimmering stones set into the top. But the necklace dazzled the eye—three strands of perfect rubies set in gold. The rubies sat like drops of blood on Helene's hair and throat, and they glittered when she laughed, as if they were laughing, too.

Afterward, Giovanna blamed herself.

"Oh, why did I not see it?" she cried. "I should have seen it. I was close to her, loved her. I should have known. I should have known."

But no one had known. There had been a terrible storm that night. The wind howled in over the sea, the lightning cracked across the cliffs. Giovanna, awakened by the fury of the storm, had discovered Helene's empty bed, and the empty jewel case. She roused the house. When they found Rafael's bed unslept in, they thought the two had run away together. The brothers were on their way to the stables when Rafael's riderless horse galloped into the courtyard. Rafael staggered in behind and fell to his knees on the stones. He was pulled to his feet by the strong arms of the waiting brothers; he clung to them desperately trying to catch his breath to speak:

"I tried to stop them . . . Helene and her lover . . . I chased after them, they were on the cliffside road, heading for the harbor, but before I reached them . . . the lightning . . . Helene's horse ran away with her, toward the cliffs . . . they went over, Helene and her horse, both of them went over. I caught him, the man, but I slipped in the mud, and he fled on his horse. I tried to chase him, but my horse threw me, and he got away."

They could see Rafael was badly hurt. His clothes were muddy and torn, his face bruised, one eye blackened. His gold hoop had been pulled from his ear, and the torn flesh bled down the side of his face and neck. His story rang with truth; he was weeping as he told it.

"Forgive me . . . forgive me, I was too late, I was too late."

He sobbed in Giovanna's arms. The family, in their own sorrow, actually tried to comfort him. The brothers' search for the lover was futile. They did not even know who they were looking for.

Giovanna was sick with grief. She went to her room, and discovered what she had missed before—a letter from Helene, and their mother's rubies. "My dear sister," the letter read. "By the time you read this, I will be far at sea with my true love. I thought to use mother's rubies to finance our new life, but found I could not. They belong here, in the house where she was born, with you. Please forgive me. Father would never permit this union. I am so happy. Love, Helene." Giovanna wept until she could weep no more.

The rain stopped. The wind changed. Giovanna sat at the window, her head on her arms. She was half-drunk with tears when she heard the whisper from the sea.

"Giovanna . . ."

She thought she was mad, but then she heard it again.

"Giovanna. Giovanna."

She put on a cloak and went out into the night. She walked the long dark road to the cliffs; the moon, buried in cloud, struggled to light the sky. Giovanna stared into the freezing water at the place where Helene had fallen. Weak with sorrow she fell on her knees in the mud. From behind her a familiar voice moaned, "Giovanna. Giovanna."

Helene took form from the mist and the moonlight, but only the moonlight put life in her eyes. She was battered and bruised. Her dark hair was darker with blood, and her shift was torn. Her face, her beautiful face, was pale and swollen and the water ran from her hair, from her fingers, from her eyes as if it had no end.

"Helene," Giovanna moaned. "Helene, who was it? Who did this to you?"

Helene held out her hand. In her palm was a simple gold ring, a golden hoop, fit for a pirate's ear.

"Avenge me," whispered Helene.

Giovanna stared past her murdered sister. Behind Helene were the shades of other women, with bodies of mist and eyes without light. Helene was not the only one. There had been others. Dawn was brightening the sky when Giovanna walked back to the house, Helene's whisper still in her ear: "Sister, avenge me. Avenge us all."

Helene's body was never recovered, but the funeral mass was held nonetheless. At the service, Rafael had the eyes of a grieving angel. The young cousins found the trovatore romantically tragic. It was all Giovanna could do not to accuse him right there in the church. Despite the family's hospitable urging, Rafael left immediately after the services, but not before Giovanna obtained his promise to return. It was easy enough. Rafael had seen the necklace around her neck, the rubies she wore as her legacy from Helene. Being the thieving raven she knew he was, she knew he would come back for them, and short weeks later, he did.

They met in secret on his return, like trysting lovers. He saw Giovanna as desirable now, she made sure of it, sighing about her loneliness, the rubies warm against her skin. It was a simple matter to bring him to his knees. Rafael chose his moment well—twilight in the rose garden, the scent of sea and blossoms. He had always loved her as a sister, he claimed, but had come to love her as a woman. Giovanna demurred, at first, but let him persuade her with promises and poetry.

"I do love you, Rafael," she lied. "But my father would never permit it. Our only hope is to run away together."

He was kneeling before her, his head bent over her hands, hiding a sudden smile.

"Giovanna, my own, do we not have the right to some happiness after such terrible grief? Surely our love is a sign of God's blessing, and an answer to my prayers."

Oh, his words were dipped in passion and poison. She told him she would run away with him.

"I will wear as many of my jewels as I can, and carry still more, so we will be able to travel far, and live well."

"Tonight," said Rafael.

Stone-hearted, Giovanna smiled at him, kissed him, and called him love.

In the middle of the night, Giovanna rose from her bed to dress. She did not dress like a lovesick woman running away with her lover, but like a priestess preparing for some dark ceremony. She wore jeweled pins in her hair, and bracelets from her wrists to her elbows; her dress was covered in tiny gems that flashed in the firelight. Around her neck she wore Helene's rubies, dark as blood. Giovanna pulled her cape up around her throat and pinned it with an emerald brooch the size of her fist; Rafael's eyes gleamed when he saw it.

They rode out of the courtyard, horses' hooves muffled, along the road that led to the harbor and the sea. Rafael stopped when they reached the crossroad leading to the cliff where Helene had fallen. A moment, he asked? A moment to ask Helene's blessing on their marriage? Giovanna could not refuse him. They dismounted, and walked to the edge, his hand on her elbow, so helpful. She drew back.

"Not so close," Giovanna said. "It's such a long way down."

Rafael turned and faced her then, his back to the sea.

"Your sister feared the edge as well, but in the end she died as easily as the six who came before her, and so will you. But you will not take to the sea what you will give to me."

Giovanna was still, so still.

"Your jewels, lady," he said. "I will have them."

Giovanna undid her cloak and it slipped to the ground. The sun was coming up over the edge of the sea, and the light caught the rubies around Giovanna's throat and set them on fire. Rafael could not take his eyes from those flaming stones Giovanna reached behind her head, and, walking towards Rafael, undid the clasp that held the rubies.

"You want them?" she said. "Catch them." And she tossed the necklace toward the edge of the cliff. With a cry Rafael lunged and snatched them from the air. His gloating did not last long. Giovanna pushed him. He clutched the rubies even as he fell. Rafael was struggling to keep his head above the waves when seven pairs of pale white arms came up out of the sea, and took him.

"There," Giovanna said. "Seven brides have you sent to the bottom of the sea, and now you will be bridegroom to them all."

Giovanna picked up her cloak and went home, and that night, and every night after, she had only peaceful dreams.

THE WHITE HORSE GIRL AND THE BLUE WIND BOY

Source: Rootabaga Stories, by Carl Sandburg. Harcourt, 1922.

Culture: American

Telling Time: 10 minutes

Audience: Ages 5 to adult

Comment: Sandburg returned from World War I saying he'd seen enough ignorance and sophistication to last him a good long while. He wrote *Rootabaga Stories* as an antidote to what he'd seen as a war correspondent in Europe. "The White Horse Girl and The Blue Wind Boy" is the *classic* story from Sandburg's classic collection of tales. The surface of his story works great magic in sound. The power of his language and rhythm of his writing can easily tip the story into a performance that spins out as one long tone poem—all the sound burying the bones of the story. Nonetheless, beneath the evocative cadences is a poignant story of a young couple who find each other on their beloved prairie. Yet together they leave the prairie and their families to find the sources of all that they love. "Their fathers and mothers and sisters and brothers and aunts and uncles" clearly do not understand why or where "their darlings" have gone. And, where have they gone? To find a home above the sea, the source of wind and wave.

When I tell this story, I seek to balance its narrative sense with its rich tones. This is one of the first stories I ever learned, and it thrilled me when a young Jane Yolen heard it and loved it. But over the years she's told me there is no *story.* Now I admire Jane Yolen's heart and head for story, but I disagree—I think the story *is* there.
　　　　　　—*Carol Birch*

Note: You can hear Carol telling "The White Horse Girl and the Blue Wind Boy" on *Sandburg Out Loud!* from August House Audio.

■

WHEN THE DISHES ARE WASHED at night time and the cool of the evening has come in summer, or the lamps and fires are lit for the night in winter, then the fathers and mothers in the Rootabaga Country sometimes tell young people the story of the White Horse Girl and the Blue Wind Boy.

The White Horse Girl grew up far in the west of the Rootabaga Country. All the years she grew up as a girl she liked to ride horses. Best of all things for her was to be straddle of a white horse loping with a loose bridle among the hills and along the rivers of the west Rootabaga Country.

She rode one horse white as snow, another horse white as new washed sheep wool, and another white as silver. And she could not tell because she did not know which of these three white horses she liked best.

"Snow is beautiful enough for me any time," she said, "new washed sheep wool, or silver out of a ribbon of the new moon, any or either is white enough for me. I like the white manes, the white flanks, the white noses, the white feet of all my ponies. I like the forelocks hanging down between the white ears of all three—my ponies."

And living neighbor to the White Horse Girl in the same prairie country, with the same black crows flying over their places, was the Blue Wind Boy. All the years he grew up as a boy he liked to walk with his feet in the dirt and the grass listening to the winds. Best of all things for him was to put on strong shoes and go hiking among the hills and along the rivers of the west Rootabaga Country, listening to the winds.

There was a blue wind of day time, starting sometimes six o'clock on a summer morning or eight o'clock on a winter morning. And there was a night wind with blue of summer stars in summer and blue of winter stars in winter. And there was yet another, a blue wind of the times between night and day, a blue dawn and evening wind. All three of these winds he liked so well he could not say which he liked best.

"The early morning wind is strong as the prairie and whatever I tell it I know it believes and remembers," he said, "and the night wind with the big dark curves of the night sky in it, the night wind gets inside of me and understands all my secrets. And the blue wind of the times between, in the dusk when it is neither night nor day, this is the wind that asks me questions and tells me to wait and it will bring me whatever I want."

Of course, it happened as it had to happen, the White Horse Girl and the Blue Wind Boy met. She, straddling one of her white horses, and he, wearing his strong hiking shoes in the dirt and the grass, it had to happen they should meet among the hills and along the rivers of the west Rootabaga Country where they lived as neighbors.

And of course, she told him all about the snow white horse and the horse white as new washed sheep wool, and the horse white as a silver ribbon of the new moon. And he told her all about the blue winds he liked listening to, the early morning wind, the night sky wind, and the wind of the dusk between, the wind that asked him questions and told him to wait.

One day the two of them were gone. On the same day of the week the White Horse Girl and the Blue Wind Boy went away. And their fathers and mothers and sisters and brothers and uncles and aunts wondered about them and talked about them, because they didn't tell anybody beforehand they were going. Nobody at all knew beforehand or afterward why they were going away, the real honest why of it.

They left a short letter. It read:

To All Our Sweethearts, Old Folks and Young Folks:
    We have started to go where the white horses come from and where the
blue winds begin. Keep a corner in your hearts for us while we are gone.
                                            The White Horse Girl.
                                            The Blue Wind Boy.

That was all they had to guess by in the west Rootabaga Country, to
guess and guess where two darlings had gone.

Many years passed. One day there came riding across the Rootabaga
Country a Gray Man on Horseback. He looked like he had come a long
ways. So they asked him the question they always asked of any rider who
looked like he had come a long ways, "Did you ever see the White Horse
Girl and the Blue Wind Boy?"

"Yes," he answered, "I saw them."

"It was a long, long ways from here I saw them," he went on, "it would
take years and years to ride to where they are. They were sitting together
and talking to each other, sometimes singing, in a place where the land runs
high and tough rocks reach up. And they were looking out across water,
blue water as far as the eye could see. And away far off the blue waters met
the blue sky."

" 'Look!' " said the Boy, " 'that's where the blue winds begin.' "

"And far out on the blue waters, jut a little this side of where the blue
winds begin, there were white manes, white flanks, white noses, white gal-
loping feet."

" 'Look!' " said the Girl, " 'that's where the white horses come from.' "

"And then nearer to the land came thousands in an hour, millions in a
day, white horses, some white as snow, some like new washed sheep wool,
some white as silver ribbons of the new moon."

"I asked them, 'Whose place is this?' " They answered, " 'It belongs to us;
this is what we started for; this is where the white horses come from; this is
where the blue winds begin.' "

And that was all the Gray Man on Horseback would tell the people of
the west Rootabaga Country. That was all he knew, he said, and if there was
any more he would tell it.

And the fathers and mothers and sisters and brothers and uncles and
aunts of the White Horse Girl and the Blue Wind Boy wondered and
talked often about whether the Gray Man on Horseback made up the story
out of his head or whether it happened just like he told it.

Anyhow this is the story they tell sometimes to the young people of the
west Rootabaga Country when the dishes are washed at night and the cool
of the evening has come in summer or the lamps and fires are lit for the
night in winter.

THE VISION IN THE WOOD

Source: Revised from *The Golden Thread: Storytelling in Teaching and Learning*, by Susan Danoff. Storytelling Arts Press. Copyright © 2005 by Susan Danoff.

Culture: Literary fairy tale

Telling time: 11 minutes

Audience: Ages 12 to adult

Comment: When I wrote this story I was thinking about how storytellers, like other artists, must have a vision to make their art form come to life. As storytellers we must see into our stories and breathe life into them, just as the woodcarver sees the figures in the wood, even before he carves it. If we invest our hearts and spirits when we share our stories with children, we can inspire them to listen, to learn, to ask questions, and to search for truth.

—*Susan Danoff*

Note: You can hear Susan tell stories from *The Golden Thread* on her award-winning recording *Women of Vision*.

THERE WAS ONCE A WOODCARVER who loved his craft so very much that the wood seemed to become as he wished almost by his touch. He could see the figure of a squirrel in a curved branch of a tree or a deer in the body of a fallen oak. The figures he saw in the wood seemed alive to him and when he had finished carving them, they seemed alive to those who saw them. The wood gleamed like satin; anyone who passed by had to lay a hand on these wooden creatures which felt warm and smooth as a baby's skin.

From an early age the woodcarver had known his vocation, as if there were no other choice. And he practiced it diligently for thirty years from the time he was allowed to hold the carving tools.

But one morning he awoke and as he looked around his studio he didn't see figures and animals waiting in the wood; he saw only wood. He tilted his head this way and that, and suddenly he realized that this was how most people saw wood. No matter how he looked at it, he couldn't see anything but wood cut from trees, motionless, lifeless.

At first he was perplexed, and then angry. He picked up one of his carving knives, grabbed a slab of wood, and carved, not with his usual grace and agility but boldly and without care. As he did so the knife slipped, severely wounding his right hand, the hand that held the knife.

Perhaps it was no accident. Perhaps the hand had allowed the knife to slip on purpose. Whatever the case, his hand could not be used again—for carving or anything else.

The woodcarver was able to survive by using his savings and by selling the carvings left from before the accident. Yet each morning he awoke wondering what to do. "I always knew I was made for carving wood," he told himself. "I am of no use to the world now." The passion that had motivated him all his life had disappeared as mysteriously as it had come and no other arrived to take its place.

He lived this way for a while, wishing the days to pass quickly and the nights slowly, when one day a young man came to his door. "I wish to become a woodcarver," he said, "and I've been told you're the best this part of the world has ever seen. Will you teach me?"

"Didn't you hear about me? I can no longer carve. I've lost the use of my hand." He didn't want to say he'd lost the vision of a woodcarver too; he'd not admitted that to anyone.

"Yes," said the young man. "I've heard about your accident. But I thought, sir, that perhaps you could teach me with words, and I will try to do as you say."

In all his working life the woodcarver had never taken an apprentice. Though he'd been asked to, he had always said he was too busy. Actually, he had no desire to have students creating works that looked like his just for the purpose of selling more. That seemed like cheating.

"I've never taught anyone in my life," said the woodcarver, "but I like you, and I'll try. I won't promise a week or a month or a year. Maybe the lesson will last only one hour. If you're willing to understand that, we can try."

"Thank you, sir. I am willing," said the young man.

They went into the studio where pieces of uncarved wood still lay, and the woodcarver said, "Pick the piece you'd like to start with, but choose it carefully."

"And how shall I know which? Shall we start big or small?"

"That I cannot say. Listen to the wood. Touch it. Watch it. Take your time and if you can find the piece that is right for you, then perhaps we'll have another lesson."

The young man walked around and around the studio. Then he sat. He sat with his eyes open and with his eyes closed. He picked up some of the wood and then put it down. Then he noticed a small gnarled piece, almost like a scrap. This was the one he wanted.

"This is the one," he said to the woodcarver.

"And why that one?" his teacher asked.

"I cannot say for sure. But somehow I know it is this one."

"If that is so," said the teacher, "you have chosen well."

Now the teacher looked at the small misshapen piece of wood, and he could see nothing in it, but he asked, "My boy, when you look at the wood, what do you see?"

"A baby, his sleeping head resting in the palm of a mother's hand."

The teacher remembered when he too could see such things, and he marveled at the vision of his student.

"The lesson is over for today," said the woodcarver. "Take the vision you have had, live with it, sleep with it, dream with it, then come again tomorrow."

That night sleep came more quickly than usual for the woodcarver and in the morning he awoke with some desire to see the new day and the student who had come the day before.

"We will put the wood aside just for now," said the woodcarver, "and I will show you the tools. We will work with one tool at a time until you know it. If your hands do not know the craft, then you can never make the wood look as you see it in your vision."

The student was clumsy at first. But his teacher was patient with him. He would not have been patient had he been the great woodcarver he once was, when the craft was so easy it came to him as in a dream. He was patient because he taught as if he too were a novice, discovering the secrets of the craft. And he really was like a novice, though his mind remembered and he used the words of memory, his hands no longer knew the secrets.

But soon a strange thing began to happen to the woodcarver. He would coach his student during the day, watching, patiently correcting. Then at night, after the student left, he would secure a slab of wood in a vice, and he would practice with his left hand as he had instructed the student to do. At first it was as if his left hand had been born with none of the dexterity or grace of the right, but in time, he tamed it. And in time too, the student learned to handle the tools and get them to do what he wished.

"Now," said the woodcarver, "it is time to find the sleeping child in the gnarled piece of wood. You have the tools, but the vision is your own. I will watch you, but I will not correct you. Go where you will and learn as you go. Your own mistakes will tell you more than I can. Accept them as your greatest teachers now."

He watched as the student carved into the wood, and it was like a miracle before his eyes: a tiny head emerged, the fingers of a hand, a body curving with the motion of the wood. The carving wasn't perfect, of course, but it had life and promise.

"You have done well, my boy," said the woodcarver. "Now look at the carving and tell me what worked for you and what you might do differently another time."

The young man did so, spurred on by his discoveries to try his hand at another carving.

Meanwhile, the woodcarver too was ready—at least his left hand had learned what his right had once known, but still when he looked at the wood, he saw only wood and not the beings in the wood that had guided his hand before. Nor did he feel the desire to create that had once fed his art.

He was perplexed but not angry or discouraged when another stranger knocked at the door. He was a blind man.

"I have heard that you are a teacher. You can see that I am blind, but if you would be patient with me, I believe that my hands could learn the craft of woodcarving."

The woodcarver looked at the man's hands, beautiful hands with long slender fingers, just the type of hands he would have carved into the sculpture of an archer once long ago.

"I will try," said the woodcarver, "for though I have the use of my eyes, I too am blind." And for the first time he revealed his secret loss.

The woodcarver taught the blind man how to use each tool, just as he had taught his first student. This man learned even more rapidly than the first. And then the time came for him to make his carving.

"Here in my studio are many pieces of wood. Explore them with your hands and find the piece you would like to carve. I cannot tell you what to carve, for though I have taught you the craft of the tools, I cannot teach you the art. That is yours alone."

The blind man examined the wood with his hands until he found a piece he wanted, and he began to carve. As the woodcarver watched, again he saw the miracle happen, for out of the wood he saw a hand emerge holding a heart.

"You are a great teacher," said the blind man, "and I understand now how to carve. I have carved this piece for you because I know you too have lost your vision. But what you do not know is that you now see with your heart. Let your heart show you where to go, and perhaps your left hand will lead you there."

"Thank you," said the woodcarver, yet he was still perplexed.

That night the woodcarver chose a piece of wood to see what would happen. He did not know at first what his hand would do but he wasn't afraid. He began to chip away and suddenly he knew what to do, not because of the vision in the wood, but from a feeling that he could not name. And the miracle happened again. Out of the wood two hands emerged: one old, gnarled, lined; the other smooth and outstretched.

And as he looked at this creation he realized that he could carve again—perhaps not as before, but that no longer troubled him. A new passion had taken the place of the old.

He was a teacher now.

THE LEGEND OF THE CHRISTMAS ROSE

Source: The Legend of the Christmas Rose, by Selma Lagerlöf, retold by Ellin Greene. Illustrated by Charles Mikolaycak. Holiday House, 1990.

Culture: Swedish

Reading Time: 17 minutes

Audience: Ages 5 to adult

Comment: There are several legends that explain the origin of the Christmas Rose. This retelling is adapted from Selma Lagerlöf's "The Legend of the Christmas Rose," published in *Good Housekeeping* in December 1907. Ms. Lagerlöf is best known to children for her books *The Wonderful Adventures of Nils* and *The Further Adventures of Nils* in which she combined the folklore, history, and geography of Sweden. Ms. Lagerlöf's lifelong interest in Swedish folklore was fostered by her grandmother's retellings of local legends and tales. In 1909 this gifted storyteller became the first woman to receive the Nobel Prize for Literature.

I have indicated Reading Time rather than Telling Time because this is a wonderful "read-aloud in the family" story, and I have preserved Ms. Lagerlöf's words as much as possible. If you decide to tell it, approach it as a literary tale. And if you are fortunate enough to find a copy with Charles Mikolaycak's magnificent illustrations (o.p.), be sure to share them with your listeners.

The Christmas Rose (Helleborus niger) is not really a rose. It is a member of the buttercup family. The pale white flower seems to rise miraculously from the cold wintry earth, serving to remind us that life is full of miracles.

—*Ellin Greene*

■

ROBBER MOTHER, WHO LIVED IN ROBBERS' CAVE UP IN GÖINGE Forest with Robber Father and their five children, went down to the village one day to beg. Robber Father did not go with her.

Years before, Robber Father had been caught stealing a neighbor's cow, and the bishop had outlawed him, threatening to put him in prison if he ever dared to show his face in the village again. But sometimes, when food was scarce or the children's clothing had worn to tatters, Robber Mother would take all five youngsters into the village to beg. When the villagers saw Robber Mother and her wild-looking brood coming down the road, they would quickly put a bundle of used clothing or a parcel of food on their doorstep and bolt their doors. No one spoke kindly to Robber Mother and her children or invited them indoors, even in the coldest weather.

On this particular day, when Robber Mother and her children were out begging, they happened to pass Ovid Cloister. The cloister was situated in a beautiful park east of the lake. The grounds were surrounded by a stone wall, but today the gate was ajar and the youngest of the Robber children scampered in. In a moment she was back, tugging at her mother's skirt and pulling her toward the open gate.

When Robber Mother entered the grounds, she found herself standing at the foot of a magnificent garden laid out in the shape of a cross. The corners of the flower beds had been rounded and a giant fountain had been set in the center of the intersecting paths. Each section of the cross had been planted with a different variety of flowers—sweetly scented roses, rosemary, rue, and other healing herbs; brilliantly colored lilies; and exotic plants. Robber Mother's stern look softened into an indulgent smile. Holding her youngest by the hand, she began walking along the stone-paved path toward the fountain. The other Robber children followed close behind.

When the lay brother who was tending the garden saw Robber Mother with all five youngsters in tow, he shouted for them to leave at once. "This is the abbot's private garden," he said, "and you have no right to be here." Robber Mother's smile changed to a scowl so fierce that it sent the lay brother reeling backwards. "I am Robber Mother from Göinge Forest," she answered sharply, "so touch me if you dare! I will leave when I have finished looking."

At this the lay brother became greatly agitated since women were not allowed in the monastery, and it was he who had left the gate open. "If you don't leave, the monks will be angry with me for forgetting to close the gate and may send me away," he pleaded. But Robber Mother paid no more attention to his pleas than to his shouts and continued walking toward the fountain.

The lay brother decided there was nothing to be done but to run to the cloister and ask for help. He returned with two monks. The monks tried to persuade Robber Mother to leave, and when she refused, they each took her by an arm and turned her toward the gate. Robber Mother planted her feet firmly on the path and began to shriek in a hoarse, strident voice. At the same time, the children threw themselves on the monks, biting and kicking. They caused such an uproar that the old abbot himself came out to see what was the matter.

The lay brother explained that Robber Mother and her children had invaded the garden and now refused to leave. The abbot scolded the monks for trying to use force and sent them back to the cloister. "Get on with your work," he ordered the lay brother. "I will see to this matter."

Meanwhile, Robber Mother had gone back to wandering among the flower beds. The abbot, certain that the woman had never seen such a splendid garden, was surprised to find her so at home. He greeted her gently and asked if the garden pleased her.

Robber Mother was expecting a different sort of welcome and now, when she looked at the abbot and noticed his white hair and frail frame, her anger left her. "It is a fine garden," she replied, "but it cannot be compared with another that I know."

The garden was the one earthly thing about which the abbot was vain. He had spent long hours cultivating his plants, many of them brought to him by sea captains who traveled to faraway lands. Robber Mother's words offended the good monk, and he replied coldly that he was not familiar with the garden of which she spoke.

"I tell you the truth," Robber Mother cried in a loud voice, her face growing crimson with rage. "You who are holy men surely ought to know that once a year on Christmas Eve a part of Göinge Forest is transformed into a beautiful garden in remembrance of the birthday of the Christ Child. And in that garden I have seen flowers far more lovely than any here."

At this the lay brother gave a scornful laugh. "The abbot has gathered plants from far and near, and there is not a lovelier garden to be found in all of Sweden."

But the abbot's heart stirred with memories of stories heard in childhood. He longed to see the Christmas garden and begged Robber Mother to send one of her children on Christmas Eve to show him the way.

At first Robber Mother refused, fearing that the abbot would betray the Robbers' hiding place. But the abbot promised he would do the Robber family no harm and even offered, in return for her kindness, to ask the bishop to grant Robber Father a pardon. In the end, Robber Mother agreed to send her eldest son on Christmas Eve to guide the old abbot through the forest. "But mind that you bring only the lay brother with you," she warned. The abbot promised, and Robber Mother went on her way.

In the autumn the bishop visited the cloister. While the two men were walking in the garden, the abbot related the story of Robber Mother's visit and the Christmas garden. "Will you not give Robber Father a pardon so that the Robber family may once more live in the village? If God allows him to see a miracle, there must be some good in the man. Surely it would be better for his children to live among the villagers than to grow up as outlaws."

The bishop smiled at the old man's simple faith. "On the day that you send me a flower from the Christmas garden," he said, "I will pardon Robber Father." The abbot thanked the bishop for his promise and said that he would send him the flower next Christmas Day.

Christmas Eve came at last. The abbot packed a parcel of food, a bottle of wine, and sweets for the Robber children. Then he and the lay brother walked through the village to the edge of Göinge Forest, where the eldest Robber son waited for them.

The abbot had set forth joyously, but the lay brother was not at all happy to be going on what seemed to him a pointless journey. He did not believe Robber Mother's story about a garden that bloomed in winter, but he was too fond of the frail old monk to refuse to accompany him. He longed for the warmth of the cloister hearth and the smell of goose roasting for the Christmas feast.

Robber Son led them through the dense forest. Sometimes the path was steep and the horses stumbled. Sometimes the lay brother had to dismount to guide them over fallen trees covered with snow. The farther they went, the colder it grew. The lay brother fretted and grumbled, but the abbot's thoughts were on the miracle he was about to witness. As the sun's rays began to weaken, they came to a forest meadow. Beyond the meadow loomed a mountain wall, and cut into the wall was a door made of thick wooden planks. Robber Son pulled back the heavy door. Inside the mountain grotto Robber Mother was seated beside a log fire that burned in the middle of the floor. Robber Father was taking a nap. The four younger Robber children were sprawled on the floor around a large pot of watery gruel. There were no signs of Christmas celebration here!

"Sit by the fire and warm yourself, Father Abbot," Robber Mother greeted him. "And if you are tired from your long journey, sleep awhile for I will wake you when it is time to see what you have come all this way to see."

The abbot thanked Robber Mother, stretched out on a pile of dried bracken beside the fire, and soon fell into a deep sleep.

The lay brother was also invited to rest, but he refused, thinking he had better keep an eye on Robber Father. Gradually, fatigue got the better of him and he, too, dozed off.

When he awoke he saw that the abbot had left his bed and was talking with Robber Mother by the fire. Robber Father sat nearby with his back to them, as though he were not interested in their conversation.

The abbot was describing the Christmas preparations taking place in the village. Robber Mother listened intently, remembering the Christmas celebrations of her youth. Suddenly, her husband turned and shook his fist in the abbot's face. "No more of this talk! Have you come to coax from me my wife and children? Don't you know that I am an outlaw and may not enter the village?"

The abbot spoke calmly. "It is my purpose to get a letter of pardon for you from the bishop." At his words, Robber Father burst out laughing—he knew well enough the kind of mercy a forest robber could expect from the bishop!

Before the abbot could tell him about the bishop's promise, their conversation was interrupted by the sound of church bells ringing in Christmas. The abbot rose and followed the Robber family to the entrance of the cave.

The forest was as dark as before but instead of an icy wind, a gentle breeze stirred from the south. The church bells stopped ringing, and in the stillness the winter darkness turned to the pale pinks of dawn. The snow vanished from the ground, the moss-turf thickened and raised itself, and the spring blossoms shot their pale-colored buds upward. The ferns unfolded their fronds that had been curled like a bishop's staff. The trees burst into leaf as suddenly as if a thousand green butterflies had lit in their branches. A pair of finches began building a nest. Baby squirrels played tag among the branches. A mother fox came out of her lair and proudly paraded her young past Robber Mother. The air was filled with birdsong and the lazy droning of bees. It seemed to the abbot that the angels themselves were singing.

Wave upon wave of light pulsed through the forest. A strong south wind scattered meadow seeds from southern lands over the forest. The seeds took root and sprang up the instant they touched the ground.

Robber Mother and Father stood transfixed, but the Robber children shrieked with delight. They gamboled in the soft grass, stuffed their mouths full of raspberries, and picked armfuls of wild flowers.

The abbot bent to pluck a wild strawberry blossom and, as he straightened up, the berry ripened in his hand. Everything was changing so rapidly that he did not have time to think of each wonder that happened. He thought of the flower he was to send to the bishop, but each new flower that appeared seemed more beautiful than the last one, and he wanted to choose the most beautiful of all.

The abbot's heart trembled with joy that he had been allowed to witness such a miracle, but the mind of the lay brother was filled with dark thoughts. He knew that no matter how hard he might work with hoe and spade, he could never bring forth such a garden. "This cannot be a true miracle since it is revealed to outlaws," he thought to himself. "It must be the work of the Evil One performed to delude us!"

All this time the birds circled around the abbot's head or rested in his hands. But they were afraid of the lay brother. No bird perched on his shoulder.

Then a little forest dove plucked up courage, flew down to the lay brother's shoulder, and laid her head against his cheek. Frightened out of his wits and thinking that the devil had come upon him, the lay brother struck the forest dove with his hand and cried in such a loud voice that it rang throughout the forest, "Go thou back to Hell from whence thou art come!"

At the sound of his words, the angels' song was hushed for the darkness in a human heart. The light and warmth vanished. Darkness sank over the earth like a coverlet, all the flowers shriveled up, the leaves fell from the trees, and the birds and animals fled. An icy wind covered the earth and trees with snow. The Robber family and the lay brother ran shivering back to the cave. But the abbot did not move. A cold anguish seized his heart as he realized what was happening. The abbot stumbled forward and at the same moment, remembering the flower he was to deliver to the bishop, clutched a handful of earth as he fell.

When the abbot did not return to the cave, the lay brother went out to look for him and found him dead under a blanket of snow. Lifting the old monk gently, he carried him back to the cloister. There the abbot was laid to rest, a radiant smile on his face.

The monks found a pair of root bulbs in the abbot's clutched hand and gave them to the lay brother. The lay brother planted them in the abbot's garden and tended them with great care. All through the spring, the summer, and the autumn, he waited in vain for the roots to send up shoots. When winter settled in, he gave up hoping that the bulbs would ever flower. But when Christmas Eve came again, he was so reminded of the abbot that he wandered into the garden to think of him. And when he came to the spot where he had planted the roots, he was astonished to see a cluster of flowers with silvery white petals and pale golden stamens. He had seen the flowers only once before on Christmas Eve in the garden at Göinge Forest.

Taking a few blossoms to the bishop, he said, "The abbot sends you a flower from the Christmas garden, as he promised." Then he told the bishop all that had happened that Christmas Eve. The bishop had long ago forgotten the abbot's promise, for he thought it was only an old man's dream. When the lay brother had finished speaking, the bishop sat thinking of his own promise to the abbot. "The abbot has faithfully kept his word, and I shall keep mine," he said. He wrote out a pardon for Robber Father and gave it to the lay brother to deliver. The lay brother departed at once for Robber's Cave.

When he reached the clearing, Robber Father saw him coming and shouted at him to go away. "Thanks to you, we have had no Christmas garden this year," he raged.

"What you say is true, Robber Father. The fault is mine alone and I would gladly die for it. But first I must deliver your pardon from the bishop. You are free to return to the village to live among your people, as the good abbot promised you."

And so the Robber family returned to the village, where they lived in harmony with the neighbors and celebrated many Christmases together.

The lay brother did not return to the cloister. He chose to stay in Robbers' Cave and live a life of meditation and prayer, hoping that his hard-heartedness might be forgiven him.

The Christmas garden never again bloomed in Göinge Forest. But each year at Christmas time the plant that the abbot plucked from the garden sends forth its green stalks and white blossoms in celebration of the birthday of the Christ Child.

It is called the Christmas Rose.

PART IV:
RESOURCES FOR THE STORYTELLER

PROFESSIONAL READING

BIBLIOGRAPHIES, DICTIONARIES, ENCYCLOPEDIA, AND INDEXES

Aarne, Antti. *The Types of the Folktale: A Classification and Bibliography.* Translated and revised by Stith Thompson. 1961, Academia Scientiarum Fennica, 1995. ISBN 0-2533-2959-0 and ISBN 9780253329592.

Ashliman, D. L. *A Guide to Folktales in the English Language: Based on the Aarne-Thompson Classification System.* Greenwood, 1987. ISBN 0-3132-5961-5 and ISBN 9780313259616.

Baughman, Ernest. *Type and Motif-Index of the Folktales of England and North America.* Mouton, 1966. ISBN 9-0279-0046-9 and ISBN 9789027900463.

Blackburn, G. Meredith. *Index to Poetry for Children and Young People, 1993–1997: A Title, Subject, Author, and First Line Index to Poetry in Collections for Children and Young People.* H. W. Wilson, 1999 (see earlier editions at www.hwwilson.com). ISBN 0-8242-0939-7 and ISBN 9780824209391.

Briggs, Katherine M. *A Dictionary of British Folk-Tales in the English Language.* Indiana University, 1991. ISBN 0-4150-6696-4 and ISBN 9780415066969.

———. *An Encyclopedia of Fairies.* Pantheon, 1978. ISBN 0-394-40918-3 and ISBN 9780394409184.

Eastman, Mary. *Index to Fairy Tales, Myths and Legends.* Faxon, 2008. Supplements 1 and 2, 1937, 1952. ISBN 1-4366-7697-5 and ISBN 9781436676977.

Greene, Ellin, and George Shannon. *Storytelling: A Selected Annotated Bibliography.* Garland, 1986. ISBN 0-824-08749-6 and ISBN 9780824087494.

Haviland, Virginia. "Storytelling," "Folktales, Myths and Legends," and "Poetry and Children." In her *Children's Literature: A Guide to Reference Sources,* pp. 183–201 "Storytelling"; pp. 201–226 "Folktales, Myths and Legends"; and pp. 235–241 "Poetry and Children." Library of Congress, 1966. Also in the first supplement to her *Children's Literature: A Guide to Reference Sources,* pp. 121–122 "Storytelling"; pp. 123–132 "Folktales, Myths, and Legends"; pp. 132–134 "Nursery Rhymes"; and pp. 134–136 "Poetry and Children." Library of Congress, 1972. ISBN 0-8444-0215-X and ISBN 9780844402154.

Ireland, Norma Olin, comp. *Index to Fairy Tales, 1949–1972, Including Folklore, Legends, and Myths in Collections.* Third Supplement. Scarecrow Press, 1973. ISBN 0-8108-2011-0 and ISBN 9780810820111.

———. *Index to Fairy Tales, 1973–1977, Including Folklore, Legends, and Myths in Collections.* Fourth Supplement. Scarecrow Press, 1985. ISBN 0-8108-1855-8 and ISBN 9780810818552.

Ireland, Norma Olin, and Joseph W. Sprug, comps. *Index to Fairy Tales, 1978–1986, Including Folklore, Legends, and Myths in Collections.* Fifth Supplement. Scarecrow Press, 1989. ISBN 0-8108-2194-X and ISBN 9780810821941.

Leach, Maria, ed. *Funk & Wagnall's Standard Dictionary of Folklore, Mythology and Legend.* 2 vols. Harper San Francisco, 1984. ISBN 0-06-250511-4 and ISBN 9780062505118.

Leeming, David A., ed. *Storytelling Encyclopedia: Historical, Cultural, and Multiethnic Approaches to Oral Traditions Around the World.* Oryx Press, 1997. ISBN 1-5735-6025-1 and ISBN 9781573560252.

MacDonald, Margaret Read. *The Storyteller's Sourcebook: A Subject, Title and Motif Index to Folklore Collections for Children.* Neal-Schuman, Gale Research, 1982. ISBN 0-8103-0471-6 and ISBN 9780810304710.

MacDonald, Margaret Read, and Brian Sturm. *The Storyteller's Sourcebook: A Subject, Title and Motif Index to Folklore Collections for Children 1983–1999.* Gale Cengage, 2001. ISBN 9780810354851. These two editions of MacDonald's *Storyteller's Sourcebook* are indispensable, both for the librarian storyteller and for strong folk- and fairy tale collection building. MacDonald's *Sourcebook* simplifies searching for folktale variants as it contains a title index as well as an ethnic and geographic index.

Marantz, Sylvia, and Kenneth A. Marantz. *The Art of Children's Picture Books: A Selective Reference Guide.* 2nd ed. Routledge, 1995. ISBN 0-8153-0937-6 and ISBN 9780815309376.

Shannon, George W. B. *Folk Literature and Children: An Annotated Bibliography of Secondary Materials.* Greenwood Press, 1981. ISBN 0-313-22808-6 and ISBN 9780313228087.

Sprug, Joseph W. *Index to Fairy Tales, 1987–1992: Including 310 Collections of Fairy Tales, Folktales, Myths, and Legends, with Significant Pre-1987 Titles Not Previously Indexed.* Scarecrow Press, 1994. ISBN 0-8108-2750-6 and ISBN 9780810827509.

Thompson, Stith. *Motif-Index of Folk-Literature: Classification of Narrative Elements in Folktales, Ballads, Myths, Fables, Medieval Romances, Exempla, Fabliaux, Jest-books, and Local Legends.* Indiana University, 1956. ISBN 0-253-33887-5 and ISBN 9780253338877.

Ziegler, Elsie B. *Folklore: An Annotated Bibliography and Index to Single Editions.* Faxon, 1973. ISBN 0-87305-100-9 and ISBN 9780873051002.

Books About Stories and Storytelling

Barton, Bob, and David Booth. *Stories in the Classroom: Storytelling, Reading Aloud and Roleplaying with Children.* Heinemann, 1990. ISBN 0-435-08527-1 and ISBN 9780435085278. This valuable guide is based on the authors' more than 30 years of experience as teachers, consultants, and storytellers. Though addressed to classroom teachers, it has much to offer anyone who works with children in a group setting. The authors discuss "why children need stories" and "why children need to story" and present ways of engaging children in storying.

Bauer, Caroline Feller. *New Handbook for Storytellers with Stories, Poems, Magic, and More.* Illus. by Lynn Gates Bredeson. ALA, 1993. ISBN 0-8389-0613-3 and ISBN 9780838906132. This revised and expanded edition of the author's popular storytelling handbook is filled with exciting ideas for multimedia story hours. It includes excerpts from the works of more than 50 well-known writers, sample programs, and updated booklists.

———. *The Poetry Break: An Annotated Anthology with Ideas for Introducing Children to Poetry.* Illus. by Edith Bingham. H. W. Wilson, 1994. ISBN 0-8242-0852-8 and ISBN 9780824208523. Part 1 of this fun-filled book explains the Poetry Break idea and suggests methods and activities to make poetry a natural part of a child's life. Part 2 is a collection of 240 poems, both classic and contemporary, for children ranging from preschool through elementary school.

Bettelheim, Bruno. *The Uses of Enchantment: The Meaning and Importance of Fairy Tales.* Knopf, 1976. ISBN 0-394-49771-6 and ISBN 9780394497716. While some of

Bettelheim's theories have been called into question, his comments on fairy tales and their impact on and importance to children are still relevant.

Birch, Carol, L. and Melissa A. Heckler, eds. *Who Says? Essays on Pivotal Issues in Contemporary Storytelling.* August House, 1996. ISBN 0-8748-3454-6 and ISBN 9780874834543.

————. *The Whole Story Handbook: Using Imagery to Complete the Story Experience.* August House, 2000. ISBN 0-87483-566-6 and ISBN 9780874835663.

Bottigheimer, Ruth, ed. *Fairy Tales and Society: Illusion, Allusion, and Paradigm.* University of Pennsylvania, 1986. ISBN 0-8122-1294-0 and ISBN 9780812212945.

Bruchac, Joseph. *Tell Me a Tale: A Book About Storytelling.* Harcourt, 1997. ISBN 0-1520-1221-4 and ISBN 9780152012212.

Bryant, Sara Cone. *How to Tell Stories to Children.* Houghton Mifflin, 1973. ISBN 0-8103-3740-1 and ISBN 9780810337404. Note: The 1915 edition is available as an e-book at http://etext.lib.virginia.edu/toc/modeng/public/BryTell.html.

Cabral, Len. *Len Cabral's Storytelling Book.* Neal-Schuman, 1997. ISBN 1-5557-0253-8 and ISBN 9781555702533.

Campbell, Joseph. *The Hero with a Thousand Faces.* Princeton University Press, 1949, 1968, 1972. ISBN 1-5773-1593-6 and ISBN 9781577315933.

Collins, Rives, and Pamela J. Cooper. *The Power of Story: Teaching Through Storytelling.* 2nd ed. Gorsuch, 1997. ISBN 1-5776-6433-7 and ISBN 9781577664338.

Cook, Elizabeth. *The Ordinary and the Fabulous.* Cambridge, 1976. ISBN 0-5210-9961-7 and ISBN 9780521099615.

Cullinan, Bernice E., Marilyn C. Scala, and Virginia C. Schroder, with Ann K. Lovett. *Three Voices: An Invitation to Poetry Across the Curriculum.* Stenhouse, 1995. ISBN 1-57110-015-6 and ISBN 9781571100153. This book is organized into three sections: developing a love of poetry, helping students discover how poetry works, and using poetry in the content areas. Written by teachers for teachers, Strategy 5 "Poetry to Enrich Stories," Strategy 31 "Storytelling and Cultures," and Strategy 32 "Performance and Poetry" hold particular interest for storytellers.

Dailey, Sheila. *Putting the World in a Nutshell: The Art of the Formula Tale.* H. W. Wilson, 1994. ISBN 0-8242-0860-9 and ISBN 9780824208608. In separate chapters, Dailey discusses the nine basic types of formula tales—chain, cumulative, circle, endless, catch, compound triad, question, air castles, and good/bad tales—and gives several examples of each type. Because formula tales are so easy to learn and tell, this is a good source book for new storytellers.

Danoff, Susan. *The Golden Thread: Storytelling in Teaching and Learning.* Storytelling Arts Press, 2006. ISBN 0-9777-2280-5 and ISBN 9780977722808.

de Vos, Gail. *New Tales for Old: Folktales as Literary Fiction for Young Adults.* Libraries Unlimited, 1999. ISBN 1-5630-8447-3 and ISBN 9781563084478.

————. *Storytelling for Young Adults: A Guide to Tales for Teens.* Libraries Unlimited, 2003. ISBN 1-56308-903-3 and ISBN 9781563089039. See also *Stories from Songs: Ballads as Literary Fictions for Young Adults.* Libraries Unlimited, 2008. ISBN 1-5915-8424-8 and ISBN 9781591584247.

de Wit, Dorothy. *Children's Faces Looking Up: Program Building for the Storyteller.* ALA, 1979. ISBN 0-8389-0272-3 and ISBN 9780838902721. This older but still valuable title explores the characteristics of a good storytelling program—balance, rhythm, pacing, and variety—and demonstrates with six sample programs.

Dundes, Alan, ed. *Cinderella: A Casebook.* University of Wisconsin, 1988. ISBN 0-299-11864-9 and ISBN 9780299118648.

Ellis, Elizabeth. *Inviting the Wolf In: Thinking About Difficult Stories.* With Loren Niemi. August House, 2001. ISBN 0-8748-3623-9 and ISBN 9780874836233.

Ellis, John M. *One Fairy Story Too Many.* University of Chicago, 1983. ISBN 0-2262-0547-9 and ISBN 9780226205472.

Estes, Clarissa Pinkola. *Women Who Run with the Wolves.* Ballantine, 1997. ISBN 0-3454-0987-6 and ISBN 9780345409874.

Frank, Arthur W. *The Wounded Storyteller.* University of Chicago Press, 1995. ISBN 0-2262-5993-5 and ISBN 9780226259932.

Gose, Elliott B., Jr. *The World of the Irish Wonder Tale.* University of Toronto, 1985. ISBN 0-8632-2074-6 and ISBN 9780863220746.

Greene, Ellin. *Books, Babies, and Libraries: Serving Infants, Toddlers, Their Parents and Caregivers.* ALA, 1991. ISBN 0-8389-0572-2 and ISBN 9780838905722. An overall view of library service to children under the age of three and their caregivers and the librarian's role in developing a love of books and reading. Covers early child development and learning, emergent literacy, library collections, program planning, networking and outreach, and planning, implementing, and evaluating library service to early childhood. Includes talks by Dorothy Butler and Jan Ormerod presented at the New York Public Library's Early Childhood Conference, April 1989.

———. *Read Me a Story: Books and Techniques for Reading Aloud and Storytelling.* Preschool Publications, 1992. ISBN 1-8814-2500-2 and ISBN 9781881425007. This concise, informative guide on storytelling and reading aloud was designed for use by early childhood teachers and caregivers. It includes a bibliography of more than 100 children's books arranged by genre or subject. Recommended for the library's parenting collection.

Haase, Donald, ed. *Fairy Tales and Feminism: New Approaches.* Wayne State University, 2004. ISBN 0-8143-3030-4 and ISBN 9780814330302.

Hallett, Martin, and Barbara Karasek, eds. *Folk and Fairy Tales.* Broadview Press, 1991. ISBN 1-5511-1495-X and ISBN 9781551114958.

Hamilton, Martha, and Mitch Weiss. *Children Tell Stories: Teaching and Using Storytelling in the Classroom.* 2nd ed. Richard C. Owen, 2005. ISBN 1-57274-663-7 and ISBN 9781572746633. Anne Izard Storyteller's Choice Award, 2006 Storytelling World Gold Award. Expanded and updated with a companion DVD that documents a storytelling unit. "Must" reading for anyone working with young storytellers.

———. *Scared Witless: Thirteen Eerie Tales to Tell.* August House, 2006. ISBN 0-8748-3796-0 and ISBN 9780874837964.

———. *Through the Grapevine: World Tales Kids Can Read and Tell.* August House, 2001. ISBN 0-8748-3624-7 and ISBN 9780874836240.

Haven, Kendall. *Story Proof: The Science Behind the Startling Power of Story.* Libraries Unlimited, 2007. ISBN 1-5915-8546-5 and ISBN 9781591585466.

Hearne, Betsy, ed. *Story: From Fireplace to Cyberspace.* GSLIS Publications, 1999. ISBN 0-8784-5105-6 and ISBN 9780878451050.

Holt, David, ed. *The Storyteller's Guide.* With Bill Mooney. August House, 1996. ISBN 0-8748-3482-1 and ISBN 9780874834826.

Kinghorn, Harriet R., and Mary Helen Pelton. *Every Child a Storyteller: A Handbook of Ideas.* Libraries Unlimited, 1991. ISBN 0-8728-7868-6 and ISBN 9780872878686.

Lane, Marcia. *Picturing the Rose: A Way of Looking at Fairy Tales*. H. W. Wilson, 1994. ISBN 0-8242-0848-X and ISBN 9780824208486. "A discussion of the nature and meaning of fairy tales with explanation of the process for preparing seven multicultural tales for telling."

Livo, Norma. *Storytelling Folklore Sourcebook*. Libraries Unlimited, 1991. ISBN 0-8728-7601-2 and ISBN 9780872876019.

———. *Storytelling: Process and Practice*. Libraries Unlimited, 1985. ISBN 0-87287-443-5 and ISBN 9780872874435.

———. *Who's Afraid . . . ? Facing Children's Fears with Folktales*. Libraries Unlimited, 1994. ISBN 0-87287950-X and ISBN 9780872879508.

Luthi, Max. *The European Folktale: Form and Nature*. Indiana University Press, 1986. ISBN 0-2532-0393-7 and ISBN 9780253203939.

———. *The Fairy Tale as Art Form and Portrait of Man*. Indiana University Press, 1987. ISBN 0-2532-0420-8 and ISBN 9780253204202.

———. *Once Upon A Time: On the Nature of Fairy Tales*. Indiana University Press, 1976. ISBN 0-2532-0203-5 and ISBN 9780253202031.

MacDonald, Margaret Read. *Storyteller's Start-Up Book*. August House, 1993. ISBN 0-8748-3305-1 and ISBN 9780874833058. See also *Twenty Tellable Tales*.

Marino, Jane. *Sing Us a Story: Using Music in Preschool and Family Storytimes*. H. W. Wilson, 1994. ISBN 0-8242-0847-1 and ISBN 9780824208479. A librarian shares her love of music by suggesting ways to integrate songs into preschool and family storytimes. The first part of the book includes 38 songs for use with children ages two and a half to four; the second part has 39 songs for use in programs where adults and children of all ages gather together. Musical arrangements are given for all of the songs.

Marino, Jane, and Dorothy F. Houlihan. *Mother Goose Time: Library Programs for Babies and Their Caregivers*. H. W. Wilson, 1992. ISBN 0-8242-0850-1 and ISBN 9780824208509. Written with warmth, enthusiasm, and the knowledge that comes from conducting baby and toddler library storytimes for more than 10 years, this practical guide covers the who, what, when, where, and why of getting started, 150+ "baby-tested and toddler-approved" rhymes classified by developmental stage and activity level, music arrangements for the rhymes, a short list of picture books to use in the programs, and a bibliography of additional resources.

Mason, Harriet. *The Power of Storytelling: A Step-by-Step Guide to Dramatic Learning in K–12*. Corwin Press, 1996. ISBN 0803964145 and ISBN 9780803964143.

Nichols, Judy. *Storytimes for Two-Year-Olds*. 3rd ed. Illus. by Lora D. Sears. ALA, 2007. ISBN 0-8389-0925-6 and ISBN 9780838909256. How to plan toddler storytimes, with 50 thematic programs including book titles, rhythms, rhymes and fingerplays, crafts, follow-up ideas for parents to pursue at home, and program notes, plus a bibliography of titles used in the programs and a discography.

Norfolk, Bobby, and Sherry Norfolk. *The Moral of the Story: Folktales for Character Development*. August House, 1999. ISBN 0-8748-3798-7 and ISBN 9780874837988.

Norfolk, Sherry, Diane Williams, and Jane Stenson. *Literacy Development in the Storytelling Classroom*. ABC-CLIO, Incorporated, 2009. ISBN 1-59158694-1 and ISBN 9781591586944.

Nuba, Hannah, Michael Searson, and Deborah Lovitky Sheiman, eds. *Resources for Early Childhood: A Handbook*. Garland, 1995. ISBN 0-8240-7395-9 and ISBN 9780824073954. A collection of essays on topics in early childhood education, from language development to social policy issues, by notable theorists in the field.

Paradiz, Valerie. *Clever Maids: The History of the Grimm Fairy Tales.* Basic Books, 2005. ISBN 0-4650-5491-9 and ISBN 9780465054916.

Pellowski, Anne. *The World of Storytelling.* H. W. Wilson, 1990. ISBN 0-8242-0788-2 and ISBN 9780824207885. This expanded and revised edition covers history, types of storytelling, format and style of telling, and the training of storytellers, with emphasis on the importance of knowing something about the culture from which a story comes. An indispensable resource for the serious student of storytelling, this title includes an extensive bibliography.

Propp, Vladimir. *The Morphology of the Fairytale.* University of Texas Press, 1968. ISBN 0-292-78376-0 and ISBN 9780292783768.

Richey, Cynthia K. *Programming for Serving Children with Special Needs.* ALA, 1994. ISBN 0-8389-5763-3 and ISBN 9780838957639. This helpful booklet offers guidance on personnel, facilities, programs, and more to make libraries more user-friendly for children with emotional or physical disabilities.

Roney, R. Craig. *The Story Performance Handbook.* Lawrence Erlbaum, 2001. ISBN 0-8058-3628-4 and ISBN 9780805836288.

Ross, Ramon Royal. *Storyteller.* August House, 1996. ISBN 0-8748-3451-1 and ISBN 9780874834512.

Sawyer, Ruth. *The Way of the Storyteller.* Viking, 1942. ISBN 0-1400-4436-1 and ISBN 9780140044362.

Sayers, Frances Clarke. *Summoned by Books: Essays and Speeches.* Compiled by Marjeanne Jenson Blinn. Foreword by Lawrence Clarke Powell. Viking, 1965. Penguin, 1968. ISBN 9780670002184.

Shedlock, Marie. *The Art of the Story-teller.* 3rd ed. Dover, 1951. ISBN 0-486-20635-1 and ISBN 9780486206356.

Sierra, Judy. *The Storyteller's Research Guide: Folktales, Myths, and Legends.* Folkprint, 1996. ISBN 0-9363-0894-0 and ISBN 9780963608949.

———. *Twice Upon a Time.* H. W. Wilson, 1989. ISBN 0-8242-0775-0 and ISBN 9780824207755.

Sima, J., and K. Cordi. *Raising Voices: Creating Youth Storytelling Groups and Troupes.* Libraries Unlimited, 2003. ISBN 1-5630-8919-X and ISBN 9781563089190.

Simpson, Martha Seif, and Lynne Perrigo. *Storycraft: 50 Theme-Based Programs Combining Storytelling Activities and Crafts for Children in Grades 1–3.* MacFarland, 2001. ISBN 0-7864-0891-X and ISBN 9780786408917.

Sobol, Joseph. *The Storytellers' Journey: An American Revival.* University of Illinois, 1999. ISBN 0-2520-2436-2 and ISBN 9780252024368.

Stenson, Jane, ed. *The Storytelling Classroom: Applications Across the Curriculum.* Libraries Unlimited, 2006. ISBN 1-5915-8305-5 and ISBN 9781591583059.

Stone, Kay. *Burning Brightly: New Light on Old Tales Told Today.* Broadview Press, 1998. ISBN 1-5511-1167-5 and ISBN 9781551111674.

Sutherland, Zena, ed. *Children and Books.* 8th ed. HarperCollins, 1990. ISBN 0-6731-5037-2 and ISBN 9780673150370. (Chapters 6 and 7).

Tales of the Punjab. An online book originally printed in 1894, this contains 43 tales and notes on the tales. Available at www.digital.library.upenn.edu/women/steel/punjab/punjab.html.

Tatar, Maria. *The Hard Facts of the Grimms' Fairy Tales.* Princeton University, 1987. ISBN 0-6910-1487-6 and ISBN 9780691014876.

———. *Off With Their Heads! Fairy Tales and the Culture of Childhood.* Princeton University, 1992. ISBN 0-6910-6943-3 and ISBN 9780691069432.

Thompson, Stith. *The Folktale.* University of California Press, 1977. ISBN 0-5200-3537-2 and ISBN 9780520035379.

Trostle-Brand, Susan, and Jeanne Donata. *Storytelling in Emergent Literacy: Fostering Multiple Intelligences.* Delmar, 2001. ISBN 0-7668-1480-7 and ISBN 9780766814806.

Vardell, Sylvia M. *Poetry Aloud Here! Sharing Poetry with Children in the Library.* ALA, 2006. ISBN 0-8389-0916-7 and ISBN 9780838909164.

Warner, Marina. *From the Beast to the Blonde: On Fairy Tales and Their Tellers.* Farrar, Straus and Giroux, 1994. ISBN 0-3745-2487-4 and ISBN 9780374524876.

Weir, Beth. *Introducing Children to Folktales.* Christopher-Gordon, 2001. ISBN 1-9290-2416-9 and ISBN 9781929024162.

Yolen, Jane. *Touch Magic: Fantasy, Faerie and Folklore in the Literature of Childhood.* Philomel, 1981. ISBN 0-3992-0830-5 and ISBN 9780399208300.

Zipes, Jack. *The Brothers Grimm: From Enchanted Forests to the Modern World.* Routledge, 1988. ISBN 0-3122-9380-1 and ISBN 9780312293802.

———. *Creative Storytelling: Building Community, Changing Lives.* Routledge, 1995. ISBN 0-4159-1272-5 and ISBN 9780415912723.

———. *Fairy Tale as Myth, Myth as Fairy Tale.* University of Kentucky, 1994. ISBN 0-8131-0834-9 and ISBN 9780813108346.

———. *Great Fairy Tale Tradition: From Straparola and Basile to the Brothers Grimm.* Norton, 2001. ISBN 0-3939-7636-X and ISBN 9780393976366.

———. *The Oxford Companion to Fairy Tales.* Oxford University Press, 2000. ISBN 0-1986-0509-9 and ISBN 9780198605096.

———. *Speaking Out: Storytelling and Creative Drama for Children.* Routledge, 2004. ISBN 0-4159-6661-2 and ISBN 9780415966610.

———. *When Dreams Come True: Classical Fairy Tales and Their Tradition.* Routledge, 1999. ISBN 0-4159-2151-1 and ISBN 9780415921510.

———. *Why Fairytales Stick: The Evolution and Relevance of a Genre.* Routledge, 2006. ISBN 0-415-97781-9 and ISBN 9780415977814.

Also see other titles by this prolific author.

RESOURCES FOR FINGERPLAYS, ACTION RHYMES, FLANNEL BOARD STORYTELLING, STORYTELLING ACTIVITIES, PARTICIPATION TALES, READER'S THEATRE AND STORY THEATRE

Defty, Jeff. *Creative Fingerplays and Action Rhymes.* Oryx, 1992. ISBN 0-8977-4709-7 and ISBN 9780897747097.

Ernst, Linda. *Baby Rhyming Time.* Neal-Schuman, 2008. ISBN 1-5557-0540-5 and ISBN 9781555705404.

Fujita, Hiroko. *Stories to Play With.* August House, 1999. ISBN 0-8748-3553-4 and ISBN 9780874835533.

Hansen, Charles A., and Cynthia S. Stilley, eds. *Ring a Ring o' Roses: Fingerplays for Preschool Children.* Flint Public Library, 2002. ISBN 0-9654589-0-3 and ISBN 9780965458900.

Livo, Norma. *Storytelling Activities.* Libraries Unlimited, 1987. ISBN 0-87287-566-0 and ISBN 9780872875661.

McBride-Smith, Barbara. *Tell It Together: Foolproof Scripts for Story Theatre.* August House, 2001. ISBN 0-87483-655-7 and ISBN 9780874836554.

MacDonald, Margaret Read. *Shake-It-Up Tales: Stories to Sing, Dance, Drum and Act Out.* August House, 2000. ISBN 0-87483-570-4 and ISBN 9780874855700.

Mayo, Margaret. *Wiggle Waggle Fun. Stories and Rhymes for the Very Young.* Knopf, 2002. ISBN 0-375-81529-5 and ISBN 9780375815294.

Miller, Teresa. *Joining In: Audience Participation Tales and How to Tell Them.* Yellow Moon, 1988. ISBN 0-9387-5621-4 and ISBN 9780938756217.

Newcome, Zita. *Head, Shoulders, Knees, and Toes and Other Action Rhymes.* Candlewick, 2002. ISBN 0-7636-1899-3 and ISBN 9780763618995.

Pellowski, Anne. *The Family Storytelling Handbook: How to Use Stories, Anecdotes, Rhymes, Handkerchiefs, Paper, and Other Objects to Enrich Your Family Traditions.* Illus. by Lynn Sweat. Macmillan, 1987. ISBN 0-02-770610-9 and ISBN 9780027706109. The why and how of storytelling within the family with more than a dozen entertaining stories ready to tell.

———. *The Story Vine: A Source Book of Unusual and Easy-to-Tell Stories from Around the World.* Illus. by Lynn Sweat. Macmillan, 1984. ISBN 0-02-770590-0 and ISBN 9780027705904. Step-by-step instructions for telling stories that require objects, such as string, picture drawing, dolls, or musical instruments.

———. *The Storytelling Handbook: A Young People's Collection of Unusual Tales and Helpful Hints on How to Tell Them.* Illus. by Martha Stoberock. Simon & Schuster, 1995. ISBN 0-689-80311-7 and ISBN 9780689803116. Addressed to children and young adults who want to learn the art of storytelling, this handbook will also serve as a guide for librarians and teachers working with young tellers.

Schimmel, Nancy. *Just Enough to Make a Story.* Sister's Choice, 1992. ISBN 0-9321-6402-1 and ISBN 9780932164025.

Shepard, Aaron. *Folktales on Stage: Children's Plays for Reader's Theater, with 16 Play Scripts from World Folk and Fairy Tales and Legends.* Shepard Publications, 2003. ISBN 0-9384-9720-0 and ISBN 9780938497202.

Sierra, Judy. *Flannel Board Storytelling Book.* H. W. Wilson, 1987. ISBN 0-8242-0747-5 and ISBN 9780824207472.

ARTICLES

Ash, Viki, and Elaine Meyers. "Every Child Ready to Read @ your library: How It All Began." *Children and Libraries: The Journal of the Association for Library Service to Children.* Vol. 7 No. 1 (Spring 2009): 3–7.

Birch, Carol. "A Storyteller's Lament: A Librarian Looks at the Rights and Wrongs of Sharing Literature Orally." *School Library Journal* (August 2007): 26–27.

Blankenship, M. E., J. E. Lokerson, and K. A. Verbeke. "Folk and Fairy Tales for the Learning Disabled: Tips for Enhancing Understanding and Enjoyment." *School Library Media Quarterly* 17 (Summer 1989): 200–205.

Bochner, A. P. "Narrative's Virtues." *Qualitative Inquiry*, 7, (2001): 131–157.

Cullinan, Bernice E., Ellin Greene, and Angela Jagger. "Books, Babies, and Libraries: The Librarian's Role in Literacy Development." *Language Arts* (November 1990): 750–755.

de Vos, Gail. "Storytelling, Folktales and the Comic Book Format," (2001) www.langandlit. ualberta.ca/archives/vol31papers/Gail%20DeVos.pdf.

Fulton, Rhonda. "Taking it to the Streets: Every Child Ready to Read on the Go." *Children and Libraries, The Journal of the Association for Library Service to Children.* Vol. 7 No. 1 (Spring 2009): 8–12.

Goble, Paul. "On Beaded Dresses and the Blazing Sun," in *Sitting at the Feet of the Past: Retelling the North American Folktale for Children.* Gary D. Schmidt and Donald R. Hettinga, eds. Greenwood, 1992.

Greene, Ellin. "A Peculiar Understanding: Re-creating the Literary Fairy Tale." *Horn Book* 59 (June 1983): 270–278.

———. "There Are No Talent Scouts . . . " *School Library Journal* 29 (November 1982): 25–27.

Hays, May Bradshaw. "Memories of My Father, Joseph Jacobs." *Horn Book* 28 (December 1952): 385–392.

Hearne, Betsy. "The Bones of Story." *Horn Book* (January/February 2005): 39–47.

———. "Cite the Source: Reducing Cultural Chaos in Picture Books, Part I." *School Library Journal* 39.7 (1993): 81–83.

———. "Once There Was and Will Be: Storytelling in the Future." *Horn Book* (November/ December 2000): 712–719.

———. "Respect the Source: Reducing Cultural Chaos in Picture Books, Part II." *School Library Journal* 39.8 (1993): 33–37.

———. "Ruth Sawyer: A Woman's Journey from Folklore to Children's Literature." *Lion and the Unicorn* 24.2 (2000): 279–307.

———. "Swapping Tales and Stealing Stories: The Ethics and Aesthetics of Folklore in Children's Literature." *Library Trends* 47 (1999): 509–528.

Horner, Beth. "Through My Voice: Telling Family History." *Storytelling Magazine* 16:4 (July/ August 2004): 21–25.

Iarusso, Marilyn Berg. "How to Promote the Love of Reading." *Catholic Library World* (March/April 1988): 212–218.

Kimball, Melanie A., Christine A. Jenkins and Betsy Hearne. "Effie Louise Power: Librarian, Educator, Author." *Library Trends* 52:4 (Spring 2004): 924–951.

Kupetz, Barbara N. "A Shared Responsibility: Nurturing Literacy in the Very Young." *School Library Journal* (July 1993): 28–30.

L'Engle, Madeleine. "What Is Real?" *Language Arts* 55 (April 1978): 447–451.

Lipman, Doug. "In Quest of the Folktale." *Yarnspinner* 14:4 (June 1990): 1–3.

McKamey, Eric S. "Storytelling for Children with Learning Disabilities: A First-Hand Account." *Teaching Exceptional Children* 23, no. 2 (Winter 1991): 46–48.

Manna, Anthony L., and Carolyn S. Brodie. "Br'er Rabbit Redux," in *Sitting at the Feet of the Past: Retelling the North American Folktale for Children*. Gary D. Schmidt and Donald R. Hettinga, eds. Greenwood, 1992.

Mellon, Constance A. "Promoting Cross-Cultural Appreciation Through Storytelling." *Journal of Youth Services in Libraries* 5:3 (Spring 1992): 306–307.

———. "Reflections on Technology, Books, and Children." *Journal of Youth Services in Libraries* 7 (Winter 1994): 207–210.

Miller-Lachmann, Lyn. "Multicultural Publishing: The Folktale Flood." *School Library Journal* 40.2 (1994): 35–37.

Mitchoff, Kate Houston. "Ignite the Story Within: A Librarian Makes a Case for Using Storytelling to Increase Literacy." *School Library Journal* (February 2005): 39–40.

Nesbitt, Elizabeth. "Hold to That Which Is Good." *Horn Book* 16 (January-February 1940): 7–15.

"Oral Tradition" Issue. *Parabola* 17 (August 1992).

Rochman, Hazel. "And Yet . . . Beyond Political Correctness." *Evaluating Children's Books: A Critical Look*. Betsy Hearne, ed. Papers presented at the Allerton Park Institute, 1993, 33–48.

Rovenger, Judith. "Learning Differences/Library Directions: Library Service to Children with Learning Differences." *Library Trends* 35 (Winter 1987): 427–435.

Ryan, Patrick. "Once Upon a Time into Altered States: Temporal Space, Liminality, and Flow." *Time Everlasting: Representations of Past, Present and Future in Children's Literature*. Papers from the IBBY/NCRCL Conference held at Roehampton University, London, November 11, 2006. NCRCL papers 13, edited by Pat Pinsent. Pied Piper Publishing Ltd., 2007.

Sayers, Frances Clarke. "From Me to You" and "The Storyteller's Art." In Sayers's *Summoned by Books: Essays and Speeches*, pp. 95–98 "From Me to You"; pp. 99–106 "The Storyteller's Art." Viking, 1965. Penguin, 1968. ISBN 9780670002184.

Shimojima, Anne. "Storytelling and the School Media Center." In *Story: From Fireplace to Cyberspace*. GSLIS Publications, 1999. ISBN 0-87845-105-6 and ISBN 9780878451050.

Stone, Kay. "Things Walt Disney Never Told Us." *Journal of American Folklore* 88 (1975): 42–50 (1992).

Stone, Kay, and Donald Davis, "To Ease the Heart: Traditional Storytelling." *National Storytelling Journal* 1 (Winter 1984): 3–6.

Sturm, Brian. "The Storylistening Trance Experience." *Journal of American Folklore* 113 (449): 287–304.

Tolkien, J. R. R. "Tree and Leaf." In *The Tolkien Reader*. Ballantine Books, 1977. ISBN 0-345-25585-2.

Wendelin, Karla H., and Kathy Everts Danielson. "New Twists on Old Tales: A Ten." *CLA Bulletin* 18 (Spring 1992): 11–14.

Werner, Craig. "A Blind Child's View of Children's Literature." In *Children's Literature* 12 (1984): 209–216.

Wilson, Anne. "Magical Thought in Story." *Signal* 36 (September 1981): 138–151.

Wolkstein, Diane. "Twenty-Five Years of Storytelling: The Spirit of the Art." *Horn Book* 68 (November-December 1992): 702–708.

Zipes, Jack. "The Contamination of the Fairy Tale: Or, The Changing Nature of the Grimms' Fairy Tales." *Journal of the Fantastic in the Arts* 11, 1 (41) (2000): 77–93.

———. "Fairy Tale Culture," *Locus,* 47, 5 (490) (2001): 8–9, 83–84.

Magazines About Folktales, Myths, and Storytelling

Journal of American Folklore
www.afsnet.org/publications/jaf.cfm

Marvels and Tales: A Journal of Fairy-Tale Studies
www.langlab.wayne.edu/marvelshome/Marvels_Tales.html

Edited by Donald Haase, Wayne State University. Includes a listing of back issues and short annotations of each article.

Parabola
www.parabola.org

Storytelling, Self, and Society
www.courses.unt.edu/efiga/SSS/Call_SSSJournal.htm

"A bi-annual, interdisciplinary, peer-reviewed journal that publishes scholarship on a wide variety of topics related to storytelling as interpersonal, performance, or public discourse."

Storytelling Magazine
www.storynet.org/Other/Magazine

Web Sources

Aaron Shepard's Storytelling Page
www.aaronshep.com/storytelling

Adaptations of Shepard's stories, a guide to storytelling, articles and quotes about storytelling, and a recommended reading list on storytelling, folklore, and mythology.

Circle of Stories
www.pbs.org/circleofstories

"Circle of Stories uses documentary film, photography, artwork, and music to honor and explore Native American storytelling."

Encyclopedia Mythica
www.pantheon.org

An online encyclopedia of mythology including Greek, Norse, Roman, and Celtic mythology and articles on legends as well as on individual gods and goddesses. Good for research.

Folk and Fairy Tales
www.pitt.edu/~dash/ashliman.html

Homepage of Professor D. H. Ashliman, containing links for an online library and other resources.

Folklinks: Folk and Fairy Tales Sites
www.pitt.edu/~dash/folklinks.html

Ashliman's links to search engines, reference works, electronic texts, directories of folk and fairy tale sites, film and fairy tales, and more.

Folklore and Mythology
www.pitt.edu/~dash/folktexts.html

Ashliman's folk and mythology electronic texts library, organized by theme, author, figure, or plot.

Library of Congress American Folklife Center
www.loc.gov/folklife

Contains collections of Native American song and dance, ancient English ballads, and stories from the lives of many people throughout the United States.

Mythology: MYTHING LINKS
www.mythinglinks.org

An annotated, illustrated collection of links on mythologies, fairy tales, and folklore.

National Council of Teachers of English Position Paper on Storytelling
www.ncte.org/about/over/positions/category/lang/107637.htm?source=gs

National Storytelling Network
www.storynet.org

The national American storytelling organization. Features lists of upcoming programs and events, resources, and pages for tellers.

Project Gutenberg
www.gutenberg.org/wiki/Main_Page

More than 25,000 free books available online.

Sources for the Analysis and Interpretation of Folk and Fairy Tales
www.folkandfairy.org/index.html#LIST

StoryArts Online
www.storyarts.org

Offers articles on storytelling in the classroom as well as lesson plans. Also includes a story library, story arts theatre, and links.

StoryDynamics.com
www.storydynamics.com

Articles about storytelling, workshops, and storytelling resources.

Storyteller.net
www.storyteller.net

Articles about storytelling, stories, a calendar of events, and teller directory. Also at Storyteller.net, free downloadable stories, www.storyteller.net/stories/audio.

Storytelling Websites and Resources
www.courses.unt.edu/efiga/STORYTELLING/StorytellingWebsites.htm

An extensive list of links concerning storytelling and storytelling resources; most are annotated or reviewed.

SurLaLuneFairytales.com
www.surlalunefairytales.com

Offers 47 fairy tales with annotations including histories, similar tales from other cultures, contemporary interpretations, and more than 1,500 illustrations. Also 40 full-text e-Books and a discussion forum.

Tell Me a Story
www.web.net/~story/mbstory.htm

An annotated "meta-bibliography" featuring books, articles, movies, and audiotapes about and for storytelling.

Tim Sheppard's Storytelling Page
www.timsheppard.co.uk/story/tellinglinks.html

An extensive annotated list of links including storytelling training, literature, and background resources.

Urban Legends Reference Pages
www.snopes2.com

Urban myths are organized into categories (e.g., autos, crime, and toxins); also lists various statements associated with urban myths. Each statement includes a rating regarding its truth.

Youth Storytelling
www.youthstorytelling.com

Features articles, tips, and links for ensemble storytelling.

FOLKTALES, LITERARY TALES, POETRY, AND SONG

FOLKTALES: COLLECTIONS

(Cultures are given in square brackets at the ends of entries)

Aardema, Verna, reteller. *Misoso: Once Upon a Time Tales from Africa*. Illus. by Reynold Ruffins. Knopf, 1994. ISBN 0-679-83430-3 and ISBN 9780679834304. Twelve *misoso* ("Once upon a time") tales from a variety of African cultures, with a glossary and illuminating note for each story, and a bibliography of sources. **[African]**

Ada, Alma Flor, and F. Isabel Campoy. *Tales Our Abuelitas Told: A Hispanic Folktale Collection*. Illus. by Felipe Davalos. Atheneum, 2006. ISBN 0-6898-2583-8 and ISBN 9780689825835. **[Hispanic]**

Adler, Naomi. *The Dial Book of Animal Tales from Around the World*. Illus. by Amanda Hall. Dial, 1996. ISBN 0-8037-2063-7 and ISBN 9780803720633. **[World]**

Aldana, Patricia. *Jade and Iron: Latin American Tales from Two Cultures*. Translated by Hugh Hazelton. Douglas & McIntyre, 1996. ISBN 0-8889-9256-4 and ISBN 9780888992567. Pre- and post-conquest tales from Latin America. **[Hispanic]**

Arnott, Kathleen. *African Myths and Legends*. Illus. by Joan Kiddell-Monroe. Oxford University Press, 1990. ISBN 0-19-274143-8 and ISBN 9780192741431. **[African]**

Asimov, Isaac. *Legends, Folklore, and Outer Space*. Gareth Stevens, 2005. ISBN 0-8368-3951-X and ISBN 9780836839517. **[World]**

Ausubel, Nathan. *A Treasury of Jewish Folklore*. Crown, 1989. ISBN 0-517-50293-3 and ISBN 9780517502938. **[Jewish]**

Badoe, Adwoa. *The Pot of Wisdom: Ananse Stories*. Illus. by Baba Wagué Diakité. Douglas & McIntyre, 2001. ISBN 0-8889-9429-X and ISBN 9780888994295. **[African]**

Baker, Augusta. *The Golden Lynx*. Lippincott, 1960. ISBN 0-3973-0495-1 and ISBN 9780397304950. **[World]**

———. *The Talking Tree*. Illus. by Johannes Troyer. Lippincott, 1955. Two collections of folktales from many lands used successfully with children, from librarian/storyteller Augusta Baker. **[World]**

Baltuck, Naomi. *Apples from Heaven: Multicultural Folk Tales About Stories and Storytellers*. Linnet, 1995. ISBN 0-2080-2434-4 and ISBN 9780208024343. **[World]**

Barchers, Suzanne, ed. *Wise Women: Folk and Fairy Tales from Around the World*. Illus. by Leann Mullineaux. Libraries Unlimited, 1990. ISBN 0-87287816-3 and ISBN 9780872878167. **[World]**

Barlow, Maisie (Yarrcali). *Jirrbal: Rainforest Dreamtime Stories*. Illus. by Michael (Boiyool) Anning. Advance Press, 2001. ISBN 1-8756-4106-8 and ISBN 9781875641062. **[Australian]**

Barton, Bob. *The Bear Says North: Tales from Northern Lands*. Illus. by Jirina Marton. Groundwood Books, 2003. ISBN 0-8889-9533-4 and ISBN 9780888995339. **[World]**

Baumgartner, Barbara, reteller. *Crocodile! Crocodile! Stories Told Around the World.* Illus. by Judith Moffatt. Dorling Kindersley, 1994. ISBN 1-56458-463-1 and ISBN 9781564584632. A children's librarian and professional storyteller has chosen six less-anthologized folktales suitable for younger listeners and retold them as she would perform them. In addition to giving her story sources, she has included a section called "Bringing the Stories to Life with Stick Puppets." **[World]**

Beck, Ian. *The Oxford Nursery Treasury.* Oxford University Press, 2000. ISBN 0-1927-8164-2 and ISBN 9780192781642. **[World]**

Bedard, Michael. *The Painted Wall and Other Strange Tales.* Tundra Books, 2003. ISBN 0-8877-6652-8 and ISBN 9780887766527. **[Chinese]**

Belpré, Pura. *The Tiger and the Rabbit, and Other Tales.* Illus. by Tomie de Paola. Lippincott, 1965. ISBN 0-39730842-6 and ISBN 9780397308422. Folktales from Puerto Rico. **[Puerto Rican]**

Bernier-Grand, Carmen T. *Shake It, Morena! And Other Folklore from Puerto Rico.* Illus. by Lulu Delacre. Millbrook, 2002. ISBN 0-7613-1910-7 and ISBN 9780761319108. **[Puerto Rican]**

Bierhorst, John. *The Dancing Fox: Arctic Folktales.* Illus. by Mary K. Okheena. Morrow, 1997. ISBN 0-6881-4406-3 and ISBN 9780688144067. **[Inuit]**

———. *Is My Friend at Home? Pueblo Fireside Tales.* Illus. by Wendy Watson. Farrar, Straus and Giroux, 2001. ISBN 0-3743-3550-8 and ISBN 9780374335502. **[Native American]**

———. *Latin American Folktales: Stories from Hispanic and Indian Traditions.* Pantheon Books, 2002. ISBN 0-3754-2066-5 and ISBN 9780375420665. **[Hispanic]**

———. *The Monkey's Haircut and Other Stories Told by the Maya.* Morrow, 1986. ISBN 0-688-04269-4 and ISBN 9780688042691. An unusual collection of folktales that includes myths, just-so-stories, witch stories, and animal tales. Contains an excellent introduction, sources, variants, and bibliography. **[Mayan]**

———. *The Naked Bear: Folktales of the Iroquois.* Morrow, 1987. ISBN 0-688-06422-1 and ISBN 9780688064228. A skillfully edited collection of excellent stories for telling. **[Native American]**

———. *The Whistling Skeleton: American Indian Tales of the Supernatural.* Collected by George Bird Grinnell. Four Winds, 1982. ISBN 0-5900-7801-1 and ISBN 9780590078016. Stories from the Pawnee, the Blackfeet, and the Cheyenne. The informative Foreword deepens understanding of the traditions and customs of the three tribes. **[Native American]**

Blecher, Lone Thygesen, and George Blecher. *Swedish Folktales and Legends.* Pantheon, 1995. ISBN 0-6797-5841-0 and ISBN 9780679758419. **[Swedish]**

Briggs, Katherine. *British Folk Tales.* Dorset Press, 1989. ISBN 0-88029-288-1 and ISBN 9780880292887. A selection from the four-volume work *A Dictionary of British Folktales,* published by Routledge & Kegan Paul Ltd., London, in 1970–1971, with new introductions. **[British]**

Brinkerhoff, Shirley. *Contemporary Folklore.* Mason Crest, 2003. ISBN 1-5908-4331-2 and ISBN 9781590843314. **[Urban Legend]**

Bruchac, Joseph, reteller. *The Boy Who Lived with the Bears and Other Iroquois Stories.* Illus. by Murv Jacob. HarperCollins, 1995. ISBN 0-06-021287-X and ISBN 9780060212872. Six Iroquois stories retold by a Native American (Bruchac also recorded the tales on Parabola's Storytime Series) and illustrated by an award-winning Native American artist. **[Native American]**

————. *Flying with the Eagle, Racing the Great Bear.* Illus. by Murv Jacob. BridgeWater, 1993. ISBN 0-8167-3026-1 and ISBN 9780816730261. **[Native American]**

Bruchac, Joseph, and Gayle Ross, retellers. *The Girl Who Married the Moon.* Illus. by S. S. Burrus. BridgeWater, 1994. ISBN 0-8167-3480-1 and ISBN 9780816734801. These companion books (the first—*Flying with the Eagle, Racing the Great Bear*—focuses on boys, the second on girls) each contain 16 coming-of-age stories from as many different Native American nations. The stories emphasize the need for courage and resourcefulness during the journey to adulthood. **[Native American]**

Bruchac, Joseph, and James Bruchac. *The Girl Who Helped Thunder and Other Native American Folktales.* Illus. by Stefano Vitale. Sterling, 2008. ISBN 1-4027-3263-5 and ISBN 9781402732638. **[Native American]**

————. *When the Chenoo Howls: Native American Tales of Terror.* Illus. by William Sauts Bock. Walker, 1999. ISBN 0-8027-7576-4 and ISBN 9780802775764. **[Native American]**

Brunvand, Jan Harold. *Encyclopedia of Urban Legends.* ABC-CLIO, 2001. ISBN 0-3933-2358-7 and ISBN 9780393323580. **[Urban Legend]**

————. *The Vanishing Hitchhiker: American Urban Legends and Their Meanings.* Norton, 1981. ISBN 0-3930-1473-8 and ISBN 9780393014730. **[Urban Legend]**

Bryan, Ashley. *Ashley Bryan's African Tales, Uh-Huh.* Retold and illustrated by Ashley Bryan. Atheneum, 1998. Includes the complete contents of *Beat the Story Drum, Pum-Pum, Lion and the Ostrich Chicks,* and *The Ox of the Wonderful Horns.* ISBN 0-689-82076-3 and ISBN 9780689820762. **[African]**

————. *Beat the Story Drum, Pum-Pum.* Retold and illus. by Ashley Bryan. Simon & Schuster, 1987. ISBN 0-689-31356-X and ISBN 9780689313561. African tales told with rhythm, humor, and vigor. **[African]**

————. *Lion and the Ostrich Chicks.* Illus. by Ashley Bryan, 1996. ISBN 0-689-80713-9 and ISBN 9780689807138. Four stories that represent different African peoples—Masai, Bushman, Angola, and Hausa. **[African]**

————. *The Ox of the Wonderful Horns and Other African Folktales.* Simon & Schuster, 1993. ISBN 0-689-31799-9 and ISBN 9780689317996. **[African]**

Caduto, Michael J., and Joseph Bruchac. *Keepers of Life: Discovering Plants Through Native American Stories and Earth Activities for Children.* Illus. by John Kahionhes Fadden and David Kanietakeron Fadden. Fulcrum, 1994. ISBN 1-55591-186-2 and ISBN 9781555911867. Companion volumes of Native American stories and activities that teach children respect for the environment and all living creatures. **[Native American]**

————. *Keepers of the Animals: Native American Stories and Wildlife Activities for Children.* Illus. by John K. Fadden. Fulcrum, 1991. ISBN 1-55591-088-2 and ISBN 9781555910884. **[Native American]**

————. *Keepers of the Earth: Native American Stories and Environmental Activities for Children.* Illus. by John K. Fadden and Carol Wood. Introduction by N. Scott Momaday. Fulcrum, 1988. ISBN 1-55591-027-0 and ISBN 9781555910273. **[Native American]**

Calvino, Italo. *Italian Folktales.* Harvest, 1992. ISBN 0-3947-4909-X and ISBN 9780394749099. **[Italian]**

Carrick, Valery. *Picture Folk-Tales.* Dover, 1992. Ten short animal tales, including "The Crab and the Jaguar." ISBN 0-4862-7083-1 and ISBN 9780486270838. **[Russian]**

Carter, Angela, ed. *Old Wives' Fairy Tale Book.* Pantheon, 1990. ISBN 0-3945-8764-2 and ISBN 9780394587646. **[World]**

Chaikin, Miriam, ed. *Angel Secrets: Stories Based on Jewish Legend*. Illus. by Leonid Gore. Henry Holt, 2006. ISBN 0-8050-7150-4 and ISBN 9780805071504. **[Jewish]**

Chase, Richard. *Grandfather Tales*. Houghton Mifflin, 2003. ISBN 0-3950-6692-1 and ISBN 9780395066928. Tales collected from the southern Appalachian folk and retold with local idioms. **[North American/Appalachian]**

————. *Jack Tales*. Houghton Mifflin, 2003. ISBN 0-3956-6951-0 and ISBN 9780395669518. Appalachian tales centered around the character Jack. **[North American/Appalachian]**

Clarkson, Atelia, ed. *World Folktales: A Scribner Resource Collection*. Scribner, 1980. ISBN 0-6841-6290-3 and ISBN 9780684162904. Includes notes, tale types, and motifs. **[World]**

Cleveland, Rob. *The Drum: A Folktale from India*. Illus. by Tom Wrenn. August House Story Cove, 2006. ISBN 0-8748-3802-9 and ISBN 9780874838022. **[Indian]**

Climo, Shirley. *Monkey Business: Stories from Around the World*. Illus. by Erik Brooks. Holt, 2005. ISBN 0-8050-6392-7 and ISBN 9780805063929. **[World]**

Cohen, Daniel. *The Beheaded Freshman and Other Nasty Rumors*. Avon Books, 1993. ISBN 0-3807-7020-2 and ISBN 9780380770205. **[Urban Legend]**

Cohn, Amy L. and Suzy Schmidt. *From Sea to Shining Sea: A Treasury of American Folklore and Folk Songs*. Illus. by Molly Bang. Scholastic, 1993. ISBN 0-5904-2868-3 and ISBN 9780590428682. **[North American]**

Cole, Joanna. *Best Loved Folktales of the World*. Anchor, 1982. ISBN 0-3851-8520-0 and ISBN 9780385185202. **[World]**

Conover, Sarah, and Freda Crane. *Ayat Jamilah (Beautiful Signs): A Treasury of Islamic Wisdom for Children and Parents*. Illus. by Valerie Wahl. Eastern Washington University Press, 2004. ISBN 0-9100-5594-7 and ISBN 9780910055949. **[Middle East]**

Courlander, Harold. *Cow-Tail Switch and Other West African Stories*. Holt, 1947, 1988. ISBN 0-8050-0288-X and ISBN 9780805002881. **[African]**

————. *Treasury of African Folklore*. Marlowe, 1996. ISBN 1-56924-811-7 and ISBN 9781569248119. **[African]**

Courlander, Harold, and Wolf Leslau. *The Fire on the Mountain and Other Stories from Ethiopia and Eritrea*. Illus. by Robert Kane. Holt, 1995. ISBN 0-8050-3652-0 and ISBN 9780805036527. An outstanding collection of sophisticated folktales, originally published in 1950 and out of print since 1968. **[African]**

Crossley-Holland, Kevin, ed. *British Folk Tales: New Versions*. Orchard, 1987. ISBN 0-531-05733-X and ISBN 9780531057339. In the first comprehensive collection of retellings in a long time, here are 55 stories of all types. Includes sources and a commentary for each tale. **[British]**

————. *Enchantment: Fairy Tales, Ghost Stories and Tales of Wonder*. Illus. by Emma Chichester Clark. Orchard, 1987. ISBN 1-8425-5032-2 and ISBN 9781842550328. **[World]**

————. *Why the Fish Laughed and Other Tales*. University Press, 2002. ISBN 0-1927-5187-5 and ISBN 9780192751874. **[World]**

Daly, Ita. *Irish Myths and Legends*. Illus. by Bea Willey. Oxford University Press, 2001. ISBN 0-1927-5454-8 and ISBN 9780192754547. **[Irish]**

D'Aulaire, Edgar Parin, and Ingri D'Aulaire. *East of the Sun and West of the Moon: Twenty-One Norwegian Folk Tales*. Viking, 1969. **[Norwegian]**

De Almeida, Livia Maria Melibeu and Ana Maria Carneiro Portella. *Brazilian Folktales.* Margaret Read MacDonald, ed. Libraries Unlimited, 2006. ISBN 1-5630-8930-0 and ISBN 9781563089305. **[Brazilian]**

Dearden, Carmen Diana, ed. *Little Book of Latin American Folktales.* Translated by Susana Wald and Beatriz Zeller. Douglas & McIntyre, 2003. ISBN 0-8889-9543-1 and ISBN 9780888995438. **[Hispanic]**

DeArmond, Dal, reteller and illustrator. *The Boy Who Found the Light.* Sierra, 1990. ISBN 0-316-17787-3 and ISBN 9780316177870. Three traditional stories from Alaska: "The Boy Who Found the Light," "The Doll," and "The Raven and the Marmot." **[Inuit]**

Doucet, Sharon Arms. *Lapin Plays Possum: Trickster Tales from the Louisiana Bayou.* Illus. by Scott Cook. Farrar, Straus and Giroux, 2002. ISBN 0-3743-4328-4 and ISBN 9780374343286. **[North American]**

Doyle, Malachy. *The Barefoot Book of Fairy Tales.* Illus. by Nicoletta Ceccoli. Barefoot Books, 2005. ISBN 1-8414-8798-8 and ISBN 9781841487984. **[World]**

———. *Tales from Old Ireland.* Illus. by Niamh Sharkey. Barefoot Books, 2000. ISBN 1-9022-8397-X and ISBN 9781902283975. **[Irish]**

Durrell, Ann, compiler. *The Diane Goode Book of American Folk Tales and Songs.* Illus. by Diane Goode. Dutton, 1989. ISBN 0-525-44458-0 and ISBN 9780525444589. Nine stories and seven songs from various regions and ethnic groups in the United States. **[North American]**

Fang, Linda. *The Ch'i-lin Purse: A Collection of Ancient Chinese Stories.* Illus. by Jeanne M. Lee. Farrar, Straus and Giroux, 1995. ISBN 0-374-31241-9 and ISBN 9780374312411. A collection of nine stories with substantial notes about the origins of the retellings and a pronunciation guide. **[Chinese]**

Faulkner, William J. *The Days When the Animals Talked: Black American Folk Tales and How They Came to Be.* Illus. by Troy Stowell. Africa World Press, 1993. ISBN 0-86543-373-9 and ISBN 9780865433731. Slave tales as well as animal stories told without dialect. Introductions are a good base for the storyteller. **[African American]**

Finger, Charles. *Tales from Silver Lands.* Doubleday, 1924, 1965. Scholastic, 1989. ISBN 0-590-42447-5 and ISBN 9780590424479. Contains several chilling stories from South America that are excellent for the Halloween story hour. A Newbery Medal winner. **[South American]**

Flood, Bo, Beret E. Strong, and William Flood. *Micronesian Legends.* Illus. by Connie J. Adams. Bess Press, 2002. ISBN 1-5730-6124-7 and ISBN 9781573061247. **[Micronesian]**

Forest, Heather. *Wisdom Tales from Around the World.* August House, 1996. ISBN 0-8748-3479-1 and ISBN 9780874834796. **[World]**

———. *Wonder Tales from Around the World.* August House, 1997. ISBN 0-8748-3427-9 and ISBN 9780874834277. **[World]**

Friedman, Amy. *Tell Me a Story: Timeless Folktales from Around the World.* Illus. by Jillian H. Gilliland. Friedman & Danziger, 2006. ISBN 0-8362-4228-9 and ISBN 9780836242287. **[World]**

Gág, Wanda. *Tales from Grimm* and *More Tales from Grimm.* Coward, 1936, 1947. Reissued (paperback eds.). University of Minnesota Press, 2006. ISBN 0-8166-4936-7 and ISBN 9780816649365; ISBN 0-8166-4938-3 and ISBN 9780816649389. **[German]**

Garcia, Emmett Shkeme. *Coyote and the Sky: How the Sun, Moon, and Stars Began.* Illus. by Victoria Pringle. University of New Mexico, 2006. ISBN 0-8263-3730-9 and ISBN 9780826337306. **[Native American]**

Garner, Alan. *Alan Garner's Book of British Fairy Tales*. Illus. by Derek Collard. Delacorte, 1985. ISBN 0-3852-9425-4 and ISBN 9780385294256. Familiar and unfamiliar folktales are told and illustrated with strength and power. **[British]**

————. *A Bag of Moonshine*. Collins Voyager, 2002. ISBN 0-00-712790-1 and ISBN 9780007127900. Stories of boggarts and hobgoblins chosen from the folklore of England and Wales. **[English/Welsh]**

————. *The Lad of the Gad*. Collins, 1980. ISBN 0-0018-4711-2 and ISBN 9780001847118. Five Gaelic stories, four drawn from *Popular Tales of the West Highlands* by J. F. Campbell (Forgotten Books, 2007; ISBN 1-6050-6173-5 and ISBN 9781605061733), and one based on an Irish manuscript, "The Adventures of the Children of the King of Norway." **[Scottish/Irish]**

Gatti, Anne, reteller. *Tales from the African Plains*. Illus. by Gregory Alexander. Dutton, 1995. ISBN 0-525-45282-6 and ISBN 9780525452829. Twelve stories of wisdom collected from different cultural groups from Africa, told with humor. **[African]**

Gerson, Mary-Joan. *Fiesta Femenina: Celebrating Women in Mexican Folktale*. Illus. by Maya Christina Gonzalez. Barefoot Books, 2005. ISBN 1-8414-8365-6 and ISBN 9781841483658. **[Mexican]**

González, Lucía M. *Señor Cat's Romance and Other Favorite Stories from Latin America*. Illus. by Lulu Delacre. Scholastic, 1997. ISBN 0-439-27863-5 and ISBN 9780439278638. **[Hispanic/Cuban]**

Greene, Ellin. *Midsummer Magic: A Garland of Stories, Charms, and Recipes*. Lothrop, 1977. ISBN 0-688-41800-7 and ISBN 9780688418007. (A limited number of copies are available from the author. To order, send a self-addressed mailing label and $35 in check or money order to Ellin Greene, 113 Chatham Lane, Point Pleasant, NJ 08742.) **[World]**

Grimm, Jacob, and Wilhelm Grimm. *About Wise Men and Simpletons*. Translated from the German by Elizabeth Shub. Simon & Schuster, 1986. ISBN 0-02-737450-5 and ISBN 9780027374506. **[German]**

————. *The Brothers Grimm: Popular Folk Tales*. Newly translated by Brian Alderson. Illus. by Michael Foreman. Doubleday, 1978. **[German]**

————. *Household Stories of the Brothers Grimm*. Translated from the German by Lucy Crane. Dover, 1986. ISBN 0-486-21080-4 and ISBN 9780486210803. **[German]**

————. *The Juniper Tree and Other Tales from Grimm*. Illus. by Maurice Sendak. Translated by Lore Segal and Randall Jarrell. Farrar, Straus and Giroux, 2003. ISBN 0-3743-3971-6 and ISBN 9780374339715. **[German]**

————. *The McElderry Book of Grimms' Fairy Tales*. Retold by Saviour Pirotta. Illus. by Emma Chichester Clark. McElderry, 2006. ISBN 1-4169-1798-5 and ISBN 9781416917984. **[German]**

Haley, Gail E., reteller. *Mountain Jack Tales*. Dutton, 1992. ISBN 0-525-44974-4 and ISBN 9780525449744. In a sly, colloquial style, the narrator, Poppyseed, relates nine adventures of Jack. Haley's background information and bibliography about the Jack tales will be of special interest to storytellers. **[North American/Appalachian]**

Hamilton, Virginia, reteller. *The Dark Way: Stories from the Spirit World*. Illus. by Lambert Davis. Harcourt Brace Jovanovich, 1990. ISBN 0-1522-2340-1 and ISBN 9780152223403. **[World]**

————. *Her Stories: African American Folktales, Fairy Tales, and True Tales*. Illus. by Leo Dillon and Diane Dillon. Scholastic, 1995. ISBN 0-590-47370-0 and ISBN 9780590473705. This stunning book "brings together narratives about females from the vast treasure store of traditional black folklore." The collection of 19 stories is divided into five sections:

Animal Tales, Fairy Tales, Tales of the Supernatural, Folkways and Legends, and True Tales with sources and notes. **[African American]**

————. *In the Beginning: Creation Stories from Around the World*. Illus. by Barry Moser. Harcourt, Brace, Jovanovich, 1988. ISBN 0-1523-8740-4 and ISBN 9780152387402. **[World]**

————. *Many Thousand Gone: African Americans from Slavery to Freedom*. Illus. by Leo and Diane Dillon. Random House, 1993. ISBN 0-6799-7936-0 and ISBN 9780679979364. **[African American]**

————. *The People Could Fly: American Black Folktales*. Illus. by Leo and Diane Dillon. Knopf, 1992. ISBN 0-679-84336-1 and ISBN 9780679843368. Twenty-four selections that represent the main body of American black folklore. Includes animal stories, John stories, and slave tales. **[African American]**

————. *Ring of Tricksters: Tales from America, West Indies and Africa*. Illus. by Barry Moser. Blue Sky, 1997. ISBN 0-5904-7374-3 and ISBN 9780590473743. **[World]**

————. *When Birds Could Talk and Bats Could Sing*. Illus. by Barry Moser. Blue Sky, 1996. ISBN 0-590-47372-7 and ISBN 9780590473729. **[African American]**

Harris, Christie. *Mouse Woman and the Mischief-Makers*. Raincoast Books, 2005. (paperback) ISBN 1-55192-751-9 and ISBN 9781551927510. **[Native American]**

Harris, Joel Chandler. *Jump! The Adventures of Brer Rabbit*. Adapted by Van Dyke Parks and Malcolm Jones. Illus. by Barry Moser. Harcourt, 1986. ISBN 0-15-241350-2 and ISBN 9780152413507. The adapters-retellers have eliminated the fictional character Uncle Remus and used standard English in this collection for younger children. **[African American]**

————. *Jump Again! More Adventures of Brer Rabbit*. Adapted by Van Dyke Parks. Illus. by Barry Moser. Harcourt, 1987. ISBN 0-15-241352-9 and ISBN 9780152413521. **[African American]**

————. *Jump on Over! The Adventures of Brer Rabbit and His Family*. Adapted by Van Dyke Parks. Illus. by Barry Moser. Harcourt, 1989. ISBN 0-15-241354-5 and ISBN 9780152413545. The second and third collections in this series maintain the same high quality as the first, both in narrative style and illustration. **[African American]**

Hausman, Gerald, and Loretta Hausman. *Cats of Myth: Tales from Around the World*. Illus. by Leslie A. Baker. Simon & Schuster, 2000. ISBN 0-6898-2320-7 and ISBN 9780689823206. **[World]**

Haviland, Virginia, ed. *The Fairy Tale Treasury*. Coward, 1972. ISBN 0-241-02207-X and ISBN 9780241022078. Thirty-two of the best-loved tales for young children. **[World]**

————. *Favorite Fairy Tales Told Around the World*. Illus. by S. D. Schindler. Little, Brown, 1985. ISBN 0-316-35044-3 and ISBN 9780316350440. A selection from the 16-volume series. Retold in simple language for children to read for themselves. **[World]**

Hayes, Joe. *Dance, Nana, Dance/ Baila, Nana, Baila: Cuban Folktales in English and Spanish*. Illus. by Mauricio Trenard Sayago. Cinco Puntos Press, 2007. ISBN 1-9336-9317-7 and ISBN 9781933693170. **[Cuban]**

————. *The Day It Snowed Tortillas/ El Día que Nevaron Tortillas: Folktales Told in Spanish and English*. Illus. by Antonio Castro Lopez. Cinco Puntos Press, 2003. ISBN 0-9383-1776-8 and ISBN 9780938317760. **[Hispanic]**

He, Liyi. *The Spring of Butterflies: And Other Folktales of China's Minority Peoples*. Translated by He Liyi. Edited by Neil Philip. ISBN 0-0018-4137-8 and ISBN 9780001841376.

Paintings by Pan Aiquing and Li Zhao. Lothrop, 1985. Traditional stories of the Tibetan, Thai, Uighur, and Bai peoples who live in China. **[Chinese]**

Hearne, Betsy. *Beauties and Beasts.* Oryx Press, 1993. ISBN 0-8977-4729-1 and ISBN 9780897747295. **[World]**

Hoberman, Mary Ann. *You Read to Me, I'll Read to You: Very Short Fairy Tales to Read Together.* Illus. by Michael Emberley. Little, Brown, 2004. ISBN 0-31614611-0 and ISBN 9780316146111. Fractured versions of eight familiar tales, such as "Little Red Riding Hood" and "Cinderella." **[World]**

Holt, David, and Bill Mooney, eds. *The Exploding Toilet: Modern Urban Legends.* August House, 2004. ISBN 0-8748-3715-4 and ISBN 9780874837155. **[Urban Legend]**

————. *More Ready-to-Tell Tales from Around the World.* August House, 2000. ISBN 0-8748-3592-5 and ISBN 9780874835922. **[World]**

————. *Ready-to-Tell Tales.* August House, 1994. ISBN 0-8748-3381-7 and ISBN 9780874833812. **[World]**

————. *Spiders in the Hairdo: Modern Urban Legends.* August House, 1999. ISBN 0-8748-3525-9 and ISBN 9780874835250. **[Urban Legend]**

Houston, James A. *James Houston's Treasury of Inuit Legends.* Harcourt, 2006. ISBN 0-1520-5930-X and ISBN 9780152059309. **[Inuit]**

Hume, Lotta Carswell. *Favorite Children's Stories from China and Tibet.* Tuttle, 1989. ISBN 0-8048-1605-0 and ISBN 9780804816052. **[Chinese; Tibetan]**

Hurston, Zora Neale. *Lies and Other Tall Tales.* Illus. by Christopher Myers. HarperCollins, 2005. ISBN 0-06-000655-2 and ISBN 9780060006556. **[African American]**

————. *The Six Fools.* Illus. by Ann Tanksley. Adapted by Joyce Carol Thomas. HarperCollins, 2006. ISBN 0-0600-0647-1 and ISBN 9780060006471. **[African American]**

————. *The Three Witches.* Illus. by Faith Ringgold. Adapted by Joyce Carol Thomas. HarperCollins, 2006. ISBN 0-0600-0649-8 and ISBN 9780060006495. **[African American]**

Hutchinson, Veronica. *Candlelight Stories.* Illus. by Lois Lenski. Minton, Balch, 1926. **[World]**

————. *Chimney Corner Stories: Tales for Little Children.* Illus. by Lois Lenski. Minton, Balch, 1925. Neumann Press, 2006. ISBN 0-20802339-9 and ISBN 9780208023391. **[World]**

————. *Fireside Stories.* Illus. by Lois Lenski. Minton, Balch, 1927. **[World]**

Jacobs, Joseph. *English Fairy Tales.* Dover, 1898. ISBN 0-486-21818-X and ISBN 9780486218182. **[English]**

Jaffe, Nina, reteller. *The Mysterious Visitor: Stories of the Prophet Elijah.* Scholastic, 1997. ISBN 0-5904-8422-2 and ISBN 9780590484220. **[Jewish]**

————. *Patakin: World Tales of Drums and Drummers.* Illus. by Ellen Eagle. Holt, 1994. ISBN 0-8050-3005-0 and ISBN 9780805030051. Available with accompanying CD. Ten folktales featuring drums; with source notes and information about types of drums and the historical importance of drums in the societies from which the stories come. **[World]**

Jaffe, Nina, and Steve Zeitlin. *While Standing on One Foot: Puzzle Stories and Wisdom Tales from the Jewish Tradition.* Illus. by John Segal. Holt, 1993. ISBN 0-8050-2594-4 and ISBN 9780805025941. Seventeen stories involving a riddle or question. **[Jewish]**

Jaquith, Priscilla, reteller. *Bo Rabbit Smart for True: Folktales from the Gullah.* Illus. by Ed Young. Putnam, 1994. ISBN 0-399-22668-0 and ISBN 9780399226687. Hilarious stories told on the Sea Islands of Georgia and South Carolina, using a modified version of a poetic, lilting pattern of speech. **[African American]**

Jiang, Ji-Li. *The Magical Monkey King: Mischief in Heaven.* Illus. by Hui Hui Su-Kennedy. HarperCollins, 2002. ISBN 1-8850-0825-2 and ISBN 9781885008251. **[Chinese]**

Johnson-Davies, Denys. *Goha the Wise Fool.* Illus. by Hag Hamdy Mohamed Fattou and Hany El Saed Ahmed. Philomel, 2005. ISBN 0-3992-4222-8 and ISBN 9780399242229. **[Middle East]**

Kallen, Stuart A. *Urban Legends.* Lucent Books, 2006. ISBN 1-5901-8830-6 and ISBN 9781590188309. **[Urban Legends]**

Keding, Dan. *Stories of Hope and Spirit: Folktales from Eastern Europe.* August House, 2004. ISBN 0-8748-3727-8 and ISBN 9780874837278. **[Eastern European]**

Krull, Kathleen. *A Pot o' Gold: A Treasury of Irish Stories, Poetry, Folklore, and (of course) Blarney.* Illus. by David McPhail. Hyperion, 2004. ISBN 0-7868-0625-7 and ISBN 9780786806256. **[Irish]**

Laird, Elizabeth. *When the World Began: Stories Collected in Ethiopia.* Oxford University Press, 2000. ISBN 0-1927-4535-2 and ISBN 9780192745354. **[Ethiopian]**

Lang, Andrew. *Blue Fairy Book.* Edited by Brian Alderson. Dover, 1969. ISBN 0-486-21437-0 and ISBN 9780486214375. **[World]**

———. *Green Fairy Book.* Edited by Brian Alderson. Illus. by Anthony Maitland. Dover, 1969. ISBN 0-486-21439-7 and ISBN 9780486214399. **[World]**

———. *Pink Fairy Book.* Edited by Brian Alderson. Illus. by Colin McNaughton, Dover, 1966. ISBN 0-486-21792-2 and ISBN 9780486217925. **[World]**

———. *Red Fairy Book.* Edited by Brian Alderson. Illus. by Faith Jacques. Dover, n.d. ISBN 0-486-21673-X and ISBN 9780486216737. **[World]**

———. *A World of Fairy Tales.* Selected and introduced by Neil Philip. Illus. by Henry Justice Ford. Dial, 1994. ISBN 0-8037-1250-2 and ISBN 9780803712508. Philip has chosen 24 of the lesser-known tales from Lang's 12-volume color fairy tale collections. The source of each story is given as well as the name of the fairy book from which it was taken. This beautiful edition, with the original artwork by Ford, is a treasure. **[World]**

———. *Yellow Fairy Book.* Edited by Brian Alderson. Illus. by Erik Blegvad. Dover, n.d. ISBN 0-486-21674-8 and ISBN 9780486216744. **[World]**

Larson, Jean Russell. *The Fish Bride and Other Gypsy Tales.* Illus. by Michael Larson. Linnet Books, 2000. ISBN 0-2080-2474-3 and ISBN 9780208024749. **[Welsh; North American]**

Lattimore, Deborah Nourse, adapter and illustrator. *Arabian Nights: Three Tales.* HarperCollins, 1995. ISBN 0-06-024585-9 and ISBN 9780060245856. Includes "Aladdin," "The Queen of the Serpents," and "The Lost City of Ubar." **[Middle Eastern]**

Leach, Maria. *Whistle in the Graveyard: Folk Tales to Chill Your Bones.* Illus. by Ken Rinciari. Puffin, 1982. ISBN 0-1403-1529-2 and ISBN 9780140315295. **[World]**

Lester, Julius. *How Many Spots Does a Leopard Have? And Other Tales.* Illus. by David Shannon. Scholastic, 1989. ISBN 0-590-41973-0 and ISBN 9780590419734. A master storyteller retells ten African and two Jewish folktales. **[African/Jewish]**

———. *The Knee-High Man and Other Tales.* Dial, 1972, 1985. ISBN 0-8037-4593-1 and ISBN 9780803745933. **[African American]**

———. *The Tales of Uncle Remus: The Adventures of Brer Rabbit*. Illus. by Jerry Pinkney. Dial, 1987. ISBN 0-8037-0271-X and ISBN 9780803702714. **[African American]**

———. *More Tales of Uncle Remus: Further Adventures of Brer Rabbit, His Friends, Enemies, and Others*. Illus. by Jerry Pinkney. Dial, 1988. ISBN 0-8037-0419-4 and ISBN 9780803704190. **[African American]**

———. *Further Tales of Uncle Remus: The Misadventures of Brer Rabbit, Brer Fox, Brer Wolf, the Doodang, and Other Creatures*. Illus. by Jerry Pinkney. Dial, 1989. ISBN 0-8037-0610-3 and ISBN 9780803706101. **[African American]**

———. *The Last Tales of Uncle Remus*. Illus. by Jerry Pinkney. Dial, 1994. ISBN 0-8037-1303-7 and ISBN 9780803713031. Lester uses modified contemporary southern black English, "which is a combination of standard English and black English," and includes some contemporary references, such as shopping malls, in his spirited retelling of Uncle Remus tales, but the story lines have not changed. His introductions are *must* reading for the storyteller. **[African American]**

Livo, Norma, ed. *Troubadour's Storybag: Musical Folktales of the World*. Fulcrum, 1996. ISBN 1-5559-1953-7 and ISBN 9781555919535. **[World]**

Livo, Norma, and Dia Cha. *Folk Stories of the Hmong: Peoples of Laos, Thailand, and Vietnam*. Libraries Unlimited, 1991. ISBN 0-8728-7854-6 and ISBN 9780872878549. **[Asian]**

Lottridge, Celia Barker. *Ten Small Tales*. Illus. by Joanne Fitzgerald. Macmillan/McElderry, 1994. ISBN 0-689-50568-X and ISBN 9780689505683. Folktales from different cultures, suitable for telling to younger children. **[World]**

Lundburgh, Holger, translator. *Swedish Folk Tales*. Illus. by John Bauer. Floris, 2004. ISBN 0-8631-5457-3 and ISBN 9780863154577. **[Swedish]**

Lunge-Larsen, Lise. *The Hidden Folk: Stories of Fairies, Dwarves, Selkies, and Other Secret Beings*. Illus. by Beth Krommes. Houghton Mifflin, 2004. ISBN 0-6181-7495-8 and ISBN 9780618174959. **[Northern European]**

———. *The Troll with No Heart in His Body and Other Tales of Trolls from Norway*. Illus. by Betsy Bowen. Houghton Mifflin, 1999. ISBN 0-3959-1371-3 and ISBN 9780395913710. **[Norwegian]**

Lupton, Hugh. *Riddle Me This! Riddles and Stories to Challenge Your Mind*. Illus. by Sophie Fatus. Barefoot Books, 2003. ISBN 1-8414-8169-6 and ISBN 9781841481692. **[World]**

———. *The Story Tree: Tales to Read Aloud*. Illus. by Sophie Fatus. Barefoot Books, 2001. ISBN 1-8414-8790-2 and ISBN 9781841487908. **[World]**

Lurie, Alison. *Clever Gretchen and Other Forgotten Folktales*. Crowell, 1980. ISBN 0-6900-3944-1 and ISBN 9780690039443. **[World]**

McCaughrean, Geraldine. *One Thousand and One Arabian Nights*. Illus. by Rosamund Fowler. Oxford University Press, 1999. ISBN 0-1927-5013-5 and ISBN 9780192750136. **[Middle Eastern]**

MacDonald, Margaret Read. *Look Back and See: Twenty Lively Tales for Gentle Tellers*. Illus. by Rozane Murphy. H. W. Wilson, 1991. ISBN 0-8242-0810-2 and ISBN 9780824208103. **[World]**

———. *Shake-It-Up Tales! Stories to Sing, Dance, Drum, and Act Out*. August House, 2000. ISBN 0-8748-3590-9 and ISBN 9780874835908. **[World]**

———. *Tom Thumb: The Oryx Multicultural Folktale Series*. Oryx Press, 1993. ISBN 0-8977-4728-3 and ISBN 9780897747288. **[World]**

———. *Twenty Tellable Tales: Audience Participation Folktales for the Beginning Storyteller*. H. W. Wilson, 1988. ISBN 0-8389-0893-4 and ISBN 9780838908938. **[World]**

———. *When the Lights Go Out: Twenty Scary Tales to Tell*. H. W. Wilson, 1988. ISBN 0-8242-0770-X and ISBN 9780824207700. **[World]**

McGill, Alice. *Sure as Sunrise: Stories of Bruh Rabbit and His Walkin' Talkin' Friends*. Illus. by Don Tate. Houghton Mifflin, 2004. ISBN 0-6182-1196-9 and ISBN 9780618211968. **[African American]**

McKissack, Patricia C. *Porch Lies: Tales of Slicksters, Tricksters and Other Wily Characters*. Illus. by Andre Carrilho. Schwartz & Wade Books, 2006. ISBN 0-3758-3619-5 and ISBN 9780375836190. **[African American]**

MacManus, Seumas. *Donegal Fairy Stories*. Dover, 1968. ISBN 0-486-21971-2 and ISBN 9780486219714. **[Irish]**

———. *Hibernian Nights*. Barnes & Noble Books, 1994. ISBN 1-5661-9361-3 and ISBN 9781566193610. **[Irish]**

Mama, Raouf. *Why Monkeys Live in Trees and Other Stories from Benin*. Illus. by Andy Jones. Curbstone Press, 2006. ISBN 1-9318-9621-6 and ISBN 9781931896214. **[Benin]**

Manitonquat (Medicine Story), reteller. *The Children of the Morning Light: Wampanoag Tales*. Illus. by Mary F. Arquette. Macmillan, 1994. ISBN 0-02-765905-4 and ISBN 9780027659054. Stories of the southeastern Massachusetts Wampanoag told in a colloquial style. **[Native American]**

Martin, Eva, and László Gál. *Tales of the Far North*. Dial, 1986. Twelve Canadian fairy tales, born of the marriage of French and English traditions. **[North American/Canadian]**

Martin, Rafe. *The Hungry Tigress: Buddhist Legends and Jataka Tales*. Parallax, 1990. ISBN 0-9380-7725-2 and ISBN 9780938077251. **[Indian]**

———. *Mysterious Tales of Japan*. Illus. by Tatsuro Kiuchi. Putnam, 1993. ISBN 0-3992-2677-X and ISBN 9780399226779. **[Japanese]**

Mayo, Margaret. *Mythical Birds and Beasts from Many Lands*. Illus. by Jane Ray. Dutton, 1997. ISBN 0-5254-5788-7 and ISBN 9780525457886. **[World]**

Mayo, Margaret, reteller. *Magical Tales from Many Lands*. Illus. by Jane Ray. Dutton, 1993. ISBN 0-525-45017-3 and ISBN 9780525450177. Fourteen tales from a variety of cultures, from Arabic to Peruvian, with source notes. **[World]**

Medearis, Angela Shelf. *Haunts: Five Hair-Raising Tales*. Illus. by Trina Schart Hyman. Holiday House, 1996. ISBN 0-8234-1280-6 and ISBN 9780823412808. **[North American/US]**

Minard, Rosemary. *Womenfolk and Fairy Tales*. Houghton Mifflin, 1975. ISBN 0-3952-0276-0 and ISBN 9780395202760. **[World]**

National Association for the Preservation and Perpetuation of Storytelling. *Best-Loved Stories Told at the National Storytelling Festival*. Introduction by Jane Yolen. National Storytelling Press, 1991. ISBN 1-879991-01-2 and ISBN 9781879991019. Published on the occasion of the twentieth anniversary of the National Storytelling Festival, founded by Jimmy Neil Smith, these 37 tales offer a sampler drawn from the hundreds of stories told over the years. Also see *More Best Stories Told at the National Storytelling Festival*. National Storytelling Press, 1992. ISBN 1-879991-09-8 and ISBN 9781879991095. **[World]**

Nic Leodhas, Sorche. *Heather and Broom: Tales of the Scottish Highlands*. Holt, 1960. ISBN 0-0303-5280-0 and ISBN 9780030352805. **[Scottish]**

Norman, Howard. *The Girl Who Dreamed Only Geese and Other Tales of the Far North*. Illus. by Leo and Diane Dillon. Harcourt, 1997. ISBN 0-1523-0979-9 and ISBN 9780152309794. **[Inuit]**

———. *Trickster and the Fainting Birds.* Illus. by Tom Pohrt. Harcourt, 1999. ISBN 0-1520-0888-8 and ISBN 9780152008888. **[Native American]**

Norman, Howard, reteller. *How Glooskap Outwits the Ice Giants: And Other Tales of the Maritime Indians.* Illus. by Michael McCurdy. Little, Brown, 1989. ISBN 0-316-61181-6 and ISBN 9780316611817. Six Glooskap stories. **[Native American]**

O'Brien, Edna. *Tales for the Telling: Irish Folk and Fairy Stories.* Illus. by Michael Foreman. Puffin, 1988. ISBN 0-14-032293-0 and ISBN 9780140322934. **[Irish]**

Olson, Arielle North. *Ask the Bones: Scary Stories from Around the World.* With Howard Schwartz. Illus. by E. M. Gist. Puffin, 2002. ISBN 0-1423-0140-X and ISBN 9780142301401. **[World]**

———. *More Bones: Scary Stories from Around the World.* With Howard Schwartz. Illus. by E. M. Gist. Viking, 2008. ISBN 0-6700-6339-8 and ISBN 9780670063390. **[World]**

O'Malley, Kevin. *Velcome.* Walker, 1997. ISBN 0-5906-3610-3 and ISBN 9780590636100. **[Urban Legend]**

Oodgeroo. *Dreamtime: Aboriginal Stories.* Illus. by Bronwyn Bancroft. Lothrop, 1993. ISBN 0-688-13296-0 and ISBN 9780688132965. About half of the stories are based on the author's childhood memories of growing up on Stradbroke Island off the Queenland coast. The other half are aboriginal tales and new stories written in traditional aboriginal form. Both the author and artist are aboriginals. **[Australian/Aboriginal]**

Osborne, Mary Pope. *Mermaid Tales from Around the World.* Illus. by Troy Howell. Scholastic, 1993. ISBN 0-590-44377-1 and ISBN 9780590443777. Twelve mermaid tales, mostly from tradition (an exception is Hans Christian Andersen's "The Little Mermaid"), with an author's note on sources and an artist's note on his approach to illustrating the stories. **[World]**

Oxenbury, Helen, reteller and illustrator. *The Helen Oxenbury Nursery Story Book.* Knopf, 1992. ISBN 0-394-87519-2 and ISBN 9780394875194. An appealing collection of ten nursery tales, including such favorites as "Henny-Penny," "The Turnip," and "Goldilocks and the Three Bears." **[World]**

Phelps, Ethel Johnston. *Maid of the North.* Holt, 1981. ISBN 0-0306-2374-X and ISBN 9780030623745. **[World]**

Philip, Neil, reteller. *The Arabian Nights.* Illus. by Sheila Moxley. Orchard, 1994. ISBN 0-531-06868-4 and ISBN 9780531068687. This handsome edition of a literary classic includes such favorites as "Aladdin" and "Ali Baba and the Forty Thieves." **[Middle East]**

———. *Fairy Tales from Eastern Europe.* Illus. by Larry Wilkes. Houghton Mifflin, 1991. ISBN 0-395-57456-0 and ISBN 9780395574560. Twenty-two stories from Eastern Europe and the former Soviet Union. **[Eastern European]**

———. *Horse Hooves and Chicken Feet: Mexican Folktales.* Illus. by Jacqueline Mair. Clarion, 2003. ISBN 0-6181-9463-0 and ISBN 9780618194636. **[Mexican]**

Power, Effie. *Bag O'Tales: A Sourcebook for Storytellers.* Illus. by Corydon Bell. Dutton, 1934. Omnigraphics, 1990. ISBN 1-558888-34-9 and ISBN 9781558888340. Dover, 1970 (paperback) ISBN 0-486-22527-5 and ISBN 9780486225272. **[World]**

Provensen, Alice. *The Master Swordsman and the Magic Doorway: Two Legends from Ancient China.* Simon & Schuster, 2001. ISBN 0-689-83232-X and ISBN 9780689832321. **[Chinese]**

Ragan, Kathleen, ed. *Fearless Girls, Wise Women, and Beloved Sisters: Heroines in Folktales from Around the World.* Norton, 1997. ISBN 0-3930-4598-6 and ISBN 9780393045987. **[World]**

Ransome, Arthur. *Old Peter's Russian Tales.* Viking, 1975. ISBN 0-14-030696-X and ISBN 9780140306965. **[Russian]**

Reneaux, J. J. *Cajun Folktales.* August House, 1992. ISBN 0-8748-3283-7 and ISBN 9780874832839. **[North American/Cajun]**

———. *Haunted Bayou and Other Cajun Ghost Stories.* August House, 1994. ISBN 0-8748-3385-X and ISBN 9780874833850. **[North American/Cajun]**

———. *How Animals Saved the People: Animal Tales from the South.* Illus. by James Ransome. HarperCollins, 2001. ISBN 0-6881-6253-3 and ISBN 9780688162535. **[North American]**

Riordan, James. *The Woman in the Moon and Other Tales of Forgotten Heroines.* Illus. by Angela Barrett. Dial, 1985. ISBN 0-8037-0194-2 and ISBN 9780803701946. **[World]**

Rockwell, Anne. *The Old Woman and Her Pig.* Crowell, 1979. ISBN 0-6900-3928-X and ISBN 9780690039283. **[World]**

———. *The Three Bears and Fifteen Other Stories.* Crowell, 1979. ISBN 0-0644-0142-1 and ISBN 9780064401425. **[World]**

Ross, Gayle, reteller. *How Rabbit Tricked Otter and Other Cherokee Trickster Stories.* Illus. by Murv Jacob. Foreword by Chief Wilma Mankiller. HarperCollins, 1994. ISBN 0-060-21285-3 and ISBN 9780060212858. Fifteen tales centered around Rabbit, retold by a descendant of John Ross, a chief of the Cherokee nation. **[Native American]**

RunningWolf, Michael B., and Patricia Clark Smith. *On the Trail of Elder Brother: Glous'gap Stories of the Micmac Indians.* Illus. by Michael B. RunningWolf. Persea, 2000. ISBN 0-8925-5248-4 and ISBN 9780892552481. **[Native American]**

San Souci, Robert D. *Sister Tricksters: Rollicking Tales of Clever Females.* Illus. by Daniel San Souci. LittleFolk, 2006. ISBN 0-8748-3791-X and ISBN 9780874837919. **[North American]**

Schram, Peninnah, reteller. *Chosen Tales: Stories Told by Jewish Storytellers.* Jason Aronson, 1995. ISBN 1-56821-352-2 and ISBN 9781568213521. Two outstanding collections by a master storyteller. The stories will appeal to a wide age range, from children to adults. **[Jewish]**

———. *Jewish Stories One Generation Tells Another.* Jason Aronson, 1987. ISBN 0-87668-967-5 and ISBN 9780876689677. **[Jewish]**

Schwartz, Alvin, reteller. *Scary Stories to Tell in the Dark.* Collected from American folklore. Drawings by Stephen Gammel. Harper, 1986. ISBN 0-397-31926-6 and ISBN 9780397319268. See other collections by this author. **[North American]**

Schwartz, Howard. *Elijah's Violin and Other Jewish Fairy Tales.* Illus. by Linda Heller. Oxford University Press, 1994. ISBN 0-1950-9200-7 and ISBN 9780195092004. **[Jewish]**

Schwartz, Howard, and Barbara Rush, retellers. *The Diamond Tree: Jewish Tales from Around the World.* Illus. by Uri Shulevitz. HarperCollins, 1991. ISBN 0-06-025239-1 and ISBN 9780060252397. Fifteen familiar and unfamiliar Jewish tales from Africa, the Middle East, and Eastern Europe. **[Jewish]**

Serwadda, W. Moses. *Songs and Stories from Uganda.* Transcribed and edited by Hewitt Pantaleoni. Illus. by Leo and Diane Dillon. World Music Press, 1987. ISBN 0-937203-17-3 and ISBN 9780937203170. **[African]**

Serwer-Bernstein, Blanche. *Let's Steal the Moon.* Illus. by Trina S. Hyman. Shapolsky Pubs., 1987. ISBN 0-933503-27-X and ISBN 9780933503274. **[Jewish]**

Shannon, George, reteller. *More Stories to Solve: Fifteen Folktales from Around the World.* Illus. by Peter Sís. Greenwillow, 1991. ISBN 0-688-09161-X and ISBN 9780688091613. **[World]**

———. *Still More Stories to Solve: Fourteen Folktales from Around the World.* Illus. by Peter Sís. Greenwillow, 1994. ISBN 0-688-04619-3 and ISBN 9780688046194. As in *Stories to Solve: Folktales from around the World* (Greenwillow, 1985), Shannon presents the tales in the form of challenging riddles. **[World]**

Sherlock, Philip M. *West Indian Folk Tales.* Oxford University Press, 1988. ISBN 0-19-274127-6 and ISBN 9780192741271. **[West Indian]**

Sherman, Josepha. *Trickster Tales.* Illus. by David Boston. August House, 1996. ISBN 0-87483-450-3 and ISBN 9780874834505. **[World]**

Sierra, Judy. *Can You Guess My Name? Traditional Tales Around the World.* Illus. by Stefano Vitale. Clarion, 2002. ISBN 0-61813328-3 and ISBN 9780618133284. **[World]**

———. *Nursery Tales Around the World.* Illus. by Stefano Vitale. Clarion, 1996. ISBN 0-3956-7894-3 and ISBN 9780395678947. **[World]**

Singer, Isaac B. *The Fools of Chelm and Their History.* Translated from the Yiddish by Elizabeth Shub. Illus. by Uri Shulevitz. Farrar, Straus and Giroux, 1973. ISBN 0-374-32444-1 and ISBN 9780374324445. **[Jewish]**

———. *When Shlemiel Went to Warsaw and Other Stories.* Illus. by Margot Zemach. Farrar, Straus and Giroux, 1992. ISBN 0-374-38316-2 and ISBN 9780374383169. Eight Yiddish tales, some traditional, some original. **[Jewish]**

Spencer, Ann. *Song of the Sea: Myths, Tales and Folklore.* Illus. by Mark Lang. Tundra, 2001. ISBN 0-8877-6487-8 and ISBN 9780887764875. **[World]**

Stoutenburg, Adrien. *American Tall Tales.* Puffin, 1976. ISBN 0-14-030928-4 and ISBN 9780140309287. **[North American]**

Taback, Simms. *Kibitzers and Fools: Tales My Zayda Told Me.* Viking, 2005. ISBN 0-6700-5955-2 and ISBN 9780670059553. **[Jewish]**

Tchana, Katrin. *Changing Woman and Her Sisters: Stories of Goddesses from Around the World.* Illus. by Trina Schart Hyman. Holiday House, 2006. ISBN 0-8234-1999-1 and ISBN 9780823419999. **[World]**

———. *The Serpent Slayer and Other Tales of Strong Women.* Illus. by Trina Schart Hyman. Little, Brown, 2000. ISBN 0-3163-8701-0 and ISBN 9780316387019. **[World]**

Tingle, Tim. *Spirits Dark and Light: Supernatural Tales from the Five Civilized Tribes.* August House, 2006. ISBN 0-8748-3778-2 and ISBN 9780874837780. **[Native American]**

Townsend, John. *Mysterious Urban Myths.* Raintree, 2004. ISBN 1-84443-233-5 and ISBN 9781844432332. **[Urban Legends]**

Vigil, Angel. *The Eagle on the Cactus: Traditional Stories from Mexico.* Libraries Unlimited, 2000. ISBN 1-5630-8703-0 and ISBN 9781563087035. **[Mexican]**

Vittorini, Domenico. *Thread of Life: Twelve Old Italian Tales.* Illus. by Mary GrandPre. Knopf, 1995. ISBN 0-5175-9595-8 and ISBN 9780517595954. **[Italian]**

Vuong, Lynette Dyer. *The Brocaded Slipper and Other Vietnamese Tales.* Illus. by Vo-Dinh Mai. Harper, 1992. ISBN 0-064-40440-4 and ISBN 9780064404402. Vietnamese variants of familiar folktales such as "Cinderella" and "The Frog Prince." **[Vietnamese]**

———. *The Golden Carp: And Other Tales from Vietnam.* Illus. by Manabu Saito. Lothrop, 1993. ISBN 0-688-12514-X and ISBN 9780688125141. Six fairy tales from the Vietnamese oral tradition, with source notes and a pronunciation guide. **[Vietnamese]**

Walker, Barbara K., adapter. *The Dancing Palm Tree and Other Nigerian Folktales.* Illus. by Helen Siegl. Texas Tech, 1990. Reissue. ISBN 0-89672-216-3 and ISBN 9780896722163. Within each of these 11 tales from the Yoruba people there is a moral, for an important purpose of storytelling in Nigeria is to teach. Walker's excellent glossary provides insight into the culture. **[African]**

Walker, Paul Robert, adapter. *Giants!* Illus. by James Bernardin. Harcourt, 1995. ISBN 0-15-200883-7 and ISBN 9780152008833. There is great variety in the type of giant stories in this collection, from the biblical story of David and Goliath to the Greek myth of the Cyclops and the nursery tale of Jack and the Beanstalk. **[World]**

Walker, Richard, adapter. *The Barefoot Book of Pirates.* Illus. by Olwyn Whelan. Barefoot Books, 1998. ISBN 1-8414-8886-0 and ISBN 9781841488868. **[World]**

Washington, Donna. *A Pride of African Tales.* Illus. by James Ransome. HarperCollins, 2004. ISBN 0-0602-4929-3 and ISBN 9780060249298. **[African]**

Williams-Ellis, Amabel, selector. *Tales from the Enchanted World.* Illus. by Moira Kemp. Little, Brown, 1988. ISBN 0-316-94133-6 and ISBN 9780316941334. Twenty-two stories from around the world, some old favorites, others less well-known, chosen from earlier collections by Williams-Ellis, who died in 1984. A rich source for the storyteller. **[World]**

Williamson, Duncan. *The Broonie, Silkies and Fairies: Travellers' Tales of the Other World.* Harmony, 1987. ISBN 0-8624-1169-6 and ISBN 9780862411695. **[Scottish]**

————. *Fireside Tales of the Traveller Children.* Harmony, 1983. ISBN 0-8624-1100-9 and ISBN 9780862411008. **[Scottish]**

————. *Tales of the Seal People: Scottish Folk Tales.* Interlink, 1998. ISBN 0-9407-9399-7 and ISBN 9780940793996. **[Scottish]**

Windham, Sophie, adapter. *Read Me a Story: A Child's Book of Favorite Tales.* Scholastic, 1991. ISBN 0-590-44950-8 and ISBN 9780590449502. Fifteen familiar nursery tales. **[World]**

Wolkstein, Diane. *The Magic Orange Tree and Other Haitian Folktales.* Drawings by Elsa Henriqueg. Schocken, 1987. ISBN 0-8052-0650-7 and ISBN 9780805206500. **[Haitian]**

Yeats, W. B. *Fairy Tales of Ireland.* Selected by Neil Philip. Illus. by P. J. Lynch. Delacorte, 1990. ISBN 0-385-30249-5 and ISBN 9780385302494. Twenty folk and fairy tales chosen from Yeats's *Fairy and Folk Tales of the Irish Peasantry* and *Irish Fairy Tales*, with a brief commentary on Yeats and notes about the stories. **[Irish]**

Yellow Robe, Rosebud. *Tonweya and the Eagles and Other Lakota Tales.* Illus. by Jerry Pinkney. Dial, 1992. ISBN 0-8037-8973-4 and ISBN 9780803789739. Ten tales of the Lakota Sioux people. **[Native American]**

Yeoman, John. *The Singing Tortoise and Other Animal Folktales.* Illus. by Quentin Blake. Tambourine, 1994. ISBN 0-688-13366-5 and ISBN 9780688133665. These 11 animal folktales capture the flavor of the cultures from which they come, from Tibet to Papua New Guinea. Some of the tales are hilarious, others are poignant. All are very tellable and will appeal to a wide age range. **[World]**

Yep, Laurence, reteller. *The Rainbow People.* Illus. by David Wiesner. HarperCollins, 1989. ISBN 0-06-026760-7 and ISBN 9780060267605. **[Chinese]**

————. *Tongues of Jade.* Illus. by David Wiesner. HarperCollins, 1991. ISBN 0-06-022470-3 and ISBN 9780060224707. These volumes of traditional tales, *The Rainbow People* and *Tongues of Jade*, were brought to America and collected in the 1930s from Chinese immigrants living in Oakland, California. They are filled with magic and mystery. **[Chinese]**

Yolen, Jane, ed. *Favorite Folktales from around the World*. Pantheon, 1988. ISBN 0-3947-5188-4 and ISBN 9780394751887. One hundred sixty tales from more than 40 different cultures. Excellent introduction. **[World]**

—————. *Mightier than the Sword: World Folktales for Strong Boys*. Illus. by Raul Colón. Silver Whistle, 2003. ISBN 0-1521-6391-3 and ISBN 9780152163914. **[World]**

—————. *Mirror, Mirror: Forty Folk Tales for Mothers and Daughters to Share*. Illus. by Heidi Stemple. Viking, 2000. ISBN 0-1402-9835-5 and ISBN 9780140298352. **[World]**

—————. *Not One Damsel in Distress: World Folktales for Strong Girls*. Silver Whistle, 2000. ISBN 0-1520-2047-0 and ISBN 9780152020477. **[World]**

FOLKTALES: PICTURE BOOKS

Aardema, Verna. *Bimwili and the Zimwi*. Illus. by Susan Meddaugh. Dial, 1985. ISBN 0-8037-0212-4 and ISBN 9780803702127. A tale from Zanzibar in which the little girl Bimwili outwits an ogre. **[African]**

—————. *Borreguita and the Coyote: A Tale from Ayutla, Mexico*. Illus. by Petra Mathers. Knopf, 1991. ISBN 0-679-80921-X and ISBN 9780679809210. A clever little lamb outwits a hungry coyote. **[Mexican]**

—————. *How the Ostrich Got Its Long Neck*. Illus. by Marcia Brown. Scholastic, 1995. ISBN 0-590-48367-6 and ISBN 9780590483674. A *pourquoi* story from Kenya, reminiscent of "The Elephant's Child" by Rudyard Kipling. **[African]**

—————. *Jackal's Flying Lesson*. Illus. by Dale Gottlieb. Knopf, 1995. ISBN 0-679-85813-X and ISBN 9780679858133. Clever Blue Crane rescues Mother Dove's babies by making Jackal think he can fly. **[South African]**

—————. *Koi and the Kola Nuts: A Tale from Liberia*. Illus. by Joe Cepeda. Schwartz/Atheneum, 1999. ISBN 0-6898-5677-6 and ISBN 9780689856778. **[African]**

—————. *Traveling to Tondo: A Tale of the Nkundo of Zaire*. Illus. by Will Hillenbrand. Knopf, 1991. ISBN 0-679-80081-6 and ISBN 9780679800811. A comical tale about a civet cat traveling with friends to his wedding. Whenever unexpected delays take place, the friends agree to wait for each other. By the time the bridegroom arrives, the bride has married and has two kittens! The cumulative action and chantable refrain invite audience participation. **[African]**

—————. *Who's in Rabbit's House?* Illus. by Leo and Diane Dillon. Dial, 1979. ISBN 0-8037-9551-3 and ISBN 9780803795518. A humorous Masai tale for younger children. **[African]**

—————. *Why Mosquitoes Buzz in People's Ears*. Illus. by Leo and Diane Dillon. Puffin, 1978. ISBN 0-8037-6089-2 and ISBN 9780803760899. **[African]**

Arnold, Katya, reteller and illustrator. *Baba Yaga*. North-South, 1993. ISBN 1-55858-208-8 and ISBN 9781558582088. With the help of a hungry gosling, young Tishka escapes from the witch Baba Yaga. Based on the story "Tereschichka," collected by Alexander Afanasyev. The illustrations by the Russian-born artist were inspired by traditional Russian *lubola* pictures, hand-colored wood engravings. **[Russian]**

Asbjørnsen, Peter C., and Jørgen E. Moe. *The Three Billy Goats Gruff*. Illus. by Marcia Brown. Harcourt, 1991. ISBN 0-15-690150-1 and ISBN 9780156901505. **[Norwegian]**

Aylesworth, Jim. *The Tale of Tricky Fox: A New England Trickster Tale*. Illus. by Barbara McClintock. Scholastic, 2001. ISBN 0-4390-9543-3 and ISBN 9780439095433. **[American]**

Bang, Molly Garrett. *Wiley and the Hairy Man.* Macmillan, 1976. ISBN 0-02-708370-5 and ISBN 9780027083705. How Wiley and his mother trick the Hairy Man. **[African American]**

Batt, Tanya Robyn. *The Faerie's Gift.* Illus. by Nicoletta Ceccoli. Barefoot, 2003. ISBN 1-8414-8998-0 and ISBN 9781841489988. **[Irish]**

Battle-Lavert, Gwendolyn. *The Shaking Bag.* Illus. by Aminah Brenda Lynn Robinson. Whitman, 2000. ISBN 0-8075-7328-0 and ISBN 9780807573280. **[African American]**

Belpré, Pura, reteller. *Perez and Martina: A Puerto Rican Folktale.* Illus. by Carlos Sanchez. Viking, 1991. Reissue (Warne, 1932). ISBN 0-670-84166-8 and ISBN 9780670841660. A favorite with Puerto Rican children who recognize and appreciate the humor in the tragic romance between the beautiful cockroach Martina and the gallant mouse Perez. Also available in Spanish. ISBN 0-670-84167-6 and ISBN 9780670841677. **[Puerto Rican]**

Birdseye, Tom, reteller. *Soap! Soap! Don't Forget the Soap! An Appalachian Folktale.* Illus. by Andrew Glass. Holiday House, 1993. ISBN 0-8234-1005-6 and ISBN 9780823410057. A much-loved tale from North Carolina about a boy who has trouble remembering and the hilarious situations he gets himself into as a result. **[North American/Appalachian]**

Brett, Jan, adapter and illustrator. *Goldilocks and the Three Bears.* Dodd, Mead, 1987. ISBN 0-399-22004-6 and ISBN 9780399220043. Adapted from *The Green Fairy Book* by Andrew Lang. **[English]**

———. *The Mitten: A Ukrainian Folktale.* Putnam, 2009. ISBN 0-399-25296-7 and ISBN 9780399252969. When too many forest creatures seek shelter in a mitten, they all tumble out onto the snow. **[Ukrainian]**

Brooke, L. Leslie, illustrator. *The Golden Goose Book.* Houghton Mifflin, 1992. ISBN 0-395-61303-5 and ISBN 9780395613030. **[English]**

Brown, Marcia, reteller and illustrator. *Once a Mouse.* Simon & Schuster, 1972. ISBN 0-684-12662-1 and ISBN 9780684126623. A fable from the Hitopadésa about big and little, set in India. **[Indian]**

Bruchac, Joseph, and James Bruchac. *How Chipmunk Got His Stripes.* Illus. by Jose Aruego and Ariane Dewey. Dial, 2001. ISBN 0-8037-2404-7 and ISBN 9780803724044. **[Native American]**

———. *Raccoon's Last Race: A Traditional Abenaki Story.* Illus. by Jose Aruego and Ariane Dewey. Dial, 2004. ISBN 0-8037-2977-4 and ISBN 9780803729773. **[Native American]**

———. *Turtle's Race with Beaver: A Traditional Seneca Story.* Illus. by Jose Aruego and Ariane Dewey. Dial, 2003. ISBN 0-1424-0466-7 and ISBN 9780142404669. **[Native American]**

Bruchac, Joseph, and Gayle Ross, retellers. *The Story of the Milky Way: A Cherokee Tale.* Illus. by Virginia A. Stroud. Dial, 1995. ISBN 0-8037-1737-7 and ISBN 9780803717374. With the help of Beloved Woman, the people frighten away the spirit dog who has been stealing their cornmeal. The white cornmeal spills from the dog's mouth as he flees across the sky—and that is how the Milky Way came to be! **[Native American]**

Bryan, Ashley, reteller and illustrator. *The Cat's Purr.* Simon & Schuster, 1985. ISBN 0-689-31086-2 and ISBN 9780689310867. How Cat lost his drum and got his purr. **[West Indian]**

———. *The Dancing Granny.* Simon & Schuster, 1987. ISBN 0-689-71149-2 and ISBN 9780689711497. Granny Anika and Spider Ananse become dancing partners. **[West Indian]**

————. *Turtle Knows Your Name*. Simon & Schuster, 1989. ISBN 0-689-31578-3 and ISBN 9780689315787. Turtle helps a little boy remember his long name. As always, Bryan's storytelling is full of rhythm and vitality. **[West Indian]**

Bushyhead, Robert H. *Yonder Mountain: A Cherokee Legend*. Illus. by Kristina Rodanas. Marshall Cavendish, 2002. ISBN 0-7614-5113-7 and ISBN 9780761451136. **[Native American]**

Casanova, Mary. *The Hunter: a Chinese Folktale*. Illus. by Ed Young. Atheneum, 2000. ISBN 0-6898-2906-X and ISBN 9780689829062. **[Chinese]**

Climo, Shirley. *The Egyptian Cinderella*. Illus. by Ruth Heller. HarperCollins, 1989. ISBN 0-690-04822-X and ISBN 9780690048223. Set in Egypt in the sixth century B.C.E., this mixture of fact and fable is one of the earliest versions of the Cinderella story. A falcon steals the tiny rose-red slippers of a Greek slave girl and carries them to the pharaoh. The pharaoh searches until he finds Rhodopis, the beautiful owner, and makes her his queen. **[Egyptian]**

————. *The Korean Cinderella*. Illus. by Ruth Heller. HarperCollins, 1993. ISBN 0-06-020432-X and ISBN 9780060204327. Pear Blossom is helped by a frog, sparrows, and an ox, rather than by a fairy godmother, in the Korean version of a favorite tale. Children will enjoy discovering other parallels—a straw sandal substitutes for the glass slipper, a handsome young magistrate for the prince. **[Korean]**

Cole, Joanna, reteller. *It's Too Noisy!* Illus. by Kate Duke. HarperCollins, 1989. ISBN 0-690-04735-5 and ISBN 9780690047356. A humorous story about a farmer's attempts to find quiet in his noisy cottage. **[Jewish]**

Compestine, Ying Chang. *The Real Story of Stone Soup*. Illus. by Stephane Jorisch. Dutton, 2007. ISBN 0-5254-7493-5 and ISBN 9780525474937. **[Chinese]**

Compton, Patricia A., reteller. *The Terrible EEK: A Japanese Tale*. Illus. by Sheila Hamanaka. Simon & Schuster, 1991. ISBN 0-671-73737-6 and ISBN 9780671737375. A funny cumulative tale that begins when an eavesdropping thief misunderstands the words "terrible leak" for "terrible eek." **[Japanese]**

Conover, Chris, reteller and illustrator. *Froggie Went A-Courting*. Farrar, Straus and Giroux, 1986. ISBN 0-374-32466-2 and ISBN 9780374324667. A retelling of an Elizabethan nursery rhyme. **[British]**

Cooper, Susan, reteller. *The Selkie Girl*. Illus. by Warwick Hutton. Simon & Schuster, 1986. ISBN 0-689-50390-3 and ISBN 9780689503900. A fine retelling in words and pictures that captures the bittersweet quality of this ancient tale about a mortal man wed to a seal woman. **[Celtic]**

————. *The Silver Cow: A Welsh Tale*. Illus. by Warwick Hutton. Simon & Schuster, 1983. ISBN 0-689-50236-2 and ISBN 9780689502361. A story about the crafty greed of a farmer and the revenge of the magic people, the Tylwyth Teg. **[Welsh]**

————. *Tam Lin*. Illus. by Warwick Hutton. Simon & Schuster, 1991. ISBN 0-689-50505-1 and ISBN 9780689505058. The last in the author's and artist's Celtic trilogy is a lyric prose retelling of the old ballad about a young girl who rescues a lad under the enchantment of the Elfin Queen. **[Scottish]**

Cowley, Joy. *The Wishing of Biddy Malone*. Illus. by Christopher Denise. Philomel, 2004. ISBN 0-399-23404-7 and ISBN 9780399234040. **[Irish]**

Croll, Carolyn, reteller and illustrator. *The Three Brothers*. Putnam, 1991. ISBN 0-399-22195-6 and ISBN 9780399221958. A farmer offers the family farm to the son who can fill the barn by the end of the day. With the help of his imagination—and a candle—the youngest son succeeds. **[German/Latvian]**

Czernecki, Stefan, and Timothy Rhodes. *The Singing Snake*. Illus. by Stefan Czernecki. Hyperion, 1993. ISBN 1-56282-399-X and ISBN 9781562823993. Old Man said he would make a musical instrument in the shape of the creature with the most beautiful singing voice. To win the contest, Snake carefully swallows Lark so that when Lark sings it appears as if her song is coming from Snake. When Snake is found out, he hides in the grass, which is why people today call someone who can't be trusted "a snake in the grass." The instrument that Old Man made is called a didgeridoo. **[Australian]**

Dasent, George Webbe, translator. *East o' the Sun and West o' the Moon*. Introduction by Naomi Lewis. Illus. by P. J. Lynch. Candlewick, 1992. ISBN 1-56402-049-5 and ISBN 9781564020499. The much-loved fairy tale about a girl and an enchanted white bear. **[Norwegian]**

Day, Nancy Raines, reteller. *The Lion's Whiskers: An Ethiopian Folktale*. Illus. by Ann Grifalconi. Scholastic, 1995. ISBN 0-590-45803-5 and ISBN 9780590458030. A kind stepmother finds a way to win the heart of her new husband's son. For a different treatment of this Ethiopian folktale, see *Pulling the Lion's Tail* by Jane Kurtz. Illus. by Floyd Cooper. Simon & Schuster, 1995. ISBN 0-671-88183-3 and ISBN 9780671881832. **[African]**

Dayrell, Elphinstone. *Why the Sun and Moon Live in the Sky*. Illus. by Blair Lent. Houghton Mifflin, 1990. ISBN 0-395-53963-3 and ISBN 9780395539637. **[African]**

de Gerez, Toni. *Louhi, Witch of North Farm: A Story from Finland's Epic Poem the Kalevala*. Illus. by Barbara Cooney. Viking, 1986. ISBN 0-670-80556-4 and ISBN 9780670805563. A vividly retold tale from "the Land of Heroes." **[Finnish]**

de Gerez, Tree. *When Bear Came Down from the Sky*. Illus. by Lisa Desimini. Viking, 1994. ISBN 0-670-85171-X and ISBN 9780670851713. All the things that happened, including the first snowfall, when Sky Father let Bear visit Earth. An unusual myth that will appeal to younger children, told with simplicity and charm. **[Finnish]**

de Regniers, Beatrice Schenk. *Little Sister and the Month Brothers*. Illus. by Margot Tomes. Lothrop, 1994. ISBN 0-688-05293-2 and ISBN 9780688052935. The 12 month brothers befriend little sister when her cruel stepmother and sister send her out to find strawberries in the snow. **[Czechoslovakian]**

Deedy, Carmen Agra. *Martina, the Beautiful Cockroach: A Cuban Folktale*. Illus. by Michael Austin. Peachtree, 2007. ISBN 1-5614-5399-4 and ISBN 9781561453993. **[Cuban]**

DeFelice, Cynthia, adapter. *Cold Feet*. Illus. by Robert Andrew Parker. Dorling Kindersley, 2000. ISBN 0-7894-2636-6 and ISBN 9780789426369. **[Scottish]**

————. *The Dancing Skeleton*. Illus. by Robert Andrew Parker. Macmillan, 1989. ISBN 0-02-726452-1 and ISBN 9780027264524. A funny ghost story about a deceased husband who tries to frustrate his wife's new romance. **[American]**

————. *One Potato, Two Potato*. Illus. by Andrea U'Ren. Farrar, Straus and Giroux, 2006. ISBN 0-3743-5640-8 and ISBN 9780374356408. **[Irish]**

DeFelice, Cynthia, and Mary DeMarsh, retellers. *Three Perfect Peaches: A French Folktale*. Illus. by Irene Trivas. Orchard, 1995. ISBN 0-531-06872-2 and ISBN 9780531068724. The princess is very near death and only three perfect peaches can save her. A romantic tale told with tongue-in-cheek humor. **[French]**

Demi, adapter and illustrator. *The Hungry Coat: A Tale from Turkey*. McElderry, 2004. ISBN 0-6898-4680-0 and ISBN 9780689846809. **[Turkish]**

————. *The Stonecutter*. Knopf, 1995. ISBN 0-517-59864-7 and ISBN 9780517598641. A stonecutter learns wisdom when an angel grants his ever-changing wish to be something else. **[Chinese]**

Diakité, Baba Wagué. *The Hatseller and the Monkeys.* Scholastic, 1999. ISBN 0-590-96069-5 and ISBN 9780590960694. **[African]**

———. *The Hunterman and the Crocodile.* Scholastic, 1997. ISBN 0-590-89828-0 and ISBN 9780590898287. **[African]**

———. *The Magic Gourd.* Scholastic, 2003. ISBN 0-4395-3960-4 and ISBN 9780439439602. **[African]**

———. *Mee-an and the Magic Serpent: A Story from Mali.* Groundwood, 2006. ISBN 0-8889-9719-1 and ISBN 9780888997197. **[African]**

Doyle, Malachy. *Hungry! Hungry! Hungry!* Illus. by Paul Hess. Peachtree, 2001. ISBN 1-56145-241-6 and ISBN 9781561452415. **[British]**

Duvall, Deborah L. *How Rabbit Lost His Tail: A Traditional Cherokee Legend.* University of New Mexico Press, 2003. ISBN 0-82633010-X and ISBN 9780826330109. **[Native American]**

———. *Rabbit Goes Duck Hunting: A Traditional Cherokee Legend.* Illus. by Murv Jacob. University of New Mexico Press, 2004. ISBN 0-8263-3336-2 and ISBN 9780826333360. **[Native American]**

Echewa, Obinkaram. *The Magic Tree: A Folktale from Nigeria.* Illus. by E. B. Lewis. Morrow, 1999. ISBN 0-6881-6232-0 and ISBN 9780688162320. **[African]**

Ehlert, Lois. *Cuckoo/Cucú: A Mexican Folktale.* Harcourt, 2000. ISBN 0-1520-0274-X and ISBN 9780152002749. **[Mexican]**

Ehlert, Lois, illustrator. *Moon Rope: A Peruvian Folktale/Un lazo a la luna: Una leyenda peruana.* Translated into Spanish by Amy Price. Harcourt, 1992. ISBN 0-15-255343-6 and ISBN 9780152553432. How fox ended up on the moon, told in Spanish and English. Illustrated with striking collages inspired by pre-Columbian artifacts. **[South American/Peruvian]**

Eilenberg, Max. *Beauty and the Beast.* Illus. by Angela Barrett. Candlewick Press, 2006. ISBN 0-7636-3160-4 and ISBN 9780763631604. **[French]**

Faulkner, William J., reteller. *Brer Tiger and the Big Wind.* Illus. by Roberta Wilson. Morrow, 1995. ISBN 0-688-12985-4 and ISBN 9780688129859. When Brer Tiger refuses to let the other animals eat from the pear tree and drink from the spring during a time of famine and drought, Brer Rabbit devises a scheme to teach Tiger the importance of sharing. **[African American]**

Forest, Heather. *Feathers: A Jewish Tale from Eastern Europe.* Illus. by Marcia Cutchin. August House, 2005. ISBN 0-8748-3755-1 and ISBN 9780874837551. **[Jewish]**

Fowles, Shelley. *The Bachelor and the Bean.* Farrar, Straus and Giroux, 2003. ISBN 0-3743-0478-5 and ISBN 9780374304782. **[Jewish]**

Galdone, Joanna. *The Tailypo: A Ghost Story.* Illus. by Paul Galdone. Houghton Mifflin, 1984. ISBN 0-395-30084-3 and ISBN 9780395300848. **[African American]**

Galdone, Paul. *What's in Fox's Sack?* Houghton Mifflin, 1987. ISBN 0-89919-062-6 and ISBN 9780899190624. A retelling, for younger children, of an old English folktale. **[English]**

Gershator, David, and Phillis Gershator. *Kallaloo! A Caribbean Tale.* Illus. by Diane Greenseid. Marshall Cavendish, 2005. ISBN 0-7614-5110-2 and ISBN 9780761451105. **[West Indian]**

Gershator, Phillis, reteller. *Tukama Tootles the Flute: A Tale from the Antilles.* Illus. by Synthia Saint James. Orchard, 1994. ISBN 0-531-06811-0 and ISBN 9780531068113. Through the power of his magic song, Tukama escapes from a two-headed giant who planned to have him for supper. **[West Indian]**

Gerson, Mary-Joan, reteller. *How Night Came from the Sea: A Story from Brazil*. Illus. by Carla Golembe. Little, Brown, 1994. ISBN 0-316-30855-2 and ISBN 9780316308557. An African sea goddess brings the gift of night to the land of bright sunshine. **[South American]**

———. *Why the Sky Is Far Away: A Nigerian Folktale*. Illus. by Carla Golembe. Little, Brown, 1992. ISBN 0-316-30852-8 and ISBN 9780316308526. In the beginning the sky was close to earth and the people did not have to grow their own food. Anyone who was hungry could cut off a piece of sky and eat it. But there was one woman who was never satisfied. **[African]**

Goble, Paul, reteller and illustrator. *Adopted by the Eagles: A Plains Indian Story of Friendship and Treachery*. Simon & Schuster, 1994. ISBN 0-02-736575-1 and ISBN 9780027365757. When two Lakota friends fall in love with the same maiden, one turns treacherous and leaves the other to die. The deserted friend is rescued by eagles and returns to marry the maiden. **[Native American/Lakota]**

———. *Iktomi and the Berries: A Plains Indian Story*. Orchard, 1989. ISBN 0-531-05819-0 and ISBN 9780531058190. See other stories about the Plains Indian trickster Iktomi, retold by Goble in a style that invites audience participation. **[Native American]**

———. *Mystic Horse*. HarperCollins, 2003. ISBN 0-0602-9814-6 and ISBN 9780060298142. **[Native American/Pawnee]**

González, Lucía M., reteller. *The Bossy Gallito/El Gallo de Bodas: A Traditional Cuban Folktale*. Illus. by Lulu Delacre. Scholastic, 1994. ISBN 0-590-46843-X and ISBN 9780590468435. This cumulative folktale is reminiscent of "The Old Woman and Her Pig." On his way to his uncle's wedding, a bossy little rooster cannot resist eating some corn near a mud puddle and dirties his beak. Only his friend the Sun can cause a chain of events that will make the grass clean his beak so he can go to the wedding. A bilingual picture book. **[Cuban]**

Greene, Ellin. *The Little Golden Lamb*. Illus. by Rosanne Litzinger. Clarion, 2000. ISBN 0-3957-1526-1 and ISBN 9780395715260. **[Hungarian]**

Greene, Ellin, reteller. *Billy Beg and His Bull*. Illus. by Kimberly Bulcken Root. Holiday House, 1994. ISBN 0-8234-1100-1 and ISBN 9780823411009. With the help of magical gifts from his bull, Billy Beg kills three multi-headed giants and a fiery dragon, and wins the hand of a princess. A male Cinderella tale. **[Irish]**

———. *Ling-Li and the Phoenix Fairy: A Chinese Folktale*. Illus. by Zong-Zhou Wang. Houghton Mifflin, 1996. ISBN 0-395-71528-8 and ISBN 9780395715284. Ling-Li's beautiful wedding robe, made by her own hand, is stolen and torn into pieces, which become the flower known as impatiens. **[Chinese]**

Greene, Jacqueline Dembar, reteller. *What His Father Did*. Illus. by John O'Brien. Houghton Mifflin, 1992. ISBN 0-395-55042-4 and ISBN 9780395550427. Herschel, a raggedy vagabond, tricks an innkeeper into providing supper by threatening to do "what my father did when he was given no supper." After he has eaten everything the innkeeper can gather from the neighbors, Herschel tells her his father "went to bed with an empty stomach"! **[Jewish]**

Gregorowski, Christopher. *Fly, Eagle, Fly! An African Fable*. Illus. by Niki Daly. McElderry, 2000. ISBN 0-6898-2398-3 and ISBN 9780689823985. **[African]**

Grimm, Jacob, and Wilhelm Grimm. *The Bremen Town Musicians*. Illus. by Bernadette Watts. Translated by Anthea Bell. North-South, 1992. ISBN 1-55858-140-5 and ISBN 9781558581401. A simple but lively retelling of an old favorite. **[German]**

———. *The Devil and the Three Golden Hairs.* Retold and illus. by Nonny Hogrogian. Knopf, 1983. ISBN 0-394-95560-9 and ISBN 9780394955605. **[German]**

———. *The Elves and the Shoemaker.* Retold and illus. by Bernadette Watts. North-South, 1986. ISBN 1-55858-035-2 and ISBN 9781558580350. Another favorite with younger children. **[German]**

———. *The Frog Prince or Iron Henry.* Translated by Naomi Lewis. Illus. by Binette Schroeder. North-South, 1989. ISBN 1-55858-015-8 and ISBN 9781558580152. Ideal for sharing in the picture-book hour. **[German]**

———. *Hansel and Gretel.* Translated by Elizabeth D. Crawford. Illus. by Lisbeth Zwerger. Penguin/Minedition, 2008. (Reissue) ISBN 0-698-40078-X and ISBN 9780698400788. **[German]**

———. *Little Red Cap.* Illus. by Lisbeth Zwerger. Penguin/Minedition, 2006. (Reissue) ISBN 0-698-40053-4 and ISBN 9780698400534. **[German]**

———. *Little Red Riding Hood.* Retold and illus. by Trina Schart Hyman. Holiday House, 1983. ISBN 0-8234-0653-9 and ISBN 9780823406531. **[German]**

———. *The Seven Ravens.* Translated by Elizabeth D. Crawford. Illus. by Lisbeth Zwerger. Simon & Schuster, 1991. ISBN 0-88708-092-8 and ISBN 9780887080920. **[German]**

———. *The Sleeping Beauty.* Retold and illus. by Trina Schart Hyman. Little, Brown, 1983. ISBN 0-316-38708-8 and ISBN 9780316387088. **[German]**

———. *Snow White and Rose Red.* Retold and illus. by Barbara Cooney. Delacorte, 1991. ISBN 0-385-30175-8 and ISBN 9780385301756. A newly designed edition of a book first published in 1965. Two loving sisters befriend a bear (a prince bewitched by a wicked dwarf) who, in turn, brings them good fortune. **[German]**

———. *Snow-White and the Seven Dwarfs.* Translated by Randall Jarrell. Illus. by Nancy Burkert. Farrar, Straus and Giroux, 1972. ISBN 0-374-37099-0 and ISBN 9780374370992. **[German]**

———. *The Wolf and the Seven Little Kids.* Illus. by Felix Hoffman. Harcourt, 1959. **[German]**

Hague, Michael. *Kate Culhane: A Ghost Story.* SeaStar, 2001. ISBN 1-5871-7058-2 and ISBN 9781587170584. **[Irish]**

Haley, Gail E. *Jack and the Bean Tree.* Crown, 1986. ISBN 0-517-55717-7 and ISBN 9780517557174. **[North American/Appalachian]**

———. *Jack and the Fire Dragon.* Crown, 1988. ISBN 0-517-56814-4 and ISBN 9780517568149. A dramatic picture-book version of the Appalachian story known as "Old Fire Dragaman" in *Jack Tales* by Richard Chase. **[North American/Appalachian]**

———. *A Story, a Story: An African Tale.* Simon & Schuster, 1970. ISBN 0-689-20511-2 and ISBN 9780689205118. **[African]**

Hamilton, Virginia. *Bruh Rabbit and the Tar Baby Girl.* Illus. by James E. Ransome. Blue Sky/Scholastic, 2003. ISBN 0-5904-7376-X and ISBN 9780590473767. **[African American]**

———. *Wee Winnie Witch's Skinny: An Original African American Scare Tale.* Illus. by Barry Moser. Blue Sky/Scholastic, 2004. ISBN 0-5902-8880-6 and ISBN 9780590288804. **[African American]**

Han, Suzanne Crowder, reteller. *The Rabbit's Escape.* Illus. by Yumi Heo. Holt. 1995. ISBN 0-8050-2675-4 and ISBN 9780805026757. **[Korean]**

————. *The Rabbit's Judgment*. Illus. by Yumi Heo. Holt, 1994. ISBN 0-8050-2674-6 and ISBN 9780805026740. Two folktales about a clever rabbit, from the author's collection *Korean Folk and Fairy Tales*. Told in English and Korean. **[Korean]**

Harper, Wilhelmina. *The Gunniwolf*. Illus. by Barbara Upton. Dutton, 2003. ISBN 0-5254-6785-8 and ISBN 9780525467854. **[American]**

Hastings, Selina, reteller. *The Firebird*. Illus. by Reg Cartwright. Candlewick, 1993. ISBN 1-56402-096-7 and ISBN 9781564020963. With the advice of his valiant horse, a brave lad wins the Princess Vasilisa. This simplified retelling of the famous Russian tale is a pleasing introduction to the ballet. Another inviting picture book is *Firebird* (Putnam, 1994; ISBN 0-399-22510-2 and ISBN 9780399225109) by Rachel Isadora, a former ballerina who used George Balanchine's version of the ballet as her inspiration. **[Eastern Europe]**

Hayes, Joe. *El Cucuy! A Bogeyman Cuento*. Illus. by Honorio Robledo. Cinco Puntos Press, 2001. ISBN 0-93831754-7 and ISBN 9780938317548. **[Hispanic]**

————. *The Weeping Woman (La Llorona): A Hispanic Legend Told in Spanish and English*. Illus. by Vicki Trego Hill and Mona Pennypecker. Cinco Puntos Press, 2004. ISBN 0-9383-1739-3 and ISBN 9780938317395. **[Hispanic]**

Heyer, Marilee. *The Weaving of a Dream: A Chinese Folktale*. Viking, 1986. ISBN 0-670-80555-6 and ISBN 9780670805556. A devoted and brave son retrieves his mother's beautiful tapestry, stolen by the fairies, and is justly rewarded. **[Chinese]**

Hodges, Margaret. *The Little Humpbacked Horse*. Farrar, Straus and Giroux, 1987. ISBN 0-374-44495-1 and ISBN 9780374444952. Based on a story by the Russian writer Peter Pavlovich Yashov. **[Russian]**

Hong, Lily Toy, reteller and illustrator. *Two of Everything*. Whitman, 1993. ISBN 0-8075-8157-7 and ISBN 9780807581575. Mr. Haktak finds a pot that duplicates whatever is put into it. The Haktaks become rich, but then Mrs. Haktak falls into the pot! What will Mr. Haktak do? **[Chinese]**

Hooks, William H. *Moss Gown*. Illus. by Donald Carrick. Houghton Mifflin, 1987. ISBN 0-89919-460-5 and ISBN 9780899194608. A traditional English tale that preserves elements of the King Lear story and "Cinderella," as told in the Tidewater section of eastern North Carolina. **[North American]**

————. *The Three Little Pigs and the Fox*. Illus. by S. D. Schindler. Macmillan, 1989. ISBN 0-02-744431-7 and ISBN 9780027444315. An Appalachian version of "The Three Little Pigs." **[North American/Appalachian]**

Hort, Lenny, reteller. *The Fool and the Fish*. Illus. by Gennady Spirin. Dial, 1990. ISBN 0-8037-0861-0 and ISBN 9780803708617. Based on Alexander Afanasyev's folktale about Ivan and a wish-granting fish. Ivan is so lazy that all he wants is to escape from work, but his wishes bring him unexpected good fortune and marriage to the tsar's daughter. **[Russian]**

Howe, John, reteller and illustrator. *Jack and the Beanstalk*. Little, Brown, 1989. ISBN 0-316-37579-9 and ISBN 9780316375795. More subdued and with more realistic illustrations than Kellogg's version, but equally satisfying. **[English]**

Hurst, Margaret M. *Grannie and the Jumbie: A Caribbean Tale*. HarperCollins, 2001. ISBN 0-0662-3632-0 and ISBN 9780066236322. **[Caribbean]**

Hurston, Zora Neale. *Roy Makes a Car*. Adapted by Mary E. Lyons. Illus. by Terry Widener. Atheneum, 2005. ISBN 0-689-84640-1 and ISBN 9780689846403. **[African American]**

Ishii, Momoko, reteller. *The Tongue-cut Sparrow.* Translated from the Japanese by Katherine Paterson. Illus. by Suekichi Akaba. Dutton, 1987. ISBN 0-525-67199-4 and ISBN 9780525671992. This retelling makes use of onomatopoeic words to bring out the pathos and humor of the much-loved folktale. **[Japanese]**

Jacobs, Joseph. *King of the Cats.* Illus. by Paul Galdone. Houghton Mifflin, 1980. ISBN 0-395-29030-9 and ISBN 9780395290309. A story for Halloween shivers. **[English]**

―――. *Tom Tit Tot.* Illus. by Evaline Ness. Scribner, 1965. The English variant of "Rumpelstiltskin." **[English]**

Jaffe, Nina, reteller. *Older Brother, Younger Brother: A Korean Folktale.* Illus. by Wenhai Ma. Viking, 1995. ISBN 0-670-85645-2 and ISBN 9780670856459. The story of two brothers as different as day and night and of the swallow and magic gourds that bring each brother his just reward. **[Korean]**

Janisch, Heinz. *The Fire: An Ethiopian Folktale.* Illus. by Fabricio VandenBroeck. Groundwood, 2002. ISBN 0-8889-9450-8 and ISBN 9780888994509. **[African]**

Jiang, Ji-Li. *The Magical Monkey King.* Illus. by Hui-Hui Su-Kennedy. HarperCollins, 2002. ISBN 0-0602-9544-9 and ISBN 9780060295448. **[Chinese]**

Johnson, Paul Brett. *Bearhide and Crow.* Holiday House, 2000. ISBN 0-8234-1470-1 and ISBN 9780823414703. **[North American/Appalachian]**

―――. *Fearless Jack.* McElderry, 2001. ISBN 0-6898-3296-6 and ISBN 9780689832963. **[North American/Appalachian]**

―――. *Jack Outwits the Giants.* McElderry, 2002. ISBN 0-689-83902-2 and ISBN 9780689839023. **[North American/Appalachian]**

Kajikawa, Kimiko. *Yoshi's Feast.* Illus. by Yumi Heo. DK Ink, 2000. ISBN 0-7894-2607-2 and ISBN 9780789426079. **[Japanese]**

Kellogg, Steven, reteller and illustrator. *Jack and the Beanstalk.* Morrow, 1991. ISBN 0-688-10250-6 and ISBN 9780688102500. The text closely follows that of its nineteenth-century collector, Joseph Jacobs, but Kellogg's energetic illustrations add much gusto to the old tale. **[English]**

Kimmel, Eric A. *Three Samurai Cats: A Story from Japan.* Illus. by Mordicai Gerstein. Holiday House, 2003. ISBN 0-8234-1877-4 and ISBN 9780823418770. **[Japanese]**

Kimmel, Eric A., reteller. *Anansi and the Moss-Covered Rock.* Illus. by Janet Stevens. Holiday House, 1990. ISBN 0-8234-0689-X and ISBN 9780823406890. When Anansi discovers a magic rock, he is able to trick the other animals out of their fruits and vegetables until little Bush Deer turns the tables on him and Anansi loses everything. (See other stories about Anansi by this author/illustrator team.) **[African]**

―――. *The Three Princes: A Tale from the Middle East.* Illus. by Leonard Everett Fisher. Holiday House, 1994. ISBN 0-8234-1115-X and ISBN 9780823411153. A story from *The Arabian Nights* about a princess who was as wise as she was beautiful. **[Middle East]**

Knutson, Barbara. *Love and Roast Chicken: A Trickster Tale from the Andes Mountains.* Lerner, 2004. ISBN 1-5750-5657-7 and ISBN 9781575056579. **[South American]**

―――. *Sungura and Leopard: A Swahili Trickster Tale.* Little, Brown, 1993. ISBN 0-316-50010-0 and ISBN 9780316500104. Sungura, the clever little hare, finds a way to save his family from the leopard with whom he shares a house. **[African]**

Kurtz, Jane. *In the Small, Small Night.* Illus. by Rachel Isadora. Greenwillow, 2005. ISBN 0-0662-3814-5 and ISBN 9780066238142. **[African]**

Kurtz, Jane, reteller. *Fire on the Mountain.* Illus. by E. B. Lewis. Simon & Schuster, 1994. ISBN 0-671-88268-6 and ISBN 9780671882686. Challenged by his rich master to spend a night in the cold mountains alone and without shelter, Alemayu keeps himself alive by imagining the warmth of a distant fire. The master accuses the poor shepherd lad of cheating because "looking at a fire on the mountain is the same as building a fire," but is shamed into honoring his promise. **[African]**

Kushner, Lawrence, and Gary Schmidt. *In God's Hands.* Jewish Lights Publishing, 2005. ISBN 1-5802-3224-8 and ISBN 9781580232241. **[Jewish]**

Laird, Elizabeth. *Beautiful Bananas.* Illus. by Liz Pichon. Peachtree, 2004. ISBN 1-5614-5305-6 and ISBN 9781561453054. **[African]**

Lang, Andrew, reteller. *Aladdin and the Wonderful Lamp.* Illus. by Errol Le Cain. Puffin, 1983. ISBN 0-14-050389-7 and ISBN 9780140503890. **[Middle East]**

Langton, Jane, reteller. *Salt: A Russian Folktale.* Translated by Alice Plume. Illus. by Ilse Plume. Hyperion, 1992. ISBN 1-56282-178-4 and ISBN 9781562821784. Based on the folktale by Alexander Afanasyev. How Ivan the Fool discovers a mountain of salt, outwits his greedy brothers, and marries a beautiful tsarevna. **[Russian]**

Lee, Jeanne M. *Toad Is the Uncle of Heaven: A Vietnamese Folktale.* Holt, 1989. ISBN 0-8050-1147-1 and ISBN 9780805011470. How it came to be that one day the King of Heaven called an ugly toad "Uncle." **[Vietnamese]**

Levine, Arthur A., reteller. *The Boy Who Drew Cats: A Japanese Folktale.* Illus. by Frédéric Clément. Dial, 1994. ISBN 0-8037-1172-7 and ISBN 9780803711723. Kenji's compulsion to draw cats saves his life when the cats come alive and battle with the Goblin Rat and its followers in the darkness of an abandoned temple. Key Japanese characters and their pronunciation and meaning are explained in a glossary. **[Japanese]**

Lewis, J. Patrick. *The Frog Princess: A Russian Folktale.* Paintings by Gennady Spirin. Dial, 1994. ISBN 0-8037-1623-0 and ISBN 9780803716230. The youngest son of the tsar, forced to marry a little green frog, discovers she is really a princess under an evil enchantment. **[Russian]**

Lexau, Joan M. *Crocodile and Hen.* Illus. by Doug Cushman. HarperCollins, 2001. ISBN 0-0602-8486-2 and ISBN 9780060284862. **[African]**

Lottridge, Celia Barber, reteller. *The Name of the Tree: A Bantu Folktale.* Illus. by Ian Wallace. Simon & Schuster, 1990. ISBN 0-689-50490-X and ISBN 9780689504907. During a drought the animals hunger for the fruit "that smelled like all the fruits of the world," but it is on a tree too high for even the giraffe to reach. The tree will yield its fruit only to those who know its name. When Gazelle and Elephant fail to bring back the name from King Lion, it is determined little Tortoise who makes the long journey and returns with the tree's name. **[African]**

Lunge-Larsen, Lise. *The Race of the Birkebeiners.* Illus. by Mary Azarian. Houghton Mifflin, 2001. ISBN 0-618-10313-9 and ISBN 9780618103133. **[Norwegian]**

McDermott, Gerald, reteller and illustrator. *Coyote: A Trickster Tale from the American Southwest.* Harcourt, 1994. ISBN 0-15-220724-4 and ISBN 9780152207243. Coyote's attempts to fly like the crows ends in disaster. A Zuni tale. **[Native American]**

―――. *The Magic Tree: A Tale from the Congo.* Holt, 1994. ISBN 0-8050-3080-8 and ISBN 9780805030808. An unloved twin discovers a magic tree that brings him wealth and happiness, but when he forgets his pledge of silence, he loses everything. **[African]**

―――. *Raven: A Trickster Tale from the Pacific Northwest.* Harcourt, 1993. ISBN 0-15-265661-8 and ISBN 9780152656614. Raven disguises himself as a human baby in order to steal the sun from the Sky God's house and bring light to the people of the world. **[Native American]**

————. *Zomo the Rabbit: A Trickster Tale from West Africa*. Harcourt, 1992. ISBN 0-15-299967-1 and ISBN 9780152999674. How Zomo the clever rabbit performs three impossible tasks set by the Sky God and earns wisdom. **[African]**

MacDonald, Amy. *Please, Malese! A Trickster Tale from Haiti*. Illus. by Emily Lisker. Farrar, Straus and Giroux, 2002. ISBN 0-3743-6000-6 and ISBN 9780374360009. **[Haitian]**

MacDonald, Margaret Read. *Conejito: A Folktale from Panama*. Illus. by Geraldo Valerio. August House, 2006. ISBN 0-8748-3779-0 and ISBN 9780874837797. **[Latin American]**

————. *Fat Cat: A Danish Folktale*. Illus. by Julie Paschkis. August House, 2001. ISBN 0-8748-3765-0 and ISBN 9780874837650. **[Danish]**

————. *Go to Sleep, Gecko! A Balinese Folktale*. Illus. by Geraldo Valerio. August House, 2006. ISBN 0-8748-3780-4 and ISBN 9780874837803. **[Balinese]**

————. *The Great Smelly, Slobbery, Small-tooth Dog: A Folktale from Great Britain*. Illus. by Julie Paschkis. August House, 2007. ISBN 0-8748-3808-8 and ISBN 9780874838084. **[British]**

————. *Little Rooster's Diamond Button*. Illus. by Will Terry. Albert Whitman, 2007. ISBN 0-8075-4644-5 and ISBN 9780807546444. **[Hungarian]**

————. *Mabela the Clever*. Illus. by Tim Coffey. Albert Whitman, 2001. ISBN 0-8075-4902-9 and ISBN 9780807549025. **[African]**

Maddern, Eric, reteller. *Rainbow Bird: An Aboriginal Folktale from Northern Australia*. Illus. by Adrienne Kennaway. Little, Brown, 1993. ISBN 0-316-54314-4 and ISBN 9780316543149. Bird Woman steals Fire from Crocodile Man and puts it into the heart of every tree so that people can make fire from dry sticks and logs. Then she puts firesticks into her tail and becomes Rainbow Bird. **[Australian/Aboriginal]**

Maggi, María Elena. *The Great Canoe: A Kariña Legend*. Illus. by Gloria Calderón. Translated by Elisa Amado. Douglas & McIntyre, 2001. ISBN 0-8889-9444-3 and ISBN 9780888994448. **[Venezuelan]**

Mahy, Margaret, reteller. *The Seven Chinese Brothers*. Illus. by Jean Tseng and Mousien Tseng. Scholastic, 1990. ISBN 0-590-42055-0 and ISBN 9780590420556. The popular Chinese folktale of look-alike brothers who possess unique abilities. This retelling lacks the rhythm and humor of Claire Bishop's *The Five Chinese Brothers* but avoids the stereotypical images that made that book so controversial. **[Chinese]**

Marshak, Samuel, reteller. *The Month Brothers: A Slavic Tale*. Translated from the Russian by Thomas P. Whitney. Illus. by Diane Stanley. Morrow, 1983. ISBN 0-688-01510-7 and ISBN 9780688015107. A traditional Czechoslovakian story about a little girl who sees all the 12 months of the year at once. **[Czechoslovakian]**

Martin, Rafe. *The Language of Birds*. Illus. by Susan Gaber. Putnam, 2000. ISBN 0-3992-2925-6 and ISBN 9780399229251. **[Russian]**

Martin, Rafe, reteller. *The Rough-Face Girl*. Illus. by David Shannon. Putnam, 1992. ISBN 0-399-21859-9 and ISBN 9780399218590. The Algonquin version of the Cinderella story. **[Native American]**

Milligan, Bryce. *The Prince of Ireland and the Three Magic Stallions*. Illus. by Preston McDaniels. Holiday House, 2003. ISBN 0-8234-1573-2 and ISBN 9780823415731. **[Irish]**

Mills, Lauren, reteller and illustrator. *Tatterhood and the Hobgoblins: A Norwegian Folktale*. Little, Brown, 1993. ISBN 0-316-57406-6 and ISBN 9780316574068. A girl with a mind of her own rescues her sister from the hobgoblins and proves the insignificance of appearances. **[Norwegian]**

Mollel, Tolowa M., reteller. *The Flying Tortoise: An Igbo Tale*. Illus. by Barbara Spurll. Houghton Mifflin, 1994. ISBN 0-395-68845-0 and ISBN 9780395688458. This pourquoi tale from the Igbo people of southeastern Nigeria tells why the tortoise has a checkered shell. **[African]**

———. *The Orphan Boy*. Illus. by Paul Morin. Houghton Mifflin, 1991. ISBN 0-89919-985-2 and ISBN 9780899199856. A star takes the shape of a young orphan boy in order to bring good fortune to an impoverished herdsman. As in "The Crane Maiden," curiosity leads to the revelation of the boy's true identity and the old man's loss. The boy returns to the sky where he appears as Venus, the morning star. A haunting story, beautifully told and illustrated. **[African]**

Mosel, Arlene, reteller. *The Funny Little Woman*. Illus. by Blair Lent. Dutton, 1972. ISBN 0-525-30265-4 and ISBN 9780525302650. A woman who loves to laugh and to make rice cakes escapes from the wicked *oni* with a magic cooking paddle and becomes the richest woman in Japan. **[Japanese]**

Nunes, Susan, reteller. *Tiddalick the Frog*. Illus. by Ju-Hong Chen. Simon & Schuster, 1989. ISBN 0-689-31502-3 and ISBN 9780689315022. When a giant frog drinks up all the fresh water in the world it is Noyang the eel who breaks the drought with wild and wonderful dancing that makes Tiddalick laugh and release the water. **[Australian/ Aboriginal]**

O'Brien, Anne Sibley, reteller and illustrator. *The Princess and the Beggar: A Korean Folktale*. Scholastic, 1993. ISBN 0-590-46092-7 and ISBN 9780590460927. Exiled by the king for her disobedience, the "weeping princess" teaches the royal arts to her illiterate beggar husband and in the process regains her self-respect and that of her father. A feminist tale from the sixth century, retold by an American who spent most of her childhood in South Korea. **[Korean]**

Olaleye, Issac O. *In the Rainfield: Who Is the Greatest?* Illus. by Ann Grifalconi. Blue Sky Press, 2000. ISBN 0-5904-8363-3 and ISBN 9780590483636. **[African]**

Olson, Arielle North, reteller. *Noah's Cats and the Devil's Fire*. Illus. by Barry Moser. Orchard, 1992. ISBN 0-531-05984-7 and ISBN 9780531059845. Why cats have eyes that gleam in the dark and fur that makes sparks. **[Romanian]**

O'Malley, Kevin. *Velcome*. Walker, 1999. ISBN 0-8027-7568-3 and ISBN 9780802775689. **[Urban Legends]**

Ormerod, Jan, and David Lloyd, retellers. *The Frog Prince*. Illus. by Jan Ormerod. Lothrop, 1990. ISBN 0-688-09568-2 and ISBN 9780688095680. This retelling of the familiar tale about an enchanted frog is based on the Grimm story and the English version known as "The Well of the World's End." **[German/English]**

Paterson, Katherine, reteller. *The Tale of the Mandarin Ducks*. Illus. by Leo and Diane Dillon. Dutton, 1990. ISBN 0-525-67203-4. In this story of love and compassion, a pair of mandarin ducks repays the couple Yasubo and Skoza for their former kindness to the drake. **[Japanese]**

Paye, Won-Ldy, and Margaret H. Lippert. *Head, Body, Legs: A Story from Liberia*. Illus. by Julie Paschkis. Holt, 2002. ISBN 0-8050-6570-9 and ISBN 9780805065701. **[African]**

———. *Mrs. Chicken and the Hungry Crocodile*. Illus. by Julie Paschkis. Holt, 2003. ISBN 0-8050-7047-8 and ISBN 9780805070477. **[African]**

————. *Talking Vegetables.* Illus. by Julie Paschkis. Holt, 2006. ISBN 0-8050-7742-1 and ISBN 9780805077421. **[African]**

Percy, Graham, illustrator. *The Cock, the Mouse, and the Little Red Hen.* Candlewick, 1992. ISBN 1-56402-008-8 and ISBN 9781564020086. A favorite nursery tale with illustrations that capture all the humor and drama. **[English]**

Philip, Neil. *Noah and the Devil: A Legend of Noah's Ark from Romania.* Illus. by Isabelle Brent. Clarion, 2001. ISBN 0-6181-1754-7 and ISBN 9780618117543. **[Romanian]**

Pitre, Felix, reteller. *Paco and the Witch: A Puerto Rican Folktale.* Illus. by Christy Hale. Dutton, 1995. ISBN 0-525-67501-9 and ISBN 9780525675013. Paco must guess the name of the evil witch or be forever in her power. The storyteller's skill and the use of many Spanish words within the English text evoke a real sense of the land and culture of Puerto Rico. **[Puerto Rican]**

Poole, Josephine. *Snow White.* Illus. by Angela Barrett. Knopf, 1991. ISBN 0-679-82656-4 and ISBN 9780679826569. Keeping to the plot, but not to the language of the Grimm tale, Poole gives readers a more contemporary set of characters, providing a new look to an old story. **[German]**

Powell, Patricia Hruby. *Ch'at to Yinilo: Frog Brings Rain.* Illus. by Kendrick Benally. Translated by Peter A. Thomas. Salina Bookshelf, 2006. ISBN 1-8933-5408-3 and ISBN 9781893354081. **[Native American]**

Puttapipat, Niroot. *The Musicians of Bremen.* Candlewick, 2005. ISBN 0-7636-2758-5 and ISBN 9780763627584. **[German]**

Quattlebaum, Mary. *Sparks Fly High: The Legend of Dancing Point.* Illus. by Leonid Gore. Farrar, Straus and Giroux, 2006. ISBN 0-37434452-3 and ISBN 9780374344528. **[American]**

Réascol, Sabina I. *The Impudent Rooster.* Illus. by Holly Berry. Dutton, 2004. ISBN 0-5254-7179-0 and ISBN 9780525471790. **[Romanian]**

Rogasky, Barbara. *The Water of Life: A Tale from the Brothers Grimm.* Holiday House, 1986. ISBN 0-8234-0552-4 and ISBN 9780823405527. The youngest son finds the Water of Life and helps save his father. **[German]**

Root, Phyllis. *Coyote and the Magic Words.* Illus. by Sandra Speidel. Lothrop, 1993. ISBN 0-688-10308-1 and ISBN 9780688103088. An original story based on southwestern Native American folklore that will have special appeal for storytellers. **[Native American]**

Ross, Gayle. *How Turtle's Back Was Cracked: A Traditional Cherokee Tale.* Illus. by Murv Jacob. Dial, 1995. ISBN 0-8037-1728-8 and ISBN 9780803717282. When a wolf chokes to death on a persimmon, Turtle takes credit, convinced he is a mighty hunter. In revenge for Turtle flaunting "wolf spoons," the other wolves capture Turtle and mean to kill him. Turtle outwits his captors, but cracks his beautiful shell when the wolves throw him into the river and he lands on a rock. **[Native American]**

Roth, Susan L., reteller and illustrator. *The Story of Light.* Morrow, 1990. ISBN 0-688-08676-4 and ISBN 9780688086763. A pourquoi story inspired by a Cherokee tale that tells how Spider brought light to the animal people. **[Native American]**

Rounds, Glen, reteller and illustrator. *Three Little Pigs and the Big Bad Wolf.* Holiday House, 1992. ISBN 0-8234-0923-6 and ISBN 9780823409235. Rounds's bold drawings and sparse text give this old tale an immediacy that will appeal to the K–3 crowd. **[English]**

San Souci, Robert D. *The Faithful Friend.* Illus. by Brian Pinkney. Simon & Schuster, 1995. ISBN 0-02-786131-7 and ISBN 9780027861310. In this West Indian variant of Grimm's "Faithful John," set on the island of Martinique, an uncle hires three zombies to cast an evil spell over his niece and her betrothed. The emphasis throughout the story is on the friendship between two youths, one black, one white. **[West Indian]**

———. *Little Pierre: A Cajun Story from Louisiana.* Illus. by David Catrow. Harcourt, 2003. ISBN 0-1520-2482-4 and ISBN 9780152024826. **[American]**

———. *Sukey and the Mermaid.* Illus. by Brian Pinkney. Simon & Schuster, 1992. ISBN 0-02-778141-0 and ISBN 9780027781410. A mermaid befriends an unhappy girl in this haunting story from the Sea Islands, South Carolina. **[African American]**

———. *The Twins and the Bird of Darkness: A Hero Tale from the Caribbean.* Illus. by Terry Widener. Simon & Schuster, 2002. ISBN 0-6898-3343-1 and ISBN 9780689833434. **[Caribbean]**

Sawyer, Ruth. *Journey Cake, Ho!* Illus. by Robert McCloskey. Puffin, 1978. ISBN 0-14-050275-0 and ISBN 9780140502756. The American variant of "The Gingerbread Boy." **[North American]**

———. *The Remarkable Christmas of the Cobbler's Sons.* Illus. by Barbara Cooney. Viking, 1994. ISBN 0-670-84922-7 and ISBN 9780670849222. This story was first published in 1941 in Ruth Sawyer's *The Long Christmas* under the title "Schnitzle, Schnotzle, and Schnootzle." The story has been slightly changed, but this lovely edition is a treasure to share with younger children. **[Austrian]**

Schlitz, Laura Amy. *The Bearskinner: A Tale of the Brothers Grimm.* Illus. by Max Grafe. Candlewick, 2007. ISBN 0-7636-2730-5 and ISBN 9780763627300. This elegant retelling of the Grimm tale "Bearskin," about a soldier who bargains with the Devil, has a softer ending. For older children and young adults. **[German]**

Shannon, George. *The Piney Woods Peddler.* Illus. by Nancy Tafuri. Greenwillow, 1981. ISBN 0-688-84304-2 and ISBN 9780688843045. An original tale that uses elements of traditional American swapping songs. **[North American]**

———. *Rabbit's Gift.* Illus. by Laura Dronzek. Harcourt, 2007. ISBN 0-15-206073-1 and ISBN 9780152060732. **[Chinese]**

Shepard, Aaron. *Master Man: A Tall Tale of Nigeria.* Illus. by David Wisniewski. HarperCollins, 2001. ISBN 0-6881-3783-0 and ISBN 9780688137830. **[African]**

Shepard, Aaron, reteller. *The Gifts of Wali Dad: A Tale of India and Pakistan.* Illus. by Daniel San Souci. Atheneum, 1995. ISBN 0-684-19445-7 and ISBN 9780684194455. A retelling of a story from Andrew Lang's *Brown Fairy Book* about a simple grass-cutter whose gift to a queen brings about an embarrassment of riches. **[Indian and Pakistani]**

Shute, Linda. *Momotaro, the Peach Boy: A Traditional Japanese Tale.* Lothrop, 1986. ISBN 0-688-05863-9 and ISBN 9780688058630. **[Japanese]**

Sierra, Judy. *The Beautiful Butterfly: A Folktale from Spain.* Illus. by Victoria Chess. Clarion, 2000. ISBN 0-3959-0015-8 and ISBN 9780395900154. **[Spanish]**

Snyder, Dianne, reteller. *The Boy of the Three-Year Nap.* Illus. by Allen Say. Houghton Mifflin, 1988. ISBN 0-395-44090-4 and ISBN 9780395440902. A lazy boy gets more than he bargained for—a rich wife *and* a good job! **[Japanese]**

So, Meilo. *Gobble, Gobble, Slip, Slop: A Tale of a Very Greedy Cat.* Knopf, 2004. ISBN 0-3758-2504-5 and ISBN 9780375825040. **[Indian]**

Steptoe, John. *Mufaro's Beautiful Daughters: An African Tale.* Morrow, 1993. ISBN 0-688-12935-8 and ISBN 9780688129354. An original story inspired by a folktale published in 1895 in Theal's *Kaffir Folktales.* **[African]**

Stewig, John Warren. *Whuppity Stoorie.* Illus. by Preston McDaniels. Holiday House, 2004. ISBN 0-8234-1749-2 and ISBN 9780823417490. **[Scottish]**

Tadjo, Véronique, reteller and illustrator. *Lord of the Dance: An African Retelling.* HarperCollins, 1989. ISBN 0-397-32351-4 and ISBN 9780397323517. The Senufo people are known for their wood-carved masks that represent invisible spirits. In this poetic retelling the mask represents the Creator. **[African]**

Taylor, Harriet Peck, reteller and illustrator. *Coyote and the Laughing Butterflies.* Macmillan, 1995. ISBN 0-02-788846-0 and ISBN 9780027888461. "Even today butterflies remember the trick that was played on coyote. They flutter high and low, to and fro, laughing too hard to fly straight, all day long in the yellow sunshine." Based on a Tewa legend. **[Native American]**

Thomas, Joyce Carol, and Zora Neale Hurston. *What's the Hurry, Fox? And Other Animal Stories.* Illus. by Brian Collier. HarperCollins, 2004. ISBN 0-0600-0643-9 and ISBN 9780060006433. **[African American]**

Thompson, Pat. *Drat That Fat Cat!* Illus. by Ailie Busby. Levine/Scholastic, 2003. ISBN 0-4394-7195-8 and ISBN 9780439471954. **[European]**

Uchida, Yoshiko, reteller. *The Wise Old Woman.* Illus. by Martin Springett. Simon & Schuster, 1994. ISBN 0-689-50582-5 and ISBN 9780689505829. An arrogant young lord decrees that everyone over the age of 70 must be taken into the mountains and left to die. But a septuagenarian is the only person able to solve the three impossible tasks that will save his village. **[Japanese]**

Washington, Donna. *A Big, Spooky House.* Illus. by Jacqueline Roger. Jump at the Sun/Hyperion, 2000. ISBN 0-7868-0349-5 and ISBN 9780786803491. **[African American]**

Wattenberg, Jane. *Henny-Penny.* Scholastic, 2000. ISBN 0-4390-7817-2 and ISBN 9780439078177. **[English]**

Whitney, Thomas P. *Vasilisa the Beautiful.* Illus. by Nonny Hogrogian. Macmillan, 1970. ISBN 0-02792540-4 and ISBN 9780027925401. The Russian Cinderella. **[Russian]**

Willey, Margaret. *Clever Beatrice.* Illus. by Heather Soloman. Atheneum, 2001. ISBN 0-6898-3254-0 and ISBN 9780689832543. **[American]**

Williams, Carol Ann. *Tsubu the Little Snail.* Illus. by Tatsuro Kiuchi. Simon & Schuster, 1995. ISBN 0-671-87167-6 and ISBN 9780671871673. This ancient Japanese folktale has elements of "Tom Thumb," but the mood is spiritual with the emphasis on honoring the divine essence in every being. **[Japanese]**

Winthrop, Elizabeth, adapter. *Vasilissa the Beautiful.* Illus. by Alexander Koshkin. HarperCollins, 1991. ISBN 0-06-021662-X and ISBN 9780060216627. With the help of a magical doll given to her by her mother before her death, Vasilissa overcomes the witch Baba Yaga and marries a tsar. **[Russian]**

Wolkstein, Diane. *Sun Mother Wakes the World: An Australian Creation Story.* Illus. by Bronwyn Bancroft. HarperCollins, 2004. ISBN 0-6881-3915-9 and ISBN 9780688139155. **[Australian]**

———. *White Wave: A Chinese Tale.* Illus. by Ed Young. Harcourt, 1996. ISBN 0-15-200293-6 and ISBN 9780152002930. **[Chinese]**

Yacowitz, Caryn, reteller. *The Jade Stone: A Chinese Folktale.* Illus. by Ju-Hong Chen. Holiday House, 1992. ISBN 0-8234-0919-8 and ISBN 9780823409198. The emperor sends Chan Lo a perfect piece of jade from which to carve a dragon, but the artist listens to the stone and carves three carp. **[Chinese]**

Yagawa, Sumiko. *The Crane Wife.* Translated from the Japanese by Katherine Paterson. Illus. by Suekichi Akaba. Peter Smith, 1992. ISBN 0-8446-6589-4 and ISBN 9780844665894. A man rescues a wounded crane and soon after marries an elegant stranger. Three times his wife weaves exquisite cloth but begs her husband not to watch. His curiosity brings about his sorrow when she resumes her crane shape and departs. **[Japanese]**

Yep, Laurence, reteller. *The Man Who Tricked a Ghost.* Illus. by Isadore Seltzer. Bridgewater, 1993. ISBN 0-8167-3030-X and ISBN 9780816730308. An amusing ghost story said to have been written down by an emperor of China in the third century A.D. **[Chinese]**

Yolen, Jane. *Tam Lin.* Illus. by Charles Mikolaycak. Harcourt, 1990. ISBN 0-15-284261-6 and ISBN 9780152842611. A longer prose rendering of the ancient Scottish ballad with dramatic and romantic illustrations. (See also Susan Cooper's version.) **[Scottish]**

Young, Ed. *Monkey King.* HarperCollins, 2001. ISBN 0-06-027919-2 and ISBN 9780060279196. **[Chinese]**

Young, Ed, translator and illustrator. *Lon Po Po: A Red-Riding Hood Story from China.* Putnam, 1989. ISBN 0-399-21619-7 and ISBN 9780399216190. Three brave young girls outwit a wolf in this smooth retelling of the Red Riding Hood story, set in China. **[Chinese]**

Zelinsky, Paul O., reteller and illustrator. *Rumpelstiltskin: From the German of the Brothers Grimm.* Dutton, 1986. ISBN 0-525-44265-0 and ISBN 9780525442653. **[German]**

Zemach, Harve. *Duffy and the Devil: A Cornish Tale.* Illus. by Margot Zemach. Farrar, Straus and Giroux, 1973. ISBN 0-374-31887-5 and ISBN 9780374318871. **[Cornish]**

Zemach, Margot. *The Little Red Hen: An Old Story.* Farrar, Straus and Giroux, 1993. ISBN 0-374-44511-7 and ISBN 9780374445119. The classic nursery story reinterpreted through humorous pictures. **[English]**

Zunshine, Tatiana. *A Little Story About a Big Turnip.* Illus. by Evgeny Antonenkov. Pumpkin House, 2003. ISBN 0-9646-0100-1 and ISBN 9780964601000. **[Russian]**

TALL TALES

Andreasen, Dan. *The Giant of Seville.* Abrams, 2007. ISBN 0-8109-0988-X and ISBN 9780810909885. **[North American]**

Calhoun, Mary. *Jack and the Whoopee Wind.* Illus. by Dick Gackenbach. Morrow, 1987. ISBN 0-688-06137-0 and ISBN 9780688061371. Jack sets out to tame the wind. **[North American]**

Doucet, Sharon Arms. *Alligator Sue.* Illus. by Anne Wilsdorf. Farrar, Straus and Giroux, 2003. ISBN 0-3743-0218-9 and ISBN 9780374302184. **[North American]**

Emberley, Barbara. *The Story of Paul Bunyan.* Illus. by Ed Emberley. Simon & Schuster, 1994. ISBN 0-671-88557-X and ISBN 9780671885571. **[North American]**

Fox, Frank G. *Jean Lafitte and the Big Ol' Whale.* Illus. by Scott Cook. Farrar, Straus and Giroux, 2003. ISBN 0-3743-3669-5 and ISBN 9780374336691. **[North American]**

Glass, Andrew, adapter and illustrator. *Mountain Men: True Grit and Tall Tales.* Doubleday, 2001. ISBN 0-3853-2555-X and ISBN 9780385325554. **[North American]**

Griffin, Kitty, and Kathy Combs. *The Foot-Stomping Adventures of Clementine Sweet.* Illus. by Mike Wohnoutka. Clarion, 2004. ISBN 0-6182-4746-7 and ISBN 9780618247462. **[North American]**

Hopkinson, Deborah. *Apples to Oregon: Being the (Slightly) True Narrative of How a Brave Pioneer Father Brought Apples, Peaches, Pears, Plums, Grapes, and Cherries (and Children) Across the Plains.* Illus. by Nancy Carpenter. Atheneum, 2004. ISBN 0-6898-4769-6 and ISBN 9780689847691. **[North American]**

Hurston, Zora Neale. *Lies and Other Tall Tales.* Christopher Myers, adapter and illustrator. HarperCollins, 2005. ISBN 0-0600-0655-2 and ISBN 9780060006556. **[North American]**

Isaacs, Anne. *Pancakes for Supper!* Illus. by Mark Teague. Scholastic, 2006. ISBN 0-4396-4483-6 and ISBN 9780439644839. Isaacs retells Helen Bannerman's "Little Black Sambo," reset in the New England woods with a heroine named Toby. **[North American]**

———. *Swamp Angel.* Illus. by Paul O. Zelinsky. Dutton, 1994. ISBN 0-525-45271-0 and ISBN 9780525452713. The amazing feats of Angelica Longrider, the greatest woodswoman in Tennessee. **[North American]**

Johnson, Paul Brett. *Fearless Jack.* Illus. by Paul Brett Johnson. Margaret K. McElderry, 2001. ISBN 1-4169-6833-4 and ISBN 9781416968337. **[North American/Appalachian]**

Kellogg, Steven, reteller and illustrator. *Paul Bunyan.* Morrow, 1992. ISBN 0-688-03849-2 and ISBN 9780688038496. Kellogg's energetic storytelling in words and paintings introduces this popular folk hero. **[North American]**

———. *Pecos Bill.* Morrow, 1986. ISBN 0-688-05871-X and ISBN 9780688058715. A simplified telling of the tall tale that is part of our American heritage. **[North American]**

Kesey, Ken. *Little Tricker the Squirrel Meets Big Double the Bear.* Illus. by Barry Moser. Viking, 1990. ISBN 0-670-81136-X and ISBN 9780670811366. A wily squirrel outwits a big hungry bear in this Ozark tall tale. **[North American]**

Kimmel, Eric A. *The Great Texas Hamster Drive: An Original Tall Tale.* Illus. by Bruce Whatley. Marshall Cavendish, 2007. ISBN 0-7614-5357-1 and ISBN 9780761453574. Pecos Bill's daughter Sal starts with a couple of pet hamsters, but soon there are thousands. **[North American]**

Krensky, Stephen. *Calamity Jane.* Illus. by Lisa Carlson. Millbrook, 2007. ISBN 0-8225-6480-7 and ISBN 9780822564805. **[North American]**

———. *Paul Bunyan.* Illus. by Craig Orback. Millbrook, 2007. ISBN 1-5750-5888-X and ISBN 9781575058887. **[North American]**

———. *Pecos Bill.* Illus. by Paul Tong. Millbrook, 2007. ISBN 0-8225-6475-0 and ISBN 9780822564751. **[North American]**

———. *Shooting for the Moon: The Amazing Life and Times of Annie Oakley.* Illus. by Bernie Fuchs. Melanie Kroupa Books, 2001. ISBN 0-3743-6843-0 and ISBN 9780374368432. This picture-book biography is a good source for details about a real-life heroine. **[North American]**

Lyons, Mary E. *Roy Makes a Car.* Based on a story collected by Zora Neale Hurston. Illus. by Terry Widener. Atheneum, 2005. ISBN 0-6898-4640-1 and ISBN 9780689846403. **[North American]**

McKissack, Patricia C. *Porch Lies: Tales of Slicksters, Tricksters, and Other Wily Characters.* Illus. by André Carrilho. Schwartz & Wade, 2007. ISBN 0-3758-3619-5 and ISBN 9780375836190. **[North American]**

Mora, Pat. *Dona Flor: A Tall Tale About a Giant Woman with a Great Big Heart.* Illus. by Raul Colón. Knopf, 2005. ISBN 0-3758-2337-9 and ISBN 9780375823374. **[Hispanic]**

Nolen, Jerdine. *Big Jabe.* Illus. by Kadir Nelson. Amistad, 2003. ISBN 0-0605-4061-3 and ISBN 9780060540616. An original tale set in slavery times with art by Caldecott Honor winner Nelson. **[African American]**

———. *Thunder Rose.* Illus. by Kadir Nelson. Silver Whistle/Harcourt, 2003. ISBN 0-1521-6472-3 and ISBN 9780152164720. **[African American]**

Osborne, Mary Pope, reteller. *American Tall Tales.* Wood engravings by Michael McCurdy. Knopf, 1991. ISBN 0-679-80089-1 and ISBN 9780679800897. Nine magnificent heroes—including Johnny Appleseed; Mose, the New York fireman; and a fantastic woman, Sally Ann Thunder Ann Whirlwind—stomp across the pages of this outsized book. **[North American]**

———. *New York's Bravest.* Paintings by Steve Johnson and Lou Fancher. Knopf, 2002. ISBN 0-3758-3841-4 and ISBN 9780375838415. The legend of real-life, nineteenth-century firefighter Mose Humphrey. **[North American]**

Pinkney, Andrea Davis. *Peggony Po: A Whale of a Tale.* Illus. by Brian Pinkney. Jump at the Sun/Hyperion, 2006. ISBN 0-7868-1958-8 and ISBN 9780786819584. **[African American]**

Root, Phyllis. *Aunt Nancy and the Bothersome Visitors.* Illus. by David Parkins. Walker, 2008. ISBN 1-4063-1058-1 and ISBN 9781406310580. Four of Root's tricksy Aunt Nancy tales under one cover. **[North American]**

San Souci, Robert D. *Cut from the Same Cloth: American Women of Myth, Legend, and Tall Tale.* Illus. by Brian Pinkney. Putnam, 1993. ISBN 0-399-21987-0 and ISBN 9780399219870. All 15 female heroes in this collection are wily and bold, including Sal Fink, Sweet Betsey from Pike, Hiiaka (from Hawaii), and the others whose names are not well known. The introductory comments for each tale establish the geographical and literary contexts, and the 11 pages of folklore sources and bibliography at the end of the book are valuable for scholars. **[North American]**

Shepard, Aaron. *Master Man: A Tall Tale of Nigeria.* Illus. by David Wisniewski. Lothrop, Lee & Shepard, 2000. ISBN 0-6881-3783-0 and ISBN 9780688137830. **[Nigerian]**

Thomassie, Tynie. *Feliciana Feydra Le Roux: A Cajun Tall Tale.* Illus. by Cat Bowman Smith. Little, Brown, 1995. ISBN 0-316-84125-0 and ISBN 9780316841252. When Grampa won't let her go alligator hunting with "all the men-children" in the family, Feliciana sneaks out to follow them and finds herself face-to-face with an alligator! This riotous tale about a spunky little girl is sure to please the picture-book crowd. **[North American]**

Walker, Robert Paul. *Big Men, Big Country: A Collection of American Tall Tales.* Illus. by James Bernardin. Sandpiper, 2000. ISBN 0-1520-2625-8 and ISBN 9780152026257. Featuring familiar and unfamiliar tall tale heroes such as John Henry, Paul Bunyan, Ol' Gabe of Yellowstone, John Darling of the Catskills, and others. **[North American]**

Wallace, Ian. *The True Story of Trapper Jack's Left Big Toe.* Roaring Brook, 2002. ISBN 0-7613-1493-8 and ISBN 9780761314936. **[North American]**

Wheeler, Lisa. *Avalanche Annie: A Not-So-Tall Tale.* Illus. by Kurt Cyrus. Harcourt, 2003. ISBN 0-7567-8536-7 and ISBN 9780756785369. **[North American]**

Willey, Margaret. *Clever Beatrice: An Upper Peninsula Conte.* Illus. by Heather Solomon. Atheneum, 2001. ISBN 0-6898-7068-X and ISBN 9780689870682. **[North American]**

Wooldridge, Connie Nordheim. *The Legend of Strap Buckner: A Texas Tale.* Illus. by Andrew Glass. Holiday House, 2001. ISBN 0-8234-1536-8 and ISBN 9780823415366. **[North American]**

Wright, Catherine. *Steamboat Annie and the Thousand-Pound Catfish.* Illus. by Howard Fine. Philomel Books, 2001. ISBN 0-3992-3331-8 and ISBN 9780399233319. **[North American]**

FABLES

Aesop. *Aesop and Company: With Scenes from His Legendary Life*. Barbara Bader, ed. Etchings by Arthur Geisert. Houghton Mifflin, 1991. ISBN 0-395-50597-6 and ISBN 9780395505977. This handsome edition of 19 favorite Aesop fables includes a scholarly introduction and facts and legends about Aesop's life. **[Greek]**

———. *Aesop's Fables*. Retold and illus. by Jerry Pinkney. SeaStar Books, 2000. ISBN 1-58717-000-0 and ISBN 9781587170003. **[Greek]**

———. *Aesop's Fables*. Retold and illus. by Brad Sneed. Dial, 2003. ISBN 0-8037-2751-8 and ISBN 9780803727519. **[Greek]**

———. *The Best of Aesop's Fables*. Retold by Margaret Clark. Illus. by Charlotte Voake. Little, Brown, 1990. ISBN 0-316-14499-1 and ISBN 9780316144995. These 27 fables, with their morals left unsaid and their lively illustrations, will appeal to younger children. **[Greek]**

———. *The Boy Who Cried Wolf*. Retold by B. G. Hennessy. Illus. by Boris Kulikov. Simon & Schuster, 2006. ISBN 0-6898-7433-2 and ISBN 9780689874338. Text and images overflow with humor in this clever retelling. **[Greek]**

———. *The McElderry Book of Aesop's Fables*. Michael Morpurgo, adapter. Illus. by Emma Chichester Clark. McElderry, 2005. ISBN 1-1469-0290-2 and ISBN 9781416902904. **[Greek]**

Bierhorst, John, adapter. *Doctor Coyote: A Native American Aesop's Fables*. Illus. by Wendy Watson. Simon & Schuster, 1987. ISBN 0-02-709780-3 and ISBN 9780027097801. **[Native American]**

Bynum, Eboni, and Roland Jackson. *Jamari's Drum*. Pictures on glazed tiles by Baba Wagué Diakité. Groundwood, 2004. ISBN 0-8889-9531-8 and ISBN 9780888995315. **[African]**

Chaucer, Geoffrey. *Chanticleer and the Fox*. Adapted and illus. by Barbara Cooney. Harper, 1982. ISBN 0-690-18561-8 and ISBN 9780690185614. The story of the proud cock and the wily fox. Adapted from "Nun's Priest's Tale" in *The Canterbury Tales*. **[English]**

Fontaine, Jean de la. *Fables*. Translated by Sir Edward Marsh. Illus. by R. de le Nézière. Everyman's Library, 2001. ISBN 0-3754-1334-0 and ISBN 9780375413346. **[French]**

———. *The Hare and the Tortoise and Other Fables of La Fontaine*. Translated by Ranjit Bolt. Illus. by Giselle Potter. Barefoot Books, 2006. ISBN 1-9052-3654-9 and ISBN 9781905236541. **[French]**

Heins, Ethel, reteller. *The Cat and the Cook: And Other Fables of Krylov*. Illus. by Anita Lobel. Greenwillow, 1995. ISBN 0-688-12310-4 and ISBN 9780688123109. Twelve droll fables from the Russian writer (1768–1844) with notes on the fabulist and sources for this collection. **[Russian]**

Lobel, Arnold. *Fables*. Harper, 1980. ISBN 0-06-023973-5 and ISBN 9780060239732. **[American]**

Young, Ed. *Seven Blind Mice*. Philomel, 1992. ISBN 0-399-22261-8 and ISBN 9780399222610. When seven blind mice meet a "strange Something," six come to the wrong conclusion about what he has found, based on partial information. Only the seventh mouse, who examines the whole creature, knows it is an elephant. This fable from India appeals to a wide age range, and Young's vibrant cut-paper artwork invites further exploration. **[Indian]**

Heroes and Heroines, Myths and Legends

Baldwin, James. *Nordic Hero Tales from the Kalevala*. Illus. by N. C. Wyeth. Dover, 2006. ISBN 0-4864-4748-0 and ISBN 9780486447483. **[Scandinavian]**

Belting, Natalie M. *Moon Was Tired of Walking on Air*. Illus. by Will Hillenbrand. Houghton Mifflin, 1992. ISBN 0-395-53806-8 and ISBN 9780395538067. Fourteen strikingly different myths from ten South American tribes. **[South American]**

Bierhorst, John. *The Hungry Woman: Myths and Legends of the Aztecs*. Morrow, 1993. ISBN 0-688-12301-5 and ISBN 9780688123017. A scholarly introduction provides background for the storyteller. **[Mexican]**

Blackwood, Gary L. *Legends or Lies?* Unsolved History Series. Marshall Cavendish Benchmark, 2006. ISBN 0-7614-1891-1 and ISBN 9780761418917. Includes the legends of Atlantis, the Amazons, El Dorado, King Arthur, and others. **[World]**

Brown, Marcia. *Dick Whittington and His Cat*. Atheneum, 1988. ISBN 0-684-18998-4 and ISBN 9780684189987. This Caldecott Honor Book relates the legend of Richard Whittington, Lord Mayor of London, and how his cat brought him fame and fortune. **[British]**

Bruchac, Joseph, reteller. *The First Strawberries: A Cherokee Story*. Illus. by Anna Vojtech. Dial, 1993. ISBN 0-8037-1331-2 and ISBN 9780803713314. When first man and first woman quarrel, the sun creates the sweet strawberry to bring the couple together again. **[Native American]**

Buff, Mary, and Conrad Buff. *The Apple and the Arrow*. Houghton, 2001. Reissue (1951) ISBN 0-618-12807-7 and ISBN 9780618128075. "The legend of William Tell as seen through the eyes of his son." **[Swiss]**

Cohen, Caren Lee. *The Mud Pony*. Illus. by Shonto Begay. Scholastic, 1988. ISBN 0-590-41525-5 and ISBN 9780590415255. Perfection Learning, 1992. ISBN 0-81247805-3 and ISBN 9780812478051. In this hero story from the Pawnee Indians, a poor boy shapes a pony out of clay and cares for it as if it were real. In times of trouble the pony comes alive and helps the boy achieve greatness. **[Native American]**

Colum, Padraic. *The Children of Odin*. Illus. by Willy Pogeny. IndyPublish, 2008. ISBN 1-4378-3630-5 and ISBN 9781437836301. **[Scandinavian]**

———. *The Children's Homer: The Adventures of Odysseus and the Tale of Troy*. Illus. by Willy Pogeny. Simon Pulse, 1982. ISBN 0-0204-2520-1 and ISBN 9780020425205. **[Greek]**

Courlander, Harold. *The Crest and the Hide: And Other African Stories of Heroes, Chiefs, Bards, Hunters, Sorcerers and Common People*. Coward, 1982. ISBN 0-698-20536-7 and ISBN 9780698205369. Twenty legends collected by the noted folklorist. With notes and sources. **[African]**

Daly, Ita, adapter. *Irish Myths and Legends*. Illus. by Bee Willey. Oxford University Press, 2001. ISBN 0-1927-5454-8 and ISBN 9780192754547. **[Irish]**

d'Aulaire, Ingri, and Edgar d'Aulaire. *Book of Greek Myths*. Doubleday, 1980. Paperback ed. Delacorte, 1992. ISBN 0-440-40694-3 and ISBN 9780440406945. Contains most of the famous gods, goddesses, mortals, and animals that children find fascinating. **[Greek]**

———. *D'Aulaire's Book of Norse Myths*. Preface by Michael Chabon. The New York Review Children's Collection, 2005. ISBN 1-59017-125-X and ISBN 9781590171257. *Norse Gods and Giants* (Doubleday, 1986) has been retitled in this handsome new edition. Faithful to the Edda. **[Scandinavian]**

dePaola, Tomie. *The Legend of the Bluebonnet: An Old Tale of Texas*. Putnam, 1983. ISBN 0-399-20937-9 and ISBN 9780399209376; Penguin, 1996. (paperback edition) ISBN

0-698-11359-4 and ISBN 9780698113596. How the bluebonnet, the state flower of Texas, came to be. Based on a Comanche Indian legend. Also in *Tomie dePaola's Big Book of Favorite Legends*. Putnam, 2007. ISBN 0-399-25035-2 and ISBN 9780399250354. **[Native American]**

―――. *The Legend of the Poinsettia*. Putnam, 1994. ISBN 0-399-21692-8 and ISBN 9780399216923. Lucinda, a child who has nothing else to offer, brings an armful of weeds to church for her Christmas gift. Miraculously, the weeds blossom into the flaming red stars of the poinsettia. Also in *Tomie dePaola's Big Book of Favorite Legends*. Putnam, 2007. ISBN 0-399-25035-2 and ISBN 9780399250354. **[Mexican]**

Gibfried, Diane. *Brother Juniper*. Illus. by Meilo So. Clarion, 2006. ISBN 0-6185-4361-9 and ISBN 9780618543618. **[Religious]**

Goble, Paul. *Her Seven Brothers*. Simon & Schuster, 1988. ISBN 0-02-737960-4 and ISBN 9780027379600. How the Big Dipper was created. A Cheyenne legend. **[Native American]**

―――. *Love Flute*. Bradbury, 1992. ISBN 0-02-736261-2 and ISBN 9780027362619. Among the Plains Indians, it was the custom for a young man to court the girl he wished to marry with a love flute. This is the story of the very first love flute, given to a shy young man by the birds and animals. **[Native American]**

Graham, Pita, adapter. *Maori Legends of the Land: Maori Tales and Traditions*. Engravings by W. L. Dittmer; photographs by Gordon Ell. Bush Press of New Zealand, 2002. ISBN 0-9086-0887-X and ISBN 9780908608874. **[New Zealand]**

Greene, Ellin. *The Legend of the Cranberry: A Paleo-Indian Tale*. Illus. by Brad Sneed. Simon & Schuster, 1993. ISBN 0-671-75975-2 and ISBN 9780671759759. This bittersweet Lenape tale explains the demise of the mastodon and the origin of the cranberry. **[Native American]**

Hamilton, Virginia. *In the Beginning: Creation Stories from Around the World*. Illus. by Barry Moser. Harcourt, 1988. ISBN 0-15-238740-4 and ISBN 9780152387402. Hamilton's comments after each of these 25 myths reveal curious similarities from culture to culture. **[World]**

Hastings, Selina, reteller. *Sir Gawain and the Loathly Lady*. Illus. by Juan Wijngaard. Lothrop, 1985. ISBN 0-688-05823-X and ISBN 9780688058234. "What is it that women most desire?" is the question that stumps King Arthur and his knights. A hideous lady has the correct answer but the price seems almost unbearably high. **[British]**

Hazeltine, Alice. *Hero Tales from Many Lands*. Abingdon, 1961. ISBN 0-687-16943-7 and ISBN 9780687169436. **[World]**

Heaney, Marie. *The Names upon the Harp: Irish Myth and Legend*. Illus. by Patrick J. Lynch. Arthur A. Levine, 2000. ISBN 0-5906-8052-8 and ISBN 9780590680523. **[Irish]**

Hodges, Margaret. *Saint George and the Dragon*. Illus. by Trina Schart Hyman. Little, Brown, 1990. ISBN 0-316-36795-8 and ISBN 9780316367950. **[British]**

Jaffrey, Madhur. *Seasons of Splendour: Tales, Myths, and Legends of India*. Illus. by Michael Foreman. Puffin, 1992. ISBN 0-14-034699-6 and ISBN 9780140346992. **[Indian]**

Kanawa, Kiri Te. *Land of the Long White Cloud: Maori Myths, Tales and Legends*. Illus. by Michael Foreman. Arcade, 1990. ISBN 1-55970-046-7 and ISBN 9781559700467. These authentic tales, based on the author's childhood memories, need the storyteller's voice to make them come alive. **[New Zealand]**

Keyser, Samuel Jay. *The Pond God and Other Stories*. Drawings by Robert Shetterly. Front Street, 2003. ISBN 1-8869-1096-0 and ISBN 9781886910966. **[Original]**

Krasno, Rena, and Yeng-Fong Chiang. *Cloud Weavers: Ancient Chinese Legends.* Illustrations from the collection of Yeng-Fong Chiang. Pacific View Press, 2003. ISBN 1-8818-9626-9 and ISBN 9781881896265. **[Chinese]**

Lester, Julius. *John Henry.* Illus. by Jerry Pinkney. Dial, 1994. ISBN 0-8037-1606-0 and ISBN 9780803716063. Lester adds contemporary details and poetic similes in this wonderful retelling of the original legend. **[African American]**

Lewis, J. Patrick. *Blackbeard the Pirate King: Several Yarns Detailing the Legends, Myths, and Real-Life Adventures of History's Most Notorious Seaman.* Told in verse. National Geographic Society, 2006. ISBN 0-7822-5585-2 and ISBN 9780792255857. **[English]**

Low, Alice. *The Macmillan Book of Greek Gods and Heroes.* Illus. by Arvin Stewart. Macmillan, 1994. ISBN 0-689-71874-8 and ISBN 9780689718748. A fine interweaving of stories and characters. **[Greek]**

Lunge-Larsen, Lise. *The Adventures of Thor the Thunder God.* Illus. by Jim Madsen. Houghton Mifflin, 2007. ISBN 0-6184-7301-7 and ISBN 9780618473014. **[Norwegian]**

———. *The Race of the Birkebeiners.* Illus. by Mary Azarian. Houghton Mifflin, 2001. ISBN 0-618-10313-9 and ISBN 9780618103133. A baby prince is saved from assassins in this true story. **[Norwegian]**

McBratney, Sam. *One Voice, Please.* Illus. by Russell Ayto. Candlewick, 2008. ISBN 0-7636-3479-4 and ISBN 9780763634797. **[World]**

McCaughrean, Geraldine. *Odysseus.* Cricket, 2004. ISBN 0-8126-2721-0 and ISBN 9780812627213. **[Greek]**

———. *Perseus.* Cricket, 2005. ISBN 0-8126-2735-0 and ISBN 9780812627350. **[Greek]**

———. *Roman Myths.* Illus. by Emma Chichester Clark. McElderry, 2001. ISBN 0-689-83822-0 and ISBN 9780689838224. **[Roman]**

———. *Theseus.* Cricket, 2005. ISBN 0-8126-2739-3 and ISBN 9780812627398. **[Greek]**

McCaughrean, Geraldine, reteller. *Greek Myths.* Illus. by Emma Chichester Clark. Simon & Schuster, 1993. ISBN 0-689-50583-3 and ISBN 9780689505836. Sixteen epic stories, retold in a contemporary style suitable for telling or reading aloud. **[Greek]**

Mandela, Nelson. *Nelson Mandela's Favorite African Folktales.* Norton, 2002. ISBN 0-393-05212-5 and ISBN 9780393052121. These 32 folktales, myths, and legends from various countries or regions in Africa (a map shows their location) were written and illustrated by others, but chosen by Mandela in the hope that "the voice of the storyteller will never die in Africa, that all the children in the world may experience the wonder of books and that they will never lose the capacity to enlarge their earthly dwelling place with the magic of stories." **[African]**

Matthews, John. *The Barefoot Book of Knights.* Illus. by Giovanni Mann. Barefoot, 2002. ISBN 1-8414-8064-9 and ISBN 9781841480640. **[World]**

Matthews, John, and Caitlin Matthews. *Trick of the Tale: A Collection of Trickster Tales.* Illus. by Tomislav Tomiâc. Candlewick, 2008. ISBN 0-7636-3646-0 and ISBN 9780763636463. **[World]**

Mayer, Marianna. *Women Warriors: Myths and Legends of Heroic Women.* Illus. by Julek Heller. Morrow Junior, 2000. ISBN 0-6881-5522-7 and ISBN 9780688155223. **[World]**

Moses, Will. *Johnny Appleseed: The Story of a Legend.* Philomel, 2001. ISBN 0-399231-53-6 and ISBN 9780399231537. **[North America]**

Oliver, Narelle, adapter and illustrator. *Mermaids Most Amazing.* Putnam, 2005. ISBN 0-3992-4288-0 and ISBN 9780399242885. **[World]**

Osborne, Mary Pope, reteller. *Favorite Greek Myths.* Illus. by Troy Howell. Scholastic, 1989. ISBN 0-590-41338-4 and ISBN 9780590413381. Twelve myths, their straightforward events enhanced by imaginative details, are followed by a list clarifying the roles of the deities and mortals, as well as useful word origins. **[Greek]**

Oughton, Jerrie. *How the Stars Fell into the Sky: A Navajo Legend.* Illus. by Lisa Desmini. Houghton Mifflin, 1992. ISBN 0-395-58798-0 and ISBN 9780395587980. First Woman wanted to write the laws in the sky with her jewels so that all the people could read them. She accepted Coyote's offer to help, but Coyote was so impatient he tossed the jewels (stars) into the sky, shattering First Woman's careful patterns. That is why there is confusion in the world today. **[Native American]**

Picard, Barbara Leonie, reteller. *French Legends, Tales and Fairy Stories.* Illus. by Joan Kiddell-Monroe. Oxford University Press, 1992. ISBN 0-19-274149-7 and ISBN 9780192741493. This fine collection of stories for older children includes four hero tales, six courtly tales of the Middle Ages, and 13 folktales or legends. **[French]**

————. *The Iliad of Homer.* Illus. by Joan Kiddell-Monroe. Oxford University Press, 1991. ISBN 0-19-274147-0 and ISBN 9780192741479. **[Greek]**

————. *The Odyssey of Homer.* Illus. by Joan Kiddell-Monroe. Oxford University Press, 1991. ISBN 0-19-274146-2 and ISBN 9780192741462. Distinguished retellings of these companion stories. **[Greek]**

————. *Tales of the Norse Gods.* Retold by Barbara Leonie Picard. Illus. by Rosamund Fowler. Oxford University Press, 2001. ISBN 0-1927-5116-6 and ISBN 9780192751164. **[Scandinavian]**

Pyle, Howard. *The Merry Adventures of Robin Hood of Great Renown in Nottinghamshire.* Dover, 1968. ISBN 0-486-22043-5 and ISBN 9780486220437. **[English]**

————. *The Story of King Arthur and His Knights.* Dover, 1965. ISBN 0-486-21445-1 and ISBN 9780486214450. **[British]**

Robinson, Gail. *Raven the Trickster: Legends of the North American Indians.* Illus. by Joanna Troughton. Atheneum, 1982. ISBN 0-6895-0247-8 and ISBN 9780689502477. Nine unusual and tellable tales about the mischievous "animal-god" of the early people of the northwest coast of the Pacific Ocean. **[Native American]**

Roza, Greg. *Incan Mythology and Other Myths of the Andes.* Rosen, 2008. ISBN 1-4042-0739-2 and ISBN 9781404207394. **[Incan]**

Sanderson, Ruth. *More Saints: Lives & Illuminations.* Eerdmans Books for Young Readers, 2007. ISBN 0-8028-5272-6 and ISBN 9780802852724. **[Religious]**

————. *Saints: Lives & Illuminations.* Eerdmans Books for Young Readers, 2003. ISBN 0-8028-5220-3 and ISBN 9780802852205. **[Religious]**

Schwartz, Howard. *Next Year in Jerusalem: 3,000 Years of Jewish Stories.* Illus. by Neil Waldman. Viking 1996. ISBN 0-670-86110-3 and ISBN 9780670861101. This outstanding anthology includes rabbinic and Hassidic legends, folktales, fairy tales, and even a vampire story. Schwartz gives sources of the 11 stories, historical facts, and background. **[Jewish]**

Sierra, Judy. *The Gruesome Guide to World Monsters.* Illus. by Henrik Drescher. Candlewick, 2005. ISBN 0-7636-1727-X and ISBN 9780763617271. Sierra's wonderful descriptions of monsters from myth and folklore will add spice to any myth-telling. **[World]**

Simpson, Margaret. *Arthurian Legends.* Illus. by Michael Tickner. Scholastic Canada, 2006. ISBN 0-4399-6358-3 and ISBN 9780439963589. Arthurian legends told with tongue in cheek and twist in text. **[British]**

Souhami, Jessica. *Mrs. McCool and the Giant Cuhullin: An Irish Tale.* Henry Holt, 2002. ISBN 0-8050-6852-X and ISBN 9780805068528. **[Irish]**

Spires, Elizabeth. *I Am Arachne: Fifteen Greek and Roman Myths.* Illus. by Mordicai Gerstein. Square Fish, 2009. ISBN 0-3125-6125-3 and ISBN 9780312561253. **[Greek/Roman]**

Synge, Ursula. *The Giant at the Ford and Other Legends of the Saints.* Macmillan, 1980. ISBN 0-689-50168-4 and ISBN 9780689501685. **[Religious]**

———. *Land of Heroes: Retelling of the Kalevala.* Macmillan, 1978. ISBN 0-68950094-7 and ISBN 9780689500947. **[Finnish]**

Turner, Pamela S. *Hachiko: The True Story of a Loyal Dog.* Illus. by Yan Nascimbene. Sandpiper, 2009. ISBN 0-5472-2755-3 and ISBN 9780547237558. **[Japanese]**

Van Laan, Nancy. *Buffalo Dance: A Blackfoot Legend.* Illus. by Beatriz Vidal. Little, Brown, 1994. ISBN 0-316-89728-0 and ISBN 9780316897280. The origin of the Buffalo Dance based on one of the earliest recorded versions of this myth. **[Native American]**

Waldherr, Kris. *Sacred Animals.* HarperCollins, 2001. ISBN 0-6881-6379-3 and ISBN 9780688163792. Fascinating facts and glittering art make this a good beginning for myth research. **[Religious]**

Yolen, Jane. *Sherwood: Original Stories from the World of Robin Hood.* Illus. by Dennis Nolan. Philomel, 2000. ISBN 0-6981-1953-3 and ISBN 9780698119536. **[English]**

Young, Ella. *The Tangle-Coated Horse.* Dufour, 1999. ISBN 0-86315517-0 and ISBN 9780863155178. **[Celtic/Irish]**

Zarin, Cynthia. *Saints Among the Animals.* Illus. by Leonid Gore. Atheneum, 2005. ISBN 0-6898-5031-X and ISBN 9780689850318. **[Religious]**

LITERARY TALES: COLLECTIONS

Andersen, Hans Christian. *Favorite Tales of Hans Andersen.* Translated by M. R. James. Checkerboard, 1988. ISBN 1-56288-253-8 and ISBN 9781562882532.

———. *Hans Christian Andersen: The Complete Fairy Tales and Stories.* Translated from the Danish by Erik Christian Haugaard, with a Foreword by Virginia Haviland. Doubleday, 1974. ISBN 0-385-01901-7 and ISBN 9780385019019.

———. *Hans Christian Andersen's Fairy Tales.* Translated by Anthea Bell. Illus. by Lisbeth Zwerger. North-South Books, 2001. ISBN 0-7358-1394-9 and ISBN 9780735813946. (Originally published in 1991.)

———. *Seven Tales by H. C. Andersen.* Translated by Eva Le Gallienne. Illus. by Maurice Sendak. HarperCollins, 1959. ISBN 0-06-023790-2 and ISBN 9780060237905.

———. *Tales of Hans Christian Andersen.* Illus. by Joel Stewart. Translated by Naomi Lewis. Candlewick, 2004. ISBN 0-7636-2515-9 and ISBN 9780763625153.

———. *Twelve Tales.* Selected, translated, and illus. by Erik Blegvad. Simon & Schuster, 1994. ISBN 0-689-50584-1 and ISBN 9780689505843.

Babbitt, Natalie. *The Devil's Storybook.* Farrar, Straus and Giroux, 1974. ISBN 0-374-31770-4 and ISBN 9780374317706.

———. *The Devil's Other Storybook.* Farrar, Straus and Giroux, 1987. ISBN 0-3743-1767-4 and ISBN 9780374317676.

Banks, Lynne Reid. *The Magic Hare.* Illus. by Barry Moser. Morrow, 1993. ISBN 0-688-10896-2 and ISBN 9780688108960. Ten unusual stories about a winsome hare.

Bianco, Margery Williams. *A Street of Little Shops*. Gregg Press children's literature series, 1981. Introduction by Augusta Baker. Seven delightful original stories set in a little country village in the 1920s. ISBN 0-8398-2725-3 and ISBN 9780839827252.

Carus, Marianne, ed. *Fire and Wings: Dragon Tales from East and West*. Illus. by Nilesh Mistry, with an introduction by Jane Yolen. Cricket Books, 2002. ISBN 0-8126-2664-8 and ISBN 9780812626643.

Chaucer, Geoffrey. *Canterbury Tales*. Adapted, selected, and translated from Middle English by Barbara Cohen. Illus. by Trina Schart Hyman. Lothrop, 1988. ISBN 0-688-06201-6 and ISBN 9780688062019. Four well-chosen tales offer a good introduction to Chaucer: "The Nun's Priest's Tale," "The Pardoner's Tale," "The Wife of Bath's Tale," and "The Franklin's Tale."

cummings, e. e. *Fairy Tales*. Illus. by Meilo So. Afterword by George James Firmage. Liveright Publishing Corporation, 2004. ISBN 0-87140-658-6 and ISBN 9780871406583. Includes "The Old Man Who Said 'Why'," "The Elephant and the Butterfly," "The House That Ate Mosquito Pie," and "The Little Girl Named I."

Dann, Jack, and Gardner Dozois, eds. *Dark Alchemy: Magical Tales from Masters of Modern Fantasy*. Bloomsbury, 2007. ISBN 0-7475-9056-7 and ISBN 9780747590569.

Datlow, Ellen, and Terri Windling. *Black Heart, Ivory Bones*. Avon, 2000. ISBN 0-7394-0892-5 and ISBN 9780739408926.

———. *The Coyote Road: Trickster Tales*. Decorations by Charles Vess. Puffin, 2009. ISBN 0-1424-1300-3 and ISBN 9780142413005.

———. *Swan Sister: Fairy Tales Retold*. Aladdin, 2005. ISBN 0-6898-7837-0 and ISBN 9780689878374.

de la Mare, Walter. *Tales Told Again*. Faber, 1980. ISBN 0-571-18013-2 and ISBN 9780571180134. Nineteen classic fairy tales retold by a literary genius.

Del Negro, Janice M. *Passion and Poison: Tales of Shape-Shifters, Ghosts, and Spirited Women*. Marshall Cavendish, 2007. ISBN 0-7614-5361-X and ISBN 9780761453611.

Farjeon, Eleanor. *The Little Bookroom: Eleanor Farjeon's Short Stories for Children Chosen by Herself*. Illus. by Edward Ardizzone. Afterword by Rumer Godden. New York Review Children's Collection, 2003. ISBN 1-5901-7048-2 and ISBN 9781590170489.

Hawes, Louise. *Black Pearls: A Faerie Strand*. Illus. by Rebecca Guay. Houghton Mifflin, 2008. ISBN 0-6187-4797-4 and ISBN 9780618747979.

Hearne, Betsy. *Hauntings, and Other Tales of Danger, Love, and Sometimes Loss*. Greenwillow, 2007. ISBN 0-0612-3910-0 and ISBN 9780061239106.

Housman, Laurence. *The Rat-Catcher's Daughter: A Collection of Stories by Laurence Housman*. Selected and with an Afterword by Ellin Greene. Atheneum, 1974. ISBN 0-689-30420-X and ISBN 9780689304200.

Hughes, Richard. *The Wonder Dog: The Collected Children's Stories of Richard Hughes*. Morrow, 1977. ISBN 0-6888-4099-X and ISBN 9780688840990.

Jones, Diana Wynne. *Spellbound: Fantasy Stories*. Kingfisher, 2007. ISBN 0-7534-6144-7 and ISBN 9780753461440.

Kennedy, Richard. *Richard Kennedy: Collected Stories*. Illus. by Marcia Sewall. HarperCollins, 1987. ISBN 0-06-023255-2 and ISBN 9780060232559. Sixteen stories for older children, originally published separately as picture books.

Kipling, Rudyard. *Just So Stories*. Illus. by David Frampton. HarperCollins, 1991. ISBN 0-06-023294-3 and ISBN 9780060232948. A handsome edition with richly colored woodcuts in harmony with the tales.

———. *Just So Stories*. Illus. by Safaya Salter. Holt, 1987. ISBN 0-8050-0439-4 and ISBN 9780805004397.

Lubar, David. *Invasion of the Road Weenies: and Other Warped and Creepy Tales*. Starscape, 2005. ISBN 0-7653-5325-3 and ISBN 9780765353252.

Maguire, Gregory. *Leaping Beauty: and Other Animal Fairy Tales*. Illus. by Chris L. Demarest. HarperCollins, 2004. ISBN 0-0605-6419-9 and ISBN 9780060564193.

Noyes, Deborah, ed. *Gothic! Ten Original Dark Tales*. Candlewick, 2004. ISBN 1-4063-0967-2 and ISBN 9781406309676.

———. *The Restless Dead: Ten Original Stories of the Supernatural*. Candlewick Press, 2007. ISBN 0-7636-2906-5 and ISBN 9780763629069.

Owen, James A. *Here, There Be Dragons*. Simon & Schuster, 2006. ISBN 1-4169-1228-2 and ISBN 9781416912286.

Peretz, I. L. *The Seven Good Years and Other Stories of I. L. Peretz*. Translated and adapted by Esther Hautzig. Jewish Publication Society of America, 1984. Reissue 2004. (paperback) ISBN 0-82760771-7 and ISBN 9780827607712.

Perrault, Charles. *The Complete Tales of Charles Perrault*. Translated by Neil Philip and Nicolette Simborowski. Illus. by Sally Holmes. Clarion, 1993. ISBN 0-395-57002-6 and ISBN 9780395570029. A new translation of all 11 of Perrault's tales, with an introduction and Afterword by Neil Philip.

Pyle, Howard. *The Wonder Clock*. Dover, 1887, 1915. Paperback ed. Starscape, 2003. ISBN 0-7653-4266-9 and ISBN 9780765342669. Twenty-four original stories in the tradition of folktales.

Sandburg, Carl. *More Rootabagas*. Collected and with a Foreword by George Hendrick. Illus. by Paul O. Zelinsky. Knopf, 1993. ISBN 0-679-80070-0 and ISBN 9780679800705. A Sandburg scholar has collected ten of the "many dozens" of unpublished "Rootabaga stories."

———. *Rootabaga Stories*. Harcourt, 1951, 1988. ISBN 0-15-269061-1 and ISBN 9780152690618.

Singer, Isaac B. *Stories for Children*. Farrar, Straus and Giroux, 1984. ISBN 0-374-37266-7 and ISBN 9780374372668. Thirty-six tales chosen from former collections.

———. *Zlateh the Goat and Other Stories*. Illus. by Maurice Sendak. Harper, 1966, 1984. ISBN 0-06-025698-2 and ISBN 9780060256982.

Springer, Nancy, ed. *Ribbiting Tales: Original Stories About Frogs*. Illus. by Tony DiTerlizzi. Philomel, 2000. ISBN 0-6981-1952-5 and ISBN 9780698119529.

Tolstoy, Leo. *Classic Tales and Fables for Children*. Edited with an introduction by Bob Blaisdell. Prometheus, 2002. ISBN 1-5739-2939-5 and ISBN 9781573929394.

Vande Velde, Vivian. *All Hallows' Eve: 13 Stories*. Harcourt, 2006. ISBN 0-1520-5576-2 and ISBN 9780152055769.

———. *The Rumpelstiltskin Problem*. Houghton Mifflin, 2000. ISBN 0-6180-5523-1 and ISBN 9780618055234.

Weiss, M. Jerry, and Helen S. Weiss, eds. *Dreams and Visions: Fourteen Flights of Fantasy*. Starscape, 2007. ISBN 0-7653-5107-2 and ISBN 9780765351074.

Wilde, Oscar. *The Fairy Tales of Oscar Wilde*. Illus. by Isabelle Brent. Introduction by Neil Philip. Viking, 1994. ISBN 0-670-85585-5 and ISBN 9780670855858. This edition, distinguished by its beautiful Persian-style artwork, includes all nine of Wilde's fairy tales for children.

————. *The Happy Prince and Other Stories*. Illus. by Charles Robinson. Morrow, 1991. ISBN 0-688-10390-1 and ISBN 9780688103903. Part of the Books of Wonder series. Includes five stories: "The Happy Prince," "The Nightingale and the Rose," "The Selfish Giant," "The Devoted Friend," and "The Remarkable Rocket," with Robinson's famous illustrations.

Yolen, Jane. *The Girl Who Cried Flowers and Other Tales*. Crowell, 1974. ISBN 0-6900-0217-3 and ISBN 9780690002171.

Yolen, Jane, and Patrick Nielsen Hayden, eds. *The Year's Best Science Fiction and Fantasy for Teens: First Annual Collection*. Tor, 2005. ISBN 0-7653-1384-7 and ISBN 9780765313843.

Zipes, Jack, ed. *The Outspoken Princess and the Gentle Knight: A Treasury of Modern Fairy Tales*. Illus. by Stephane Poulin. Bantam, 1994. ISBN 0-553-09699-0 and ISBN 9780553096996. An anthology of stories by 15 modern writers, including Ernest Hemingway, Richard Kennedy, Jack Sendak, Catherine Storr, and Jane Yolen.

LITERARY TALES: PICTURE BOOKS

Alexander, Lloyd. *The Fortune-Tellers*. Illus. by Trina Schart Hyman. Dutton, 1992. ISBN 0-525-44849-7 and ISBN 9780525448495. An unhappy carpenter who consults a fortune-teller, and hears only what he wants to hear, achieves wealth and fame when he is mistaken for a fortune-teller himself.

————. *The House Gobbaleen*. Illus. by Diane Goode. Dutton, 1995. ISBN 0-525-45289-3 and ISBN 9780525452898. Gladsake, a wise and cunning cat, teaches his master how to make his own luck instead of relying on "the Friendly Folk." An amusing story made even funnier by the droll illustrations.

Andersen, Hans Christian. *The Emperor's New Clothes*. Retold and illus. by John A. Rowe. Penguin/Minedition, 2004. ISBN 0-698-40000-3 and ISBN 9780698400009.

————. *The Fir Tree*. Illus. by Bernadette Watts. North-South, 1990. ISBN 1-55858-093-X and ISBN 9781558580930.

————. *The Nightingale*. Translated by Anthea Bell. Illus. by Lisbeth Zwerger. Simon & Schuster, 1991. ISBN 0-907234-57-7 and ISBN 9780907234579.

————. *The Nightingale*. Translated by Eva Le Gallienne. Illus. by Nancy Burkert. Harper, 1965. ISBN 0-06-443070-7 and ISBN 9780064430708.

————. *The Princess and the Pea*. Retold by John Cech. Illus. by Bernhard Oberdieck. Sterling, 2007. ISBN 1-40273065-9 and ISBN 9781402730658.

————. *The Princess and the Pea*. Retold by Lauren Child. Illus. by Polly Borland. (fractured version) Hyperion, 2006. ISBN 0-7868-3886-8 and ISBN 9780786838868.

————. *The Snow Queen*. Retold by Naomi Lewis. Illus. by Christian Birmingham. Candlewick, 2008. ISBN 0-7636-3229-5 and ISBN 9780763632298.

————. *The Steadfast Tin Soldier*. Translated by Naomi Lewis. Illus. by P. J. Lynch. Harcourt, 1992. ISBN 0-15-200599-4 and ISBN 9780152005993.

————. *The Swineherd*. Translated by Anthea Bell. Illus. by Lizbeth Zwerger. North-South, 1995. ISBN 1-55858-428-5 and ISBN 9781558584280.

———. *Thumbelina.* Retold and illus. by Lauren Mills. Little, Brown, 2005. ISBN 0-316-57359-0 and ISBN 9780316573597.

———. *The Tinderbox.* Illus. by Warwick Hutton. Simon & Schuster, 1988. ISBN 0-689-50458-6 and ISBN 9780689504587.

———. *The Ugly Duckling.* Retold by Stephen Mitchell. Illus. by Steve Johnson and Lou Fancher. Candlewick, 2008. ISBN 0-7636-2159-5 and ISBN 9780763621599.

———. *The Ugly Duckling.* Retold and illus. by Jerry Pinkney. HarperCollins, 1999. ISBN 0-688-15932-X and ISBN 9780688159320.

———. *The Wild Swans.* Retold by Amy Ehrlich. Illus. by Susan Jeffers. Dial, 1987. ISBN 0-8037-9381-2 and ISBN 9780803793811.

Chekhov, Anton. *Kashtanka.* Adapted from a new translation by Ronald Meyer. Illus. by Gennady Spirin. Harcourt, 1995. ISBN 0-15-200539-0 and ISBN 9780152005399. Kashtanka, a young chestnut-colored dog, becomes separated from her master during a heavy snowfall. She is adopted by a kindhearted circus clown and learns to perform in his act. On opening night there is a wonderful surprise and Kashtanka is reunited with her family. Spirin's paintings are a perfect match for this heartwarming story. A good read-aloud.

Daly, Niki. *Pretty Salma: A Little Red Riding Hood Story from Africa.* Clarion, 2007. ISBN 0-6187-2345-5 and ISBN 9780618723454.

de la Mare, Walter, reteller. *The Turnip.* Illus. by Kevin Hawkes. Godine, 1992. ISBN 0-87923-934-4 and ISBN 9780879239343. Not the familiar Russian nursery tale, but a story from Grimm about two brothers, one kind and generous, the other selfish and greedy, and how their lives are changed by a turnip.

Del Negro, Janice. *Lucy Dove.* Illus. by Leonid Gore. DK Ink, 1999. ISBN 0-7894-2514-9 and ISBN 9780789425140.

———. *Willa and the Wind.* Illus. by Heather M. Solomon. Marshall Cavendish, 2005. ISBN 0-7614-5232-X and ISBN 9780761452324.

Derby, Sally. *Two Fools and a Horse.* Illus. by Robert Rayevsky. Cavendish, 2003. ISBN 0-7614-5119-6 and ISBN 9780761451198.

Dickens, Charles. *The Magic Fish-Bone.* Illus. by Robert Florczak. Harcourt, 2000. ISBN 0-1520-1080-7 and ISBN 9780152010805.

Ernst, Lisa Campbell. *The Gingerbread Girl.* Dutton, 2006. ISBN 0-5254-7667-9 and ISBN 9780525476672. A gender-bending retelling of the traditional tale.

Farjeon, Eleanor. *Elsie Piddock Skips in Her Sleep.* Illus. by Charlotte Voake. Candlewick, 2008. ISBN 0-7636-3810-2 and ISBN 9780763638108.

Fleming, Candace. *Gator Gumbo: A Spicy-Hot Tale.* Illus. by Sally Anne Lambert. Farrar, Straus and Giroux, 2004. ISBN 0-3743-8050-3 and ISBN 9780374380502.

French, Fiona. *Anancy and Mr. Dry-Bone.* Little, Brown, 1991. ISBN 0-316-29298-2 and ISBN 9780316292986. This original trickster tale based on characters from African and Caribbean folklore is told in street-smart, jazzy language.

Gogol, Nikolai. *The Nose.* As retold for children by Catherine Cowan. Illus. by Kevin Hawkes. Lothrop, 1994. ISBN 0-688-10464-9 and ISBN 9780688104641. The high-spirited words and pictures make a romp of Gogol's absurd satire about a nose with a life of its own.

Goldin, Barbara Diamond. *The Magician's Visit: A Passover Tale.* Illus. by Robert Andrew Parker. Viking, 1993. ISBN 0-670-84840-9 and ISBN 9780670848409. Adapted from a story by I. L. Peretz.

Gregory, Valiska. *Through the Mickle Woods*. Illus. by Barry Moser. Little, Brown, 1992. ISBN 0-316-32779-4 and ISBN 9780316327794. A king honors his dying queen's last request: "Into the dark and mickle woods go forth to find the bear . . ." And the bear gives him three stories that both sadden and help to heal him. A picture storybook for older readers.

Hearne, Betsy. *Seven Brave Women*. HarperCollins, 2006. ISBN 0-0607-9921-8 and ISBN 9780060799212.

Hodges, Margaret. *Gulliver in Lilliput*. Retold from *Gulliver's Travels* by Jonathan Swift. Illus. by Kimberly Bulcken Root. Holiday House, 1995. ISBN 0-8234-1147-8 and ISBN 9780823411474. Hodges retells Part I as Gulliver might have told the first of his adventures to children. Root's marvelous watercolor paintings are as riveting as the tale.

Icenoggle, Jodi. *'Til the Cows Come Home*. Illus. by Normand Chartier. Boyds Mills, 2004. ISBN 1-5639-7987-X and ISBN 9781563979873. A retelling of the Jewish tale about the button, also known as "Just Enough to Make a Story," set in the American West.

Kasza, Keiko. *The Mightiest*. Putnam, 2001. ISBN 0-3992-3586-8 and ISBN 9780399235863.

Kimmel, Eric A. *Gershon's Monster: A Story for the Jewish New Year*. Illus. by Jon J Muth. Scholastic, 2000. ISBN 0-4391-0839-X and ISBN 9780439108393.

———. *Grizz!* Illus. by Andrew Glass. Holiday House, 2000. ISBN 0-8234-1469-8 and ISBN 9780823414697. A Grimm tale reset in the American West about a cowboy who, to win a deal with the devil, doesn't bathe for seven years.

———. *Hershel and the Hanukkah Goblins*. Illus. by Trina Schart Hyman. Holiday House, 1989. ISBN 0-8234-0769-1 and ISBN 9780823407699. An original story based on Yiddish folklore about Hershel Ostropolier.

Kipling, Rudyard. *The Elephant's Child*. North-South, 1995. ISBN 1-55858-369-6 and ISBN 9781558583696.

Lagerlöf, Selma. *The Legend of the Christmas Rose*. Retold by Ellin Greene. Illus. by Charles Mikolaycak. Holiday House, 1990. ISBN 0-8234-0821-3 and ISBN 9780823408214. Once, long ago in Sweden, there was a garden that bloomed every Christmas Eve in remembrance of the Christ Child. The garden was destroyed by evil in the human heart, but a bulb was rescued and from it grew the flower we call the Christmas Rose. Based on Swedish folklore and written by the first woman to receive the Nobel Prize for Literature.

LeGuin, Ursula K. *A Ride on the Red Mare's Back*. Illus. by Julie Downing. Orchard, 1992. ISBN 0-531-05991-X and ISBN 9780531059913. With the help of an inspired toy horse, a girl rescues her younger brother from trolls. A journey story reminiscent of Hans Christian Andersen's "The Snow Queen."

Lester, Julius. *Sam and the Tigers: A Retelling of Little Black Sambo*. Illus. by Jerry Pinkney. Dial, 1996. ISBN 0-8037-2028-9 and ISBN 9780803720282.

———. *What a Truly Cool World*. Illus. by Joe Cepeda. Scholastic, 1999. ISBN 0-5908-6468-8 and ISBN 9780590864688.

———. *Why Heaven Is Far Away*. Illus. by Joe Cepeda. Scholastic, 2002. ISBN 0-4391-7871-1 and ISBN 9780439178716.

MacDonald, George. *Little Daylight*. Adapted by Anthea Bell. Illus. by Dorothée Duntze. North-South, 1987. ISBN 0-200-72912-8 and ISBN 9780200729123. The princess is doomed to wax and wane with the cycles of the moon until she is kissed by a prince who does not know who she is.

Osborne, Mary Pope. *The Brave Little Seamstress*. Illus. by Giselle Potter. Atheneum, 2002. ISBN 0-6898-4486-7 and ISBN 9780689844867.

Peretz, I. L. *The Magician*. Illus. by Uri Shulevitz. Macmillan, 1985. ISBN 0-02-782770-4 and ISBN 9780027827705.

Perrault, Charles. *Cinderella, or the Little Glass Slipper*. Illus. by Marcia Brown. Simon & Schuster, 1971. ISBN 0-684-12676-1 and ISBN 9780684126760.

———. *Puss in Boots*. Translated by Malcolm Arthur. Illus. by Fred Marcellino. Farrar, Straus and Giroux, 1990. ISBN 0-374-36160-6 and ISBN 9780374361600.

Pyle, Howard. *Bearskin*. Illus. by Trina Schart Hyman. Afterword by Peter Glassman. Morrow Junior Books, 1997. ISBN 0-6880-9837-1 and ISBN 9780688098377.

Ray, Jane. *The Happy Prince*. Dutton, 1994. ISBN 0-525-45367-9 and ISBN 9780525453673. An abridged version of Oscar Wilde's fairy tale, with shimmering illustrations.

Rees, Douglas. *Grandy Thaxter's Helper*. Illus. by S. D. Schindler. Atheneum, 2004. ISBN 0-6898-3020-3 and ISBN 9780689830204. Death comes for Grandy Thaxter, but she keeps him so busy he finally gives up!

Roberts, Lynn. *Little Red: A Fizzlingly Good Yarn*. Illus. by David Roberts. Abrams, 2005. ISBN 0-8109-5783-3 and ISBN 9780810957831.

Salley, Colleen. *Epossumondas Saves the Day*. Illus. by Janet Stevens. Harcourt, 2006. ISBN 0-1520-5701-3 and ISBN 9780152057015. A retelling of the American folktale "Sody Saleratus."

Sandburg, Carl. *The Huckabuck Family and How They Raised Popcorn in Nebraska and Quit and Came Back*. Illus. by David Small. Farrar, Straus and Giroux, 1999. ISBN 0-3743-3511-7 and ISBN 9780374335113.

Scieszka, Jon. *The True Story of the Three Little Pigs, by A. Wolf as told to Jon Scieszka*. Illus. by Lane Smith. Viking, 1989. ISBN 0-670-82759-2 and ISBN 9780670827596. The old nursery tale sounds entirely different when the wolf gives it his spin. A fractured tale for children already familiar with the traditional version.

Shannon, Margaret. *The Red Wolf*. Houghton Mifflin, 2002. ISBN 0-6180-5544-4 and ISBN 9780618055449.

Stockton, Frank R. *The Bee Man of Orn*. Illus. by Maurice Sendak. HarperCollins, 2005. ISBN 0-06-029729-8 and ISBN 9780060297299. The Bee Man sets out to find his original form and has many adventures.

———. *The Griffin and the Minor Canon*. Illus. by Maurice Sendak. HarperCollins, 2005. ISBN 0-06-029731-X and ISBN 9780060297312. Middle-grade children will enjoy this highly imaginative story.

Storace, Patricia. *Sugar Cane: A Caribbean Rapunzel*. Illus. by Raúl Colón. Jump at the Sun/Hyperion, 2007. ISBN 0-7868-0791-1 and ISBN 9780786807918.

Thurber, James. *The Great Quillow*. Illus. by Steven Kellogg. Harcourt, 1994. ISBN 0-15-232544-1 and ISBN 9780152325442. Kellogg's ebullient paintings are a perfect match for Thurber's story about a clever toymaker who outwits a giant.

———. *Many Moons*. Illus. by Marc Simont. Harcourt, 1990. ISBN 0-15-251872-X and ISBN 9780152518721. First published in 1943 with pictures by Louis Slobodkin for which he received the 1944 Caldecott Medal. This new edition has been illustrated with charming pastel watercolors by an artist who knew Thurber personally and has included him in one of the drawings.

———. *Many Moons*. Illus. by Louis Slobodkin. Harcourt, 1943. ISBN 0-15-251873-8 and ISBN 9780152518738.

Walter, Mildred Pitts. *Brother to the Wind.* Illus. by Diane and Leo Dillon. Lothrop, 1985. ISBN 0-688-03812-3 and ISBN 9780688038120. An original story that draws on many beliefs and symbols of the African culture.

Wilde, Oscar. *The Happy Prince.* Illus. by Ed Young. Simon & Schuster, 1992. ISBN 0-671-77819-6 and ISBN 9780671778194. The complete text with exquisite impressionistic artwork.

————. *The Nightingale and the Rose.* Illus. by Freire Wright and Michael Foreman. Oxford University Press, 1981. ISBN 0-19-520231-7 and ISBN 9780195202311.

Willard, Nancy. *The Sorcerer's Apprentice.* Illus. by Leo and Diane Dillon. Scholastic, 1993. ISBN 0-590-47329-8 and ISBN 9780590473293. This modern version of the magical tale is told in rhyming text and features a contemporary heroine.

Yolen, Jane. *The Girl in the Golden Bower.* Illus. by Jane Dyer. Little, Brown, 1994. ISBN 0-316-96894-3 and ISBN 9780316968942. A sorceress obsessed with finding a powerful charm does not know that a little girl possesses it—a brown comb that shimmers for a moment as the child puts it into her hair, and then turns to gold. And "no one could tell where the hair ended and the comb began."

————. *The Sleeping Beauty.* Illus. by Ruth Sanderson. Knopf, 1986. ISBN 0-394-55433-7 and ISBN 9780394554334. A beautiful retelling of a classic love story.

POETRY AND SONG

Adoff, Arnold. *I Am the Darker Brother: An Anthology of Modern Poems by African Americans.* Foreword by Charlemae Hill Rollins. Macmillan, 1969. Revised and updated edition (paperback), Simon Pulse, 1997. ISBN 0-689-80869-0 and ISBN 9780689808692.

————. *The Poetry of Black America: Anthology of the Twentieth Century.* Introduction by Gwendolyn Brooks. Harper, 1973. ISBN 0-0602-0089-8 and ISBN 9780060200893.

Alarcón, Francisco X. *Animal Poems of the Iguazú/Animalario del Iguazú: Poemas.* Children's Book Press, 2008. ISBN 0-8923-9225-8 and ISBN 9780892392254.

————. *Poems to Dream Together/Poemas para soñar juntos.* Lee & Low, 2005. ISBN 1-5843-0233-X and ISBN 9781584302339.

Argueta, Jorge. *Talking with Mother Earth/Hablando con Madre Tierra.* Groundwood, 2006. ISBN 0-8889-9626-8 and ISBN 9780888996268.

Bauer, Caroline Feller. *Rainy Day: Stories and Poems.* Harper, 1986. ISBN 0-397-32105-8 and ISBN 9780397321056.

————. *Snowy Day: Stories and Poems.* Harper, 1986. ISBN 0-397-32177-5 and ISBN 9780397321773.

Begay, Shonto. *Navajo: Visions and Voices Across the Mesa.* Scholastic, 1995. ISBN 0-590-46153-2 and ISBN 9780590461535. Begay has written original poetry and prose to accompany 20 of his paintings to make a portrait of Navajo life. The result is a stunning, moving experience.

Berry, James. *When I Dance.* Illus. by Karen Barbour. Harcourt, 1991. ISBN 0-15-295568-2 and ISBN 9780152955687. A collection of poems for young people by the celebrated Jamaican poet. The poems reflect two cultures: the rural Caribbean and inner-city Britain.

Bierhorst, John, comp. *On the Road of Stars: Native American Night Poems and Sleep Charms.* Illus. by Judy Pederson. Macmillan, 1994. ISBN 0-02-709735-8 and ISBN 9780027097351. Lullabies and poems to bring good dreams.

————. *The Sacred Path: Spells, Prayers and Power Songs of the American Indians.* Morrow, 1983. ISBN 0-688-01699-5 and ISBN 9780688016999.

Bober, Natalie S. *Let's Pretend: Poems of Flight and Fancy.* Illus. by Bill Bell. Viking, 1986. ISBN 0-14-032132-2 and ISBN 9780140321326.

Bodecker, N. M. *Hurry Hurry, Mary Dear! And Other Nonsense Poems.* Simon & Schuster, 1976. ISBN 0-689-50066-1 and ISBN 9780689500664. Nonsense poems that reflect a variety of moods from wistful to ridiculous.

Bontemps, Arna. *Hold Fast to Your Dreams.* Wilcox & Follett, 1979. ISBN 0-69543770-4 and ISBN 9780695437701.

Booth, David, comp. *Til All the Stars Have Fallen: A Collection of Poems for Children.* Illus. by Kady MacDonald Denton. Viking, 1990. ISBN 0-670-83272-3 and ISBN 9780670832729. The 76 poems in this diverse and delightful collection are by Native American and Canadian poets.

Brenner, Barbara, ed. *The Earth Is Painted Green: A Garden of Poems About Our Planet.* Illus. by S. D. Schindler. Scholastic, 1994. ISBN 0-590-45134-0 and ISBN 9780590451345. Includes nearly 100 poems by such award-winning poets as Aileen Fisher, Myra Cohn Livingston, and Valerie Worth.

Brooks, Gwendolyn. *Bronzeville Boys and Girls.* Illus. by Faith Ringgold. Amistad, 2006. ISBN 0-0602-9505-8 and ISBN 9780060295059.

Brooks, Jeremy. *A World of Prayers.* Eerdmans, 2006. ISBN 0-8028-5285-8 and ISBN 9780802852854. Prayers from different religions and countries that reflect the universal themes of love, forgiveness, and hope.

Bryan, Ashley. *All Night, All Day: A Child's First Book of African-American Spirituals.* Musical arrangements by David Manning Thomas. Macmillan, 1991. ISBN 0-689-31662-3 and ISBN 9780689316623. The artist has selected 20 of the best-known and best-loved spirituals and captured their spirit in colorful double-spread paintings.

————. *Ashley Bryan's ABC of African American Poetry.* Atheneum, 1997. ISBN 0-689-81209-4 and ISBN 9780689812095.

————. *Let it Shine: Three Favorite Spirituals.* Atheneum 2007. ISBN 0-6898-4732-7 and ISBN 9780689847325. "This Little Light of Mine," "Oh, When the Saints Go Marching In," and "He's Got the Whole World in His Hands" are brilliantly illustrated in this award-winning book.

————. *Sing to the Sun.* HarperCollins, 1992. ISBN 0-06-020829-5 and ISBN 9780060208295. Wilder Medal-winner Bryan's first book of original poetry is a joyful celebration of life that sets the heart singing. Illustrated with jewel-colored paintings that look like stained glass windows.

Carlson, Lori Marie. *Red Hot Salsa: Bilingual Poems on Being Young and Latino in the United States.* Holt, 2005. ISBN 0-8050-7616-6 and ISBN 9780805076165.

Carroll, Lewis. *Lewis Carroll's Jabberwocky.* Illus. by Jane Breskin Zalben. Boyds Mills, 1992. ISBN 1-56397-080-5 and ISBN 9781563970801. The poem and Humpty Dumpty's explanation to Alice of the meaning of portmanteau words.

————. *The Walrus and the Carpenter.* Illus. by Jane Breskin Zalben. Holt, 1986. ISBN 0-8050-0071-2 and ISBN 9780805000719.

Carter, Anne, comp. *Birds, Beasts, and Fishes: A Selection of Animal Poems.* Illus. by Reg Cartwright. Macmillan, 1991. ISBN 0-02-717776-9 and ISBN 9780027177763. This fine collection for middle-grade children features 53 poems in diverse voices, from Lear to Sandburg.

Christie, Jason. *I-Robot: Poetry*. EDGE Science Fiction and Fantasy Pub., 2006. ISBN 1-8940-6324-4 and ISBN 9781894063241.

Clark, Ann Nolan. *In My Mother's House*. Illus. by Velino Herrera. Viking, 1991. ISBN 0-14-054496-8 and ISBN 9780140544961. These poems reflect the world as seen through the eyes of five young children of Tesuque Pueblo, near Santa Fe, New Mexico. Originally published in 1941.

Clark, Emma Chichester, comp. and illus. *I Never Saw a Purple Cow and Other Nonsense Rhymes*. Little, Brown, 1991. ISBN 0-316-14500-9 and ISBN 9780316145008. An exuberant collection of more than 100 nonsense rhymes about animals. With the exception of entries by Hilaire Belloc, Gelett Burgess, Lewis Carroll, and Samuel Goodrich, the selections come from tradition.

Clarke, Gillian. *The Whispering Room: Haunted Poems*. Kingfisher, 1996. ISBN 1-8569-7363-8 and ISBN 9781856973632.

Clinton, Catherine. *I, Too, Sing America: African American Poetry*. Houghton Mifflin, 1998. ISBN 0-3958-9599-5 and ISBN 9780395895993.

Cole, William. *A Zooful of Animals*. Illus. by Lynn Munsinger. Houghton Mifflin, 1992. ISBN 0-395-52278-1 and ISBN 9780395522783. A playful collection of 45 poems about animals, by American and British poets.

Collins, Billy, ed. *Poetry 180: A Turning Back to Poetry*. Random House, 2003. ISBN 0-8129-6887-5 and ISBN 9780812968873.

Cullinan, Bernice E., ed. *I Heard a Bluebird Sing: Children Select Their Favorite Poems by Aileen Fisher*. Illus. by Jennifer Emery. Wordsong, 2002. ISBN 1-56397-191-7 and ISBN 9781563971914.

———. *A Jar of Tiny Stars: Poems by NCTE Award-Winning Poets: Children Select Their Favorite Poems*. Illus. by Andi MacLeod. Portraits by Marc Nadel. Wordsong, 1996. ISBN 1-56397-087-2 and ISBN 9781563970870.

cummings, e. e. *hist whist*. Illus. by Deborah Kogan Ray. Crown, 1989. ISBN 0-517-57360-1 and ISBN 9780517573600. Poems just scary enough to please children in the primary grades.

de Gasztold, Carmen Bernos. *Prayers from the Ark: Selected Poems*. Translated from the French by Rumer Godden. Illus. by Barry Moser. Viking, 1992. ISBN 0-670-84496-9 and ISBN 9780670844968. This selection of 13 poems from an international bestseller first published in 1962 has been illustrated with hauntingly beautiful paintings.

de la Mare, Walter. *Peacock Pie: A Book of Rhymes*. Illus. by Louise Brierley. Holt, 1989. ISBN 0-8050-1124-2 and ISBN 9780805011241. A newly illustrated edition of a classic work first published in 1913.

de Regniers, Beatrice Schenk, et al. *Sing a Song of Popcorn: Every Child's Book of Poems*. Scholastic, 1988. ISBN 0-590-40646-0. A handsome collection, arranged by themes, such as "Mostly People," "Story Poems," and "Spooky Poems." Each section is illustrated by a different artist.

Demi, comp. and illus. *In the Eyes of the Cat: Japanese Poetry for All Seasons*. Translated by Tze-si Huang. Holt, 1992. ISBN 0-8050-1955-3 and ISBN 9780805019551. Seventy-seven Japanese nature poems, arranged by the seasons.

Dunning, Stephen, et al. *Reflections on a Gift of Watermelon Pickle . . . and Other Modern Verse*. Lothrop, 1966. ISBN 0-688-41231-9 and ISBN 9780688412319.

Elledge, Scott, comp. *Wider than the Sky: Poems to Grow Up With.* HarperCollins, 1990. ISBN 0-06-021786-3 and ISBN 9780060217860. An American literature professor emeritus compiled this anthology of 200 poems with his ten-year-old niece in mind.

Evans, Dilys, comp. *Monster Soup and Other Spooky Poems.* Illus. by Jacqueline Rogers. Scholastic, 1992. ISBN 0-590-45208-8 and ISBN 9780590452083. Deliciously scary poems about monsters, ghosts, and other fabulous creatures.

Farjeon, Eleanor. *Eleanor Farjeon's Poems for Children.* HarperCollins, 1984. ISBN 0-397-32091-4 and ISBN 9780397320912. The complete text of four volumes of verse by Eleanor Farjeon: *Sing for Your Supper, Over the Garden Wall, Joan's Door, Come Christmas,* and 20 poems from her *Collected Poems* heretofore published only in England.

Feelings, Tom, comp. and illus. *Soul Looks Back in Wonder.* Dial, 1993. ISBN 0-8037-1001-1 and ISBN 9780803710016. The artist has chosen poems by African American authors, including Maya Angelou, Lucille Clifton, and Langston Hughes, to accompany his stunning collages made from blueprints, colored pencils, spray paints, cutouts, and colored paper.

Fleischman, Paul. *I Am Phoenix: Poems for Two Voices.* Illus. by Ken Nutt. HarperCollins, 1985. ISBN 0-06-021881-9 and ISBN 9780060218812.

Florian, Douglas. *Handsprings: Poems and Paintings.* Greenwillow, 2006. ISBN 0-06-009280-7 and ISBN 9780060092801. The last in Florian's series of seasonal poetry. Companion titles include *Winter Eyes, Summersaults,* and *Autumnblings.*

George, Christine O'Connell. *The Great Frog Race and Other Poems.* Illus. by Kate Kiesler. Sandpiper, 2005. ISBN 0-6186-0478-2 and ISBN 9780618604784.

Giovanni, Nikki. *Spin a Soft Black Song.* Illus. by George Martins. Hill and Wang, 1985. ISBN 0-8090-8796-0 and ISBN 9780809087969. Reissue of the 1971 edition in a new format.

Goldstein, Bobbye S., comp. *Inner Chimes: Poems on Poetry.* Boyds Mills, 1992. ISBN 1-56397-040-6 and ISBN 9781563970405. An anthology of poems about poetry, by such diverse writers as Eleanor Farjeon, Eve Merriam, and Nikki Giovanni.

Gordon, Ruth, comp. *Peeling the Onion: An Anthology of Poems.* HarperCollins, 1993. ISBN 0-06-021727-8 and ISBN 9780060217273. Thought-provoking poems on diverse subjects, for the middle grades and up.

———. *Pierced by a Ray of Sun: Poems About the Times We Feel Alone.* HarperCollins, 1995. ISBN 0-06-023613-2 and ISBN 9780060236137. These poems about feeling alone and different speak to all of us but especially to young adults.

Greenberg, Jan. *Side by Side: New Poems Inspired by Art from Around the World.* Abrams, 2008. ISBN 0-8109-9471-2 and ISBN 9780810994713.

Greenfield, Eloise. *Daydreamers.* Illus. by Tom Feelings. Dial, 1981. ISBN 0-8037-2137-4 and ISBN 9780803721371.

———. *Honey, I Love and Other Love Poems.* Illus. by Diane and Leo Dillon. HarperCollins, 1978. ISBN 0-690-01334-5 and ISBN 9780690013344.

———. *Under the Sunday Tree.* Illus. by Amos Ferguson. HarperCollins, 1988. ISBN 0-06-022254-9 and ISBN 9780060222543. Poems and paintings that evoke native life in the Bahamas.

Grimes, Nikki. *At Jerusalem's Gate: Poems of Easter.* Eerdmans, 2005. ISBN 0-8028-5183-5 and ISBN 9780802851833.

———. *It's Raining Laughter.* Photographs by Myles C. Pinkney. Boyds Mill Press, 1997. ISBN 1-59078-077-9 and ISBN 9781590780770.

Hague, Michael, selector and illus. *The Book of Fairy Poetry*. HarperCollins, 2004. ISBN 0-688-14004-1 and ISBN 9780688140045. Forty-nine poems about fairy folk by poets ranging from Shakespeare to Jack Prelutsky.

Hall, Donald. *The Oxford Book of Children's Verse in America*. Oxford, 1985. ISBN 0-19-503539-9 and ISBN 9780195035391.

Harrington, Janice. *Even the Hollow My Body Made Is Gone*. BOA, 2007. ISBN 1-9299-1889-5 and ISBN 9781929918898.

Hart, Jane, ed. *Singing Bee! A Collection of Favorite Children's Songs*. Illus. by Anita Lobel. Lothrop, 1989. ISBN 0-688-41975-5 and ISBN 9780688419752.

Heide, Florence Parry. *Grim and Ghastly Goings On*. Lothrop, 1992. ISBN 0-6880-8319-6 and ISBN 9780688083199.

Ho, Minfong, comp. *Maples in the Mist: Children's Poems from the Tang Dynasty*. Lothrop, 1996. ISBN 0-6881-2044-X and ISBN 9780688120443.

Hopkins, Lee Bennett, comp. *Rainbows Are Made: Poems by Carl Sandburg*. Wood engravings by Fritz Eichenberg. Harcourt, 1982. ISBN 0-15-265480-1 and ISBN 9780152654801.

———. *Small Talk: A Book of Short Poems*. Illus. by Susan Gaber. Harcourt, 1995. ISBN 0-15-276577-8 and ISBN 9780152765774. Moments of significance caught by such writers as Carl Sandburg, Langston Hughes, and Eve Merriam.

———. *Wonderful Words: Poems About Reading, Writing, Speaking, and Listening*. Illus. by Karen Barbour. Simon & Schuster, 2004. ISBN 0-689-83588-4 and ISBN 9780689835889.

Hughes, Langston. *The Dream Keeper and Other Poems*. Illus. by Brian Pinkney. Knopf, 1994. ISBN 0-679-84421-X and ISBN 9780679844211. A new edition, with seven additional poems (66 poems in all), a new introduction by Lee Bennett Hopkins, and scratchboard illustrations by Brian Pinkney. Originally published in 1932.

Issa, Kobayashi. *Today and Today*. Illus. by G. Brian Karas. Scholastic, 2007. ISBN 0-4395-9078-7 and ISBN 9780439590785. Haiku from the eighteenth-century Japanese poet.

Janeczko, Paul B., comp. *A Foot in the Mouth: Poems to Speak, Sing and Shout*. Candlewick, 2009. ISBN 0-7636-0663-4 and ISBN 9780763606633.

———. *A Poke in the I: A Collection of Concrete Poems*. Illus. by Chris Raschka. Candlewick. ISBN 0-7636-0661-8 and ISBN 9780763606619.

———. *Seeing the Blue Between: Advice and Inspiration for Young Poets*. Candlewick, 2002. ISBN 1-5907-8383-2 and ISBN 9781590783832. Leading American poets share advice and poems with potential young poets.

Janeczko, Paul B., and J. Patrick Lewis. *Wing Nuts: Screwy Haiku*. Little, Brown, 2006. ISBN 0-3166-0731-2 and ISBN 9780316607315.

Johnson, Angela. *The Other Side: Shorter Poems*. Scholastic, 2000. ISBN 0-5310-7167-7 and ISBN 9780531071670.

Johnson, James Weldon. *The Creation*. Illus. by James E. Ransome. Holiday House, 1994. ISBN 0-8234-1069-2 and ISBN 9780823410699. Johnson's powerful free-verse poem is based on the biblical story.

———. *God's Trombones: Seven Negro Sermons in Verse*. Introduction by Maya Angelou. Penguin Classics, 2008 (paperback). ISBN 0-14-310541-8 and ISBN 9780143105411. An excellent introduction discusses the folk sermon. For older children and adults.

Jones, Hettie, comp. *The Trees Stand Shining: Poetry of the North American Indians*. Illus. by Robert Andrew Parker. Dial, 1993. ISBN 0-8037-9083-X and ISBN 9780803790834. "The poems in this book are really songs."

Katz, Alan. *Where Did They Hide My Presents? Silly Dilly Christmas Songs*. McElderry, 2005. ISBN 1-4169-6830-X and ISBN 9781416968306.

Kennedy, Caroline. *A Family of Poems: My Favorite Poetry for Children*. Paintings by Jon J Muth. Hyperion, 2005. ISBN 0-7868-5111-2 and ISBN 9780786851119.

Kennedy, X. J. *The Beasts of Bethlehem*. Illus. by Michael McCurdy. Simon & Schuster, 1992. ISBN 0-689-50561-2 and ISBN 9780689505614. The thoughts of each of the animals present at the birth of Christ are expressed with quiet reverence in these 19 poems and drawings.

Kennedy, X. J., and Dorothy M. Kennedy, comps. *Talking Like the Rain: A First Book of Poems*. Illus. by Jane Dyer. Little, Brown, 1992. ISBN 0-316-48889-5 and ISBN 9780316488891. The title of this joyous anthology comes from Isak Dinesen's *Out of Africa* ("Speak again. Speak like rain"). The more than 120 poems are about important moments in a child's life, from dressing up and birthday parties to splashing in puddles and discovering "the lovely whiteness of snow."

Koch, Kenneth, and Kate Farrell. *Talking to the Sun: An Illustrated Anthology of Poems for Young People*. Metropolitan Museum of Art and Holt, 1985. ISBN 0-8050-0144-1 and ISBN 9780805001440.

Kuskin, Karla. *Green as a Bean*. Laura Geringer Books, 2007. ISBN 0-0607-5332-3 and ISBN 9780060753320.

———. *Moon, Have You Met My Mother? The Collected Poems of Karla Kuskin*. Illus. by Sergio Ruzzier. Geringer/HarperCollins, 2003. ISBN 0-06-027173-6 and ISBN 9780060271732.

Lalicki, Barbara. *If There Were Dreams to Sell*. Illus. by Margot Tomes. Simon & Schuster, 1994. ISBN 0-02-751251-7 and ISBN 9780027512519. A reissue of an unusual alphabet poetry book. Originally published in 1984.

Larios, Julie. *Yellow Elephant: A Bright Bestiary*. Illus. by Julie Paschkis. Harcourt, 2006. ISBN 0-1520-5422-7 and ISBN 9780152054229.

Larrick, Nancy, comp. *Cats Are Cats*. Illus. by Ed Young. Philomel, 1988. ISBN 0-399-21517-4 and ISBN 9780399215179. "Truly these cats are cats that inspire wonder, the imagination, and a sensitivity to perfectly matched visual and verbal images" (from Kay E. Vandergrift's review in *School Library Journal*, December 1988).

———. *Mice Are Nice*. Illus. by Ed Young. Philomel, 1990. ISBN 0-399-21495-X and ISBN 9780399214950. A few cats have managed to find their way into this companion piece, in which we meet a meadow mouse, a house mouse, a mouse in a rocket, and others.

———. *Piping Down the Valleys Wild: Poetry for the Young of All Ages*. Illus. by Ellen Raskin. Dell, 1982. ISBN 0-440-46952-X and ISBN 9780440469520.

———. *To the Moon and Back: A Collection of Poems*. Illus. by Catharine O'Neill. Delacorte, 1991. ISBN 0-385-30159-6 and ISBN 9780385301596. Rhythmic verse that appeals to the imagination from such well-known poets as e. e. cummings and David McCord along with lesser-known selections from Native American and Inuit poetry.

Lawrence, Jacob. *Harriet and the Promised Land*. Simon & Schuster, 1993. ISBN 0-671-86673-7 and ISBN 9780671866730. The story of the daring black slave who led her people to freedom, told in rhythmic verse and powerful paintings by the acclaimed artist.

Lear, Edward. *Of Pelicans and Pussycats: Poems and Limericks*. Illus. by Jill Newton. Dial, 1990. ISBN 0-8037-0728-2 and ISBN 9780803707283. These seven poems and six limericks are a pleasing introduction to Lear.

———. *The Owl and the Pussycat*. Illus. by Jan Brett. Putnam, 1991. ISBN 0-399-21925-0 and ISBN 9780399219252. This beguiling rendition of a childhood favorite is set in the colorful tropics.

Levy, Constance. *Splash! Poems of Our Watery World*. Illus. by David Soman. Orchard, 2002. ISBN 0-4392-9318-9 and ISBN 9780439293181.

Lewis, Claudia. *Up in the Mountains and Other Poems of Long Ago*. Illus. by Joel Fontaine. HarperCollins, 1991. ISBN 0-06-023810-0 and ISBN 9780060238100. And *Long Ago in Oregon*. Illus. by Joel Fontaine. HarperCollins, 1987. ISBN 0-06-023839-9 and ISBN 9780060238391. A beloved teacher of children's literature recalls growing up in Oregon.

Lewis, J. Patrick, and Paul B. Janeczko. *Birds on a Wire: A Renga 'round Town*. Illus. by Gary Lippincott. Wordsong, 2008. ISBN 1-5907-8383-2 and ISBN 9781590783832.

Lewis, Richard. *In the Night, Still Dark*. Illus. by Ed Young. Simon & Schuster, 1988. ISBN 0-689-31310-1 and ISBN 9780689313103. A skillful abridgement of the Hawaiian creation chant traditionally recited over a newborn child to help bond the new life to all other living things.

Livingston, Myra Cohn, comp. *Animal, Vegetable, Mineral: Poems About Small Things*. HarperCollins, 1994. ISBN 0-06-023008-8 and ISBN 9780060230081. Langston Hughes, Karla Kuskin, William Carlos Williams, and other fine poets illuminate things in our everyday world that often go unnoticed.

———. *Call Down the Moon: Poems of Music*. Simon & Schuster, 1995. ISBN 0-689-80416-4 and ISBN 9780689804168. These traditional and contemporary poems "range in mood from amusing to moving, serious to sublime."

———. *How Pleasant to Know Mr. Lear! Edward Lear's Selected Works with an Introduction and Notes*. Stemmer House, 1994. ISBN 0-88045-126-2 and ISBN 9780880451260.

Livingston, Myra Cohn, and Leonard Everett Fisher. *Celebrations*. Holiday House, 1985. ISBN 0-8234-0550-8 and ISBN 9780823405503. Poems and paintings to mark 16 important days throughout the year, including Martin Luther King Day.

Longfellow, Henry Wadsworth. *Paul Revere's Ride*. Illus. by Ted Rand. Dutton, 1990. ISBN 0-525-44610-9 and ISBN 9780525446101. Full-color paintings capture the drama of the well-known poem.

McCord, David. *One at a Time*. Little, Brown, 1986. ISBN 0-316-55516-9 and ISBN 9780316555166. The collected poems of David McCord, with a subject index and index of first lines.

McNaughton, Colin. *Making Friends with Frankenstein*. Walker, 2003. ISBN 0-7445-9666-1 and ISBN 9780744596663.

Martin, Bill, Jr., ed., with Michael Sampson. *The Bill Martin Jr. Big Book of Poetry*. Foreword by Eric Carle. Afterword by Steven Kellogg. Simon & Schuster, 2008. ISBN 1-4169-3971-7 and ISBN 9781416939719. Nearly 200 of Bill Martin's favorite poems illustrated by award-winning artists including Aliki, Ashley Bryan, Steven Kellogg, Chris Raschka, Nancy Tafuri, and Dan Yaccarino.

Merriam, Eve. *The Singing Green: New and Selected Poems for All Seasons*. Illus. by Kathleen Collins Howell. Morrow, 1992. ISBN 0-688-11025-8 and ISBN 9780688110253. A joyous collection by a distinguished American poet. See other collections by this prolific author.

Milne, A. A. *The Complete Poems of Winnie-the-Pooh.* Illus. by Ernest H. Shepard. Dutton, 1998. ISBN 0-525-46077-2 and ISBN 9780525460770. All the poems from *When We Were Very Young* and *Now We Are Six.*

Mitchell, Stephen. *The Wishing Bone and Other Poems.* Illus. by Tom Pohrt. Candlewick, 2003. ISBN 0-7636-1118-2 and ISBN 9780763611187.

Moore, Lilian. *Beware, Take Care: Fun and Spooky Poems.* Illus. by Howard Fine. Holt, 2006. ISBN 0-8050-6917-8 and ISBN 9780805069174.

———. *Mural on Second Avenue, and Other City Poems.* Illus. by Roma Karas. Candlewick, 2005. ISBN 0-7636-1987-6 and ISBN 9780763619879.

———. *Poems Have Roots.* Illus. by Tad Hills. Atheneum, 1997. ISBN 0-6898-0029-0 and ISBN 9780689800290.

———. *Sunflakes: Poems for Children.* Illus. by Jan Ormerod. Houghton Mifflin, 1992. ISBN 0-395-58833-2 and ISBN 9780395588338. The 82 verses in this appealing anthology were chosen with young children in mind.

Myers, Walter Dean. *Here in Harlem: Poems in Many Voices.* Holiday House, 2004. ISBN 0-8234-2212-7 and ISBN 9780823422128.

Nicholls, Judith, comp. *The Sun in Me: Poems About the Planet.* Illus. by Beth Krommes. Barefoot, 2003. ISBN 1-84148-058-4 and ISBN 9781841480589. "Nature through the eyes of wonder and curiosity, as a child might see it." Illustrated with striking artwork combining scratchboard and watercolor.

Niven, Penelope. *Carl Sandburg: Adventures of a Poet with Poems and Prose by Carl Sandburg.* Illus. by Marc Nadel. Harcourt, 2003. ISBN 0-15-204686-0 and ISBN 9780152046866.

Nye, Naomi Shihab. *Is This Forever, or What? Poems and Paintings from Texas.* Greenwillow, 2004. ISBN 0-0605-1178-8 and ISBN 9780060511784.

———. *A Maze Me: Poems for Girls.* Illus. by Terre Maher. Greenwillow, 2005. ISBN 0-0605-8189-1 and ISBN 9780060581893.

———. *Nineteen Varieties of Gazelle.* Greenwillow, 2002. ISBN 0-0600-9766-3 and ISBN 9780060097660.

Nye, Naomi Shihab, comp. *This Same Sky: A Collection of Poems from Around the World.* Simon & Schuster, 1992. ISBN 0-02-768440-7 and ISBN 9780027684407. Older children and young adults will be pulled into the lives of these extraordinary, talented poets, none of whom were born in the United States. Nearly all of the 129 poems present common ideas in uncommonly fresh ways.

Once Upon a Poem: Favorite Poems That Tell Stories. Foreword and Afterword by Kevin Crossley-Holland. Illus. by Peter Bailey, Sian Bailey, Carol Lawson, and Chris McEwan. The Chicken House, 2004. ISBN 0-439-65108-5 and ISBN 9780439651080. Sixteen poems of wide variety, from "The Owl and the Pussycat" to "The Highway Man."

O'Neill, Mary. *Hailstones and Halibut Bones.* Illus. by John Wallner. Doubleday, 1989. ISBN 0-385-24484-3 and ISBN 9780385244848. A reissue of a popular book, with fresh new illustrations.

Perry, Andrea. *Here's What You Do When You Can't Find Your Shoe (Ingenious Inventions for Pesky Problems).* Atheneum, 2003. ISBN 0-6898-3067-X and ISBN 9780689830679.

Philip, Neil, ed. *Songs Are Thoughts: Poems of the Inuit.* Illus. by Maryclare Foa. Orchard, 1995. ISBN 0-531-06893-5 and ISBN 9780531068939. Poems that introduce children to the Inuit way of life.

Plotz, Helen. *Imagination's Other Place: Poems of Science and Mathematics*. HarperCollins, 1987. ISBN 0-690-04700-2 and ISBN 9780690047004.

Pomerantz, Charlotte. *Halfway to Your House*. Illus. by Gabrielle Vincent. Greenwillow, 1991. ISBN 0-688-11804-6 and ISBN 9780688118044. Delicate watercolors illustrate these whimsical poems for the young child.

———. *The Tamarindo Puppy and Other Poems*. Illus. by Byron Barton. Greenwillow, 1993. ISBN 0-688-80251-6 and ISBN 9780688802516. The inclusion of Spanish words within the predominately English text is a pleasing introduction to the Spanish language.

Prelutsky, Jack. *Awful Ogre Running Wild*. Illus. by Paul O. Zelinsky. Greenwillow, 2008. ISBN 0-06-623866-8 and ISBN 9780066238661. Awful Ogre is back again!

———. *Be Glad Your Nose Is on Your Face: And Other Poems: Some of the Best of Jack Prelutsky*. HarperCollins, 2008. ISBN 0-0615-7653-0 and ISBN 9780061576539.

———. *My Dog May Be a Genius*. Illus. by James Stevenson. Greenwillow Books, 2008. ISBN 0-0662-3862-5 and ISBN 9780066238623.

———. *Nightmares: Poems to Trouble Your Sleep*. Mulberry, 1993. ISBN 0-6880-4589-8 and ISBN 9780688045890.

Prelutsky, Jack, comp. *Beauty of the Beast*. Illus. by Meilo So. Knopf, 2006. ISBN 0-6798-7058-X and ISBN 9780679870586.

Radley, Gail, comp. *Rainy Day Rhymes*. Illus. by Ellen Kandoian. Houghton Mifflin, 1992. ISBN 0-395-59967-9 and ISBN 9780395599679. An appealing collection of 17 poems about rain by Rachel Field, Robert Louis Stevenson, Aileen Fisher, and others.

Read, Herbert. *This Way Delight*. Illus. by Juliet Kepes. Pantheon, 1956. ISBN 0-394-91741-3 and ISBN 9780394917412.

Rex, Adam. *Frankenstein Makes a Sandwich*. Harcourt, 2006. ISBN 0-1520-5766-8 and ISBN 9780152057664.

Rogasky, Barbara, comp. *Winter Poems*. Illus. by Trina Schart Hyman. Scholastic, 1994. ISBN 0-590-42872-1 and ISBN 9780590428729. Twenty-five poems, some new, some more than a thousand years old, celebrate the winter season without reference to any holidays.

Rollins, Charlemae Hill, comp. *Christmas Gif': An Anthology of Christmas Poems, Songs, and Stories Written by and About African-Americans*. Illus. by Ashley Bryan. Introduction by Augusta Baker. Morrow, 1993. ISBN 0-688-11667-1 and ISBN 9780688116675. A reissue of a classic anthology first published in 1963.

Rosen, Michael, comp. *Poems for the Very Young*. Illus. by Bob Graham. Kingfisher, 1993. ISBN 1-85697-908-3 and ISBN 9781856979085. A collection of modern and traditional poems with pleasing wordplay and sounds.

Rylant, Cynthia. *God Went to Beauty School*. HarperCollins, 2003. ISBN 0-0600-9435-4 and ISBN 9780060094355. For young adults and adults.

Schertle, Alice. *How Now, Brown Cow*. Illus. by Amanda Schaffer. Browndeer/Harcourt, 1994. ISBN 0-15-276648-0 and ISBN 9780152766481.

Schwartz, Alvin. *And the Green Grass Grew All Around: Folk Poetry from Everyone*. Illus. by Sue Truesdell. HarperCollins, 1992. ISBN 0-06-022757-5 and ISBN 9780060227579. Children's folk poetry—funny, irreverent, bursting with energy—collected in schoolyards and other places where children gather.

Service, Robert. *The Cremation of Sam McGee*. Paintings by Ted Harrison. Greenwillow, 1987. ISBN 0-688-06903-7 and ISBN 9780688069032. A classic poem about gold rush days.

Shaw, Alison, comp. *Until I Saw the Sea: A Collection of Seashore Poems*. Holt, 1995. ISBN 0-8050-2755-6 and ISBN 9780805027556. Nineteen poems with color photographs of seashore scenes taken on Martha's Vineyard by the compiler, an award-winning photographer.

Sidman, Joyce. *Butterfly Eyes and Other Secrets of the Meadow*. Houghton Mifflin, 2006. ISBN 0-6185-6313-X and ISBN 9780618563135.

———. *Song of the Water Boatman and Other Pond Poems*. Houghton Mifflin, 2004. ISBN 0-6181-3547-2 and ISBN 9780618135479.

Sidman, Joyce, comp. *The World According to Dog: Poems and Teen Voices*. Houghton Mifflin, 2003. ISBN 0-6182-8381-1 and ISBN 9780618283811.

Silverstein, Shel. *Where the Sidewalk Ends: the poems and drawings of Shel Silverstein*. HarperCollins, 2004. 30th Anniversary edition. ISBN 0-06-057234-5 and ISBN 9780060572341.

Simon, Seymour, ed. *Star Walk*. Morrow, 1995. ISBN 0-688-11887-9 and ISBN 9780688118877. A collection of poetry (and some prose) about stars and space, accompanied by awe-inspiring photographs.

Sky-Peck, Kathryn. *Who Has Seen the Wind? An Illustrated Collection of Poetry for Young People*. Rizzoli, 1991. ISBN 0-8478-1423-8 and ISBN 9780847814237. Classic poems illustrated with reproductions of paintings from the Museum of Fine Arts in Boston.

Sneve, Virginia Driving Hawk, comp. *Dancing Teepees: Poems of American Indian Youth*. Illus. by Stephen Gammell. Holiday House, 1989. ISBN 0-8234-0724-1 and ISBN 9780823407248. Selections from the oral tradition of North American Indians and contemporary tribal poets.

Soto, Gary. *Neighborhood Odes*. Illus. by David Diaz. Harcourt, 1992. ISBN 0-15-256879-4 and ISBN 9780152568795. These 21 poems celebrate everyday life in a Hispanic neighborhood. For children in the middle grades.

Stevenson, Robert Louis. *A Child's Garden of Verses*. Illus. by Henriette Willebeek le Mair. Philomel, 1991. ISBN 0-399-21818-1 and ISBN 9780399218187. A new edition of a book first published in 1926 with additional illustrations by this well-known artist.

Strauss, Gwen. *Trail of Stones*. Illus. by Anthony Browne. Knopf, 1990. ISBN 0-6799-0582-0 and ISBN 9780679905820.

Strickland, Michael R., comp. *Poems that Sing to You*. Illus. by Alan Leiner. Boyds Mills, 1993. ISBN 1-56397-178-X and ISBN 9781563971785. Poems that capture the rhythms of music.

Thomas, Joyce Carol. *The Blacker the Berry*. Illus. by Floyd Cooper. Joanna Cotler Books, 2008. ISBN 0-0602-5375-4 and ISBN 9780060253752.

———. *Brown Honey in Broomwheat Tea*. Illus. by Floyd Cooper. HarperCollins, 1993. ISBN 0-06-021087-7 and ISBN 9780060210878. Poems about family and pride of heritage.

———. *Gingerbread Days*. Illus. by Floyd Cooper. HarperCollins, 1995. ISBN 0-06-023469-5 and ISBN 9780060234690. This companion volume to *Brown Honey in Broomwheat Tea* celebrates family love throughout the months of the year.

Treece, Henry. *The Magic Wood*. Illus. by Barry Moser. HarperCollins, 1992. ISBN 0-06-020802-3 and ISBN 9780060208028. A ghost poem for children old enough to enjoy the macabre.

Turner, Ann. *Grass Songs*. Illus. by Barry Moser. Harcourt, 1993. ISBN 0-1563-6477-8 and ISBN 9780156364775.

Vecchione, Patrice. *The Body Eclectic.* Holt, 2002. ISBN 0-8050-6935-6 and ISBN 9780805069358.

———. *Faith and Doubt: An Anthology of Poems.* Holt, 2006. ISBN 0-8050-8213-1 and ISBN 9780805082135.

Volavkova, H., ed. *I Never Saw Another Butterfly: Children's Drawings and Poems from Theresienstadt Concentration Camp, 1942–1944.* Schocken, 1994. ISBN 0-8052-1015-6 and ISBN 9780805210156.

Walker, Alice. *There Is a Flower at the Tip of My Nose Smelling Me.* Illus. by Stefano Vitale. HarperCollins, 2006. ISBN 0-06-057080-6 and ISBN 9780060570804.

Watts, Bernadette, selector and illustrator. *Fly Away, Fly Away Over the Sea: And Other Poems for Children by Christina Rossetti.* North-South, 1992. ISBN 1-55858-101-4 and ISBN 9781558581012. Twenty-three short lyrical poems by a poet who understood early childhood.

Westcott, Nadine Bernard. *Never Take a Pig to Lunch.* Orchard, 1994. ISBN 0-5310-8684-4 and ISBN 9780531086841.

Whipple, Laura, compiler. *Eric Carle's Animals, Animals.* Illus. by Eric Carle. Philomel, 1989. ISBN 0-399-21744-4 and ISBN 9780399217449. A wide range of poetry about the animal kingdom, selected from sources as diverse as the Bible, Shakespeare, Japanese haiku, Lewis Carroll, Ogden Nash, and Pawnee Indian. Illustrated with brilliantly colored tissue paper collages.

———. *Eric Carle's Dragons Dragons and Other Creatures That Never Were.* Illus. by Eric Carle. Philomel, 1991. ISBN 0-399-22105-0 and ISBN 9780399221057. A companion volume with poems about dragons and other mythological creatures.

———. *A Snowflake Fell: Poems About Winter.* Illus. by Hatsuki Hori. Barefoot, 2003. ISBN 1-84148-033-9 and ISBN 9781841480336.

Wilner, Isabel. *The Poetry Troupe: An Anthology of Poems to Read Aloud.* Simon & Schuster, 1977. ISBN 0-684-15198-7 and ISBN 9780684151984.

Wong, Janet S. *The Rainbow Hand: Poems About Mothers and Children.* BookSurge, 2008. ISBN 1-4392-0700-3 and ISBN 9781439207000.

Worth, Valerie. *All the Small Poems and Fourteen More.* Illus. by Natalie Babbitt. Farrar, Straus and Giroux, 1996. ISBN 0-3744-0345-7 and ISBN 9780374403454.

———. *At Christmastime.* Illus. by Antonio Frasconi. HarperCollins, 1992. ISBN 0-06-205019-2 and ISBN 9780062050199. A lovely collection for younger children.

Yolen, Jane, selector. *Mother Earth, Father Sky: Poems of Our Planet.* Illus. by Jennifer Hewitson. Boyds Mills, 1995. ISBN 1-56397-414-2 and ISBN 9781563974144. This handsome anthology reminds us of our responsibilities as caretakers of planet Earth.

Zemach, Margot, comp. *Some from the Moon, Some from the Sun: Poems and Songs for Everyone!* Farrar, Straus and Giroux, 2001. ISBN 0-374-39960-3 and ISBN 9780374399603. Twenty-seven traditional rhymes illustrated in glorious watercolors. Includes a mini-autobiography with sketches, writings, and photos of this gifted artist who died in 1989.

STORIES OF SPECIAL APPEAL

STORIES FOR THREE- TO FIVE-YEAR-OLDS

"The Acorn Tree." In *The Acorn Tree and Other Folktales* by Anne Rockwell. Greenwillow, 1995. ISBN 0-688-10746-X and ISBN 9780688107468.

"The Bed." In *The Tiger and the Rabbit and Other Tales* by Pura Belpré. Lippincott, 1965. ISBN 0-3973-1591-0 and ISBN 9780397315918.

The Big Wide-Mouthed Frog: A Traditional Tale. Written and illus. by Ana Martín Larrañaga. Candlewick, 1999. ISBN 0-7636-0808-4 and ISBN 9780763608088.

Book! Book! Book! by Deborah Bruss. Illus. by Tiphanie Beeke. Scholastic, 2001. ISBN 0-439-13525-7 and ISBN 9780439135252.

"The Cat and the Parrot." In *How to Tell Stories to Children* by Sara Cone Bryant. Omnigraphics, 1979. ISBN 1-55888-994-9 and ISBN 9781558889941.

Circle Dogs by Kevin Henkes. Illus. by Dan Yaccarino. HarperCollins, 2001. ISBN 0-0644-3757-4 and ISBN 9780064437578.

The Cow Who Clucked, written and illus. by Denise Fleming. Holt, 2006. ISBN 0-8050-7265-9 and ISBN 9780805072655.

Cows in the Kitchen by June Crebbin. Illus. by Katharine McEwen. Houghton Mifflin, 2005. ISBN 0-6180-3649-0 and ISBN 9780618036493.

"The Elegant Rooster" retold by Judy Sierra and Robert Kaminski. In *MultiCultural Folktales: Stories to Tell Young Children.* Oryx, 1991. ISBN 0-8977-4688-0 and ISBN 9780897746885.

The Elves and the Shoemaker by Jacob Grimm and Wilhelm Grimm. Retold by Bernadette Watts. North-South, 1986. ISBN 1-55858-035-2 and ISBN 9781558580350.

The Enormous Potato retold by Aubrey Davis. Illus. by Dušan Petričić. Kids Can, 1999. ISBN 1-5507-4669-3 and ISBN 9781550746693.

The Fierce Yellow Pumpkin by Margaret Wise Brown. Illus. by Richard Egielski. HarperCollins, 2006. ISBN 0-0644-3534-5 and ISBN 9780064435345.

The Gigantic Turnip by Aleksei Tolstoy. Illus. by Niamh Sharkey. Barefoot, 2009. ISBN 1-8468-6298-1 and ISBN 9781846862984.

The Gingerbread Boy retold by Richard Egielski. HarperCollins, 2000. ISBN 0-0644-3708-6 and ISBN 9780064437080.

The Gingerbread Girl. Told and illus. by Lisa Campbell Ernst. Dutton, 2006. ISBN 0-5254-7667-9 and ISBN 9780525476672.

"The Gingerbread Man" retold by Judy Sierra. In *Nursery Tales from Around the World.* Clarion, 1996. ISBN 0-395-67894-3 and ISBN 9780395678947 (see p. 279).

The Gunniwolf retold by Wilhelmina Harper. Dutton, 1970. ISBN 0-525-31139-4 and ISBN 9780525311393. Also in *Nursery Tales Around the World*, selected and retold by Judy Sierra. Clarion, 1996. ISBN 0-395-67894-3 and ISBN 9780395678947.

Henny-Penny retold by Jane Wattenberg. Scholastic, 2000. ISBN 0-4390-7817-2 and ISBN 9780439078177.

Jack and the Beanstalk retold by Richard Walker. Illus. by Niamh Sharkey. Barefoot, 1999. ISBN 1-9022-8313-9 and ISBN 9781902283135.

"La Hormiguita" retold by Judy Sierra and Robert Kaminski. In *MultiCultural Folktales: Stories to Tell Young Children*. Oryx Press, 1991. ISBN 0-8977-4688-0 and ISBN 9780897746885.

"The Little Boy Who Turned Himself into a Peanut." In *Ten Small Tales by Celia Lottridge*. Simon & Schuster, 1994. ISBN 0-689-50568-X and ISBN 9780689505683. Also in *Nursery Tales Around the World*, retold by Judy Sierra under the title "The Boy Who Tried to Fool His Father." Clarion, 1996. ISBN 0-395-67894-3 and ISBN 9780395678947.

The Little Old Lady Who Was Not Afraid of Anything by Linda Williams. HarperCollins, 1986. ISBN 0-690-04584-0 and ISBN 9780690045840.

The Little Red Hen retold and illus. by Jerry Pinkney. Dial, 2006. ISBN 0-8037-2935-9 and ISBN 9780803729353.

Lizard's Song by George Shannon. Illus. by Jose Aruego and Ariane Dewey. Greenwillow, 1981. ISBN 0-688-80310-5 and ISBN 9780688803100.

"The Magic Pot." In *Diane Goode's Book of Silly Stories and Songs*. Dutton, 1992. ISBN 0-5254-4967-1 and ISBN 9780525449676.

Millions of Cats by Wanda Gág. Putnam, 1977. ISBN 0-698-20091-8 and ISBN 9780698200913.

The Mitten: A Ukrainian Folktale adapted and illus. by Jan Brett. 20th Anniversary Edition. Putnam, 2009. ISBN 0-399-25296-7 and ISBN 9780399252969.

Mockingbird retold by Allan Ahlberg. Illus. by Paul Howard. Walker, 1999. ISBN 0-7636-0439-9 and ISBN 9780763604394.

"More, More, More," Said the Baby: Three Love Stories by Vera B. Williams. Greenwillow, 1990. ISBN 0-688-09173-3 and ISBN 9780688091736.

Muncha! Muncha! Muncha! by Candace Fleming. Schwartz/Atheneum, 2002. ISBN 1-4169-0968-0 and ISBN 9781416909682.

No Dinner! The Old Lady and the Pumpkins by Jessica Souhami. Frances Lincoln Publishers, 2000. ISBN 0-7112-1459-X and ISBN 9780711214590.

The Old Woman and Her Pig: An Old English Tale by Rosanne Litzinger. Harcourt, 1993. ISBN 0-15-257802-1 and ISBN 9780152578022.

The Owl and the Pussycat by Edward Lear. Illus. by Jan Brett. Putnam, 1991. ISBN 0-399-21925-0 and ISBN 9780399219252.

Owl Moon by Jane Yolen. Illus. by John Schoenherr. Twentieth Anniversary Edition. Philomel, 2007. ISBN 0-399-24799-8 and ISBN 9780399247996.

"Pickin' Peas: A Folktale from Alabama" retold by Margaret Read MacDonald. In *Shake-It-Up Tales! Stories to Sing, Dance, Drum, and Act Out*. August House, 2000. ISBN 0-87483-570-4 and ISBN 9780874835700.

"Pooh Goes Visiting and Gets into a Tight Place." In *The Complete Tales of Winnie-the-Pooh* by A. A. Milne. Illus. by Ernest H. Shepard. Dutton, 1994. ISBN 0-525-45723-2 and ISBN 9780525457237.

"Rabbit's Snow Dance." In *The Boy Who Lived with the Bears and Other Iroquois Stories* by Joseph Bruchac. HarperCollins, 1995. ISBN 0-06-021288-8 and ISBN 9780060212889.

"The Rooster and the Mouse" retold by Judy Sierra. In *Nursery Tales Around the World*. Clarion, 1996. ISBN 0-395-67894-3 and ISBN 9780395678947.

The Singing Chick by Victoria Stenmark. Illus. by Randy Cecil. Holt, 1999. ISBN 0-439-11354-7 and ISBN 9780439113540.

"Sody Saleratus" retold by Barbara Baumgartner. In *Crocodile! Crocodile! Stories Told Around the World*. Illus. by Judith Moffatt. Dorling Kindersley, 1994. ISBN 1-56458-463-1 and ISBN 9781564584632. Also in *Nursery Tales Around the World*, retold by Judy Sierra. Clarion, 1996. ISBN 0-395-67894-3 and ISBN 9780395678947.

"Star Money." In *The Three Bears and 15 Other Stories* by Anne Rockwell. HarperCollins, 1975. ISBN 0-690-00598-9 and ISBN 9780690005981.

"The Story of the Three Little Pigs." In *English Fairy Tales* by Joseph Jacobs. CreateSpace, 2008. ISBN 1-4404-1845-4 and ISBN 9781440418457.

"The Sweet Porridge." In *More Tales from Grimm* by Wanda Gág. University of Minnesota, 2006. ISBN 0-8166-4938-3 and ISBN 9780816649389.

The Tale of Peter Rabbit by Beatrix Potter. Penguin, 2002. ISBN 0-7232-4770-6 and ISBN 9780723247708. Also in *The Complete Tales* by Beatrix Potter. Penguin, 2006. The 23 original Peter Rabbit books. ISBN 0-7232-5804-X and ISBN 9780723258049.

The Talking Vegetables retold by Won-Ldy Paye and Margaret H. Lippert. Illus. by Julie Paschkis. Holt, 2006. ISBN 0-8050-7742-1 and ISBN 9780805077421.

The Three Bears and Goldilocks retold by Margaret Willey. Illus. by Heather M. Solomon. Atheneum, 2008. ISBN 1-4169-2494-9 and ISBN 9781416924944.

The Three Billy Goats Gruff by Peter C. Asbjørnsen and Jørgen E. Moe. Illus. by Marcia Brown. Harcourt, 1991. ISBN 0-15-690150-1 and ISBN 9780156901505.

The Three Silly Girls Grubb by John Hassett. Sandpiper, 2006. ISBN 0-6186-9334-3 and ISBN 9780618693344.

"The Turnip." In *The Helen Oxenbury Nursery Story Book* by Helen Oxenbury. Harcourt, 1993. ISBN 0-517-13398-9 and ISBN 9780517133989.

What James Likes Best by Amy Schwarz. Atheneum, 2003. ISBN 0-689-84059-4 and ISBN 9780689840593. Four short stories, filled with the kind of details young children love, invite the listener to guess what James likes best about each of his favorite adventures.

Why Mosquitoes Buzz in People's Ears retold by Verna Aardema. Dial Books, 1975. ISBN 0-8810-3079-1 and ISBN 9780881030792.

Why the Sun and Moon Live in the Sky retold by Elphinstone Dayrell. Illus. by Blair Lent. Houghton Mifflin, 1990. ISBN 0-395-53963-3 and ISBN 9780395539637.

Wilfrid Gordon McDonald Partridge by Mem Fox. Illus. by Julie Vivas. Kane/Miller, 1985. ISBN 0-916291-04-9 and ISBN 9780916291044.

STORIES FOR FIVE- TO EIGHT-YEAR-OLDS

"Alligator's Sunday Suit" retold by Priscilla Jacquith. In *Bo Rabbit Smart for True: Folktales from the Gullah*. Putnam, 1994. ISBN 0-399-22668-0 and ISBN 9780399226687.

"Baba Yaga and the Little Girl with the Kind Heart." In *Old Peter's Russian Tales* by Arthur Ransome. Viking, 1975. ISBN 0-14-030696-X and ISBN 9780140306965.

Baby Rattlesnake told by Te Ata. Adapted by Lynn Moroney, illus. by Mira Reisberg. Children's Book Press, 2003. ISBN 0-8923-9111-1 and ISBN 9780892391110.

"Better Wait Till Martin Comes" by Virginia Hamilton. In *The People Could Fly: American Black Folktales*. Knopf, 1985. ISBN 0-3948-6925-7 and ISBN 9780394869254.

Borreguita and the Coyote: A Tale from Ayutla, Mexico retold by Verna Aardema. Illus. by Petra Mathers. Knopf, 1991. ISBN 0-679-80921-X and ISBN 9780679809210.

The Bossy Gallito/El Gallo de Bodas: A Traditional Cuban Folktale retold by Lucía M. González. Illus. by Lulu Delacre. Scholastic, 1994. ISBN 0-590-46843-X and ISBN 9780590468435.

"The Boy and the North Wind" retold by Lise Lunge-Larsen. In *The Troll with No Heart in His Body and Other Tales of Trolls, from Norway.* Illus. by Betsy Bowen. Houghton Mifflin, 1999. ISBN 0-3959-1371-3 and ISBN 9780395913710.

"The Bremen Town Musicians" by Jacob Grimm and Wilhelm Grimm. Adapted by Doris Orgel. In *The Bremen Town Musicians and Other Animal Tales from Grimm.* Illus. by Bert Kitchen. Roaring Brook, 2004. ISBN 1-5964-3010-9 and ISBN 9781596430105.

The Day It Snowed Tortillas/El día que nevaron tortillas retold by Joe Hayes. Cinco Puntos Press, 2003. ISBN 0-9383-1776-8 and ISBN 9780938317760.

"'Dear Deer!' Said the Turtle" retold by Isabel F. Campoy and Alma Flor Ada. In *Tales Our Abuelitas Told: A Hispanic Folktale Collection.* Atheneum, 2006. ISBN 0-6898-2583-8 and ISBN 9780689825835.

Dick Whittington and His Cat retold by Margaret Hodges. Illus. by Mélsande Potter. Holiday House, 2006. ISBN 0-8234-1987-8 and ISBN 9780823419876.

The Eye of the Needle: Based on a Yupik Tale Told by Betty Hoffman retold and illus. by Teri Sloat. Dutton, 1990. ISBN 0-525-44623-0 and ISBN 9780525446231.

"The Frog Prince." In *Tales from Grimm* by Wanda Gág. University of Minnesota, 2006. ISBN 0-8166-4936-7 and ISBN 9780816649365.

The Frog Prince, Continued by Jon Scieszka. Illus. by Steve Johnson. Viking, 1991. ISBN 0-6708-3421-1 and ISBN 9780670834211.

The Hatseller and the Monkeys retold and illus. by Baba Wagué Diakité. Scholastic, 1999. ISBN 0-5909-6071-7 and ISBN 9780590960717.

How Chipmunk Got His Stripes: A Tale of Bragging and Teasing retold by Joseph Bruchac and James Bruchac. Pictures by Jose Aruego and Ariane Dewey. Dial, 2001. ISBN 0-6062-7431-6 and ISBN 9780606274319.

The Huckabuck Family and How They Raised Popcorn in Nebraska and Quit and Came Back by Carl Sandburg. Illus. by David Small. Farrar, Straus and Giroux, 1999. ISBN 0-3743-3511-7 and ISBN 9780374335113.

"I'm Tipingee, She's Tipingee, We're Tipingee, Too." In *The Magic Orange Tree and Other Haitian Folktales* by Diane Wolkstein. Schocken, 1987. ISBN 0-8052-0650-7 and ISBN 9780805206500.

"The Impudent Little Bird." In *The Singing Tortoise and Other Animal Folktales* by John Yeoman. Morrow, 1994. ISBN 0-688-13366-5 and ISBN 9780688133665.

Jabuti: The Tortoise, A Trickster Tale from the Amazon retold and illus. by Gerald McDermott. Harcourt, 2001. ISBN 0-1520-5374-3 and ISBN 9780152053741.

Jack and the Beanstalk retold by Richard Walker. Illus. by Niamh Sharkey. Barefoot, 2006. ISBN 1-9012-2337-X and ISBN 9781901223378.

"Jack and the Robbers" retold by Margaret Read MacDonald. In *Twenty Tellable Tales: Audience Participation Folktales for the Beginning Storyteller.* Illus. by Roxanne Murphy. ALA, 2004. ISBN 0-8389-0893-4 and ISBN 9780838908938.

"Jack and the Two-Bullet Hunt." In *From Sea to Shining Sea: a Treasury of American Folklore and Folk Songs* by Amy L. Cohn and Suzy Schmidt. Illus. by Molly Bang. Scholastic, 1993. ISBN 0-5904-2868-3 and ISBN 9780590428682 (see p. 303).

Kiss the Cow by Phyllis Root. Illus. by Will Hillenbrand. Candlewick, 2000. ISBN 0-7636-0298-1 and ISBN 9780763602987.

"Koala." In *Magical Tales from Many Lands* by Margaret Mayo. Dutton, 1993. ISBN 0-525-45017-3 and ISBN 9780525450177.

"Leelee Goro." In *Misoso: Once Upon a Time Tales from Africa* retold by Verna Aardema. Knopf, 1994. ISBN 0-679-83430-3 and ISBN 9780679834304.

"The Little Half-Chick." In *Señor Cat's Romance and Other Favorite Stories from Latin America* retold by Lucía M. González. Scholastic, 1997. Also in *Storytelling: Art and Technique,* 3rd ed., by Ellin Greene. Bowker, 1996. ISBN 0-8352-3458-4 and ISBN 9780835234580.

"The Little Rooster and the Turkish Sultan." In *The Good Master* by Kate Seredy. Puffin, 1986. ISBN 0-14-030133-X and ISBN 9780140301335. See also Eric Kimmel's retelling, *The Valiant Red Rooster: A Story from Hungary.* Illus. by Katya Arnold. Holt, 1995. ISBN 0-8050-2781-5 and ISBN 9780805027815.

Little Sister and the Month Brothers by Beatrice Schenk de Regniers. Illus. by Margot Tomes. Morrow, 1994. ISBN 0-688-05293-2 and ISBN 9780688052935.

"Little Snot Nose Boy" retold by Margaret Read MacDonald. In *Celebrate the World: Twenty Tellable Folktales for Multicultural Festivals.* H. W. Wilson, 1994. ISBN 0-8242-0862-5 and ISBN 9780824208622.

"The Magic Orange Tree." In *The Magic Orange Tree and Other Haitian Folktales* by Diane Wolkstein. Schocken, 1997. ISBN 0-8052-1077-6 and ISBN 9780805210774.

Martina the Beautiful Cockroach: A Cuban Folktale retold by Carmen Agra Deedy. Illus. by Michael Austin. Peachtree, 2007. ISBN 1-5614-5468-0 and ISBN 9781561454686.

"The Mischievous Girl and the Hideous Creature" by Beth Horner. In *Ready-to-Tell Tales: Sure-Fire Stories from America's Favorite Storytellers.* David Holt and Bill Mooney, eds. August House, 1994. ISBN 0-87483-381-7 and ISBN 9780874833812.

"Molly Whuppie." In *English Fairy Tales* by Joseph Jacobs. CreateSpace, 2008. ISBN 1-4404-1845-4 and ISBN 9781440418457.

"Mr. Miacca." In *English Fairy Tales* by Joseph Jacobs. CreateSpace, 2008. ISBN 1-4404-1845-4 and ISBN 9781440418457.

"Nana Miriam" retold by Jane Yolen. In *Not One Damsel in Distress.* Silver Whistle, 2000. ISBN 0-1520-2047-0 and ISBN 9780152020477.

"The Nungwama" retold by Judy Sierra. In *Twice Upon a Time: Stories to Tell, Retell, Act Out and Write About.* H. W. Wilson, 1989. ISBN 0-8242-0775-0 and ISBN 9780824207755.

"One-Eye, Two-Eyes, and Three-Eyes." In *The Complete Grimm's Fairy Tales* by Jacob Grimm and Wilhelm Grimm. Pantheon, 1976. ISBN 0-394-49415-6 and ISBN 9780394494159.

"Punia and the King of the Sharks" retold by Margret Read MacDonald. In *Twenty Tellable Tales: Audience Participation Folktales for the Beginning Storyteller.* Illus. by Roxanne Murphy. ALA, 2004. ISBN 0-8389-0893-4 and ISBN 9780838908938.

"Puss in Boots" retold and illus. by Anne Rockwell. In *Puss in Boots and Other Stories.* Simon & Schuster, 1988. ISBN 0-02-777781-2 and ISBN 9780027777819.

"The Roof of Leaves" retold by Donna L. Washington. In *A Pride of African Tales.* Illus. by James Ransome. HarperCollins, 2004. ISBN 0-0602-4932-3 and ISBN 9780060249328.

Saint Francis and the Wolf written and illus. by Richard Egielski. Laura Geringer Books, 2005. ISBN 0-0662-3870-6 and ISBN 9780066238708.

Snow-White and the Seven Dwarfs: A Tale from the Brothers Grimm. Translated by Randall Jarrell. Farrar, Straus and Giroux, 1972. ISBN 0-374-37099-0 and ISBN 9780374370992.

"The Steadfast Tin Soldier." In *Twelve Tales: Hans Christian Andersen.* Selected, translated, and illus. by Erik Blegvad. Simon & Schuster, 1994. ISBN 0-689-50584-1 and ISBN 9780689505843. Also available in various picture-book editions.

"The Sun Catcher" by Pleasant DeSpain. In *Eleven Nature Tales: A Multicultural Journey.* August House, 1996. ISBN 0-8748-3458-9 and ISBN 9780874834581.

The Teeny Tiny Woman retold and illus. by Paul Galdone. Clarion/Ticknor & Fields, 1984. ISBN 0-8991-9463-X and ISBN 9780899194639.

"The Three Little Pigs." In *The Golden Goose Book* by L. Leslie Brooke. Houghton Mifflin, 1992. ISBN 0-395-61303-5 and ISBN 9780395613030.

"Unanana and the Enormous One-Tusked Elephant." In *Magical Tales from Many Lands* by Margaret Mayo. Dutton, 1993. ISBN 0-525-45017-3 and ISBN 9780525450177.

The Wedding Procession of the Rag Doll and the Broom Handle and Who Was in It by Carl Sandburg. Harcourt, 1978. ISBN 0-15-695487-7 and ISBN 9780156954877.

What's in Fox's Sack? retold by Paul Galdone. Houghton Mifflin, 1982. ISBN 0-89919-062-6 and ISBN 9780899190624.

Whuppity Stoorie retold by John Stewig. Holiday House, 2004. ISBN 0-8234-1749-2 and ISBN 9780823417490.

Why the Sun and the Moon Live in the Sky retold by Niki Daly. Lothrop, Lee, & Shepard, 1995. ISBN 0-6881-3331-2 and ISBN 9780688133313.

"Why the Waves Have Whitecaps." In *The Knee-High Man and Other Tales* by Julius Lester. Dial, 1985. ISBN 0-8037-4593-1 and ISBN 9780803745933.

"Wiley, His Mama, and the Hairy Man." In *The People Could Fly: American Black Folktales* by Virginia Hamilton. Knopf, 1985. ISBN 0-394-86925-7 and ISBN 9780394869254.

STORIES FOR EIGHT- TO ELEVEN-YEAR-OLDS

"Anansi's Hat-Shaking Dance." In *The Hat-Shaking Dance and Other Ashanti Tales from Ghana* by Harold Courlander and Albert K. Prempeh. Harcourt, 1957. ISBN 0-15233615-X and ISBN 9780152336158.

"The Baker's Daughter." In *A Street of Little Shops* by Margery Bianco. Gregg, 1981. ISBN 0-83982725-3 and ISBN 9780839827252.

"Bedtime Snacks." In *The Rainbow People* by Laurence Yep. HarperCollins, 1989. ISBN 0-06-026760-7 and ISBN 9780060267605.

"The Best and Worst in All the World" by Hugh Lupton. In *Riddle Me This! Riddles and Stories to Challenge Your Mind.* Illus. by Sophie Fatus. Barefoot, 2007. ISBN 1-9052-3692-1 and ISBN 9781905236923.

The Boy Who Drew Cats: A Japanese Folktale by Arthur A. Levine. Illus. by Frédéric Clément. Dial, 1994. ISBN 0-8037-1172-7 and ISBN 9780803711723.

"Chenoo" retold by Joseph Bruchac and James Bruchac. In *When the Chenoo Howls: Native American Tales of Terror.* Illus. by William Sauts Bock. Walker, 1998. ISBN 0-8027-7576-4 and ISBN 9780802775764.

Clever Tom and the Leprechaun by Linda Shute. Lothrop, 1988. ISBN 0-688-07488-X and ISBN 9780688074883.

Cold Feet retold by Cynthia DeFelice. Illus. by Robert Andrew Parker. Dorling Kindersley, 2000. ISBN 0-7894-2636-6 and ISBN 9780789426369. See also Billy Teare's version, "The Piper's Revenge," in *More Ready-To-Tell Tales from Around the World*. David Holt, ed. August House, 2000. ISBN 0-8748-3583-6 and ISBN 9780874835830.

"The Dripping Cutlass" retold by Arielle North Olson. In *Ask the Bones: Scary Stories from Around the World*. Puffin, 2002. ISBN 0-14-230140-X and ISBN 9780142301401.

Feathers, a Jewish Tale from Eastern Europe retold by Heather Forest. Illus. by Marcia Cutchin. August House, 2005. ISBN 0-87483-755-3 and ISBN 9780874837551.

Finn MacCoul and His Fearless Wife: A Giant of a Tale from Ireland retold and illus. by Robert Byrd. Dutton, 1999. ISBN 0-5254-5971-5 and ISBN 9780525459712.

"The First Story" retold by Dan Keding. In *Stories of Hope and Spirit: Folktales from Eastern Europe*. August House, 2004. ISBN 0-8748-3727-8 and ISBN 9780874837278.

"The Goat Well." In *The Fire on the Mountain and Other Stories from Ethiopia and Eritrea* by Harold Courlander and Wolf Leslau. Holt, 1995. ISBN 0-8050-3652-0 and ISBN 9780805036527.

"The Graveyard Voice." In *The Ghost and I: Scary Stories for Participatory Telling.* Jennifer Justice, ed. Yellow Moon Press, 1992. ISBN 0-938756-37-0 and ISBN 9780938756378.

"Hafiz, the Stone-Cutter." In *The Art of the Story-teller* by Marie Shedlock. Dover, 1951. ISBN 0-486-20635-1 and ISBN 9780486206356. See also *The Stone Cutter: A Japanese Folk Tale* by Gerald McDermott. Viking, 1975. ISBN 0-67067074-X and ISBN 9780670670741.

"He Lion, Bruh Bear, and Bruh Rabbit." In *The People Could Fly: American Black Folktales* by Virginia Hamilton. Knopf, 1985. ISBN 0-394-86925-7 and ISBN 9780394869254.

"How Boots Befooled the King." In *The Wonder Clock* by Howard Pyle. Starscape, 2003. ISBN 0-7653-4266-9 and ISBN 9780765342669.

"How to Break a Bad Habit" retold by Margaret Read MacDonald. In *Twenty Tellable Tales: Audience Participation Folktales for the Beginning Storyteller*. Illus. by Roxanne Murphy. ALA, 2004. ISBN 0-8389-0893-4 and ISBN 9780838908938.

"The Hungry Old Witch." In *Tales from Silver Lands* by Charles J. Finger. Scholastic, 1989. ISBN 0-590-42447-5 and ISBN 9780590424479.

Kate Culhane: A Ghost Story retold and illus. by Michael Hague. Chronicle, 2001. ISBN 1-5871-7059-0 and ISBN 9781587170591. See also "Mary Culhane and the Dead Man" in *The Goblins Giggle and Other Stories* selected by Molly Bang. Peter Smith, 1988. ISBN 0-8446-6360-3 and ISBN 9780844663609.

"King Arthur and His Sword." In *The Story of King Arthur and His Knights* by Howard Pyle. Signet Classics, 2006. ISBN 0-4515-3024-1 and ISBN 9780451530240.

"The Legend of the Bodhran." In *Patakin: World Tales of Drums and Drummers* by Nina Jaffe. Holt, 1994. ISBN 0-8050-3005-0 and ISBN 9780805030051.

Ling-Li and the Phoenix Fairy: A Chinese Folktale retold by Ellin Greene. Clarion, 1996. ISBN 0-3957-1528-8 and ISBN 9780395715284 (see p. 314).

Lucy Dove by Janice M. Del Negro. Illus. by Leonid Gore. DK Ink, 1999. ISBN 0-7894-8084-0 and ISBN 9780789480842.

"The Magic Ball." In *Tales from Silver Lands* by Charles J. Finger. Scholastic, 1989. ISBN 0-590-42447-5 and ISBN 9780590424479.

"The Magic Pomegranate." In *Jewish Stories One Generation Tells Another* retold by Peninnah Schram. Aronson, 1993. ISBN 0-87668-967-5 and ISBN 9780876689677.

The Magic Tree: A Tale from the Congo retold and illus. by Gerald McDermott. Holt, 1994. ISBN 0-8050-3080-8 and ISBN 9780805030808.

"Mary Culhane and the Dead Man." In *The Goblins Giggle and Other Stories* selected by Molly Bang. Peter Smith, 1988. ISBN 0-8446-6360-3 and ISBN 9780844663609.

"The Mischievous Girl and the Hideous Creature." In *Ready-to-Tell Tales.* David Holt and Bill Mooney, eds. August House, 1994. ISBN 0-8748-3381-7 and ISBN 9780874833812.

"Mouse Woman and Porcupine Hunter." In *Mouse Woman and Mischief-Makers* by Christie Harris. Atheneum, 1977. ISBN 0-689-30554-0 and ISBN 9780689305542. Raincoast Books, 2005 (paperback). ISBN 1-55192-751-9 and ISBN 9781551927510.

"The Nungwama" retold by Judy Sierra and Robert Kaminski. In *Twice Upon a Time: Stories to Tell, Retell, Act Out and Write About.* H. W. Wilson, 1989. ISBN 0-8242-0775-0 and ISBN 9780824207755.

"Paul Bunyan: The Winter of the Blue Snow." In *Paul Bunyan Swings His Axe* by Dell J. McCormick. Caxton, 1936. ISBN 0-87004-093-6 and ISBN 9780870040931.

"The Princess Golden-Hair and the Great Black Raven." In *The Wonder Clock* by Howard Pyle. Starscape, 2003. ISBN 0-7653-4266-9 and ISBN 9780765342669.

"Rabbit and Coyote." In *The Monkey's Haircut and Other Stories Told by the Maya* compiled by John Bierhorst. Illus. by Robert A. Parker. Morrow, 1986. ISBN 0-688-04269-4 and ISBN 9780688042691.

"The Rat-Catcher's Daughter." In *The Rat-Catcher's Daughter: A Collection of Stories* by Laurence Housman, selected and with an Afterword by Ellin Greene. Atheneum, 1974. ISBN 0-689-30420-X and ISBN 9780689304200.

"Robin Hood: The Shooting-Match at Nottingham Town." In *The Merry Adventures of Robin Hood* by Howard Pyle. Book Jungle, 2008. ISBN 1-6059-7793-4 and ISBN 9781605977935.

"The Rooster, the Hand Mill and the Swarm of Hornets." In *The Golden Lynx and Other Tales* selected by Augusta Baker. Lippincott, 1960. ISBN 0-3973-0495-1 and ISBN 9780397304950.

The Rough-Face Girl retold by Rafe Martin. Illus. by David Shannon. Putnam, 1998. ISBN 0-6981-1626-7 and ISBN 9780698116269.

"The Stinky Cheese Man." In *The Stinky Cheese Man and Other Fairly Stupid Tales* by Jon Scieszka. Illus. by Lane Smith. Viking, 1992. ISBN 0-670-84487-X and ISBN 9780670844876.

"The Talking Stone." In *The Hungry Woman: Myths and Legends of the Aztecs.* John Bierhorst, ed. Morrow, 1993. ISBN 0-688-12301-5 and ISBN 9780688123017.

Tatterhood and the Hobgoblins: A Norwegian Folktale retold and illus. by Lauren Mills. Little, Brown, 1993. ISBN 0-316-57406-6 and ISBN 9780316574068.

"Ticky-Picky Boom-Boom." In *Anansi, the Spider Man Jamaican Folktales* retold by Philip M. Sherlock. Illus. by Marcia Brown. Crowell, 1954. ISBN 0-690-08905-8 and ISBN 9780690089059.

"The Tinderbox." In *Twelve Tales: Hans Christian Andersen* selected, translated, and illus. by Erik Blegvad. Simon & Schuster, 1994. ISBN 0-689-50584-1 and ISBN 9780689505843. A picture-book version of *The Tinderbox* is beautifully illustrated by Warwick Hutton. Simon & Schuster, 1988. ISBN 0-689-50458-6 and ISBN 9780689504587.

"Turtle Goes Hunting." In *The Naked Bear: Folktales of the Iroquois.* John Bierhorst, ed. Illus. by Dirk Zimmer. Morrow, 1987. ISBN 0-688-06422-1 and ISBN 9780688064228.

"Two Giants." In *Tales for the Telling: Irish Folk and Fairy Stories* by Edna O'Brien. Illus. by Michael Foreman. Puffin, 1988. ISBN 0-14-032293-0 and ISBN 9780140322934.

Wee Winnie Witch's Skinny: An Original African American Scare Tale by Virginia Hamilton. Engravings by Barry Moser. Blue Sky Press, 2004. ISBN 0-5902-8880-6 and ISBN 9780590288804.

"The Woman Who Flummoxed the Fairies." In *Heather and Broom: Tales of the Scottish Highlands, by Sorche Neodhas.* Holt, 1960. ISBN 0-03-035280-1 and ISBN 9780030352805. See also Ellin Greene's *Clever Cooks: A Concoction of Stories, Charms, Recipes and Riddles.* Illus. by Trina Schart Hyman. Lothrop, Lee & Shepard, 1973. ISBN 0-6885-1519-3 and ISBN 9780688515195.

"The Wonderful Brocade." In *The Spring of Butterflies and Other Chinese Folk Tales* by He Liyi. Lothrop, 1985. ISBN 0-0018-4137-8 and ISBN 9780001841376.

Yeh-Shen: A Cinderella Story from China retold by Ai-Ling Louie. Illus. by Ed Young. Putnam, 1990. ISBN 0-399-20900-X and ISBN 9780399209000.

"The Yellow Ribbon" by Maria Leach. In *Juba This and Juba That,* 2nd ed., selected by Virginia A. Tashjian. Little, Brown, 1995. ISBN 0-316-83234-0 and ISBN 9780316832342.

S TORIES FOR E LEVEN- TO F IFTEEN-Y EAR-O LDS

"The Black Prince." In *Ready-To-Tell Tales.* David Holt and Bill Mooney, eds. August House, 1994. ISBN 0-8748-3381-7 and ISBN 9780874833812.

"The Cat Bride." In *Dream Weaver* by Jane Yolen. Collins, 1979. ISBN 0-5290-5517-1 and ISBN 9780529055170.

"Childe Roland." In *English Fairy Tales* by Joseph Jacobs. CreateSpace, 2008. ISBN 1-4404-1845-4 and ISBN 9781440418457.

"The Children of Lir." In *A Storyteller's Choice* by Eileen Colwell. Walck, 1964. See also the picture book *The Children of Lir* by Sheila MacGill-Callahan. Illus. by Gennady Spirin. Dial, 1993. ISBN 0-8037-1121-2 and ISBN 9780803711211.

"Count Alaric's Lady." In *Midsummer Magic* by Ellin Greene. Lothrop, 1977. ISBN 0-688-41800-7 and ISBN 9780688418007. Also in *Storytelling: Art and Technique,* 3rd ed., by Ellin Greene. Bowker, 1996. ISBN 0-8352-3458-4 and ISBN 9780835234580.

"The Cow-Tail Switch." In *The Cow-Tail Switch and Other West African Stories* by Harold Courlander and George Herzog. Holt, 1988. ISBN 0-8050-0288-X and ISBN 9780805002881.

The Crane Wife retold by Odds Bodkin. Illus. by Gennady Spirin. Sandpiper, 2002. ISBN 0-1521-6350-6 and ISBN 9780152163501.

"The Devil and Old John" retold by Jane Yolen. In *Favorite Folktales from around the World.* Pantheon, 1988. ISBN 0-3947-5188-4 and ISBN 9780394751887.

"The 11:59" by Patricia C. McKissack. In *The Dark-Thirty: Southern Tales of the Supernatural.* Illus. by Brian Pinkney. Knopf, 1992. ISBN 0-6798-8335-5 and ISBN 9780679883357.

"Eyes of Jade." In *Tongues of Jade* by Laurence Yep. HarperCollins, 1991. ISBN 0-06-022470-3 and ISBN 9780060224707.

The Fire: An Ethiopian Folk Tale retold by Heinz Janisch. Illus. by Fabricio VandenBroeck. Groundwood, 2002. ISBN 0-8889-9450-8 and ISBN 9780888994509. See also "The Fire on the Mountain" in *The Fire on the Mountain and Other Stories from Ethiopia and Eritrea* retold by Harold Courlander and Wolf Leslau. Holt, 1995. ISBN 0-8050-3652-0 and ISBN 9780805036527 and the picture book *Fire on the Mountain* retold by Jane Kurtz. Illus. by E. B. Lewis. Simon & Schuster, 1994. ISBN 0-671-88268-6 and ISBN 9780671882686.

"The Four Footed Horror" retold by Arielle North Olsen and Howard Schwartz. In *Ask the Bones: Scary Stories from Around the World.* Puffin, 2002. ISBN 0-1423-0140-X and ISBN 9780142301401.

"Fowler's Fowl." In *Grimm's Grimmest* by the Brothers Grimm. Illus. by Tracy Arah Dockray. Chronicle Books, 2005. ISBN 0-8118-5046-3 and ISBN 9780811850469.

"A Friend's Affection." In *The Golden Carp and Other Tales from Vietnam* by Lynette Dyer Vuong. Lothrop, 1993. ISBN 0-688-12514-X and ISBN 9780688125141.

"The Girl Who Cried Flowers." In *The Girl Who Cried Flowers and Other Tales* by Jane Yolen. Crowell, 1974. ISBN 0-6900-0216-5 and ISBN 9780690002164.

"The Girl Who Married the Moon." In *The Girl Who Married the Moon* by Joseph Bruchac and Gayle Ross. BridgeWater, 1994. ISBN 0-8167-3480-1 and ISBN 9780816734801.

"Godfather Death." In *Grimms' Tales for Young and Old: The Complete Stories.* Translated by Ralph Manheim. Anchor, 1983. ISBN 0-3851-8950-8 and ISBN 9780385189507. See also "La Muerta: Godmother Death" in *Ready-to-Tell Tales.* David Holt and Bill Mooney, eds. August House, 1994. ISBN 0-8748-3381-7 and ISBN 9780874833812.

"The Hairy Hands" retold by Robert D. San Souci. In *A Terrifying Taste of Short and Shivery: Thirty Creepy Tales.* Dell, 2004. ISBN 0-4404-1878-X and ISBN 9780440418788.

"Hansel's Eyes" by Garth Nix. In *A Wolf at the Door and Other Retold Fairy Tales.* Ellen Datlow and Terri Windling, eds. Simon & Schuster, 2000. ISBN 0-6898-2139-5 and ISBN 9780689821394.

"Hershel and the Nobelman." In *While Standing on One Foot: Puzzle Stories and Wisdom Tales from the Jewish Tradition* by Nina Jaffe and Steve Zeitlin. Holt, 1993. ISBN 0-8050-2594-4 and ISBN 9780805025941.

"In Bad Taste" by Vivian Vande Velde. In *The Rumpelstiltskin Problem.* Scholastic, 2002. ISBN 0-6180-5523-1 and ISBN 9780618055234.

"Jamie Freel and the Young Lady." In *Fairy Tales of Ireland* by W. B. Yeats. Illus. by P. J. Lynch. Delacorte, 1990. ISBN 0-385-30249-5 and ISBN 9780385302494.

"Keewahkee" retold by Joseph Bruchac and James Bruchac. In *When the Chenoo Howls: Native American Tales of Terror.* Illus. by William Sauts Netamuâxwe Bock. Walker, 1998. ISBN 0-8027-7576-4 and ISBN 9780802775764.

"The King's Child" retold by Judith Black. In *Ready-to-Tell Tales.* David Holt and Bill Mooney, eds. August House, 1994. ISBN 0-87483-380-9 and ISBN 9780874833805.

La Llorona / The Weeping Woman: A Hispanic Legend Told in Spanish and English by Joe Hayes. Cinco Puntos Press, 2004. ISBN 0-9383-1702-4 and ISBN 9780938317029.

"The Lass That Couldn't Be Frightened." In *Heather and Broom: Tales of the Scottish Highlands* by Sorche Nic Leodhas. Holt, 1960. ISBN 0-03-035280-0 and ISBN 9780030352805.

"The Magic Fruit." In *Magical Tales from Many Lands* retold by Margaret Mayo. Dutton, 1993. ISBN 0-525-45017-3 and ISBN 9780525450177.

"The Magic Garden of the Poor." In *Earth Care: World Folktales to Talk About* retold by Margaret Read MacDonald. August House, 2005. ISBN 0-8748-3784-7 and ISBN 9780874837841.

"The Mixed-Up Feet and the Silly Bridegroom." In *Zlateh the Goat and Other Stories* by Isaac Bashevis Singer. Illus. by Maurice Sendak, HarperCollins 2001 ISBN 0-06-028477-3 and ISBN 9780060284770.

"The Nightingale and the Rose." In *The Happy Prince and Other Stories* by Oscar Wilde. Morrow, 1991. ISBN 0-688-10390-1 and ISBN 9780688103903.

"Owl." In *The Magic Orange Tree and Other Haitian Folktales* by Diane Wolkstein. Schocken, 1987. ISBN 0-688-10390-1 and ISBN 9780688103903.

"The Porcelain Man." In *Richard Kennedy: Collected Stories*. HarperCollins, 1987. ISBN 0-06-023255-2 and ISBN 9780060232559.

"A Pretty Girl in the Road" by Vance Randolph. In *Favorite Folktales from around the World*. Jane Yolen, ed. Pantheon, 1986. ISBN 0-394-75188-4 and ISBN 9780394751887.

"The Princess Who Stood on Her Own Two Feet" by Jeanne Desy. In *Don't Bet on the Prince: Contemporary Feminist Fairy Tales in North America and England* by Jack Zipes. Methuen, 1986. ISBN 0-416-01371-6 and ISBN 9780416013719.

"The Promise." In *Here There Be Witches* by Jane Yolen. Harcourt, 1995. ISBN 0-15-200311-8 and ISBN 9780152003111.

"The Ranee and the Cobra." In *The Singing Tortoise and Other Animal Folktales* by John Yeoman. Morrow, 1993. ISBN 0-688-13366-5 and ISBN 9780688133665.

"Raw Head, Devil and the Barefoot Woman" retold by Mary E. Lyons. In *Raw Head, Bloody Bones: African-American Tales of the Supernatural*. Aladdin, 1995. ISBN 0-6898-0306-0 and ISBN 9780689803062.

"Rubies." In *Passion and Poison: Tales of Shape-Shifters, Ghosts, and Spirited Women* by Janice M. Del Negro. Marshall Cavendish, 2007. ISBN 0-7614-5361-X and ISBN 9780761453611 (see p. 318).

The Selkie Girl retold by Susan Cooper. Illus. by Warwick Hutton. Margaret K. McElderry, 1986. ISBN 0-6895-0390-3 and ISBN 9780689503900.

"The Sloogey Dog and the Stolen Aroma: A Fang Tale." In *Misoso: Once Upon a Time Tales from Africa* retold by Verna Aardema. Knopf, 1994. ISBN 0-679-83430-3 and ISBN 9780679834304.

"The Story of Washing Horse Pond." In *The Spring of Butterflies and Other Chinese Folktales* by He Liyi. Lothrop, 1985. ISBN 0-00-184137-8 and ISBN 9780001841376.

"Strength" retold by Margaret Read MacDonald. In *Ready-to-Tell Tales: Sure-Fire Stories from America's Favorite Storytellers*. David Holt and Bill Mooney, eds. August House, 1994. ISBN 0-87483-381-7 and ISBN 9780874833812.

Tam Lin by Jane Yolen. Harcourt, 1990. ISBN 0-15-284261-6 and ISBN 9780152842611.

"The Tell-Tale Heart." In *Edgar Allan Poe: Complete Tales and Poems*. Castle Books, 2003. ISBN 0-87483-380-9 and ISBN 9780874833805.

"Those Three Wishes." In *A Taste of Quiet* by Judith Gorog. Philomel, 1982. ISBN 0-399-20922-0 and ISBN 9780399209222. Carol Birch's retelling can be found in *Ready-to-Tell Tales* edited by David Holt and Bill Mooney. August House, 1994. ISBN 0-87483-380-9 and ISBN 9780874833805.

"Tia Miseri." In *From Sea to Shining Sea: A Treasury of American Folklore and Folk Songs* by Amy L. Cohn and Suzy Schmidt. Scholastic, 1993. ISBN 0-590-42868-3 and ISBN 9780590428682.

Tristan and Iseult by Rosemary Sutcliff. Peter Smith, 1994. ISBN 0-8446-6773-0 and ISBN 9780844667737. Tell as a cycle story, or read aloud a few chapters at a sitting.

"The Vision in the Wood." In *The Golden Thread: Storytelling in Teaching and Learning* by Susan Danoff. Storytelling Arts Press, 2006. ISBN 0-9777-2280-5 and ISBN 9780977722808 (see p. 325).

"When the Girl Rescued Her Brother." In *The Girl Who Married the Moon* by Joseph Bruchac and Gayle Ross. BridgeWater, 1994. ISBN 0-8167-3480-1 and ISBN 9780816734801.

"Wicked John and the Devil." In *Grandfather Tales* by Richard Chase. Houghton Mifflin, 2003. ISBN 0-6183-4691-0 and ISBN 9780618346912.

"The Woodcutter of Gura." In *The Fire on the Mountain and Other Stories from Ethiopia and Eritrea* by Harold Courlander and Wolf Leslau. Holt, 1995. ISBN 0-8050-3652-0 and ISBN 9780805036527.

"The Wooing of the Maze." In *The Rat-Catcher's Daughter: A Collection of Stories* by Laurence Housman, selected by Ellin Greene. Atheneum, 1974. ISBN 0-689-30420-X and ISBN 9780689304200.

STORIES FOR A MIXED-AGE GROUP

"Aladdin." In *Arabian Nights: Three Tales* retold by Deborah Nourse Lattimore. HarperCollins, 1995. ISBN 0-06-024585-9 and ISBN 9780060245856.

Anansi and the Moss-Covered Rock by Eric Kimmel. Illus. by Janet Stevens. Holiday House, 1988. ISBN 0-8234-0689-X and ISBN 9780823406890.

Billy Beg and His Bull: An Irish Tale retold by Ellin Greene. Holiday House, 1994. ISBN 0-8234-1100-1 and ISBN 9780823411009.

"Catalina the Fox" in *Tales Our Abuelitas Told: A Hispanic Folktale Collection*. F. Isabel Campoy and Alma Flor Ada, compilers. Atheneum, 2006. ISBN 0-6898-2583-8 and ISBN 9780689825835.

The Cat's Purr by Ashley Bryan. Simon & Schuster, 1985. ISBN 0-689-31086-2 and ISBN 9780689310867. Also in *Storytelling: Art and Technique*, 3rd ed., by Ellin Greene. Bowker, 1996. ISBN 0-8352-3458-4 and ISBN 9780835234580.

"Coyote, Iktome and the Rock" retold by Judy Sierra. In *Twice Upon a Time: Stories to Tell, Retell, Act Out and Write About*. H. W. Wilson, 1989. ISBN 0-8242-0775-0 and ISBN 9780824207755.

"The Crab and the Jaguar." In *Picture Folk-Tales* by Valery Carrick. Dover, 1992. ISBN 0-486-27083-1 and ISBN 9780486270838. Also in *Storytelling: Art and Technique*, 3rd ed., by Ellin Greene. Bowker, 1996. ISBN 0-8352-3458-4 and ISBN 9780835234580.

"The Elephant's Child." In *Just So Stories* by Rudyard Kipling. Holt, 1987. ISBN 0-8050-0439-4 and ISBN 9780805004397.

"The Freedom Bird." In *Ready-to-Tell Tales: Surefire Stories from America's Favorite Storytellers*. David Holt and Bill Mooney, eds. August House, 1994. ISBN 0-87483-380-9 and ISBN 9780874833805.

Go to Sleep, Gecko! A Balinese Folktale retold by Margaret Read MacDonald. Illus. by Geraldo Valerio. August House, 2006. ISBN 0-8748-3780-4 and ISBN 9780874837803.

Hansel and Gretel retold and illus. by James Marshall. Dial, 1990. ISBN 0-8037-0828-9 and ISBN 9780803708280.

"Hic! Hic! Hic!" retold by Margaret Read MacDonald. In *Twenty Tellable Tales*. H. W. Wilson, 1986. ISBN 0-8242-0719-X and ISBN 9780824207199.

"How Anansi Got a Small Waist" retold by Judy Sierra. In *Twice Upon a Time: Stories to Tell, Retell, Act Out and Write About*. H. W. Wilson, 1989. ISBN 0-8242-0775-0 and ISBN 9780824207755.

"How the Farmer's Wife Took Care of Things," an Icelandic folktale translated and adapted by Mary Buckley. Originally published in *Cricket* magazine. Also in *Storytelling: Art and Technique,* 3rd ed., by Ellin Greene. Bowker, 1996. ISBN 0-8352-3458-4 and ISBN 9780835234580.

"How the Lizard Lost and Regained His Farm." In *The Hat-Shaking Dance and Other Tales from the Gold Coast* by Harold Courlander. Also in *Storytelling: Art and Technique,* 3rd ed., by Ellin Greene. Bowker, 1996. ISBN 0-8352-3458-4 and ISBN 9780835234580.

How the Turtle's Back Was Cracked: A Traditional Cherokee Tale retold by Gayle Ross. Illus. by Murv Jacob. Dial, 1995. ISBN 0-8037-1728-8 and ISBN 9780803717282.

"How to Tell Corn Fairies When You See 'Em." In *Rootabaga Stories* by Carl Sandburg. Harcourt, 1988. ISBN 0-15-269061-1 and ISBN 9780152690618.

"It Could Always Be Worse." In *Favorite Folktales from around the World*. Jane Yolen, ed. Pantheon, 1986. ISBN 0-3947-5188-4 and ISBN 9780394751887.

"Jazzy Three Bears" selected by The Folktellers. In *Storytelling: Art and Technique*, 3rd ed., by Ellin Greene. Bowker, 1996. ISBN 0-8352-3458-4 and ISBN 9780835234580.

John Henry: An American Legend by Ezra Jack Keats. Knopf, 1987. ISBN 0-394-99052-8 and ISBN 9780394990521.

"The Lion and the Rabbit . . . A Fable from India" adapted by Heather Forest. In *Joining In: An Anthology of Audience Participation Stories and How to Tell Them*. Teresa Miller, compiler. Yellow Moon Press, 1988. ISBN 0-938756-21-4 and ISBN 9780938756217.

"The Little Old Woman Who Hated Housework" by Margaret Read MacDonald. In *Shake-It-Up Tales! Stories to Sing, Dance, Drum, and Act Out*. August House, 2000. ISBN 0-8748-3570-4 and ISBN 9780874835700.

"The Little Rooster and the Turkish Sultan." In *The Good Master* by Kate Seredy. Puffin, 1986. ISBN 0-14-030133-X and ISBN 9780140301335.

"The Lord's Daughter and the Blacksmith's Son." In *The Serpent Slayer and Other Stories of Strong Women* retold by Katrin Tchana. Illus. by Trina Schart Hyman. Little, Brown, 2000. ISBN 0-316-38701-0 and ISBN 9780316387019.

The Month Brothers: A Slavic Tale by Samuel Marshak. Translated by Thomas P. Whitney. Illus. by Diane Stanley. Morrow, 1983. ISBN 0-688-01510-7 and ISBN 9780688015107.

"The Mosquito." In *The Story Vine* by Anne Pellowski. Simon & Schuster, 1984. ISBN 0-02-770590-0 and ISBN 9780027705904. (Another fascinating string story in this book is "The Farmer and the Yams.")

"Mr. Sampson Cat." In *Picture Tales from the Russian* by Valery Carrick. Blackwell, 1969. ISBN 0-631-08630-7 and ISBN 9780631086307.

"The Old Woman Who Lost Her Dumpling" from *Japanese Fairy Tale Series No. 24*, rendered into English by Lafcadio Hearn. T. Hasegawa, 1902. See also *Clever Cooks:*

A Concoction of Stories, Charms, Recipes and Riddles compiled by Ellin Greene. Illus. by Trina Schart Hyman. Lothrop, Lee & Shepard, 1973. ISBN 0-6885-1519-3 and ISBN 9780688515195 (see p. 288).

"Peterkin and the Little Grey Hare." In *The Wonder Clock* by Howard Pyle. Dover, 1887. ISBN 0-486-21446-X and ISBN 9780486214467.

"The Pumpkin Child." In *Persian Folk and Fairy Tales* retold by Anne Sinclair Mehdevi. Knopf, 1965. Also in *Storytelling: Art and Technique,* 3rd ed., by Ellin Greene. Bowker, 1996. ISBN 0-8352-3458-4 and ISBN 9780835234580.

"The Race Between Toad and Donkey." In *Favorite Folktales from around the World,* Jane Yolen, ed. Pantheon, 1986. ISBN 0-3947-5188-4 and ISBN 9780394751887.

Rikki-Tikki-Tavi by Rudyard Kipling. Illus. by Lambert Davis. Harcourt, 1992. ISBN 0-15-267015-7 and ISBN 9780152670153.

"The Seventh Princess." In *The Little Bookroom* by Eleanor Farjeon. Illus. by Edward Ardizzone. New York Review of Books Children's Collection, 2003. ISBN 1-5901-7048-2 and ISBN 9781590170489.

"Soap, Soap, Soap." In *Grandfather Tales* by Richard Chase. Houghton Mifflin, 1973. ISBN 0-395-06692-1 and ISBN 9780395066928. Also see Tom Birdseye's retelling, *Soap! Soap! Don't Forget the Soap! An Appalachian Folktale.* Illus. by Andrew Glass. Holiday House, 1993. ISBN 0-8234-1005-6 and ISBN 9780823410057.

"Sody Sallyraytus." In *Grandfather Tales* by Richard Chase. Houghton Mifflin, 1973. ISBN 0-395-06692-1 and ISBN 9780395066928.

Stone Soup by Marcia Brown. Simon & Schuster, 1947. ISBN 0-684-92296-7 and ISBN 9780684922966.

A Story, a Story: An African Tale by Gail Haley. Simon & Schuster, 1970. ISBN 0-689-20511-2 and ISBN 9780689205118.

"The Three Sillies." In *English Fairy Tales* by Joseph Jacobs. CreateSpace, 2008. ISBN 1-4404-1845-4 and ISBN 9781440418457.

"Three Whiskers from a Lion's Chin." In *The Serpent Slayer and Other Stories of Strong Women* adapted by Katrin Tchana. Illus. by Trina Schart Hyman. Little, Brown, 2000. ISBN 0-3163-8701-0 and ISBN 9780316387019.

"Two Giants" retold by Edna O'Brien. In *Tales for the Telling: Irish Folk and Fairy Stories.* Puffin, 1986. ISBN 1-8579-3746-5 and ISBN 9781857937466.

"Wait Till Emmett Comes" retold by James Haskins. In *The Headless Haunt and Other African-American Ghost Stories.* Illus. by Ben Otero. Trophy, 1995. ISBN 0-0644-0602-4 and ISBN 9780064406024.

What a Wonderful World by George David Weiss and Bob Thiele. Simon & Schuster, 1995. ISBN 0-689-80087-8 and ISBN 9780689800870.

"White Wave." In *Homespun.* Jimmy Neil Smith, ed. Crown, 1988. ISBN 0-517-56936-1 and ISBN 9780517569368. Also available as a picture book, *White Wave: A Chinese Tale* retold by Diane Wolkstein. Illus. by Ed Young. Harcourt, 1996. ISBN 0-15-200293-6 and ISBN 9780152002930.

"Why Dogs Hate Cats." In *The Knee-High Man and Other Tales* by Julius Lester. Dial, 1985. ISBN 0-8037-4593-1 and ISBN 9780803745933.

Willa and the Wind by Janice M. Del Negro. Marshall Cavendish, 2005. ISBN 0-7894-2514-9 and ISBN 9780789425140 (see p. 305).

"The Woman Who Flummoxed the Fairies" by Sorche Nic Leodhas. In *Womenfolk and Fairy Tales*. Rosemary Minard, ed. Houghton Mifflin, 1975. ISBN 0-395-20276-0 and ISBN 9780395202760.

"The Young and Dashing Princess." In *More Ready-to-Tell Tales from Around the World*. David Holt and Bill Mooney, eds. August House, 2000. ISBN 0-8748-3583-6 and ISBN 9780874835830.

Stories for the Family Evening Storytelling Program

"Ananse the Spider in Search of a Fool." In *The Ox of the Wonderful Horns and Other African Folktales* retold and illus. by Ashley Bryan. Atheneum, 1971. Also in *Ashley Bryan's African Tales, Uh-Huh* retold and illus. by Ashley Bryan. Atheneum, 1998. ISBN 0-689-82076-3 and ISBN 9780689820762 (see p. 299).

"The Boy Who Lived with the Bears." In *The Boy Who Lived with the Bears and Other Iroquois Stories* by Joseph Bruchac. HarperCollins, 1995. ISBN 0-06-021288-8 and ISBN 9780060212889.

"Buzzard and Wren Have a Race." In *A Ring of Tricksters: Animal Tales from America, the West Indies, and Africa* adapted by Virginia Hamilton. Blue Sky, 1997. ISBN 0-5904-7374-3 and ISBN 9780590473743.

"Cap o' Rushes." In *English Fairy Tales* by Joseph Jacobs. CreateSpace, 2008. ISBN 1-4404-1845-4 and ISBN 9781440418457.

"Clever Mandy" retold by Judy Sierra. In *Silly and Sillier: Read Aloud Tales from Around the World*. Knopf, 2002. ISBN 0-3758-0609-1 and ISBN 9780375806094.

"Clever Manka." In *The Shoemaker's Apron* by Parker Fillmore. Harcourt, 1920. Also in *Storytelling: Art and Technique,* 3rd ed., by Ellin Greene. Bowker, 1996. ISBN 0-8352-3458-4 and ISBN 9780835234580.

"The Clever Monkey." In *Folk Tales and Fables of the World*. Barbara Hayes and Robert Ingpen, compilers. Portland House, 1987. ISBN 1-8695-3667-3 and ISBN 9781869536671.

The Dancing Granny by Ashley Bryan. Simon & Schuster, 1987. ISBN 0-689-71149-2 and ISBN 9780689711497 (see p. 292).

"Don't Blame Me." In *The Wonder Dog: The Collected Children's Stories of Richard Hughes*. Morrow, 1977. ISBN 0-6888-0099-8 and ISBN 9780688800994.

Elsie Piddock Skips in Her Sleep by Eleanor Farjeon. Illus. by Charlotte Voake. Candlewick, 2000. ISBN 0-7637-0790-8 and ISBN 9780763707906.

Flossie and the Fox by Patricia McKissack. Dial, 1986. ISBN 0-8037-0250-7 and ISBN 9780803702509.

"The Forgotten Gifts." In *The Golden Thread: Storytelling in Teaching and Learning* by Susan Danoff. Storytelling Arts Press, 2006. ISBN 0-9777-2280-5 and ISBN 9780977722808.

"Gubrand-on-the-Hillside." In *East o' the Sun and West o' the Moon* by George W. Dasent. Dover, 1970. ISBN 0-486-22521-6 and ISBN 9780486225210.

"A Handful of Mustard Seed." In *Still More Stories to Solve: Fourteen Folktales from Around the World* by George Shannon. Greenwillow, 1994. ISBN 0-688-04619-3 and ISBN 9780688046194. Also in *Storytelling: Art and Technique,* 3rd ed., by Ellin Greene. Bowker, 1996. ISBN 0-8352-3458-4 and ISBN 9780835234580.

"Kaleeba." In *Songs and Stories from Uganda* by W. Moses Serwadda. Illus. by Leo Dillon. World Music Press, 1987. ISBN 0-937203-17-3 and ISBN 9780937203170.

"Krencilpal and Krencilpalka" adapted by Virginia Haviland. In *Favorite Fairy Tales Told in Poland.* HarperCollins, 1995. ISBN 0-6881-2602-2 and ISBN 9780688126025.

"Language of the Birds" adapted by Jane Yolen. In *Mightier Than the Sword: World Folktales for Strong Boys.* Harcourt, 2003. ISBN 0-15-216391-3 and ISBN 9780152163914.

The Legend of the Christmas Rose by Selma Lagerlöf. Retold by Ellin Greene. Holiday House, 1990. ISBN 0-8234-0821-3 and ISBN 9780823408214 (see p. 329).

The Little Juggler by Barbara Cooney. Hastings, 1961. ISBN 0-80384239-2 and ISBN 9780803842397.

"Living in Wales." In *The Wonder Dog: The Collected Children's Stories of Richard Hughes.* Morrow, 1977. ISBN 0-688-80099-8 and ISBN 9780688800994.

"A Lover of Beauty." In *Greek Myths* by Olivia E. Coolidge. Illus. by E. Sandoz. Houghton Mifflin, 1949. ISBN 0-395-06721-9 and ISBN 9780395067215.

"More Than Salt" retold by Patrick Ryan (see p. 310).

"Oranges and Lemons." In *Italian Peepshow* by Eleanor Farjeon. Stokes, 1926.

Ouch! retold by Natalie Babbitt. Illus. by Fred Marcellino. HarperCollins, 1998. ISBN 0-0620-5066-4 and ISBN 9780062050663.

"The Palace on the Rock." In *The Wonder Dog: The Collected Children's Stories of Richard Hughes.* Morrow, 1977. ISBN 0-6888-0099-8 and ISBN 9780688800994.

"Patrick O'Donnell and the Leprechaun" adapted by Kathleen Krull in *A Pot O'Gold: A Treasury of Irish Stories, Poetry, Folklore, and (of Course) Blarney.* Hyperion, 2004. ISBN 1-4231-1752-2 and ISBN 9781423117520.

Perez and Martina by Pura Belpré. Viking, 1991. Reissue (Warne, 1932). ISBN 0-670-84166-8 and ISBN 9780670841660 (see p. 283).

"Perfection." In *The Devil's Storybook* by Natalie Babbitt. Farrar, Straus and Giroux, 1974. ISBN 0-374-31770-4 and ISBN 9780374317706.

"The Pixie at the Grocer's." In *Twelve Tales by Hans Christian Andersen.* Selected, translated, and illus. by Erik Blegvad. Simon & Schuster, 1994. ISBN 0-689-50584-1 and ISBN 9780689505843.

"Prince Rooster." In *While Standing on One Foot: Puzzle Stories and Wisdom Tales from the Jewish Tradition* by Nina Jaffe and Steve Zeitlin. Holt, 1993. ISBN 0-8050-2594-4 and ISBN 9780805025941.

"The Princess on the Pea." In *Fairy Tales of Hans Christian Andersen.* Illus. by Isabelle Brent. Collected and with an introduction by Neil Philip. Viking, 1995. ISBN 0-670-85930-3 and ISBN 9780670859306. Also see the picture book *The Princess and the Pea* illus. by Dorothée Duntze. North-South, 1985. ISBN 0-03-005738-8 and ISBN 9780030057380.

Raspberries by Jay O'Callahan. Illus. by Will Moses. Philomel, 2009. ISBN 0-399-25181-2 and ISBN 9780399251818. The book includes a CD of O'Callahan reading the story.

The Remarkable Christmas of the Cobbler's Sons by Ruth Sawyer. Illus. by Barbara Cooney. Viking, 1994. ISBN 0-670-84922-7 and ISBN 9780670849222. Also in *The Long Christmas* by Ruth Sawyer under the title "Schnitzle, Schnotzle, and Schnootzle." Viking, 1941.

"The Snooks Family" by Harcourt Williams. In *Juba This and Juba That,* 2nd ed., selected by Virginia A. Tashjian. Little, Brown, 1995. ISBN 0-316-83234-0 and ISBN 9780316832342.

"Talk." In *The Cow-Tail Switch and Other West African Stories* by Harold Courlander and George Herzog. Holt, 1988. ISBN 0-8050-0288-X and ISBN 9780805002881.

"Three Strong Women." In *The Woman in the Moon and Other Tales of Forgotten Heroines* by James Riordan. Dial, 1985. ISBN 0-8037-0194-2 and ISBN 9780803701946.

"Two of Everything." In *The Scott, Foresman Anthology of Children's Literature* by Zena Sutherland and Myra Cohn Livingston. Scott, Foresman, 1984. ISBN 0-673-15527-7 and ISBN 9780673155276. *Two of Everything*, a picture book by Lily Toy Hong, is a simpler retelling. Whitman, 1993. ISBN 0-8075-8157-7 and ISBN 9780807581575.

"Uncle Bouqui Rents a Horse." In *Uncle Bouqui of Haiti* by Harold Courlander. Morrow, 1942. Also in *Storytelling: Art and Technique,* 3rd ed., by Ellin Greene. Bowker, 1996. ISBN 0-8352-3458-4 and ISBN 9780835234580.

"The Voyage of the Wee Red Cap." In *The Long Christmas* by Ruth Sawyer. Viking, 1941. Also in *Storytelling: Art and Technique,* 3rd ed., by Ellin Greene. Bowker, 1996. ISBN 0-8352-3458-4 and ISBN 9780835234580.

"What Is Trouble?" In *The Knee-High Man and Other Tales* by Julius Lester. Dial, 1985. ISBN 0-8037-4593-1 and ISBN 9780803745933.

"The White Horse Girl and the Blue Wind Boy." In *Rootabaga Stories* by Carl Sandburg. Sandpiper, 2003 (paperback). ISBN 0-15-204714-X and ISBN 9780152047146 (see p. 322).

Why the Sky Is Far Away: A Folktale from Nigeria retold by Mary-Joan Gerson. Little, Brown, 1992. ISBN 0-316-30852-8 and ISBN 9780316308526.

"The Wise Old Woman." In *The Sea of Gold and Other Tales from Japan* by Yoshiko Uchida. Scribner, 1965. Also in *Storytelling: Art and Technique,* 3rd ed., by Ellin Greene. Bowker, 1996. ISBN 0-8352-3458-4 and ISBN 9780835234580. See also the picture book *The Wise Old Woman* by Yoshiko Uchida. Illus. by Martin Springett. Simon & Schuster, 1994. ISBN 0-689-50582-5 and ISBN 9780689505829.

"The Wooden Bowl" adapted by Domenico Vittorini in *The Thread of Life: Twelve Old Italian Tales.* Crown, 1995. ISBN 0-5175-9594-X and ISBN 9780517595947.

"The Yellow Ribbon" by Maria Leach. In *Juba This and Juba That,* 2nd ed., selected by Virginia A. Tashjian. Little, Brown, 1995. ISBN 0-316-83234-0 and ISBN 9780316832342.

"The Yellow Thunder Dragon." In *Magical Tales from Many Lands* retold by Margaret Mayo. Dutton, 1993. ISBN 0-525-45017-3 and ISBN 9780525450177.

"Young Kate." In *The Little Bookroom* by Eleanor Farjeon. New York Review Books, 2003. ISBN 1-5901-7048-2 and ISBN 9781590170489.

"Zlateh the Goat." In *Zlateh the Goat and Other Stories* by Isaac B. Singer. HarperCollins, 1966. ISBN 0-06-025699-0 and ISBN 9780060256996.

READ-ALOUDS:
100 PERSONAL FAVORITES

Alderson, Brian, reteller. *The Arabian Nights: Or Tales Told by Sheherezade During a Thousand Nights and One Night*. Illus. by Michael Foreman. Morrow, 1995. ISBN 0-688-14219-2 and ISBN 9780688142193.

Alexander, Lloyd. *The High King*. Revised ed. Holt, 1999. ISBN 0-8050-6135-5 and ISBN 9780805061352.

Almond, David. *My Dad's a Birdman*. Illus. by Polly Dunbar. Candlewick, 2007. ISBN 0-7636-3667-3 and ISBN 9780763636678.

Amato, Mary. *The Chicken of the Family*. Putnam, 2008. ISBN 0-3992-4196-5 and ISBN 9780399241963.

Andersen, Hans Christian. *The Snow Queen*. Translated by Naomi Lewis. Christian Birmingham. Candlewick, 2008. ISBN 0-7636-3229-5 and ISBN 9780763632298.

Armstrong, Jennifer. *Shipwreck at the Bottom of the World*. Crown, 2000. ISBN 0-3758-1049-8 and ISBN 9780375810497.

Avi. *Poppy*. HarperCollins, 2005. ISBN 0-3807-2769-2 and ISBN 9780380727698.

Babbitt, Natalie. *Tuck Everlasting*. Square Fish, 2007. ISBN 0-3123-6981-6 and ISBN 9780312369811.

Bang-Campbell, Monika. *Little Rat Makes Music*. Harcourt, 2008. ISBN 0-15-206360-9 and ISBN 9780152063603.

Belton, Sandra. *Ernestine and Amanda*. Aladdin, 1998. ISBN 0-6898-0847-X and ISBN 9780689808470.

Birdsall, Jeanne. *The Penderwicks: A Summer Tale of Four Sisters, Two Rabbits, and a Very Interesting Boy*. Yearling, 2007. ISBN 0-4404-2047-4 and ISBN 9780440420477.

Bond, Michael. *A Bear Called Paddington*. Illus. by Peggy Fortnum. Houghton Mifflin, 1960, 2008. (First in series) ISBN 0-547-13351-0 and ISBN 9780547133515.

Brown, Margaret Wise. *Sneakers: Seven Stories About a Cat*. Illus. by Jean Charlot. HarperCollins, 1985. ISBN 0-201-00625-1 and ISBN 9780201066254.

Bruchac, Joseph. *The Winter People*. Dial, 2002. ISBN 0-8037-2694-5 and ISBN 9780803726949.

Burnett, Frances Hodgson. *The Secret Garden*. Illus. by Graham Rust. Godine, 1987. ISBN 0-87923-649-3 and ISBN 9780879236496.

Byars, Betsy. *Keeper of the Doves*. Viking, 2002. ISBN 0-1424-0063-7 and ISBN 9780142400630.

Carroll, Lewis. *Alice's Adventures in Wonderland*. Illus. by John Tenniel. Morrow, 1992. ISBN 0-688-11087-8 and ISBN 9780688110871. Also see *Alice's Adventures in Wonderland* by Lewis Carroll. Illus. by Arthur Rackham. Seastar, 2002. ISBN 1-58717-152-X and ISBN 9781587171529.

Chaucer, Geoffrey. *Canterbury Tales.* Selected, translated from Middle English, and adapted by Barbara Cohen. Illus. by Trina Schart Hyman. Lothrop, 1988. ISBN 0-688-06201-6 and ISBN 9780688062019.

Cleary, Beverly. *The Mouse and the Motorcycle.* HarperCollins, 1990. ISBN 0-688-21698-6 and ISBN 9780688216986.

Cooper, Susan. *The Boggart.* Aladdin, 2004. ISBN 0-689-86930-4 and ISBN 9780689869303.

Creech, Sharon. *Love that Dog.* Scholastic, 2001. ISBN 0-06-029287-3 and ISBN 9780060292874.

Curtis, Christopher Paul. *Elijah of Buxton.* Scholastic, 2009. ISBN 0-4390-2345-9 and ISBN 9780439023450.

Cushman, Karen. *Catherine, Called Birdy.* Houghton Mifflin, 1994. ISBN 0-395-68186-3 and ISBN 9780395681862.

Dahl, Roald. *The BFG.* Puffin, 2007. ISBN 0-1413-2262-4 and ISBN 9780141322629.

DiCamillo, Kate. *The Tale of Despereaux.* Candlewick, 2006. ISBN 0-7636-2529-9 and ISBN 9780763625290.

Dunrea, Olivier. *Hanne's Quest.* Philomel, 2006. ISBN 0-399-24216-3 and ISBN 9780399242168.

Erdrich, Louise. *The Birchbark House.* Hyperion, 2002. ISBN 0-7868-1454-3 and ISBN 9780786814541.

Farjeon, Eleanor. *Elsie Piddock Skips in Her Sleep.* Illus. by Charlotte Voake. Candlewick, 2000. ISBN 0-7636-0790-8 and ISBN 9780763607906.

Fox, Paula. *The One-Eyed Cat.* Illus. by Irene Trivas. Atheneum, 2002. ISBN 0-689-86193-1 and ISBN 9780689861932.

Gaiman, Neil. *Coraline.* Harper Perennial, 2006. ISBN 0-0611-3937-8 and ISBN 9780061139376.

George, Jean C. *Julie of the Wolves Treasury.* Illus. by John Schoenherr. HarperCollins, 2001. Includes *Julie of the Wolves, Julie,* and *Julie's Wolf Pack.* ISBN 0-06-000239-5 and ISBN 9780060002398.

Gerstein, Mordicai. *Leaving the Nest.* Foster/Farrar, 2007. ISBN 0-3743-4369-1 and ISBN 9780374343699.

Godden, Rumer. *Four Dolls: Impunity Jane, the Fairy Doll, Holly, Candy Floss.* Illus. by Pauline Baynes. Greenwillow, 1984. ISBN 0-688-02801-2 and ISBN 9780688028015.

Goudge, Elizabeth. *Linnets and Valerians.* Puffin, 2001. ISBN 0-1423-0026-8 and ISBN 9780142300268.

Grahame, Kenneth. *The Reluctant Dragon.* Abridged and illus. by Inga Moore. Candlewick, 2004. ISBN 0-7445-8638-0 and ISBN 9780744586381.

Hale, Shannon. *Princess Academy.* Bloomsbury, 2009. ISBN 0-7475-9801-0 and ISBN 9780747598015.

Harley, Bill. *The Amazing Flight of Darius Frobisher.* Peachtree, 2006. ISBN 1-5614-5381-1 and ISBN 9781561453818.

Harrington, Janice N. *Going North.* Illus. by Jerome Lagarrigue. Kroupa/Farrar, 2004. ISBN 0-3743-2681-9 and ISBN 9780374326814.

Hastings, Selina, reteller. *Reynard the Fox.* Illus. by Graham Percy. Morrow, 1991. ISBN 0-688-09949-1 and ISBN 9780688099497.

Hearne, Betsy. *Canine Connection: Stories About Dogs and People.* Simon Pulse, 2007. ISBN 1-4169-6817-2 and ISBN 9781416968177.

Hendry, Frances Mary. *Quest for a Maid.* Farrar, Straus and Giroux, 1992. ISBN 0-3744-6155-4 and ISBN 9780374461553.

Henkes, Kevin. *Words of Stone.* Greenwillow, 1992. ISBN 0-688-11356-7 and ISBN 9780688113568.

Hoban, Russell. *The Mouse and His Child.* Illus. by David Small. Scholastic, 2001. ISBN 0-439-09826-2 and ISBN 9780439098267.

Hodges, Margaret, adapter. *Don Quixote and Sancho Panza* by Miguel de Saavedra Cervantes. Illus. by Stephen Marchesi. Simon & Schuster, 1992. ISBN 0-684-19235-7 and ISBN 9780684192352.

Hoffman, E. T. A. *Nutcracker.* Illus. by Maurice Sendak. Random House, 2003. ISBN 0-517-55285-X and ISBN 9780517552858.

Howe, James. *Bunnicula.* Aladdin, 2006. ISBN 1-4169-2817-0 and ISBN 9781416928171.

Hughes, Shirley. *Stories by Firelight.* Lothrop, 1993. ISBN 0-688-04568-5 and ISBN 9780688045685.

Hunter, Mollie. *The Mermaid Summer.* HarperCollins, 1988. ISBN 0-06-022628-5 and ISBN 9780060226282.

Ibbotson, Eva. *Journey to the River Sea.* Macmillan, 2008. ISBN 0-3303-9715-X and ISBN 9780330397155.

Jarrell, Randall. *The Animal Family.* Illus. by Maurice Sendak. HarperCollins, 1995. ISBN 0-06-205084-2 and ISBN 9780062050847.

Jimenez, Juan Ramon. *Platero y yo/Platero and I.* Selected, translated, and adapted from the Spanish by Myra Cohn Livingston and Joseph F. Dominguez. Illus. by Antonio Frasconi. Houghton Mifflin, 1994. ISBN 0-685-71523-X and ISBN 9780685715239.

Keehn, Sally M. *Magpie Gabbard and the Quest for the Buried Moon.* Philomel, 2007. ISBN 0-3992-4340-2 and ISBN 9780399243400.

Kimmel, Eric A., adapter. *Sword of the Samurai.* HarperCollins, 2000. ISBN 0-0644-2131-7 and ISBN 9780064421317.

King-Smith, Dick. *The Water Horse.* Yearling, 2007. ISBN 0-3758-4231-4 and ISBN 9780375842313.

Kipling, Rudyard. *The Jungle Book.* Illus. by Jerry Pinkney. Morrow, 1995. ISBN 0-688-09979-3 and ISBN 9780688099794.

Konigsburg, E. L. *From the Mixed-Up Files of Mrs. Basil E. Frankweiler.* Simon & Schuster, 1970. ISBN 0-689-20586-4 and ISBN 9780689205866.

Lagerlöf, Selma. *The Legend of the Christmas Rose.* Retold by Ellin Greene. Illus. by Charles Mikolaycak. Holiday House, 1990. ISBN 0-8234-0821-3 and ISBN 9780823408214 (see p. 329).

Lawrence, Iain. *The Wreckers.* Yearling, 1999. ISBN 0-4404-1545-4 and ISBN 9780440415459.

LeGuin, Ursula K. *Catwings.* Illus. by Stephen D. Schindler. Orchard, 1988. (First in series.) ISBN 0-531-08359-4 and ISBN 9780531083598.

L'Engle, Madeleine. *A Wrinkle in Time.* Square Fish, 2007. ISBN 0-3123-6754-6 and ISBN 9780312367541.

Lester, Julius. *What a Truly Cool World.* Scholastic, 1999. ISBN 0-5908-6468-8 and ISBN 9780590864688.

Lewis, C. S. *The Lion, the Witch and the Wardrobe.* Illus. by Pauline Baynes. HarperCollins, 1994. (First in series.) ISBN 0-06-023481-4 and ISBN 9780060234812.

Lowry, Lois. *The Giver.* Houghton Mifflin, 1993. ISBN 0-395-64566-2 and ISBN 9780395645666.

McClements, George. *Night of the Veggie Monster.* Bloomsbury, 2008. ISBN 1-5999-0061-0 and ISBN 9781599900612.

McGill, Alice, adapter. *Way Up and Over Everything.* Houghton Mifflin, 2008. ISBN 0-6183-8796-X and ISBN 9780618387960.

MacGrory, Yvonne. *The Secret of the Ruby Ring.* Illus. by Terry Myler. Milkweed, 1994. ISBN 0-915943-92-1 and ISBN 9780915943920.

McKay, Hilary. *Forever Rose.* Aladdin, 2009. ISBN 1-4169-5487-2 and ISBN 9781416954873.

McKissack, Patricia C. *The Dark-Thirty: Southern Tales of the Supernatural.* Illus. by Brian Pinkney. Knopf, 1992. ISBN 0-679-81863-4 and ISBN 9780679818632.

MacLachlan, Patricia. *Sarah, Plain and Tall.* HarperCollins, 1985. ISBN 0-06-024101-2 and ISBN 9780060241018. (First in series, ending with *Grandfather's Dance.* HarperCollins, 2006. ISBN 0-06-027560-X and ISBN 9780060275600).

Mayne, William. *Hob and the Goblins.* Illus. by Norman Messenger. Dorling Kindersley, 1994. ISBN 1-56458-713-4 and ISBN 9781564587138.

Murphy, Shirley Rousseau. *The Song of the Christmas Mouse.* Illus. by Donna Diamond. HarperCollins, 1990. ISBN 0-06-024357-0 and ISBN 9780060243579.

Naylor, Phyllis. *Shiloh.* Atheneum, 1991. ISBN 0-689-31614-3 and ISBN 9780689316142 (First of a trilogy).

Norton, Mary. *The Borrowers.* Illus. by Joe Krush and Beth Krush. Harcourt, 1953. (First in series.) ISBN 0-15-209990-5 and ISBN 9780152099909.

Park, Linda Sue. *A Single Shard.* Clarion, 2001. ISBN 0-395-97827-0 and ISBN 9780395978276.

Paterson, Katherine. *Bridge to Terabithia.* Illus. by Donna Diamond. HarperCollins, 1977. ISBN 0-690-01359-0 and ISBN 9780690013597.

Paulsen, Gary. *Lawn Boy.* Yearling, 2009. ISBN 0-5534-9465-1 and ISBN 9780553494655.

Pearce, Philippa. *Tom's Midnight Garden.* HarperCollins, 1992. ISBN 0-397-30477-3 and ISBN 9780397304776.

Peck, Richard. *A Year Down Yonder.* Puffin, 2002. ISBN 0-1423-0070-5 and ISBN 9780142300701.

Perkins, Lynn Rae. *The Cardboard Piano.* Greenwillow, 2008. ISBN 0-0615-4265-2 and ISBN 9780061542657.

Pratchett, Terry. *The Wee Free Men.* Harper Teen, 2004. ISBN 0-0600-1238-2 and ISBN 9780060012380.

Pyle, Howard. *Otto of the Silver Hand.* Wilder, 2008. ISBN 1-6045-9556-6 and ISBN 9781604595567.

Rawls, Wilson. *Summer of the Monkeys.* Yearling, 1998. ISBN 0-4404-1580-2 and ISBN 9780440415800.

Reynolds, Aaron. *Metal Man*. Charlesbridge, 2008. ISBN 1-58089-150-0 and ISBN 9781580891509.

Riordan, Rick. *The Lightning Thief*. Miramax, 2006. ISBN 0-7868-3865-5 and ISBN 9780786838653.

Rowling, J. K. *Harry Potter and the Sorcerer's Stone*. Illus. by Mary Grandpre. Scholastic, 1998. (First in series.) ISBN 0-590-35340-3 and ISBN 9780590353403.

Rylant, Cynthia. *Henry and Mudge: The First Book of Their Adventures*. Illus. by Suçie Stevenson. Simon & Schuster, 1987. (First in series.) ISBN 0-02-778001-5 and ISBN 9780027780017.

Sachar, Louis. *Holes*. Farrar, Straus and Giroux, 2008. ISBN 0-3743-3266-5 and ISBN 9780374332662.

Smee, Nicola. *Clip-Clop*. Sterling/Boxer, 2006. ISBN 1-9054-1704-7 and ISBN 9781905417049.

Stevenson, Robert Louis. *Treasure Island*. Illus. by Robert Ingpen. Palazzo Editions, 2006. ISBN 0-95451036-4 and ISBN 9780954510367.

Stewart, Mary. *A Walk in Wolf Wood: A Tale of Fantasy and Magic*. Illus. by Emanuel Schongut. Morrow, 1980. ISBN 0-688-03679-1 and ISBN 9780688036799.

Tate, Eleanora E. *Celeste's Harlem Renaissance*. Little, Brown, 2009. ISBN 0-3161-1362-X and ISBN 9780316113625.

Temple, Frances. *The Ramsay Scallop*. HarperCollins, 1995. ISBN 0-0644-0601-6 and ISBN 9780064406017.

Thomas, Gwyn, and Kevin Crossley-Holland. *Tales from the Mabinogion*. Illus. by Margaret Jones. Gollancz, 1985. ISBN 0-575-03531-5 and ISBN 9780575035317.

Thurber, James. *The Great Quillow*. Illus. by Steven Kellogg. Harcourt, 1994. ISBN 0-15-232544-1 and ISBN 9780152325442.

Vande Velde, Vivian. *Now You See It . . .* Harcourt, 2005. ISBN 0-1520-5461-8 and ISBN 9780152054618.

White, E. B. *Charlotte's Web*. 50th Anniversary Retrospective Edition. Illus. by Garth Williams. Additional artwork by Rosemary Wells. Afterword by Peter F. Newmeyer. HarperCollins, 2002. ISBN 0-06-000698-6 and ISBN 9780060006983.

White, Terence H. *The Sword in the Stone*. Illus. by Dennis Nolan. Putnam, 1993. ISBN 0-399-22502-1 and ISBN 9780399225024.

Wilce, Ysabeau S. *Flora Segunda*. Magic Carpet, 2008. ISBN 0-1520-5439-1 and ISBN 9780152054397.

Williams, Vera. *Scooter*. HarperCollins, 2001. ISBN 0-0644-0968-6 and ISBN 9780064409681.

Woodson, Jacqueline. *The Other Side*. Putnam, 2001. ISBN 0-3992-3116-1 and ISBN 9780399231162.

A SAMPLING OF STORYTELLING RECORDINGS

Many freelance storytellers distribute their own recordings through personal websites, which are noted where applicable.

Abiyoyo and Other Story Songs for Children. Smithsonian/Folkways SF 45001. Sung by Pete Seeger. Available as an MP3, CD, and cassette. www.folkways.si.edu.

Abraham and Isaac: Sacrifice at Gettysburg. Syd Lieberman, storyteller. Levyland Studio. "President Abraham Lincoln and Private Isaac Taylor could have been a father and his son. Both hailed from Illinois, were steeped in the King James Bible, and shared a passion to preserve the Union. In 1863, President Lincoln would honor Isaac and his fellows who had fought at Gettysburg." *Storytelling World* Magazine Award Winner. www.sydlieberman. com/store.

Aesop: Alive and Well. Diane Ferlatte, storyteller. From Diane Ferlatte. CD 9-01010-1. Ferlatte delivers the fables in a rich, powerful voice with guitar accompaniment and occasional sound and vocal effects. Includes *The Boy Who Cried Wolf*, the greedy dog who drops his bone in the water, crane and the crow inviting each other to eat from dishes they can't use, and a small creature rescuing a big one. For ages five to ten.

Anansi Time. Bobby Norfolk, storyteller. August House. CD. ISBN 0-87483-748-0 and ISBN 9780874837483. NAPPA Gold Award; Parents' Choice Award (Silver Title); Parent's Guide to Children's Media. Norfolk's energetic storytelling overflows with humor and sound effects. Includes "How Wisdom Came into the World," "Why Spider Has a Small Waist," and "Anansi and the Tug o' War."

Ananzi. Len Cabral, storyteller. From Len Cabral. Traditional folktales delivered with uncommon energy. Includes several tales of Ananzi, the trickster figure from West Africa. Additional recordings include *Nho Lobo*. www.lencabral.com.

The Animals Could Talk: Aesop's Fables Retold in Song. Heather Forest, storyteller. August House. CD. ISBN 0-8748-3750-2 and ISBN 9780874837506. Nineteen classic fables from Aesop are retold in poetry and song and shared troubadour style with guitar, bass, and cello accompaniment. For ages four to eight.

An Anthology of African American Poetry for Young People. Smithsonian/Folkways SF 45044. Arna Bontemps reads poems from his anthology *Golden Slippers*. www.folkways.si.edu.

Ashley Bryan: Poems and Folktales. Audio Bookshelf. ISBN 9780976193227. A vibrant presentation of "Ananse the Spider in Search of a Fool," "The Cat's Purr," "Turtle Knows Your Name," and "The Story of Lightning and Thunder," plus poems from Bryan's collection *Sing to the Sun.*

Ashley Bryan's Beautiful Blackbird and Other Folktales. Ashley Bryan, storyteller. Audio Bookshelf. ISBN 9781883332990. In his inimitable style Bryan delivers the text of "Beautiful Blackbird" plus four folktales from *African Tales, Uh Huh*: "Why Frog and Snake Never Play Together," "Tortoise, Hare, and the Sweet Potatoes," "Hen and Frog," "Frog and His Two Wives," and "How Animals Got Their Tails."

Baby Hawk Learns to Fly. Bobby Norfolk, storyteller. CD. August House. ISBN 0-87483-747-2 and ISBN 9780874837476. Parents' Choice 2005 Gold Award Winner. Six traditional stories delivered with humor and zest include tales from Aesop, the African American experience, and Japan.

Beatrix Potter: Artist, Storyteller and Countrywoman. Weston Woods Author Documentary DVD 445. Based on the biography by Judy Taylor. Narrated by Lynn Redgrave.

The Best of Syd Lieberman. Syd Lieberman, storyteller. CD. A selection of audience favorites including "The Tell-Tale Heart," "The Debate in Sign Language," and "Challahs in the Ark." www.sydlieberman.com/store.

The Boy Who Lived with the Bears and Other Iroquois Stories. Harper Children's Audio. ISBN 1-55994-541-9 and ISBN 9781559945417. Joe Bruchac, accompanying himself with drumming and chanting, relates stories from his collection. This recording is part of the outstanding Parabola Storytime Series: Traditional Tales by Traditional Storytellers.

Cajun Ghost Stories. J. J. Reneaux, storyteller. August House Audio. These unusual stories, available only as a download from www.audible.com, are hauntingly told by Cajun storyteller Reneaux. Includes a story of a ghost girl who comes back to frighten her miser father to a well-deserved death. For older children and adults.

Children Telling Stories. Companion DVD to *Children Tell Stories: Teaching and Using Storytelling in the Classroom* by Martha Hamilton and Mitch Weiss. 2nd ed. Richard C. Owen Publishers, Inc., 2005. ISBN 9781572746633. The author team, known as Beauty and the Beast Storytellers, plus teachers and a children's literature specialist talk about the values of storytelling in this film documentation of a storytelling unit. Older students, including a high school senior, are featured tellers.

Chillers. The Folktellers/Mama-T Artists MTA-2. The Folktellers tell "Mary Culhane and the Dead Man" and other chilling tales.

Chrysanthemum. Weston Woods Studios. CD WCD369RA. ISBN 9781555929053. Meryl Streep gives an extraordinary, sensitive rendition of Kevin Henkes's endearing story about a little girl mouse who agonizes about her unusual name.

Cockroach Party: Folktales to Sing, Dance and Act Out. Margaret Read MacDonald, storyteller. Music by Richard Scholtz. August House Audio. CD. ISBN 0-8748-3769-3 and ISBN 9780874837698. A charming collection of unfamiliar stories for young children, with music and refrains. Includes *Teeny Weeny Bop*, a trading story about a determined old lady. For ages four to six.

Crazy Gibberish and Other Story Hour Stretches. Naomi Baltuck, storyteller. Parents' Choice Gold Award, 1994. Eighteen audience participation songs, stretches, chants, and other surefire material to use with young children. *Crazy Gibberish Too! More Story Hour Stretches* was released in 2006. www.naomibaltuck.com.

The Dancing Granny and Other African Stories. Caedmon TC 1765. In his powerful, rhythmic style, Ashley Bryan tells "The Dancing Granny" and three other trickster tales.

D'Aulaires' Book of Greek Myths. Airplay Inc. Audio CD. ISBN 9781885608154. Unabridged edition of the D'Aulaires' book read by Paul Newman, Sidney Poitier, Kathleen Turner, and Matthew Broderick.

The Dragons Are Singing Tonight. Listening Library. ISBN 0-8072-0222-3 and ISBN 9780807202227. Jack Prelutsky reads and sings excerpts from his book of the same name.

Dream and Illusions: Tales of the Pacific Rim. Brenda Wong Aoki, storyteller. Rounder Select, 1992. www.firstvoice.org/BrendaWongAoki/index.html.

Dreams and Other Realities. Angela Lloyd, storyteller. CD. At Last Productions, 1997. NAPPA Gold Award Winner. Lloyd's storytelling has both whimsy and charm, and the addition of bells, washboard, and guitar gives vibrancy to the mix of traditional and literary pieces.

Dunbar Out Loud: The Poetry of Paul Lawrence Dunbar Performed by Bobby Norfolk. August House Audio. CD. ISBN 0-8748-3721-9 and ISBN 9780874837216. Norfolk performs in the dialect of the period, skillfully cadenced to clarify the narratives and illuminate the close relationship to today's speech. Includes poems of love, mourning, and hope, along with story poems full of social observation. For older children and adults.

Elsie Piddock Skips in Her Sleep. Stories and Poems by Eleanor Farjeon. Ellin Greene, storyteller. A Gentle Wind. GW1025. CD. ISBN 0-93906574-6 and ISBN 9780939065745. Greene's personality and style are uniquely suited to the romantic tales of the beloved British author. Includes "Elsie Piddock Skips in Her Sleep," "The Sea Baby," and "Nella's Dancing Shoes." For ages seven to adult.

An Evening at Cedar Creek. Wellspring CS 4902. Beth Horner tells "The Mousedeer and the Buffalo Chip," "Phantom Black Carriage," and five other stories. Country music performed by Win and Paul Grace.

Everywhere Everywhere Christmas Tonight. Marianne McShane. In a gentle, quiet voice McShane gives her listeners a gift of six Christmas stories, including "The Little Clockmaker" from Ruth Sawyer's *This Way to Christmas* and "The Three Magi" from *The Tiger and the Rabbit and Other Tales* by Pura Belpré.

Eyes of the Wise. Eth-Noh-Tec, storytellers. DVD. Robert Kikuchi-Yngojo and Nancy Wang are Eth-Noh-Tec, "kinetic story theater" with a concentration on tales from Asia and the Asian American experience. This DVD features nine traditional tales, including "Eyes of the Wise," "The Man Who Planted Onions," and "Bird of Happiness." See also the DVD *Fools, Frogs, and Folktales.* www.ethnohtec.org.

The Fabrics of Fairy Tale: Stories Spun from Far and Wide. Retold and narrated by Tanya Robyn Batt. Barefoot. Two-CD set. ISBN 1-84148-407-5 and ISBN 9781841484075. In a pleasant voice with a slight British accent, Batt tells stories from around the world, all having to do with fabrics. With pleasant musical selections between the stories, this is a complete, unabridged recording of the book by the same name. For ages five to ten.

Faster than Sooner: Tales of an Immigrant's Son. Antonio Sacre, storyteller. "The title story from this CD, about the father/son relationship, won a 'Best in Fringe Festival Award' at the 1999 New York International Fringe Festival." Additional recordings by Sacre include *Brown and Black and White All Over* and *Tribes and Bridges.* www.antoniosacre.com/id1. html.

Fat Cat and Friends. Read by Margaret Read MacDonald; musical accompaniment by Richard Scholtz. August House Audio, 2002.

Feathers in the Wind and Other Jewish Tales. Susan Stone, storyteller. CD. Interesting, mostly unfamiliar stories, nicely told. The title story uses feather pillows to teach a lesson on the impossibility of recalling hurtful gossip. For ages seven to twelve.

Fireside Tales. Dovie Thomason, storyteller. Seven stories told by Dovie Thomason, plus six Iroquois social songs by Micky Sickles. "Traditionally, these stories would be told by an older relative, in the cold season, to teach the history, memories, culture, and values of the people to the next generation, while simultaneously reminding the older generation of the proper way to live in harmony with the Earth and all who share it." Additional recordings by Dovie Thomason include *Lessons from the Animal People* and *Wopila: A Giveaway.* www.doviethomason.com.

The Flood and Other Lakota Stories. Harper Children's Audio. ISBN 1-55994-677-6 and ISBN 9781559946773. Kevin Locke, a Lakota of the Standing Rock Reservation of South Dakota, incorporates the Lakota language and sounds of his flute in a compelling presentation. This recording is part of the outstanding Parabola Storytime Series: Traditional Tales by Traditional Storytellers. See also www.kevinlocke.com.

Folk Tales from West Africa. Smithsonian/Folkways 7103. Harold Courlander reads the title story and four others from his book *The Cow-Tail Switch.*

Folktales of Strong Women. Yellow Moon Press. CD. Doug Lipman retells "The Chicken Woman," "The Woman Who Saved the City," "The Young Woman of Vietnam," "The One with the Star on Her Forehead," and "Godmother Death." A companion cassette is *Milk from the Bull's Horn: Tales of Nurturing Men,* six stories that come from Jewish, Persian, Irish, and Appalachian sources.

Forbidden. Susan Klein, storyteller. Four rites-of-passage stories with female protagonists from Alaska (Sedna), Greece (Persephone), South Africa (the Star Sister), and Vietnam (the Crystal Teacup). Each story contains a forbidden element that the protagonist must challenge.

Four Legged Tales. Animal Stories from Here and Away. Laura Simms, storyteller. CD. Stories for young children featuring kindness, friendship, compassion, loyalty, and some foolishness. Includes some how and why stories, some tales of magic. These deceptively simple stories contain wise thoughts, and are beautifully told with effective musical background by the Real Myth Ensemble. For ages three to five.

From the Back of the Bus. Bill Harley, storyteller. CD. ISBN 0-87483-441-4 and ISBN 9780874834413. Life in elementary school, complete with theme song. Storytelling World Award. www.billharley.com.

Getting to Know Mo Willems. Weston Woods/Scholastic Author Documentary DVD. ISBN 0-545-13437-4 and ISBN 9780545134378. Live-action, 23-minute film. The author discusses his art and the source of inspiration for his popular books about Trixie and her beloved Knuffle Bunny. For ages eight to adult.

Getting to Know Simms Taback. Weston Woods/Scholastic Author Documentary DVD. ISBN 9780439828215. Live-action, 15-minute film. Simms Taback charms us with stories about his life and work and ends with singing the words of his Caldecott-winning book *Joseph Had a Little Overcoat.* Delightful listening for all ages.

Graveyard Tales. National Storytelling Network. CD. ISBN 1-87991-29-2. A live recording from the National Storytelling Festival that includes Gayle Ross telling the cannibalistic *Skeleton Woman,* and the Folktellers offering Jack Prelutsky's poem "Ghoul." Also included are Katherine Wyndham's regional ghost story, *The Hole That Would Not Stay Filled*; Mary Carter Smith's *Dead Aaron*; Laura Simms and Steve Gorn, musician, with *The Woodcutter*; and Jackie Torrence with *The Monkey's Paw.* For ages seven to adult.

The Hairyman and Other Wild Tales. High Windy Audio HW1202. David Holt, accompanied by banjo, harmonica, fiddle, guitar, and buck dancing, entertains with "The Hairyman," "The Apple Tree," and four other tales. This is a good example of the performance type of storytelling in which different voices are used for different characters. Excellent pacing and relaxed style.

Hans Christian Andersen: Classic Stories. August House Audio. CD. ISBN 9780874837677. Diane Wolkstein tells six Andersen stories with accompaniment on kazoo, kalimba, and guitar. Includes "Hans Clodhopper," "The Goblin and the Grocer," "The Ugly Duckling," "The Emperor's New Clothes," "The Nightingale," and "Dance, Dance Dolly Mine." For ages five to ten.

Harry Potter series. Listening Library. Audiobook CD/CS Recipient of Audio Hall of Fame Award (2006) and numerous other awards. Performed by Jim Dale.

Hoop of Life: Lakota Stories of the Nobility of the Human Spirit. Four ancient stories and one personal narrative accompanied by Kevin Locke's flute and additional Lakota-language narrative. www.kevinlocke.com.

Hoot Owl Blues: Tales and Tunes to Conjure Up a Mood. CD. Available from Jeslyn Wheeless. 2000 ALSC Notable Children's Recording. Storyteller-folksinger Jeslyn Wheeless, accompanied on the guitar by her son Ben, sings an original blues song, "Hoot Owl Blues," and tells scary tales including "The Conjure Wives," "Jack and the Haunted House," "Wiley and the Hairy Man," and "The Strange Visitor."

How and Why Stories: World Tales Kids Can Tell. August House. CD 51200. 2000 Gold Award—National Parenting Publications Awards (NAPPA). Martha Hamilton and Mitch Weiss tell four stories from the companion book. They are joined by eight youngsters, ages nine to fourteen, who tell fourteen other tales. For ages seven to twelve.

How I Learned to Love Liver and Other Tales Too Tall to Tell. Joel ben Izzy, storyteller. Old City Press. CD. ISBN 0-9631129-7-X and ISBN 9780963112972. Parents' Choice Silver Award. Tall tales of Paula Bunyan, Moose Turd Pie, and more. www.storypage.com.

How Rabbit Tricked Otter and Other Cherokee Animal Stories. Harper Children's Audio. ISBN 1-55994-542-7 and ISBN 9781559945424. Gayle Ross tells stories from her collection in a clear, calm, expressive voice. This recording is part of the outstanding Parabola Storytime Series: Traditional Tales by Traditional Storytellers.

If the Shoe Fits . . . Cinderella Stories from Around the World. Milbre Burch, storyteller. Kind Crone Productions. CD. 2006 NAPPA Honors Award. These stories—from Egypt, Iraq, Ireland, and North America—are retold combining facts and folklore. www.kindcrone. com.

In a Dead Man's Company: Dark Spirits and Savage Truths. Dan Keding, storyteller. CD. 2001 Storytelling World Winner Award. www.dankeding.com.

Irish Wonder Tales. Volumes One and Two. The Storyteller's School, Toronto. Told by master storyteller Alice Kane who says she has been influenced by the rhythms, the feeling, and the ancient qualities of the stories told by Padraic Colum and Ella Young. Volume One includes "The Golden Fly," "The Birth of Usheen," and "Usheen Returns to Ireland." Volume Two is a 55-minute telling of Ella Young's "The Wondersmith and His Son."

Jack's First Job. Donald Davis. August House Audio. Available only as a download from www.audible.com. A collection of stories about the Appalachian folktale hero, including the favorite, *Jack and the Robbers.* For ages seven to adult.

Jeux d'Enfants (Children's games). CD 5170434. Also includes *The Sorcerer's Apprentice, Dolly Suite, The Musical Box, Nutcracker Suite, The Pied Piper, Themes for Narnia,* and *Brazileira.* Excellent recording to use in multimedia musical storytelling programs. Available from Musical Heritage Society, Inc.

Joe Bruchac: Iroquois Stories. Good Mind Records, 2001. CD. Bruchac's tales, including animal stories and two longer stories about brave women, are told with sympathy and compassion. Pleasant commentary on the place of storytelling in the culture and on the role and importance of women. With some chanting and drumming between the stories. All ages.

John Henry. Brad Kessler, adapter. Read by Denzel Washington. Rabbit Ears/Simon & Schuster, 2000.

The Johnstown Flood of 1889. Syd Lieberman. Syd Lieberman Store. CD. S.L. 104. The town invited Lieberman to retell the story of the flood's destruction along with the brave, inspiring rebuilding that followed. Lieberman brings the riveting story of an awesome tragedy to life with the selection of well-chosen details; music introduces and ends the story. For older children and adults.

Lakota Love Songs and Stories. Kevin Locke, storyteller. Locke's voice and his flute music evokes Paul Goble's story, *The Love Flute.*

Laura Simms: Making Peace—Heart Uprising. From Laura Simms. CD. This vivid performance of stories about transforming aggression into compassion is a testimonial to the power of storytelling. Simms shares touching and haunting tales from world folklore and from her life, with spectacular use of music and song to create mood and texture. For older children, teens, and adults.

Lessons from the Animal People. Dovie Thomason. Yellow Moon Press. CD, ISBN 0-938756-51-6 and ISBN 9780938756514. Audiotape, ISBN 0-938756-50-8 and ISBN 9780938756507. Little-known stories from a variety of Native American tribes with music by Ulali. Buffalo challenges turtle to a race, a wiggly little chipmunk keeps a bear from hibernating, and trickster fox is punished by the animals and helped by the birds, "because sometimes our kindness needs to be saved for those who need to learn kindness." For ages six to ten.

Lights and Laughter: Joel ben Izzy Spins Hanukkah Tales. Old City Press. CD. NAPPA Gold Award; Parents' Choice Gold Award. The story of Hanukkah plus "seven other tales to keep you smiling all eight nights." www.storypage.com.

Listening for the Crack of Dawn. Donald Davis, storyteller. August House Audio. CD. ISBN 0-87483-608-5 and ISBN 9780874836080. A master storyteller recalls the Appalachia of the 50s and 60s. Includes a tender story about his maiden aunt, Laura, who moved from house to house in the family as she grew old; "LSMFT," a story about the handicapped boy they taunted as children; and a wrenching story of a friend who ran away from Vietnam. For older children and adults.

Looking for Papito: Family Stories from Latin America. Antonio Sacre, storyteller. CD. Parents' Choice Gold Award 1996; NAPPA Gold Award 1999. Available in English and Spanish.

Lou Gehrig. The Story of a Great Man. Written and told by Carol Birch. From Carol Birch. CD SBP200. Birch provides a moving portrait of a shy and gentle man who experienced blazing heights of success and a tragic death. For older children and adults.

Love Flute. Drumbeat Indian Arts, Inc. Cassette/CD DAK 101. Based on the book by Paul Goble. Narrated by Tom Bee with Dakota flute music by Brian Akipa.

Making the Heart Whole Again: Stories for a Wounded World. Milbre Burch, storyteller. Kind Crone Productions. CD. 2007 Grammy Nominee. "Features international folktales and personal stories promoting peace, justice, and reconciliation." www.kindcrone.com.

Maynard Moose Tales. Willy Claflin, storyteller. August House. CD. ISBN 0-87483-699-9 and ISBN 9780874836998. Maynard Moose, the alter-ego of storyteller Willy Claflin, tells not-so-traditional versions of familiar folktales. See also *Sleeping Beastly.*

Medusa and Other Good Ol' Greeks. Barbara McBride Smith, storyteller. Pandora Productions 102. CD. Retellings of "Medusa and Perseus," "The Trojan War: The Beginning," "Demeter," and "Baucis and Philemon" seen through an irreverent lens in a humorous manner suited to young adults and adults.

The Minstrel and the Storyteller. Stories and songs of the Jewish people. Gerard Edery and Peninnah Schram. Sefarad Records. CD 5761. An appealing selection of thoughtful, often reverent stories from Schram's books, including the *Innkeeper's Clever Daughter,* an Elijah story, and the tale of an artist who searches for something beautiful enough to paint, and finds it at home in the faces of his family. Choral and solo performances in various languages, including Spanish, Italian, Hebrew, and Arabic are included. For older children and adults.

Once Upon a Time. Stories from the Bahamas. Derek Burrows, storyteller. Yellow Moon Press. ISBN 0-938756-25-7 and ISBN 9780938756255. Folklorist and storyteller Burrows introduces the folklore of the Bahamas, including riddles, songs, and characters like B'Rabby and B'Bouki. Natural, low-key storytelling, with wonderful traditional beginnings and endings for the tales, is enhanced by some a capella offerings of intriguing songs. For ages seven to ten.

One Righteous Man: The Story of Raoul Wallenberg. Syd Lieberman, storyteller. This straightforward telling combines events from Wallenberg's life and his rescue of Jews in Budapest during World War II. Includes reminiscences from Lieberman's aunt, who lived on a farm until she was taken by the Nazis. For older children and adults. www. sydlieberman.com/store.

The People Could Fly. Knopf/Random House. Twelve tales from Virginia Hamilton's book. Narrated by Virginia Hamilton and James Earl Jones.

Peter and the Wolf by Serge Prokofiev. Narrated by Boris Karloff. CD 5171273. A Vanguard Classic CD distributed by Musical Heritage Society. Includes Haydn's "Toy Symphony" and Tchaikovsky's *Nutcracker Suite.*

Poetry Speaks to Children. Sourcebooks MediaFusion, 2005. ISBN 9781402203299. CD and book, edited by Elise Paschen. Fifty poems read by 34 poets, of which 29 read their own work. The CD and handsomely illustrated book offer children ages four and older a wonderful introduction to poetry.

Sandburg Out Loud. A selection of Carl Sandburg's *Rootabaga Stories*, poetry, and folksongs collected in *The American Songbag.* Carol Birch, Bill Harley, and Angela Lloyd, with David Holt. August House. CD, ISBN 0-87483-676-X and ISBN 9780874836769. Cassette, ISBN 0-87483-677-8 and ISBN 9780874836776. Three storytellers, telling together and individually, share stories and songs with humor, some yearning, and much delight. A superbly paced recording with appealing musical pieces performed by David Holt. All ages.

Shakespeare's Storybook. Barefoot, 2001. CD. ISBN 9781841484143. A complete, unabridged recording of *Shakespeare's Storybook: Folk Tales That Inspired the Bard*, retold and narrated by Patrick Ryan.

Silent Night. Susan Klein, storyteller. Susan Klein, 1999. 2000 Parents' Guide Award; 2000 Storytelling World Winner. Christmas collection of folklore, literary, and autobiographical stories. Includes "The Night Before Christmas" and "Star Mother's Youngest Child." www.susanklein.net.

The Silver Spurs: A True Story of the American Civil War. Beth Horner, storyteller. DVD. Available from Beth Horner. This beautifully told story, based on family history, is not to be missed!

Sisters All . . . and One Troll. Mary Hamilton, storyteller. 2007 Storytelling World Award for Storytelling Recordings. 2006 iParenting Media Award; 2006 Parents' Choice Gold Award. Stories with active heroines including "Kate Crackernuts" and "Eleven Cinderellas." www.maryhamilton.info/StoryStore/recordings.

Sleeping Beastly and Other Tales. Willy Claflin, storyteller. August House. ISBN 0-87483-703-0 and ISBN 9780874837032. Parents' Choice Award (Classic Title); ALA Notable Children's Recording.

Sop Doll and Other Tales of Mystery and Mayhem. Milbre Burch, storyteller. Kind Crone. CD. 2003 Film Advisory Board Inc Award of Excellence; 2004 Storytelling World Award. "Stories inspired by Jack and the witches, murder ballads, Wolf Man movies and Snow White—all written by Milbre. Plus a bonus tale by Jane Yolen." www.kindcrone.com.

Spirits Walk: Chilling Tales for Teenagers and Adults. Connie Regan-Blake. StoryWindow Productions, 1999. CD. ISBN 1-929415-06-0 and ISBN 9781929415069. Stories range from spooky to scary and have musical touches. Includes "Two White Horses," about a woman buried alive, and "Mary Culhane," who has to carry a dead man on her back from the graveyard. For older children and adults.

Stories for the Road and to Grow On. Connie Regan-Blake and Barbara Freeman. StoryWindow Productions. CD. 37101-15823-4. Selections from two award-winning recordings from Regan-Blake's and Freeman's days of working as the Folktellers demonstrate their skill in telling in tandem, as well as their appealing individual styles. Together they tell *Come Again in the Spring*, *The King at the Door*, and their well-known *Jazzy Three Bears*. For ages four to twelve.

Stories from the Enchanted Loom: Musical Stories for Children Ages 4 to 12. Marcia Lane, storyteller. A Gentle Wind. CD and cassette. GW1040. Favorite traditional stories entertainingly told by a storyteller with a beautiful and expressive voice. Includes stories of why the sun and moon live in the sky, a courtship that begins with shooting an arrow into the forest, and a tale of a fisherman and a genie.

Stories from the Other Side. Dan Keding, storyteller. Turtle Creek Recordings. TC 1003. A broodingly well-told collection of supernatural tales. Listen for the style of telling a suspense story as well as for the stories themselves.

Stories in My Pocket: Tales Kids Can Tell. CD. Available from Beauty and the Beast Storytellers Mitch Weiss and Martha Hamilton. 1998 Parents' Choice Recommendation. 1998 National Parenting Publications Awards Gold Award. Eighteen stories from the companion book, told by Martha Hamilton, Mitch Weiss, and five guest kid tellers. These short tellable tales are from many cultures and range from jump tales to trickster/fool tales to more serious folktales such as "The Stonecutter." For ages seven to twelve.

Storytelling: Tales for Children and Techniques for Teachers. StoryWindow Productions. DVD. A combination of two earlier videos—*Pennies, Pets and Peanut Butter* and *Storytelling: Tales and Techniques*—that were recorded live by PBS. This set includes the former storytelling duo the Folktellers, telling stories to children as well as telling abbreviated versions to adults to illustrate many helpful hints for successful storytelling and ways to involve and intrigue children and young people. Several fine examples of Connie Regan-Blake and Barbara Freeman telling stories together are included.

A Storytelling Treasury. National Storytelling Network. Four CDs. ISBN 1-879991-25-X. In this live recording from the 20th National Storytelling Festival, 37 storytellers, including Joseph Bruchac, Johnny Moses, Len Cabral, Pleasant DeSpain, Linda Goss, Rafe Martin, Jay O'Callahan, Elizabeth Ellis, Nancy Schimmel, and many others provide a fine cross-section of contemporary American storytelling. For older children and adults.

Tales for Scary Times. Jackie Torrence. Earwig Music Company. Cassette 4908CS. The renowned storyteller (d. 2004) effectively tells a selection of suspenseful stories, including "The Golden Arm," a version of the vanishing hitchhiker tale, and a story of a stranded couple who meet a headless ghost. For older children and adults.

Tales from an Irish Hearth. The Storytellers School of Toronto. Alice Kane tells ten traditional Irish tales taken from the works of Patrick Kennedy, T. Crofton Croker, and others.

Tales from Cultures Far and Near. Greathall Productions. Storyteller Jim Weiss relates tales from a wide range of cultures, from the Lakota Sioux to Senegal, unified by inherent morals that give a clear sense of the ideals of each culture.

The Tales of Peter Rabbit. Harper Children's Audio. Cassette, 4 tapes. ISBN 1-55994-795-0 and ISBN 9781559947954. Nineteen stories by Beatrix Potter read by Claire Bloom.

Tales of Womenfolk. Heather Forest, storyteller. StoryArts. CD. In minstrel style, Heather Forest tells five folktales featuring resourceful heroines: "The Squire's Bride," "Janet and Tamlin," "The Hedley Kow," "Three Strong Women," and "The Lute Player." www.storyarts.org.

The Tell-Tale Heart and Other Terrifying Tales. SL Productions SL105. Syd Lieberman tells six terrifying tales adapted from Poe, Bierce, Chaucer, and the first adventure of Beowulf. His adaptations are good examples of how to edit a long story for oral presentation.

Tío Conejo. Olga Loya, storyteller. August House. CD. ISBN 0-87483-580-1 and ISBN 9780874835809. Also available on audio and video are *Animal Stories* and *Magic Tales*. www.olgaloya.com/books_videos.html.

Tom Lee Telling Stories. Volume 1. Red Branch Audio. CD. 112360. A fine recording of less-well-known traditional stories, with musical interludes. Lee tells in a measured and expressive way that makes the stories engrossing. Includes "The Twelve Windows," the romantic story of an independent princess and her persistent suitor.

Touch Magic . . . Pass It On! Milbre Burch, storyteller. Kind Crone Productions. CD. 2000 Parents' Choice Classic Award. Burch's first recording of stories and poems by Jane Yolen includes "The Cat Bride," "Sleeping Ugly," "Princess Heart O'Stone," and five other stories by the popular Yolen. See also *The Ready Heart*. Milbre Burch, storyteller. Kind Crone Productions. CD. 1995 Parents' Choice Gold Award Winner. A second collection of Yolen's stories and poems told by Burch, including "The Fisherman's Wife" and "Silent Bianca."

Troubling Trouble. Donna Washington, storyteller. 2007 Parents' Choice Gold Award. "Fun, fast-paced collection of African and African American tales about the perils of troubling with trouble." www.dlwstoryteller.com.

Tuck-Me-In Tales: Bedtime Stories from Around the World. Margaret Read MacDonald. August House Audio. CD, ISBN 0-87483-770-7 and ISBN 9780874837704. Cassette, ISBN 0-87483-511-9 and ISBN 9780874835113. Sweet and soothing stories including "Kanji-jo," a Liberian tale of baby birds looking for their mother; "The Old Woman Who Lived in a Vinegar Bottle"; and a Siberian tale about a bird's lullaby. Songs, chants, and music performed by Richard Scholtz. For ages three to seven.

Uncle Bouqui of Haiti. Smithsonian/Folkways. Folkways 07107. Augusta Baker tells "Uncle Bouqui and Godfather Malice," "Uncle Bouqui Rents a Horse," and "Uncle Bouqui Gets Whee-Ai" from Harold Courlander's book.

Virginia Lee Burton: A Sense of Place. Weston Woods/Scholastic Author Documentary. DVD 1322. Live action, 30 minutes. "Lindsay Crouse narrates this richly textured portrait."

Water Torture, the Barking Mouse and Other Tales of Wonder. Antonio Sacre, storyteller. Sacre tells folktales learned while traveling throughout Mexico, including "The Rabbit in the Moon," "The Virgin of Guadalupe," "La Llorona (The Weeping Woman)," and "The Barking Mouse," a tale of how important it is to speak another language.

When the Chenoo Howls: Native American Tales of Terror. Joseph and Jim Bruchac, storytellers. www.josephbruchac.com.

When the Troupe Tells Tales: The Story of the Roosevelt Middle School Tellers. DVD. 45 minutes. Directed by Robert Rubinstein. Available from Robert Rubinstein.

Why Mosquitoes Buzz in People's Ears and Other Tales. Harper Children's Audio. ISBN 0-69451-187-0. Ruby Dee and Ossie Davis perform stories from Africa.

Why the Dog Chases the Cat: Great Animal Stories. High Windy. ISBN 0-942303-07-5 and ISBN 9780942303070. Storyteller cousins David Holt and Bill Mooney delight listeners with amusing pourquoi stories, many adapted from *The Complete Tales of Uncle Remus*.

Women of Vision. Stories told by Susan Danoff. Music by Brad Hill. From Susan Danoff. CD. Danoff's thoughtful and reflective women-centered retellings of traditional and tradition-based tales are gentle but compelling. Musical backgrounds enhance the moods of the stories. 2008 Gold Parents' Choice Award; 2008 Gold NAPPA (National Parenting Publication) Award. For older children and adults.

Women to Remember. Kathryn Tucker Windham. August House Audio. CD. ISBN 0-8748-3691-3 and ISBN 9780874836912. The noted southern writer and storyteller, known for telling personal stories, recalls memorable women in her life including Aunt Bet, who made cakes and wine during Prohibition, and the teller's own mother. Extremely enjoyable listening as the chuckling storyteller remembers times long past. For older children and adults.

World Tales of Wisdom and Wonder. Heather Forest. August House Audio. CD. ISBN 0-8748-3673-5 and ISBN 9780874836738. Intriguing stories filled with gentle lessons on making peace, keeping one's word, and the importance of friends. Includes stories of a magical brocade, and the mullah whose fine clothes go to dinner. For ages six to ten.

SOURCES

Audio Bookshelf, 44 Ocean View Drive, Middletown, RI 02842. 800-234-1713. www.audbkshf@agate.net.

August House Audio, 3500 Piedmont Road N.E., #310, Atlanta, GA 30305. 800-284-8784, 404-442-4420. www.augusthouse.com. All August House recordings can also be downloaded from www.audible.com.

Barefoot Books, 2067 Massachusetts Avenue, Cambridge, MA 02140. 617-576-0660. 866-417-2396. www.barefoot-books.com/us/site/pages/home.php.

Beauty and the Beast Storytellers Martha Hamilton and Mitch Miller, 954 Coddington Road, Ithaca, NY 14850. 607-277-0016. www.beautyandthebeaststorytellers.com.

Carol Birch, P.O. Box 32, Southbury, CT 06488. 203-264-3800. www.carolbirch.com/store.

Susan Danoff, 116 Clover Lane, Princeton, NJ 08540. 609-439-6467. www.susandanoff.com.

Drumbeat Indian Arts, Inc., 4143 North 16th Street, Phoenix, AZ 85016. 800-895-4859, 602-266-4823. www.drumbeatindianarts.com.

Earwig Music, Farwell Avenue, Garden Unit, Chicago, IL 60645. 773-262-0285. www.earwigmusic.com.

Diane Ferlatte, 5836 Ocean View Drive, Oakland, CA 94618. 510-655-2719. www.dianeferlatte.com. All of Diane's recordings are available for download from cdbaby.com and the newest titles are also available from iTunes.com.

A Gentle Wind, Box 3103, Albany, NY 12203. 518-482-9023, 888-386-7664. www.gentlewind.com.

Greenfield Review Press, P.O. Box 3008, Greenfield Center, NY 12833. 518-584-1728. www.nudatlog@earthlink.net.

Kevin Locke, P.O. Box 241, Mobridge, SD 57601. www.kevinlocke.com. Recordings by Kevin Locke are also available from Drumbeat Indian Arts, Inc.

Musical Heritage Society, Inc., 1710 Highway 35, Oakhurst, NJ 07755. 800-777-6105, 732-531-7003.

National Storytelling Network, 101 Courthouse Square, Jonesborough, TN 37659. 800-525-4514. www.storynet.org.

Red Branch Audio, P.O. Box 150, Chester, CT 06412. 860-526-4600, 888-659-3052. www.tomleestoryteller.com or tellingstories@msn.com.

Richard C. Owens Publishers, P.O. Box 585, Katonah, NY 10536. 914-232-3903. www.RCOwen.com.

Robert Rubinstein, 90 E. 49th Avenue, Eugene, OR 97405. 800-493-3005, 541-344-8176. www.robertrubinstein.net bambarer@hotmail.com.

Nancy Schimmel, Sisters Choice. www.sisterschoice.com nancy@sisterschoice.com.

Sefarad Records, 392 Central Park West, Suite 17Y, New York, NY 10025. 212-662-9712. www.sefaradrecords.com.

Laura Simms, 814 Broadway, New York, NY 10013. 212-674-3477. www.laurasimms.com. Some of Simms's recordings, including *Women and Wild Animals* and *Dance Without End* are available online from BetterListen!.com on iTunes, under spoken word. Her children's recordings will soon be on the "kids" list there.

Sourcebooks MediaFusion, P.O. Box 4410, Naperville, IL 60567-4410. 630-962-3900.

Susan Stone, 1320 Wesley Avenue, Evanston, IL 60201. 847-328-8159. www.momteller@ yahoo.com.

StoryWindow Productions. P.O. Box 2898, Asheville, NC 28802. 800-864-0299. www. storywindow.com.

Syd Lieberman Store, 2522 Ashland, Evanston, IL 60201. www.sydlieberman.com/store.

Weston Woods Studios, 143 Main Street, Norwalk, CT 06851. 800-243-5020, 203-845-0197. www.teacher.scholastic.com/products/westonwoods/faq.htm.

Jeslyn Wheeless, 34 Kings Hill Ct., Summit, NJ 07901. 908-522-0416 wheelessj@aol.com.

Yellow Moon Press, P.O. Box 381316, Cambridge, MA 02238. 800-497-4385, 617-776-2230. www.yellowmoon.com.

GLOSSARY

Ballad—A narrative song, e.g., "Tam Lin."

Circular story—A story in which the main character ends up in the same place or condition from which he started, e.g., *Once a Mouse* by Marcia Brown.

Cumulative tale—A repetitive tale that builds on the last action, characterized by minimum plot and maximum rhythm, e.g., "The Gingerbread Boy."

Droll—A humorous story about sillies or numbskulls, e.g., *When Shlemiel Went to Warsaw* by Isaac Bashevis Singer.

Epic—A cycle of tales centered around one hero, e.g., *The Green Hero: Early Adventures of Finn McCool* by Bernard Evslin.

Fable—A brief story that teaches a moral lesson, e.g., *Aesop's Fables*, retold by Jerry Pinkney. Usually the main characters are animals that speak as humans.

Fairy tale—A story involving the "little people" (fairies, elves, pixies, gnomes, dwarfs, brownies, leprechauns), e.g., "The Woman Who Flummoxed the Fairies."

Folklore—The traditional creations of the folk or common people, comprising beliefs and superstitions, customs, recipes, weather lore, proverbs, riddles, songs and dances, arts and crafts, etc.

Folktale—A narrative story that comes from the oral tradition. Equivalent to "Traditional tale."

Formula tale—A story with a predictable pattern that makes it easy to learn and to tell, e.g., "Toads and Diamonds." See *Putting the World in a Nutshell* by Sheila Dailey.

Fractured fairy tale—A traditional tale retold from a different point of view to create a parody, e.g., *The True Story of the 3 Little Pigs! by A. Wolf as told to Jon Scieszka.*

Hero tale—A tale that recounts the exploits of a human hero who embodies the ideals of a culture, e.g., *The Story of King Arthur and His Knights* by Howard Pyle.

Jump tale—A tale with an unexpected ending that startles the listener, e.g., "The Teeny Tiny Bone."

Legend—A narrative about a person, place, or event involving real or pretended belief, e.g., *Johnny Appleseed: The Story of a Legend* by Will Moses.

Literary fairy tale—A story that uses the form of a traditional folktale or fairy tale but has an identifiable author, e.g., the stories of Eleanor Farjeon.

Märchen or wonder tale—A traditional story in which quite ordinary people have extraordinary adventures involving magical objects, transformations, talking animals, e.g., "East o' the Sun and West o' the Moon."

Motif—The smallest element that persists in a traditional tale, e.g., the favorite youngest child.

Myth—A story about the gods or culture heroes, e.g., *Theseus and the Minotaur* by Warwick Hutton. Creation myths attempt to explain natural phenomena, e.g., "Persephone," or the origins of a people.

Nursery tale—A simple folktale appropriate for telling to young children, e.g., "The Three Billy Goats Gruff."

Pourquoi story—A narrative that explains the origin of a physical or cultural phenomenon, e.g., *The Cat's Purr* by Ashley Bryan.

Realistic story—A story that is true to life. It may be a biography, historical fiction, an adventure tale, or an animal story, e.g., *Julie of the Wolves* by Jean George.

Religious tale—A story that uses elements of religious belief, e.g., "The Juggler of Notre Dame."

Romance—A medieval story in verse or prose based on chivalrous love and adventure, e.g., *Sir Gawain and the Loathly Lady* by Selina Hastings.

String story—A tale told using string to form figures in the story, e.g., "The Mosquito" in Anne Pellowski's *The Story Vine*.

Talking animal tale—A story that teaches a moral lesson but so subtly that we are not aware of it, e.g., "The Three Little Pigs."

Tall tale—Exaggerated story about extraordinary persons or events, e.g., *Swamp Angel* by Anne Isaacs.

Traditional tale—A story that has been handed down from one generation to another, either in writing or by word of mouth. There is no identifiable author.

Trickster tale—A traditional tale with a trickster as the main character, e.g., *The Tales of Uncle Remus: The Adventures of Brer Rabbit* by Julius Lester.

Type—A recognizable tale for which variants are known.

Variant—A different version of the same tale, e.g., "Tom Tit Tot" is the English version of the German "Rumpelstiltskin."

Wishing candle—A candle lit at the beginning of the storytime to help the children focus. At the end of the program, the children make a wish and blow out the candle. (Be sure to use a dripless candle.)

COPYRIGHT ACKNOWLEDGMENTS

Belpré, Pura. "Perez and Martina" from *Perez and Martina: A Puerto Rican Folktale* by Pura Belpré. Copyright © 1932, renewed 1960 by Pura Belpré White. Used by permission of Viking Children's Books, A Division of Penguin Young Readers Group, A Member of Penguin Group (USA) Inc., 345 Hudson Street, New York, NY 10014.

Bryan, Ashley. "The Dancing Granny" from *The Dancing Granny*. Text and illustrations by Ashley Bryan. Copyright © 1977 by Ashley Bryan. Atheneum, 1977. Reprinted by permission.

Freeman, Judy. *Books Kids Will Sit Still For 3: A Read-Aloud Guide*, Judy Freeman. Copyright © 2006 by Judy Freeman. Reproduced with permission of ABC-CLIO, LLC, Santa Barbara, CA.

Ghoting, Saroj Nadkarni, and Pamela Martin-Diaz. *Early Literacy Storytimes @ Your Library: Partnering with Caregivers for Success.* American Library Association, 2006. Reprinted with permission from the American Library Association.

Ryan, Patrick. "Once Upon a Time into Altered States: Temporal Space, Liminality, and Flow." First published in *Time Everlasting: Representations of Past, Present and Future in Children's Literature*. Pinsent, P. (ed.)

Sierra, Judy. "The Gingerbread Man" from *Nursery Tales from Around the World* by Judy Sierra. Text copyright © 1996 by Judy Sierra. Reprinted by permission of Clarion Books, an imprint of Houghton Mifflin Harcourt Publishing Company.

INDEX

About the Authors

ELLIN GREENE, PhD, is an internationally known storyteller, lecturer, workshop leader, and conference director. A former associate professor at the University of Chicago Graduate Library School and assistant coordinator of children's services/storytelling and group work specialist at the New York Public Library, Greene coauthored the first two editions of *Storytelling: Art and Technique* with her mentor Augusta Baker and was the sole author of the third edition. She has written 13 professional books and retold 11 folktales for children. In 2002, she received the Lifetime Achievement Award from the National Storytelling Network. Greene is a Distinguished Alumna of Douglass College, Rutgers, and is profiled in several Marquis *Who's Who* volumes and *The World Who's Who of Women*, Cambridge, England.

JANICE M. DEL NEGRO, PhD, is assistant professor at the Graduate School of Library and Information Science at Dominican University, River Forest, IL. Her first picture book, *Lucy Dove*, won the Anne Izard Storytelling Award. Her second picture book, *Willa and the Wind*, was an ALA Notable Book. Del Negro's latest book, *Passion and Poison*, is a collection of supernatural tales for young adults. Del Negro has been a featured storyteller at the National Storytelling Festival, the Bay Area Storytelling Festival, the Illinois Storytelling Festival, the Fox Valley Folk Festival, and many others. She has conducted workshops on various aspects of storytelling for librarians, teachers, parents, storytellers, and other educators in a variety of settings, including the National Storytelling Network Annual Conference, the Illinois School Library Media conference, the University of Illinois, the University of Wisconsin, and the University of San Diego. She is currently working on her fourth recording, *Fortune's Daughters: Folktales and Ghost Tales*, to be released in 2010.